Term	Conditions	Procedure	Process / Result
[11] Interoceptive conditioning	An interoceptive signaling stimulus, e.g. a novel taste, and an interoceptive US, e.g. illness	Present signaling stimulus and US in association	Signaling stimulus acquires appetitive or aversive properties, depending on nature of US
[12] Sign tracking	A localized CS, a US and a freely-moving subject	Repeatedly pair CS and US, or make US contingent upon CS in some other way	CS is approached and contacted or withdrawn from, depending on nature of US
[13] Stimulus generalization	A response, an appropriate reinforcer, and a discriminative stimulus S^D	S^D: $R \to S^+$, then test responding in presence of other stimuli, similar to S^D	Responding generalizes to related stimuli
[14] Discrimination	A response, an appropriate reinforcer two stimulus conditions, S^D and S^Δ	S^D: $R \to S^+$ S^Δ: $R \nrightarrow$	Responding becomes restricted to S^D Responding to S^Δ is inhibited
[15] Escape	An aversive stimulus S^-, an appropriate response, R	S^-: $R \to \cancel{S}^-$	R increases in frequency and/or reduces in late[r]
[16] Avoidance	An aversive stimulus, S^-, an appropriate response, R	Arrange for R to cancel, postpone, or reduce frequency of S^-	R increases in frequency
[17] Punishment	A previously reinforced response R, an aversive stimulus, S^-	$R \to S^-$	R decreases in frequency
[18] L-set	Appropriate discrimination contingencies	Present a series of related discrimination problems	The individual discrimination processes change gradual to rapid
[22] Satiation	A previously reinforced response, R, an appropriate reinforcer, S^+, established through deprivation	$R \to S^+$	A steady rate of response is followed by abrup[t] cessation of responding

PRINCIPLES OF BEHAVIORAL ANALYSIS

J. R. MILLENSON
University of Brasilia

JULIAN C. LESLIE
The New University of Ulster

Principles
of
Behavioral
Analysis

SECOND EDITION

Macmillan Publishing Co., Inc.
New York

Collier Macmillan Publishers
London

Macmillan Publishing Co., Inc.
866 Third Avenue, New York, New York 10022

Collier Macmillan Canada, Ltd.

Library of Congress Cataloging in Publication Data

Millenson, John R.   (date)
    Principles of behavioral analysis.

    Bibliography: p.
    Includes index.

    1. Behaviorism.   2.   Conditioned response.
    3. Psychology.   I.   Leslie, Julian C., joint author.
    II. Title.
BF199.M48   1979   150'.19'43   78–17469
ISBN 0–02–381280–X

Printing: 1 2 3 4 5 6 7 8   Year: 9 0 1 2 3 4 5

ACKNOWLEDGMENTS

We wish to thank the following for permission to reproduce copyrighted material.

Academic Press: Figure 7.2 from B. R. Moore and Fig. 7.3, from P. Sevenster, both in R. A. Hinde and J. Stevenson-Hinde (eds.): *Constraints on Learning*, 1973. Fig. 9.4 from Horn, G., and Hill, R. M.: Responsiveness to sensory stimulation of units in the superior colliculus and subadjacent tectotegonental regions of the rabbit. *Experimental Neurology* 14: 199–233, 1966. Figures 12.2 and 12.3 from Hearst, E., in G. M. Bower (ed.): *The Psychology of Learning and Motivation*, vol. 9, 1975. Figure 18.3 from Warren, J. M. in A. M. Schrier et al. (eds.): *Behavior of Nonhuman Primates*, 1965. Figure 22.12 from Gray, J. A.: *Elements of a Two Process Theory of Learning*, 1975.
American Association for the Advancement of Science: From *Science*: Figure 10.4 from Gormezano, I., et al.: Nictitating membrane: classical conditioning and extinction in the albino rabbit. 138: 33–34, 1962. Figure 15.7 from Weitzman, E. D. et al., Behavioral method for study of pain in the monkey. 133: 37–38, 1961. Figure 22.9 from Hodos, W.: Progressive ratio as a measure of reward strength. 134: 943–944, 1961. Figure 24.5 from Skinner, B. F.: Teaching machines, 128: 969–977, 1958.
American Institute of Biological Sciences: Figure 21.8 from Richter, C.: Animal behavior and internal drives, *Quarterly Review of Biology*, 2: 307–343, 1927.
American Journal of Psychology: Figure 8.5 from Jacobson, E.: The electrophysiology of mental activities. 44: 677–694, 1932. Figures 16.1 and 16.2 from Brogden, W. J., et al.: The role of incentive in conditioning and extinction. 51: 109–117, 1938.
American Psychological Association: (1) From *Journal of Comparative and Physiological Psychology*: Figure 3.7 from Capehart, J., et al.: The effect of effort upon extinction. 51: 505–507, 1958. Figure 8.2 from Zimmerman, D. W.: Sustained performance in rats based on secondary reinforcement. 52: 353–358, 1959. Figure 10.6 from Rescorla, R. A.: Probability of

shock in the presence and absence of CS in fear conditioning. 66: 1–5, 1968. Figure 12.6 from Wasserman, E. A., et al.: Pavlovian appetitive contingencies and approach vs. withdrawal to conditioned stimuli in pigeons. 86: 616–627, 1974. Figure 14.1 from Herrick, R. M., et al.: Changes in S^D and S^Δ rates during the development of an operant discrimination. 52: 359–363, 1959. Figure 15.5 from Kaplan, M.: The effects of noxious stimulus intensity and duration during intermittent reinforcement of escape behavior. 45: 538–549, 1952. Figure 16.8 from Boren, J. J. and Sidman, M. A.: A discrimination based upon repeated conditioning and extinction of avoidance behavior. 50: 18–22, 1957. Figure 17.7 from Hunt, H. F. and Brady, J. V.: Some effects of electroconvulsive shock on a conditioned emotional response ("anxiety"). 44: 88–98, 1951. Figure 21.4 from Young, P. T. and Richey, H. W.: Diurnal drinking patterns in the rat. 45: 80–89, 1952. Figure 22.2 from Siegel, P. S.: The relationship between voluntary water intake, body weight loss and numbers of hours of water privation in the rat. 40: 231–238, 1947. Figure 22.11 from Olds, J. and Milner, P.: Positive reinforcement produced by electrical stimulation of septal area and other regions of rat brain. 47: 419–427, 1954. ——— (2) From *Journal of Experimental Psychology*: Figure 3.11 from Bullock, D. H., and Smith, W. C.: An effect of repeated conditioning extinction upon operant strength. 46: 349–352, 1953. Figure 10.9 from Grant, D. A. and Norris, E. B.: Eyelid conditioning as influenced by the presence of sensitized beta-responses. 37: 423–433, 1947. Figure 14.5 from Hanson, H. M.: Effects of discrimination training on stimulus generalization. 58: 321–334, 1959. Figure 21.2 from Webb, W. B.: Antecedents of sleep. 53: 162–166, 1957. ——— (3) Figure 17.2 from Dunham, P. J.: Punishment: method and theory. *Psychological Review* 78: 58–70, 1971. ——— (4) From *Journal of Personality and Social Psychology*: Figure 20.1 from Bandura, A.: Influence of model's reinforcement contingencies on the acquisition of imitative responses. 1: 589–595, 1965. Figure 20.2 from Bandura, A. and Menlove, F. L.: Factors determining vicarious extinction of avoidance behavior through symbolic modelling. 8: 99–108, 1968. Figure 25.3 from Bandura, A. et al.: The relative efficacy of desensitization and modelling approaches for induced, behavioral, affective and attitudinal change. 13: 173–199, 1969. ——— (5) Figure 24.11 from Bayley, N.: On the growth of intelligence. *American Psychologist* 10: 805–818, 1955.

American Physiological Society: Figure 21.3 from Anliker, J. and Mayer, J.: Operant conditioning technique for studying feeding patterns in normal and obese mice. *Journal of Applied Physiology* 8: 667–670, 1956.

American Speech and Hearing Association: Figure 2.9 from Irwin, O. C.: Infant speech: development of vowel sounds. *Journal of Speech and Hearing Disorders* 17: 269–279, 1952.

Ballière Tindall: Figure 9.3 from Cook, A.: Habituation of a freshwater snail (*Limnaea stagnalis*). *Animal Behaviour* 19: 463–474, 1971.

Cambridge University Press: Figure 13.12 from Staddon, J. E. R.: Limitations on temporal control: generalization and the effects of context. *British Journal of Psychology* 66: 229–246, 1975.

Canadian Journal of Psychology: Figure 16.5 from Kamin, L. J.: The effects of termination of the CS and avoidance of the US on avoidance learning: an extension. 11: 48–56, 1957.

Columbia University Press: Figure 22.8 from Warden, J. C.: *Animal Motivation Studies*. 1931.

R. Gerbrands and Company: Figure 2.3.

Harcourt Brace Jovanovich: Figure 24.12 from Cronbach, L. J.: *Educational Psychology*. New York, 1963.

Harper & Row: Figure 21.7 from Gross, C. G.: General activity. In Weiskrantz, L. (ed.): *Behavioral Change*. New York, 1968.

Houghton Mifflin Co.: Figures 18.9 and 18.11 from Gibson, J. J.: *The Perception of the Visual World*. Cambridge, Mass.: The Riverside Press, 1950. Figure 24.9 from Neisworth, J. T. and Smith, R. M.: *Modifying Retarded Behavior*. Boston, Mass.: Houghton Mifflin, 1973.

The Jester: Figure 2.10 from *The Jester* of Columbia College.

Journal of Applied Behavior Analysis: Figures 24.1 and 24.2 from McAllister, L. W., et al.: The application of operant conditioning techniques in a secondary school classroom. 2: 277–285, 1969.

Lawrence Erlbaum Associates: Figure 12.4 from Boakes, R. A.: Performance on learning to associate a stimulus with positive reinforcement. In Davis, H. and Hurwitz, H. M. B. (eds.): *Operant-Pavlovian Interactions*. Hillside, N.J.: Lawrence Erlbaum, 1977.

Macmillan Journal Limited (London): Figure 19.9 from Dennis, I., et al.: New problems in concept formation. *Nature* 243: 101–102, 1973.

McGraw-Hill, Inc.: Figure 7.1 from Skinner, B. F.: A case history in scientific method. In Koch. S. (ed.): *Psychology: A Study of a Science*, volume 2. New York: McGraw-Hill, 1959.

Methuen & Company Ltd.: Figure 7.4 from Blackman, D. E.: *Operant Conditioning: An Experimental Analysis of Behavior*. London: Methuen, 1974.

The New Yorker: Figure 3.19: Drawing by Opie, ©1961 by *The New Yorker* Magazine, Inc.

Pergamon Press: Figure 25.6 and Table 25.1 from Stuart, R. B.: A three-dimensional program for the treatment of obesity. *Behaviour Research and Therapy* 9: 177–186, 1971.

Plenum Publishing Company: Figure 25.5 from Baltzer, V., and Weiskrantz, L.: Antidepressant agents and reversal of diurnal activity cycles in the rat. *Biological Psychiatry* 10: 199–209, 1975.

Prentice-Hall, Inc.: Figure 1.4 from Garrett, H.: *Great Experiments in Psychology*. Appleton Century Crofts, 1951. Figures 2.4, 3.1, 3.10, 3.12, 8.1, 17.1, and 22.3 from Skinner, B. F.: *The Behavior of Organisms*. Appleton Century Crofts, 1938. Figures 3.9 and 4.2 from Hull, C. L.: *Principles of Behavior*. Appleton Century Crofts, 1943. Figures 5.3, 5.11, and 5.12 from Ferster, C. B. and Skinner, B. F.: *Schedules of Reinforcement*. Appleton Century Crofts, 1957. Figure 5.14 from Catania, A. C.: Concurrent operants. In Honig, W. K. (ed.): *Operant Behavior: Areas of Research and Application*. Appleton Century Crofts, 1966. Figure 13.5 from Lewis, D. J.: *Scientific Principles of Psychology*. Prentice-Hall, 1963. Figure 13.11 from Mackintosh, N. J.: Stimulus control. In Honig, W. K. and Staddon, J. E R. (eds.): *Handbook of Operant Behavior*. Prentice-Hall, 1977. Figure 14.7 from Rilling, M.: Stimulus control and inhibitory processes. In Honig and Staddon, *Handbook of Operant Behavior*. Prentice-Hall, 1977. Figure 16.7 from Sidman, M.: Avoidance behavior. In W. K. Honig (ed.): *Operant Behavior: Areas of Research and Application*. Appleton Century Crofts, 1966. Figure 17.3 from Rachlin, H., and Herrnstein, R. J.: Hedonism revisited: on the negative law of effect. In Campbell, B. A. and Church, R. M. (eds.): *Punishment and Aversive Behavior*. Prentice-Hall, 1969. Figure 17.4 from Azrin, N. H. and Holz, W. C.: Punishment. In Honig, W. K. (ed.): *Operant Behavior: Areas of Research and Application*. Appleton Century Crofts, 1966. Figure 17.6 from Morse, W. H. and Kelleher, R. T.: Schedules as fundamental determinants of behavior. In Schoenfeld, W. N. (ed.): *The Theory of Reinforcement Schedules*. Appleton Century Crofts, 1970. Figure 18.10 from Hochberg, J. E.: *Perception*. Prentice-Hall, 1964. Figure 23.6 from Blackman, D. E.: Conditioned suppression and the effects of classical conditioning on operant behavior. In Honig, W. K. and Staddon, J. E. R. (eds.): *Handbook of Operant Behavior*. Prentice-Hall, 1977. Figure 24.3 from Tribble, A., and Hall, R. V.: Effects of peer approval on completion of arithmetic assignments. In Clark, F. W. et al., (eds.): *Implementing Behavioral Programs for Schools and Clinics*. Champaign, Illinois: Research Press, 1972. Figure 25.4 from Maier, S. F. et al.: Pavlovian fear conditioning and learned helplessness: effects on escape and avoidance behavior. In Campbell, B. A. and Church, R. M. (eds.): *Punishment and Aversive Behavior*. Appleton Century Crofts, 1969.

Psychological Reports: Figure 13.8 from Guttman, N. The pigeon and the spectrum and other complexities. 2: 449–460, 1956. Figure 15.5 from Barry, J. J. and Harrison, J. M.: Relations between stimulus intensity and strength of escape responding. 3: 3–8, 1957. Figure 22.5 from Crocetti, C. P.: Drive level and response strength in the bar-pressing apparatus. 10: 563–575, 1962.

Quarterly Journal of Experimental Psychology: Figure 3.2 from Hurwitz, H. M. B.: Periodicity of response in operant extinction. 9: 177–184, 1957.

Random House/Alfred A. Knopf, Inc.: Figures 21.10 and 21.11 from Rosenzweig, M.: The mechanisms of hunger and thirst. in Postman, L. (ed.): *Psychology in the Making*. New York: Knopf, 1962.

The Ronald Press: Figures 18.6, 23.7, and 24.10 from Kimble, G. A. and Garmezy, N.: *Principles of General Psychology*. New York: Ronald Press, 1963.

Scott, Foresman and Co.: Figures 5.9 and 5.15 from Reynolds, G. S.: *A Primer of Operant Conditioning*, second edition. Glenview, Ill.: Scott, Foresman, 1975.

Society for Child Development: Figure 24.13 from McCall, R. B., et al.: Developmental changes in mental performance. *Child Development Monographs* 38(3): 1–84, 1973.

Society for Exceptional Children: Figures 24.4 and Table 24.1 from Alexander, R. N. and Apfel, C. H.: Altering schedules of reinforcement for improved classroom behavior. *Exceptional Children* 43: 97–99, 1976.

Society for the Experimental Analysis of Behavior: all from *Journal of the Experimental Analysis of Behavior*: Figures 3.5 from Eckerman, D. A. and Lanson, R. N.: Variability of response location for pigeons responding under continuous reinforcement, intermittent reinforcement and extinction. 12: 73–80, 1969. Figure 3.6 from Azrin, N. H. et al.: Extinction-induced aggression. 9: 191–204, 1966. Figure 3.18 from Shimp, C. P.: Short-term memory in the pigeon: relative recency. 25: 55–61, 1976. Figure 4.5 from Herrick, R. M.: The successive differentiation of a lever displacement response. 7: 211–215, 1964. Figure 4.7 from Hefferline, R. F. and Keenan, B.: Amplitude-induction gradient of a small-scale (covert) operation. 6: 307–315, 1963. Figure 5.4 from Cumming, W. W. and Schoenfeld, W. N.: Behavior under extended exposure to a high-value fixed interval reinforcement schedule. 1: 245–263, 1958. Figure 6.3 from Catania, A. C. and Reynolds, G. S.: A quantitative analysis of the responding maintained by interval schedules of reinforcement. 11: 327–383, 1968. Figures 6.4 and 6.5 from Herrnstein, R. J.: Relative and absolute strength of response as a function of frequency of reinforcement. 4: 267–272, 1961. Figure 7.5 from Schwartz, B. and Williams, D. R.: Discrete trials space responding in the pigeon: the dependence of efficient performance on the availability of a stimulus for collateral pecking. 16: 155–160, 1971. Figure 8.3 from Kelleher, R.: Conditioned reinforcement in second-order schedules. 9: 475–485, 1966. Figure 12.1 from Brown P. L., and Jenkins, H. M.: Autoshaping of the pigeon's key peck. 11: 1–8, 1968. Figure 12.5 from Jenkins, H. M. and Moore, B. R.: The form of the auto-shaped response with food or water reinforcers. 20: 163–181, 1973. Figure 13.10 from Blough, D.: The shape of some wavelength generalization gradients. 4: 31–40, 1961. Figure 14.6 from Thomas, D. R. and Williams, J. L.: A further study of stimulus generalization following three-stimulus discrimination training. 6: 171–176, 1963. Figure 14.8 from Hearst, E. et al.; Inhibition and the stimulus control of operant behavior. 14: 373–409, 1970. Figures 15.4 and 15.5 from Dinsmoor, J. A. and Winograd, E.: Shock intensity in variable interval escape schedules. 1: 145–148, 1958. Figure 16.6 from Verhave, T.: Avoidance responding as a function of simultaneous and equal changes in two temporal parameters. 2: 185–190, 1959. Figure 16.9 from Badia, P., et al.; Choice of longer or stronger signalled shocks over shorter or weaker unsignalled shock. 19: 25–32, 1973. Figure 16.10 from Herrnstein, R. J. and Hineline, P. N.: Negative reinforcement as shock-frequency reduction. 9: 421–430, 1966, Figure 16.11 from deVilliers, P. A.: The law of effect in avoidance: a quantitative relationship between response rate and shock frequency reduction. 21: 223–235, 1974. Figure 16.14 from Gardner, E. T. and Lewis, P.: Negative reinforcement with shock-frequency increase. 25: 3–14, 1976. Figure 17.5 from Bradshaw, C. M., et al.: Effects of punishment on human variable-interval performance. 27: 275–280, 1977, Figure 17.8 from Blackman, D. E.: Conditioned suppression or acceleration as a function of the behavior baseline. 11: 53–61, 1968. Figure 20.3 from Gladstone, E. W. and Cooley, J.: Behavioral similarity as a reinforcer for preschool children. 23: 357–368, 1975. Figure 20.4 from Baer, D. et al.: The development of imitation by reinforcing behavioral similarity to a model. 10: 405–416, 1967. Figure 22.1 from Reese, T. W. and Hogenson, M. J.: Food satiation in the pigeon. 5: 239–245, 1962. Figure 22.4 from Clark, F. C.: The effect of deprivation and frequency of reinforcement on variable interval responding. 1: 221–228, 1958. Figure 23.4 from Dove, L. D. et al.: Development and maintenance of attack in pigeons during variable-interval reinforcement of key pecking. 21: 563–570, 1974. Figure 23.5 from Hynan, M. T.: the influence of the victim on shock-induced aggression in rats. 25: 401–409, 1976. Figure 25.1 from Ayllon, T. and Azrin, N. H.: The measurement and reinforcement of behavior of psychotics. 8: 357–383, 1965.

Teachers College Press, Teachers College of Columbia University: Figure 25.3 from Jersild, A. T. and Holmes, F. B.: *Children's Fears*, 1935.

University of Chicago Press: Figure 21.1 from Kleitman, N.: *Sleep and Wakefulness*. University of Chicago Press, 1963.

University of Wisconsin and H. F. Harlow: Figure 18.4.

D. Van Nostrand Co., Inc.: Figure 3.16 from Guilford, J. P.: *General Psychology*. Princeton: Van Nostrand, 1939.

Wadsworth Publishing Company: Figure 21.9 from Sanford, F.: *Psychology, A Scientific Study of Man*. Belmont, Calif.: Wadsworth Publishing Company, 1961.

John Wiley & Sons, Inc.: Figures 13.4 and 13.6 from Boring, E. G., et al.: *Foundations of Psychology*, 1948. Figure 19.8 from Bruner, J. S., et al.: *A Study of Thinking*, 1956. Figure 23.1 and Table 23.3 from Young, P. T.: *Motivation and Emotion*, 1961. Figure 24.7 from Lysaught, J. P. and Williams, C. M.: *A Guide to Programmed Instruction*, 1963.

TO DIANE

PREFACE TO THE SECOND EDITION

Like its predecessor, the aim of this second edition of *Principles of Behavioral Analysis* is to provide a rigorous, data-oriented introduction to behavioral psychology. The success of the first edition confirmed our view, only a speculation in 1967, that a vacuum existed for an undergraduate introductory text offering a systematic grounding in the concepts and methods of The Experimental Analysis of Behavior (TEAB). Now, more than a decade later, TEAB has established itself solidly within the mainstream of experimental psychology and has proliferated widely through far-reaching applications to education, industry, the mental health clinic, and the design of communities.

The instructor now has a number of modern texts from which to choose. Still, the systematic fashion with which *Principles of Behavioral Analysis* integrated the wide field from conditioning and learning to intelligence and problem solving via perception and motivation remained unique. Even so, no scientific text bearing the date 1967 can postpone obsolescence indefinitely, especially one in a field that has burgeoned so rapidly and extensively as TEAB. New data have poured in from all the areas represented by the chapter headings of the first edition of this text. In turn, new concepts have crystallized, virgin areas have opened up, and significant shifts in theoretical perspective have occurred. For some time now these events and developments have supplied pressure for a thoroughgoing revision of the first edition.

The present edition, therefore, grows out of this need to accommodate significant change, while retaining the unity and coherence of the original text. Thus, this edition preserves the basic principle that early chapters serve to introduce basic concepts and methods that the later chapters build on in their discussions of more sophisticated and complex areas of psychology. With one major exception this edition adheres closely to the chapter sequence of the first edition. We have found it expedient to discuss operant paradigms at length before turning to classical conditioning. So much of the new data on association has arisen as byproducts of operant conditioning that it cannot readily be understood without a background in operant methodology.

The expansion of this edition to include many new experimental areas and concepts has resulted in seven entirely new chapters. In order to keep the text manageable for a two-semester undergraduate course we elected to delete the statistical and notational sections of the first edition. The material of both of these sections is readily available elsewhere from a variety of specialized texts. In compensation, the second edition offers substantially expanded and modernized discussions of associative processes, aversive contingencies, and behavior modification. The latter, a hopeful promise in 1967, has become a vigorous technology of behavior in the '70s.

Entirely new chapters have been created to integrate sign tracking, modeling, and interoceptive conditioning into the basic framework, which remains that of the first edition: translating the principal concepts of psychology into the language of behavior. We have brought other chapters up to date by inclusion of new experimental data on adjunctive behavior, operant conditioning of autonomic responses, safety signals, learned helplessness, response and reinforcer preparedness, and a discussion of the quantification of the law of effect.

A modern revision of any textbook in this field requires, however, considerably more than a mere appending of recent empirical findings to an unchanging conceptual base. About a decade ago the landscape of behavioral analysis began to undergo a radical and thoroughgoing change. In 1967, TEAB meant reinforcement theory. And reinforcement theory meant B. F. Skinner. The first edition of *Principles of Behavioral Analysis* primarily represented an introduction to the principles of operant behavior and scientific method drawn from Skinner's ground-breaking work begun in the early 30s of this century. "Skinner for beginners," some wag quipped. J. D. Keehn (Gilbert and Keehn, 1972) rightly identified *Principles of Behavioral Analysis* as the first textbook to employ the law of effect as a scientific paradigm (Kuhn, 1970) in which reinforcement, no longer taken as a problem for explanation, had become the keystone explaining a host of animal and human activities. In our compendium of "normal science" we set up reinforcement as a primitive concept, examined all of the phenomena of our science in terms of it, and boldly interpolated the laboratory principles to the real world wherever plausible. In 1967 the law of effect reigned supreme in the land of behavioral analysis. Few insiders could see effective challenges to its continuing hegemony, and it appeared that the future for some time to come would remain dominated by its systematic elaboration, expansion, and application.

Strangely enough, this prediction was fulfilled, yet at the same time the law of effect became displaced as the monolithic explanatory mechanism in TEAB. By 1967, the value of Pavlov's principles, which had dominated the scene of learning theory throughout the early part of the century, had become so eroded that we used them primarily to describe a handful of apparently isolated and relatively unimportant autonomic reflexes. Knee jerks and salivary secretions seemed a long way from concept learning, problem solving, discrimination performances, and skills acquisition. Some modern theorists had attempted to use Pavlovian mechanisms to explain motivation, emotion, and even language, but the accounts bore a highly speculative flavor, not readily palatable to the new generation of empiricists eager to demonstrate the great power of reinforcement schedules to control and manipulate behavior.

In ten years all this was to change, for as the contents of this current edition attest, Pavlov's star is once more in ascendency. Two-factor theory—Skinner's learning by the consequences of action combined with Pavlov's acquisition of new stimulus properties by association—has grown to impressive dimensions in D. Anger's elegant explication of avoidance and punishment (in press), and by its natural application to conditioned reinforcement. In this past decade, too, we have discovered and elaborated new associative phenomena—sign tracking, autoshaping, interoceptive conditioning, adjunctive behavior—that markedly influence those behaviors we once called operant and imagined were susceptible only to reinforcement. These influences and their interactions justify Pavlov's early enthusiasm for conditioning as a fundamental principle of behavioral analysis, germane to all human and higher animal behavior.

A revolution has been occurring in behavioral analysis. Reinforcement as the sole explanatory paradigm has had to make room for association as a companion explanatory principle. And both of these ontogenetic factors have had to yield ground to phylogenetic concepts capturing the importance of the organism's wired-in structure, long neglected by psychologists. This structure has highly prepared the organism to learn some responses with some reinforcers but not others, and it has provided a high degree of inherent selectivity in the association of stimuli (Seligman, 1970). The action of reinforcement is not like mechanical action (Shettleworth, 1973) and to understand the processes of discrimination and motivation we cannot ignore the context of the species' evolutionary development and its particular ecological niche. While remaining couched in the objective language of science, our theories have begun to reflect the biological fact that the organism is an information processor.

Yet along with the new emphasis on association and the renewed respect for the organism's biology, reinforcement theory has not remained quiescent. The early preoccupation with impressive feats of control of rat and pigeon outputs has given way to a deeper study of the quantitative nature of the law of effect and the rise of a true calculus of choice behavior (Herrnstein, 1970). Reinforcement may aptly be said in 1979 to explain relatively fewer things than it did in 1967, yet to explain those fewer far more comprehensively. Moreover, the extension of reinforcement mechanisms to the autonomic nervous system represents an important new growth area for the law of effect, one that completes the symmetry of reciprocal encroachment of associative and reinforcement mechanisms on each other's once sovereign territories.

As this second edition illustrates, TEAB is alive and well and flourishing in many new and all the old areas of experimental psychology. Its applications continue to expand in education and mental health fields, and the early exaggerated concern with control has begun to yield to humanistic pressures demanding the controllee's active participation and cooperation with the controller.

In this volume we have preserved the unified flavor of the first edition by interweaving the new with the old, by continuing to emphasize conceptual issues at the expense of exhaustive coverage, and by retaining the original thoroughgoing objective stance. Behavior remains our primary datum, and the principles continue to come from environmental manipulations. But we speak now of intervening variables, of interactions of processes, of multiply determined repertoires. Gone are the days of heroic optimism and their fantasy that the complexity of man's behavior might yield to a complete explanation in terms of a few elementary principles of reinforcement. Our touchstone now is the fundamental question: "What are the reinforcement, associative, and structural factors germane to this or that particular piece of observed behavior?" Though the world of behavioral analysis appears more complex, more scattered, and with far more loose ends in 1979 than it did in 1967, that can only augur for the better.

Over the past decade, invaluable interactions with John Falk, Dore Gormezano, Dick Herrnstein, Dick Solomon, John Staddon, and Dave Williams have significantly shaped our thinking about behavior science, and their influences are reflected in this edition. While we know that many of the strengths of this volume are due to them, we hope they will forgive whatever distortions of their ideas we may have inadvertently introduced. We owe a special debt to June Anderson and Margaret Beckett who typed the entire manuscript, and to Paul Poots and Sabrina Campbell who critically read it. Michael Keenan, Stuart Margulies, Paula Pasquali, Jill Sharpe, Teresa Arauja Silva, Steve Pinker, João Claudio Todorov, Peter de Villiers, Alina Wydra, and our ever congenial editor, Clark Baxter, all contributed in various essential ways in bringing this edition to fruition.   J. R. M.
                                                                    J. C. L.

CONTENTS

Chapter 6
Quantifying the Law of Effect   111

Chapter 7
Species-Typical Behavior and Operant Conditioning   131

Chapter 8
Conditioned Reinforcement and Chaining   145

PART THREE: ASSOCIATIVE PROCESSES
Chapter 9
Reflexes   167

REMARKS TO STUDENTS

Introductory psychology may be construed as an introduction to the methods and principles of the scientific analysis of behavior. Although older definitions of psychology emphasized the "mental processes," for reasons that will be made clear throughout this text a modern approach to psychology takes the *behavior* of humans as well as lower animals as its subject matter. Holding fast to the canon that only what can be observed can be studied scientifically, this modern viewpoint attacks traditional psychological problems through the medium of behavioral analysis. In the course of the text we shall find ourselves studying and representing in the language of behavior such topics as learning and memory, problem solving and intelligence, sensation and perception, and emotion and motivation.

The organization of this book will permit you to arrive at a preliminary understanding of the basic principles of human behavior. Although many of the fundamental concepts and paradigms that are treated in detail were originally derived from laboratory experiments with animal subjects, they are by no means limited to animals. We employ animal subjects in psychological research for pragmatic reasons: a twentieth-century human being would be unlikely to submit freely to the long-range environmental control necessary for a scientific study; and even if he would, society would not permit him.

In order to acquire an understanding of the causes of human and animal behavior, you will first have to acquire a technical vocabulary and a thorough familiarity with the basic concepts of psychology. There is no known short-cut to this vocabulary. You must learn it in much the same way that, in preparation for playing winning chess, you must learn the names and permissible moves of the pieces, the most common openings, and the basic principles of attack and defense.

When approaching psychology, you may suffer a peculier handicap that is absent in your initial learning of chess. Certain preconceived opinions and views about the causes of behavior that are a standard part of the everyday common-sense interpretation of the world may first have to be unlearned. Unfortunately, this common-sense view of human nature is not always the most useful for formulating a systematic science of the relations between behavior and its controlling variables. You will do well, therefore, to try to put aside your preconceptions about people's actions, and in particular your representation system of their so-called inner mental processes. Try rather to approach the subject matter with a fresh point of view, contending yourself initially with merely asking simple-minded questions such as "What was the organism observed to do?" and "What is related consistently to its doing that?" Your progress may seem slow at first, but it will always be sure.

J. R. M.
J. C. L.

PART ONE

Introduction

CHAPTER 1

The Scientific Approach to Behavior

When Socrates heard about the new discoveries in anatomy that purported to prove that the causes of bodily movement were due to an ingenious mechanical arrangement of muscle, bone, and joints, he remarked: "That hardly explains why I am sitting here in a curved position . . . talking to you" (Kantor,1963). It is 2,300 years since Socrates' complaint, and in the intervening centuries the causes of human behavior have been attributed to the tides, the divine soul, the position of the stars, and frequently simply to caprice. The last hundred years have seen the rise of a *science* of behavior bringing with it a fresh conceptual framework with new attitudes toward the causes of behavior. A brief history of the events which led to the development of this science makes an apt prelude to its study. For just as there is no better way to understand the present activities of a person than through an acquaintance with his or her past history, so too there is no better way to understand the present activities of a science than through an acquaintance with its past.

1.1

Early Attempts to Explain Human Behavior

It is never possible to identify precisely the moment at which interest in a particular subject began, but we do know that by 325 B.C. in ancient Greece, Aristotle had combined observation and interpretation into a naturalistic, if primitive, system of behavior. Aristotle sought the causes of (1) body movements, and (2) the discriminations made by organisms. He described many categories of behavior, such as sense perception, sight, smell, hearing, common sense, simple and complex thinking, appetite, memory, sleep, and dreaming. His topics ring familiar to us today, for they are still to be found in some form or other in nearly every comprehensive text of psychology. Aristotle was less interested in the prediction and control of nature than we are today, and consequently, his explanations of behavior have a less modern flavor. Aristotle was concerned with explaining the various activities of an individual by showing them to be specific instances of general "qualities", such as appetite, passion, reason, will, and sense-ability (Toulmin and Goodfield, 1962).

The observations and classifications of Aristotle and the Greek investigators who followed him represented a substantial beginning in a naturalistic attempt to understand the causes of human and animal behavior. But the new science declined with the demise of Hellenic civilization. The early Christian era and the Middle Ages produced an intellectual climate poorly suited to observation and investigation: man turned his attention to metaphysical matters. The Church Fathers began, and the medieval theologians completed, a conceptual transformation of Aristotle's purely abstract "quality" of mind into a supernatural entity named the soul. The causation of human behavior was entirely attributed to the soul, but the soul was regarded as *non*-material, *in*-substantial and *super*-natural. This *dualistic* doctrine stated that there was no direct connection between soul and body, and that each inhabited a separate realm. By locating the causes of behavior in the unobservable realm of the spirit or soul, dualism inhibited a naturalistic study of behavior, and for a very long time, no interest was taken in an empirical or observational approach to behavior. We have to jump forward to the seventeenth century, the time of Galileo and the rise of modern physics, to pick up the threads that were eventually to be rewoven into a scientific fabric.

The work of René Descartes (1596–1650), the French philosopher and mathematician, represents a critical point in the development of a science of behavior. Although Descartes produced one of the clearest statements of the dualistic position, he also advanced psychological science by suggesting that bodily movement might be the result of mechanical, rather than super-natural, causes.

Descartes was familiar with the mechanical figures in the royal gardens at Versailles that could move and produce sounds, and observations of these probably prompted him to put forward a mechanical account of behavior. The machines in the royal gardens worked on mechanical principles. Water was pumped through concealed tubes to inflate the limbs of the figures, producing movement, or was conducted through devices that emitted words or music as the water flowed by. Descartes imagined that animals and man might be a kind of complex machine, analogously constructed. He substituted animal spirits, a sort of intangible, invisible elastic substance, for the water of the Royal Figures and supposed the spirits to flow in the nerves in such a way as to enter the muscles, thereby causing them to expand and contract, and in turn make the limbs move.

Some of the Royal Figures were so arranged that if passersby chanced to tread on hidden tiles, hydraulic mechanisms caused the figures to approach or withdraw. Descartes took this mechanical responsiveness as a model for explaining how an external environmental *stimulus* might cause a bodily movement. An illustration (see Figure 1.1) in one of his works shows a

FIGURE 1.1.

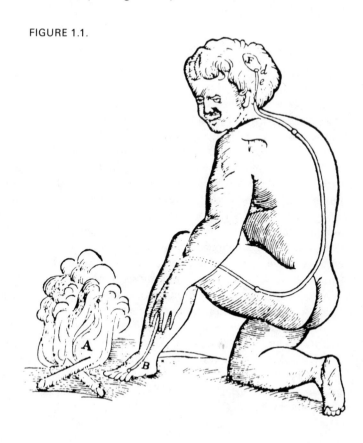

withdrawal of a human limb from a flame. According to Descartes, the "machine of our body is so formed that the heat of the flame excites a nerve which conducts that excitation to the brain. From the brain, animal spirits are then passed out, or *reflected* back via that nerve to the limb, enlarging the muscle, and so causing a contraction and withdrawal" (Fearing, 1930).

Descartes' willingness to view human behavior as determined by natural forces was only partial. He confined his mechanical hypotheses to certain "involuntary" activities and supposed the rest to be governed by the soul, located in the brain. The soul guided even the mechanisms of the "involuntary" activities, much in the way an engineer might have directed the workings of the Royal Figures.

In spite of this dualism, and in spite of his choice of a hydraulic principle, Descartes' formulation represented an advance over earlier thinking about behavior. The theory of the body as a specific kind of machine *was one that was testable by observation and experiment*. That was the property so conspicuously lacking in medieval explanations. In reestablishing the idea that at least some of the causes of animal and human behavior might be found in the observable environment, Descartes laid the philosophical foundations that would eventually lead to an experimental approach to behavior.

1.2
Reflex Action

Descartes' views symbolize the new interest in mechanism that was to lead to experimentation on "reflected" animal action. Even so, a century elapsed before a Scottish physiologist, Robert Whytt, experimentally rediscovered and extended Descartes' principle of the stimulus in 1750. By observing systematic contraction of the pupil of the eye of light, salivation to irritants, and various other *reflexes*, Whytt was able to state a necessary relationship between two separate events: an external stimulus (for example, a light) and a bodily response (for example, a pupil contraction). Moreover, Whytt's demonstration that a number of reflexes could be elicited in the decapitated frog weakened the attractiveness of a soul explanation. Yet the eighteenth century was not quite able to regard the stimulus alone as a sufficient cause of behavior in an intact, living organism. The soul, thought Whytt, probably diffused itself throughout the spinal cord and the brain, thereby retaining master control of reflexes.

In the ensuing 150 years, more and more reflex relationships were discovered and elaborated, and the concept of the stimulus grew increasingly powerful. At the same time, nerve action became understood as an electrical system and the older hydraulic or mechanical models were discarded. By the end of the nineteenth century, spiritual direction had become superfluous for "involuntary action," and Sir Charles Sherrington, the celebrated English physiologist, could summarize the principles of reflex behavior in quantitative stimulus-response laws. These laws relate the speed, magnitude, and probability of the reflex response to the intensity, frequency, and other measurable properties of the stimulus.

The anatomy of an example of the simplest type of reflex, consisting of two nerve cells or *neurons*, is shown in Figure 1.2. One neuron (the afferent) transmits neural impulses resulting from the stimulus to the spinal cord and the other (the efferent) runs from the spinal cord back to the muscle. Firing of the efferent neuron results in a motor response of the muscle.

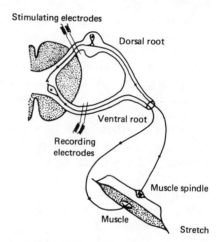

FIGURE 1.2.
A simple reflex and its connections to the spinal cord.

By 1900, there could be no doubt that reflexive behavior was a suitable subject for scientific analysis and that analysis was well advanced. However, reflexes clearly accounted for only a small proportion of the behavior of human beings and higher animals, and it had yet to be established that the remainder could be subjected to the same sort of analysis.

1.3
Acquired or Conditioned Reflexes

Just before the beginning of the twentieth century, Ivan Pavlov, the Russian physiologist, was investigating the digestive secretions of dogs. In the course of these experiments, he noticed that while the introduction of food or acid into the mouth resulted in a flow of saliva, the mere appearance of the experimenter bringing food would also elicit a similar flow. Pavlov was by no means the first man to make observations of this sort; but he seems to have been the first to suspect that their detailed study might provide a clue to the understanding of adjustive and adaptive behavior of organisms. It was this insight that led him to a systematic study of these reflexes, which he called *conditional reflexes*, because they depended or were conditional upon some previous events in the life of the organism. The appearance of the experimenter had not originally elicited saliva. It was only after his appearance had been frequently associated with food or acid that it had this effect. Pavlov's unique contribution was to show experimentally how conditioned reflexes came to be acquired, how they could be removed (extinguished), and what range of stimuli was effective in their production. In time, Pavlov was to lay down a general law of conditioning: after repeated temporal association of two stimuli, the one that occurs first comes eventually to elicit the response that is normally elicited by the second stimulus. Somewhat modified, this law is with us today.

Three general aspects of Pavlov's work deserve our close attention. First, he was not satisfied merely to observe the gross aspects of conditioning, as many others had done before him (c.f. Hall and Hodge, 1890). Instead, he proceeded to verify the generality of the phenomenon using many stimuli and many dogs. It was only after numerous demonstrations that he encoded what he had discovered in a law—applicable, he thought, to all stimuli and all higher organisms. Second, Pavlov concerned himself with the measurable, or quantitative, aspects of the phenomenon. His measurable quantities, such as amount of salivation and number of reflex pairings, proved useful in providing a detailed analysis of conditioning. A third aspect of Pavlov's work concerned its systematic nature. By confining his studies to the effects of numerous conditions on a single quantity (amount of salivation), Pavlov assured that his experimental findings would be interrelated, and therefore, more meaningful.

Pavlov saw clearly how the explanation of behavior must proceed.

> The naturalist must consider only one thing: what is the relation of this or that external reaction of the animal to the phenomena of the external world? This response may be extremely complicated in comparison with the reaction of any inanimate object, but the principle involved remains the same.
>
> Strictly speaking, natural science is under obligation to determine only the precise connection which exists between a given natural phenomenon and the response of the living organism to that phenomenon . . . (Pavlov, 1928, p. 82).

And yet, in spite of his own stated interest in the relation of environment and response, Pavlov increasingly came to regard conditioning as a study of brain function. His explanations tended to be in terms of hypothetical brain processes. But in fact, Pavlov rarely measured any actual relationships between brain and behavior, so that these explanations were as fictional as the earlier soul explanations. In trying to explain away behavior by appealing to unknown brain functions, he was avoiding a direct description of behavior itself, thus violating one of his own dicta: that we need only determine "the precise connection which exists between a given natural phenomenon and the response of the living organism to that phenomenon."

Very often, major advances in a field are the result of, or are accompanied by, methodological innovations. This is certainly true in the case of Pavlov and conditioned reflexes. Pavlov's typical experimental arrangement is illustrated in Figure 1.3. Pavlov discovered that *controlled conditions* were essential for successful behavioral experimentation. His dogs had to be kept in steady temperatures and in sound-proof chambers for the experiments, during which stimuli were presented in a controlled fashion and responses recorded in ways which did not interfere too much with the subject. He also realized that only dogs in good general health made satisfactory subjects.

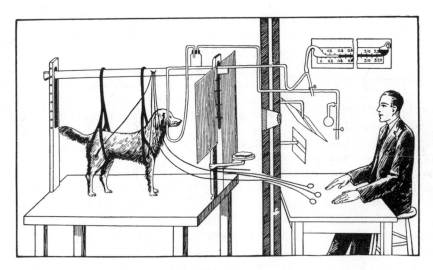

FIGURE 1.3. A typical experimental arrangement for conditioning salivation in Pavlov's laboratory. The dog is restrained and isolated so that experimental stimuli can be carefully presented and irrelevant stimuli excluded.

1.4

Evolutionary Theory and Adaptive Behavior

Pavlov's work showed how "new" reflexes could be acquired to supplement those "built-in" reflexes that the organism possesses prior to any appreciable experience of the world. As such, it represents the culmination of Descartes' mechanistic view of reflex behavior. However, only those responses that form part of an existing reflex can become conditioned reflexes, and thus, much nonreflexive behavior still remains to be scientifically analyzed. This behavior comes into the category traditionally described as voluntary, or under the control of the will, and it is just this category that Descartes assigned to the control of an unobservable soul. Descartes' maneuver only postponed a scientific inquiry, however, because we are now faced with the difficult problem of describing the relations between the soul which we cannot observe, and the patterns of behavior, which we do observe.

The view that voluntary human behavior was not a suitable subject for a scientific study was assailed in 1859. In that year, Charles Darwin proposed his theory of evolution, holding that man was a member of the animal kingdom, and that differences between man and other animals were quantitative and matters of degree. As a distinguished historian of psychology put it:

> The theory of evolution raised the problem of animal psychology because it demands continuity between different animal forms and between man and the animals. In a vague way the Cartesian (Descartes') notion still prevailed. Man possessed a soul and the animals were believed to be soulless; and there was, moreover, little distinction then made between a soul and a mind. Opposition to the theory of evolution was based primarily upon its assumption of continuity between man and the brutes, and the obvious reply to criticism was to demonstrate the continuity. The exhibition of mind in animals and of the continuity between the animal and the human mind thus became crucial to the life of the new theory (Boring, 1929, pp. 462–463).

Darwin's theory derived support from the many careful observations that he had made of fossils and the structure of flora and fauna living in isolated areas of the earth. In addition, he had investigated the behavior by which animals adapted to their environments. Darwin's behavioral observations were so comprehensive and detailed as to mark the first systematic attempt at a comparative animal psychology (see Darwin, 1873).

Darwin's interest in behavior was, as Boring noted, based on what it could reveal about mind. Thus, the demonstration of complexity and variety in adaptive behavior of animals in relation to their changing environments seemed to prove that they, like men, must also think, have ideas, and feel desires. Eventually, Darwin was to be criticized for his *anthropomorphism*, that is, for trying to explain animal behavior in terms of mentalistic concepts. But few thought at the time to raise the far more radical methodological question: whether the traditional mentalistic concepts (thoughts, ideas, desires) have explanatory value even for human behavior.

Darwin's friend, George John Romanes, an English writer and popularizer of science, wrote a book on animal intelligence (Romanes, 1886) in which he compared the behavior of various species of animals. Romanes gathered material from careful observation of animals, but he also took evidence from popular accounts of pets and circus animals. For this reason, his method has come to be called *anecdotal*. The anthropomorphic and anecdotal methods of Darwin and Romanes, respectively, marked the renewal of interest in adaptive animal behavior and its relation to human behavior, and therefore, represent important historical precursors of a truly *experimental* analysis of behavior. The crucial conceptual change had occurred. Animal and human behavior was now approached from a scientific point of view and in a biological context.

1.5
Analyzing "Voluntary" Behavior

In 1898, Edward L. Thorndike of Columbia University published the results of a number of laboratory studies on kittens, dogs, and chicks. His methods departed radically from those of the casual observers who had preceded him. Thorndike's apparatus is shown in Figure 1.4. The behavior studied was escape from a confining enclosure, and the acts, such as pulling a string, moving a latch, pressing a lever, or prying open a lock, were chosen for their convenience and reliability of observation. Since any of these responses could be arranged to be instrumental in producing escape from the box, Thorndike classed them as *instrumental behavior*.

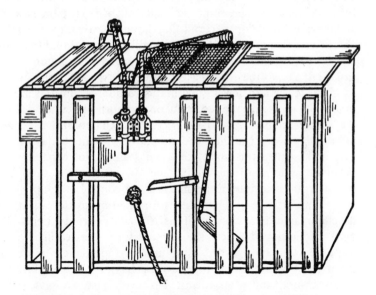

FIGURE 1.4. Thorndike's puzzle box for studying instrumental behavior of animals. Escape from the box was made contingent on various responses (Garrett, 1951).

Four aspects of Thorndike's work on instrumental behavior gave it a modern quality not seen in earlier investigations.

1. He recognized the importance of making observations of animals whose *past histories were known* and were more or less uniform. Thus,

he raised his animals in the laboratory, where they would obtain similar environmental conditions prior to experimentation.

2. Thorndike understood the necessity for making *repeated observations* on individual animals, and making observations on more than one animal in more than one species. In only this way, could he be sure the results he obtained were applicable to animals in general.
3. Thorndike saw that unless he considered more than one particular response, his conclusions would hold only for the single bit of behavior he chose. Thus, he examined *diverse* responses in several different pieces of apparatus.
4. Still another quality of Thorndike's work, and one which we have come to recognize as characteristic of science, was his attempt to make a *quantitative presentation* of his findings.

From his work with animals in puzzle boxes, Thorndike derived a number of principles or general laws of behavior which he believed held for many species and for many kinds of behavior. One of these, in a somewhat modified form, has come down to us today. Thorndike noticed that when animals were first put into the puzzle box, they made many diffuse struggling responses. Eventually, one of these responses would chance to trip the escape mechanism and the door would open, permitting the animal to escape from the box and to obtain a small quantity of food. Thorndike observed that the behavior which first let the animal out was only one of many that the animal made in the situation. Yet, as the animal was repeatedly exposed to the situation, it came to make fewer and fewer superfluous responses, until eventually, it made practically none save the successful ones. Thorndike concluded from this that the successful past results or *effects* of behavior must be an important influence in determining the animal's present behavioral tendencies. Thorndike called this ability of the past effects of behavior to modify the behavior patterns of the animal the *law of effect*. It survives today as a fundamental principle in the analysis and control of adaptive behavior.

The importance of Thorndike's formulation of the law of effect for the development of behavioral analysis lies in its generality. Unlike Pavlov's laws of the conditioned reflex, the law of effect was readily applied to those responses usually regarded as voluntary. Indeed, it is more applicable to that type of behavior than to reflexive behavior which is relatively insensitive to its consequences or effects. However, just as Pavlov presented his behavioral findings wrapped up in superfluous neurophysiological speculations, Thorndike claimed that "effects," such as escaping from a box or receiving food, did not influence behavior directly. Rather, they were supposed to be influential because they resulted in pleasure or satisfaction, and the burden of explanation was passed onto these hypothetical mental states which were regarded as the true causes of changes in behavior. For Thorndike, as for his contemporaries, the behavior of the cat in escaping from the puzzle box was not important as behavior, but only as a means of shedding light on the mental processes and associations of ideas of the animal. Nevertheless, just as Pavlov's laws of the conditioned reflex are important independent of his neurophysiological theory, so Thorndike's law of effect remains an important behavioral principle, even when Thorndike's mentalistic assumptions are removed.

Thorndike went along with his times and traditions in viewing behavior as interesting principally for what it revealed about some other system. The constraints by which the times and traditions bind even the most original of thinkers are often referred to as the *Zeitgeist*. The great men of an era will rise above their *Zeitgeist* in some ways, yet be bound by it in others. Descartes rose above it when he propounded an original mechanistic theory of bodily movement. That he was bound by the *Zeitgeist* is evident in his retention of the earlier "soul-body" dualism. We see the *Zeitgeist* in Whytt, who rediscovered the principle of the stimulus, but was unable to relinquish the soul as the final cause of the reflexes he observed. Pavlov studied conditioned reflexes, a phenomenon whose importance had been neglected for centuries. Yet, Pavlov was bound by the *Zeitgeist*; he held the view that conditioned reflexes, though manifestly a behavioral phenomenon, were of interest for the understanding of the brain rather than behavior. Now we see the *Zeitgeist* in Thorndike, who performed some of the earliest experiments in "voluntary" behavior, but explained away his findings by appeal to the association of ideas. In fact, the *Zeitgeist* principle is so pervasive in all of science that we may take as a general rule that every scientist's work will be colored by the accepted theories and viewpoints of their time. Thus, while a particular person's greatness is that they free themself from certain established modes of thinking and sees what no one before them has seen as clearly or in the same way, they will not completely escape the social, philosophical, and cultural climate in which they work. This chapter charts the evolution of the psychological *Zeitgeist* from its prescientific origins to its present state.

1.6
The Behaviorist Revolution

Thorndike initiated the laboratory study of behavior which is adaptive; that is, behavior which enables an organism to adjust rapidly to the prevailing environmental conditions, and comes into the category often described as "voluntary." In so doing, he discovered the law of effect and this discovery has had a profound influence on the subsequent development of behavioral analysis. However, Thorndike's own interest in behavior arose from his concern as a psychologist with mental processes. It will, therefore, be instructive at this point to describe the discipline of psychology in which Thorndike was immersed, and which began to merge early in the twentieth century with other tributaries of behavioral science.

Experimental psychological research began in the middle of the nineteenth century as a discipline growing out of the physiology of the sense organs. In fact, its early pioneers, Hermann Helmholtz, Johannes Müller, and Wilhelm Wundt, were all physicists and physiologists. These early experimental psychologists adopted the categories of behavior described by Aristotle, but unlike Aristotle, they were interested in behavior only as it threw light on mental processes. Thus, the work of the early psychologists represents an attempt to make the naturalistic experimental methods introduced by Galileo compatible with metaphysical doctrines developed in the Middle Ages.

It was Wundt who, in 1879, founded the first psychological laboratory in Leipzig. We may take his system as representative of the activities of this new discipline, which was less than twenty years old when Thorndike was performing his experiments with cats and chicks at Columbia. Wundt held that psychology was the science of *experience*; and, as such, its subject matter comprised feelings, thoughts, and sensations. He laid down the doctrine that the method of psychology was introspective, an examination of the conscious processes of the experiencing organism. Thus, Wundt outlined the problem of psychology as "(1) the analysis of conscious processes into elements, (2) the determination of the manner of connection of these elements, and (3) the determination of the laws of connection" (Boring, 1929, p. 328, ital. omitted). The experiments that Wundt and his followers performed give a better picture of the content of this psychology than do Wundt's definitions. Much of the work was classified under human sensation and concerned the visual sense in particular. Numerous experiments measured the minimum intensities of light that an observer could detect under various conditions. Others concerned themselves with the smallest environmental changes needed for an observer to report just noticeable changes in brightness, color, and distance of objects. Such investigations came to be called threshold experiments in *psychophysics*. Psycho—because sensations were considered to be under study; physics— because physical changes in the environment were manipulated and measured in the experiments. Hearing, touch, taste, smell, and the sense of time, were also investigated, as were reaction time, attention, and feeling. The memorization of nonsense syllables of various sorts was a method used for treating the association of ideas and deducing the properties of memory.

Though psychology asserted that it was a science of mental contents, mental processes, and mental acts, in fact it investigated behavior. Associations of ideas were inferred from the learning of nonsense syllables; identical sensations were inferred from observations of behavior when a human subject matched two different environmental objects in different contexts (for example, two samples of gray paper under different conditions of illumination); speed of the mental process was inferred from an individual's reaction time. So it was no paradox that when Thorndike came to make a closer investigation of the association of ideas, he was at liberty to choose animal subjects. If the behavior of human organisms could lead to inferences about mental processes, why not the behavior of animals? Thus, it happened that Thorndike's work helped to bring animal research methods into psychology. There they have remained, side by side with methodological descendants of the classical sensory and introspective psychology of the nineteenth century.

Despite Thorndike's innovations, the man who did the most to clarify the relationship between behavior and psychology was John B. Watson. The earliest work of this American psychologist was concerned with the sense-modalities that the rat uses in learning a maze. As Watson carried on his animal studies, he came to be more and more disturbed by the prevailing view that behavior possessed significance only as it shed light on mental or conscious processes. It occurred to Watson that the data of behavior were valuable in their own right and that the traditional problems of psychology—imagery, sensation, feeling, association of ideas—could all be studied by strictly behavioral methods.

In 1913, Watson published a now classic paper defining psychology as the science of behavior and naming this new psychology "behaviorism." Watson argued in this paper that the study of behavior could achieve an independent status within science. The goal of such a science could be the prediction and control of the behavior of *all* animals, and no special preference need be given human beings. The behaviorist, claimed Watson, need relate his studies of rats and cats to human behavior no more (nor less) than the zoologist need relate his dissections on frogs and earthworms to human anatomy. By his doctrine, Watson was destroying the homocentric theory of man's importance in the behavioral world just as effectively as Copernicus had destroyed the geocentric (earth-centered) theory of the universe, four hundred years earlier.

Watson's main theme was that psychology must be objective—that is, it must have a subject matter which, like that of the other sciences, remains independent of the observer. Classical psychology, in attempting to take as its subject matter *self-observation*, lacked an independent observer located outside of the system being considered. Watson realized that this meant that conflicts about the contents of consciousness between different introspectionist psychologists could not be resolved *in principle*. There were no grounds for preferring one person's report over another's. This, he argued, made that approach unscientific, but the problem could be resolved if behavior itself was treated as the primary subject matter of psychology. If we take "behavior" to include only those human or animal activities that are, in principle, observable, then any statement about behavior made by one observer or experimenter can be verified by another person repeating the observations.

Watson's program for the new science of behavior was far-reaching and, for its time, remarkably sophisticated. In its insistence on behavior as an independent subject matter of a science aimed at the prediction and control of *behavior*, and in its stress on a microscopic analysis of the environment and behavior into stimuli and responses as the way to eventual understanding of complex patterns of behavior, Watson's program laid the basis for our modern viewpoints.

1.7
The Experimental Analysis of Behavior

Thorndike's early experiments on animal behavior and Watson's definition of psychology as a science of behavior established animal research in psychology. Even so, the scientific status of the new psychology was precarious. In Pavlov's principle of conditioned reflexes, Watson thought he saw an explanatory mechanism for the many complex and subtle adjustments that adult organisms, including man, make to their environments. But the attempt to force *all* behavior into the reflex mold was to prove a failure. Watson failed to appreciate the significance of Thorndike's law of effect, largely one might guess, because of the excess conceptual baggage with which Thorndike had encumbered it. Watson's view, that the task of a predictive science of behavior is the compilation of all the hereditary and acquired stimulus-response correlations that a given organism exhibits, distracted attention from the search for *general* laws of behavior. In this theoretical vacuum, traditional mentalistic concepts continued to survive. The experimental rigor of behaviorism was unquestioned, but its methodology was in danger of proving barren.

> Twenty years of the "natural science method" heralded by Behaviorism had failed to provide a consistent and useful systematic formulation. The . . . experimental data reflected many arbitrary properties of the apparatus. Acceptable conclusions of any degree of generality referred to aspects, characteristics, or limiting capacities. While many of these were valid enough, few were logically compelling, and individual preferences had led to many individual "sciences" of behavior (Skinner, 1944, p. 276).

In a series of papers beginning in 1930, B. F. Skinner proposed a formulation of behavior which arose out of observations made on single organisms responding in a carefully controlled and highly standardized artificial experimental situation. Skinner's organism was the white rat, and his apparatus consisted of a box containing a small lever which, if depressed by the rat, resulted in the delivery of a small pellet of food to a cup located directly under the lever (see Figure 1.5). Under these experimental conditions, a hungry rat left alone in the box would soon come to press the lever at a sustained moderate rate until the number of food pellets delivered had begun to satiate the animal. Skinner's experimental situation and his approach to the problems of behavior were unique in many respects. Skinner saw the necessity for making available a sensitive and reliable dependent variable; that is, some quantitative aspect of behavior which could vary over a wide range and enter into lawful and orderly relationships with past and present environmental, or independent, variables. His discovery that the frequency of occurrence of the lever-press response during a given interval of time (its

FIGURE 1.5. An experimental chamber based on the box originally developed by B. F. Skinner for the study of instrumental behavior (Will Rapport).

rate) satisfied these conditions was a major step towards a sophisticated analysis of individual behavior.

Skinner's approach to the problems of behavior differed in certain ways from those of both his predecessors and his contemporaries working in animal psychology. As a fundamental proposition, he held that a science of behavior could be what he called descriptive or functional; that is, it could limit itself to the discovery of relationships or correlations between measurable variables. He maintained that the identification of such *functional relationships* between aspects of behavior and parameters of the environment should be the goal of a science of behavior. Skinner also argued that the investigations must be systematic, in that the relationships obtained be linked by a common thread. By confining his observations to the ways that a single dependent variable (the frequency per unit time of an arbitrary, yet representative act) changed with varied environmental conditions, Skinner kept his own work highly systematic.

A subject matter often awaits instruments to bring the observer into better contact with it. Skinner invented a recording device which made a visual record of successive responses by a slight vertical displacement of a pen moving horizontally in time. As the actual experiment progressed, a graph was thus drawn of cumulative responses against time. This cumulative-response recorder makes available a fine-grained qualitative record of behavioral processes for immediate inspection, and has functioned for the behaviorist in a way not unlike the way the microscope has functioned for the biologist.

Skinner's actual methodological contributions to modern behavior science are numerous, and we can only sketch some of the more important here. He recognized a methodological analogy between particle emission in physics and the *emitted* character of spontaneous voluntary action. Skinner adopted the unique strategy of scientifically studying these emitted behaviors, even though their immediate antecedents remained unknown. Treating instrumental acts (he called them *operants*, because they generally operate upon the environment to change it) as an emission phenomenon, Skinner was able to explore their systematic and quantitative relation to motivational variables, and to a host of reward and punishment (or *reinforcement*) parameters. He formulated a precise vocabularly whose terms were defined by reference to the observable properties of the stimuli used and the behavior recorded, and coined the phrase, "the experimental analysis of behavior," to describe the type of research characterized by the methods and objectives outlined above. From the outset, Skinner emphasized the importance of detailed prediction and control of individual behavior rather than gross differences between groups of animals. His own researches were invariably characterized by a great many measurements on very few organisms, with the reproducibility of the process under study as the test for reliability. Skinner's focus on the rate of a representative operant response has avoided many of the problems associated with more indirect measures of behavior. Thorndike had observed the number of errors made and the time taken to achieve success in his puzzle box, but neither of these was a property of the instrumental behavior that was being acquired. If we wish to train a dog to jump through a hoop, for instance, we are not interested in the errors he makes, but in the hoop jumping itself. Errors are a measure of response other than those we are in the process of investigating. Interesting questions about whether or not a given act will occur, or how often it will occur, could never be answered in terms of errors or time scores. Skinner's basic datum, rate of response, is closely related to the probability of occurrence of behavior, and has been especially useful in providing answers to questions of response probability.

The empirical basis of the experimental analysis of behavior has been gradually, but steadily, broadened. Starting from the lever-pressing of rats for food, many other responses; reinforcers and species have been examined; and it has been possible to thereby show that principles derived from the original situation can be generalized to many other superficially dissimilar situations and to man himself. Clearly the scope of the experimental analysis of behavior would be limited and its progress very slow if it had turned out that principles coming from one experimental situation did not apply to substantially different situations and had no relevance to ourselves.

It should not be presumed that the experimental analysis of behavior, whose preoccupation until recently has been the elaboration of the law of effect, has solved all behavioral mysteries or penetrated all the traditional areas of psychology. However, its scope continues to expand, and alongside it, a behavioral technology has developed. This technology, which is the direct result of progress in behavioral analysis, is increasingly used in education, clinical treatment of abnormal behavior, drug research, cultural design, physiological investigations, and has even led to critiques of the traditional philosophical concepts of freedom and control.

1.8
The Biological Context

The great figures in the development of twentieth century behavioral science—Pavlov, Thorndike, Watson, and Skinner—were all aware that the study of behavior is a *biological* science. Indeed, Pavlov insisted that his work on conditioned reflexes was a contribution to physiology, and many early students of learning processes believed that, in the last analysis, behavior would be described in terms of physiological processes. Nevertheless, as the experimental analysis of behavior evolved as an approach to psychology, there was a strong tendency to stress the *ontogenetic* influences on behavior at the expense of the *phylogenetic* influences. To put it in terms of a traditional distinction, behaviorists were more interested in "learning," the ways in which specific experiences of an individual in the environment changes its behavior, than they were in "instinct", the behavioral predispositions that an individual organism possesses by virtue of its membership in a particular species.

This bias seems hardly surprising, since it is the ontogenetic, or individual past historical factors that have traditionally comprised the special domain of the psychologist. However, the interactions between ontogenetic and phylogenetic influences remain so tightly intertwined that the one cannot easily be studied without fully taking into account the effects of the other. Yet only very recently have behavioral psychologists begun to examine ontogenetic influences within the context of the "biological constraints" which limit and modulate the influence of the conditioning processes studied by Pavlov, Watson, and Skinner. This recent development within psychology constitutes a considerable advance in our aim to provide a complete account of behavior for it integrates the two most fundamental categories of behavioral influences.

Biologically oriented behavioral research of this kind has turned up some unexpected specificities concerning which responses can be affected by which reinforcer, constraints on which behavioral acts can serve as operants, and inherent limitations on the degree to which "pure" instrumental (Thorndikian) or associative (Pavlovian) conditioning can be isolated in a particular experimental situation. These biologically oriented contributions to the study of behavior have already shaken some of our most cherished assumptions and they promise to effect considerable changes in the conceptual landscape of the science in the coming years.

1.9
Objectives

In this chapter, we have traced several strands in the historical development of behavioral science. In later chapters we will describe the present "state of the art" and its applications. Throughout, the question of our objectives must be borne in mind: what are we trying to find out?

In other, better-established sciences, this question is less important. The physical sciences have highly sophisticated technologies and methodologies which have established a welter of phenomena. These jointly define the subject matter and the objectives of the science. In psychology, there are still choices to be made. The shift to the study of behavior was a very important step, but it did not settle all of the issues. How shall we deal with the aspects of behavior that are apparently inaccessible to our simple measuring techniques? Are there phenomena of psychological significance that will never yield to a behavioral analysis? Behavioral science has recently been criticized for being "manipulative" and for providing techniques that enable the strong to influence the weak. Is this true, and if it is, is it a truth about behavior or about the way the subject has been approached?

Partial answers to these questions will be provided by the theoretical and technological developments that will be described. The answers will only be partial, because behavioral science is still in a dynamic, transitional stage. Both practioners and students should remember that the direction taken by a science is neither random nor irrevocably determined. Rather, it is jointly determined by the theoretical and technical ingenuity shown in the solution of its problems, and by the problems its practitioners choose to solve.

1.10
Summary

Aristotle (fourth century B.C.) classified behavior in ways that are familiar in psychology today, but his suggestions did not lead directly to an objective study of behavior. Rather, a theologically-based doctrine, or assumption that human behavior is guided by free will and not susceptible to a scientific analysis, held sway until the seventeenth century. Interest in understanding behavioral mechanisms was revived by Descartes (1596–1650) who suggested that mechanical principles governed those types of behavior we now call reflexes. Whytt and several subsequent generations of physiologists showed that a reflex is a very precise relationship between a piece of behavior and certain environmental events, and that this behavioral unit obeys certain laws.

Pavlov (1849–1936) extended the reflex concept to include environment-behavior relationships which are conditional upon a particular history of the organism. These conditional reflexes make possible an analysis of some of the behavior that an organism acquires during its lifetime. Behavior that is spontaneous or "voluntary" was not subjected to a scientific analysis until Thorndike (1874–1949). By relating various motor responses of small animals to their consequences, he produced certain qualitative laws that differ from the laws of reflexes.

The traditional assumption that the proper subject matter of psychology is mental processes was challenged by Watson (1878–1958). He maintained that psychology could only be put on a scientific footing if behavior was taken as its primary data, rather than as a means to examining mental processes. Watson's campaign to establish a science of behavior was given substance by Skinner's study of operant behavior and reinforcement processes. Skinner (b. 1904) showed how an account of many aspects of behavior could be developed from systematic study of a simple, spontaneously emitted response. He called this study the experimental analysis of behavior.

Recent research has shown that, while the experimental analysis of behavior has established behavioral principles of considerable generality, the phylogeny of the species must also be taken into account in order to successfully predict the behavior of an individual organism. Behavioral science is, thus, in transition from emphasizing only the external determinants of behavior to taking more account of the structure that the organism brings to the situation.

The direction taken by a young science is determined, in part, by the objectives its practitioners choose to pursue. In opting to study behavior, psychologists took an important step, but many other important decisions will have to be made as the science evolves.

References for Chapter 1

Boring, E. G. *A history of experimental psychology*. New York: The Century Company, 1929.

Darwin, C. R. *The expression of the emotions in man and animals*. London: Murray, 1873.

Dennis, W. *Readings in the history of psychology*. New York: Appleton-Century, 1948. (Chapters 3, 45, 48, and 50).

Fearing, F. *Reflex action: a study in the history of physiological psychology*. Baltimore: Williams and Wilkins, 1930.

Garrett, H. *Great experiments in psychology.* New York: Appleton-Century-Crofts, 1951.

Hall, G. S., and Hodge, C. F. A sketch of the history of reflex action. *American Journal of Psychology*, 1890, **3**, 71–86; 149–173; 343–363.

Kantor, J. R. *The scientific evolution of psychology.* Vol. 1. Chicago: Principia Press, 1963.

Pavlov, I. P. *Lectures on conditioned reflexes.* New York: International Publishers, 1928.

Romanes, G. J. *Animal intelligence.* (4th ed.) London: Kegan Paul, 1886.

Skinner, B. F. A review of C. L. Hull's Principles of behavior. *American Journal of Psychology*, 1944, **57**, 276–281.

Thorndike, E. L. Animal intelligence. *Psychological Review Monograph Supplement*, 1898, No. 8.

Toulmin, S., and Goodfield, June. *The architecture of matter.* New York: Harper and Row, 1962.

Watson, J. B. Psychology as the behaviorist views it. *Psychological Review*, 1913, **20**, 158–177.

PART TWO

Operant Behavior

B. F. Skinner's (1938) suggestion that we distinguish between responses, or behavioral acts, that are *elicited* by a stimulus and those that are *emitted* in the presence of a stimulus has proved very important in the development of a science of behavior. Previously, it had been assumed that all behavior is elicited, and thus, eliciting stimuli were presumed to exist even when none could be readily observed. This had the unfortunate consequence that observation and description of behavior and its environment were frequently abandoned in favor of appeal to unobserved events. If, for example, a nervous student in an examination frequently stops work and chews the end of a pen, it is most unlikely that an observer could identify a stimulus that preceded and elicited each bout of chewing. We could, therefore, only describe the hypothesized eliciting stimulus in terms of the behavior it has been invoked to explain. Skinner realized that we could avoid this vicious circularity by dropping the assumption that a response can only occur when elicited by a stimulus. He proposed that there exists an alternative relationship, whereby the response can be viewed as *emitted*, from time to time, in the presence of an environmental stimulus. The stimulus still *controls* the response, because the frequency (or probability) of the response alters when the stimulus is present, but its onset does not elicit the response.

The analysis of elicited and emitted behavior have developed in semi-independent fashion. The chief tools in the study of elicited behavior have been the classical conditioning techniques developed by Pavlov, and the behavioral processes they have been used to analyze are described in Part Three "Associative Processes." Emitted behavior has come to be called, "operant behavior" and its quantitative study originated with Skinner's pioneer work on operant conditioning; although this, in turn, was an implementation of Thorndike's Law of Effect. The present section outlines the basic procedures and findings of operant conditioning.

Parts Two and Three should be seen as complementary, and together form the basis of our knowledge of behavioral analysis.

CHAPTER 2

Operant
Conditioning

There is much behavior that apparently occurs at the instigation of the individual, rather than being elicited by the onset of an external stimulus. This includes those actions of man traditionally described as voluntary, purposeful, spontaneous, or willful, and it is just this class of behavior that, until the turn of the twentieth century, was thought to be beyond the pale of a scientific or experimental analysis. The relationship between this sort of behavior and reflexive behavior is well illustrated by the following passage:

> . . . when a cat hears a mouse, turns towards the source of the sound, sees the mouse, runs toward it, and pounces, its posture at every stage, even to the selection of the foot which is to take the first step, is determined by reflexes which can be demonstrated one by one under experimental conditions. *All the cat has to do is to decide* whether or not to pursue the mouse; everything else is prepared for it by its

postural and locomotor reflexes (Skinner, 1957, p. 343; italics added).

The cat's behavior in this situation has an essential, nonreflexive ingredient, although reflexes are vital for the success of its attempt to catch the mouse. Hidden in the simple statement, "all the cat has to do is to *decide*," lies the point of departure for an analysis of *purposive behavior*, whose occurrence is not related to the presence of an eliciting stimulus, either as a result of the history of the species or as a result of the history of the individual.

2.1
Purposive Behavior

In any research area in psychology, scientific explanation and understanding comes about by a progressive discovery and elaboration of the relations between certain aspects of behavior (the dependent response variables) and certain aspects of the environment (the independent stimulus and past-history variables). Each discovery of such a new relationship or law of behavior becomes a prized event in the history of the science. As the laws began to pile up and intermingle, we begin to speak about a partial understanding of the area.

The experimental analysis of so-called purposive behavior has proceeded in exactly this fashion. Starting with Thorndike's extensive pioneer work on learning in cats and chicks, psychologists have searched for relationships between purposive behavior and other events. Consider the problems in beginning such an analysis: how do we go about finding variables or events to which purposive behavior might be significantly related? Initially, we must proceed by intuition and crude observation. Very often, forward-looking philosophical speculation precedes scientific investigation of a problem, and in this case, the British philosopher, Herbert Spencer wrote:

> Suppose, now, that in putting out its head to seize prey scarcely within reach, a creature has repeatedly failed. Suppose that along with the group of motor actions approximately adapted to seize prey at this distance . . . a slight forward movement of the body [occurs]. Success will occur instead of failure . . . On recurrence of the circumstances, these muscular movements that were followed by success are likely to be repeated: what was at first an accidental combination of motions will now be a combination having considerable probability (Spencer, 1878).

Here, a quarter of a century before Thorndike, Spencer suggests that the effect of an action is all important in determining its subsequent occurrence: "those muscular movements that were followed by success are likely to be repeated." This is the key idea that led Thorndike to the law of effect and

Skinner to a thoroughgoing experimental analysis of behavior.

If a piece of behavior has a purpose, then that purpose can be described by the usual consequences or effect of that behavior. Indeed, we could almost say that purposive behavior is that behavior which is *defined* by its consequences. Consider the examples in Table 2.1. In every case, the purpose of the behavior is closely related to its consequences. We say that we tie a shoelace to keep our shoe on, but an equivalent statement is that we tie a shoelace, and on previous occasions when we tied it, it did stay on. Furthermore, we identify instances of shoelace tying by their effects: if the shoe stays on, then this counts as an example of "shoelace tying"; otherwise, it does not.

Apparently, we have two ways in our language to represent the same behavior. These are: (1) the purposive, in which we use the term *to* (or, *in order to*) and imply the future tense; or (2) the descriptive, in which we state the present behavior and conjoin it with what happened in the past. Which is more appropriate for use in a scientific analysis of behavior? Consider the following example:

> During the war the Russians used dogs to blow up tanks. A dog was trained to hide behind a tree or wall in low brush or other cover. As a tank approached and passed, the dog ran swiftly alongside it, and a small magnetic mine attached to the dog's back was sufficient to cripple the tank or set it afire. The dog, of course, had to be replaced (Skinner, 1956, p. 228).

In this example, the dog's behavior can be explained by reference to past events—it presumably had been rewarded for running to tanks by food, petting, and the like—but not by reference to its purpose. We can immediately reject the idea that the dog ran to the tank in order to be blown up. This extreme case illustrates the general principle that the future does not determine behavior. When we use "purposive language," we are drawing on our knowledge of the effects of our behavior on earlier occasions; it is the latter that determines behavior.

In brief, a very real and important class of behavior, arising out of

TABLE 2.1. Some "purposive" behaviors of animals and men, their so-called purposes, and their actual past consequences.

Behavior	Purpose	Consequences
Tie a shoelace	*To* keep shoe on	Shoe stays on
Buy a raincoat	*To* keep rain off	Rain stays off
Enter a restaurant	*To* eat lunch	You get lunch
Turn on faucet	*To* get water	Water appears
Write a letter	*To* secure a reply	Reply obtained
Dig a hole	*To* escape the cold	Warmth obtained

situations that seem to involve choice or decision, is called purposive behavior. Such behavior, it should be apparent at once, falls into Descartes' category of "voluntary" and constitutes action that is often called "willful." Our present analysis indicates that this behavior is in some way related to, and thus governed by, its consequences. For that reason we shall henceforth replace the older term, purposive, with Thorndike's term, "instrumental," or Skinner's term, "operant." Calling behavior "instrumental" or "operant" suggests that, by operating on the environment, the behavior is instrumental in obtaining consequences. Neither of these terms implies the confusing conceptual scheme that "purposive" does, yet both attempt to capture the fundamental notion that the past consequences of such behavior are one of its important determinants.

2.2

A Prototype Experiment: A Rat in the Skinner Box

If a hungry laboratory rat is put in the box shown in Figure 2.1 and certain procedures are instituted, a number of interesting changes in the behavior of the rat may be observed.

For present purposes, the significant features of the box are (1) a tray for delivery of a small pellet of food to the rat; and (2) a lever or bar, protruding from the front wall that, when depressed downward with a force of about 10 gm, closes a switch, permitting the automatic recording of this behavior. The significant features of the rat are as follows: (1) It is healthy and has been accustomed to eating one meal each day at about the same hour as it now finds itself in the box. (2) It has previously been acclimatized to this box, during which time food was occasionally delivered into the tray; it now readily approaches the food tray and eats food whenever it is available.

Consider the following experiment. The rat is left in the box for an

FIGURE 2.1. The Skinner box is situated in a sound-attenuating housing to exclude extraneous stimuli.

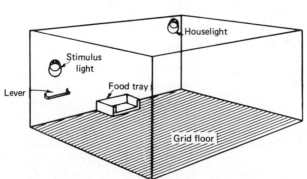

observation period of 15 min. During this time, no food is delivered, but the rat engages in a lot of exploratory behavior. It noses the corners, noses the food tray, occasionally depresses the lever, rears up against the walls, and so forth. Other activities observed are sniffing and grooming. None of these responses are reflexive. That is, no specific eliciting stimulus can be identified for any of them. Thus, we call them *emitted responses*. Clearly, there are stimuli present that are related to the occurrence of these responses, the general construction of the box obviously determines which responses can occur, for example, but none of the stimuli elicits specific responses at specific times.

The rate and pattern of the emitted responses of an animal, in an environment in which no special consequences are being provided for any response, defines the *operant-level* of those responses. Operant-level recordings will provide an important *baseline* against which we shall later compare the effects of providing special consequences for one or a number of the emitted responses.

After the observation period, the following procedure is initiated. Each time the rat presses the lever, a pellet of food is delivered into the tray. As the rat has previously learned to retrieve food pellets and eat them as soon as they are delivered, each lever-pressing response is now immediately followed by the rat eating a food pellet. We have introduced a *contingency* between the lever-pressing response and the delivery of food pellets. Provided the operant-level pressing is above zero—that is, lever presses occur from time to time—this new contingency will rapidly have an effect. Soon the rat is busily engaged in lever pressing and eating pellets. Some very marked changes in its behavior have occurred in a relatively short period of time.

In common parlance, the rat is said to have learned to press the lever to get food. Such a description adds little to the statement that the rat is pressing the lever frequently now and getting food. What we wish to do is to describe in detail, and as quantitatively as possible, the changes in behavior that result from the simple operation of providing a special consequence for only one of an individual's normal ongoing activities in a situation. To do that, we shall consider four complementary ways of viewing the changes in the rat's behavior when, as here, one of its behaviors is selected out and given a favorable consequence:

1. the increase in response frequency
2. changes in other behavior
3. sequential changes in responding
4. changes in response variability.

2.3

Monitoring the Increase in Response Frequency: The Cumulative Record

The experiment we have described is an instance of the prototype experiments on operant behavior by B. F. Skinner in the 1930's. The most striking change in behavior that occurs when food is presented to a hungry rat as a consequence of lever pressing is that lever pressing dramatically increases in rate. This is an example of *operant conditioning*, because the increase in rate is a result of the *contingency* between the lever-pressing response and the food. If there is a contingency between two events, *A* and *B*, this means that *B* will occur if, and only if, *A* occurs. We say that *B* is dependent on *A*, or that *A* predicts *B*, because when *A* occurs, *B* occurs; but if *A* does not occur, *B* will not occur. Sequences of events in which *B* is contingent upon *A* and when *B* is independent of *A* are illustrated in Figure 2.2. In our present example, food (*B*) is contingent upon lever pressing (*A*). Another way of saying this is that food (*B*) is a consequence of lever pressing (*A*).

Changes in rate are most clearly seen on the ink recorder developed by Skinner: the Cumulative Recorder illustrated in Figure 2.3. The pen moves continuously across the paper in one direction at fixed speed, and this axis thus records elapsed time. Whenever a response occurs, the pen moves in a perpendicular direction by a small step of fixed size. The resulting *cumulative record* shows the number of responses and the time during which they occurred, and so illustrates the pattern of behavior. Examples of actual records from subjects exposed to the aforementioned procedure are shown in Figure 2.4. When a contingency between lever pressing and food was established for these subjects, there was a relatively abrupt transition to a high rate of response. It should be noted that the time spent in the experiment before this transition varied and, in the examples in Figure 2.4, could be up to 30 min. Once the transition had occurred, the rate of responding was fairly constant; this is shown by the steady slopes of the graphs.

FIGURE 2.2. Time lines illustrating a contingency between, or independence of, (A) and (B). In an operant conditioning experiment, event (A) might represent lever presses and event (B) food delivery.

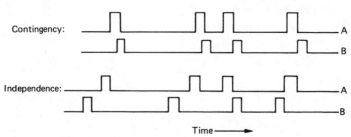

FIGURE 2.3. Cumulative recorder (Courtesy of Ralph Gerbrands Co. Inc.).

FIGURE 2.4. Cumulative records obtained from four hungry rats on their first session of operant conditioning. Lever presses were reinforced with food. Each lever press produced an incremental step of the pen (Skinner, 1938).

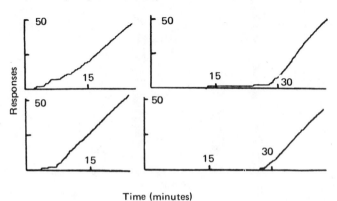

2.4

Concomitant Changes in Other Responses

If the rat begins to spend a large part of its time lever pressing, retrieving and eating food pellets, there must necessarily be a reduction in the frequency of some of the responses (R's) that were previously occurring in the Skinner box. For example, in an undergraduate classroom demonstration of lever-press operant conditioning at Carnegie—Mellon University, the following behaviors of a hungry rat were recorded over 15 min of operant level, and then over a subsequent 15 min of conditioning the lever pressing:

R_L = lever pressing
R_S = sniffing
R_C = pulling of a small chain that dangled into the box from overhead
R_T = nosing the food tray
R_B = extending a paw to a lead block that rested in one of the far corners
R_I = remaining approximately immobile for 10 consecutive seconds.

The frequencies of these activities during operant level and during operant conditioning are represented in the histograms of Figure 2.5. It is clear that, while lever pressing and tray nosing increase, the other responses that are not associated with eating decline. Indeed, the operant conditioning process can be seen as one of selection. Those responses that are selected increase in relative frequency, while most of the remainder decline.

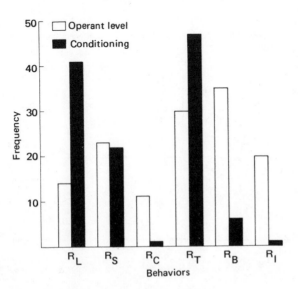

FIGURE 2.5.
Relative frequencies of several behaviors occurring in a Skinner box before and after conditioning of lever pressing.

2.5

Sequential Changes in Responding

The behavior changes that result from a contingency being established between a response and food extend beyond that response to many other activities. In particular, other activities involved in food getting increase in frequency, but this is not the only change that takes place. A sequence of responses is rapidly established and maintained. In the lever pressing example, the sequence might be:

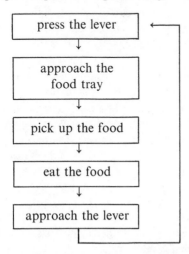

This continuous loop of behavior is quite different from that seen in operant level. Two members of the established loop will serve to illustrate the point. Let us ignore, for the moment, all the other possible behavior in the situation and confine our attention to (1) pressing the lever and (2) approaching the food tray. Prior to conditioning the lever press, these two responses occur in such a way that, when the animal performs one of them, it is likely to repeat that one again rather than perform the other (Frick and Miller, 1951). Thus, a fairly typical operant-level sequence of lever press (R_L) and tray-approach responses (R_T) might be

$$R_L R_L R_T R_L R_L R_L R_T R_T R_T \ldots$$

During conditioning, this sequence quickly changes to the alternation

$$R_L R_T R_L R_T R_L R_T \ldots$$

with hardly any other pattern to be seen (Millenson and Hurwitz, 1961). This reorganization of behavior probably takes place as soon as rapid responding begins.

2.6
Changes in Response Variability

"The rat presses the lever" describes an effect the rat has on the environment, not a particular pattern of movements by the rat. There is a wide range of movements that could have the specified effect. Presses can be made with the right paw, with the left, with nose, shoulder, or even, tail. We group all of these instances together and say that the class of responses that we call lever pressing is made up of all the possible ways of pressing a lever. However, not all members of the class are equally likely to occur in an experiment nor, on the other hand, does the same member occur repeatedly.

Several processes interact to determine exactly which forms of the response are observed. First, there is a tendency for the *topography* of the response to become *stereotyped* under certain conditions. By "topography," we mean the pattern of muscular movements that make up the response; when this becomes stereotyped, the response looks exactly the same on each occasion that it occurs. One situation in which stereotypy develops is when very little effort is required to make the response. Guthrie and Horton (1946) took photographs of cats and dogs who were required to make a pole-tilting response to get out of a box. Some of these are reproduced in Figure 2.6, which shows that successive instances of the response made by particular

FIGURE 2.6. Sequences of the stereotyped responses emitted by two cats and a dog in the Guthrie and Horton (1946) pole-tilting experiment.

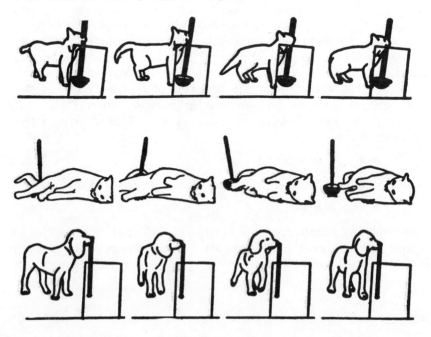

individuals were strikingly similar. A remarkable example of human stereotypy in a rather different response is illustrated in Figure 2.7.

A second process involved is described by Skinner's (1938) "law of least effort." This states that the form of the response made will tend to be that which requires the least effort. In the experiment described above, it is typically found that, while different subjects start out by pressing the lever in various ways, as the experiment progresses, they show an increasing tendency to use an economical paw movement to press the lever.

More recently, attention has been directed to a third process that influences the form of the response. This is the "preparedness" of the subject to associate the response (in the present case, lever pressing) with the consequence provided for it (in this case, food pellets). Seligman (1970) noted that, if the subject is prepared to associate a particular response and consequence, then the contingency will rapidly affect the frequency of the response. If, however, the subject is unprepared, or actually contraprepared, to associate response and consequence, the contingency will be less effective. This process has the result that the operant response occurs more vigorously in a form that the subject is prepared to associate with the consequence. For example, Thorndike (1911) made escape from the puzzle box contingent upon the licking or scratching by cats. He found that, even though these are common responses; that is, they have a high operant level, operant conditioning proceeded erratically. Also, the responding lacked vigor:

There is in all these cases a noticeable tendency . . . to diminish the

FIGURE 2.7.
Ted Williams getting his 2,000th hit in the first inning and 2,001st hit in the fifth inning of a game played at Yankee Stadium, August 11, 1955 (©The New York Times and Patrick A. Burns).

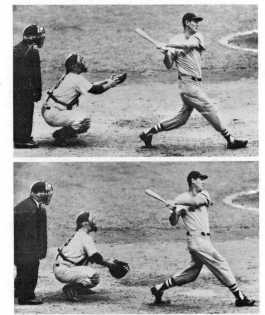

act until it becomes a mere vestige of a lick or scratch . . . the licking degenerated into a mere quick turn of the head with one or two motions up and down with tongue extended. Instead of a hearty scratch, the cat waves its paw up and down rapidly for an instant. Moreover, if sometimes you do not let the cat out after the feeble reaction, it does not at once repeat the movement, as it would do if it depressed a thumb piece, for instance, without success in getting the door open (Thorndike, 1911, p. 48).

In Seligman's terms, Thorndike discovered that cats are *contraprepared* to associate licking or scratching with the consequence of escaping from a puzzle box. However, he also found that they were *prepared* to associate string pulling, button pressing ("depressing a thumb piece"), or lever pressing with this consequence.

The three processes described act together during operant conditioning to produce a response that tends to be: (1) stereotyped, (2) easy to make (little effort required), (3) one that a subject of that species is prepared to make for the consequence arranged. Normally, these three requirements are compatible with each other, but cases in which they are incompatible will be discussed later. Whatever the resultant form of the response, response variability decreases as operant-conditioning proceeds; successive instances of the response resemble each other more and more as the topography becomes more restricted.

2.7
Operants and Reinforcing Stimuli

In summary, operant conditioning strengthens a response in four ways:

1. the rate of that response increases relative to its operant or base level,
2. the rate of that response increases relative to the rate of other responses occurring in the situation,
3. the pattern or sequence of behavior changes to a loop involving that response and this loop is repeated again and again,
4. the form or topography of that response becomes stereotyped, while requiring a minimum effort and being influenced by the subject's preparedness to associate the response with the consequence arranged for it.

Lever pressing, string pulling, and pole tilting, represent convenient acts chosen by experiments to study the effects of environmental consequences on behavior. The suitability of these responses for studying operant conditioning depends critically upon their ability to be modified as described. Formally, responses are defined as *operants* if they can be increased in frequency and strengthened in the four stated ways by making certain consequences contingent upon them. The selection of the operant response is often said to be arbitrary, in that the experimenter is generally not interested in lever pressing *per se*, but only as an example of a response that can be modified by its consequences. We have already seen, in the case of Thorndike's attempts to train cats to lick and scratch themselves, that not every simple piece of behavior can be assumed to be an operant, and to this extent, the selection of an operant response is nonarbitrary. However, research in operant conditioning has primarily concerned itself with the discovery of general principles that apply to all operant behavior. In general, lever pressing and other simple pieces of animal behavior are chosen for the experiments because they are easily observed and measured by the experimenter, and can be executed at various rates and in various patterns by the organism. Throughout this book, we will continuously extend the applicability of the principles of operant conditioning and the term "operant" well beyond lever presses and rats. But we must remember that laboratory experiments represent idealized cases and there may be surprises when we move to more complex situations and organisms.

Which are the consequences of behavior that will produce operant conditioning? This is a central issue that we have carefully avoided this far. In his law of effect, Thorndike stressed the importance of "satisfiers." If a satisfier, or satisfying state of affairs, was the consequence of a response, then that response would be "stamped in," for example, increased in frequency. At first sight, Thorndike seems to have provided an answer to the question we posed, but actually, he merely leaves us with another: which events will act as satisfiers? It seems obvious that food may be satisfying to a hungry organism, and "armchair reflection" might produce a list of events likely to prove satisfying in general, such as warmth, activity, play, contact, power, novelty, and sex. We might also notice that there are some events that become very satisfying once the organism has been appropriately *deprived*. Food comes into this category, along with water when thirsty, air when suffocating, and rest when fatigued. But so far, we are only guessing; how can we establish whether these events are satisfying? One way is to see whether they have the consequence specified by the law of effect, that of strengthening operant response; but according to Thorndike's definition, they *must* have this property. A plausible alternative suggestion was made by Hull (1943). He said that all such events reduce a basic need or drive of the organism and that this *drive reduction* is crucial to their response-strengthening effect. Subsequent research has failed, however, to support Hull's suggestion, for there are many satisfiers whose ability to reduce a basic need seems questionable (see Chapter 21).

Thorndike's term, "satisfier," carries the implication that such events will be pleasurable—things that we like. But this does not help us to identify them in practice. It simply changes the form of the problem again: how do I know what you like? The things we like are, in the final analysis, the things that we will work for. But this again takes us back to the law of effect, because to say that we will work for them is just another way of saying that we will do for them what our rat will do "for" food. At this point, we shall prefer to exchange Thorndike's term, "satisfier," for Skinner's less introspective, *reinforcing stimulus*, or simply, *reinforcer*. The operation of presenting a reinforcer contingent upon a response we will denote as *reinforcement*.

The foregoing discussion can be summarized as follows. A reinforcing stimulus can be defined as an event that, in conjunction with at least some behavior of an individual, has the effects specified by the law of effect and listed at the beginning of this section.

Note that we lack an independent method of identifying reinforcers other than by their effects on behavior. Moreover, the work of Premack (1965) suggests that this represents an inherent limitation. In a series of ingenious experiments, Premack established that the property of being a reinforcer is a relative one, that for any pair of responses, the less probable response can be reinforced by the opportunity to carry out the more probable response, and that this relationship is reversible. He made these surprising findings by breaking some of the unwritten "rules of the game." For example, in one experiment, Premack studied rats making the operant response of turning an activity wheel and being reinforced with water delivery. (The apparatus is shown in Figure 2.8). To insure that water acted as a reinforcer, the rats were made thirsty at the time of the experiment and this made water a reinforcer for wheel turning. Wheel turning duly increased in frequency. In another part of the experiment, however, Premack (1962) reversed the relationship: he allowed the rats continuous access to water, but prevented access to the activity wheel except for 1 hr/day.

FIGURE 2.8. Apparatus at which drinking and wheel-running can be either freely available or contingent upon another response (Premack, 1971).

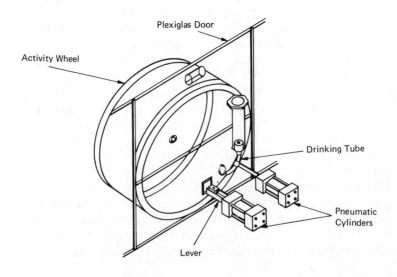

In this unusual situation, he found that if the opportunity to run in the wheel was made contingent upon licking water from a tube, the rats spent between three and five times as long drinking during that hour than they did when this contingency was not in effect. He thus established that it is not a "law of nature" that wheel turning by rats can be reinforced with water. Instead, this result depends on the usual practice of depriving rats of water, but not activity, prior to the experiment. If the conditions are reversed, then running in the wheel can be shown to reinforce drinking.

The concept of "a reinforcer" is evidently a relative one; a fact that we should especially bear in mind before uncritically calling any particular stimulus in the everyday world a reinforcer. We should also take care in the laboratory not to presume that a stimulus will necessarily continue to be a reinforcer if the conditions are radically changed.

2.8
The Simple Operant Conditioning Paradigm

The matters that we have been discussing in this chapter are variously referred to in the literature of psychology as simple selective learning, trial-and-error learning, effect learning, instrumental learning, instrumental conditioning, operant learning, and operant conditioning. We prefer to restrict the term, simple operant conditioning, to the situation where a reinforcing stimulus is made contingent upon a response that has a nonzero frequency of occurrence prior to the introduction of reinforcement. Nevertheless, when reading the literature it is important to realize that all of the terms listed are used in a roughly similar way.

Formally, the simple operant conditioning paradigm is defined as follows. Each emission of a selected behavioral act or sequence is followed by the presentation of a particular stimulus. If this arrangement results in an increase in response frequency, relative to operant level and relative to other behavior occurring in the situation, the incorporation of the response into a behavioral loop and the narrowing of the topography of the response, then we say that the selected behavior is an operant response, that the stimulus functions as a reinforcer for that operant, and that what occurred was operant conditioning. The operation can be represented diagrammatically.

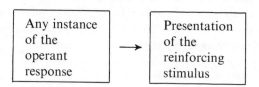

The arrow stands for "leads to" or "produces." This diagram can, in turn, be summarized as:

$$R \rightarrow S^+$$

where R represents an operant response class and S$^+$ the reinforcing stimulus it produces. S$^+$ is used to denote a *positive* reinforcer. The distinction between positive and another class of significant environmental events, called negative reinforcers, will be explained in Part Five.

2.9
Changing the Subject Matter: Vocal Operants.

This section is included partly to illustrate the breadth of application of simple operant conditioning and partly to direct our attention to some characteristically human behavior. The usual elements of all languages are sounds produced by the vibration of expelled air from the lungs, moving through and across a set of muscles in the larynx called the vocal chords. The tension of these muscles, a major determinant of the sound produced, is under the same kind of neural control as movements of the other parts of the body, and the emitted sound patterns can be considered as examples of operant behavior. The jaws, lips, and tongue act in combination with the larynx to mold the sounds and produce the more than forty different humanoid sounds known as *phonemes* that are used in various combinations in languages. Because the sounds of phonemes are directly dependent on the movements of the vocal apparatus, measurement of phoneme production constitutes an indirect measure of behavior, in the same way that measurement of the depression of a lever constitutes an indirect measure of the movements used by the rat in depressing that lever.

Human language evolves from the crude sounds emitted by infants. Surprisingly, the human infant during the first 5 months of life emits every sound used in every human language—French nasals and trills, German gutturals, and so on (Osgood, 1953). These sounds are emitted independently of eliciting stimuli, and are to be distinguished from the actual crying of a baby. During the early months of life, a baby exhibits a very high operant level of sound production. He or she may lie for hours producing gurgling sounds, sputterings, whistles, squeaks, and snorts. The technical term *babbling* is used to denote the spontaneous emission of these behaviors. An important advance in babbling occurs at about the sixth month, when the sequential structure of babbling is altered so that the infant tends to repeat its own vocal production (uggle-uggle, oodle-oodle, luh-luh-luh, and so forth).

The changes that occur from babbling to speaking are complex, and no single graph could describe the progress with any completeness. However, one important change that takes place is the change in relative frequency of the different sounds uttered as the baby grows older. Thus, in France, the phonemes involved in the French *r* and the nasal vowels are strengthened by the reinforcing community—the child's parents, its playmates, and eventually, its teachers. In English-speaking countries, a different set of phonemes is shaped into words by a different reinforcing community. The result of this strengthening can be inferred from a set of histograms similar to that of Figure 2.5, but more complicated. In Figure 2.9, histograms of the relative frequencies of 12 vowel phonemes are shown for infants at various ages and the adult. The pronunciations of the phonemes are given in Table 2.2. We may infer that reinforcement of these sounds is adjusting their frequency to that of the adult community.

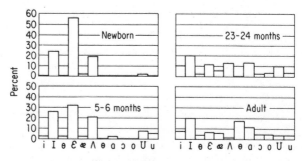

FIGURE 2.9. Frequency profiles of vowel-phonemes in vocal behavior, showing the gradual shifts toward the adult pattern characteristic of, and reinforced by, the particular community (Irwin, 1952).

More direct evidence of the effects of reinforcing infant sounds comes from laboratory experiments. In one experiment, the behavior of 3-month-old babies was observed while they lay in their cribs. During two observation sessions, an adult experimenter leaned over the crib, at a distance of a little more than a foot from the child, and remained relatively motionless and

TABLE 2.2.

Symbol	Example
j	the *y* in yet
I	the *y* in hymn
e	the *a* in alone
ε	the *a* in dare
æ	the *a* in hat
ʌ	the *o* in son
θ	the *a* in rain
a	the *a* in father
ɔ	the *a* in tall
o	the *o* in toe
U	the *o* in wolf
u	the *o* in move

expressionless. During this time, a second observer recorded the frequency of sounds produced by the infant. In two subsequent sessions, the procedure was the same, except that the first experimenter followed each noncrying sound with a "broad smile, three 'tsk' sounds, and a light touch applied to the infant's abdomen with thumb and fingers of the hand opposed" (Rheingold, Gewirtz, and Ross, 1959, p. 28). This is, of course, just:

$$R_{(babble)} \rightarrow S^+_{(smile, clucking, touch of abdomen)}$$

The effect of the procedure was to raise the frequency of babbling well above its operant-level rate during these conditioning sessions.

Even more striking were the findings of Routh (1969), working with 2 to 7-month-old infants. Using the same reinforcing stimuli, he reinforced either vowel or consonant sounds rather than all vocalizations. He found that vocalizations increased under both conditions, but infants differentially increased the responses in the reinforced class. Experiments of this type provide ample evidence that human vocal behavior is susceptible to control by operant conditioning.

Experiments with other animals have verified that the barking of dogs, the meowing of cats, and some of the sounds of birds are reinforceable. In these cases, the frequency of sound production can be markedly raised by special consequences. The largely unsuccessful attempts to teach speech sounds to apes (Hayes, 1951), and the much more successful attempts to teach them sign languages (Gardner and Gardner, 1969), or language using visual symbols (Premack and Premack, 1974) will be discussed in Chapter 6. It will suffice here to point out that, while human babies babble a great deal so that the reinforcing community of parents and others can reinforce particular sounds, baby chimpanzees are more or less silent at a comparable developmental stage. Clearly, a nonzero operant level is essential for simple operant conditioning; otherwise, there is no behavior to reinforce. A suitable class of behavior in apes that has a nonzero operant level is hand and finger movements, and this activity provides the basis of the sign languages that they have successfully acquired.

2.10
Simple Operant Conditioning of Complex Human Behavior

Operant conditioning is a phenomenon which is by no means limited to the simple animal and infant behaviors we have discussed so far. We study the animal because we can rigorously control its environment, past and present. But operant behavior—that is, behavior that can be strengthened by its consequences—constitutes a large proportion of the everyday activities of humans. When we kick a football, sew up a hem, give a lecture, discuss the latest in fashions, bemoan the weather, and wash the dishes, we are constantly emitting operant behavior. True, our complex skills entail much more complicated sequences than the simple repetitive loop of the rat, described earlier; but as we shall see in later chapters, surprising complexity can also be generated at the level of the rat, cat, pigeon, and monkey.

It is not difficult to demonstrate simple operant conditioning in humans. Given the conditions of the simple operant conditioning paradigm, we can perform demonstrations on our friends without great difficulty. We are apt to find the demonstration more dramatic and convincing if we prevent our human subject from "becoming aware" that we are performing such an experiment. For the subject to "become aware" is a way of saying that he or she is able to verbalize the procedure that is being followed. This verbal "awareness" is a sure index that the behavior which we are trying to strengthen will now be under the powerful control of years of past history, against which the application of a conditioning paradigm for 30 min or so with a weak reinforcer will have little possibility of competing.

In a novel experimental design, based on early work by W. Verplanck (1955), an undergraduate research assistant was employed as an "actor" to try to strengthen certain conversational behavior in fellow undergraduate subjects (Centers, 1963). The assistant and subject were confined to a room, both ostensibly waiting to be called for a psychological experiment. Actually, this was the experiment. During this time, the assistant engaged the unsuspecting subject in ordinary conversation, but at various periods, reinforced several types of conversational content, such as opinion statements, information statements, and questions, with agreement and special attention. Meanwhile, unknown to the subject, the conversation was being taped and observed through a one-way screen.

The experimental "conversation" lasted 30 min, broken up into three, 10-min portions. During the first portion, or operant level, the assistant refrained from expressing agreement or providing informative answers to the subject's opinions and questions. During the second 10 min, the behavioral strengthening period, the assistant agreed with or paraphrased favorably all opinion statements that were voiced by the subject. The assistant further expressed attention, sympathy, and understanding to all information statements, and reinforced all questions by either giving the information solicited, or giving agreement or approval, if that was what the question indicated was desired. During the final 10 min, the assistant either disagreed with the subject's opinions or remained silent after they were verbalized, ignored information statements, and was as noncommittal as possible to questions.

The results of agreement reinforcement indicated clearly that the frequency of opinion and information statements relative to all statements increased. Furthermore, no subject noted this conditioning of his or her behaviors. For reasons not well understood by the experimenters, the question statements did not show any increase and, therefore, according to our definition, either they do not constitute an operant class relative to this reinforcer, or else they may already have been at their maximum strength.

A great many other studies of simple operant conditioning of complex human behavior have been carried out and numerous examples can be found in the chapters on behavior modification later in this book (Part Eight).

Scientists, themselves, are engaged in an enterprise that often demands the emission of much operant behavior, only a small part of which may be reinforced. Behaviors that bring about the statement of new relationships, or a new order among concepts, or the discovery of a new phenomenon are reinforced by the scientific community. Among the prominent reinforcers for the behaviorist, is the order observed when some behavior of an individual is seen to be lawfully related to its consequences, as was the lever pressing of the rat in Section 2.2. This reminder that human investigators are just, themselves, behaving organisms, subject to the laws of operant conditioning, characterizes the cartoon shown in Figure 2.10.

The verification of the laws of operant conditioning on human behavior is important, for it shows that despite very great apparent differences between man and animal, certain functional similarities exist. It is these similarities that, in the end, justify our study of a significant domain of psychology through the behavior of lower organisms. After all, the psychologist is interested principally in human behavior. We very often utilize animal subjects in our experimental work for pragmatic reasons. We can more easily control an animal's immediate and past environment. We can deprive it of agents, such as food and water, in order to dole these agents out later as powerful reinforcers. Finally, we can continuously observe the animal for very long periods of confinement.

Of course, the use of animals in experimentation has important limitations. There is always a possibility that the findings of a particular study involving animal subjects will turn out not to be generalizable to other species and human behavior, because the behavior shown by the subjects is species-typical, that is, it involves a behavioral pattern shown only by members of that species.

However, the use of animals in psychological research follows a long and respected tradition in science of isolating relevant conditions in unnatural settings, in order to reveal the basic lawfulness in nature. Perhaps our most

FIGURE 2.10.
"Boy do we have this guy conditioned. Every time I press the bar down he drops a pellet in." (Adapted by permission from *Jester*, Columbia College).

important class of independent variables in psychology is concerned with the past history of the individual. A human subject comes to us with a long, complicated, and incompletely known past history. The fact that an hour or so of weak reinforcement of an only partially specified operant can result in detectable behavioral modification, as in the Centers (1963) experiment, must be taken as a tribute to the fundamental nature of the processes that we have isolated from animal study.

2.11
Operant Conditioning of Autonomic Responses

It was pointed out earlier that operant conditioning has been used to analyze and influence categories of behavior that have been traditionally described as *voluntary*, while Pavlov's classical conditioning has been applied to behavior regarded as *involuntary*. It has also been frequently assumed that the voluntary/involuntary distinction corresponds to the division between responses produced by the *skeletal* muscles (those connected to the skeleton) and controlled by the somatic nervous system, and responses of "smooth" muscles and glands under the control of the *autonomic* nervous system. This has had the consequence that most operant-conditioning studies have involved skeletal responses, while classical conditioning studies have involved autonomic responses.

This restricted application of each conditioning procedure to a different response class led to the belief (for example, by Kimble, 1961) that *only* skeletal responses were susceptible to operant conditioning, while only autonomic responses could be classically conditioned. However, there have now been numerous demonstrations of the influence of operant procedures on autonomic responses.

The Galvanic skin response (GSR) is a fluctuation in the electrical resistance of the skin that is elicited by emotional events, such as sudden noises, electric shocks, and frightening situations. The GSR is controlled by the autonomic nervous system and is readily classically conditioned using the techniques developed by Pavlov. Recent studies have also shown that the GSR can be used as an operant response (see Kimmel, 1973), but these effects may, in some cases, have been produced indirectly because nonautonomic bodily movements can elicit GSR's. A study which ruled out the *mediation by skeletal responses* was carried out by Van Twyver and Kimmel (1966). They reinforced GSR's, while concurrently monitoring skeletal activity and respiration. The reinforcing stimulus was a 1-sec presentation of a dim light to a subject otherwise in total darkness. Even when all GSR's, occurring close in time to skeletal movements and respiratory irregularities, were eliminated, they found a considerable increase in GSR frequency when the reinforcement contingency was in operation.

A more dramatic type of demonstration of operant conditioning of autonomic responses is provided by the work of Neal Miller and his associates (Miller, 1969). They attempted to rule out any involvement of skeletal muscles by paralyzing rats with curare and then reinforcing changes in autonomic responses. Initially, Trowill (1967) demonstrated small, but reliable, changes in heart rate, both increases and decreases. Subsequently, the operant conditionability of a number of other autonomic responses was demonstrated. These included intestinal contraction, blood pressure, and even vasodilation of one ear but not the other. However, the remarkable size of the response changes reported in some of these studies has proved difficult to replicate (Miller and Dworkin, 1974), and while it seems reasonable to conclude that autonomic responses are indeed susceptible to reinforcement contingencies, they may not be as easily modified as skeletal responses. This is unsurprising, as our current ignorance of their internal physiological consequences makes it impossible for us to manipulate those consequences directly as reinforcers.

References for Chapter 2

Centers, R. A laboratory adaptation of the conversational procedure for the conditioning of verbal operants. *Journal of Abnormal and Social Psychology*, 1963, **67**, 334–339.

Frick, F. C., and Miller, G. A. A statistical description of operant conditioning. *American Journal of Psychology*, 1951, **64**, 20–36.

Gardner, R., and Gardner, B. Teaching sign language to a chimpanzee. *Science*, 1969, **165**, 664–672.

Guthrie, E. R., and Horton, G. P. *Cats in a puzzle box*. New York: Rinehard, 1946.

Hayes, C. *The ape in our house*. New York: Harper and Row, 1951.

Hull, C. L. *Principles of behavior*. New York: Appleton-Century-Crofts, 1943.

Irwin, O. C. Infant speech: development of vowel sounds. *Journal of Speech and Hearing Disorders*, 1952, **17**, 269–279.

Kimble, G. A. *Hilgard and Marquis' conditioning and learning*. New York: Appleton-Century-Crofts, 1961.

Kimmel, H. Instrumental conditioning. In W. F. Prokasy and D. C. Raskin (Eds.) *Electrodermal activity in psychological research*. New York: Academic Press, 1973.

Millenson, J. R., and Hurwitz, H. M. B. Some temporal and sequential properties of behavior during conditioning and extinction. *Journal of the Experimental Analysis of Behavior*, 1961, **4**, 97–105.

Miller, N. E. Learning of visceral and glandular responses. *Science*, 1969, **163**, 434–445.

Miller, N. E., and Dworkin, B. R. Visceral learning: recent difficulties with curarized rats and significant problems for human research. In P. A. Obrist, *et al* (Eds.) *Cardiovascular Psychophysiology*, Chicago: Aldine, 1974.

Osgood, C. E. *Method and theory in experimental psychology*. New York: Oxford University Press, 1953.

Premack, D. Reversibility of the reinforcement relation. *Science*, 1962, **136**, 255–257.

Premack, D. Reinforcement theory. In D. Levine (Ed.) *Nebraska symposium on motivation*. Lincoln, Nebraska: University of Nebraska Press, 1965.

Premack, D. Catching up with commonsense or two sides of a generalization: Reinforcement and punishment. In R. C. Glaser (Ed.) *The nature of reinforcement*. New York: Academic Press, 1971.

Premack, D., and Premack, A. J. Teaching visual language to apes and language-deficient persons. In R. L. Schiefelbusch and L. L. Lloyd (Eds.). *Language perspectives-acquisition, retardation and intervention*. New York: Macmillan, 1974.

Rheingold, H. L., Gewirtz, J. L., and Ross, H. W. Social conditioning of vocalizations in the infant. *Journal of Comparative and Physiological Psychology*, 1959, **52**, 68–73.

Routh, D. K. Conditioning of vocal response differentiation in infants. *Developmental Psychology*, 1969, **1**, 219–226.

Seligman, M. E. P. On the generality of the laws of learning, *Psychological Review*, 1970, **77**, 406–418.

Skinner, B. F. *The behavior of organisms*, New York: Appleton-Century, 1938.

Skinner, B. F. A case history in scientific method. *American Psychologist*, 1956, **11**, 221–233.

Skinner, B. F. The experimental analysis of behavior. *American Scientist*, 1957, **45**, 343–371.

Spencer, H. *The principles of psychology*. New York: D. Appleton, 1878.

Thorndike, E. L. *Animal intelligence: experimental studies*. New York: Macmillan, 1911.

Trowill, J. A. Instrumental conditioning of the heart rate in the curarized rat. *Journal of Comparative and Physiological Psychology*. 1967, **63**, 7–11.

Van Twyver, H. B., and Kimmel, H. D. Operant conditioning of the GSR with concomitant measurement of two somatic variables. *Journal of Experimental Psychology*, 1966, **72**, 841–846.

Verplanck, W. S. The control of the content of conversation. *Journal of Abnormal and Social Psychology*, 1955, **51**, 668–676.

CHAPTER 3

Extinction and Reconditioning

"So long as life endures, a creature's behavior is a clay to be molded by circumstances, whimsical or planned. Acts added to it, and other acts which fall out, are the means by which it is shaped. Like the two hands of an artisan, busily dabbing and gouging, are the processes, *reinforcement* and *extinction*."

F. S. Keller and W. N. Schoenfeld, *Principles of Psychology*, 1950

Operant conditioning results in changes in the behavioral repertoire. It provides a method by which the organism can adapt to its own circumstances by selectively increasing the frequency of responses that are followed by reinforcing stimuli. It is not surprising to find that, if a previously reinforced operant is no longer followed by its usual reinforcing consequence, the frequency of the operant declines. In parallel with Pavlovian conditioning, this process is called *extinction*. However, we shall see that, while operant extinction has the same overall effect as Pavlov's classical extinction—the reduction in frequency of a specific response—there are various associated phenomena specific to operant extinction.

What constitutes extinction? The normal operation is to cease presenting the reinforcing stimulus at all, and most of the findings reported herewith are based on this procedure, but there is an alternative. If it is the particular relationship, or contingency between operant response and reinforcer that defines operant conditioning, then any operation that breaks the contingency will constitute extinction. Thus, a procedure in which the reinforcing stimulus continues to occur but is no longer dependent on occurrences of the operant response could result in extinction.

Note carefully that the word "extinction" is used by psychologists in two different ways. Extinction refers to the experimental procedure, or *operation*, of breaking the contingency between response and reinforcer. But it is also a name for the observed resulting decline in the frequency of the response when that operation is carried out. We call this change in behavior the extinction *process*. So, a response is said to be *extinguished* if the frequency has fallen too close to its operant level as a result of there no longer being a contingency between it and its reinforcer. There are, of course, other methods of reducing the frequency of a response (satiation, punishment, and others discussed in later chapters), but these are not called extinction.

3.1
Changes in Response Rate During Extinction

The decline in the rate of the once-reinforced response is the best-documented effect of extinction. The changes in rate are clearly seen in a cumulative curve, where they appear as wavelike fluctuations, superimposed on a general negative acceleration. In Figure 3.1, such an extinction curve appears for the lever-press response of a rat, previously accustomed to receiving a food pellet for each lever press. The response rate is highest at the

FIGURE 3.1. Cumulative record of responding in extinction of a lever press response, previously reinforced with food (From Skinner, 1938, data of F. S. Keller and A. Kerr).

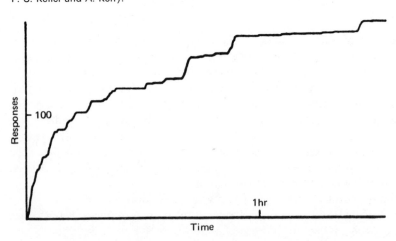

start (just after reinforcement is withdrawn), and gradually diminishes over the period of an hour and a half. By the end of 90 min, the rat is responding at a rate only slightly higher than its operant-level rate. As Figure 3.1 shows, the extinction curve is very irregular and contains many periods of high activity interspersed with periods of low activity (the flat portions of the curve). The latter becomes more prominent towards the end of extinction. Some workers have supposed that the extinction process is due principally to a gradual increase in the number of these inactive periods over time, and that when the organism responds, it does so at its usual high rate. Hurwitz (1957) has presented suggestive data in support of this notion. He analyzed a number of curves similar to Figure 3.1, breaking them into successive 2-min time intervals. He then divided the intervals into two classes, depending on how many responses were in them. Those containing zero, or only a single response, he called "silent," and those containing two or more responses, he called "active." He found that the number of responses in the active periods failed to decline as extinction progressed, but that more intervals became "silent." His results for a group of animals are summarized as Figure 3.2. Hurwitz analyzed the data in terms of *time allocation*. The idea is that the amount of time the subject allocates to an activity is the primary determinant of how often that activity occurs.

Accompanying the overall decline in response rate in extinction, there is often seen a transitory *increase* in rate at the very beginning of extinction. This can be seen at the beginning of the cumulative record in Figure 3.3. The reason for this transient effect is suggested by the results of another procedure in which the contingency between the response (lever pressing) and the reinforcer (food pellets) is broken. Figure 3.3 shows cumulative records for two rats given food reinforcement for 100 lever presses, and then shifted to a procedure where food pellets were delivered automatically at approximately the same intervals at which they had been obtained during reinforcement.

FIGURE 3.2. Two measures of responding in extinction (After Hurwitz, 1957).

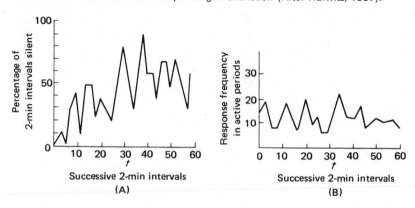

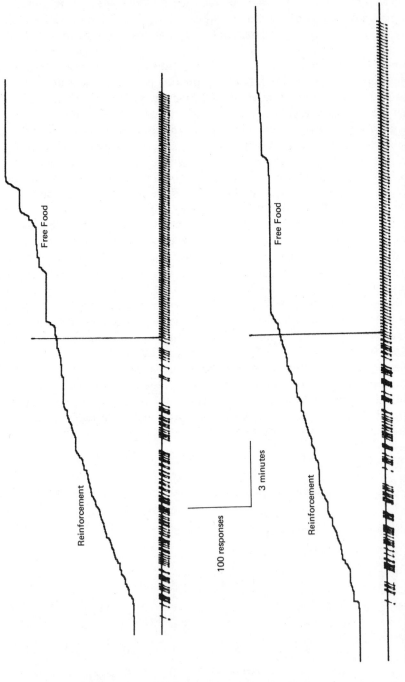

FIGURE 3.3. Cumulative records for two rats reinforced one hundred times for lever pressing and then transferred to a response-independent food presentation schedule. The vertical line indicates the transition from reinforcement to "free food" at an equivalent rate (Data collected by M. Keenan).

This "free food" procedure was effective in reducing response rates, which rapidly declined to near zero, but the transient increase in rate was slight for one subject and non-existent for the other. We may conclude that the transient rate increase is related to the shift to a procedure in which the reinforcer is no longer presented.

"Time allocation" proves a useful concept in describing this finding. During reinforcement for lever pressing, rats typically spend a great deal of time retrieving and consuming the reinforcers. This leaves comparatively little time available for making the operant response. If they are subsequently transferred to a procedure in which no reinforcing stimuli occur, the time spent on retrieval and consumption is "released" for other activities such as the operant response. The transient increase in rate described above may thus reflect the allocation of more time to lever pressing at the beginning of extinction than was available during reinforcement.

3.2
Topographical and structural Changes in Extinction

The effects of extinction are by no means confined to frequency changes in the selected response. In particular, marked changes occur in the form of the behavior during extinction. In a study by Antonitis (1951), in which a rat's poking its nose through a slot in the wall was the operant under study, the effects of several sessions of extinction interspersed with reinforcement were measured. One wall of the chamber used by Antonitis contained a horizontal slot, 50 cm long. Whenever the rat poked its nose into the slot, a light beam was broken, causing a photograph of the rat to be made at the exact instant of the response. The position along the slot where the animal was at that moment, and the angle that its body made with the slot, were measured. Figure 3.4 illustrates the apparatus.

By reinforcing nose poking with food, the frequency of this behavior was first increased above operant level. Subsequently, nose poking was extinguished, reconditioned, reextinguished, and reconditioned again. Confirming Guthrie and Horton's (1946) results with pole tilting of cats and dogs, Antonitis found that response position and angle tended to become stereotyped during reinforcement: the animal confined its responses to a rather restricted region of the slot. Extinction, however, produced variability in nose poking at least as great as that observed during operant level; the animal varied its responses over the entire length of the slot. Finally, reconditioning resulted in even more stereotypy (more restricted responses) than the original conditioning had produced.

A similar study was carried out with pigeons by Eckerman and Lanson (1969), using an apparatus in which the pigeon could peck at an area 10 in long and 3/4 in high (the equivalent of the slot through which the rat poked its nose in the Antonitis experiment). Recordings were made of the position

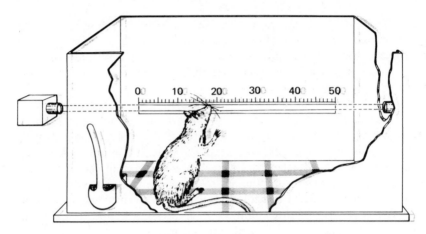

FIGURE 3.4. Apparatus used by Antonitis (1951) to reinforce nose poking.

at which pecks occurred. Figure 3.5 shows how pecks were distributed along the 10 in strip for the three birds in the experiment during reinforcement, and during a subsequent session of extinction. During extinction, pecks were distributed over a much wider area than during reinforcement.

The loop or chain of behavior established by reinforcement degenerates when reinforcement no longer follows the operant response. Frick and Miller (1957) gave rats 300 reinforcements over a period of five sessions in a modified Skinner box. This box had a lever on one wall and a food tray on the opposite wall. This increased the distance between lever and food tray, and made the two responses topographically and spatially distinct, and thus, easy to record separately. These were denoted R_L, lever press and R_T, tray visit. During extinction, Miller and Frick observed the degeneration of the strengthened $R_L R_T R_L R_T \ldots$ loop. As extinction progressed, lever presses began to follow lever presses ($R_L R_L$, and so on), and tray visits began to follow tray visits ($R_T R_T$, and so on). There was very little tendency for the pattern to become random during extinction. Rather, the strengthened pattern of $R_L R_T R_L R_T \ldots$ gradually gave way to the operant-level pattern of repeated occurrences of the same response. Notice that this result was by no means logically inevitable, for the loop of behavior could simply have declined in frequency during extinction, yet remained intact.

To summarize, the extinction procedure instigates a behavioral process whose effects include decline in frequency of the operant response, an increase in its variability, and a breakdown in the sequential structure of the behavior. These important properties of extinction will subsequently be invoked to explain other phenomena.

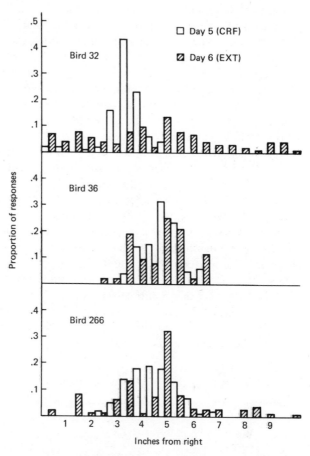

FIGURE 3.5. Data from 3 pigeons reinforced for pecking a 10-inch "key." Variability was greater during extinction (Day 6) than during the preceding reinforced session on Day 5 (Eckerman and Lanson, 1969).

3.3

Extinction-Induced Aggression

We have described some changes in the formerly reinforced response resulting from extinction. What happens to the other behaviors that do not have a history of reinforcement in the experiment? Not surprisingly, some responses that are reduced in frequency when an operant is reinforced, such as grooming and investigatory behavior, increase again during extinction. More surprisingly, some "new" behavior may be seen. That is, responses occur that were not seen during reinforcement and had effectively zero operant level prior to reinforcement.

The most remarkable of these is aggression. Azrin, Hutchinson and Hake (1966) trained a hungry bird to peck a disk for food. When the experimental bird had acquired key-pecking behavior, a second "target" bird, immobilized in a specially designed box, was introduced into the experimental compartment (Figure 3.6). The box holding the target bird was mounted on an assembly that caused a switch underneath to close whenever the box was jiggled vigorously. The assembly was carefully balanced so that normal spontaneous movements of the target bird were insufficient to close the microswitch, whereas any forceful attacks that the experimental bird might direct against the exposed body of the target bird would be recorded. Attacks occurred predictably. Whenever its reinforcement contingencies were abruptly changed from reinforcement of pecking to extinction, the experimental bird invariably attacked the target bird. The attacks were vicious and aggressive, lasting up to 10 min.

Other experiments have established a considerable degree of generality for this result by demonstrating that extinction-induced aggression can be obtained with various species and reinforcers. The important point to remember is that these attacks do not occur simply because no reinforcement is available, but because reinforcement was previously available and has now been discontinued. It turns out that aggression is one of a class of *adjunctive behaviors* that occur during periods of extinction or nonreinforcement, and these will be further discussed in Chapter 5.

FIGURE 3.6. Apparatus used for measuring attack (Azrin, Hutchinson and Hake, 1966).

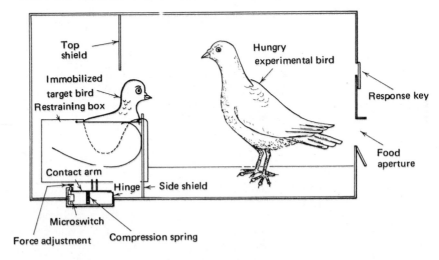

3.4

Resistance to Extinction

Were the extinction process allowed to go to completion, the operant-level state might eventually be reached. The time taken for this to occur is apparently an index of the individual's persistence in the face of extinction. In actual experiments, a return to operant level is rarely, if ever, reached. Hence, more convenient and practical measures of persistence are based on how fast the response rate declines during extinction. For instance, the number of responses emitted, or the amount of time up until the point at which some low rate criterion is met, are called resistance-to-extinction measures.

Resistance to extinction provides a quantitative behavioral index, which is related in an interesting way to a number of experimental operations. On occasion, we shall refer to studies in which resistance to extinction is the principal behavioral variable. In everyday life, we are often interested in how persistent a person will be in the face of no reward. A person whose resistance to extinction is low is said to "give up too easily" or to lack "perserverance" at a difficult task. On the other hand, too much resistance to extinction is sometimes counterproductive. The man or woman who spends too much time fruitlessly trying to patch up a broken love affair may miss a good chance for a new and better relationship.

One of the variables that has been shown to affect resistance to extinction is the number of previous reinforcements. It seems plausible that if many strengthening reinforcements have been given, resistance to extinction will be greater than if only a few have been given. This general hypothesis has been confirmed by several experiments (Williams, 1938; Perin, 1942; Hearst, 1961) which indicate that the resistance to extinction of an operant is low when only a few reinforcements have been given in conditioning, then gradually increases reaching a maximum.

Another variable that would seem likely to affect the persistence of a response in extinction is the effortfulness of the response. Mowrer and Jones (1943) hypothesized that responses that required great effort to make would extinguish more quickly than would responses requiring less effort. This prediction has been confirmed in a study by Capehart, Viney, and Hulicka (1958), who trained rats to press a bar for food. They varied the force necessary to depress the bar during conditioning, so that on some sessions, a heavy bar was present, and on others, it was light or intermediate. The animals were then divided into three groups, one of which was extinguished on the heavy bar, another on the light bar, and the last on the intermediate bar. Using a criterion of no responses in 5 min as the index of resistance to extinction, they obtained the function shown in Figure 3.7.

The design of this experiment is rather different from any we have considered up to the present. In the graphical representations of behavioral effects in this and previous chapters, we have presented data obtained from

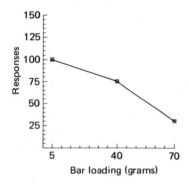

FIGURE 3.7.
Resistance to extinction of lever pressing as a function of the weight of the bar (after Capehart, Viney and Hulicka, 1958).

individual subjects. Sometimes the graphical representations have been averages of several subjects but, in all cases, every subject underwent an identical and complete procedure. By complete, it is meant that the behavior of the subject was measured at every employed value of the independent variable. The use of several subjects and the averaging of the results was merely an attempt to cancel out random errors of measurement that perturb every experiment. In certain behavioral studies, however, it is impossible to subject the same individual to more than one value of the independent variable without introducing new confounding variables. Such is generally the case when resistance to extinction is the dependent variable. To measure the values of resistance to extinction for each of several values of our independent variable, we would have to get several extinction curves from the organism. But after original strengthening at a given value of the independent variables, there exists only one extinction curve. To get another one, we would either have to recondition the behavior or to use another subject. The first course is justified only if successive extinction curves, after repeated reinforcement and reconditionings, are identical. It turns out, however (see Section 3.6), that they are not; in fact, they are systematically different. Thus, we are usually left no recourse but to adopt the device of using a different subject or group of subjects for each experimental condition.

Hence, Capehart, Viney, and Hulicka extinguished one rat at a 5-gm loading, another at a 40-gm loading, and a third at a 70-gm loading. In this way, they avoided the problem of how to get initial extinction curves from the same rat at all 3 bar weights. But in so doing, they introduced a new source of measurement error; that of individual differences among subjects due to such factors as genetic differences or uncontrolled differences in past history. To average out these individual differences among subjects, which might obscure whatever effect effort of response might have, the investigators essentially replicated their experiment 9 more times and averaged their results, thus using a total of 27 subjects altogether (9 rats per condition times 3 different conditions). Although the smoothness of their function relating resistance to extinction to bar loading attests to the success of their strategy, their results (and all such similar results) must be interpreted with caution. In their experiment, no single subject ever experienced all three values of the independent variable in extinction. Hence, the generalization of the result to any individual organism depends upon the assumption that, if it were possible to obtain initial extinction curves for three different values of the independent variable in a single individual, the results of such a procedure would correspond to the results obtained by subjecting different individuals to the different experimental conditions. In general, we tend to avoid this assumption whenever possible and thus resort to such group functions (of which Figure 3.7 is an example) only when, as in this case, we seem to have no choice. Whenever we have a choice, it is usually preferable to perform a complete experiment on an individual subject, exposing him or her to all the conditions in which we are interested. Reliability of our results can then be assessed by complete replications of our experiment on additional subjects.

The Skinner Box, and related pieces of apparatus, allow *free-operant responses* to occur. That is, the operant can be emitted at any time. In contrast to this are apparatuses for recording operant behavior on a *discrete-trial* basis. In these, the subject's opportunities to omit the operant response are limited to particular moments in time, or trials. The most frequently used apparatus of this latter type is the *runway*, or alley, illustrated in Figure 3.8.

On a trial, the subject is placed in the start box, the door is opened, the subject runs to the goal box and consumes whatever reinforcer has been provided. After sufficient time has elapsed for consumption of the reinforcer, the subject is removed from the apparatus by the experimenter. This apparatus enables the experimenter to control exactly the number of opportunities the subject has to make the operant response. It is often used to study resistance to extinction, and the criterion employed is usually the number of trials run in extinction before the subject takes more than a specified time, for example, two minutes, to traverse the runway. The effects

FIGURE 3.8.

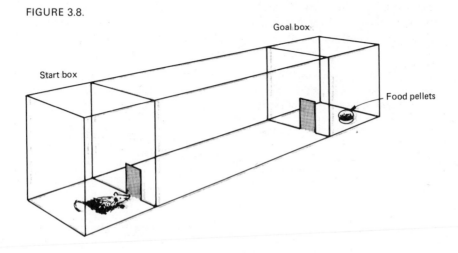

Goal box

Start box

Food pellets

of numerous parameters of reinforcement on resistance to extinction have been examined in this apparatus and, as an example, the results of a study of the effects of different numbers of food pellets given as reinforcement is shown in Figure 3.9. Studies of this type have generally used the method of employing groups tested under different conditions, similar to Capehart, Viney, and Hulicka (1958).

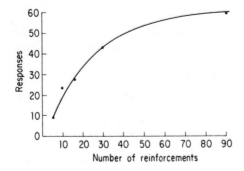

FIGURE 3.9.
Average number of responses in extinction, a measure of resistance to extinction, for groups of rats given differing numbers of food reinforcements for traversing a runway (adapted from Perin, 1942, and Williams, 1938).

3.5

Spontaneous Recovery

Extinction may be extended until the rate of a formerly strengthened operant has reached a low level. If the subject (for example, a rat in a Skinner box) is then removed from the situation and returned a bit later, another (smaller) extinction curve will be obtained (see Figure 3.10). Even though no reconditioning has taken place between the two extinction sessions, a certain amount of spontaneous increase in responding has occurred.

The amount of spontaneous recovery (as measured by the resistance to extinction in the second extinction session) depends on the time lapse between the end of the first extinction and the beginning of the second one. With food reinforced operants, spontaneous recovery has been observed

FIGURE 3.10. Spontaneous recovery from extinction of a rat's lever-press response. The portions of the curve to the right and left of the vertical line were separated by 47 hr out of experimental session (Skinner, 1938).

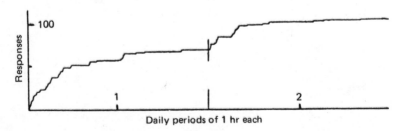

Daily periods of 1 hr each

after as little as 15 min, and seems to reach a maximum after about two hours.

The existence of spontaneous recovery supports a conclusion from the schedule-induced aggression findings: once a response has been extinguished, the organism is not returned to the state it was in before conditioning was started. Further support for this hypothesis will be found in the next section.

3.6

Successive Conditioning and Extinction

The first extinction after original reinforcement is a unique phenomenon. Later extinctions (after reconditioning by the reintroduction of reinforcement) differ by being more rapid and containing fewer total responses. The effect was documented by Bullock and Smith (1953). They exposed rats to 10 daily sessions of a procedure that reinforced the first 40 lever responses, followed directly by 1 hr of extinction. When the extinction curves were examined, it was found that they became progressively smaller over sessions 1 to 10. The effect is shown in Figure 3.11. Whereas in session 1, the average resistance to extinction in 1 hr was 50 responses, by session 10, this had dropped to only 10 responses.

These results can be extrapolated beyond ten sessions. It would seem that only a few more sessions would be needed before the animals would reach what is called one-trial extinction. In one-trial extinction, only a single response is emitted following the withdrawal of reinforcement. The change in behavior has become abrupt, and it seems reasonable to conclude that the organism has come to discriminate the extinction procedure as such. Few responses in extinction are the rule at the human level. Many of our own responses show a rapid decrement when reinforcement ceases. We do not continue to insert coins into a faulty cigarette or candy machine when we fail

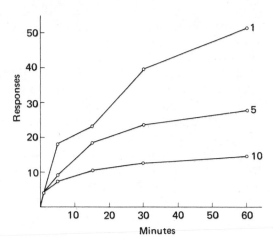

FIGURE 3.11.
Averaged cumulative response curves for 1 hr of extinction. The numbers to the right of each curve designate the session (after Bullock and Smith, 1953).

to receive the payoff. When we open the mailbox and discover it is empty, we do not keep opening it. Like Bullock and Smith's rats, we have learned to wait for our reinforcement.

3.7
Are Irreversible Processes Involved?

We have seen that repeated cycles of conditioning and extinction result in both processes becoming quicker and more "efficient." This might be taken to imply that, during initial conditioning, an irreversible change takes place that cannot be eradicated by extinction and that facilitates reconditioning. It is possible that this is a correct conclusion, but Sidman (1960) argues that the change in the subject's behavior is not, in principle, irreversible, but that in practice, the procedure used is inadequate to produce complete reversion to operant-level behavior.

He points out that the lever pressing of a rat reinforced with food, for example, involves a sequence or *chain* of behaviors (chaining is discussed in Chapter 7) that may include approaching the lever, reaching towards it, pressing it, releasing it, approaching the food tray, picking up the food pellet, and swallowing it. This chain has been acquired because its successful completion results in reinforcement, and it is a new piece of the behavioral repertoire.

When the procedure is changed from reinforcement to extinction, the frequency of completed chains declines after a time. However, the chain is not extinguished piece by piece. Rather, the rat approaches and presses the lever but this is not followed by its usual consequence of a pellet being delivered into the food tray. Consequently, either the rat does not approach the tray, or else it approaches it but finds nothing there. After a number of these "abortive" lever approach-lever press sequences, these early members of the chain extinguish. Note, however, that the later members of the chain (approach food tray, picking up pellet, swallowing it) did not occur. Consequently, they were not extinguished, as *a response can only be extinguished if it occurs.* Thus, Sidman argues, when reinforcement is reintroduced, only the first part of the behavior chain making up the operant response has to be reacquired, and the process will be quicker than the original acquisition. The conclusion here is that extinction normally is only applied to some of the components in the sequence that make up a simple reinforced operant and that, consequently, other components remained unextinguished and so occur with high frequency when reinforcement is reintroduced. If Sidman is right and, in principle, no irreversibility is involved, it may still be true in practice that total reversal cannot be achieved.

3.8
The Operant Extinction Paradigm

The extinction procedure gives rise to the extinction process. As we have seen, the extinction process consists, in part, of a decline in response rate. A number of other behavioral processes, such as fatigue, habituation, satiation, and punishment, entail a similar decline, and we must be careful to distinguish them. If a decline in rate of response is all we, happen to observe, we are likely to find it difficult to say which decay process is operating. As we will wish to use the extinction process later in this text to explain more complex processes, it is important that we understand both its specific procedure and the various characteristics of its resulting process. We will then be able to distinguish those instances of decline in response rate that are the result of extinction from those that reflect other processes.

Formally, the operant extinction paradigm is defined as follows. The contingency between a previously-reinforced operant response and its reinforcer is broken by either (a) ceasing to present the reinforcing stimulus, or (b) presenting that stimulus independent of the occurrence of the response. This has the following effects:

1. A gradual, somewhat irregular decline in response rate marked by progressive increases in frequency of relatively long periods of nonresponding. This may be preceded by a transient increase in response rate.
2. An increase in the variability of the form and magnitude of the response.
3. A disruption of the loop or sequence of behavior that characterized the reinforced operant.

The decline in rate continues until the operant level is approached as a limiting value.

3.9
Forgetting and Extinction

Because extinction and forgetting are both associated with a weakening of behavior, they are often confused. In extinction, the weakening is associated with the emission of unreinforced responses in the situation previously associated with reinforcement. In forgetting, the effect of reinforcement is weakened simply by the passage of time, during which the individual is not in the situation previously associated with conditioning. Forgetting can be studied by first conditioning an operant, then allowing a considerable period of time to elapse, and finally, extinguishing that operant. When this is done under the controlled conditions of the Skinner box, the resulting extinction curve is very similar to those obtained just after conditioning. Figure 3.12 shows a comparison between two averaged cumulative-response curves, one obtained from a group of rats extinguished 1 day after original conditioning, the other obtained from rats extinguished 45 days after original strengthening. The 44 days' difference in time lapse seems to have had only a very small effect compared with the effect of the actual procedure itself.

Even more impressive results are available in support of the notion that the mere passage of time between conditioning and extinction has surprisingly little effect. A group of pigeons was trained in the Skinner box shown in Figure 3.13 to peck a lighted key or disk for food. After strengthening of the key-peck response, the birds were transferred to the usual living quarters. Four years later, they were returned to the apparatus and tested under the extinction procedure. Although the birds had not seen the disk for over 1,400 days, they began to peck it immediately and gave hundreds of responses in extinction (Skinner, 1950).

Much literature exists on the forgetting of human verbal behavior. Before the turn of the twentieth century, Ebbinghaus memorized lists of what are called nonsense syllables (see Figure 3.14) and noted what percentage of the syllables he could remember after various time lapses. The use of nonsense syllables rather than words was an attempt to eliminate factors of meaning and familiarity that might influence the results if ordinary words were used. Ebbinghaus found (see Figure 3.15) that a marked drop in retention occurred during the first 8 hr after learning the lists; after that, the forgetting process very slowly approached an asymptote. Almost as much could be remembered 31 days after learning as 2 days after learning.

Nonsense syllables are easily forgotten. Other verbal materials are not lost so quickly. Figure 3.16 shows forgetting curves for three types of materials: poetry, prose, and nonsense syllables.

Why is it that the animal extinction curves show such small effects after extended lapses, whereas a human may forget more than half of what he or she learns in a few hours? Is this an unsuspected superiority of the rat and pigeon over humans? It may be, but a more convenient explanation lies in a

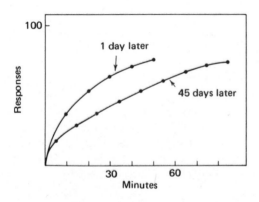

FIGURE 3.12.
Cumulative records in extinction after an interval of one or 45 days since conditioning (Skinner, 1938).

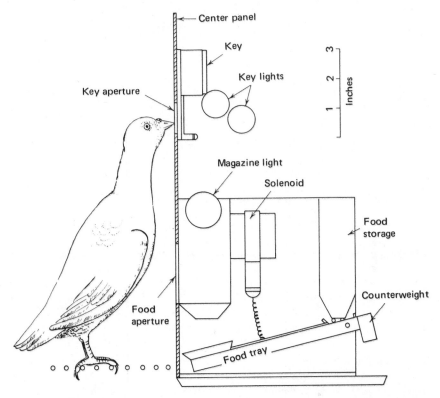

FIGURE 3.13. The operating panel of a pigeon Skinner box.

FIGURE 3.14.
Nonsense syllables used for the study of verbal learning and forgetting.

BIK	NAX
ZUR	KIB
JEK	VOD
ZOT	MEF
YIN	BEW

FIGURE 3.15. Ebbinghaus' data on forgetting of nonsense syllables (after Ebbinghaus, 1913, from Keller and Schoenfeld, 1950).

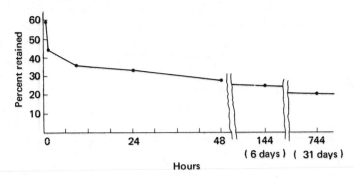

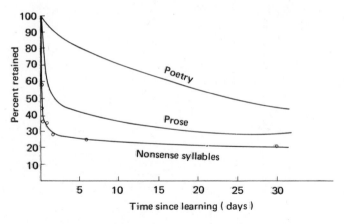

FIGURE 3.16. Retention of different kinds of material over long periods (after Guilford, 1939, and Kendler, 1963).

consideration of the activity that intervenes during the time lapse in the two kinds of experiments. In the animal experiments, the animal is removed from the experimental situation and has little chance to make responses that resemble the strengthened operant. In its usual living quarters, the animal does not experience any situations which closely resemble its training box. The human, on the other hand, after memorizing passages of words—be they nonsense words, prose, or poetry—is not then abruptly removed from his or her verbal environment. Rather, humans continue to use the words they learned and to experience situations in some degree similar to the environment in which they did the original memorizing. Whenever situations do change radically after acquisition, forgetting is not so great. Typewriting skills are only a little affected after a year or so of disuse. Away from the typewriter, the chances of a person's being called upon to execute responses similar to typewriting are small. Swimming and riding a bicycle are two further illustrations of skills that are retained over long periods of disuse.

Whenever a special response is conditioned in a novel environment that is different from any found in the everyday situation, forgetting is reduced. This is true for both human and animal. It is difficult to transport a human abruptly from the learning situation to another, completely different environment. An attempt to do this was made by Jenkins and Dallenbach (1924), whose subjects learned a list of nonsense syllables just before going off to sleep. The subjects were then awakened at various intervals after learning and asked to recall the list they had learned earlier. The results (Figure 3.17) were compared with those obtained from a group of subjects who did not go to sleep after learning the list, but continued with their usual daily activities. Apparently, what one does during the time lapse is critical in determining how much forgetting takes place. We can usefully consider that in the most extreme case of "forgetting," normal and complete extinction

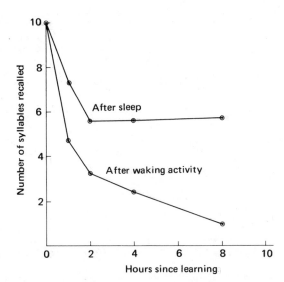

FIGURE 3.17.
The number of syllables recalled after sleep or waking, as a function of the retention interval (adapted from Jenkins and Dallenbach, 1924).

takes place; that is, the response is emitted over and over, but without reinforcement until it ceases to occur. In other everyday cases, some weakening takes place due to the similarity of other behaviors with the learned behavior, and due to the similarity of the environments during conditioning and forgetting.

The pigeon's apparent superiority at retention is eroded when it is put into a situation in which forgetting occurs without extinction. Shimp (1976) trained hungry pigeons in a Skinner box similar to that shown in Figure 3.13, except that there were three response keys mounted in a horizontal row. It was a discrete-trial procedure with two phases. In the first phase, a dim white "X" appeared on one of the side keys (left or right) and remained on until the pigeon pecked that key. The "X" then appeared again on the left or right key until pecked, and then again. Thus there was a three "item" list—peck left, peck left, peck right. There followed a retention interval (in which no stimuli were presented) before the second phase began. A cue was presented on the center key. This was a red, blue, or white light. When this was pecked, it went out and lights of the same color appeared on both keys. (The purpose of this technique was to have the pigeon standing roughly in the middle). The color of the lights indicated which response was now "correct." Red meant repeat the first response or item in the preceding list (left key in our example). Blue meant the second item, and white meant the third item. A "correct" response was reinforced with grain and the trial ended. Shimp found that recall (that is, the probability of a correct response) was a function of list position and retention interval. The last item was recalled best, and recall of all items declined as the interval lengthened. His results are shown in Figure 3.18. Note that recall fell away sharply as a function of both variables. While the last (most recent) item was almost always correct at the shorter retention

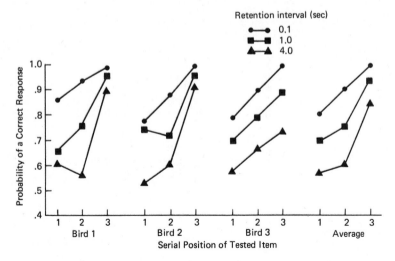

FIGURE 3.18. The probability of a peck on the correct side key in the second phase of a trial as a function of the serial position of the tested item in the first phase of that trial (from Shimp, 1976).

intervals, the first (earliest) item at the longest retention interval (4 sec) was correct only slightly more than 50 per cent of the time, and the pigeon would get 50 per cent if it responded at random.

Comparing this with Skinner's (1950) results mentioned earlier, we may conclude that while a pigeon forgets little about a simple reinforced operant in 1,400 days, it forgets a lot about a complex response sequence in 4 sec.

3.10
Extinction Outside the Laboratory

The author of the cartoon in Figure 3.19 is not an experimental psychologist but he has caricatured the way extinction can influence human behavior. Many instances can be identified in which the frequency or probability of certain behavior declines because it is no longer reinforced. In ordinary language, this decline in response probability may be attributed to other causes, but to the experimental psychologist, the role of extinction is clear:

> An aspiring writer who has sent manuscript after manuscript to the publishers only to have them all rejected may report that "he can't write another word". He may be partially paralyzed with what is called "writer's cramp". He may still insist that he "wants to write", and we may agree with him in paraphrase: his extremely low probability of response is mainly due to extinction. Other variables

FIGURE 3.19. The power of extinction. (Drawing by Opie, © 1961, The New Yorker Magazine, Inc.).

are still operative which, if extinction had not taken place, would yield a high probability (Skinner, 1953, pp. 71–72).

The task of the psychologist is easy when he or she merely provides *post hoc* analyses of everyday terms and situations, but we have already seen how, in this case, laboratory studies have already provided us with an account of the extinction process that goes well beyond that which can be extracted from casual observation. In later chapters on behavior modification, we will discover how this knowledge has been used effectively to deal with behavior problems in the world outside the laboratory.

While there are many other ways of affecting operant-response frequency, the two we have dealt with so far, reinforcement and extinction, can give us a considerable degree of understanding of response frequency, both inside and outside the laboratory. The relevance for psychology of studying the ways in which response frequency, or *strength*, can be controlled is emphasized by a consideration of the use that is made of words involving it in our descriptions of behavior:

> We say that someone is "enthusiastic" about bridge when we observe that he plays bridge often and talks about it often. To be "greatly interested" in music is to play, listen to, and talk about music a good deal. The "inveterate" gambler is one who gambles frequently. The camera "fan" is to be found taking pictures, developing them, and looking at pictures made by himself and others. The "highly sexed" person frequently engages in sexual behavior. The "dipsomaniac" drinks frequently (Skinner, 1953, p. 62).

After all, our descriptions of other people rely in the last analysis on our repeatedly observing them engaging in certain behaviors, and our account becomes more sophisticated when we can accurately specify the frequency of those behaviors.

References for Chapter 3

Antonitis, J. J. Response variability in the white rat during conditioning, extinction, and reconditioning. *Journal of Experimental Psychology*, 1951, **42**, 273–281.

Azrin, N. H., Hutchinson, R. R., and Hake, D. I. Extinction-induced aggression. *Journal of the Experimental Analysis of Behavior*, 1966, **9**, 191–204.

Bullock, D. H., and Smith, W. C. An effect of repeated conditioning-extinction upon operant strength. *Journal of Experimental Psychology*, 1953, **46**, 349–352.

Capehart, J., Viney, W. and Hulicka, I. M. The effect of effort upon extinction. *Journal of Comparative and Physiological Psychology*, 1958, **51**, 505–507.

Ebbinghaus, H. *Memory* (Translated by H. A. Ruger and C. E. Bussenius). New York: Teachers College, 1913.

Eckerman, D. A., and Lanson, R. N. Variability of response location for pigeons responding under continuous reinforcement, intermittent reinforcement, and extinction. *Journal of the Experimental Analysis of Behavior*, 1969, **12**, 73–80.

Frick, F. S., and Miller, G. A. A statistical description of operant conditioning. *American Journal of Psychology*, 1951, **64**, 20–36.

Guilford, J. P. *General psychology*. Princeton: D. Van Nostrand, 1939.

Guthrie, E. R., and Horton, G. P. *Cats in a puzzle box*. New York: Rinehart, 1946.

Hearst, E. Resistance-to-extinction functions in the single organism. *Journal of the Experimental Analysis of Behavior*, 1961, **4**, 133–144.

Hurwitz, H. M. B. Periodicity of response in operant extinction. *Quarterly Journal of Experimental Psychology*, 1957, **9**, 177–184.

Jenkins, J. G., and Dallenbach, K. M. Oblivescence during sleep and waking. *Journal of Experimental Psychology*, 1924, **35**, 605–612.

Keller, F. S., and Schoenfeld, W. N. *Principles of psychology*. New York: Appleton-Century-Crofts, 1950.

Kendler, H. H. *Basic psychology*. New York: Appleton-Century-Crofts, 1963.

Mowrer, O. H., and Jones, H. M. Extinction and behavior variability as functions of effortfulness of task. *Journal of Experimental Psychology*, 1943, **33**, 369–386.

Perin, C. T. Behavior potentiality as a joint function of the amount of training and the degree of hunger at the time of extinction. *Journal of Experimental Psychology*, 1942, **30**, 93–113.

Shimp, C. P. Short-term memory in the pigeon: relative recency. *Journal of the Experimental Analysis of Behavior*, 1976, **25**, 55–61.

Sidman, M. *Tactics of scientific research*. New York: Basic Books, 1960.

Skinner, B. F. *The behavior of organisms*. New York: Appleton-Century, 1938.

Skinner, B. F. Are theories of learning necessary? *Psychological Review*, 1950, **57**, 193–216.

Skinner, B. F. *Science and human behavior*. New York: Macmillan, 1953.

Williams, J. B. Resistance to extinction as a function of the number of reinforcements. *Journal of Experimental Psychology*, 1938, **23**, 506–522.

CHAPTER 4

Response
Specification

In the previous chapter, we restricted our interest in operant behavior to those responses that already existed at some frequency in the behavioral repertoire prior to conditioning. We now want to remove this arbitrary restriction and deal with the acquisition of "new" behavior that is not in the organism's repertoire at all, prior to conditioning. This aspect of operant conditioning corresponds more closely to the ordinary language usage of the term, "learning."

Before expanding our analysis in this way, we need to examine the nature of an operant response more closely.

4.1
The Definition of Response Classes

One of the reasons that the science of behavior has been late in developing lies in the nature of its subject matter. Unlike kidney tissue, salt crystals, batteries, and rock formations, behavior cannot easily be held still for observation. Rather, the movements and actions of organisms appear to flow in a steady stream with no clear-cut beginning or end. When a rat moves from the front to the back of its cage, when you drive 500 miles nonstop in your car, when you sew on a button, it is difficult to identify points at which the continuous *behavior stream* can be broken into natural units. A further complication is that no two instances of an organism's actions are ever exactly the same, because no response is ever exactly repeated.

The problem of extracting fundamental units from a continuous, nonrepetitive behavioral stream lies at the very foundation of the science and corresponds to the problem of taxonomy in other biological sciences. In order to subject behavior to a scientific analysis, we must partition our subject matter in such a way that something fixed and repeatable can be conceptualized. The methods of science are reserved for repeatable events. Both the term *event* and its qualifier *repeatable* are primitive scientific concepts. Thunderstorms, electric charges, fluids, molecules, planets, social institutions, and so on, are the stuff of sciences. Although no two thunderstorms are exactly alike and no two democratic governments the same, it is necessary to group similar—though not identical—events into a single class and call them "thunderstorms" or "democratic governments." Through the use of such artifices, not only meteorology and political science, but all sciences establish concepts in terms of which to frame their laws, generalizations, and predictions. Conceptualization of behavior in terms of such classes, analogous to the class concepts of other sciences is, therefore, a prerequisite for a science of behavior capable of making laws, predictions, and generalizations. The way in which we classify and partition behavior is not a matter of arbitrary choice: an inappropriate system for analyzing the subject matter can be a great obstacle to scientific progress. For example, no real progress was made in astronomy between Ptolemy's description of the universe, which placed the Earth at the center, and Copernicus's, which was centered on the sun. About 1,400 years elapsed between the writings of these two men.

In behavior, we can sometimes begin by classifying into a single category a set of behaviors that are correlated with the same stimulus. Thus, we can observe successive flexions of the leg in response to a well-defined tap on the knee and, although noting their differences, decide to call the knee-jerk response the class (set) of all movements (say) that occur with a duration between the limits of 1/5 to 1 sec and that fall into the range of angles (α) 5 to 30 degrees (see Figure 4.1). In adopting this class, our hope is to include all, or nearly all, the behaviors that are in fact correlated with that particular, eliciting stimulus. We have obtained the successive movements by repeated elicitation, using the same eliciting stimulus with a fixed intensity, duration, locus, and so on. Although the class that is so formed appears to be a grouping of apparently similar movements, its formal definition is merely the class of movements that occurs to a given stimulus.

In defining such classes of behavior, it is necessary to conceptualize certain

FIGURE 4.1.
Schematic diagram of the movement range
defined as including all "knee jerks."

dimensions along which behaviors can be described and measured. Just as a table is exhaustively described by measuring its length, width, height, number of legs, color, weight, density of wood, number of drawers, and so forth, a sample of behavior can be exhaustively described by measuring the position and orientation of the organism in reference to parts of its environment, the movements that are occurring, the time span they occupy, the intensity and frequency with which they occur, and so forth. Particular tables and particular samples of behavior can thus be described by their unique configuration of dimensional values. It appears, therefore, that the classes "tables" and "behavioral samples of type X" are established by setting *restrictions*, *limits*, and *requirements* along certain dimensions so that all "things" that we might conceivably wish to call tables and type-X behaviors, respectively, would fall naturally into our classes. Thus, tables must have, say, one or more legs (a requirement), be made of solid rather than liquid or gaseous material (a restriction), have a flat top (a restriction), be greater than 1 ft, but less than 40 yd long (a limit), and so forth. Similarly, behaviors of type X might include, say, any downward movement (a restriction) of the left arm (a requirement) that is between 15 and 100 gm in force (a limit) and that does not exceed 1/2 sec duration (a restriction), and so on.

We have mentioned examples of behavioral dimensions, such as position of response and duration of response, in earlier sections. These dimensions were used to describe the variability of behavior under operant level, conditioning, and extinction. Some of the dimensions, such as position, angle, location, and orientation of behavior, are said to be *topographical* dimensions, since a listing of their values at any given time will specify the precise form of the behavior. Specifying the value of these dimensions at any moment gives the kind of information provided by a photograph of the organism caught in action. Having captured the static form of the behavior by the topographical variables, we can use dynamic dimensions, such as speed, force, duration, and repetition rate of the behavior, to further describe a particular sample of behavior. In principle, a sample of behavior could be completely described by a statement of the values of all pertinent behavioral dimensions. It would, of course, stand in precisely the same relation to a more complete account that a snapshot stands to a film. In practice, an exhaustive description of behavior is rarely attempted. When topography or form is of primary interest, recourse may be made to photographing the behavior, but a quantitative account of one or two representative behavioral dimensions will often be preferred. In the case of the knee jerk, specification of the class of behavior in terms of just two dimensions seems to suffice for a useful approximation. One of these dimensions constitututes the angle of the leg from the resting position; the other dimension is the duration of the movement. In general, the experimental specification of a piece of behavior is never more than partial, with the values of many dimensions left indeterminate.

To form the classes or units for expressing the laws, generalizations, and predictions of emitted behavior, a strategy different from that used to define elicited behavior must be adopted. In operant behavior, we may proceed at first to define a somewhat arbitrary set of behaviors that meet certain restrictions and requirements and that fall within certain limits along specified response dimensions. Our original criteria for grouping certain samples of behavior may be based on little more than superficial observation that the set of behaviors falling into what we described as type X might be a class of some interest. Having formed this arbitrary class, appeal must now be made—not to an eliciting stimulus, for there is none—to a reinforcer for confirmation that the class we arbitrarily selected will, indeed, function as a unit. That is, we proceed to apply the reinforcing operation to successive instances of the type-X behavior, as defined. Each instance of the class will, of course, be a little different from any other and for that reason is called a *variant*. We prepared ourselves for such differences by specifying *limits* (and not exact values) within which we would reinforce. If reinforcement now affects behavior in such a way as to selectively strengthen a class of behaviors, we are justified in speaking of this class as an *operant-response class*, or more simply, as an operant.

Consider some examples. We might define the limits of a certain class of movements—those of the right arm, for example—and attempt to reinforce all movements within the specified limits. If reaching movements then occur, are reinforced, and increase in frequency, we can conclude that reaching (with the right arm) is an operant. Words are prominent examples of the formation of culturally-determined response classes. All sounds that fall within certain acceptable limits (hence are made by muscular activity within certain limits) make up the spoken word "*please*". When a child enunciates and pronounces the word correctly (emits a variant falling in the desired class), reinforcement is provided and the class of movements that produce *please* are increased in frequency.

In nature, it seems unlikely that reinforcement is ever contingent on a restricted set of topographical limits in the way just described. In the laboratory, reinforcement *could* be made contingent on a restricted subset of behaviors defined by dimensional limitations. But even there, units are more usually approximated by classing together all the movements that act, by the laws of simple mechanics, to produce a specified change in the environment. We call this a *functionally-defined operant*. It is defined as consisting of all the behaviors that could effect a particular environmental change. It contrasts with a *topographically-defined operant* which would be defined as consisting of movements of the organism that fall within certain physical limits. The arm-movement example would fall into this latter category.

These two definitions are not logically independent: a functionally-defined operant can, in principle, be translated into topographic terms, because there is a limit to the number of movements that an organism can make that have a specified effect on the environment. However, the use of functionally-defined operants greatly facilitates analysis, because not only do such units closely correspond to the way in which we talk about behavior ("he missed the train" or "shut the door"), but also, measurement is made easier. When a rat is placed in a conventional Skinner box, it is easy to measure how many times the lever is depressed by a certain amount; it is much more difficult to record how many paw movements of a certain type occur.

While we can alter the specifications of an operant for our convenience, it must be remembered that *the only formal requirement of an operant is that it be a class of behaviors that is susceptible, as a class, to reinforcement.* If we specify a class that fails to be strengthened or maintained by reinforcing its members, such a class does not constitute an operant response; its members are not response variants, and presumably, it is not suitable for use in the study of operant behavior. This is true whether a specification of the boundaries of the behavior was in terms of dimensional limitations, or some necessary environmental change that the behavior must produce. Operants, or operant responses (responses for short, *if* you remember that response does not mean "response-to"), then, are the reinforceable classes of behavior that form the fundamental units of analysis of a large portion of human and animal actions.

In the definition of operants as classes of behaviors amenable to reinforcement, no logic bars the definition of subclasses or superclasses of operants contained in, or containing any particular, previously defined operant class. This flexibility, in the way the basic behavioral "packages" may be subdivided into smaller "packages" or combined to form larger "packages," will be of great importance when we examine the extreme limits to which operant concepts can be extended. In itself, the definition of an operant, therefore, places no restriction on how "big" or how "small" a response class may be in terms of the amount of behavior entering into it. As we shall see, classes consisting of muscle twitches, too minute to be observable by the subject emitting them, may come to function as operants. At the other extreme, lengthy sequences of actions appear to function as single operant classes. Under some conditions, it may be possible to speak of knitting a sweater, writing a book, or walking to work as operants. Extensions of the concept of the operant to such large-scale operants are only recently being explored in the laboratory.

It is sometimes held that the terms, operant and reinforcement, are circular. It appears that each is defined in terms of the other. Reinforcers appear to be defined as those events that strengthen operants; but operants appear to be defined as those behaviors that are strengthenable by reinforcers. The little "thought experiment" which follows shows how the circularity can be broken.

Consider a naive experimenter faced with a Martian. The experimenter observes an "organism" he or she has never seen before. The organism does something. The experimenter, from his or her bag of consequences, presents one at random. Does the organism perform that behavior again more frequently, or does the consequence have no effect? If not, perhaps the experimenter tries again with another consequence, or perhaps he or she tries the same consequence, but selects another behavior. By a process of trial and error, the experimenter may discover certain consequences and certain behaviors that function in the ways described in the previous sections. Having discovered one special consequence, the experimenter can go on to use it to discover other operants; having found one operant, he or she can go on to use it to discover other consequences. Little by little, the persistent experimenter would build up his or her concepts of Martian "reinforcers" and Martian "operants" by just such operations.

4.2
Response Differentiation

The reinforcement of only those instances of behavior that fall within the limits, and that meet the restrictions and requirements set on behavioral dimensions, is known as *response differentiation*. Thus, the conditioning of such responses as disk pecks by pigeons, lever presses by rats, and picking up of toys by children involves response differentiation. What we have been calling simple operant conditioning is a special case of response differentiation. To appreciate the various quantitative aspects of response differentiation, consider a case in which the specification of the behavioral class to be reinforced is in terms of a single behavioral dimension.

In the definition of the lever press of a rat, the minimum force required to depress the lever may often be specified. This minimum force is an example of a lower limit of a behavioral dimension. If the minimum force is low enough, the operant level of lever pressing will be greater than zero, and strengthening of the lever-press operant class will proceed exactly as described in Chapter 2. Hays and Woodbury (cited in Hull, 1943) conducted such an experiment, using a force minimum of 21 gm. After the conditioning process had stabilized, they obtained responses distributed along the force dimension as shown by the upper histogram of Figure 4.2. Figure 4.2A shows no more than the familiar variability that characterizes behavior, even when every response is reinforced. In (A), the forces emitted are distributed approximately symmetrically about a point some 8 gm above the lower limit of the operant-response class. Notice that a few presses (represented by the open circles of Figure 4.2) do not adequately meet the criterion for a response and are, therefore, not reinforced. When the experimenters were satisfied that Figure 4.2A represented the final stabilized state of the behavior under their conditions, they raised the minimum force requirement to 36 gm. The result of this change in the response class was the adjustment of the behavior of the rat to that shown by the histogram of Figure 4.2B. The distribution of forces has moved upward and is now centered at approximately 41 to 45 gm. Conditioning of this new class of behavior has been successful; the necessary condition for conferring upon the class the status of an operant response has been met. There has been a further important consequence of this conditioning. Novel emitted forces, never before seen in the animal's repertoire (those over 45 gm), are now occurring with moderate frequency.

The differentiation procedure has resulted in the appearance and stabilization of a set of novel behaviors. How did this occur? Two complementary processes appear responsible. First, observe that, at the time

FIGURE 4.2. Distribution of response forces when (A) all forces above 21 g and (B) above 36 g were reinforced (after Hays and Woodbury, cited in Hull, 1943).

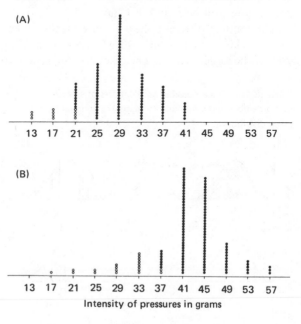

it was put into effect, the new requirement of 36 gm encompassed some existing forces (see the right tail of Figure 4.2A). The strengthening of these greater-than-36-gm force behaviors would be expected to maintain them. Had this condition not been met, normal extinction would almost certainly have occurred. Then, second, the 36-gm minimum excluded many forces previously reinforced. When lever presses of these previously reinforced were emitted under the 36-gm minimum procedure, they were extinguished. Recall that one of the results of the extinction procedure is an increase in the variability of behavior. Extinction of the previously reinforced 21 to 36-gm forces would, accordingly, tend to produce new forces, both higher and lower than those usually emitted. The emission of very low forces would be of no consequence in the present experiment, but the emission of very high forces would be met with reinforcement, and hence, increased in frequency. Eventually, these two processes—(1) differential extinction and (2) differential conditioning—interacting along the force dimension, led to behavioral stabilization in the form of histogram (B) of Figure 4.2.

Extinction has played a crucial dual role in this differentiation of more forceful lever depressions. (1) It has acted to bring about novel and exceptional response variants, some of which may be reinforced. (2) It has acted to weaken the behavior along the portion of the dimensions where reinforcement is being witheld.

The response differentiation procedure can be applied in other ways than in the Hays-Woodbury example. Figure 4.3 gives several possibilities. The Hays-Woodbury experiment is an example of procedure (A). An example of (B) is provided by Blough (1958), who reinforced pigeons for standing still. Examples of (C) and (D), where the behavioral dimension is rate of responding, will be found in Chapter 5.

The limit of differentiation is only reached when the range of behavior reinforced is so narrow that other behaviors, that fall outside the range, form part of the same operant. The response "precision" that can be achieved can

FIGURE 4.3. Some possible applications of selective reinforcement and extinction to response variants from the same distribution.

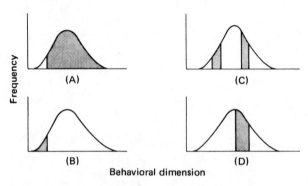

FIGURE 4.4. Herrick's (1964) lever-displacement apparatus.

FIGURE 4.5.
Lever-displacement distributions as a function of the size of the reinforced region (shaded bars). (Data from Herrick, 1964.)

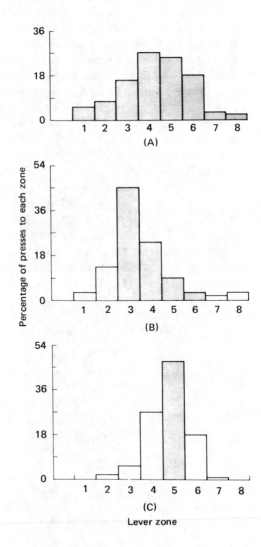

be striking. Herrick (1964) used the lever shown in Figure 4.4. Rats were reinforced for lever presses that moved the pointer into (a) any of zones 1 to 8, (b) zones 3 to 6, (c) zone 5. The results for one rat are shown in the corresponding panels of Figure 4.5. An initial broad range of behavior was narrowed in accordance with the contingencies. Note that when the range was zones 3 to 6, most of the responses were in zone 3. It appears that the rat expended the "least effort" necessary to meet the criterion for reinforcement.

4.3
Successive Approximation

The great power of the differentiation procedure lies in its ability to generate and then sustain behaviors hitherto unobserved in the animal's repertoire. This power is extended very much further in cases in which progressive and gradual differentiations can be made to take place over time. In the Hays-Woodbury example and the examples from Figure 4.3, a one-step differentiation was assumed. But a second differentiation procedure can be applied to the results of the first, and so forth, to produce, eventually, behaviors which may be very different from the original forms. Unless the successive differentiation history was known, accounting for the appearance of these behaviors would be difficult.

We call this method of introducing new behavior into the repertoire, *response shaping by successive approximation*. The process is represented schematically in Figure 4.6. By the nth differentiation, a distribution of response variants has emerged that, to the casual observer, might appear to bear no relation to the original response distribution. Nevertheless, the origins of the nth distribution lie in the successive conditioning and extinction of the ancestors of those variants. Without that causal history, the

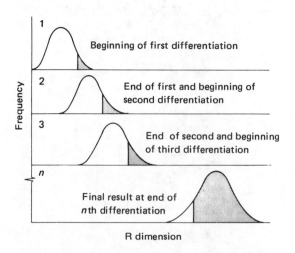

FIGURE 4.6.
Schematic representation of progressive discriminations (successive approximation) along a quantitative response dimension. Shaded areas are reinforced.

final distribution in Figure 4.6 would never have emerged. Successive differentiation must have an upper limit, determined by the capacity of the organism. But within the confines of these capacity restrictions, successive approximation to a final form of behavior is an extremely powerful method for producing behavior. By such a process of successive approximation on the lever-force dimension, Skinner (1938) was able to train 200-gm rats to perform the Herculean feat of pressing a bar requiring a 100-gm minimal force.

Response shaping by successive approximation has a straightforward and very important use in the operant-conditioning laboratory. Suppose an experimenter wishes to reinforce the pecking of a key or disk by pigeons with food (see Figure 3.13). This response often has zero operant-level frequency and thus must be shaped. The experimenter successively approximates the desired form of the behavior, beginning with a form that may not resemble key pecking at all. For example, all movements in the vicinity of the key may first be reinforced. Once these movements have increased in relative frequency, reinforcement is made contingent on head movements directed towards the key. Once such movements are frequent, reinforcement is made contingent upon striking the key with the beak, and finally, upon depressing the key with the beak. The process of instating a response not previously in the repertoire can be very easy or very difficult. The degree of difficulty experienced probably reflects the preparedness of the organism to associate the specified response and reinforcer (see Section 1.8), as well as the stringency of the response differentiation required by the experimenter.

4.4
Processes Involved in Response Specification

Various examples have been given of the ways in which an operant response can be specified, both when the required response does and does not exist in the behavioral repertoire prior to training. In every case, both *selective reinforcement* and *extinction* are involved, so response specification can be described in terms of these more basic processes. However, there is one characteristic common to reinforcement and extinction that is particularly important for response specification. It is that both induce *behavioral variation*.

If we wish to select particular response variants, we must reinforce them. But only if behavior varies along appropriate dimensions, will the opportunity arise to reinforce particular response variants or to shape behavior in the direction of those variants. The "side effects" of the reinforcement and extinction can both produce such variation. It may seem paradoxical to say this of reinforcement, which was earlier defined as producing a *narrower* range of behavior and more stereotypy. However, if the response dimension is a continuous one, such as the examples of the amount of lever displacement given in this chapter, then it is clear that shifting the peak of the distribution of response along the dimension results in some nonreinforced response variants becoming more frequent (see Figure 4.5 for example of this).

4.5

Specification of "Unconscious" Operants

There are a great many human motor performances, both simple and complex, that must be practiced before they can be carried out successfully on every occasion. Examples are: opening a door, opening a can, driving a car, or playing a musical instrument. One feature of these skills is that performance will only be improved if responses are influenced by their consequences; that is, if accurate performance is selectively reinforced in some way. In each example, some "feedback" is provided that could provide reinforcement for accurate performance. However, one of the interesting features of motor skills is that, while feedback and reinforcement are undoubtedly necessary (it is impossible to keep a car on the road in darkness and with no proprioceptive feedback from your limbs), the performer may be unable to say how he or she adjusts his or her behavior in accordance with its success. For example, if you watch someone throw a ball, 60 yards, to land in the hands of a waiting catcher and then ask, "How did you do that?", the person will probably be unable to answer, and if the person does answer, he or she is unlikely to mention the sources of proprioceptive feedback and his or her own history of throwing balls, but these are both important factors in the person's performance.

Can we arrange experimental demonstrations of human operant behavior being reinforced without the awareness of the subject? Indeed, we can. Hefferline and Keenan (1963) have investigated a "miniature" operant, so small that electronic amplification must be employed to detect it. They have reinforced responses so small in amplitude that the subject is generally not able to report observing his or her own responses. In one experiment, muscle-twitch potentials were recorded from the thumb of human subjects. Dummy electrodes were placed at other points on the subject's body to distract attention from the thumb response. Subjects were seated comfortably in a triply shielded, air-conditioned, sound-deadened cubicle, and were under instructions only to relax. They were advised that reinforcements, in the form of counts on a counter located near them, might occur and that each count was worth 5 cents. But the subjects were never told how to produce counts. In one subject, thumb twitches, generating potentials in the range of 25 to 30 microvolts, were reinforced and then extinguished. Histograms, for 10 min of operant level, followed by 6 successive blocks of 10 min of conditioning, followed by a final 10 min of extinction, are shown in Figure 4.7. The conditioning histograms show that the differentiation procedure was

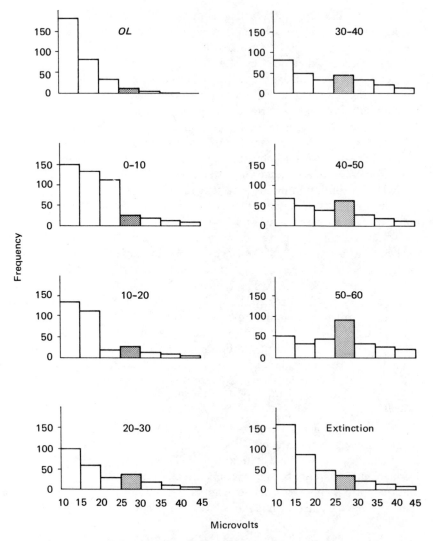

FIGURE 4.7. Histograms of various categories of thumb contractions (measured in microvolts) during operant level, conditioning and extinction. The reinforced category is shaded (after Hefferline and Keenan, 1963).

successful in selectively strengthening the reinforced class of behavior, and that even 10 min of extinction caused a marked weakening in the class. Cumulative records taken of the reinforced muscle twitch show a typical rate of increase of the reinforced class but—as might be expected with an operant of such limited dimensions—the process is a gradual one, extending throughout the 60 min of conditioning. It differs, therefore, from the rather abrupt strengthening curves of the rat's lever press (Figure 2.2).

Hefferline and Keenan's results are important in our analysis of behavior for a number of reasons. First, they show the lower limits to which our concept of operant may be pushed, and yet still denote a functional unit of behavior. Second, they demonstrate that the subject's inability to verbalize the reinforcement contingencies in no way affects the lawful nature of conditioning and extinction. A third empirical phenomenon, and one we have already noted as important in response specification, is demonstrated. In the muscle-twitch operant, the response class was defined as twitches between 25 and 30 microvolts. But close inspection of the histograms of Figure 4.7 will show that neighboring classes of behavior, though actually unreinforced, were also somewhat strengthened. This is another example of behavioral variation induced by selective reinforcement.

Many examples of human subjects successfully increasing the frequency of an operant response, without apparently having "voluntary" control over the response, can be found in *biofeedback* literature. Work on biofeedback developed as a result of the discovery that animals could produce reinforced changes in autonomic responses that were independent of changes in skeletal behavior (see Section 2.11). The biofeedback paradigm involves providing visual or auditory feedback to the subject, as the subject's heart rate, blood pressure, or other autonomic response changes. A study by Weiss and Engel (1971) illustrates the general method. Their objective was to see whether they could demonstrate operant conditioning of heart rate in patients suffering from premature ventricular contractions that produce cardiac arhythmias. It was hoped that if the subjects acquired the ability to produce heart rate changes, this would enable them to reduce the premature ventricular contractions.

During experimental sessions, the subject lay in a hospital bed with recording instruments attached to his or her chest. At the foot of the bed was a vertical display of three, colored lights. These provided the subject with feedback information about his or her cardiac function. The top light (green) and the bottom light (red) were cue lights. The middle light (yellow) was the reinforcer, and came on while the subject was producing the "correct" heart rate.

Each session started with a baseline period of 20 min, where no stimuli were presented, followed by 34 min in which either heart rate acceleration or heart rate slowing was reinforced, or acceleration and slowing were alternately reinforced in the presence of the green or red lights (this is a *multiple schedule*; see Section 5.6). This is called "differential training" in Table 4.1, which gives the results for a number of subjects. The Table simply shows that all subjects were fairly successful in the "slow" and "differential" conditions, but success was only partial in the "speed" condition, where they were required to accelerate heart rate.

This study provides evidence for the operant control of an autonomically modulated response (although the control for mediation by other responses

TABLE 4.1. Ratios of sessions during which each patient kept their heart rate in the required range for more than 50 per cent of the time to total number of sessions (after Weiss and Engel, 1971).

| Patient | Heart rate contingency | | |
	Speed	Slow	Differential
1	4/9	4/6	7/9
2	11/14	5/7	9/9
3	5/11	9/10	8/10
4	6/10	5/10	10/10
5	1/10	9/9	12/14
6	1/6	5/11	—
7	2/8	7/10	—
8	—	16/18	—
	0.40	0.73	0.89

is not as stringent as in the animal studies) and also suggests that heart rate deceleration is easier to reinforce than acceleration.

The clinical objective was to enable the subjects to reduce the frequency of premature ventricular contractions that occur predominately during slow heart rate. Latter parts of the study involved reducing the proportion of time during the session that feedback was provided about the heart rate changes achieved by the subject. Subjects sustained their ability to keep heart rate in a specified range when feedback was provided only for 1 min in 8.

This type of study shows that the processes of response specification can be applied to classes of behavior previously thought to be entirely involuntary, and thus beyond the control of reinforcement contingencies. A subject who has acquired the ability to accelerate or decelerate his or her own heart rate, without resorting to drugs, has acquired a new piece of behavior in a very real sense.

References for Chapter 4

Blough, D. S. New test for tranquilizers. *Science*, 1958, **127**, 586–587.
Hefferline, R. F., and Keenan, B. Amplitude-induction gradient of a small-scale (covert) operant. *Journal of the Experimental Analysis of Behavior*, 1963, **6**, 307–315.
Herrick, R. M. The successive differentiation of a lever displacement response. *Journall of the Experimental Analysis of Behavior*, 1964, **7**, 211–215.

Hull, C. L. *Principles of behavior*. New York: Appleton-Century-Crofts, 1943.

Skinner, B. F. *The behavior of organisms*. New York: Appleton-Century, 1938.

Weiss, T., and Engel, B. T. Operant conditioning of heart rate in patients with premature ventricular contractions. *Psychosomatic Medicine*. 1971, **33**, 301–321.

CHAPTER 5

Intermittent Reinforcement

So far, we have considered only examples of operant responses that are *continuously reinforced*; that is, every occurrence of the response is followed by delivery of the reinforcing stimulus. If we change the conditions so that the reinforcing stimulus occurs only after *some* of the designated responses, we have defined the procedure of *intermittent reinforcement*. In intermittent reinforcement, the response is still a *necessary* condition, but no longer a *sufficient* condition, for the delivery of the reinforcer.

Early experimental studies of learned behavior, concerned as they were with the *acquisition* of behavior, took little interest in intermittent reinforcement. Although learning is usually most effective when each and every response gets reinforced, it is also true that intermittent reinforcement procedures produce reliable and distinctive patterns of behavior, which are extremely resistant to extinction. It is this latter property that gives them very great utility as stable, long-term baselines of learned behavior against which to study the effects of drugs, physiological manipulations, emotional stimuli, and motivational factors.

Intermittent reinforcement also connects closely with many situations in the everyday world where behavior is maintained by a reinforcer that occurs only occasionally. A scavenging dog may knock the lid off several trash cans before finding food, a gambler may place many bets before picking a winner, pacifists had to demonstrate many times before they achieved any social change, and the bored student may glance up at the clock a number of times before seeing that it is time to go home.

5.1
Schedules of Reinforcement

We refer to those experimental procedures that specify which instances of an operant response shall be reinforced as *schedules of reinforcement*. Thus, continuous reinforcement is a schedule in which every response is reinforced whenever it occurs. A host of schedules have been devised and studied in which reinforcement is noncontinuous, or intermittent. Each of these schedules specifies the particular condition or set of conditions that must be met before the next response is reinforced.

If we consider the relatively simple situation where only one response is to be examined and the stimulus conditions are constant, there are two things we have to specify: the number of responses that must occur, and the time that must elapse. Schedules involving a required number of responses are called *ratio schedules* (referring to the ratio of responses to reinforcers); and schedules specifying a period of time are called *interval schedules* (referring to the imposed intervals between reinforcement).

Schedules can also be either *fixed* (where every reinforcer is delivered after the *same* ratio or interval), or *variable* (where the ratios and intervals can vary within the schedule). In the latter case, the schedule is described by its mean value; for example, "variable interval 20 sec" refers to an interval schedule in which the mean time from one reinforcer to the availability of the next is twenty seconds, while on "variable ratio 20," it is on the average, the twentieth response following reinforcement that is reinforced.

Each of the four schedules we have defined generates a characteristic performance, or behavioral steady state. These states can be easily identified by looking at cumulative records (see Figure 5.1). Recall from Section 2.3 that the cumulative recorder steps vertically, a small and fixed amount, each time a response occurs, while continuously moving horizontally at a fixed speed. So the slope of the record at any point reflects the rate of response; cessation of responding produces a flat record, while a very high response rate produces a steep one. Vertical marks on the record indicate the delivery of reinforcers.

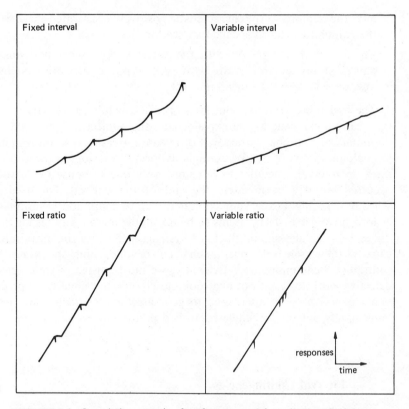

FIGURE 5.1. Cumulative records of performance on four simple schedules.

Although the records in Figure 5.1 are hypothetical, they are in no sense idealized. Reinforcement schedules exert such powerful control over behavior that even a previously "untrained" rat, placed in a Skinner box by an "untrained" student, could generate one of these records after a few hours. Significantly, these performance patterns have been produced in many species, and with a variety of operant responses.

Consider the characteristics of performance generated by each schedule:

Fixed ratio (*FR*) A high rate of response is sustained until reinforcement occurs. This is followed by a relatively lengthy *postreinforcement pause*. This pause increases with the ratio of responses required for reinforcements, and can occupy the greater part of the subject's time.

Variable ratio (*VR*) In common with the fixed ratio schedule, this procedure generates a high rate of response, but regular pausing for any length of time is very uncommon.

Fixed interval (*FI*) This procedure also produces a postreinforcement pause, but responding at other times occurs at a lower rate than on ratio schedules, except towards the end of the interval, where it accelerates to meet the reinforcer. The characteristic positively-accelerated curve seen on the cumulative record is called a "scallop."

Variable interval (*VI*) As with the variable ratio schedule, consistent pauses of any length are rare. However, response rates are moderate to low, depending on the mean interval.

The first thing to note about intermittent schedule performances is that they cannot, in general, be explained as the subject adopting the most "optimal" or "rational" strategy. For instance, treating operant responding as analogues to working (for example, laboring), we would expect response rates on interval schedules to fall until only one response per reinforcer occurred, emitted at precisely the end of the interval. On fixed ratio schedules, we might expect a maximum rate to be continuously sustained for as long as possible. There seems to be no simple reason why response rates under *VI* schedules should fluctuate systematically with the mean interval. Clearly then, schedule phenomena go beyond, and sometimes even contradict, "commonsense." Evidently, we must engage in some scientific detective work to ferret out and look closely at what underlying processes might conceivably be interacting to generate these characteristic, but not immediately obvious, schedule-controlled performances.

5.2
Interval Contingencies

As a point of departure, recall the procedure of successive conditioning and extinction (see Section 3.6). Here, a piece of behavior first receives continuous reinforcement (*CRF*) for a few reinforcements, and then receives none during a long period of extinction. Abruptly, extinction is terminated and *CRF* is briefly reinstated, followed again by a long extinction. This cycle is carried out repeatedly.

Consider now a variation of this procedure, in which only a *single* emission of a response is reinforced, followed by one minute of extinction. Then the response is once more reinforced, and extinguished. When this cycle is repeated over and over, many cycles of conditioning and extinction are effectively compressed into a single session, yielding the characteristic series of behavioral changes that are shown in Figure 5.2.

At first, abbreviated, negatively accelerated extinction curves follow each reinforcement (stage *a*). The response that is reinforced is often the last of a train of low-rate responses. This picture is transitory, however, and after a number of reinforcements have occurred, a moderate and steady rate develops (stage *b*). This is transient, too, for it, in turn, gives way to a third stage (*c*), in which a pause after reinforcement is followed by a gradual or abrupt transition to a moderately high rate of response that is sustained until the end of the interval. The transition from state *b* and *c* is illustrated with actual data

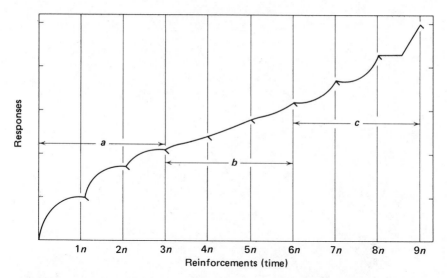

FIGURE 5.2. Stylized curve of the transition from continuous reinforcement to intermittent reinforcement on *FI*. The use of *n* to label the abscissa suggests that the successive response segments need not be from successive reinforcements, but rather from successive multiples of reinforcements. For example, if $n=5$, the segments would be from the 5th, 10th, 15th, and so on, reinforcement.

from a bird pecking a disc for grain reinforcement in Figure 5.3. The records here have been "stacked" so that they can be readily compared. It is clear that the pigeon in this experiment changed from a fairly steady rate throughout the interval in session 2 to a pronounced pause-accelerate pattern by session 4.

The principal effects of a fixed-interval schedule can be summarized as follows:

1. The behavior of the individual shows a gradual adjustment to the procedure.
2. The final pattern is "scalloped," with a period of no responding after each reinforcement.
3. Behavior can be maintained for long periods with fixed intervals from a few seconds up to several hours in duration.
4. A great many responses are generated.

Three aspects of this performance require explicit explanation:
a. why is there a postreinforcement pause?
b. why is there a "scallop"?
c. why is there so much responding?

Answers to a. and b. are suggested by an experiment of Cumming and Schoenfeld (1958). Hungry pigeons were trained on an *FI* 30-min (fixed minimum interreinforcement interval of 30 minutes) schedule of food

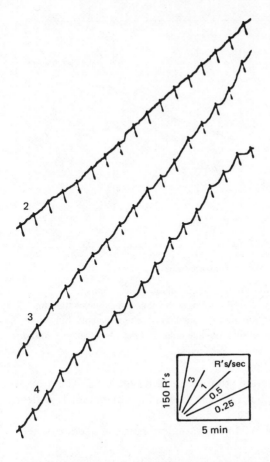

FIGURE 5.3.
Development of *FI*–1 min in a pigeon (Ferster and Skinner, 1957).

reinforcement for 16 hr a day for 144 consecutive days. Cumulative records from one bird, for sessions early, middle, and late in the experiment, are shown in Figure 5.4. These show changes from an "unreliable" scallop, to a "good" scallop, to a different pattern consisting of a much longer pause followed by a sudden switch to a steady high rate of responding.

These results seem to say that the period immediately following a reinforcer during *FI* acts like a stimulus associated with extinction, and provides the subject with a cue to cease responding during that time. We might call this process *discriminated extinction*, because the subject has learned to discriminate that period of nonreinforcement which invariably follows reinforcement. As the interval proceeds, however, the subject gets closer and closer to the time at which a response can be reinforced. The behavior appropriate to that moment is rapid responding, but since the subject's ability to tell the exact time without a clock is limited, he or she starts to respond prior to the actual moment when reinforcement is scheduled. However, his or her frequency of response is greater at points closer in time to the moment of reinforcement, and greatest at the exact time

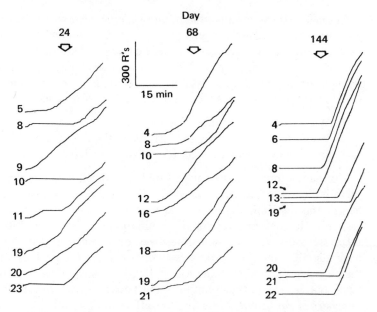

FIGURE 5.4. Stages in the development of behavior under a 30-min *FI* schedule. The number at the left of each segment gives the ordinal reinforcement number terminating that segment (Cumming and Schoenfeld, 1958).

when reinforcement is available. We might say that the subject's tendency to respond seems to vary with his or her uncertainty about when reinforcement is due. In any case, this gradation of responding away from the exact point of reinforcement constitutes an instance of what we shall call a *generalization gradient*.

With very long periods of training (in Cumming and Schoenfeld's experiment, up to 1,300 hr were given), the period of discriminated extinction in each interval may increase to a point where almost no responding occurs until very late in the interval. When this happens, nearly all responding tends to be at the "maximum" rate appropriate to the end of the interval, and the generalization gradient seems absent.

It remains for us to try to explain why there is simply so much responding—often, the number of responses per reinforcement is several hundred; sometimes, several thousands. This "excessive" aspect is characteristic of many types of schedule-controlled performances. From one point of view, however, it may be a pseudoproblem created by our tendency to view operant behavior as analogues to work and drudgery. In the schedules we have dealt with here, a particular operant response is the *only* appropriate and adaptive behavior. Why should the subject not allocate a great deal of time to it? If the response, itself, is relatively effortless and takes very little time to complete, and these are features of most simple repetitive operants, then it is not surprising that very large numbers of operant responses occur.

Let us now turn our attention to interval schedules, where the length of the interval between reinforcements varies from one interval to the next. Such variable-interval (*VI*) schedules generate fairly steady rates of responding. Figure 5.5 shows data from 3 pigeons on early and later sessions of *VI* reinforcement. In the latter sessions, their response rates are higher and show less fluctuation. Questions we can ask of this performance are:

1. Why are response rates so stable?
2. Why are response rates so high, when the lower rates shown in early sessions are adequate to obtain all the available reinforcements?

To the first question, we might simply say that the rate is steady because there is no reason for it to vary. On *FI* schedules, the predictability (and hence, the discriminability) of the time of reinforcement resulted in the response fluctuations we call discrimination and generalization affecting response rate. On *VI* schedule, the occurrence of reinforcement is unpredictable, and these processes do not operate to control response rate. In fact, a more detailed examination of *VI* performance reveals that there is a brief, but consistent, postreinforcement pause, at least in rats (J. C. Leslie, *unpublished data*), but this is an after effect of consuming the reinforcer. A more detailed answer, and an answer to the second question, requires us to go beyond cumulative records to a more sophisticated analysis of the behavior.

FIGURE 5.5. Cumulative records of pigeons at early and later sessions on *VI* 4-min. Sessions numbers are shown (Millenson, 1963).

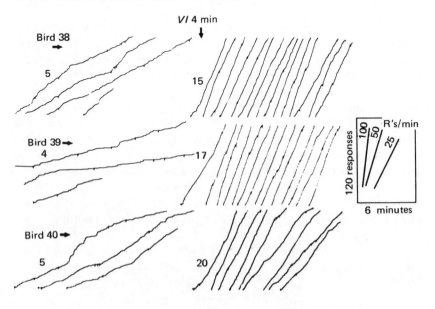

5.3

The Analysis of Interresponse Times

The cumulative record is an excellent method of looking at *sequential patterning* of responses. It draws our attention to periods of acceleration and deceleration, of high and low response rates. If, however, we display the same information on a simpler device that simply makes a mark on a horizontal line each time a response occurs, as in Figure 5.6, our attention may turn instead to the intervals between responses, or interresponse times (*IRT*'s). After all, the description of operant behavior as a sequence of responses separated by *IRT*'s is just as valid as describing it in terms of fluctuations in response rate. Indeed, the analysis of *IRT*'s is, in a sense, prior, as the analysis of response rates is begun by working out average *IRT*'s.

If we look only at the succession of *IRT*'s, then we are simply providing an alternative to the cumulative record. There is, however, an alternative method of analyzing *IRT*'s and it is one that seems particularly appropriate for studying *VI* performance, where sequential effects do not appear to be so important. This method is to examine the *IRT distribution*. Over a period of minutes or hours on the schedule, the number of *IRT*'s that fall into different time intervals is counted, and these numbers are converted into a relative-frequency histogram. An example for a rat on *VI* 30-sec is given in Table 5.1 and Figure 5.7.

The relative-frequency distribution shown in the histogram has a characteristic shape. It shows that a very large percentage of responses are preceded by very short *IRT*'s. (Note that this is not a necessary consequence of the overall response rate. In this session the average *IRT* was greater than 1 sec). The Table also shows how many reinforcements occurred following *IRT*'s in each category. Again, most fall in the first category. We might, therefore, be led to conclude that the short *IRT*'s are relatively frequent, because they are reinforced most often. This conclusion, however, would be both invalid and counterintuitive. It would be invalid, because we do not know whether the high rate of reinforcement caused the high frequency of short *IRT*'s or *vice versa*. It is counterintuitive, because an obvious feature of *VI* schedules is that the longer the subject waits between responses (for

FIGURE 5.6. A 2-channel event recording for monitoring the occurrence of responses and the delivery of reinforcements on a *VI* schedule (hypothetical data).

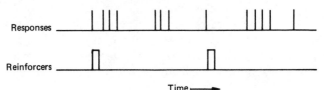

TABLE 5.1. Distribution of *IRT*'s of lever presses by a rat in one 50-min session. Sucrose reinforcement was delivered on a *VI* 30-sec schedule (J. C. Leslie, *unpublished data*).

IRT duration	Number of responses	Number of reinforced responses
<1 sec	2128	42
1–2	188	11
2–3	151	16
3–4	63	11
4–5	14	1
5–6	35	4
6–7	36	5
7–8	6	2
8–9	6	1
9–10	3	2
>10 sec	17	6

example, the longer the *IRT*), the greater the probability of reinforcement for the next response.

This raises the following questions:

1. Is the high rate of reinforcement of short *IRT*'s a cause or an effect of the preponderance of short *IRT*'s?
2. Do *VI* schedules selectively reinforce longer *IRT*'s?
3. More generally, can specific classes of *IRT*'s be selectively reinforced?

Answers to these questions are provided by studies in which more complex schedules are used, specifying that a member of a particular class of *IRT*'s must be emitted to collect the *VI* reinforcement. An example is given in Table 5.2 and Figure 5.8. In this instance, sucrose reinforcements were provided for a rat on a *VI* 30-sec schedule for lever presses, preceded by an *IRT* of between 4.0 and 7.9 sec. Data are presented from a single session of training under these conditions, when behavior had reached a stable (nontransition) state.

Clearly, the shape of the *IRT* distribution has changed considerably from that produced on the "unconstrained" *VI* in Figure 5.7. We now have a *bimodal* distribution, with one peak, as before, at the shortest *IRT* band, and another at the shortest of the reinforced bands. We can, therefore, conclude that selective reinforcement of particular *IRT*'s does work—it substantially increases their relative frequency—and that the preponderance of short *IRT*'s is not solely the result of their being reinforced. Remember that, in this situation, no *IRT*'s shorter than 4 sec were ever reinforced. The best explanation of the high frequency of short *IRT*'s and their persistence,

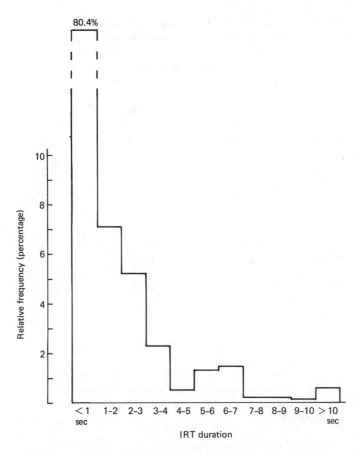

FIGURE 5.7. Relative frequency histograms for the data in Table 5.1. The "bump" at 5–7 sec represents the characteristic postreinforcement pause on this schedule.

even when explicitly nonreinforced, is probably that they result from aspects of the situation other than the schedule itself. Gilbert (1958) coined the term *tempo* to describe the natural frequency of an activity. He applied it to licking, which is obviously rhythmic, but it can plausibly be maintained that a simple operant, such as a lever press or key peck, has an invariant tempo. This will be determined by physical aspects of the apparatus, and the physical abilities and predispositions of the subject. The overall pattern of behavior we observe will then consist of bursts of responses at a fixed tempo interspersed with pauses. On this model, the high frequency of short *IRT*'s is the result of the tempo of simple operants being fast.

The remaining question, whether simple *VI* schedules selectively reinforce longer *IRT*'s, takes us on to a comparison of interval and ratio schedules.

TABLE 5.2 Distribution of *IRT*'s in one 50 min session for a rat, lever pressing for sucrose, on a paced (4.0–7.9 sec *IRT*) *VI* 30-sec schedule (J. C. Leslie, *unpublished data*). See text for details.

IRT duration	Number of responses	Number of reinforced responses
< 1 sec	471	0
1–2	30	0
2–3	21	0
3–4	87	0
4–5	195	54
5–6	173	30
6–7	31	8
7–8	12	4
8–9	3	0
9–10	2	0
> 10 sec	8	0

FIGURE 5.8. Relative frequency histogram for the data in Table 5.2. The shaded area indicates those IRT's that fell within the reinforced range.

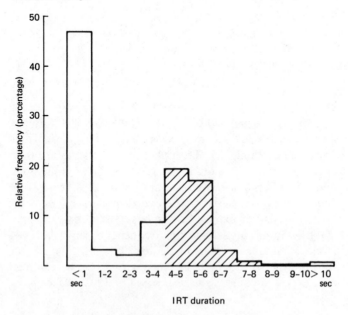

5.4
Yoked Interval and Ratio Schedules

Let us now attempt to answer the question of whether simple *VI* schedules selectively reinforce longer *IRT's* by making a comparison of interval and ratio schedules.

Suppose we have two subjects in identical Skinner boxes. The behavior of the first subject (*A*) is reinforced on a variable-ratio (*VR*) schedule, but the second subject's (*B's*) responses are only reinforced when a reinforcement has become available for the first subject. Note that subject *B* is on a variable-interval (*VI*) schedule, because there is no relationship between the number of responses it emits and the number of reinforcements it receives. Thus, if both subjects respond, we have two subjects obtaining the same *rate of reinforcement*, but one is on *VR* and the other is on *VI*. And because *A's* behavior controls *B's* reinforcement, the two subjects are said to be "yoked."

The resultant behavior is shown on cumulative records in Figure 5.9 for two hungry birds, key pecking for grain. Both respond steadily, but *A* responds over four times faster than *B*. This response-rate differential shows that, given the same rate of reinforcement, a subject will emit more long *IRT's* on interval contingencies. This seems quite reasonable, since on interval schedules, the longer the subject pauses between responses, the greater the probability of reinforcement for the next response.

FIGURE 5.9.
Cumulative records of yoked pigeons on variable ratio (*VR*) and variable interval (*VI*) schedules (from Reynolds, 1974).

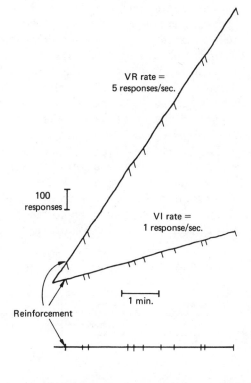

VR rate =
5 responses/sec.

100 responses

VI rate =
1 response/sec.

1 min.

Reinforcement

5.5
Ratio Contingencies

Earlier in this chapter, we describe the transition from continuous reinforcement to *FI* 1 min. It is possible for subjects of many species to make this type of transition successfully; for example, responding does not extinguish, because reinforcements will be made available each minute, even if responding falls to a very low rate. However, if we wished to transfer a subject from continuous reinforcement to a fixed ratio of forty responses per reinforcement (*FR*40), it might be unwise to transfer directly from one to the other without any intervening steps. This is because overall response rate is generally an increasing function of reinforcement rate. If we increase the response requirement suddenly from one to forty, there will be a large drop in reinforcement rate, which will probably result in a decrease in response rate. This, in turn, will further lower reinforcement rate, and so on. This type of interaction is called a *positive feedback loop* and is illustrated in Figure 5.10a.

Effects seen in the Stock market often resemble positive feedback loops. An increase in confidence results in an increase in value of stocks. This, in turn, produces an increase in confidence, and so the spiral starts. The spiral can go up or down, and in our ratio training example, it is likely to continue until extinction results. For this reason, the strategy usually adopted to achieve high ratio performance is to increase the ratio from one only gradually up to the number required. This is an example of shaping by successive approximation where the desired operant is a multiple of a simple operant. The ratio is not increased beyond a particular value until the subject reliably executes that ratio in a short time with few pauses. As with other examples of shaping, changes in the sequential organisation of behavior occur as a larger ratio is shaped. Exploratory movements and grooming, common under continuous reinforcement, decrease and visits to the food tray in the middle of the ratio requirement also decline. However, as the reinforced operant behavior becomes more frequent and orderly, the *post-reinforcement pause* also becomes more reliable and longer.

The *FR* post-reinforcement pause occurs for the same reason as in *FI* schedules, since there is a period of time following reinforcement in which reinforcement is never available. It might be objected that there is no *scheduled* delay between reinforcements and that if the subject responded as fast as possible, the rate of reinforcement would be greatly increased. While this is true, it is also irrelevant. The behavior of organisms lacking clocks,

FIGURE 5.10. The role of positive feedback in ratio performance.

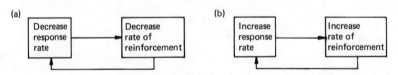

counters, and symbolic mediators is largely controlled by simpler behavioral processes. Indeed, the elimination of the familiar supports we humans use and take for granted is one primary way of revealing and studying these simpler processes.

In the case in point, we learn that since any *FR* requirement takes some time to execute, the time immediately after reinforcement becomes associated with extinction. This short extinction period discourages responding which produces another increase in the time taken to acquire each reinforcement. This positive feedback process is kept from going to complete extinction by the opposing control exerted by an increase in reinforcement rate when response rate chances to increase (see Figure 5.10b). In any *FR* schedule that actually does maintain responding these two positive feedback processes have opposing effects that balance each other out.

FR behavior, then, consists of a pause whose length is directly proportional to ratio size, followed by a sustained high rate of responding. A typical cumulative record of a pigeon key-pecking for grain on this schedule is shown in Figure 5.11. The sustained high rate is produced because pausing (long *IRT*'s) is not selectively reinforced and bursts of responding at the natural tempo are likely to be reinforced; and because high rates of response increase reinforcement rate which in turn raises response rate. The *FR* requirement produces a behavioral unit made up of a run of responses that, once initiated, is executed at a fixed tempo.

Behavior on variable-ratio (*VR*) schedules can be explained without introducing any new concepts or processes. *VR* lacks the regularity of *FR* and, as can be seen in Figure 5.9, responding is maintained at a high rate without any temporal patterning. Encouragement of high response rates exists as in *FR* schedules, but since reinforcement may occur at any time relative to the last reinforcement, the pause after reinforcement is extremely abbreviated.

FIGURE 5.11. Final performance of a pigeon on *FR* 120 (Ferster and Skinner, 1957).

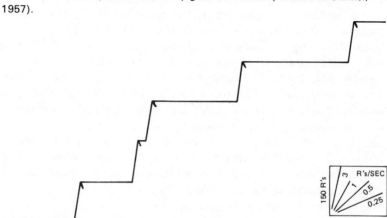

5.6
Multiple and Concurrent Schedules

We have described and analyzed four simple, or basic, schedules, *FI*, *VI*, *FR*, and *VR*, and also, schedules in which certain classes of *IRT*'s are reinforced. A special case of the latter schedule, called *differential reinforcement of low rates* (*DRL*), provides for the reinforcement of only *IRT*'s greater than a specified minimum value. On *DRL* 10 sec, for example, a response is reinforced if, and only if, it occurs more than ten seconds after the previous one. *DRL* is often treated as a fifth simple schedule, and it has been extensively investigated as a means for studying both an animal's ability to time intervals precisely, and also as a test for "patience", since waiting is required.

In our discussion of schedules so far, a given procedure has been held in effect throughout an entire experimental session. Consider now a more complex schedule, where two or more schedules are programmed within the same session. Thus, we might alternate two different schedules for the same operant response (a *multiple schedule*); or we might simultaneously have two different schedules programmed, one for each of two different operant responses (a *concurrent schedule*).

Multiple and concurrent schedules represent examples of the control of behavior by more complex schedules, and provide information about the ways in which schedules interact. An important feature of a multiple schedule is that each component schedule has an associated *discriminative stimulus*. For example, in a *mult FI FR*, a tone might signal the *FI* component, while white noise is on during the *FR*. Once stable performance is established, we say that behavior is under *stimulus control*, because each stimulus produces a distinctive performance when presented. (Stimulus control is the subject of Part Four.) An example of the development and maintenance of rat behavior on *mult FI 5-min FR20* is shown in Figure 5.12. The rat had previously been trained on simple *FR* and evidence of this is seen in the first session (Record *A*), but by the end of this session (*B*), control by both components of the schedule is evident and becomes clearer by 11 hours of training (*C*). After 38 hours, behavior is fairly stable (*D*), although bursts of *FR*-type responding occur occasionally during *FI* (at *d* and *e*). The lower panel of Figure 5.12 shows performance after much more training with this rat, when the ratio has been changed to 40. This example shows how multiple-schedule performance develops from the previous performance and how, as training proceeds, control by both components becomes stronger and inappropriate behavior less common. It is a very important general feature of schedule-controlled performance that its acquisition, and sometimes the actual nature of the performance, is strongly influenced by the subject's previous experience. Where the previous experience is known, we can see how it affects performance.

On a multiple schedule, discriminative stimuli signal different schedules

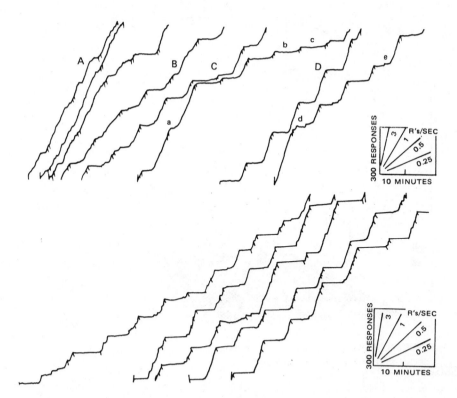

FIGURE 5.12. Cumulative records from a rat on *FI* 5-min *FR* 20 (upper panel) and *FI* 5-min *FR* 40 in lower panel (Ferster and Skinner, 1957).

for one response. Conversely, in a concurrent schedule, two or more independent reinforcement schedules are simultaneously applied to two response classes. Unlike a multiple schedule, the subject in a concurrent schedule determines when to switch from one schedule to the other. A typical concurrent responding situation is illustrated in Figure 5.13. In this example of a pigeon Skinner box, the two keys are equally accessible, although only one can be contacted at a time, and both are available all the time. Each key has an independent reinforcement schedule associated with it; this means that responding on key *B* has no effect on the programming or delivery of reinforcements for responding on key *A*.

After adequate training on a concurrent schedule, the subject divides its time between the two schedules and produces appropriate behavior on each. An example of stable performance on *conc FR* 100 *FI* 5 min of a hungry pigeon, key pecking for grain, is shown in Figure 5.14. Characteristic *FI* and *FR* performances are seen alternating with each other. The only new feature seen is a "staircase" effect, from time to time, in the *FI* component. This is produced by the subject responding on the *FI* key during postreinforcement pauses on the *FR* key.

FIGURE 5.13. A two-key pigeon Skinner box for the study of concurrent reinforcement schedules.

FIGURE 5.14. Cumulative records for two concurrent key peck responses. The schedule is *conc FR* 100 *FI* 5-min and the *FR* record is placed above the *FI* record (Catania, 1966).

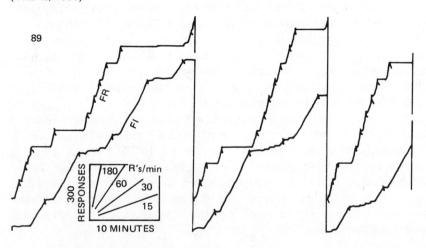

5.7

Extinction Following Intermittent Reinforcement

In Chapter 3, we saw that the amount of responding in extinction was affected by the number of reinforcers, and the effortfulness of the operant response during the preceding period of reinforcement. An even more powerful influence on resistance to extinction is the schedule on which the reinforcers were previously delivered. Indeed, the fact that any intermittency of reinforcement increases resistance to extinction has generated a large research area of its own. This phenomenon, termed the *partial reinforcement extinction effect*, has been used as a baseline to study the effects of drugs and physiological manipulations believed to affect emotional processes taking place during extinction (see Gray, 1975, for a review).

From a purely behavioral standpoint, the introduction of extinction, once a schedule-controlled performance has been established, provides further evidence of the powerful control of behavior by schedules, because the pattern of behavior in extinction depends on the nature of the preceding schedule. This is illustrated in Figure 5.15. *VI* experience produces what might be expected as an "extinction curve," but note that a large number of responses may be emitted. For example, a pigeon tested by Skinner (1950) emitted over 3,000 responses in more than 8 hours. The other performances

FIGURE 5.15.
Hypothetical cumulative records of responding in extinction after training on *VR*, *FR*, *VI* and *FI* schedules (from Reynolds, 1974).

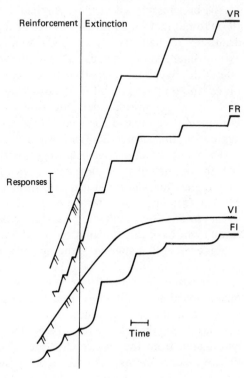

are distinctive, and reflect a gradual breakdown of the schedule-controlled behavior. The *VR* experience tends to produce the largest number of responses—this is the principle of the one-armed bandit.

Roughly speaking, it is the generalization between reinforcement and extinction that maintains behavior, and the transition from *VR* to extinction produces the least cues to aid discrimination. However, it is also clear that all these schedules give the subject experience of "intermittent extinction," and thus lead to remarkable perseveration of behavior.

5.8
Schedule-Induced Behavior

So far in this chapter, we have been concerned with the patterns of behavior generated by schedules, but we have restricted our attention to the operant responses reinforced by the schedules. There is, of course, a variety of other behavior occurring at the same time. Much of this behavior is simply the "natural" behavior that the subject brings to the situation. However, a number of behaviors have been identified that become excessive; that is, they occur with a much greater frequency within schedule-controlled performance than when the schedule is not in effect, although they are not reinforced by the schedule. These are called *schedule-induced* or *adjunctive* behaviors.

The best researched of these is schedule-induced polydipsia. Falk (1961, 1971) found that on *VI* food-reinforcement schedules, nonthirsty rats would drink up to half their own body weight of water in $3\frac{1}{2}$ hours! This extraordinary result depends on the reinforcer being available for a short time intermittently, on the intervals between reinforcer deliveries being in a certain range, and on the availability of a drinking tube. Polydipsia is not unique in that similar conditions generate other adjunctive behaviors if the environmental context is changed. These include grooming, wheel running, aggression, and overeating (with water as reinforcer).

The reality of adjunctive behaviors is well established, and it can be shown that the opportunity for them can act as a reinforcer, but their origin is not fully understood. The best generalization at present is that they are elicited when a stimulus associated with the absence of the reinforcer is present during intermittent reinforcement. Many background stimuli and temporal stimuli can have this function on schedules of reinforcement.

It is evident that an understanding and account of adjunctive behavior will be necessary to fully describe behavior on reinforcement schedules, and this is emphasized by Iversen's (1976) findings. He provided rats, lever pressing on *FR* schedules, with access to a drinking tube. In different phases of the experiment, the tube produced nothing, water, or sucrose solution when licked. Licking the tube increased from the "nothing" to "water" conditions and, again, from the "water" to "sucrose" conditions. More importantly, there were concomitant increases in postreinforcement pauses and time taken to complete the ratio requirement. Clearly, then, we cannot fully describe the behavior of the rats in this experiment without taking the adjunctive behavior into account.

The most curious feature of adjunctive behavior remains its excessiveness. Animals will expend great amounts of energy on behaviors that appear biologically unnecessary and which did not occur prior to the introduction of intermittent reinforcer delivery. Laboratory scientists have stumbled here upon a bizarre but powerful influence on behavior. Such chance findings are often the most important, and we will undoubtedly have a fuller understanding of the way behavior is energized and organized once the origin and maintaining conditions for adjunctive behavior have been fully analyzed.

5.9
Conclusion

The primary objectives of this chapter have been to give the reader a basic knowledge of reinforcement schedules and to explain their importance for a science of behavior. To the first end, the effects of simple schedules were described, and the processes involved in generating those effects were outlined. There are many types of schedules and aspects of schedule-controlled performances that were not discussed. Rather, attention was restricted to those that are simplest, that are best understood, and that will be encountered as applied to a variety of problems in other parts of this book.

In pursuit of the second objective, we pointed out that schedules control highly reliable and distinctive behavior patterns in individual organisms, that more complex patterns can be generated by combining schedules, and that experience on a schedule is an important determinant of subsequent behavior. We would argue that any new science must start by finding ways of controlling and predicting the phenomena that are its subject matter, and that work on schedules provides such a beginning. In subsequent chapters, we will see reinforcement schedules as techniques used for analyzing diverse problems.

It is sometimes said that the conditions under which we study schedule-controlled performances seem so artificial (so far from those of the real world) that any discoveries will be of doubtful relevance to behavior outside the laboratory. While it is possible that many other processes operating on behavior in natural settings will obscure schedule effects, this type of argument is not generally accepted in science. The principles of atomic physics or molecular biology are not doubted, nor is their significance diminished because they cannot be observed to operate except under controlled conditions. Furthermore, the scientific community does not insist that only certain sorts of apparatus or procedure are suitable for studying these subjects. Rather, the scientist is expected to take any necessary steps that enable him to reliably measure and control the phenomena of interest. The value of the techniques used is measured by the success in attaining these objectives, and in the long-term, schedules of reinforcement will be assessed in this way. In the meantime, schedules provide reliable and powerful techniques for the control of behavior.

References for Chapter 5

Catania, A. C. Concurrent operants. In W. K. Honig (Ed.) *Operant behavior: areas of research and application.* New York: Appleton-Century-Crofts, 1966.

Cumming, W. W., and Schoenfeld, W. N. Behavior under extended exposure to a high-value fixed interval reinforcement schedule. *Journal of the Experimental Analysis of Behavior*, 1958, **1**, 245–263.

Falk, J. L. Production of polydipsia in normal rats by an intermittent food schedule. *Science*, 1961, **133**, 195–196.

Falk, J. L. The nature and determinants of adjunctive behavior. *Physiology and Behavior*, 1971, **6**, 577–588.

Ferster, C. B., and Skinner, B. F. *Schedules of reinforcement.* New York: Appleton-Century-Crofts, 1957.

Gilbert, T. F. Fundamental dimensional properties of the operant. *Psychological Review*, 1958, **65**, 272–282.

Gray, J. A. *Elements of a two-process theory of learning.* London: Academic Press, 1975.

Iversen, I. H. Interactions between reinforced responses and collateral responses. *The Psychological Record*, 1976, **26**, 399–413.

Millenson, J. R. Random interval schedules of reinforcement. *Journal of the Experimental Analysis of Behavior*, 1963, **6**, 437–443.

Reynolds, G. S. *A primer of operant conditioning.* Second Edition. Glenview, Ill.: Scott, Foresman, 1975.

Skinner, B. F. Are theories of learning necessary? *Psychological Review*, 1950, **57**, 193–216.

CHAPTER 6

Quantifying the Law of Effect

6.1
Theory in the Experimental Analysis of Behavior

It is necessary to organize facts in such a way that a simple and convenient description can be given, and for this purpose a structure or system is required (1938).

Behavior can only be satisfactorily understood by going beyond the facts themselves. What is needed is a theory of behavior . . . . Whether particular experimental psychologists like it or not, experimental psychology is properly and inevitably committed to the construction of a theory of behavior. A theory is essential to the scientific understanding of behavior as a subject matter (1947).

Beyond the collection of uniform relationships lies the need for a formal representation of the data reduced to a minimal number of terms. A theoretical construction may yield greater generality than any assemblage of facts. But such a construction will not refer to another dimensional system . . . . It will not stand in the way of our search for functional relationships because it will arise only after relevant variables have been found and studied. Though it may be difficult to understand, it will not be easily misunderstood (1950).

The above statements, which are only a sample of a view maintained consistently throughout all his writings, come from an eminent behavior scientist, often thought to have opposed theory in the experimental analysis of behavior. His name is B. F. Skinner. We need, of course, no appeal *ex cathedra* to justify theory, for when we look at every science, we see that each one moves inexorably towards higher and higher generality of its concepts, accompanied by an increased economy of representation of its laws. As this process evolves, we commonly find a growing reliance on mathematical representation. It is in this firm tradition that the quantitative law of effect, proposed by Herrnstein (1970, 1971, 1974), stands.

The quantification of the law of effect constitutes at once both an attempt to reduce the great complexity in our empirical observations to a single formulation (model), and at the same time, to refine our ideas about the concept of reinforcement. In particular, it emphasizes and gives form to the important idea of *reinforcement value* as a critical determinant of *response strength*, the latter being a concept meant to capture the fundamental notion of how probable or dominant a piece of behavior is in a given situation. Behavior strength concepts arose out of attempts to measure the outcomes of "learning" experiments, where an organism comes to do something it formerly did not do. Nowadays, we are inclined to view learning as a special case of a transition from one behavioral steady state to another, and in that newer framework, the concept of response strength takes on a new and expanded meaning.

6.2

Reinforcing Value and Response Strength: Two sides of the Same Conceptual Coin

In the steady state, we are in an especially favorable position, with behavior occurring for many hours, to observe numerous variables affecting response frequency, only some of which seem to fit our intuitions about what should affect "strength" of behavior. We see that operant-response rate can be sensitively changed by parameters of reinforcement (such as frequency or density, magnitude, and immediacy), by the temporal distribution (proximity) of reinforcements, by the definition of the response (such as when one bar press is defined in a higher-order operant, say a *FR50*; or in a chain of barpress plus chainpull), and by explicit shaping contingencies (such as pacing, or *DRL*).

Even though behavior may be a function of many variables, not all high-probability behaviors seem to represent "strong" behaviors. Men frequently go to wars, work long hours at dull jobs, and engage in social obligations that they admittedly dislike. Unless we wish simply to equate response strength to response frequency (a strategy some theorists have indeed adopted), we shall have to sort out the classes of controls over frequency, with the aim of finding one particular class whose distinctive effects on behavior correspond in some significant way to our rough intuitions about what we mean by changes in behavior strength.

The parameters of reinforcement that modulate the "reward" value, the "attractiveness," or the "utility" of the reinforcer seem to stand out as potentially appropriate for this class. One meaning of a strong behavior equates it with strongly motivated behavior, and another way of saying this is to say that a behavior is strong when its maintaining reinforcer is very powerful. Conversely, in this scheme, a behavior tendency is weak when its reinforcement is weak. These equations imply that to quantify response strength in any given situation, we shall have to be able to measure the reinforcement strength, or *value*, in that situation. This may be possible because we know that a number of the parameters of reinforcement possess a unity of function in the similar way that they affect behavior, in their functional exchangeability within themselves, and in their relative independence from the other variables of which behavior is a function.

These then are the initial intuitions and elementary correspondences that justify our classing these parameters together, and then creating a theoretical concept, *reinforcement value*, to summarize their functional equivalence, to which changes in response strength can be conceptually coordinated.

Why is response strength a more basic, or more fundamental, or even a more useful, datum than, for instance, rate of response which, thanks to the pioneer work of Skinner, we now so easily observe and measure? Although the ultimate success of our conceptual analysis will stand or fall on its ability to order old data and to suggest new experiments and empirical correspondences, we can with profit defer a detailed answer to this question, and instead, first examine how another science progressed from raw data to theory.

6.3
The Quantification of Heat and Temperature in Physics

The development of the concepts of heat and temperature provide a striking parallel with our evolving concepts of reinforcement value and response strength. Crude observation suffices to identify some objects as hot and some cold; and some hotter than others. How could these intuitions be "measured"? That is, how might we create a scale that would allow us to equate two different objects for equal "hotness," to be able to tell how many times hotter or colder one object is from another, and in general, to secure all the advantages that measurement affords (Stevens, 1951)?

Primitive man could hardly have failed to notice that objects expand when they get hot and contract when they cool; and the ancient Greeks utilized that principle in the construction of toys. Even so, it was not until the seventeenth century that the expansion of liquids, confined to thin capillary tubes which could be carried around from place to place, was exploited to give an indication of the degree of this thing called "heat." Notice that "heat" (or its degree, "temperature") so defined does not represent a *thing*. We do not directly observe "it"; yet we would not want to refer to heat as hypothetical. Heat, quite simply, represents a concept. Thus, neither in its theoretical structure nor in its conceptual status does heat differ from those critical concepts that we have in psychology which we would so like to define and measure: intelligence, emotion, motivation, response strength. And just as we find ourselves often inclined to reify these psychological properties into things (traits, pleasure centers, drive reduction, S–R bonds), so too, physics had to free itself from thinking of heat as a thing called "caloric."

Galileo was one of the first to construct a "thermoscope", employing the principle of heat-produced liquid expansion. Galileo's device used water, so it required a large container, which rendered it extremely cumbersome. But even worse, the "thermoscope" proved impractical because it gave different readings in different places. We would say today, since we know what Galileo did not, that the device was affected by both temperature and pressure. The situation reminds us of our use of response rate to measure response strength. In many procedures, response rate shows itself affected both by reinforcement value and schedule parameters (compare *VI* and *VR* schedules, for instance). "Hotness" measuring devices began to improve when the technology of sealed tube glass blowing advanced. These new tubes effectively isolated their heat measuring liquids—water, glycerine, colored alcohol, or mercury—from atmospheric pressure variations, thereby making possible the first true "thermometers" (see Figure 6.1.).

About this same time, it occurred to several ingenious people that by making two marks, *a* and *b*, on the tube corresponding to two "standard" hotnesses, and then dividing the space between them into equal intervals, they could create a scale of hotness. This clever idea immediately raised the problem of what particular "hotnesses" should serve for *a* and for *b*. Some workers used melted snow for *b* and melted butter for *a*. Others suggested salt-ice mixture for *b* and the temperature of a healthy human body for *a*. Still others used the "coldest winter day" and the "hottest summer day" for *a* and *b*. In addition to these uncertainties, considerable confusion existed concerning which of several possible liquids to use in these tubes, for each one gave a different hotness reading for the same object being measured.

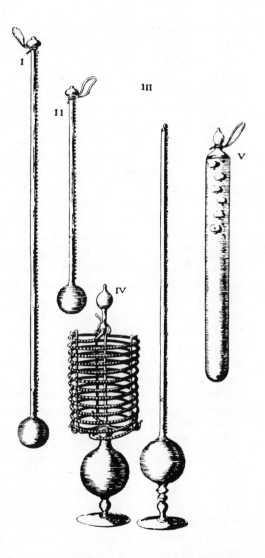

FIGURE 6.1.
Thermometers of the Academia del
Cimento (after Conant, 1957).

Our quantification of response strength presents similar problems. Which
of the various schedules, variable interval (*VI*), variable ratio (*VR*), fixed
interval (*FI*), or fixed ratio (*FR*), should we use to "measure" response
strength? All of them generate response rates that vary to some degree with
reward parameters, but each one has unique features and idiosyncrasies.
How can we choose? Or why even bother to pursue this elusive concept of
response strength? Why not just be content with the various observed
functional relationships? Our discontent with the empirical relations alone
seems to grow as the empirical base of our science grows. When there exist
few data, we find little pressure to order the data with a theoretical concept.
As a jungle of facts grows up, we seek economy in generalizations. We, like

the physicists, make that inevitable transition to theory that Skinner (1947) says, like it or not, we experimental psychologists find ourselves "properly and inevitably committed."

The way physics eventually solved its temperature measurement problem contains a lesson for us. The choice of how to mark *b* and *a* was eventually settled arbitrarily for ice water and boiling water, simply because these were so easily obtained. Standardizing the expanding liquid proved more difficult. Mercury seemed the easiest liquid to use in the tubes since it had a wider range between its own boiling and freezing points (beyond which the liquid in the tube could not be read) and could, therefore, measure a wider range of objects than could alcohol or glycerine. So for a long time, the purely pragmatic considerations dictated the choice. Perhaps analogous considerations account for the extensive use of *FI* schedules to assess drug effects in the field of behavioral pharmacology. An *FI* schedule gives, within one single scallop, a wide range of rates to be selectively affected by a given drug (but compare Branch and Gollub, 1974). However, psychopharmacologists have rarely faced the question of whether these different rates reflect different response strengths. This reluctance to go beyond "pointer readings" conjures up to us an imaginary eighteenth century physicist, impatiently dismissing the "philosophical" question of whether his tubes were or were not measuring anything called temperature, claiming that his interest lay only in describing the empirical relations between how high various liquids rose in sealed tubes under operationally defined conditions.

The moral seems clear. We, as psychologists, *are* truly interested in response strengths, not response rates. So the question of their relation to reinforcement parameters—which is the systematic question of scaling or measuring reinforcement value—cannot be avoided indefinitely. This is not to say that Skinner was not perfectly correct in first confining attention to an extensive investigation of response rates, alone. We must remember that he arrived on the stage at a time when psychology abounded in speculation. In 1930, behavior interested psychologists principally for what it allowed them to infer about inner hypothetical entities. There was a paucity of rigorous data and parametric empirical relationships. In that milieu, Skinner's program of descriptive behaviorism set the occasion for the solid empirical base upon which, only now, do we find it appropriate and perhaps possible to attempt a more "formal representation" (Skinner, 1950).

To return to temperature, the question of arbitrariness in what to use as the expanding substance (this is something like what operant ought best to measure response rate) was eventually settled by using gases. Notice though, that the idea of "gases" and their mixtures was something that was only gradually and partially independently evolving at this same time. There was thus no way that Galileo could have known that gas in his tube would have made a "better" thermometer than water. So to say that Galileo erred in how to measure temperature is to see thermometry with twentieth century eyes.

Gas turned out to be best for several reasons, the most important of which proves extremely instructive for our problem. It was only when degree of hotness was "measured" by gas thermometers that simple laws of heat exchange and thermodynamics were discovered; laws that had remained obscured by extraneous properties of the earlier alcohol and glycerine instruments.

Just as many practical and theoretical criteria entered into the selection of the way "temperature" was finally "measured," so too, analogous considerations are certain to enter into how we come eventually to measure response strength. Therefore, to answer our questions of what we will agree to call response strength, and why we will prefer it to any of its so-called "indicants" (of which free operant response rate is the principal one), is to do nothing more nor less than to find an appropriate conceptualization and quantification of reinforcement theory which will provide us with the same kind of explanatory and interpretational power that eighteenth century thermometry and calorimetry were to provide for the next century's thermodynamics.

6.4

Measurement Considerations: When Does an Indicant Become a Measure?

Like hotness and coldness, ideas about reinforcement strength must be very ancient. Man has probably always had strong intuitions about the value or utility of objects and situations. Can science classify and systematize reinforcement value in the same general way as it has done with heat? Of course, utility is the province of psychology and social science, and so we must expect the techniques of quantification to differ in details. It appears that this science began its qualitative stage with the gradual acceptance— beginning with John Stewart Mill and the social Darwinians and passing through Thorndike to Skinner—that the law of effect is our most potent technique of behavior modification. That is, we have come to see that behavior is powerfully affected by its consequences and we have begun to ask experimental questions about how and when this happens. Our answers make up the domain of empirical reinforcement study.

The primitive idea that something about behavior ought to be proportional to amount (and perhaps rate) of reinforcement has probably always been a strong intuitional component underlying the empirical expansion, and is perhaps the main pressure now towards quantification. Skinner (1938) himself tried one of the simplest ways to quantify this idea when he suggested that lever-pressing response rate (R) of hungry rats working on *FI* schedules might be directly proportional (k) to the rate of food pellets (r) delivered by various different *FI*'s. This is nothing more than a way of saying that

$$R = kr \tag{1}$$

but as Skinner (1940) later noted, the equation unfortunately did not generally hold true.

Why was *FI* (and later *VI*) selected as the schedule that Skinner gave attention to as the possible candidate for his attempt at quantification? Why not *FR* or *VR*, or any of the myriad of schedules (see Ferster and Skinner, 1957)? The reason why ratio schedules, at any rate, had to be rejected is that the rate of reinforcement they give is largely under the control of the subject, varying directly with the rate of response. With *VR*'s as different as 10, 100, or even 1,000, the organism could adjust its responding to these various *VR* schedules to give unpredictable rates of reinforcement. So to try to use a fixed or variable ratio response rate as a measure of reinforcement value, and see how it might be affected by something else (say a drug, or a drive operation), would be difficult; since if the something else changed the response rate, then the response-coupled reinforcement rate would also change. Such a confounding interaction is not unlike (though opposite in effect) a thermometer with a stem made of a superconductive glass that would draw out so much heat from the thing being measured that the object never remained at its initial temperature, so could never, in fact, be accurately measured.

Reinforcement rate has to remain constant in our measuring instrument whenever we want precisely to measure how any *other* condition affects response strength. And this, of course, is what we often want to do. *FI* or *VI* are clever schedules in this respect, because as long as our subject makes at least one response per minimum interval, it will obtain all the reinforcements, but never more than the maximum set by the schedule. So the subject's response rate can vary over a wide range, while reinforcement rate will stay constant. We can represent this property of our "reinforceometer" by Figure 6.2. It is only at extremely low response rates that our instrument becomes rather unreliable. This is a useful schedule, then, but we must not forget that it, rather like the mercury thermometer, has some important limitations.

Granted the usefulness of interval schedules, which should we use, *FI* or *VI*? Again, this question finds a parallel in the question that eighteenth century chemists asked in their debate about what fluid to use in thermometer tubes. *FI* seems a simpler schedule for many reasons. It contains only one interval, and so conveniently avoids the interactions between different intervals that seem to make *VI* a more difficult schedule to analyze. Then too, *VI* is not really one determinant schedule the way *FI* is. Because there are many ways to construct a *VI* schedule, depending on how the overall distribution and sequencing of intervals is to be arranged, *VI* really comprises a class of schedules. Finally, technical convenience, which has played a decisive role in the evolution of more than one fundamental

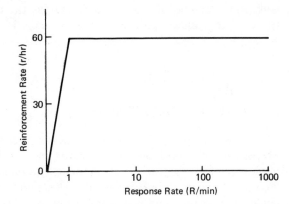

FIGURE 6.2.
The variation in reinforcement
rate with response rate on an
FI 1-min reinforcement
schedule.

scientific concept, clearly favors the *FI* schedule, with its ease of programming by a single simple clock.

However, what appears simple from one vantage point may, in science, be complex from a different (later to be called with hindsight, more fundamental) vantage point. As we saw in the *FI* scallops of Chapter 5, the response rate that is produced on *FI* schedules is far from homogeneous. This variation in interreinforcement response rate contaminates our measurement of response strength in just the way that transporting Galileo's water thermometer from Pisa to Padua disturbed the reliable measurement of the temperature of a body. Indeed, the temporal control exhibited in *FI* is so great a contaminant, and one so little understood as yet (Staddon, 1972), that we are obliged to return and reconsider our *VI* schedule, to see if we cannot use it despite its complexities.

If we were somehow to construct a *VI* schedule possessing a variety of short, medium, and long intervals, well mixed so that the subject could not discriminate them, we might succeed in eliminating most of the temporal variations in responding that characterize *FI* performance. We might still not understand how the different intervals within the *VI* are interacting to determine their final effect, but at least they could not be acting systematically, as they might if we used (say) only two intervals (what Ferster and Skinner, 1957, call a mixed schedule). Well and good. We have succeeded in confounding, if not isolating, the interactions of the intervals in our *VI*. But which particular distribution of all the many diverse ones that could and have been used should we employ? It turns out that we can devise a *VI* schedule whose interval lengths are so completely randomized that the probability of a reinforcement assignment stays always uniformly constant. (Millenson, 1963; Farmer, 1963). This random interval (*RI*) schedule altogether removes any predictive basis for temporal discriminations, so it seems the ideal choice here. However, *RI* is technically difficult to implement, requiring Geiger counters, random noise devices, or computers. Fortunately, Fleshler and Hoffman (1962) demonstrated that a close approximation to the truly random schedule can be punched for the commonly available tape timer, so that the procedure we want actually is within the scope of every laboratory.

6.5

Towards Quantification

At this point, armed with a tool that seems to possess some of the properties we regard as necessary for measuring response strengths at various reinforcement rates, magnitudes, and immediacies, we return to the laboratory and do some experiments. Alas, that simple equation, $R = kr$, still eludes us and our reinforcement rate *vs.* response rate data (Catania and Reynolds, 1968) come out looking like Figure 6.3. The failure to find a straight line function between these two variables, and in fact, the general insensitivity of *RI* rate to wide changes in reinforcement rate, creates a kind of impasse for our analysis and development of response strength. It is at this point that we may be inclined to invent a hypothetical concept, say habit strength, or expectancy, that we will assume behaves simply in the way that our observed indicant does not. This strategy is always an option open to the

FIGURE 6.3. Rate of responding as a function of the rate of reinforcement for each of six subject on variable interval schedules. The first number in each panel is k in responses per minute, and the second is r_o in reinforcements per hour for the various smooth curves (from Catania and Reynolds, 1968).

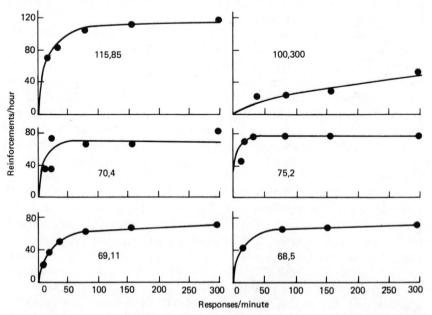

scientist, and there are times when it is successful. But in the history of psychology, too often, it has become a substitute for and deterrent to empirical development; and for this reason, the tradition that Skinner set in the experimental analysis of behavior has consistently avoided the postulation of such hypothetical entities.

If we turn our attention back to data, we find yet another procedure in which, for reasons that were at first obscure, a simple relationship between reinforcement and responding did actually emerge. This procedure, the two-response concurrent *VI* (here, and in the sequel, we use *VI* to mean "approximation to *RI*") schedule, was first studied by Ferster and Skinner (1957). Herrnstein, as early as 1961, had shown with hungry pigeons that under certain conditions this schedule generates key-pecking rates that are directly proportional to food reinforcement rates. In the concurrent schedule, the subject has two keys, and two independent *VI* schedules are in force at the same time. The subject can choose at any time where to direct its pecks, but obviously cannot peck both keys at the same time. This feature is preserved in rat experiments by keeping the response levers far enough apart so that the subject cannot use both paws simultaneously. Herrnstein varied the *VI* on one key (left) between 0 and 40 reinforcements/hr, and between 40 and 0 reinforcements/hr on the other (right) key. Notice the convention of denoting the *VI* schedules by their hourly reinforcement rate, which is just the reciprocal of the more familiar, average interreinforcement interval.

Scheduled reinforcements/hr	
Left key VI	*Right key VI*
0	40
5	35
10	30
20	20
30	10
35	5
40	0

Behavior was stabilized at each *VI* pair, and then the subject was shifted to a new pair, until eventually all pairs had been studied. The results of this experiment were interesting for their unusual simplicity. Let us agree to call the left key, R_1, and the right key, R_2, and their corresponding reinforcer rates, r_1 and r_2. Then Figure 6.4 shows what was found. Here, a simple linear relation turns up between the rate of one of the responses and its rate of reinforcement. How had Herrnstein succeeded in finding this linearity when in simple *VI*, the relation is curvilinear, and usually even in *VIVI* concurrents (Catania, 1966), curvilinear relationships between responding and re-

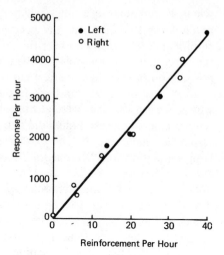

FIGURE 6.4.

The rate of responding for each of two alternatives in a two-choice procedure as a function of the rate of reinforcement for each. Variable interval schedules were used for both (from Herrnstein, 1961).

inforcement are the rule? The key to achieving the simplicity was the procedural wrinkle of holding $r_1 + r_2$ constant; in this case, equal to 40 reinforcements/hr. Under these conditions, responding did turn out to fit equation (1). But why?

Let us try to reconstruct the probable evolution of Herrnstein's thought. First, he noticed that since $r_1 + r_2 = 40 = $ constant (c), the straight line data he found for one key could be represented by the equation:

$$R_1 = \frac{kr_1}{r_1 + r_2} \tag{2}$$

which expresses the idea that the response rate on one key is relative to the *total* programmed reinforcement in the concurrent situation, not just governed by its own reinforcement. This equation reduces to:

$$R_1 = \frac{kr_1}{c} \tag{3}$$

and thence, to ar_1, where a is just a new constant, equal to k/c. Since the constants, at this stage at any rate, have no substantive meaning anyway, equation (3) is as good as equation (1) as an equation of strength. The trouble is, it can only be obtained in one special type of concurrent; that is, when $r_1 + r_2 = c$.

We may assume that Herrnstein occasionally thought about this perplexing correspondence during the years 1961 to 1970, during which time the empirical data base of concurrent and multiple schedules expanded greatly. One other simple relationship which had also come out of his data was repeatedly confirmed, and this one did not depend on the two concurrent reinforcers summing to a constant, c. He had found that when the *relative* rates of response were plotted against the *relative* rates of reinforcement, a simple linear function with slope of 45° and intercept of zero also emerged, as shown in Figure 6.5.

Figure 6.5 is the now famous "matching law," and it became solidly established in the decade of the 1960's for concurrent *VI* schedules. It says simply that the relative rate of responding in concurrent *VI* schedules matches their relative reinforcement rates. Notice that this has to be so if equation (3) is true as long as the a for R_1 is the same a as for R_2. Since $R_1 = ar_1$, and $R_2 = ar_2$, then $R_1/R_1 + R_2$, the relative rate, must

$$= \frac{ar_1}{ar_1 + ar_2} \qquad = \frac{r_1}{r_1 + r_2}. \qquad (4)$$

It is at this point that we possess all the information that Herrnstein had when he made the creative leap to theory in 1970. He did *not*, by the way, mechanically induce the law we are about to describe from the data, as some philosophers of science would like us to believe. The data themselves do not force the notion that occurred to him or else nine years would not have elapsed before its "discovery." Rather, Herrnstein had to look at the concurrent data that yielded (3) and (4), and the single key data that yielded the curvilinear relationship of Figure 6.3, and come up with a formula that would deal with both. And this, he did.

He accomplished this feat by concluding that, although the idea of "choice" is very explicit in concurrents (where it clearly occurs between the two scheduled operants), it is none the less *implicit* in single schedules. But in single key schedules, choice is occurring between a single scheduled operant and other unknown behavior—call them R_o (o for *other*)—with their own unknown, but existent, reinforcers, r_o. We do not have the record as to whether this imaginative leap came, like Archimedes' principle, as a sudden flash of insight in his bath; or rather, whether it emerged slowly and tortuously over that nine-year period from 1961 to 1970. Suffice it to say, that we may regard it as a significant step in the direction of that inevitable committment to theory that Skinner noted thirty years ago, but which, in

FIGURE 6.5.

The relative frequency of responding to one alternative in a two-choice procedure as a function of the relative frequency of reinforcement thereon. Variable interval schedules governed reinforcements for both alternatives. The diagonal line shows matching between the relative frequencies (from Herrnstein, 1961).

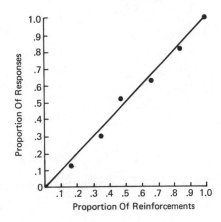

1950, he was obliged to admit still, "We do not seem to be ready for this kind of theory."

By assuming an unknown source of reinforcement, r_o, and that all behavior is choice behavior in a concurrent situation, Herrnstein at once elevated the concurrent reinforcement schedule of Ferster and Skinner to a central theoretical position in the experimental analysis of behavior. That is, although this schedule is not the simplest to program and to understand, it turns out to simplify greatly our understanding of what, at first sight, appear simpler schedules. This is like the early gas thermometer, which also, at first sight, appeared to be a far more complex device than the "simple" expansion of water in tubes.

What are the consequences for our equations by assuming that *all* behavior exists in a concurrent framework or setting? First of all, it means that instead of writing equation (1) for simple schedules, we always have to write:

$$R = \frac{kr}{r+r_o} \tag{5}$$

Equation (5) is the heart of the new theory. It says that all responding is relative to the rate of that response's reinforcement in the context of all other (r_o) reinforcers in the situation, known or unknown. k still remains a constant. When Herrnstein applied equation (5) to the graph of single schedule *VI*'s, he found good fits (see Figure 6.3). Recently, de Villiers (1977) has examined a wide range of experiments from runways, T mazes, and Skinner boxes to show that this equation (5) (and some of its consequences) has a remarkable generality across species, apparatus, and responses.

How do we fit data to equation (5)? One way (Cohen, 1973) is to plot reciprocals of our obtained response and reinforcement rates on graph paper, and then try to fit a straight line to them, extracting the unknown parameters, r_o and k, from this fit. Thus, if

$$R = \frac{kr}{r+r_o} \tag{5}$$

Then,

$$\frac{1}{R} = \frac{r+r_o}{kr}, \text{ or}$$

$$\frac{1}{R} = \frac{r}{kr} + \frac{r_o}{kr}, \text{ or}$$

$$\frac{1}{R} = \frac{1}{k} + \left(\frac{r_o}{k}\right)\frac{1}{r} \tag{6}$$

Recalling that a straight line is an equation of the form,

$$y = mx + b \tag{7}$$

where m is the slope and b the y intercept; we see that equation (6) is in the form of equation (7) with

$y = 1/R$, $x = 1/r$,

$m = r_o/k$ (slope), and $b = 1/k$ (the y intercept).

This form allows us to evaluate k, and then r_o, from any set of points obtained in a single schedule when a range of reinforcement rates (r's) and response rates (R's) are available for plotting.

Once Herrnstein had his fundamental equation (5), it was easy for him to see why matching of relative reinforcement rates and responses had to occur. For, in a general two-key concurrent schedule (that is, one where $r_1 + r_2$ not necessarily $= c$), the rates of R_1 and R_2 would be:

$$R_1 = \frac{kr_1}{r_1 + r_2 + r_o}$$

$$R_2 = \frac{kr_2}{r_2 + r_1 + r_o} \tag{8}$$

But it follows from these equations that

$$\frac{R_1}{R_2} = \frac{\dfrac{kr_1}{r_1 + r_2 + r_o}}{\dfrac{kr_2}{r_2 + r_1 + r_o}} = \frac{r_1}{r_2} \tag{9}$$

which is just another form of equation (4), the matching law.

6.6

The "Leaky Bucket" Model of Herrnstein's Equations

It often helps to be able to picture one physical process in terms of another. Thus, we see in physics books pictures of waves that are meant to represent the vibrations of light; and little billiard balls that are supposed to represent molecules in ideal gases bouncing about. The models make concrete what is, at first, a new and unfamiliar abstract process; helping us, by analogy and metaphor, to understand what by equations appears colorless and seemingly impoverished of meaning. The model described in this section mimics enough properties of Herrnstein's equations to make it useful until the equations, themselves, assume enough familiarity for them alone to become the new common sense and intuition of the law of effect.

Consider the leaky bucket shown in Figure 6.6. A quantity of liquid is poured into the bucket, wherein it is dyed (transformed) by a complex inner process. We arrange to recollect the transformed liquid under the bucket by piercing the bottom of the bucket with small pinholes and funneling the

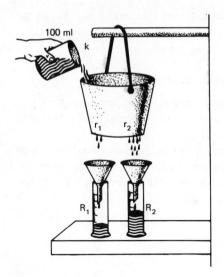

FIGURE 6.6.
The leaky, transforming bucket model of Herrnstein's equations.

liquid into graduate cylinders, where we can measure how much we get out. Imagine (*a*) that we can place any number of funnels from 1 to *n* under the bucket; (*b*) that any funnel can collect from several pinholes; (*c*) that we can make as many holes above any funnel as we wish, but that all holes are identical in size, and are small relative to the total size of the bottom of the bucket; (*d*) these holes can be sealed over and new ones pierced whenever we desire; and (*e*) this bucket leaks from some unknown place (we know not where), and the liquid lost there is not recoverable or directly measurable.

Now, suppose we first put two funnels below our bucket, piercing 30 holes above the right one, and 10 holes above the left one. Then we pour 100 ml of water into this magic bucket. We wait for a time until all the colored liquid has collected in our graduates and measure it. Suppose we discover that we collect about 22 ml in the left funnel (which we shall call R_1 amount) and about 67 ml in the right funnel (which we call R_2 amount). Evidently, we lost about 11 ml to the leak(s). (Now one discrepancy between our physical model and the theory of reinforcement becomes clear: in the model we know immediately that our leak is worth five pinholes [do you see why?] since we know we poured in exactly 100 ml to start with. In considering the behavior of organisms in concurrent choice situations, we don't know how much we "pour in" to begin with. We only know what we get out, R_1 and R_2. But let's proceed.) We now seal up the 40 holes we made, and make some new ones. Let's say we make 20 on the left and 20 on the right. The number of holes on each side, let us call r_1 and r_2, respectively. Now we repeat the pouring operation, and notice that we get out slightly over 44 ml on both sides. Again, the leak claimed its 11 ml.

Let us continue this procedure for several more pairs so that we carry out these operations for the following pairs of holes, with the following results.

Holes on left	Holes on right	Liquid collected (ml)	
		Left	Right
(r_1)	(r_2)	(R_1)	(R_2)
5	35	12	78
10	30	22	67
20	20	44	44
30	10	67	22
35	5	78	12
40	0	89	0

You will not fail to note that the left half of this table looks suspiciously like the table of VIVI pairs that Herrnstein first used in 1961, when he held $r_1 + r_2$ constant at 40 reinforcements per hour. And indeed, the correspondence is intentional. For, happily, if we now plot either the right or left output from our magic bucket against the number of holes on that side, we get what Herrnstein got, a straight line. We also note that the total output of $R_1 + R_2 = 89$ at all combinations of 40 holes, and that, too, is analogous to what Herrnstein found. So far, so good; our system does model the Herrnstein (1961) result.

Now, let us do yet another experiment in which we use only one funnel. Taking values of holes from 1 to 100, we get:

Holes	Volume collected (approximately) (ml)
1	16
2	30
4	44
10	67
50	81
100	95

Several things seem to be happening as we make more holes. First of all, the effect of increasing holes is having less and less effect as their number grows larger. Thus, while the first 50 holes got us 81 ml, the next 50 got us only $95 - 81 = 14$. Secondly, this leak is keeping us from getting all the possible liquid, even though we do get more of it by increasing the number of holes we make. But even if we make 1,000 collecting holes, we still only get 99 ml, which allows us to see that clearly 100 ml is emerging as some kind of asymptote. We have to think of the bottom of our bucket as having some high upper limit as to the number of holes we can pierce there. When we plot the amount of liquid out (R_1), we find it conforms nicely to the rule:

$$R_1 = \frac{100\,(r_1)}{r_1 + 5} \tag{10}$$

as indeed it should, since that is how your authors constructed this bucket. Note that r_o, the leak, is identified nicely by the data; so, too, is k, the total amount of water coming in from the beaker pour on each trial. Neither of these could be identified from our first (and Herrnstein's first) experiments with two funnels.

What now are the useful features of our physical model? First of all, the 100 ml in the beaker corresponds to Herrnstein's k. It is the upper limit of behaving we can expect to get out of our organism in the given experimental situation; that is, given the construction of manipulanda, the size of the chamber, and perhaps, though we are not quite so sure, drive level. The holes we make are the reinforcements we give, and the funnels are the operants we define. Moving the holes from one funnel to another, but keeping their number constant, corresponds to shifting behavior from one key to another, when total reinforcement rate is held constant across keys. The leaky bucket model gives us a feeling for why response rate is curvilinearly related to reinforcement rate in the single key (funnel) experiment; and yet linearly related when there are two keys (funnels) whose reinforcement rates (collecting holes) always sum to a constant.

References for Chapter 6

Branch, M. N., and Gollub, L. R. A detailed analysis of the effects of d-Amphetamine on behavior under fixed interval schedules. *Journal of the Experimental Analysis of Behavior*, 1974, **21**, 519–539.

Catania, A. C. Concurrent operants. In W. K. Honig (Ed.) *Operant Behavior: areas of research and application*. New York: Appleton-Century-Crofts, 1966.

Catania, A. C. Reinforcement schedules and psychophysical judgements: A study of some temporal properties of behavior. In W. N. Schoenfeld (Ed.) *The theory of reinforcement schedules*. New York: Appleton-Century-Crofts, 1970.

Catania, A. C., and Reynolds, G. S. A quantitative analysis of the responding maintained by interval schedules of reinforcement. *Journal of the Experimental Analysis of Behavior*, 1968, **11**, 327–383.

Cohen, I. A note on Herrnstein's equations. *Journal of the Experimental Analysis of Behavior*, 1973, **19**, 529–530.

Conant, J. B. (Ed.) *Harvard case histories in experimental science*. Cambridge: Harvard University Press, 1957.

de Villiers, P. A. Choice in concurrent schedules and a quantitative formulation of the law of effect. In W. K. Honig and J. E. R. Staddon (Eds.) *Handbook of operant behavior*. Englewood Cliffs, New Jersey: Prentice-Hall, 1977.

Farmer, J. Properties of behavior under random interval reinforcement schedules. *Journal of the Experimental Analysis of Behavior*, 1963, **6**, 607–616.

Ferster, C. B., and Skinner, B. F. *Schedules of reinforcement.* New York: Appleton-Century-Crofts, 1957.

Fleshler, M., and Hoffman, H. S. A progression for generating variable-interval schedules. *Journal of the Experimental Analysis of Behavior,* 1962, **5**, 529–530.

Herrnstein, R. J. Relative and absolute strength of response as a function of frequency of reinforcement. *Journal of the Experimental Analysis of Behavior,* 1961, **4**, 267–272.

Herrnstein, R. J. On the law of effect. *Journal of the Experimental Analysis of Behavior,* 1970, **13**, 243–266.

Herrnstein, R. J. Quantitative hedonism. *Journal of Psychiatric Research,* 1971, **8**, 399–412.

Herrnstein, R. J. Formal properties of the matching law. *Journal of the Experimental Analysis of Behavior,* 1974, **21**, 159–164.

Millenson, J. R. Random interval schedules of reinforcement. *Journal of the Experimental Analysis of Behavior,* 1963, **6**, 437–443.

Skinner, B. F. *The behavior of organisms.* New York: Appleton-Century-Crofts, 1938.

Skinner, B. F. The nature of the operant reserve. *Psychological Bulletin,* 1940, **37**, 423.

Skinner, B. F. *Current trends in experimental psychology.* Pittsburgh: University Press, 1947.

Skinner, B. F. Are theories of learning necessary? *Psychological Review.* 1950, **57**, 193–216.

Staddon, J. E. R. Temporal control and the theory of reinforcement schedules. In R. M. Gilbert and J. R. Millenson (Eds.) *Reinforcement: Behavioral analysis.* New York: Academic Press, 1972.

Stevens, S. S. Mathematics, measurement, and psychophysics. In S. S. Stevens (Ed.) *Handbook of experimental psychology.* New York: John Wiley, 1951.

CHAPTER 7

Species-Typical Behavior and Operant Conditioning

So far, we have considered many examples of operant behavior and many ways in which the environment can modify that behavior, but we have been primarily concerned with "successes." By "success," we mean that the behavior selected for study by the investigator turned out to be an operant response—defined (Section 2.8) as behavior that is susceptible to reinforcement as a class. A "failure" could be either the finding that the behavior does not increase in frequency at all when a reinforcing stimulus is made contingent upon it, or that some elements of the response class increased while others did not. Both results would show that the response class originally selected by the experimenter was not an operant; in the latter case, the operant could be redefined as those elements of the class that were increased by reinforcement.

Following Skinner's (1938) suggestion, the operants studied have generally been picked as arbitrary, yet representative, acts. The objective has not been to document the details of lever pressing by rats or key pecking by pigeons. Rather, these behaviors were picked because they were easy to train, easy to record, and could be emitted at high or low frequencies over long periods without the physical exertion tiring the subject. If we are developing a meter to monitor some phenomenon, we concern ourselves with the sensitivity, accuracy, and reliability of the meter, and discard versions that do not have these virtues. The preceding five chapters of this book are tribute to the success of Skinner's strategy of developing a *behavior meter*, and then using it to test the effects of a wide variety of environmental variables.

One feature of this approach, discussed in Section 4.1, is that it leads to the use of functionally defined operants. The response class is defined as all acts that have a particular *effect* on the environment; for example, the downward depression of a lever with a force of 10 g or more. This has led to great success in between-species comparability. Skinner (1959) was able to point to Figure 7.1. and ask the reader which cumulative record came from a rat, which from a monkey, and which from a pigeon. These diverse species produced identical records when responding on the same schedule. This is a remarkable success for Skinner's strategy: the operant really does seem to be arbitrary.

This, however, is not the whole story. In Section 1.8, we noted that Thorndike (1896) had already discovered that some responses are conditioned more easily than others, and we introduced Seligman's (1970) notion of "preparedness". The idea is that for a given species, there are degrees of *associability* between various responses and reinforcers, ranging from connections that the members of the species are prepared to make, through those that are unprepared, to those that are contraprepared. Seligman and others (for instance, Moore, 1973) have asserted that because the response-reinforcer pairs studied in operant-conditioning laboratories have been selected for convenience, our knowledge is based almost entirely on prepared responses, while those that are unprepared or contraprepared may not follow the same laws.

If we wish to move towards a science of behavior that takes account of all variables affecting behavior, and not just those that are species-independent,

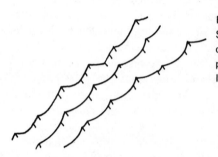

FIGURE 7.1.
Skinner's (1959) famous example of cumulative records on *mult FI FR* from a pigeon, rat and monkey. "... which is which? It doesn't matter." (Skinner, 1959, p. 374).

then we must consider the ways in which species characteristics, or *species-typical behaviors*, interact with operant behavior.

7.1

"Animal Misbehavior" and Instinctive Drift

Impetus to research in this area was provided by a report of Breland and Breland (1961) entitled, "The Misbehavior of Organisms." They had spent a number of years attempting to apply the behavior technology derived from operant conditioning to animal training. They had met with much success, using over 6,000 animals of 38 species to provide demonstrations of conditioned behavior for many commercial applications, but they also encountered a persistent pattern of failures.

Their catalogue of failures includes a number of cases where acquisition of operant behavior proceeded satisfactorily, initially, but then other behavior developed and persisted that interfered with the reinforced response. In one case, pigs were trained to carry wooden "coins" several feet and deposit them in a large "piggy bank." This behavior was reinforced with food on *FR* 4 or 5. They repeatedly found that, although a high response rate developed in early sessions, the pigs then began to slow down. They would drop the coin they were carrying and "root" it along the ground, pick it up, drop it, root it, and so on. This behavior became so persistent that it could take 10 min for a pig to carry four coins a distance of six feet.

Through various control procedures, the Brelands established that this type of outcome was not the result of inadequate operant-conditioning techniques, but must reflect another behavioral process. They named this, "instinctive drift." They suggested that when the conditioned response is closely related to instinctive behavior, the topography of the conditioned response will "drift" towards that of the instinctive behavior. This will occur even if the change in topography greatly reduces the efficiency or frequency of the operant behavior.

The importance of these findings is that they demonstrate that a *limit* can be reached where an operant reinforcement contingency becomes ineffective and other aspects of the situation control behavior. This means that any attempt to explain *all* aspects of an organism's behavior in operant terms is doomed to failure: we will have to take account of other processes, even when we set out to study operant conditioning explicitly. More specifically, the Brelands made a suggestion about the nature of the limit. We will evaluate this by considering findings from related research areas.

7.2
Effects of the Reinforcer on Response Topography

Wolin (1948) noted that, in pigeons, food- and water-reinforced operant responses resemble the corresponding consummatory behaviors. He described food-reinforced pecks, like eating behavior, as "rapid, short powerful thrusts of the head with the beak open," while water-reinforced pecks and drinking behavior involved a "slow, long, easy pushing motion with the beak almost closed." Smith (1967) provided detailed data on the form of food-reinforced pecking by filming it at 200-frames/sec. His results showed clearly that the beak springs open just before contact, closes about 25 msec after contact, and then the head is retracted. This pattern is just that required to eat grain.

It seems then that when a pigeon is required to operate a key as a functionally defined operant, the pecking that occurs is closely related to the nature of the reinforcer. Similar findings for rats have been reported by Hull (1977). He found that rats made many more lever-press responses in which they contacted the lever for more than 1 sec when reinforced with food pellets than when given water. This effect was durable and observers identified sniffing and pawing as components of the food-reinforced response, whereas the water-reinforced response was a quick "mechanical" movement.

Given that these differences exist, do they persist when reinforcement contingencies are introduced that should eliminate them? A study by J. Warren (reported by Moore, 1973) suggests that pecking topography is fairly persistent. Twelve pigeons were reinforced for pecking a key, half were reinforced with water and half with food, and half of each of these groups were reinforced for short- and half for long-duration pecks, using a progressive shaping technique. The results are shown in Figure 7.2. As can be seen, the contingency had some effect with food or water reinforcement, but water produced much longer "long" responses and rather longer "short" responses. However, there was comparatively little change in individual subjects' behavior in the two food groups and the "short" water group. It, therefore, seems that the reinforcer-peck duration link is quite resistant to reinforcement contingencies. In contrast, indirect evidence for the malleability of rat lever-press durations comes from the fact that, while food reinforcement in Hull's (1977) experiment produced quite long durations, very high rates of response (and hence short durations) can be generated on ratio schedules. However, shortening a food-reinforced lever press may depend on not using the continuous reinforcement schedule that was used in the studies of topography we have reviewed.

As these effects of reinforcers on response topographies represent failures to comply with operant-conditioning procedures, or at least, the acquisition of behavior not specified by the contingencies, operant-conditioning principles, alone will not explain them. The most parsimonious explanation is in terms of a classical conditioning process. Classical conditioning is the

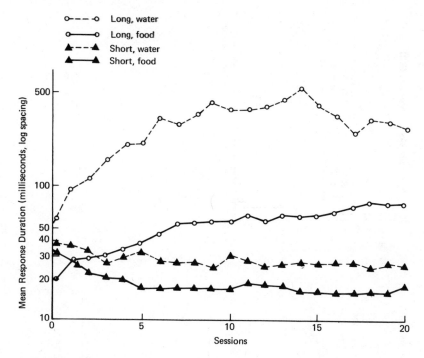

FIGURE 7.2. Mean peck durations for the groups of pigeons in J. Warren's experiment (Moore, 1973).

subject of Part Three, and we will come back to this problem in Chapter 12. In the meantime, we will merely state that the interfering behavior in these cases, and in the Brelands' "misbehaving" animals, is *species-typical appetitive behavior* which, through classical conditioning, comes to be elicited by stimuli associated with the food-reinforced response. This behavior may facilitate or interfere with the operant, depending upon its topography.

7.3

Response-Reinforcer Incompatibility

We have considered cases where species-typical behavior modifies the conditioned operant, but there are also instances where it prevents conditioning from taking place at all.

Sevenster (1973) established that both the opportunity to fight with a male and the opportunity to court a ripe female could act as reinforcers for a male, three-spined stickleback. In both cases the conspecific was presented behind glass for 10 sec. He then attempted to use each of these stimuli to reinforce two responses: swimming through a gray plastic ring (diameter 5 cm) and biting the end of a rod (diameter 0.5 cm). The results are shown in

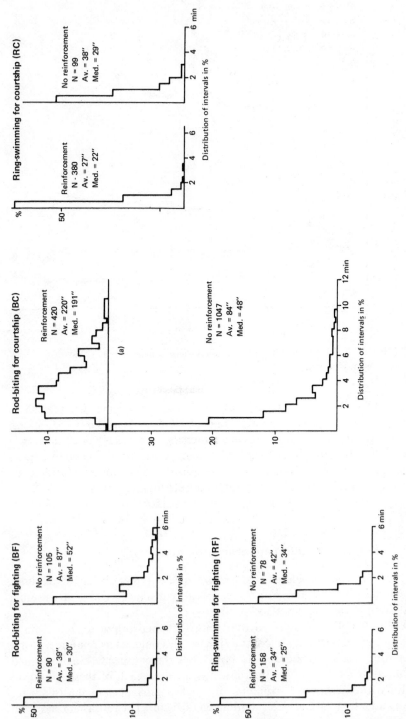

FIGURE 7.3. *IRT* distributions during reinforcement and extinction in the 4 response-reinforcement combinations of Sevenster's (1973) experiment.

the four panels of Figure 7.3. Three panels give a similar picture. For ring swimming, reinforced by fighting or courtship, and rod biting, reinforced by fighting, the interresponse time (*IRT*) distributions are highly peaked in reinforcement and diminish during extinction. When rod biting is reinforced with courtship, however, the picture is quite different. *IRT*'s are much longer and actually *shorten* dramatically during extinction. Paradoxically, removal of reinforcement appears to increase the frequency of response.

Through additional experiments and measurements, Sevenster was able to establish the causes of this strange effect. He found that for several minutes after courtship, reinforcement rod biting was severely inhibited, while there was no such effect of fighting reinforcement. However, if rod approaches were examined, there was no such difference. Because the operant level or rod approach and rod bite was very low prior to the introduction of reinforcement, but high during extinction, Sevenster concluded that the rod bite→courtship reinforcement contingency was effective; for example, an increase in the operant occurred, but the rod bite that concluded the operant response was specifically inhibited when courtship had recently occurred. Sevenster suggested that the reason for the inhibition is that the rod, through association with the female, is treated like a "dummy female," especially just after courtship. This can be restated as the rod coming through classical conditioning to elicit species-typical behavior (associated with courtship) that is incompatible with rod biting. A key point is that rod biting, but not ring swimming, is unlike any of the components of courtship behavior.

Related results employing quite different species, behaviors, and reinforcers were obtained by Shettleworth (1973). She attempted to reinforce hungry golden hamsters with food for lever pressing, open rearing, scrabbling, digging, face washing, scratching with a hind leg, or scent marking. All of these showed appropriate changes under reinforcement, except face washing, scratching with a hind leg, and scent marking, which showed only very small increases and sometimes increased more in extinction. These activities can be distinguished from the others because they are behaviors that would not normally be effective in obtaining food. Their failure to increase under reinforcement could either be because they are inhibited by food-related stimuli, or because hamsters are contraprepared to associate food with these behaviors and reinforcement is, therefore, much less effective.

The moral of Sevenster's and Shettleworth's findings is that we must look at the normal function of a behavior of an organism to understand why reinforcement does not always result in the characteristic increase in response frequency. We may also need to consider the natural sequences in which the response that we are trying to reinforce occurs.

7.4
Schedule-Controlled Performances

In a simple way, we have already considered the role of species-typical behavior in schedule-controlled performances. In Chapter 5, we concluded that an operant response has a natural frequency of occurrence that is not determined by the reinforcement contingencies arranged by the experimenter, but by various other factors. These are primarily the relationship between the species-typical behavioral repertoire that the subject brings to the experiment, and the apparatus used to monitor its behavior. Thus, if a gerbil is provided with a roll of paper to shred, its response rate will be higher than if it lever presses for food. The rate of either of these responses will decline if it is made more effortful, or if the floor of the apparatus is made a good deal larger (because this increases the reinforcing value of other activities, see Section 6.5).

Can we demonstrate a more specific role for species-typical behavior in schedule-controlled performances? There seems to be evidence for its importance in differential reinforcement of low rate (*DRL*) performance. Let us consider the *DRL* behavior of two, well-researched species: the rat and the pigeon.

Figure 7.4 shows the *IRT* distribution of a rat on a *DRL* 15-sec schedule. Note that, while the peak occurs in the 15 to 18-sec category, there is a subsidiary peak in the first category. Now "rational" behavior would be to only emit *IRT*'s greater than 15 sec, although we would expect some variability leading to "errors" of *IRT* below 15 sec. Why then are there lots of short *IRT*'s? One reason is that, although the *DRL* schedule reinforces slowing down of response rate, a direct effect of reinforcement is to speed it

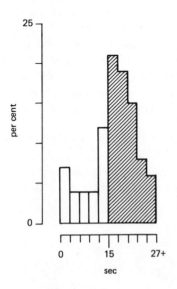

FIGURE 7.4.
Relative frequencies of *IRT*'s of different durations for a rat on *DRL* 15 sec schedule (Blackman, 1974).

up. However, another reason is that the rat's lever pressing has a species-typical natural frequency that is very high relative to the *DRL* requirement. Once responding is initiated, it tends to continue at that frequency (see Section 5.3).

The behavior of rats on *DRL* schedules is far more closely governed by the schedule contingencies than that of pigeons. Several studies (reviewed by Kramer and Rilling, 1970) found that only 2 per cent of responses met the reinforcement criterion on *DRL* 20 sec or 30 sec, although there is evidence that pigeons can readily discriminate time intervals of this length. This "inefficiency" is curious, given the reliable performances of pigeons on other schedules, but it is elucidated by several studies that varied the conditions of the *DRL* experiment. Hemmes (1975) trained pigeons to press a treadle for grain reinforcement. These subjects then performed efficiently on *DRL*'s of up to 35 sec. Dews (1960) required pigeons to emit two *IRT*'s longer than 10 sec, and then delivered reinforcement after a pause (not pecking) of 10 sec. There were always at least 10 sec from a peck to reinforcement and, under these conditions, spaced responding was rapidly acquired. Both these studies seem to show that it is when pecking is immediately followed by food reinforcement that *DRL* performance is disrupted. The reason for this is suggested by a study by Schwartz and Williams (1971).

They trained pigeons on *DRL* 6 sec for 45 daily sessions, and obtained the customary poor performance. It was a discrete trial procedure; this meant that after a period with the key darkened, it was illuminated with green light. If the pigeon pecked at it before 6 sec had elapsed, the stimulus went off, terminating that trial without reinforcement. If no peck occurred for 6 sec, the first peck turned off the stimulus and was reinforced. After the forty-fifth session, the procedure was changed so that when the green key came on, another key was illuminated with blue light. Pecks on that key had no effect, but the two keys were darkened simultaneously.

The results are shown in the left panel of Figure 7.5. Three out of four pigeons now produced *IRT*'s that were mostly long enough to be reinforced. The same three pigeons pecked frequently (more than 10 times/trial) at the blue, irrelevant, key light. It appears that the extra key enabled them to redirect their pecking, and thus increase their rate of reinforcement. The importance of the second key is shown by the right panel of Figure 7.5, which presents data from the first session in which it was removed and subjects were returned to the original training conditions. Their performance deteriorated dramatically, hardly any reinforcements being obtained.

Once again, the most parsimonious explanation of these results is in terms of classical conditioning. Stimuli (for example, key lights) paired with food reinforcers come to elicit pecking in pigeons; this is a species-typical appetitive behavior. This pecking can facilitate operant performance (for example, on *VR*), but on *DRL* it tends to interfere with it. However, if another stimulus is provided that precedes food delivery just as often (the blue key in Schwartz and Williams' study), the selective reinforcement for *not*

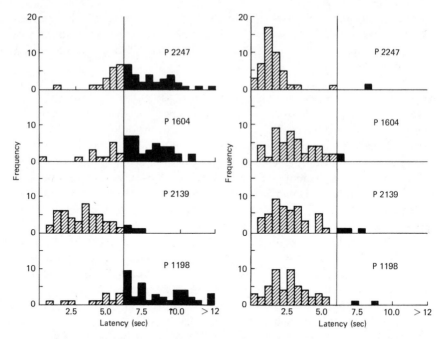

FIGURE 7.5. Performance of four pigeons in Schwartz and Williams (1971) study (see text for procedural details). Left panel: data from final session with irrelevant key. Right panel: data from first session without it. Only latencies > 6.0 sec were reinforced; these are indicated by solid bars.

pecking the operant key too soon results in pecks being directed at this other stimulus. If pecking is never immediately followed by food (Dews, 1963), or the operant response is not pecking (Hemmes, 1975), *DRL* performance is greatly improved.

7.5
Overview

This chapter has reviewed a variety of situations in which behavior has developed, unbidden by the experimenter, that interferes with or totally abolishes operant responding. We have argued that a process of classical conditioning of appetitive species-typical behavior is responsible for most of these results and this type of process will be a subject of Chapter 12.

The discovery of the phenomena reviewed here aroused great interest, because operant conditioning had not been considered to be concerned with response topographies or natural response-reinforcer relationships. It had been assumed that it was concerned solely with experimentally arranged relationships between arbitrary operant responses and reinforcers. It remains true that operant conditioning is primarily concerned with response-reinforcer relationships that are independent of particular species, response topographies, and reinforcing stimuli, but it has come to be realized that these three "extraneous" variables can jointly exert a tremendous influence on the outcome of particular experiments. This means that the experimenter disregards them at his or her peril. The experimenter must not claim that his or her result holds for *all* operant behavior until he or she has established that it is not a species-typical characteristic of rats, pigeons, hamsters, or whatever animals the experimenter has been studying.

The importance of species-typical behavior interactions with operant behavior varies with the particular area of investigation and with the orientation of the investigator. There is no doubt that many operant phenomena have been identified in which the influence of species, response topography, and reinforcing stimulus is genuinely small. Investigators interested in obtaining the greatest generality for their results will focus on these areas, while those interested in the ways the biology and ecology of particular species affect their operant behavior will direct their attention to situations where the role of species-typical behavior is evident.

In this chapter, we have described the behavior of various nonhuman species. We have been unable to relate the findings to human behavior directly because of a dearth of information. While there is an increasing number of reports of successful maintenance of human performance on schedules, we do not know enough about "species-typical human behavior" to explain unexpected behavior in those terms. However, the lesson is clear enough. The experimental analysis of human behavior will fail to progress if it is assumed that two or three simple processes account for all behavior. One type of behavior that very likely involves "special" processes is language, and it is this that we will now consider.

7.6
Species Characteristics and Communication

In many species, there is communication between individuals, but the systems used vary enormously, both in the sense modalities they use and in the "design features" they have. Honeybees perform dances, crickets chirrup, and nesting sea birds call raucously to each other. As all of these systems involve a type of language, it is not true to say that language is unique to humans. However, some features of human language are uncommon in the communication systems of other species. For example: "[Prevarication] connotes the ability to lie or talk nonsense with deliberate intent. It is highly characteristic of the human species and hardly found at all in animals" (Thorpe, 1972). Perhaps more importantly, human language seems to be vastly more complicated than other systems.

The development of operant conditioning and other behavior-acquisition techniques opened up the intriguing possibility that nonhumans could be taught human-type language. Successful acquisition would suggest that the difference in "language ability" between humans and other species is not as great as has been supposed.

The obvious candidates for these experiments were chimpanzees, the most amenable of the great ape family. Early attempts to train vocal utterances were total failures. For example, a young chimpanzee ("Vicki") learned only four sounds that approximated to English words, despite six years of assiduous training (Hayes and Hayes, 1955). However, these attempts ignored the fact that, compared with humans, chimps are relatively "nonvocal", there was thus a zero-operant level which apparently was not raised by subsequent training.

Gardner and Gardner (1969) recognized this problem and attempted to teach an infant female chimp ("Washoe"), American sign language (ASL). This is widely used for communication between deaf people and involves manual gestures. Chimps have a high operant level of "manual behavior", and Washoe was able to acquire a large "vocabulary" and produce strings that in some ways resemble sentences. Similar success was reported by Premack and Premack (1974), who used operant techniques to teach Sarah, a five-year-old female chimp, a language involving visual symbols (colored plastic shapes).

These findings with chimps resemble others discussed in this chapter. Aspects of the species-typical behavioral repertoire influence the acquisition of new behavior. It is very likely that species-typical behaviors (or behavioral predispositions) are crucial in the acquisition of language by humans.

The mechanism of language acquisition in children has been hotly debated by "nativists", such as Chomsky (1959), who believe that acquisition proceeds more or less independently of environmental stimuli, and "environmentalists," such as Skinner (1957), who lay great emphasis on the ways the verbal environment shapes verbal behavior (language). This debate has been needlessly long and vituperative. It now seems clear that while verbal behavior is shaped and maintained by its environment, there are aspects of language *acquisition* that require additional explanatory principles. These are: (1) development of the complex phenomena of language occurs very quickly and early in life; (2) each child acquires essentially the same language, although experiences differ; (3) language acquisition is systematic and productive of new utterances (Slobin, 1971). We may, therefore, conclude that the acquisition of language is an area of human behavior where species-typical behavior and dispositions interact with environmental contingencies to determine the behavioral outcome.

References for Chapter 7

Breland, K., and Breland, M. The misbehavior of organisms. *American Psychologist*, 1961, **61**, 681–684.

Chomsky, N. A review of Skinner's Verbal Behavior. *Language*, 1959, **35**, 26–58.

Dews, P. B. Free-operant behavior under conditions of delayed reinforcement. I CRF-type schedules. *Journal of the Experimental Analysis of Behavior*, 1960, **3**, 221–234.

Gardner, R. A., and Gardner, B. T. Teaching sign language to a chimpanzee. *Science*, 1969, **165**, 664–672.

Hayes, K. J., and Hayes, C. In G. J. D. Wayne (Ed.), *The non-human primates and human evolution*. Detroit: Detroit University Press, 1955.

Hemmes, N. Pigeon's performance under differential reinforcement of low rates schedules depends upon the operant. *Learning and Motivation*, 1975, **6**, 344–357.

Hull, J. H. Instrumental response topographies of rats. *Animal Learning and Behavior*, 1977, **5**, 207–212.

Kramer, T. J., and Rilling, M. Differential reinforcement of low rates: A selective critique. *Psychological Bulletin*, 1970, **74**, 225–254.

Moore, B. R. The role of directed Pavlovian reactions in simple instrumental learning in the pigeon. In R. A. Hinde and J. Stevenson-Hinde (Eds.), *Constraints on Learning*. London: Academic Press, 1973.

Premack, D., and Premack, A. J. Teaching visual language to apes and language-deficient persons. In R. L. Schiefelbusch and L. L. Lloyd (Eds.) *Language perspective-acquisition, retardation and intervention*. New York: Macmillan, 1974.

Schwartz, B., and Williams, D. R. Discrete-trials spaced responding in the pigeon: the dependence of efficient performance on the availability of a stimulus for collateral pecking. *Journal of the Experimental Analysis of Behavior*, 1971, **16**, 155–160.

Seligman, M. E. P. On the generality of the laws of learning. *Psychological Review*, 1970, 77, 406–418.

Sevenster, P. Incompatibility of response and reward. In R. A. Hinde and J. Stevenson-Hinde (Eds.) *Constraints on Learning*. London: Academic Press, 1973.

Shettleworth, S. J. Food reinforcement and the organization of behavior in the golden hamster. In R. A. Hinde and J. Stevenson-Hinde (Eds.), *Constraints on Learning*. London: Academic Press, 1973.

Skinner, B. F. *The behavior of organisms*. New York: Appleton-Century-Crofts, 1938.

Skinner, B. F. *Verbal behavior*. New York: Appleton-Century-Crofts, 1957.

Skinner, B. F. A case history in scientific method. In S. Koch (Ed.) *Psychology: a study of a science*. Volume 2. New York: McGraw-Hill, 1959.

Slobin, D. I. (Ed.) *The ontogenesis of grammar*. New York: Academic Press, 1971.

Smith, R. F. Behavioral events other than key striking which are counted as responses during pigeon pecking. Doctoral dissertation, Indiana University, 1967.

Thorndike, E. L. Animal intelligence. *Psychological Review Monograph Supplement*, 1898, No. 8.

Thorpe, W. H. The comparison of vocal communication in animals and man. In R. A. Hinde (Ed.) *Non-verbal communication*. Cambridge: Cambridge University Press, 1972.

Wolin, B. R. Difference in manner of pecking a key between pigeons reinforced with food and water. Paper read at conference on the Experimental Analysis of Behavior, 1948.

CHAPTER 8

Conditioned Reinforcement and Chaining

It is apparent from even a cursory examination of the world about us that some of the special consequences that we have been calling reinforcers have a more natural or biological primacy than others. Few would dispute that food, water, and sex fall into a different—more "basic"—category than books, money, and automobiles. Yet organisms, at one time or another, work for all of these. We can distinguish between these two categories by the manner in which the organism comes to possess a reinforcement suscepti-bility. For each individual, there exists a class of reinforcers whose powers are a biological consequence merely of the individual's membership in a certain species. These reinforcers are as much a property of the species as are the leopard's spots, the cat's fur, the dog's tail. Reinforcement susceptibilities which come built into the organism this way define the *primary* or *unconditioned* reinforcers; they are discussed in subsequent chapters under

Motivation. For the present, we address ourselves to a second group of "secondary" reinforcers, which appear more variable and less predictable from individual to individual than the primary set.

Money, cars, pencils, newspapers, prestige, honor, and the countless other arbitrary things that human beings work for constitute a vast source of reliable and potent reinforcers. But these things have no value for us at birth. Clearly, they must have *acquired* their capacity to reinforce at some time during each individual's past history. A particular past history is a prerequisite; witness the occasional adult for whom some of the conventional reinforcers seem to hold no value. Moreover, gold has little importance for a Trappist monk, primitive man would hardly have fought for a copy of the *New York Times*, not everybody likes Brahms. The context is also important. The business executive may enjoy a telephone call from his wife when work is slack, but be irritated by it occurring during an important meeting.

Money, newsprint, and the works of particular composers lack the universal value of food, water, and sex; yet for any given individual, their appeal may seem equally strong. As the following shows, the acquired reinforcers get their power to strengthen and maintain behavior by virtue of a past history of association with primary reinforcers. It is their dependence upon this *conditional* history for their power to reinforce that gives them the name of *conditioned* reinforcers.

Conditioned reinforcers appear to be especially pervasive in the maintenance of human behavior; indeed, they are tied up with the very notion of human culture. Nevertheless, they are easily cultivated with animal subjects in the laboratory, where the exact conditions of their establishment and the precise measurement of their relative strengths can be quantitatively studied.

8.1

The Three-Term Relation

In order to discuss conditioned reinforcement, we must introduce a very important aspect of operant behavior that we have not yet explicitly mentioned. This is the *stimulus control* of operant behavior. We have extensively discussed response-reinforcer relationships, but every one of these exists in the context of stimuli that may or not be explicitly arranged by the experimenter. Consider a rat reinforced for lever pressing in a Skinner box. The complex of stimuli arising from "being in the Skinner box" stand in an obvious relation to reinforced lever pressing; after all, this is the only location the rat has the opportunity to lever press. The experimenter may also arrange that a *discriminative stimulus* (S^D) is provided that signals when lever pressing is reinforced. This may simply be the houselight in the Skinner box, or maybe an additional auditory or visual cue. In either case, the situation is actually a multiple schedule in which *the S^D sets the occasion for* *reinforcement*. The S^D is thus a stimulus that does not elicit responding, but in its presence, responses are emitted and reinforced (either continuously or intermittently). When the S^D is effective, and response rates are higher in its presence than in its absence, we may say that it exerts stimulus control. The analysis of stimulus control is a very large part of the experimental analysis of behavior and is the subject of Part Four of this book.

The *three-term relation* is between the discriminative stimulus, operant response, and reinforcing stimulus, and is written thus:

$$S^D : R \rightarrow S^+$$

For our present example:

$$S^D_{\text{houselight}} : R_{\text{lever-press}} \rightarrow S^+_{\text{food-pellet}}$$

The use of an S^D implies that at times during the experiment, this stimulus is not present. It may simply be absent (for example, houselight switched off), or may be replaced with a different one (for example, houselight flashing rather than steady). In either case, we refer to the alternate stimulus situation, which generally signals extinction, as S^Δ. S^D and S^Δ are often referred to as positive and negative discriminative stimuli.

8.2
The Reinforcing Properties of Positive Discriminative Stimuli

Prior to conditioning the lever-press response of a hungry rat or the disk peck of a hungry pigeon, care is generally taken to precede each instance of food delivery with a brief click and a light flash emanating from the place where food is delivered. Since food is only available following the click-light combination, this procedure suffices to make the click-light a positive discriminative stimulus for the food-tray approach response. But in addition to making the click-light situation an S^D, an inevitable by-product of this discrimination procedure is to give the click and light the power to reinforce. This power is exploited by permitting lever pressing or disk pecking to produce the S^D. In this way, more immediate consequences can be provided for the response than is possible with food itself. It takes some time for the rat to move from the lever to the food tray and eat; but the click-light stimulus may reach it before it has even lifted its paw from the lever. This kind of immediate reinforcement, provided by the click-light conditioned reinforcer, is essential to produce rapid operant conditioning (see Figure 2.2).

The procedure for demonstrating the reinforcing power of the click-light combination may be represented as a two-phase notation: (1) Establish the click-light as an S^D by the usual discrimination method:

$$S^D : R_1 \rightarrow S^+ \text{ and } S^\Delta : R_1 \nrightarrow$$

where

S^D = click-light
S^Δ = absence of click-light
S^+ = food
R_1 = approach tray
$\rightarrow$ = leads to
$\nrightarrow$ = has no consequences

(2) Then, in S^Δ, permit a previously unstrengthened response, for instance, lever pressing, to produce the positive discriminative stimulus, S^D, at the same time, withhold the final primary reinforcer.

$$S^\Delta : R_2 \rightarrow S^D \text{ (and } S^\Delta : R_1 \rightarrow, \ S^D : R_1 \nrightarrow)$$

where

R_2 = lever press.

To test the effectiveness of the click-light S^D as an independent reinforcing agent, the primary reinforcer must be absent. As long as food occurs at the end of the sequence, strengthening of a new operant (here, lever pressing) may be due entirely to the action of the primary reinforcer; the click-light may be irrelevant.

It is apparent that, during the test, extinction of the food-tray approach response will proceed concurrently with any strengthening effects the procedure might be exerting on the lever press. Yet the experimental result is unequivocal. The lever-press response, previously existing at a low operant-level rate, is quickly strengthened by the click-light S^D, alone. The lever response is conditioned, *despite the fact that no food is being presented*, and despite the fact that the tray response is simultaneously undergoing extinction. In Figure 8.1, cumulative curves are shown for four rats on this procedure. For the first time in the rats' conditioning history, each lever press produced a special consequence—the S^D for food approach. During the time that Figure 8.1 was recorded, food, itself, was never forthcoming. Compared with curves of strengthening by primary (for example, food) reinforcement, the curves are more variable and more negatively accelerated (see Figure 2.2). From observation of the overall increase in rate of lever pressing seen in Figure 8.1, however, there is no doubt that making the S^D contingent upon the lever press serves temporarily to condition the operant. The curves of strengthening by the click-light, alone, take the general shape of extinction curves. This is hardly surprising for, simultaneously with the conditioning of $R_{2 \text{ (lever press)}}$ by S^D, $R_{1 \text{ (tray approach)}}$ is being extinguished. Therefore, S^D is concurrently losing its power to act as an S^D for R_1 and, by inference, its acquired reinforcing value as well. That loss is an inevitable consequence of testing for conditioned reinforcement in this way.

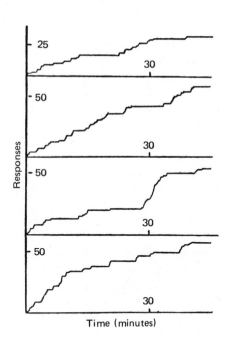

Responses

25

30

50

30

50

30

50

30

Time (minutes)

FIGURE 8.1.
Conditioning of lever pressing in four hungry rats when the only reinforcement is an S^D that previously set the occasion for approaching the food tray (Skinner, 1938).

8.3
Increasing the Durability of Conditioned Reinforcers

The principle of acquired reinforcement was received enthusiastically by the early behaviorists, who saw in it the key to the explanation of those complex social activities which, in man, seem to thrive in the absence of primary reinforcement. Conditioned reinforcement seemed a ready explanation for social behaviors, such as gregariousness or co-operation, and social values, such as the achievement of prestige, power, or wealth. But in the rush to extrapolate the laboratory concepts of conditioned reinforcement to the social field, it was rarely made clear that powerful experimental demonstrations of conditioned reinforcement remained conspicuously absent. Skinner's (1938) curves (Figure 8.1) were a genuine enough demonstration that S^D's do become conditioned reinforcers. But the output of behavior sustained by the S^D as a conditioned reinforcer was on the order of some 50 responses over 45 min—a paltry yield, indeed; certainly not a very convincing demonstration that the conditioned reinforcers of the laboratory might even remotely underlie the social incentives of human life. For some time, attempts by investigators, using runways, mazes, and levers, to produce more powerful conditioned reinforcers, which would shape and sustain behavior over long periods without primary reinforcers, met with little success. It is only relatively recently that techniques have been discovered for amplifying the durability of conditioned reinforcers to a level where the experimental concept could reasonably be assigned a major role in a theory of human activity.

The ability to demonstrate acquired reinforcement in a convincing way awaited the development of intermittent reinforcement procedures; that is, schedules of reinforcement, and higher-order operant specifications. Intermittency plays two critical roles in amplifying the effects of conditioned reinforcers. (1) Used to schedule primary reinforcement (for example, food) for a discriminative operant in S^D—S^Δ training, it can build up a high resistance to extinction of the discriminative operant. The method is simply to alternate the set of contingencies $S^D: R_1 \xrightarrow{p} S^+$ and $S^\Delta: R_1 \nrightarrow$ where p=probabilistically, some R_1's produce S^+. The result is to confine the emission of R_1 to S^D and moreover, since the contingency is probabilistic, to develop a very strong potential resistance to extinction of R_1 in S^D. (2) Used in testing the reinforcing value of the S^D, an intermittency imposed between the new R to be conditioned and the contingent S^D conserves the power of the conditioned reinforcer. The method is simply to let the new R produce S^D probabilistically, $R_2 \xrightarrow{p} S^D$; or alternately, incorporate R into a higher-order operant, $nR \rightarrow S^D$. A well-chosen intermittency here will not only conserve the power of S^D, but will also maintain a high rate of R_2. The conservation of power of S^D in this procedure derives from its infrequency of occurrence. S^D will not lose its control over R_1 until a certain number of instances of R_1 have occurred (without reinforcement) in the presence of S^D. If S^D appears infrequently, R_1 has only infrequent opportunities to weaken.

In a variant of this method, used by Zimmerman (1957, 1959), hungry rats were first trained to run down a runway, obtaining food in a goal box at the end. A runway trial began when the rat was placed in the start box. A buzzer was briefly sounded, the door to the runway alley raised, and the rat allowed to run to the goal box. The running time between the buzzer's sounding and the response of entering the goal box was measured. So far, this procedure is just:

$$S^D : R_1 \rightarrow S^+$$

where

S^D = buzz in start box and door opened
R_1 = run to goal box
S^+ = food

When the running time had become asymptotically short (after about 30 trials), food was omitted on some trials; that is, the discriminative running operant was placed on a probabilistic reinforcement schedule:

$$S^D : R_1 \xrightarrow{p} S^+$$

Over the next 60 trials, this probability was gradually lowered from 0.5 to about 0.2. That is, by the end of the 90 trials of runway training, only about one run in five ended with food. On the other four runs, the rat found an empty goal box. Yet the running time to the buzzer remained short; the buzzer-door opening continued to act as an S^D for vigorous and speedy runway responding. The situation at this point is reminiscent of our own behavior in answering a ringing telephone. Though only a few of the calls may actually be directed to us, answering behavior remains (like the running behavior of Zimmerman's rats) at high strength.

Following these 90 trials of runway training, food was permanently removed and a lever installed in the start box. A trial began with the rat being placed in the start box as usual, but now the buzzer and door opening were made contingent solely upon lever pressing. Using the buzzer-door opening S^D as the only reinforcement, Zimmerman progressively shaped an *FR* operant of 15 lever presses over three 90-min sessions. During the following 11 sessions, *FR*-15 responding was maintained completely by the contingent S^D; meanwhile, on each trial, the subsequent runway behavior was slowly weakening due to its extinction. This stage is represented as

$$S^\Delta : R_2 \rightarrow S^D : R_1 \nrightarrow$$

where

$S^D =$ buzz in start box and door opened
$S^\Delta =$ no buzz in start box, door closed
$R_1 =$ run to goal box
$R_2 =$ 15 lever presses

Except for the differences in specific elements, the procedures here and in Skinner's experiment are identical. Yet before the power of the conditioned reinforcer was depleted, Zimmerman's rats had emitted thousands of lever presses and continued working for 20 hr spaced over several sessions. Cumulative curves of lever pressing in the start box on sessions 1, 5, 11, and 14 are shown in Figure 8.2. The shape of these curves indicates clearly that the use of the S^D in Zimmerman's procedure acted in a manner similar to primary reinforcement, in *generating and maintaining* the characteristic effects of an *FR* response specification. Pauses followed by high rates of pressing are seen. As extinction continues, the pauses increase; yet when the organism responds, the entire *FR* operant is typically run off quickly and smoothly.

The performances sustained by Zimmerman's rats are to be contrasted with the behavior of Skinner's rats (Figure 8.1), who emitted only about 50 presses for the S^D, and by the end of 45 min had ceased to respond. The difference in potency between the conditioned reinforcers in the two cases may be attributed to the double intermittency used by Zimmerman in training and testing. (1) The probabilistic connection between the discriminative operant (R_1) and its primary reinforcement (food) in Zimmerman's runway training greatly increased the resistance to extinction of the runway response to the S^D (buzzer-door opening). Thus, the S^D, itself, remained in control of behavior for a much longer period of time following continuous

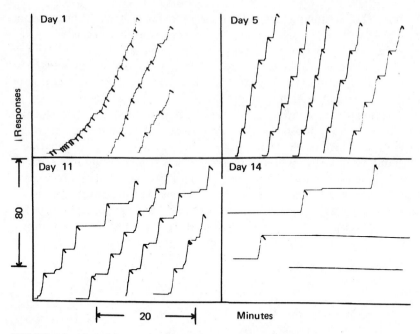

FIGURE 8.2. *FR*-15 lever-pressing based on conditioned reinforcement only. The pips represent buzzer and door opening. The recorder ran only while the rat was in the start box prior to producing the S^D (Zimmerman, 1959).

reinforcement and, therefore, retained its conditioned reinforcing power far longer. Zimmerman's results imply that Skinner would have obtained more lever presses had he probabilistically reinforced tray approach to click-light. (2) By incorporating individual lever presses into a higher-order operant made up of 15 elements, the overall behavioral output, as measured by the number of lever-press elements emitted, was greatly increased (Weissman and Crossman, 1966). At the same time, the infrequency of occurrence of S^D conserved its discriminative function in controlling running.

Zimmerman's results suggest that, so long as the conditioned reinforcer remains potent, the effects of making it contingent on a response appear indistinguishable from the effects of making a primary reinforcer contingent on the response. The results of other experiments concur. Kelleher (1961) made the operating click of a food magazine an S^D for magazine-approach behavior in pigeons. When the click, alone, was used as a reinforcer for key pecking on *FI*, *FR*, or *DRL* schedules, the birds generated patterns of responding typical of these procedures under primary reinforcement.

8.4

Second-Order Schedules

Zimmerman followed each completion of an *FR* requirement with an S^D that had previously been associated with primary reinforcement. Similar results can be obtained by following the behavior specified by a schedule with a brief stimulus that is occasionally paired with primary reinforcement, or simply occurs in place of reinforcement. For example, Findley and Brady (1965) were able to maintain behavior in the chimpanzee and monkey on *FR* 4,000 by presenting a brief food-hopper light after each 400 responses. Technically, this is described as *a second-order schedule of brief (or feedback) stimulus presentation* of *FR* 10 (*FR* 400:S). The statement inside brackets described the response unit of 400, which was followed by a feedback stimulus (the food-hopper light).

These schedules are very important, because they result in a vast increase in the amount of behavior controlled by the schedule and, as mentioned above, the behavior controlled by the component schedule that terminates only with a feedback stimulus is appropriate to that schedule. A good example is shown in Figure 8.3. The upper and lower records show a pigeon's behavior on *FR* 15 (*FI* 4 min : S); that is, reinforcement occurred only once per hour, but responding produced a feedback stimulus on an *FI* 4-min

FIGURE 8.3.
Effects of a brief white (W) light feedback stimulus presented on a *FI* 4 min schedule (Kelleher, 1966).

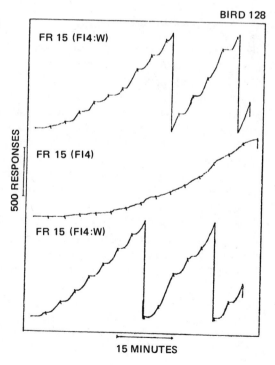

BIRD 128

FR 15 (FI4:W)

FR 15 (FI4)

500 RESPONSES

FR 15 (FI4:W)

15 MINUTES

schedule. The records look exactly as though primary reinforcement occurred on *FI* 4 min. The middle record shows data from an interpolated session in which the feedback stimulus was omitted. The pigeon now shows behavior appropriate to *FI* 60 min and makes less than half the number of responses.

A remarkable feature of these schedules is that behavior is maintained at roughly the same level if the feedback stimulus is *never* paired with the primary reinforcer. This is problematic for traditional views of conditioned reinforcement, which regard it as an attribute of a stimulus arising from its direct association with primary reinforcement. The results suggest that we should view conditioned reinforcement as a property of a *schedule* rather than simply of a *stimulus*. We will return to this point in Section 8.8. The literature on second-order schedules shows that a primary function of feedback stimuli is a *discriminative* one: on an *FI* or *FR* component schedule, the subject pauses after the feedback stimulus, because responses at that time are never reinforced, while primary reinforcement sometimes occurs at the end of the component. Staddon (1974) has shown the same effect in simple *FI* or *FR* schedules. If the reinforcement is omitted when it is due, the subject simply continues to respond at the high rate characteristic of the end of the schedule requirement until reinforcement is eventually received.

8.5
Token Rewards

While the expanding literature on second-order schedules is modifying our view of conditioned reinforcement, there are studies showing effects of pairing a stimulus with a reinforcer that have an appealing parallel with conventional views of the role of conditioned reinforcers in human behavior. In these studies, poker chips ("tokens") were used to reward primates (Wolfe, 1936; Cowles, 1937). The chips were made S^D's for various manipulative responses, including the act of inserting them into the slot of a vending machine to produce grapes, oranges, peanuts, and other primary reinforcers. It was this history of association with primary reinforcement that transformed the chips into "tokens" (money) possessing the power to reinforce.

In some of Wolfe's (1936) experiments, chimpanzees were trained to insert a white chip into a vender and thereby produce a grape. The insertion response was shaped through successive approximation. A token was inserted partway in the vender slot by the experimenter, and any operant-level push by the chimp that caused the token to drop produced a grape. The shaping procedure continued until the animals would retrieve white chips from the floor and insert them into the grape vender.

$$S_F : R_2 \rightarrow S_W : R_1 \rightarrow S^+$$

where

S_W = white chip in hand
S_F = white chip on floor
S^+ = grape
R_1 = insert chip in vender
R_2 = pick up chip

The animals were later taught to pull a weighted lever to produce chips, a task they learned to do easily.

S_o : $R_3 \rightarrow S_F$: $R_2 \rightarrow S_W$: $R_1 \rightarrow S^+$
S_o = no chips present
R_3 = pull lever

Later, a further discrimination was established between brass chips which were worthless—they did not operate the vender if inserted—and the white chips. A brief history with this set of contingencies sufficed to make the animals indifferent to the brass chips.

In other experiments (Cowles, 1937), animals learned pattern and spatial discriminations where the only reinforcement consisted of tokens. In Cowles' experiments, the response was merely to push aside a card depicting the correct pattern. Vending machines were located in another room where, *after* the discrimination had been learned, the accumulated chips could be exchanged.

In these various experiments, the chimps acquired new behaviors when the only immediate reinforcement was the chips. The chips are distinguishable from any other conditioned reinforcer only by their physical properties, which make them manipulable, storable, and so forth. Of course, not only is a "token" the S^D for an inserting response; it also provides the actual physical means by which such a manipulative response can be emitted. A chip both implies reinforcement for inserting and makes inserting possible. Nevertheless, "tokens", like buzzers and clicks, come to be S^D's simply because a certain response is reinforced in their presence.

The idea that a token can be employed to bridge the gap between behavior and reinforcement has found practical application in the *token economy* (Ayllon and Azrin, 1968, and see Part Eight). This is a system for modifying human behavior in which tokens are provided for socially acceptable behavior, attainment of educational objectives, or other desired behavioral changes, and these can be later traded for privileges, improved living conditions, and so on.

8.6

Generalized Reinforcers

Many positive discriminative stimuli set the occasion for more than a single kind of response to be emitted and reinforced. Some S^D's, in fact, control numerous responses, each of which may lead to a different primary reinforcer. Outside the laboratory, such situations are encountered frequently. Money is the prime example. Having money, many responses can be made, each leading to its own distinct reinforcer.
Thus:

$$S_{money} : \begin{array}{l} R_{(buy\ theater\ tickets)} \rightarrow S_1^+ \\ R_{(purchase\ new\ coat)} \rightarrow S_2^+ \\ R_{(order\ a\ meal)} \rightarrow S_3^+ \end{array}$$
and so forth.

Tokens in token economies have similarly diverse functions; the difference is that not all the reinforcers that can be purchased will be available in exchange for tokens.

"Attention" is sometimes used as a name for a similar kind of S^D; in order to obtain reinforcement for various verbal responses, it is often necessary for a person to obtain another's "attention." When the attention S^D has been procured, many responses (requests, demands, and so on) may then be emitted which stand a chance of being reinforced. In the absence of "attention," we would say that such requests go unheard, or unnoticed, which is the equivalent of saying that they are being subjected to extinction.

Discriminative stimuli that can set the occasion for more than one response-reinforcement sequence are based upon a history of association with more than one primary reinforcer. In our diagram, for instance, money has previously been associated, through S^D–S^Δ training, with entertainment, warmth, food, and so forth. Discriminative stimuli, associated in this manner with more than a single primary reinforcer and whose availability is then made contingent upon new behavior, are termed *generalized reinforcers*. Although they appear to play an important role in mediating complex human behavior, such generalized reinforcers have not been extensively studied in the laboratory.

8.7

Observing Responses

Discriminative stimuli are sometimes said to have the property of carrying information, regarding the state of the environmental contingencies effective at a given time. Thus, when a rat's lever presses are reinforced only in the presence of a light, the light may be said to provide the information that a certain reinforcement contingency is in effect. Similarly, the presence of an all-clear siren conveys the information that enemy bombers have retired, and it is safe to come out. Token reinforcers carry information as well, but here the informative function is overshadowed by the physical properties of the tokens which make possible the actual responses. When the automatic lock of an apartment door buzzes after you ring the bell, you are informed both that you may open the door and that, when you do, you will find somebody at home.

A different kind of information is provided by signs indicating "out of order" and "gone to lunch," red traffic lights, and busy signals. These are notices that certain behaviors will go unreinforced; as such, they constitute S^Δ's for these behaviors. Can the information about reinforcement provided by the S^D's and S^Δ's in these examples be thought of as reinforcing, itself? The answer may best be given by reference to experiments.

Herrick, Myers, and Korotkin (1959) trained rats to discriminate between randomly alternating light and dark periods. The contingencies were VI reinforcement during S^D (light) and extinction during S^Δ (darkness). Imagine that instead of being provided automatically with a bright light as S^D and darkness as S^Δ, another group of animals was trained in a midway condition of dim illumination, *which did not change when each period of VI began and ended, nor when each period of extinction began and ended.* In the vernacular, these animals might be said to have no way of telling whether they were in VI or in extinction. If the extinction period is not too prolonged, rats trained under these conditions will adjust by producing a fairly constant rate of response in both VI and extinction.

Suppose that after such stabilization, a new contingency is introduced for the first time. If now, the rat should happen to pull a cord located in his compartment, the dim light would immediately be replaced, either by darkness (S^Δ) or by the bright light (S^D), depending on the contingency which happens to be in effect at that moment. What we have done is to give the organism the *option* of producing discriminative stimuli. The behavioral result of the option is clear. The contingency acts quickly to condition the cord-pull response (Wyckoff, 1952).

When a response enables an organism to observe a situation correlated with the state of its reinforcement contingencies, we speak of it as an *observing response.* In merely observing an aspect of its environment correlated with certain reinforcement contingencies, the animal does not modify any of them, but it now has the opportunity to refrain from unreinforced responding.

Observing responses are among the most common of our own daily activities. In discriminating a genuine bill from one that is counterfeit, certain very detailed observing responses are required. A large part of the training of counterfeit and fingerprint experts involves the strengthening of observing responses which usually remain unconditioned in the layman. The expert must learn which aspects of a situation to study in order to distinguish between different stimuli which may be present. In the same way that the rat can check significant aspects of its environment by pulling a cord which produces S^D or S^Δ, so the counterfeit expert can check the significant print on a banknote which will identify it as genuine or fake. In both cases, the observing response, pulling the cord or examining the print, enables the organism to make a discrimination which increases the probability of its being reinforced.

The ability of experts to make discriminations, be it between wines, fingerprints, or paintings, is often viewed with some astonishment by the novice. For the latter, two cases reliably discriminated by the expert look, sound, or taste "alike." Observing behavior in the novice has not been strengthened, enabling him or her to "know where to look for the differences." In strengthening observing behavior in the human, we may often successfully "point out" the differences in situations. In pointing to the aspects of the situation on which the differences between S^D and S^Δ depend, we capitalize on a past history in which reinforcement has previously been contingent on looking in the direction the finger points.

Analogous contingencies shape up listening responses, as well as observing behavior in other sense modalities. In general, a principal characteristic of an observing response is that it enhances the probability of reinforcement for behavior. This is certainly true of the rat given the option of producing its S^D's and S^Δ's. If the animal's discrimination is good, S^D and S^Δ presentations will at least enable responding to be confined to S^D. This has the effect of increasing the overall probability of reinforcement for responding well above what it would be if no distinctive S^D and S^Δ were available. The batter, who observes a minute but characteristic movement of a pitcher about to throw a curve ball, stands a better chance of a hit than he or she would without such an S^D. Often, the S^D's and S^Δ's produced by observing behavior are crucial for the occurrence of any reinforcement at all. Try to thread a needle blindfolded, or answer an examination question without first reading it. In both examples, probability of reinforcement is so small as to be effectively zero in the absence of appropriate observing behavior.

Observing behavior is often covert, as when a person sits silently in the presence of a radio. Is the person listening or not? That is, is he or she observing or not? In general, the answer can only be obtained by setting reinforcement contingencies in which the probability that the individual might emit certain words would be negligibly small in the absence of prior observing behavior. If we ask what was said on the radio, the response of repeating what was, in fact, said is taken as *prima facie* evidence that observing behavior must have occurred.

8.8

What Makes Conditioned Reinforcement Effective?

We have described various procedures in which conditioned reinforcement clearly occurs: behavior is maintained by schedules of stimulus presentations that clearly do not involve primary reinforcement. However, the question as to what establishes the conditioned reinforcing power of a stimulus, or schedule of stimulus presentation, remains a difficult one.

Three plausible candidates for the solution are: (1) the *pairing hypothesis*, which states that pairing a stimulus with a primary reinforcer is effective; (2) the *delay reduction hypothesis*, stating that a stimulus has conditioned reinforcing properties if it signals a reduction in the time to primary reinforcement; (3) the *uncertainty reduction hypothesis*, stating that the stimulus is reinforcing to the extent that it provides information about the occurrence of primary reinforcement; that is, reduces uncertainty (Fantino, 1977).

Problems are raised for the pairing hypothesis by experiments such as that by Schoenfeld, Antonitis and Bersh (1950). Rats were trained to approach their food tray for a pellet of food. After the rat had picked up the pellet and was already eating it, a brief (1 sec) light was presented. One hundred light-food pairings failed to import any reinforcing value to the light, for in subsequent testing, the rats would not press a lever to produce this light alone. It appeared to be the *redundancy* of the light that made it ineffective and this led to the uncertainty reduction hypothesis.

Egger and Miller (1962) showed that a stimulus paired with reinforcement will not become a conditioned reinforcer if it is uninformative. Figure 8.4 shows the two experimental conditions. In Condition A, S_2 (a light) was

FIGURE 8.4. Diagram of Egger and Miller's (1962) two conditions. In condition (A), S_1 is uninformative, but in condition (B) it signals reinforcement. See text for the outcome of this experiment.

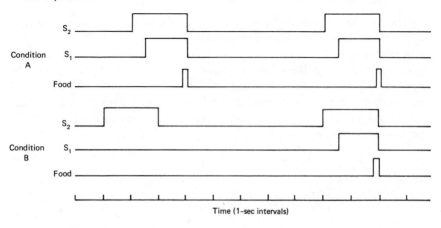

Time (1-sec intervals)

paired with food and came on for 2 sec immediately before food presentation. S_1 (a tone) came on half a second after S_2 and remained on for $1\frac{1}{2}$ sec. In condition B, S_2 was only followed by food on those trials where S_1 came on half a second later. Thus, S_1 was much more informative of when food was due in Condition B than in Condition A. Correspondingly, S_2 was found to have more conditioned reinforcing value in Condition A, while S_1 was more effective in Condition B. This result supports the uncertainty reduction hypothesis, but other experiments have shown that only when a stimulus brings "good news" rather than "bad news", and is positively associated with reinforcement, does it become a conditioned reinforcer.

After reviewing the literature, Fantino (1977) favors the delay reduction hypothesis; this says that conditioned reinforcement accrues when a stimulus signals a reduction in delay of reinforcement. This hypothesis can account for the many findings that stimuli, *correlated* with primary reinforcement, become conditioned reinforcers, and thus for the aforementioned results. Observing responses, on this account, are maintained by conditioned reinforcement because they produce stimuli associated with reduction in delay of reinforcement.

This hypothesis does not account easily for the maintenance of behavior by second-order schedules of brief stimulus presentation, in which the stimulus is never paired with primary reinforcement. However, as pointed out earlier, the *discriminative* properties of these stimuli are as important as their reinforcing properties, and this is also true of primary reinforcers in simple schedules.

8.9
Behavioral Chains

In this chapter, we have used this type of diagram several times:

$$S_1 : R_1 \rightarrow S_2 : R_2 \rightarrow \text{and so on.}$$

This is the way we represent a chain of operant behavior; this is a sequence of operant responses and discriminative stimuli such that each R produces the S^D for the next R. The successive R's in a chain are its *members*; the successive S^D's are its *links*. In the simplest chains, the number of members and the number of links are identical. The loop of behavior involving lever pressing and approaching a food tray, our prototype of operant conditioning, constitutes such a simple repetitive chain. The behavior of the rat is established by the procedure:

$$\rightarrow S_3 : R_3 \rightarrow S_2 : R_2 \rightarrow S^+ : R \rightarrow$$

where

$$S_3 = \text{no food} \qquad R_3 = \text{press lever}$$

$$S_2 = \text{click-light} \qquad R_2 = \text{approach tray}$$
$$S^+ = \text{food} \qquad R_1 = \text{eat}$$

This loop is a special case of a behavioral chain; one in which the chain is repeated indefinitely. A loop may be regarded as a chain that is "closed" by permitting the "last" response to produce the S^D for the "first". In this example, eating is the last response and produces the S^D, no food, for the first response, pressing the lever.

Our loop is represented as being composed of three response members. Thus, it is conventionally described as a three-membered chain. But the actual number of members used to represent a behavioral sequence is arbitrary, being dictated principally by descriptive convenience. In discussing the behavior observed and reinforced, three members serve adequately to illustrate the chained nature of the act. At the same time, three members are not too many to overwhelm us with a mass of details. Still, for other purposes, we may wish to represent the act as being made up of more members. For example, in further resolving the topography of the act, we could double the number of members considered and expand it to:

$$\rightarrow S_6 : R_6 \rightarrow S_5 : R_5 \rightarrow S_4 : R_4 \rightarrow S_3 : R_3 \rightarrow S_2 : R_2 \rightarrow S^+ : R_1$$

where

$S_6 = \text{no food}$	$R_6 = \text{rise up on lever}$
$S_5 = \text{on lever}$	$R_5 = \text{depress lever}$
$S_4 = \text{click-light, lever down}$	$R_4 = \text{release lever}$
$S_3 = \text{click-light, lever up}$	$R_3 = \text{enter tray}$
$S_2 = \text{in tray}$	$R_2 = \text{seize food}$
$S^+ = \text{food in paw}$	$R_1 = \text{put in mouth}$

This diagram represents the same behavior and the same set of contingencies as before, but the magnification power has been doubled. With attention to still more subtle topographical details, and to still more minute stimulus changes, the resolution could easily be extended further. In general, the composition of a behavior chain may be represented as an indefinite number of operants. The number is not infinite, because a point will inevitably be reached in successive conceptual subdivision where specification of two adjacent topographical classes will be so nearly similar that the two classes cannot be observed to function independently of each other. That is, their members will show complete overlap; the animal cannot be brought under any conditions to differentiate them. At that point, we will have reached a logical limit to response resolution. In the main, behavior is subdivided to a level which serves illustrative and procedural purposes best. Without any special instrumentation, lever presses and tray approaches are easily observed, measured, and reinforced. In the last analysis, these are the considerations that justify their status as conceptually discrete units.

8.10

Covert Behavioral Chains

One of John B. Watson's (1914, 1920) most intriguing theories was the equation of the phenomenon known as thinking with covert behavior chains. Watson was able to cite, in support of this theory, the fact that children, if not punished for it, often think out loud. In fact, a history of successively approximating ever more silent responses is necessary to get children to "talk to themselves." Furthermore, when adults solve difficult problems, their lips often move, and if the problem is very hard, the individual may resort to open talking. Watson reasoned that evidence of covert speech would probably be found by sensitive instruments attached to the very muscles that are used in everyday speech. He suggested that in thinking about such activities as riding a bicycle and driving a car, small-scale responses ought to be found in the muscles of the body normally used in these activities.

Watson's theory was not without historical precedents. Plato had observed that thought and language were closely allied, and several nineteenth-century commentators came close to anticipating Watson. But nobody before Watson had dared advance the thesis that *all thought* was covert responding. Viewed from the modern vantage point, Watson's position may appear more or less extreme, depending on one's philosophical preconceptions. But scientifically speaking, the proposed equation between thought and muscle twitches is unnecessary, and perhaps even untestable. However, the notion that chains of behavior can become reduced in magnitude until they are unobservable with the naked eye stands as a scientific proposition capable of generating experiments, whether or not all, some, or no "thought" is to be identified with these chains. It is in this sense that Watson's hypothesis stands as an important creative development in the history of behavioral science.

Unfortunately, little conclusive experimentation has resulted from Watson's hypothesis. In his own time, sensitive recording devices had not been perfected to the extent necessary to make the required measurements. Two experiments, however, done in the 1930's, provide some preliminary evidence that covert responding goes on in appropriate muscles when instructions to "think" are given to subjects.

In one experiment, electrodes were attached to various parts of the subject's body (right and left biceps) and the subject was instructed to imagine movement of a limb (Jacobson, 1932). Electrical responses of muscles were recorded on fast-moving kymographs (of the noncumulative type). In Figure 8.5, records taken from the right biceps are juxtaposed with the various instructions preceding them. The instructions clearly had a selective effect on muscle activity and, as record (B) shows, the effect was located in the right arm only when the right arm was to be "imagined." During the recording of (A), (B), and (C), the experimenter was unable to

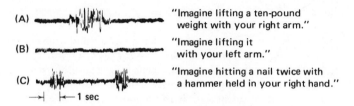

(A)	"Imagine lifting a ten-pound weight with your right arm."
(B)	"Imagine lifting it with your left arm."
(C)	"Imagine hitting a nail twice with a hammer held in your right hand."

→| |←1 sec

FIGURE 8.5. Muscle potentials recorded from the right biceps after several kinds of instructions (after Jacobson, 1932).

detect any actual movement of the arm with the naked eye.

In another experiment, electrodes were attached to the muscles of the tongue and underlip. Under instructions to "imagine" counting, or recalling poems or songs, or multiplying numbers, muscle potentials occurred in the speech musculature. The form of the electrical activity, though reduced in amplitude, was much like that of the electrical activity that took place when the instruction "imagine" was replaced by the instruction "whisper."

In other independent experiments, electrodes were attached to the arms of deaf-mute subjects, whose language takes the form of gestures with the hands and fingers. When the mutes were instructed to "think" words or solve multiplication problems covertly, muscle potentials generally appeared in the forearm region. Muscle potentials from subjects who could hear and speak were used as a basis of comparison. Under similar instructions to the normals, potentials were absent in their forearm regions (Max, 1937).

References for Chapter 8

Ayllon, T., and Azrin, N. H. *The token economy.* New York: Appleton-Century-Crofts, 1968.

Cowles, J. T. Food-tokens as incentives for learning by chimpanzees. *Comparative Psychology Monographs*, 1937, **14**, 1–96.

Egger, M. D., and Miller, N. E. Secondary reinforcement in rats as a function of information value and reliability of the stimulus. *Journal of Experimental Psychology*, 1962, **64**, 97–104.

Fantino, E. Conditioned reinforcement: Choice and information. In W.K. Honig and J. E. R. Staddon (Eds.) *Handbook of operant behavior*. Englewood Cliffs N.J.: Prentice Hall, 1977.

Findley, J. D., and Brady, J. V. Facilitation of large ratio performance by use of conditioned reinforcement. *Journal of the Experimental Analysis of Behavior*, 1965, **8**, 125–129.

Herrick, R. M., Myers, J. L., and Korotkin, A. L. Changes in S^D and S^Δ rates during the development of an operant discrimination. *Journal of Comparative and Physiological Psychology*, 1959, **52**, 359–363.

Jacobson, E. The electrophysiology of mental activities. *American Journal of Psychology*, 1932, **44**, 677–694.

Kelleher, R. Schedules of conditioned reinforcement during experimental extinction. *Journal of the Experimental Analysis of Behavior*, 1961, **4**, 1–5.

Kelleher, R. Conditioned reinforcement in second-order schedules. *Journal of the Experimental Analysis of Behavior*, 1966, **9**, 475–485.

Max, L. W. Experimental study of the motor theory of consciousness. IV. Action-current responses in the deaf during awakening, kinaesthetic imagery and abstract thinking. *Journal of Comparative Psychology*, 1937, **24**, 301–344.

Schoenfeld, W. N., Antonitis, J. J., and Bersh, P. J. A preliminary study of training conditions necessary for secondary reinforcement. *Journal of Experimental Psychology*, 1950, **40**, 40–45.

Skinner, B. F. *The behavior of organisms.* New York: Appleton-Century, 1938.

Staddon, J. E. R. Temporal control, attention and memory. *Psychological Review*, 1974, **24**, 541–551.

Watson, J. B. *Behavior, an introduction to comparative psychology.* New York: Holt, 1914.

Watson, J. B. Is thinking merely the action of language mechanisms? *British Journal of Psychology*, 1920, **11**, 87–104.

Weissman, N. W., and Crossman, E. K. A comparison of two types of extinction following fixed-ratio training. *Journal of the Experimental Analysis of Behavior*, 1966, **9**, 41–46.

Wolfe, J. B. Effectiveness of token-rewards for chimpanzees. *Comparative Psychology Monographs*, 1936, **12**, 1–72.

Wyckoff, L. B., Jr. The role of observing responses in discrimination learning: Part I. *Psychological Review*, 1952, **59**, 431–442.

Zimmerman, D. W. Durable secondary reinforcement: method and theory. *Psychological Review*, 1957, **64**, 373–383.

Zimmerman, D. W. Sustained performance in rats based on secondary reinforcement. *Journal of Comparative and Physiological Psychology*, 1959, **52**, 353–358.

PART THREE

Associative Processes

We saw in the Introduction that two major approaches to behavioral science have evolved. One of these developed from the work of Thorndike on the law of effect and of Skinner on reinforcement contingencies into the study of operant behavior, and this was reviewed in Part Two. The other approach derives from the attempts of a number of theorists, early in the twentieth century, to account for behavior in terms of reflex connections between stimuli and responses. Their ideas were given empirical substance by Pavlov's experiments on conditioned reflexes.

Classical conditioning, the procedure devised by Pavlov, results in a previously neutral stimulus coming to elicit a change in behavior because of it's association with another stimulus. Other procedures, more recently devised, also result in stimuli producing behavioral changes because the organism has a history in which those stimuli have been associated with other significant events. The generic term *associative processes* is applied to the results of all of these procedures.

The chapters in Part Three trace the development of our knowledge of the role of associative processes in behavior. We start with an account of reflexes, because Pavlov used the

behavioral concept of the reflex to
explain conditioned reflexes, the first
associative phenomenon to be
examined.

CHAPTER 9

Reflexes

The primary concern of behavioral science is the relationship between behavior and the environment in which it occurs. Historically, the first, and perhaps the simplest, type of environment-behavior relationship to be identified was the reflex.

The reflex was discovered by physiologists and to them, the reflex is a phenomenon to be explained. The physiologist will be interested in the anatomical structures underlying the reflex and the bodily events that occur between the eliciting stimulus and the response. His or her interest lies in the composition or *analysis* of the reflex. For the psychologist, on the other hand, the reflex is a phenomenon that can be used in explaining other behaviors. The psychologist will be interested in showing that complex behavior patterns are composed of, or can be *synthesized* from, reflexes. The analysis-synthesis distinction shows at once the common meeting ground and point of departure of the two sciences. From the reflex, the two disciplines move off in different directions. As psychologists, we may be able to use the reflex as an explanatory principle, or as a unit of analysis of more complex behavior. Accordingly, we must understand some of the quantitative and conceptual properties of reflexes.

9.1

The S-R Formula

As we have seen in considering reflexive behavior in Chapter 1, both Descartes and Whytt represented the environment with the concept of the *stimulus*. And they represented behavior in terms of the organism's movements or *response* to that stimulus. These concepts have continued to be useful for the description of lawful relationships between the environment and behavior. In this chapter, as in Part Two, we shall designate the stimulus in the reflex relationship by the symbol S, and the response by the symbol R. The lawfulness exhibited in the relationship between environmental events and reflex actions may thus be summarized in the formula $R_1 = f(S_1)$.

This states that a particular reflex response, R_1, is a function of (depends upon) a stimulus event, S_1. This formula expresses an important relationship or correlation between two events, one an aspect of the environment and the other, a piece of behavior. We say that S_1 *elicits* R_1, meaning that an occurrence of S_1 gives rise immediately to an occurrence of R_1, and represent this as

$$S_1 \rightarrow R_1$$

The first objective of this chapter is to examine the properties of the correlation between S_1 and R_1.

To illustrate the nature of a reflex, let us examine one of Sherrington's (1906) experiments. He connected one of the leg muscles of a cat to a device for measuring the contraction of that muscle. Earlier, under anesthesia, the cat's brain had been severed from the spinal cord. (In the study of reflexes, influences that are not directly under the control of the experimenter are often surgically removed. In this case, severing brain from cord removes any possible effects the brain might have on the muscle being studied.) Brief electric shocks of various strengths were then applied to a sensory nerve known to be involved in a reflex arc to that muscle. The term "reflex arc" denotes the neural connections known or presumed to be involved in an observed behavioral reflex.

Figure 9.1 illustrates hypothetical results of the kind that Sherrington might have obtained if he had gradually stepped up the shock intensity over seven successive trials. Some of the properties of a typical reflex are represented: for example, if we observe in Figure 9.1 that the time line moves from left to right, we can see, first of all, that the weakest shock (the shortest

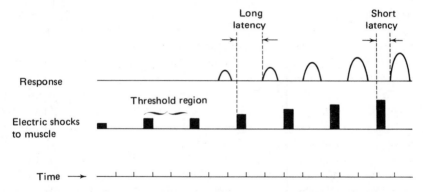

FIGURE 9.1. Hypothetical experiment in which increasingly intense stimuli are presented. The heights of the responses represent their magnitudes and the heights of the shocks represent their intensity. The "time line" simply marks off equal intervals.

and leftmost shock) does not elicit a response at all. Values of shock, too low to elicit a response, are said to be *subliminals*. The next value of shock still seems too weak to elicit a reflex response. But to be certain, we present the same value of shock again on trial 3. This time we get a response. This value of shock lies in what we shall call the "penumbra" or threshold region: its strength is such that it sometimes elicits a response and sometimes does not. Continuing our shock presentations at yet greater strengths, we observe a number of interesting effects: (1) Each shock presentation is followed by (elicits) a response, (2) stronger shocks are followed by stronger responses, (3) responses occur more rapidly following the stronger eliciting stimuli; that is, the time between shock and response, called the *latency*, is shorter when the shock is stronger.

The discovery of relations and properties such as those illustrated in Figure 9.1 is one of the persistent goals of science. When relationships that hold between the values of one event (such as shock intensities) and the values of another event (such as the magnitude or rapidity of muscle movement) can be isolated and reproduced, day after day, experiment after experiment, we often speak of the lawfulness or orderliness of nature. Figuratively, we are saying that nature appears to be bound by certain laws, whose discovery is a prime aim of scientific research.

We must carefully qualify this latter statement, however, for it seems certain that nature's relationships or laws are not like sea shells on a beach, waiting for us to come along and gather them into a scientific basket. Before we can establish laws relating our concepts, we must have formulated our concepts, at least to a first approximation. The discovery of the properties of the reflex was preceded by nearly three hundred years of a gradual evolution of the concept of the stimulus, beginning with Descartes. Thus, science is a bootstrap operation. In prescientific stages, our intuitions and crude experience lead us to suspect that a certain order exists in nature, and we speculate as to the nature of that order. (For example, consider Descartes' guess that involuntary behavior was machinelike.) Then we begin to perturb nature a bit, by doing experiments and thereby changing the natural course of events, so that we can get a better idea of what can happen with a particular phenomenon.

To do even a first, exploratory, experiment we need to define our phenomenon more precisely, so as to decide just what to alter, and just where to look for the effects of our experimental alteration. The results of our first experiment will enable us to define our terms even more accurately. In this way we continually modify our concepts. At the same time we enrich them by relating them to other things that are known. Moreover, having refined our concepts on the basis of experiment, we are led to new experiments. A good experiment is sometimes said to answer one old question and raise two new ones. There is no endpoint to this process (which is science) since we are continually refining and redefining our concepts, and continually relating one to another.

9.2
The Primary Properties of the Reflex

Figure 9.1 illustrates some orderly, or lawful, relationships between stimuli and responses linked together in reflexes. Because the reflex is a behavioral unit, any general principles, or laws, that can be derived from the study of reflexes will be behavioral laws. Scientists attempt to formulate their laws as generally as possible. They would not be satisfied to have one law for the effect of electric shocks on leg muscle, another for the effect of acids in the mouth on salivation, and yet another for the pupillary reflex. They prefer to express their laws in terms of certain properties common to all these relations, so that they encompass as wide a range of phenomena as possible. So, when Sherrington studied reflexes he made a study of many reflexes involving different eliciting stimuli and responses. From experiments of this sort, he formulated three laws summarizing the basic properties of the reflex. These laws are not stated in terms of any particular stimulus such as electric shock, or any particular response such as a given muscle movement. They are stated *generally* in terms of eliciting stimuli and responses. In so stating them, we obtain a pleasing generality, but at a sacrifice of particular details. For instance, the exact relation between stimulus intensity and response magnitude varies from reflex to reflex. Sometimes the relationship is very nearly directly proportional, so that over a wide range of stimulus intensities, doubling the stimulus intensity will double the response magnitude, and so on. In other reflexes, a tenfold increase in stimulus intensity may be required to produce a doubling of response magnitude. Our primary reflex laws are written in such a way that these differences are hidden.

Eliciting stimuli may always be specified on an intensity dimension. Thus, shock may be weak, moderate, or strong in intensity. Light stimuli that elicit pupillary responses may vary, from faint intensities that we can just see to intensities so high that the light is painful. As we have noted, energies below a certain level on the intensity dimension are insufficient to elicit any response. As the intensity is gradually raised, a region is found about which values of intensity *may or may not* elicit a movement. This region of indeterminacy, where the intensity may or may not be strong enough to elicit a response, is the threshold penumbra region. We may state this information more specifically:

1. There is a range of intensities below which no response will occur and above which a response will always occur. Within this range itself, responses will occur with some uncertainty. An arbitrary point within this uncertainty region (say, that intensity which elicits the response 50 per cent of the time) is called the threshold, and intensities above that point are called *eliciting stimuli.*

As the stimulus is raised further in intensity, the response now occurs each time, and appears graded in relation to the stimulus. Thus, strong stimuli rapidly elicit strong and long-lasting responses. Weak eliciting stimuli are followed more slowly by weak and shorter-lasting responses. Most of this information may be represented by two reflex laws:

2. As the eliciting stimulus intensity is increased, the magnitude of the elicited response also increases.
3. As the eliciting stimulus intensity is increased, the time (latency) between the onset of the eliciting stimulus and the onset of the response decreases.

These three "laws of the reflex" relate the stimulus intensity to 1. the probability that a response will occur, 2. the magnitude of the response, and 3. the latency of the response, respectively. A reflex may be said to be a correlation between stimulus and response that conforms to these laws. They can be taken as *defining properties* of the reflex. For this reason, we have described them as "primary" or "basic". Reflexes have other properties and one of these, habituation, has proved very important in the study of behavior.

9.3
Habituation

If a reflex is repeatedly elicited by an appropriate stimulus, the magnitude of the response declines and the response may cease to occur at all. This effect is called *habituation*: the response to the stimulus habituates. It can be thought of as analagous to the fatigue that occurs when a piece of behavior, such as touching one's toes, is repeated over and over again. An example of habituation in a very lowly organism, the protozoa *spirostomum ambiguum*, is shown in Figure 9.2. The stimulus was a 4 g weight dropped from a constant height onto the slide on which the protozoa was mounted. This was repeated ever 10 sec, and elicited a response of contraction. The result was that the probability of a contraction, initially high, declined fairly steadily to near zero.

Habituation is a pervasive phenomenon and has been demonstrated in many response systems in organisms throughout the animal kingdom. It is dependent on the rate of stimulus presentation and this is demonstrated for the pond snail *Limnaea stagnalis* in Figure 9.3. Like fatigued responses, habituated responses recover with the time since the eliciting stimulus was

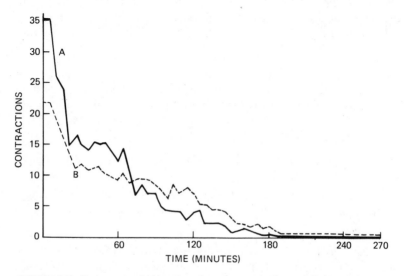

FIGURE 9.2. Group mean habituation data on contractions of *Spirostomum ambiguum*. Group (A) were stimulated irregularly, 6–12 times per min. Group (B) were stimulated regularly, 6 times per min (Wawrzyncyck, 1937).

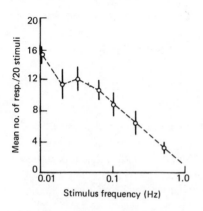

FIGURE 9.3.
The relationship between the frequency of stimulation and habituation for a group of 10 pond snails *Limnaea stagnalis* (Cook, 1971).

last applied. This is elegantly demonstrated in Figure 9.4. This shows the recovery of a neural response in the visual cortex of a rabbit between series of visual stimuli. Note that the longer the interval between habituation and renewed stimulation, the greater the next response. The stimulus in this case was a person walking across the visual field.

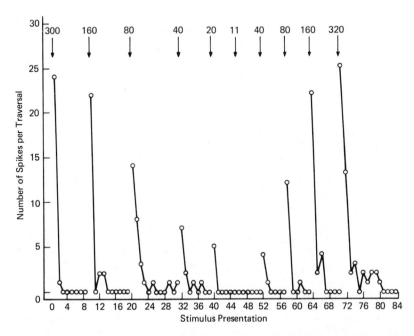

FIGURE 9.4. Response of rabbit visual neural unit to the experimenter walking back and forth across the animals visual field. The interval between traversals was 4 sec, except where the gaps in the graph occur. The interval then (in sec) is shown above the arrow at the top of the figure. Note that after stimulus presentation 45, an 11-sec interval occurred, and this was insufficient to evoke a response (Horn and Hill, 1966).

9.4
The Orienting Response

The *orienting response* (or orientation reaction) is a pattern of behavioral changes that is reflexly elicited by a *novel stimulus*. Pavlov called this the investigatory or "what-is-it?" reaction:

It is this reflex which brings about the immediate response in man and animals to the slightest changes in the world around them, so that they immediately orientate their appropriate receptor organ in accordance with the perceptible quality in the agent bringing about the change, making a full investigation of it. The biological significance of this reflex is obvious. If the animal were not provided with such a reflex its life would hang at any moment by a thread (Pavlov, 1927).

Lynn (1966) summarizes the components of the orienting response as follows:

1. Increase in sensitivity of sense organs.
2. Changes in the skeletal muscles to orient the sense organs towards the source of the stimulus.
3. Changes in general skeletal musculature.
4. Changes in the electrical activity of the brain, reflected in electro-encephalogram (EEG) changes.
5. Autonomic nervous system changes affecting the circulation of the blood, the electric resistance of the skin, respiration rate, and heart rate.

This complex pattern of reflex changes and its habituation has been extensively studied by Sokolov (1963) and other Russian investigators. In a typical experiment, a simple stimulus—for example a tone of specified physical properties is presented while one or a number of the components of the orienting response are monitored. In humans, the EEG and the electric resistance of the skin are often measured. The stimulus is presented repeatedly until the orienting response has habituated. If the procedure is then changed slightly, various effects can be observed. These (reviewed by Gray, 1975) include:

1. A small change in the physical properties of the stimulus reinstates the orienting response. If this new stimulus is repeated, habituation again takes place.
2. If a long time elapses without stimulus presentation, the response recovers from habituation.
3. Presentation of a second novel stimulus, just before the habituated stimulus, leads to a recurrence of orienting responses to the habituated stimulus.

These three phenomena all have clear parallels in classical conditioning, as we shall see in the next chapter. This points to the general importance of habituation as a behavioral process. Indeed, while Pavlov was correct to stress the adaptive significance of the orienting response, its habituation is equally important. It is the process of habituation that enables the organism to respond selectively to new or important stimulus. A nonhabituating, orienting response would be worse than useless, as the organism would be in a constant state of agitation resulting from the thousands of stimuli impinging upon it.

9.5
Some Examples of Reflexes

The observations that are summarized as the laws of the reflex are most easily made on muscles isolated surgically from influences other than those of the elicitor study. Although we study reflexes in surgically prepared muscles to obtain precision of control, reflexes are easily seen in qualitative form in the intact behavior of all animals, from man to the lowliest of species. Descartes' example of the withdrawal of a human limb from a flame is one such intact human reflex. Others are the elicitation of tears by onion juice, of sneezing by pepper in the nose, of jerking of the knee by a tap on the patellar tendon, of discharge of saliva by food placed in the mouth, of change in heart beat by a loud sound, and so on. All of these reflexes conform to our fundamental model, or *paradigm*, S→R, where some stimulus, S, elicits some response, R; and if the reflex could be properly isolated, a relation like that in Figure 9.1 would be obtained. Some examples of stimulus-response sequences are shown in Table 9.1. All of the correlations in Table 9.1 are reflexes. Some involve skeletal muscles (sneezes, knee jerks, shivering), some involve cardiac muscles (heart-rate changes), some involve glands (salivation, tears), and some involve smooth muscles (blanching of skin, pupillary changes). All have been called involuntary reflexes at one time or another. The term "involuntary" is a historical term, used to crudely express the automatic, elicited nature of certain behaviors. Since Sherrington's quantitative analysis of the reflex, the original conception of elicitation has been greatly refined. It seems judicious, therefore, to replace the older and vaguer term "involuntary" with the more exact "elicited," which encompasses all the reflex laws in its definition. This eventual replacement of a poorly specified term, which was often associated with a prescientific frame of reference, is a common and typical occurrence in

TABLE 9.1. Common reflex sequences.

Name of reflex	Elicitor stimulus	Leads to	Response
Tearing	Onion juice in the eye	→	Tearing of the eye
Sneeze	Feather in the nose	→	Sneeze
Patellar	Tap to knee	→	Knee jerk
Salivary	Food in mouth	→	Salivation
Startle	Loud sound	→	Heart rate speeds up, skeletal muscles contract, pupils dilate, etc.
Shiver	Cold	→	Shivering, blanching of skin
Pupillary	Light in eye	→	Pupil contraction

science. On the other hand, sometimes a scientific analysis will retain the old word, but rededicate it with a new and precise meaning. Science has retained the words "force" in physics, "element" in chemistry, and "motive" in psychology from the vernacular, but has greatly changed and expanded their meanings. But it is not always easy to slough off the connotations of prescientific concepts, and sometimes a new word aids the conceptual shift. The old word will then be left to die the slow death of disuse. Such is the fate of the word "involuntary" in psychology.

References for Chapter 9

Cook, A. Habituation of a freshwater snail (Limnaea stagnalis). *Animal Behaviour,* 1971, **19**, 463–474.

Gray, J. A. *Elements of a two-process theory of learning.* London: Academic Press, 1975.

Horn, G., and Hill, R. M. Responsiveness to sensory stimulation of units in the superior colliculus and subadjacent tectotegonental regions of the rabbit. *Experimental Neurology,* 1966, **44**, 199–223.

Lynn, R. *Attention, arousal and the orientation reaction.* Oxford: Pergamon, 1966.

Pavlov, I. P. *Conditioned reflexes.* London: Oxford University Press, 1927.

Sherrington, C. *The integrative action of the nervous system.* New Haven, Conn.: Yale University Press, 1906 (Second Edition, 1947).

Sokolov, Y. N. *Perception and the conditioned reflex.* Oxford: Pergamon Press, 1963.

Wawrzyncyck, S. Badania and parecia *Spirostomum ambiguum* major. *Acta Biologica Experimentalis* (Warsaw), 1937, **11**, 57–77.

CHAPTER 10

Classical Conditioning: The Pavlovian Tradition

Around 1903, Pavlov, the Russian physiologist, became interested in the phenomenon that he at first called "psychic secretions." Pavlov describes the point of departure of his investigations in the following quotation:

> If food or some rejectable substance finds its way into the mouth, a secretion of saliva is produced. The purpose of this secretion is in the case of food to alter it chemically, in the case of a rejectable substance to dilute and wash it out of the mouth. This is an example of a reflex due to the physical and chemical properties of a substance when it comes into contact with the mucous membrane of the mouth and tongue. But, in addition to this, a similar reflex secretion is evoked when these substances are placed at a distance from the dog and the receptor organs affected are only those of smell and sight. Even the vessel from which the food has been given is sufficient to

evoke an alimentary reflex complete in all its details; and, further, the secretion may be provoked even by the sight of the person who brought the vessel, or by the sound of his footsteps (Pavlov, 1927, p.13).

It was clear to Pavlov, from the beginning, that some kind of *association* between the salivary reflex and such arbitrary events as food containers and footsteps was responsible for the ability of the latter to evoke "psychic secretions." Pavlov's first major contribution to behavioral science was his description and elaboration of the necessary and sufficient conditions for this association. Through systematic study of the salivation of dogs, Pavlov discovered that if any arbitrary environmental change directly and reliably preceded the eliciting stimulus for salivation, that environmental change could itself come to produce salivation.

10.1
Conditioned Reflexes and the Nature of an Experiment

We will examine in detail an experiment by one of Pavlov's students (Anrep, 1920) as an example of the Pavlovian method and results which led to this important conclusion. Figure 10.1 depicts the experimental situation used by Pavlov and his colleagues at the Institute of Experimental Medicine in Petrograd (later, Leningrad). It is well described by Keller and Schoenfeld:

First, a normal dog is familiarized with the experimental situation until he shows no disturbance when placed in harness and left alone

FIGURE 10.1. Apparatus for classical conditioning of the salivary response in a dog (Pavlov, 1928).

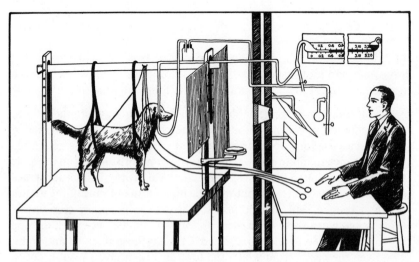

in a room especially designed to cut off unwanted outside stimuli. A small opening or fistula is made in the dog's cheek near the duct of one of the salivary glands. When the fistula is healed, a glass funnel is carefully cemented to the outside of the cheek so that it will draw off the saliva whenever the gland is activated. From the funnel, the saliva then flows into a glass container or falls, drop by drop, upon a lightly balanced recording platform. The magnitude of responses to various stimuli can be measured by the total volume or the number of drops secreted in a given unit of time. The experimenter, who sits in an adjoining room, can make his measurements, apply what stimuli he desires (including food), and observe the dog's behavior through a window (Keller and Schoenfeld, 1950, pp. 16–17)

The experimenter is thus in a position to measure the salivary reflex precisely. He or she is also able to carefully control the presentations of various stimulus events to the organism.

In an experiment by Anrep (1920), a tone was sounded in the animal's room for 5 sec. Then, 2 or 3 sec later, a bit of food was given to the dog. This *pairing* of tone with food was repeated after intervals ranging from 5 to 35 min. In order to observe the effect of the tone alone, the experimenter occasionally presented it for 30 sec, unpaired with food. Over the course of 16 days, 50 tone-food associations and 6 tone-alone tests were made. The principal data of Anrep's experiment were obtained during the 6 tone-alone tests. During these tests, he carefully measured both the total drops of saliva and the time between the onset of the 30-sec test tone and the first drop of saliva. Table 10.1 presents the data.

It is seen in Table 10.1 that, after 1 tone-food pairing, presentation of the tone alone produced no salivation at all. After 10 such pairings, however, 6 drops appeared in the tone-alone test, and the first of these 6 drops came 18 sec after the onset of the test tone. After 20 such pairings, 20 drops were produced, the first drop coming now at only 9 sec. From 30 pairings onward,

TABLE 10.1. Acquisition of a salivary response to a tone (Data from Anrep, 1920).

Number of previous tone-food pairings X	Drops of saliva Y	Time elapsing between onset of tone and ensuing salivation (seconds) Z
1	0	—
10	6	18
20	20	9
30	60	2
40	62	1
50	59	2

approximately 60 drops of saliva were obtained during each test, and they begàn to appear in the first second or two after the onset of the test tone. The results of the experiment are clearcut. Salivation occurs reliably to an arbitrarily selected tone after the tone is paired with food 30 times.

The process by which a tone comes to *acquire* the ability to produce a salivary response of its own, as pairings with food are increased, is called "conditioning". Pavlov saw the close resemblance between this new correlation of tone with salivation and ordinary reflex action, and was led, therefore, to call the new correlation a conditional reflex (usually translated as a "conditioned reflex"). Why he did so is apparent from these words:

> I have termed these new reflexes *conditioned reflexes* to distinguish them from the inborn or *unconditioned reflexes*. The term "conditioned" is becoming more and more generally employed, and I think its use is fully justified in that, compared with the inborn reflexes, these new reflexes actually do *depend on very many conditions* (ital. added) both in their formation and in the maintenance of their physiological activity. Of course, the terms "conditioned" and "unconditioned" could be replaced by others of arguably equal merit. Thus, for example, we might retain the term "inborn reflexes", and call the new type "acquired reflexes"; or call the former "species reflexes" since they are characteristic of the species, and the latter "individual reflexes" since they vary from animal to animal in a species, and even in the same animal at different times and under different conditions (Pavlov, 1927, p. 25).

The process which Pavlov investigated has come to be called *classical conditioning*, to distinguish it from operant conditioning. We will follow this convention here.

10.2
The Classical Conditioning Procedure

Pavlov and his associates did far more than simply establish the existence of classical conditioning. They experimented extensively with variations in the procedure, while usually sticking to the method of presenting visual or auditory stimuli followed by stimuli that would elicit salivation. They thus provided a highly interrelated body of results.

Figure 10.2 presents some varieties of the procedure that have been examined. In the Figure, CS stands for *conditioned stimulus* and US stands for *unconditioned stimulus*. This again follows conventional usage, where an unconditioned stimulus is one that elicits a response (an unconditioned response) prior to any conditioning, and a conditioned stimulus is the event which is arranged to precede the US. In Pavlov's experiments, CS's were typically, lights, tones, and buzzers, and US's were food or acid. Five variations of the procedure are shown in Figure 10.2.

The first case, simultaneous conditioning, is the "basic" version, in which the CS precedes the US by a very short period and may or may not overlap the US in time. Evidence that conditioning has occurred with this procedure is usually obtained by occasionally presenting the CS alone, to see whether a response is elicited. The second procedure was called "delay conditioning" by Pavlov, because of the interval that elapses between the onset of the CS and the onset of the US, but note that the CS is presented continuously in the interval. Like simultaneous conditioning, this procedure results in conditioning. The maximum delay interval possible is a function of many experimental parameters, such as the nature and intensity of the US, the response and species studied, and so forth. The fact that the third procedure, "trace conditioning," is effective was thought remarkable by Pavlov and other early workers because the CS is not present when the US occurs. Again, the interval that can elapse between CS and US is dependent on many parameters of the experiment.

The fourth procedure, illustrated in Figure 10.2, "backward conditioning," is rather curious. The US is presented *before* CS. Our intuition that this will not result in conditioning is supported by most of the experimental findings. As an example, Figure 10.3 illustrates results of Wolfle (1932) on the conditioning of finger retraction elicited by an electric shock. He varied the interval between CS and US, from + 3 sec to − 2 sec (when US preceeded CS by 2 sec), and found that significant results with this response system were

FIGURE 10.2.
Five possible procedures for classical conditioning. The "backward" procedure does not generally result in the acquisition of a response to the CS.

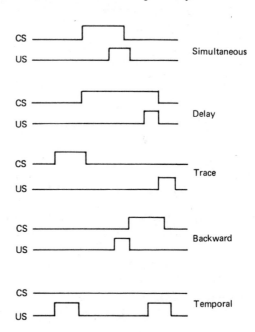

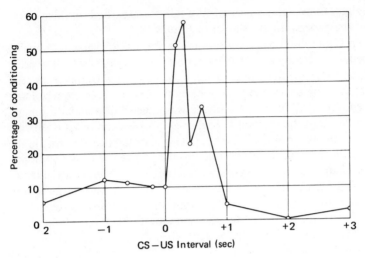

FIGURE 10.3. Relative conditionability of finger retraction as a function of CS–US interval (Wolfle, 1932).

only obtained with CS—US intervals of 0 to 1 sec. A clearer understanding of the backward conditioning procedure will follow from the theoretical considerations later in this chapter.

The final procedure in Figure 10.2 is "temporal conditioning." Hence, no CS is presented and the US is simply presented at regular time intervals. Interestingly, this still produces conditioning. In one experiment, Pavlov fed a dog regularly every 30 min. No stimulus change preceded feeding. When this feeding routine had been well established, food was withheld altogether and the effects measured. Under these conditions, salivation was observed to commence at approximately the end of the 30-min period, the time when food would ordinarily have come. Pavlov called this procedure "temporal conditioning" on the analogy that the time interval since the previous feeding comes to act in some way as a CS.

10.3
Phenomena of Classical Conditioning

The preceding section outlines varieties of the basic procedure and their effectiveness, but various other phenomena have been observed in that procedure, and in related ones, beyond the simple fact of acquisition of a response to the CS.

The simplest and most important one is *extinction*. In parallel with operant conditioning, classical extinction occurs if the CS—US pairing is broken. This is usually achieved by repeatedly presenting the CS without the

US. The result is a fairly steady diminution of the response to the CS. An example for the rabbit's eyelid is illustrated in Figure 10.4.

Various *inhibitory phenomena* were discovered in the experiments of Pavlov and his associates. This is interesting because, although Pavlov, being trained as a neurophysiologist, presumed that inhibitory (response-suppressing) processes as well as excitatory (response-eliciting) processes will occur in conditioning, it is not inevitable that inhibitory concepts will be needed to explain behavior. After all, a response either occurs or fails to occur; we need not infer from its absence that it is inhibited, it might simply be that the stimulus no longer elicits a response. This point will be made clearer by considering three phenomena demonstrated by Pavlov that show

FIGURE 10.4. Mean percentages of nictitating membrane responses (CR's) for groups of rabbits given paired (experimental) or unpaired (control) CS and US presentations. The course of extinction over 8 days is shown on the right (Gormezano, Schneiderman, Deaux and Fuentes, 1962).

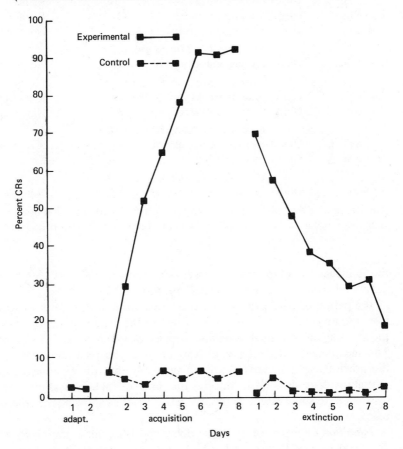

TABLE 10.2. Two experiments with dogs by Dr. Gubergritz (from Pavlov, 1927).

Time	Stimulus applied during 30 secs	Salivary secretion recorded by divisions of scale · (5 div. = 0.1 c.c.) during 30 secs	Remarks
	Experiment of 15th February, 1917.		
3.13 p.m.	Object rotating clockwise	27	Reinforced.
3.25 p.m.	Object rotating anti-clockwise	7	Not reinforced.
	Experiment of 16th February, 1917.		
1.4 p.m.	Object rotating clockwise	24	Reinforced.
1.14 p.m.	Object rotating clockwise	26	Reinforced.
1.25 p.m.	Object rotating clockwise	27	Reinforced.
1.34 p.m.	Object rotating anti-clockwise	10	Not reinforced.
	Experiment of 17th February, 1917.		
2.45 p.m.	Object rotating anti-clockwise	12	Not reinforced.
	Experiment of 18th February, 1917.		
2.48 p.m.	Object rotating clockwise	19	Reinforced.
3.33 p.m.	Object rotating anti-clockwise	34	Not reinforced.
	Experiment of 20th February, 1917.		
3.7 p.m.	Object rotating anti-clockwise	26	Not reinforced.
3.28 p.m.	Object rotating clockwise	26	Reinforced.
	Experiment of 21st February, 1917.		
3.0 p.m.	Object rotating anti-clockwise	12	Not reinforced.

The strength of the reflex which is undergoing differential inhibition now diminishes progressively with small fluctuations until it reaches a permanent zero.

the influence of inhibitory processes: spontaneous recovery, inhibition of delay and the development of differentiation.

If a period of time elapses after the extinction of a classically conditioned response and then the subject is returned to the experimental situation and the CS is again presented, a certain amount of *spontaneous recovery* occurs. This means that a higher level of responding is observed than at the end of the previous session. Pavlov argued plausibly that this demonstrates that inhibition had developed during the first extinction session and had dissipated, to some extent, before the next test, thus allowing the response to recover.

Inhibition of delay occurs in the delay-and trace-conditioning paradigms described earlier. Pavlov and subsequent investigators showed that, after

TABLE 10.2. Continued.

Time	Stimulus applied during 30 secs	Amount of saliva recorded by divisions of scale (5 div. = 0.1 c.c.) during 30 secs	Remarks
Experiment of 12th October, 1917.			
12.28 p.m.	Tone	30	Reinforced.
1.0 p.m.	Tone	35	Reinforced.
1.10 p.m.	Semitone	9	Not reinforced.
Experiment of 13th October, 1917.			
12.54 p.m.	Tone	36	Reinforced.
1.5 p.m.	Tone	36	Reinforced.
1.12 p.m.	Semitone	32	Not reinforced.
2.1 p.m.	Semitone	16	Not reinforced.
2.18 p.m.	Tone	29	Reinforced.

The reflex to the semitone continues to fluctuate. gradually diminishing in strength until at the thirteenth repetition it has fallen to zero.

prolonged experience of these procedures, conditioned responding occurs only just before US onset. Is the lack of responding during the CS (or early in the CS) a result of inhibition? The procedure of presenting a novel stimulus between the CS and US, or early in a long CS, provides an answering to this question. It turns out that a novel stimulus presented in this way elicits much more responding than if it is presented alone. Pavlov called this phenomenon *disinhibition*, presuming that it is the result of a reduction in inhibition.

The whole area of *environmental control* (discussed in Part Four) was opened up by Pavlov's studies of *differentiation*. Differentiation was achieved by pairing one stimulus with food (this is termed the CS+) and, once the CS+ has begun to reliably elicit conditioned salivation, introducing another stimulus (CS−), which is not followed by food. CS− is presented randomly, alternating with the CS+. The results of two experiments are reported in Table 10.2. In the first, CS+ is a rotating disk and CS− is the same object, rotating in the other direction. In the second, the two stimuli are a tone and its semitone. In both experiments, before the start of this phase, CS+ had been established as an elicitor of salivation. When CS− is introduced, salivation to it is, at first, slight. With continued presentations of both CS+, followed by food, and of CS−, not followed by food, salivation to CS−

increases until it approaches that to CS+. Following this rise, there is a decline in salivation to CS— until it reaches zero. The ability of CS+ to elicit salivation continues undiminished, and a discrimination is established between the two stimuli. According to Pavlov, the process of differentiation involves inhibition because of the phasic nature of its development. The similarity of CS+ and CS— induces a response to CS—, but subsequently, the fact that the US does not follow the CS— results in inhibition of responding developing to that stimulus.

A full review of the phenomena of classical conditioning would be beyond the scope of this book, but those described here well illustrate the advantages of the "Pavlovian method" of detailed study of one set of experimental conditions. The salivation of dogs to various visual and auditory stimuli has provided us with a great many general principles. In particular, it has established the reality of inhibitory processes in conditioning.

10.4
Contiguity or Contingency?

Pavlov asserted that the essential element of the classical conditioning procedure was the pairing of CS and US. Simple though the pairing operation seems, it actually confounds two distinct features—*temporal contiguity* and *contingency*. The CS is contiguous with the US if the US occurs *immediately* after the CS, and the US is contingent upon the CS if the occurrence of the CS *predicts* the occurrence of the US. This distinction is illustrated in Figure 10.5. Panel (*a*) shows the conventional pairing procedure involving both contiguity and contingency, Panel (*b*) shows a procedure that

FIGURE 10.5. Variations in contiguity and contingency of CS and US.

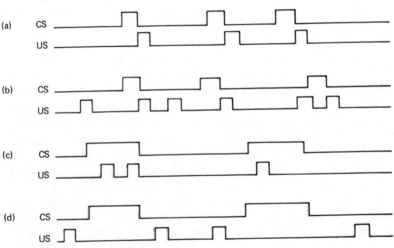

gives contiguity while minimizing contingency, Panel (c) gives contingency with minimal contiguity, and Panel (d) shows a procedure in which US *never* follows CS, thus giving no contiguity and a *negative* contingency. It is a negative contingency because the CS now predicts when the US will *not* occur.

We can make predictions about the outcomes of the various procedures in Figure 10.5. If contiguity is all-important, then (a) and (b) should produce conditioning, the effect of (c) will be weak, and (d) will have no effect. If contingency is the crucial factor, then (a) and (c) will produce conditioning, while (b) is ineffective and (d) might produce an inhibitory CS. The data show that contingency is more important: procedure (c) is effective, while (b) often is not. For example, Rescorla (1968) manipulated the probability of a shock US occurring in each 2 min, both within the CS and in the intertrial interval, the interval between CS's. He found that conditioning only occurred when the probability of the US occurring was greater during the CS than in its absence. Also, the greater the difference in probability, the greater the conditioned response. These results are shown in Figure 10.6.

Rescorla's results underline the role of contingency, but contiguity cannot be totally ignored because the overall temporal parameters are important. Lengthening CS and intertrial interval durations can drastically reduce the amount of conditioning.

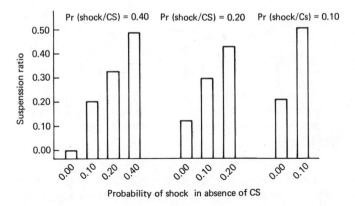

FIGURE 10.6. Effect of probability of US during CS (Pr[Shock/CS]) and in the absence of CS on a conditioned response (suppression ratio). The probability of shock is calculated for 2-min periods. A suppression ratio of 0.5 indicates no conditioning (Rescorla, 1968).

10.5

The Classical Conditioning Paradigm

The matters considered in the preceding section complicate attempts to provide an exact definition of the procedure for classical conditioning. We will fall back on stating *sufficient* (rather than *necessary*) conditions.

The procedure and result can then be formally stated as follows. If a CS and US are repeatedly paired, the CS will gradually come to elicit a response that it did not elicit prior to conditioning. Conventionally, a "neutral" CS is selected—that is, one that does not elicit any large responses prior to conditioning—along with a US that elicits a strong and measurable response. While it is necessary that the US elicits a measurable response, it is not necessary to have a "weaker" CS. Long (1941) used a 1/7-sec tone as CS, followed by a brief flash of light as the US. Both stimuli initially elicited eyelid blinks in the human subjects used, but after pairing, the tone CS elicited two successive blinks when presented. An example of this remarkable, experimental *tour de force* is shown in Figure 10.7.

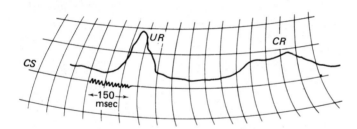

FIGURE 10.7. Eyelid responses when a 150 msec tone is presented alone after 30 tone-light pairings. Note that the tone elicits both a conditioned response (CR) and an unconditioned response (UR) (Long, 1941).

Note that we have not specified the nature of the conditioned response. It turns out that it is not possible, from a knowledge of the CS and US, to exactly specify the form of the conditioned response. A later section of this chapter outlines the sorts of generalizations about the conditioned response that can be made.

10.6

Higher-Order Conditioning

In his early writings, Watson, following Pavlov, suggested that *all* human behavior that is not innate might be acquired through classical conditioning. Apart from the problem raised earlier—that all behavior does not conform to the reflex model—this view also entails that *higher-order* classical conditioning takes place. By this, it is meant that a stimulus (call it CS_1) established as a CS in one situation can subsequently act as a US to establish a response to a second stimulus (call it CS_2). The procedure is illustrated in Figure 10.8.

Figure 10.8 shows second-order conditioning. Third-order conditioning would then be obtained by pairing CS_2 with a new stimulus, CS_3, and so on. If Watson or Pavlov's view was correct, such procedures would have to be effective in conditioning responses to CS_2, CS_3 and so on, because many stimuli that influence behavior are not directly paired with US's.

Does higher-order conditioning "work"? Early results were discouraging and led, in part, to the decline in Watson's influence and the increase in interest in Skinner's operant-conditioning methods. Keller and Schoenfeld (1950) commented that, "the influence of higher order conditioning could hardly be expected to play much of a part in the everyday behavior of organisms" (p. 32). However, recent work by Rescorla and associates has largely "rehabilitated" second-order conditioning at least. They have shown (see, for example, Rescorla, 1973) that a strong conditioned response to CS_2 can be established, and that this response is to some extent independent of the conditioned response to CS_1. These and other results establish that higher-order conditioning can be most effective, and that its possible use as a tool for behavioral analysis should not be neglected.

FIGURE 10.8. Possible sequence of conditions for second-order, classical conditioning experiment. Condition 1 is first-order conditioning. Condition 2 tests the effectiveness of CS_1. Condition 3 is second-order conditioning. Condition 4 tests the effectiveness of CS_2. In Conditions 2 and 4 occasional nontest trials are included to prevent extinction of conditioned responses.

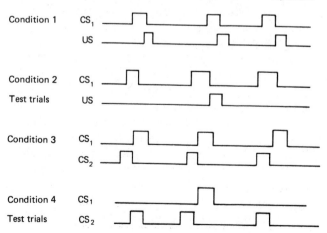

10.7

The Nature of the Conditioned Response

So far, we have studiously avoided discussing the form that a conditioned response takes. Unlike operant conditioning, where the experimenter sets up a contingency between a particular class of responses and a reinforcer, the response to be conditioned is not specified by the experimenter in classical-conditioning situations. Of course, the experimenter usually knows enough about the likely outcome of a particular procedure to successfully record the conditioned response, but he or she has no guarantee of its form.

This lack of predictability was neither discovered nor predicted by Pavlov. He observed that in his experiments, the conditioned response was apparently the same as the unconditioned response elicited by the US, and he formulated a *stimulus substitution theory.* On this account, the mechanism of classical conditioning is very simple: as a result of CS-US pairings, a "new reflex" is established. In the experimental situation, there was previously one reflex, for example:

$$S_{dry\ food} \rightarrow R_{salivation}$$

but because the dry food US has been paired with a bell CS, a new reflex relationship has been established:

$$S_{bell} \rightarrow R_{salivation}$$

Stimulus substitution theory states that *the CS comes to elicit the same response as the US.* If this were true, there would be no indeterminancy about the conditioned response, it would be wholly determined by the US. Unfortunately, this theory has not stood the tests of time and experiment.

An experiment by Notterman, Schoenfeld, and Bersh (1952), employing human subjects, is illustrative. In their study, the CS was an audible tone and the US was a mild electric shock delivered to the subject's left hand. These investigators measured the heart-rate response with a variation of the machine known as an electrocardiograph, familiar in many physicians' offices. Instead of constraining their subjects in the Pavlovian fashion, they sat them in an ordinary chair, instructing them to remain as quiet as possible for about 90 min. During this time, the experimenters recorded the heart rate of their subjects during presentation of tones and shocks. Notterman, Schoenfeld, and Bersh found clear-cut evidence for a conditioned heart-rate response after 11 pairings of shock and tone. However, whereas the unconditioned response to shock was a heart-rate acceleration, the conditioned response involved a deceleration. Although later work (Zeaman and Smith, 1965) indicates that differences between heart-rate conditioned and unconditioned responses are closely related to corresponding respiration differences, the disparity remains.

Extreme examples, such as this one, have led us to take a new look at classical conditioning. In nearly all cases of supposed stimulus substitution, marked differences between the two responses exist. In many cases, they were hidden by the crude measures taken when investigators were only interested in conditioning as a substitution phenomenon.

The brief history of stimulus substitution is an interesting example of the continual ferment of science. A concept may hold sway for a few years or decades because it seems to provide intellectual comfort and promise ordering of nature. But unless it lives up to its promises, it will eventually give way to the weight of experimental evidence. During its heyday, however, such a concept may direct research in ways which effectively blind scientists to the weaknesses of the concept. It is almost as though, to give the concept a "chance," we ignore for a time certain discrepancies, certain fuzzinesses in its definition. This temporary permissiveness at the early stage of exploration is justified over the long run, because many of our well-established concepts went through just such an initiation and emerged stronger and clearer for it. The reflex itself is a good example of this, and so many concepts of physical science that have survived the test of time.

We are left with out original question: what determines the conditioned response? There is no simple answer: Gray (1975) argues that a "modified stimulus-substitution rule," that all responses conditioned to the CS are components of the response to the US, accounts for most of the data. However, other effects often modify an observed classically-conditioned response. These include: (1) the generalized effects of arousing or aversive stimuli, and (2) the modification of the response by reinforcement contingencies. To take up the later point, the fact that an experiment involves classical conditioning does not preclude operant-reinforcement effects. For example, if a dog salivates to a tone that precedes the delivery of dry food, this may improve the taste and reinforce the salivation, making salivation more probable on subsequent tone presentations.

10.8

What Is "Learned"?

The demise of stimulus-substitution theory throws in doubt Pavlov's contention that conditioned reflexes are established in classical conditioning. Apart from the fact that the CS reliably elicits a response, does this relationship have any of the other properties of a reflex? There is very little experimental evidence we can bring to bear on the matter, but what little we have, indicates that it is not, in fact, a true reflex.

In the first place, increases in the intensity of the CS do not result in increases in the response magnitude, or in decreases in its latency. Rather, the maximum magnitude and minimum latency of the conditioned response are obtained *at the precise value of the CS used in conditioning* (Mostofsky, 1965). Values, more or less intense, result in weaker responses. On the other hand, recall from Chapter 9 that the laws of reflex magnitude and latency specify a simple proportionality between stimulus intensity and response strength.

Second, the latency of the response acquired to the CS is generally longer than the latency of reflexive responses associated with that same CS. This may be demonstrated by pairing a light (CS) with an air puff to the eyelid (US). Originally, both CS and US elicit eye blinks. As a result of pairing, the CS comes to evoke two distinct eye blinks. Using this procedure with human subjects, Grant and Norris (1947) identified several modal latency regions, as the histogram of Figure 10.9 shows. The investigators called the region between 50 and 110 milliseconds (msec) the "true reflex" range, while the region between 250 and 450 msec represents the conditioned response range.

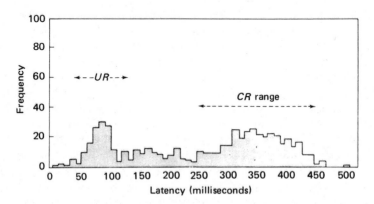

FIGURE 10.9. Latency distribution of all eyelid responses elicited by a strong light during the course of a conditioning experiment with human subjects (Grant and Norris, 1947).

Although there are clear parallels, spontaneous recovery and disinhibition occur both in conditioned responses and reflexes, as we saw in Chapter 9; it is safe to conclude that the relationship between the CS and conditioned response is not exactly the same as between the stimulus and response in a reflex. It remains an open question as to whether a connection is established between the CS and conditioned response, or whether it is one between the CS and US that results in the organism responding to the CS as if it were the US.

10.9

The Pavlovian Tradition

The research carried out by Pavlov and his associates over many years and reported in his book, "Conditioned Reflexes" (1927), produced a mass of interrelated facts about classical conditioning. Variables investigated included the duration, frequency, and sense modality of the CS, the nature of the US, extinction, differention, and methods of producing inhibition. Most importantly, they were all variables that could be studied within the standard Pavlovian experimental set-up described at the beginning of this chapter. American investigators adopted Pavlov's methods, either directly to study salivation in dogs, or in a modified fashion, to study eyelid conditioning or heart-rate conditioning in human subjects. In the latter case, the subjects were effectively restrained and the same variables were studied that Pavlov had examined with dogs. The effect was that a "Pavlovian tradition" was inherited: not only did later experimenters benefit from Pavlov's many methodological innovations and his meticulous attention to detail, but they also adopted his assumptions about the appropriate variables to study. Interestingly, Western workers did not take much interest in Pavlov's physiological speculations, although their Russian counterparts still reiterate them.

The result of the "Pavlovian tradition" was that research in classical conditioning, between 1930 and 1960, remained rigidly within the aforementioned confines. It was impeccably scientific, but became rather arid. This situation has changed dramatically in the last ten years, with developments in two directions: the use of unrestrained subjects that can move either towards or away from the CS, and the examination of the effects of US's that are purely internal, such as the illness following poisoning. These interesting developments are discussed in the next two chapters. Let us give Pavlov the last word on his contribution, with this summary of his research strategy:

> A scientific investigation of biological phenomena can be conducted along several different lines each of which would treat the problem from a different point of view. For instance, one may have in view the purely physico-chemical aspect, analyzing the elements of life by the methods of physics and chemistry. Again, keeping in view the fact of evolution of living matter one can try to elucidate the functions of complex biological structures by studying the functions of individual cells and of elementary organisms. Finally, one can make an attempt to elucidate the activities of complex structures in their fullest range directly, seeking for rigid laws governing this activity, or, in other words, trying to define all those conditions which determine the form this activity takes at every instant and in all its variations. The line of inquiry which has been adopted in the present investigation obviously belongs to the third point of view (1927, p. 377).

10.10
Classical Conditioning and Operant Conditioning

It is partly historical accident that the term "conditioning" is used for both the classical and operant procedures. It was not immediately realized that there were important differences between them, and "conditioning" was used as an all-embracing term. However, we have gone to the opposite extreme, and assumed that the procedures and associated processes are distinct, without producing any evidence to support this. We must now look at the similarities and differences.

In general terms, the modifications of behavior seen in both paradigms *are conditional upon* some prior past history. In one case, the history is a pairing of CS with US; in the other, it is the repeated following of a response by a reinforcing stimulus. It is this similarity that justifies both procedures being called conditioning. However, there are some much more specific similarities and these, along with some differences, are summarized in Table 10.3. The similarities have led to suggestions that both procedures reflect the operation of one conditioning or learning process, and that the observed differences are only due to procedural differences. For example, perhaps the dog salivates during the CS in a classical-conditioning experiment because this improves the taste of the food which follows the US, and the food thus acts as a reinforcing stimulus in an operant-conditioning paradigm. This issue can only be resolved by devising experiments in which different behavioral outcomes are predicted by the operant-conditioning analysis and the classical-conditioning analysis. Two of these are described herewith:

1. Omission Training. Sheffield (1965) classically conditioned dogs to salivate to an auditory CS and then, to show that salivation was not occurring simply because it was a reinforced operant, he introduced a new contingency. The food US was now only delivered after the US if there was no salivation on that trial. This is called *omission training* because the reinforcement contingency is that food will only be delivered if the response (salivation in this case) is omitted. Sheffield found that dogs continued to salivate on many trials, despite the loss of food deliveries that ensued. Salivation in this phase of the experiment cannot be the result of operant reinforcement, it must be a "genuine" classically-conditioned response, resulting from the CS-US relationship.

2. Having established the independence of classical conditioning, it might be argued that all operant conditioning is a disguised form of classical conditioning, in which stimuli associated with making the operant response (for example, proprioceptive feedback from the movements involved in lever pressing) become CS's paired with the US (the reinforcing stimulus) that follows them. One of the key features of classical conditioning enables us to test this idea. We saw earlier that, while the classically-conditioned response is not always the same as the

TABLE 10.3. Similarities and Differences in Classical and Operant Conditioning.

	This is true of:	
	operant conditioning	classical conditioning
Response strength increases in early part of training.	Yes	Yes
Conditioned responses can be brought under stimulus control.	Yes	Yes
If the reinforcer (US) occurs at regular intervals, behavior shows temporal patterning.	Yes	Yes
Stimuli associated with absence of reinforcer (US) inhibit responding.	Yes	Yes
Breaking the contingency results in extinction of the response.	Yes	Yes
Breaking the contingency produces a short-term increase in responding.	Yes	No
Intermittent reinforcement (US presentation) results in greater resistance to extinction.	Yes	No
A lapse of time following extinction results in some spontaneous recovery of responding.	Yes	Yes
Complex skeletal behavior is readily conditioned.	Yes	No
Autonomic response changes are readily conditioned.	No	Yes
The conditioned response is usually a component of behavior elicited by the reinforcer (US).	No	Yes
The experimenter specifies the nature of the conditioned response.	Yes	No

unconditioned response, the form of the classically-conditioned response is still determined by the US. If an electric shock to the fingers (US) of a human subject is preceded by a CS, a conditioned response of vasoconstriction (restriction of blood supply) develops. If attempts at operant conditioning were really forms of classical conditioning, we would expect the "operant" responses conditioned with a particular reinforcing stimulus to be identified with those responses that can be classically conditioned, using that stimulus as US. In this example, we would expect that vasoconstriction could be reinforced by avoidance of electric shock (for a discussion of this type of operant conditioning, see Chapter 16), but vasodilation could not be reinforced in this way. However, Lisina (1958) found that vasodilation in the finger could be reinforced by shock dilation.

The independent status of both classical conditioning and operant conditioning is, therefore, established, but this does not mean that only one will operate in a particular situation. Even very simple situations are likely to provide simultaneously, a contingency between a response and reinforcer, and a contingency between a CS and US (which may be identical with the reinforcer).

References for Chapter 10

Anrep, G. V. Pitch discrimination in the dog. *Journal of Physiology*, 1920, **53**, 367–385.

Gormezano, I., Schneiderman, N., Deaux, E. B., and Fuentes, I. Nictitating membrane: Classical conditioning and extinction in the albino rabbit. *Science*, 1962, **138**, 33–34.

Grant, D. A., and Norris, E. B. Eyelid conditioning as influenced by the presence of sensitized Beta-responses. *Journal of Experimental Psychology*, 1947, **37**, 423–433.

Gray, J. A. *Elements of a two-process theory of learning.* London: Academic Press, 1975.

Keller, F. S., and Schoenfeld, W. N. *Principles of psychology.* New York: Appleton-Century-Crofts, 1950.

Lisina, M. I. The role of orientation in converting involuntary to voluntary responses. In L. G. Voronin *et al.* (Eds.) *The orienting reflex and exploratory behavior.* Moscow, 1958.

Long, Lillian D. An investigation of the original response to the conditioned stimulus. *Archives of Psychology.* (New York) 1941, No. 259.

Mostofsky, D. (Ed.) *Stimulus generalization.* Stanford: Stanford University Press, 1965.

Notterman, J., Schoenfeld, W. N., and Bersh, P. J. Conditioned heart rate response in human beings during experimental anxiety. *Journal of Comparative and Physiological Psychology*, 1952, **45**, 1–8.

Pavlov, I. P. *Conditioned reflexes.* London: Oxford University Press, 1927.

Pavlov, I. P. *Lectures on conditioned reflexes.* New York: International Publishers, 1928.

Rescorla, R. A. Probability of shock in the presence and absence of CS in fear conditioning. *Journal of Comparative and Physiological Psychology*, 1968, **66**, 1–5.

Rescorla, R. A. Second-order conditioning: Implications for theories of learning. In F. J. McGuigan and D. B. Lumsden (Eds.) *Contemporary approaches to conditioning and learning.* Washington, D.C.: Winston, 1973.

Sheffield, F. D. Relation between classical conditioning and instrumental learning. In W. F. Prokasy (Ed.) *Classical conditioning.* New York: Appleton-Century-Crofts, 1965.

Wolfle, H. M. Conditioning as a function of the interval between the conditioned and the original stimulus. *Journal of General Psychology*, 1932, **7**, 80–103.

Zeaman, D., and Smith, R. W. Review of some recent findings in human cardiac conditioning. In W. F. Prokasy (Ed.), *Classical conditioning.* New York: Appleton-Century-Crofts, 1965.

CHAPTER 11

Interoceptive Conditioning

A survey of the history of psychology shows that the innovator of a research area has not only given the subject new techniques and new interests, but has often also determined the directions that research in that area should take. Perhaps this is inevitable; after all, a new research area is developed because the investigator is interested in approaching the subject in a particular way and it is, thus, not surprising that subsequent workers in the same area direct their attention to the same goals. Nowhere is this process more obvious than in classical conditioning. It is not a great exaggeration to say that post Pavlovian investigators used Pavlov's surgical preparations, recording apparatus, subjects, and procedures to study the effects of the same stimuli on the same response systems. More accurately, we can say that where they deviated from Pavlov's procedures, the changes were small and they continued to study the questions defined by Pavlov's results.

As an introduction to a research area in which the unwritten Pavlovian "code of conduct" is breached, consider the following situation. A farmer is suffering damage from rats in his grain store. He purchases some commercial rat poison from the store and leaves it in the area the rats frequent. He knows they will eat it because it is flavored to taste attractive to rats. By daily checks, he discovers that a number of rats quickly succumb to the poison. However, the effectiveness of the poison rapidly diminishes and the bait is no longer eaten: the local rats have become "bait-shy". The farmer returns to the store and purchases a different rat poison with a different flavor. Once again, the rats take the bait and a number are killed.

The question is, why do the rats stop eating the poisoned bait? The answer comes from a consideration of what happens when it is first put down. The manufacturers have produced a taste which is very attractive to rats and overcomes their innate rejection of new foods. Thus, let us assume, all the rats eat some bait. Those that eat a large amount become sick and die. Those that eat a little *become sick but do not die*. It is those individuals that survive and become bait-shy.

Consider a different example. You eat out at an Italian restaurant and this is a novel experience for you. You eat lasagna and enjoy it; however, later that night, you are extremely ill. You discover subsequently that the taste, the smell, and even the thought of pasta dishes makes you feel sick. Most people have had at least one experience of this type (not necessarily with Italian food!). Both the rat poison and the lasagna examples involve a *conditioned taste aversion*, established, we will argue, through classical conditioning. In each case, *a novel taste* has been followed by *sickness* and this has resulted in the subject rejecting that taste on subsequent test.

It might be objected that, in the human case, no conditioning mechanism need be postulated, as the subject's knowledge that the food upset him or her is sufficient to produce an aversion. The reliability of this type of explanation is questioned by cases such as this:

> Sauce Béarnaise is an egg-thickened, tarragon flavored concoction, and it used to be my favorite sauce. It now tastes awful to me. This happened several years ago, when I felt the effects of the stomach flu about six hours after eating filet mignon with sauce Béarnaise. I became violently ill and spent most of the night vomiting. The next time I had sauce Béarnaise, I couldn't bear the taste of it. At the time, I had no ready way to account for the change, although it seemed to fit a classical conditioning paradigm: CS (sauce) paired with US (illness) and unconditioned response (vomiting) yields conditioned response (nauseating taste). *But if this was classical conditioning it violated at least two Pavlovian laws:* The delay between tasting the sauce and vomiting was about 6 hours, and classical conditioning isn't supposed to bridge time gaps like that. In addition, neither the filet mignon, nor the white plates off which I ate the sauce, nor *Tristan und Isolde*, the opera that I listened to in the interpolated time, nor my

wife, Kerry, became aversive. Only the sauce Béarnaise did. Moreover, unlike much of classical conditioning, it could not be seen as a "cognitive" phenomenon, involving expectations. For I soon found out that the sauce had not caused the vomiting and that a stomach flu had: Steve Maier and I had been working together at the lab for the previous week, and 3 days after the sauce Béarnaise I picked up the phone to ask him what had happened in the interim. A groan answered: "How should I know, I've been sick with the stomach flu for 3 days and was about to call you and ask". This information, combined with the fact that Kerry (who also ate the sauce Béarnaise) did not get sick, convinced me that it was not the sauce but the flu that was the culprit. Yet in spite of this knowledge, I could not later inhibit my aversion (Seligman, 1972, p. 8).

If we accept the premise that taste aversion is a conditioning phenomenon, and conceptualize it as $CS_{taste} \rightarrow US_{sickness}$, resulting in a conditioned aversion to food with that taste, then, as Seligman suggests, traditional accounts of classical conditioning are in difficulty. The problems arising are:

1. there has only been one CS-US trial, but normally many are required.
2. more importantly, the CS and US are not *paired* in the usual sense. As Seligman says, why is he averse to sauce Béarnaise, when a long interval elapsed between it and sickness, and many other events occurred closer in time to the sickness?

In order to deal with these problems, we need some nonanecdotal information about taste aversion.

11.1

The Bright, Noisy Water Experiment

In a series of studies, begun to determine the effects of X-irradiation (which causes sickness), Garcia and his colleagues made some very important discoveries about taste aversion. Following a number of studies in which the acquisition of taste aversion was demonstrated, despite long delays between ingestion and sickness, Garcia and Koelling (1966) carried out a study designed to contrast the associability of tastes with sickness and pain with the associability of *exteroceptive stimuli* with sickness and pain. Exteroceptive stimuli, such as lights and noises, are the traditional tools of the classical-conditioning laboratory, and it seemed from the taste aversion experiments, that tastes functioned quite differently.

Garcia and Koelling monitored rats drinking tap water from a tube. For some rats, the water was flavored with saccharin, while for the others, each lick at the tube produced a flash of light and a noise as well as water ("bright, noisy water"). After initial training, half of each group was given electric shock immediately after drinking, while the other half was given X-irradiation, resulting in later sickness. The design of the experiment and the predicted results are shown in Table 11.1 The predictions are based on the view that there is an *exteroceptive conditioning system*, which has been extensively studied in the laboratory and involves events external to the organism (lights, sounds, shocks, food presentations and so on), and an *interoceptive conditioning system* which involves internal events. It is maintained that the "laws of classical conditioning" have only been established for the exteroceptive system, and they may be different for the interoceptive system. Furthermore, organisms are *contraprepared* (see Section 1.8 and 7.1) for "cross-system" conditioning.

TABLE 11.1. Design of the Bright, Noisy Water Experiment
(Garcia and Koelling,1966).

Type of CS	US	Expected result
Flavor	Illness	Aversion
Exteroceptive cues	Illness	No aversion
Flavor	Shock	No aversion
Exteroceptive cues	Shock	Aversion

The results are shown in Figure 11.1. The predictions were fully confirmed, the CS only being associated with the relevant US in each case. This establishes that not all CS's and US's are equally associable, and lends support to the exteroceptive/interoceptive distinction. If there is a distinct interoceptive system with different properties, then we may be able to escape the apparent embarrassment of a classical-conditioning effect that occurs in one trial, with CS and US hours apart.

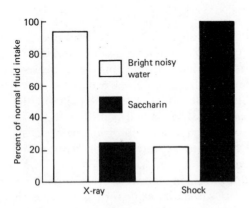

FIGURE 11.1.
Results of the bright, noisy water experiment. Aversion is measured by the reduction in intake below 100 per cent (Garcia and Koelling, 1966).

11.2

The Parameters of Interoceptive Conditioning

Many of the early studies of taste aversion examined the CS-US interval because it was so different from that in other conditioning situations. After all, it was believed for many years that a CS-US interval response-reinforcer interval could not be more than a few seconds, if conditioning is to take place. Smith and Roll (1967) carried out a typical taste-aversion experiment, demonstrating a different relationship. Groups of rats were given saccharin to drink and then X-irradiated, 0, 0.5, 1, 2, 3, 6, 12 or 24 hours later. Twenty-four hours after irradiation, a two-day preference test was carried. Figure 11.2 shows the results. A maximum aversion was obtained for all intervals up to six hours. Only then, does the degree of aversion decline.

Given the reliable aversion obtained with delays of several hours, how does it happen? Someone wishing to explain the phenomenon in traditional classical-conditioning terms might suggest that, at the time of sickness, *a trace* of the taste remains which acts as a CS directly paired with the US. This is implausible, because the length of time involved is sufficient for the substance ingested to be fully digested. Furthermore, Nachman (1968) found that rats, allowed to drink warm tap water and then injected with lithium chloride (which causes sickness), developed an aversion to warm water, while Garcia, Green, and McGowan (1969) obtained an aversion when the rat consumed a meal in the one-hour interval between the taste and X-irradiation. These and other studies have firmly established that taste aversion develops, even when no trace of the taste is present during sickness.

The Garcia *et al.* result is a pointer to a remarkable feature of the mechanism—even when other food was consumed, poisoning was associated with the *novel* taste. Revusky and Garcia (1970) propose that this is a key feature of the mechanism:

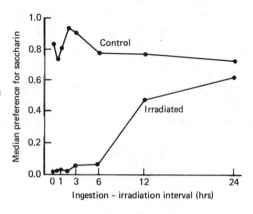

FIGURE 11.2.

Preference for saccharin solution relative to unflavored water during a two-day test for groups of irradiated and control rats. The independent variable is the time between ingestion of saccharin (CS) and X-irradiation (US), or sham-irradiation for the controls. Note that the controls have a very large preference for saccharin, measured as saccharin intake divided by total fluid intake (Smith and Roll, 1967).

It has been shown that only relevant stimuli are easily associated with toxicosis. Therefore, events such as exteroceptive stimuli and motor responses intervening between ingestion and toxicosis do not usually interfere with an association between the flavor of the ingested substance and toxicosis. But stimulus relevance cannot account for the occurrence of a learned aversion to a flavor when relevant stimuli intervene. For example, many of the aversions to saccharin in which rats were deprived of water but dry chow was continually available. The rats almost certainly ate during the delay because the saccharin solution was substituted for their daily water ration, and rats under a thirst deprivation schedule eat shortly after drinking their daily water ration. If so, why did not an association of the toxicosis with the flavor of the chow prevent the association with saccharin solution consumed prior to the chow? Furthermore, other relevant stimuli, such as smells and internal stimulus changes, are bound to occur during a long delay. More generally, one might expect the omnivorous feeding behavior of rats to interfere with their avoidance of slow-acting poisons. Since rats are likely to consume a number of substances prior to toxicosis, how can they detect which of the substances actually produced the toxicosis? Avoidance of all of these substances would hardly be an ideal solution because the rats would starve to death.

The logical solution is for the rat not to associate familiar, relevant stimuli with a novel toxicosis, if novel, relevant stimuli also occur; for if the familiar substances were poisonous, the rat would probably be dead already. (Revusky and Garcia, 1970, p. 32).

Experiments have indeed shown that aversions to novel tastes are more readily acquired than aversions to familiar tastes.

To summarize:

1. Only relevant stimuli (for example, tastes) are associated with interoceptive unconditioned stimuli.
2. Aversions develop more easily to novel or unfamiliar tastes.
3. Aversions develop even when an interval of several hours elapses between taste and illness.

Revusky and Garcia point out that while the exteroceptive world is a frantic hurly-burly of stimuli, things happen fairly slowly in the interoceptive system. Thus, if we abandon our belief that events must be contiguous in time to be associated, it is quite easy to accept that an illness can result in an aversion to a taste to the degree that it is novel and recent. Where "recent" refers to the number of tastes or other interoceptive events intervening, six hours can still be recent.

11.3

The Other Side of the Coin: Specific Hungers

So far, we have discussed only *aversions*. Can the interoceptive-conditioning mechanism generate preferences, can it cause "likes" rather than "dislikes"? Indeed, it can. It turns out that it accounts for a phenomenon with a venerable history in medical science: specific hungers.

If an animal has a vitamin deficiency and is given a choice between foods, one of which contains the appropriate vitamin, it rapidly develops a preference for that food. Furthermore, if the vitamin-rich food is distinctively flavored and that flavor is then switched to another food, most subjects select the "wrong" food in the second phase. This suggests that they have *learned* to select a particular flavor. The alternative explanation is that the animal has an innate preference for substances containing necessary nutrients. However, every species would have to be equipped with many such mechanisms to be able to show all the specific hungers that have been discovered.

Rozin and his colleagues (see Rozin and Kalat, 1971) carried out an extensive series of experiments with thiamine-deficient rats. After 21 days on the deficient diet, the rats showed clear signs of deficiency, and when given a choice, they strongly preferred thiamine-enriched food. Rozin and Kalat raise four theoretical problems arising out of these experiments:

1. *Delay*. This simply parallels the taste-aversion problem. How do rats learn to select a food which improves their health, but has no immediate effects?
2. *Preference after recovery*. As preference persists, it cannot be a direct effect of the deficiency.
3. *Which food?* Recovery from deficiency may follow ingestion of several foods; how does the rat select the "correct" thiamine-enriched substance?
4. *Why food?* Many other nonfeeding behaviors occur in proximity to recover from deficiency. Why are these not associated with recovery?

These problems clearly parallel those arising out of taste aversion, which leads us to suspect that the same or similar mechanisms are involved. Indeed, it turns out that taste aversion itself is involved. Vitamin-deficient rats actually develop an aversion to their regular diet, which reduce their built-in suspicion of novel foods. In general, the assumption that we are dealing with the same type of interoceptive-conditioning mechanism copes well with Rozin and Kalat's problems. Problems 4. and 1. are solved because only appropriate stimuli can be associated with recovery, and because the event-rate is very slow in the interoceptive system. Preference after recovery can be explained as a lasting aversion to the familiar, deficient diet. "Which food"? is the most complicated problem. The primary method by which the rat selects the enriched food appears to be by a type of sampling. Only a few foods are eaten on any one day, and only one food at any one meal, thus allowing the rat to associate each food with its consequences. Rozin (1969) found that in deficient rats, the emergence of a strong preference was always preceded by a clearly defined meal of the enriched food.

11.4
Is it Really Classical Conditioning?

We have sketched the outlines, and they are only outlines, of an interoceptive-conditioning system. Our approach has been to treat it as a version of classical conditioning, and we have identified CS's, and US's and the results of conditioning. However, we have had to admit that, in various ways, the process under study is quite unlike exteroceptive classical conditioning, at least superficially. Are we justified in treating it as classical conditioning at all?

There are certainly grounds for saying that we are not justified. When considering Pavlovian classical conditioning in Chapter 9, we stressed the CS-US contingency as a defining feature. The idea of a contingency has to be drastically modified to incorporate the relationship between events involved in the experiments described in this chapter. The process of selecting the most recent, distinctive, novel taste and associating it with illness is obviously built into the subject. The species-specificity of these effects is highlighted by a study on bobwhite quail (Wilcoxon, Dragoin, and Kral, 1971). This bird feeds by day and selects its food by visual cues. It turns out that it *will* associate a visual cue with subsequent illness. This finding, which incidently casts doubt on the generality of interoceptive/exteroceptive distinction, shows that the CS-US combinations that will be effective vary with the species. Whether or not the experimenter arranges a contingency between them is relatively unimportant, as many of the experiments involve only one presentation of CS and US.

Some remarkable findings of Garcia, McGowan, and Green (1972) illustrate the irrelevance of experimenter-arranged contingencies. They found that injections of a nitrogen mustard that produces illness reduced the amount of saccharine solution drunk immediately afterwards, although water consumption was unaffected. This means that the US (illness) produced an aversion to the CS (saccharin), although it was presented first! This is what has been called "backward conditioning" (see Figure 10.2). Any effect produced is normally regarded as nonassociative; that is, not caused by conditioning. However, given the loose connection between CS and US that produces taste aversion, there is every reason to suppose that this experiment tapped the same process as those in which the CS preceded the US.

Our problems in formally analyzing interoceptive conditioning are aggravated by the nature of the US. While the CS remains under the experimenter's control, as in conventional experiments, the US is a temporally-extended event, determined by the subject's physiology, and it may not even be perceived by the subject. Indirect evidence for conditioning with an imperceptible US comes from a study by Garcia, Kimmeldorf, and Hunt (1961). Rats developed a pronounced aversion to saccharine after a dose of X-irradiation, well below that which would be perceived by humans.

The various difficulties we have noted mean that if we wish to treat interoceptive conditioning as a form of classical conditioning, this will involve a liberal, expanded, interpretation of the latter. Nonetheless, we can safely conclude the following at present:

1. Taste aversion and specific hungers are conditioned phenomena. Particular histories of individual organisms are responsible for aversions to and preferences for certain flavors.
2. Many aspects of these conditioning phenomena follow different laws from the various other classes of conditioning phenomena traditionally studied in psychology laboratories.

While the details of interoceptive conditioning mechanisms remain to be explicated, we already know enough about them to realize that they are powerful influences on behavior and of great adaptive significance. The actuarial notion of contingency, so important in the areas we reviewed earlier, seems irrelevant here and this throws important light on conditioning mechanisms in general. Conditioning mechanisms are methods by which individual organisms adapt to their own environments. This is the sole criterion by which they can be judged; if they are not effective in this way, then natural selection will eliminate them. We should, therefore, expect to find that the mechanism for a particular type of conditioning is appropriate for the "problems" set by the environment. Where stimulus events occur at very high frequency, as exteroceptive stimuli do, then the best mechanisms will be ones which can isolate predictive relationships between stimuli, or between responses and stimuli. That is, a statistical mechanism that detects CS-US contingencies over a long run of events will be extremely useful for this system. On the other hand, when critical stimulus events are comparatively rare and novel stimuli rarer still, as in the interoceptive system, the best mechanism will be a collocating process that can pick up a lone CS-US pair, even if their temporal association is extremely loose.

11.5

Applications

The sauce Béarnaise example, and children's long-lasting hatreds of particular foods, suggest that taste aversion is a potent influence on human behavior and might be a powerful therapeutic tool. Obesity is the biggest health problem in the western world and results primarily from overindulgence in tasty foods (Schacter, 1971). Treatments such as those Garcia used to persuade rats to "give up saccharin" should prove very useful in altering human eating habits.

This approach has already been used to deal with the practical problem of predation of sheep by coyotes. Gustavson, Garcia, Hankins, and Rusiniak (1974) fed coyotes one or two meals of minced lamb flesh, skin, and wool infused with lithium chloride, and induced lithium illness. After this experience, the coyotes not only refused to attack lambs, but actually ran away from the lambs and retched! As coyotes continued to attack rabbits, this treatment succeeded in protecting the sheep, without starving or killing the coyotes. Garcia, Hankins, and Rusiniak (1975) suggest that similar, applied ecological programs could be used to change the food preferences of species whose food supply is endangered.

References for Chapter 11

Garcia, J., Green, K. F., and McGowan, B. K. X-ray as an olfactory stimulus. In C. Pfaffman (Ed.), *Taste and olfaction*, Volume 3. New York: Rockefeller University Press, 1969.

Garcia, J., Hankins, W. G., and Rusiniak, K. W. Behavioral regulation of the milieu inteme in man and rat. *Science*, 1975, **185**, 824–831.

Garcia, J., Kimmeldorf, D. J., and Hunt, E. L. The use of ionising radiation as a motivating stimulus. *Psychological Review*, 1961, **68**, 383–395.

Garcia, J., and Koelling, R. A. Relation of cue to consequence in avoidance learning. *Psychonomic Science*, 1966, **4**, 123–124.

Garcia, J., McGowan, B. K., and Green, K.F. Biological constraints on conditioning. In A. H. Black and W. F. Prokasy (Eds.) *Classical conditioning II*. New York: Appleton-Century-Crofts, 1972.

Gustavson, C. R., Garcia, J., Hankins, W. G., and Rusiniak, K. W. Coyote predation control by aversive conditioning. *Science*, 1974, **184**, 581–583.

Nachman, M. Some stimulus conditions affecting learned aversions produced by illness. Paper read at 3rd International Conference on the Regulation of Food and Water Intake, Philadelphia, 1968.

Revusky, S. H. and Garcia, J. Learned associations over long delays. In G. Bower (Ed.) *The psychology of learning and motivation*, Volume 4. New York: Academic Press, 1970.

Rozin, P. Central or peripheral mediation of learning with long CS-UCS intervals in the feeding system. *Journal of Comparative and Physiological Psychology*, 1969, **67**, 431–429.

Rozin, P., and Kalat, J. W. Specific hungers and poison avoidance as adaptive specializations of learning. *Psychological Review*, 1971, **78**, 459–486.

Schacter, S. Some extraordinary facts about obese humans and rats. *American Psychologist*, 1971, **26**, 129–144.

Seligman, M. E. P. Introduction. In M. E. P. Seligman and J. L. Hager (Eds.) *Biological Boundaries of Learning*. New York: Meredith, 1972.

Smith, J. C., and Roll, D. L. Trace conditioning with X-rays as the aversive stimulus. *Psychonomic Science*, 1967, **9**, 11–12.

Wilcoxon, H. C., Dragoin, W., and Kral, P. A. Illness induced aversions in rat and quail: Relative salience of visual and gustatory cues. *Science*, 1971, **171**, 826–828.

CHAPTER 12

Sign Tracking

Chapter 7 discussed some intriguing misbehaviors of trained animals. Pigs taught to put coins in slots for food began, after a time, to root with their coins and to toss them about in the dirt instead of carrying them directly over to their slot machine and inserting them for food. This rooting became so persistent that it sharply increased the animals' delay of reward, and considerably reduced reinforcement frequency. Then too, some chickens who had learned elaborate dance patterns to get grain began to emit incompatible flapping and pecking that interfered with the skills they had been taught. Not very surprisingly, the misbehaviors dismayed the animals' trainers, who had dutifully followed the rules of operant conditioning and hence expected "to get what they had reinforced."

Although rather mysterious from the point of view of the law of effect, these misbehaviors do have something in common with the following homely example. If you have a cat, you may find that at feeding time your pet follows you about, mewing. This regularly results in your cat being fed, perhaps a little earlier than it would have been if this behavior had not occurred. Such behavior of household pets is generally regarded as "intelligent," "sensible," and "cute." We find ourselves inclined to impute rationality to the animal and describe its behavior in the same terms that we tend to apply to human behavior. Of course, describing our feline friend as intelligent does not explain the causes of its behavior. It is more like assigning cats a high rank in their adaptability compared with other animals, or high marks in solving problems we consider important. Nevertheless, we are interested in the analysis of behavior, and in particular, the general type of behavior that this cat is exhibiting. So we have to see whether what seems to be going on in these anecdotal examples corresponds to any of the conditioning paradigms we have studied. The presupper behavior might plausibly be a *discriminative operant*:

$$S^D \; : \; R \to S^+$$

where

$$S^D \; = \; \text{stimulus complex consisting of presence of owner and internal cues signaling meal times}$$
$$R \; = \; \text{following owner about and mewing}$$
$$S^+ \; = \; \text{meal.}$$

Or, the behavior might conceivably be maintained by a *classical-conditioning* process:

$$CS_{\text{owner at meal times}} \to US_{\text{food}}$$

resulting in mewing and following being evoked, eventually, by the CS.

Both processes might be operating, of course, or even one process for mewing and another for following; but let us consider the feasibility of each explanation as a complete account of its own. While we can certainly identify S^D, R, and S^+ to fit an operant account, it is not obvious that either mewing or following will actually be reinforced. If you own a cat, you will know that the mewing and persistent following can sometimes be rather annoying. You may even have tried to extinguish mewing by delaying the meal until the cat becomes quiet, and found that you extinguished before your pet. Anyway, it is clear that the cat gets its supper even when it does not mew, so why should this unnecessary behavior be so persistent? The evidence for this type of premeal behavior being *selectively* reinforced seems pretty scanty.

If we look at the possibility that these behaviors are classically conditioned, we can readily identify a CS and US as in the preceding diagram. However, there are problems here in considering either the following behavior or mewing to be classically-conditioned responses. As the unconditioned response to food is eating it, we might expect the prefood conditioned response to involve salivation, approach to the bowl where the food US is delivered, and other preparatory behaviors. In fact, the most characteristic feature of the cat's premeal behavior is that it follows *us* around; that is, it approaches the CS rather than the US.

So far, our "armchair" behavioral analysis in terms of our two fundamental conditioning processes seems to produce as many problems as it solves. We had perhaps better return to the laboratory to ask whether there exist any other experimental models that might help us account for both these misbehaviors, and some rather ordinary behaviors, as well.

12.1
An Experimental Analogue

In 1968, Brown and Jenkins published the results of an experiment with pigeons that was originally designed to discover a convenient way of automatically shaping the key pecking of hungry pigeons. Like many experimental breakthroughs in science, their procedure differed only slightly, but crucially, from that of many previous experiments. A key feature of the Brown and Jenkins' study was that, while it contained a basically classical-conditioning procedure, it was carried out with unrestrained subjects, free to roam about in a Skinner box. Pavlov, we may recall, had always taken great care to restrain his subjects, in order to obtain recordings free from "artifacts".

Brown and Jenkins began by, first, magazine-training their pigeons. The birds learned to approach and eat grain from an automatic feeder as soon as the feeder operated. A light came on in the feeder when it operated to cue this approach behavior. Following this initial training, the birds were exposed to one of a number of conditions in which *key light presentations* were associated in various ways with *food delivery*. Figure 12.1 shows the procedures used. In each procedure, there was an intertrial interval of between 30 and 90 sec (mean = 60 sec), followed by key light and food presentations. All food presentations last 4 sec and key light presentations were 8 sec, except in "Tray only-constant light" and "3-sec Trial" conditions.

"Forward pairing—fixed trial" corresponds to a conventional classical-conditioning procedure, with key light as CS and food as US. Key pecks, if emitted, had absolutely no effect, but they were recorded. On the other hand, if the pigeon pecked the key when lit in any of the other three, forward pairing conditions, this peck was reinforced by immediate food delivery.

This operant-reinforcement contingency was included because Brown and Jenkins were endeavoring to find an "autoshaping" technique, whereby the pigeon could train itself to peck a key for food, and so save experimenters the trouble of laboriously shaping key pecks by successive approximation.

The results of the Brown and Jenkins experiment appear in Table 12.1. With the exception of the dark key procedure, all of the forward-pairing procedures reliably generated key pecking. The procedure that failed to

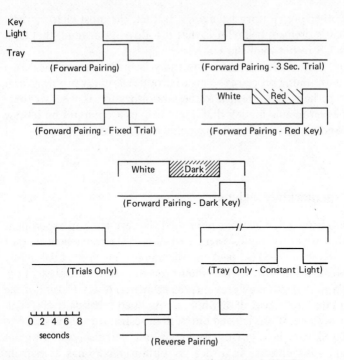

FIGURE 12.1. Procedures used in Brown and Jenkins' (1968) experiments. "Reverse pairing," "trials only," and "tray only" correspond to the control conditions typically used in classical conditioning experiments.

TABLE 12.1. The Results of Brown and Jenkin's (1968) Experiments.

Procedure	Per cent of subjects pecking the key when lit within 160 trials	Mean trial on which first peck occurred
Forward pairing	100	45
Forward pairing—3 sec trial	95	47
Forward pairing—red key	100	33
Forward pairing—fixed trial	92	55
Forward pairing—dark key	33	141
Trials only	0	—
Tray only—constant light	33	—
Reverse pairing	17	54

The mean trial of first peck is calculated only for those subjects who made some pecks.

generate pecking, the dark-key procedure, involved a relatively long period of key illumination (mean = 60 sec), followed by a relatively short period (8 sec) of darkness, immediately prior to food presentation. Key darkness thus reliably predicted food, and so the procedure resembles in some ways Pavlov's trace-conditioning procedure (see Figure 10.2). We shall not attempt to explain the failure of this dark-key condition for the moment, but will simply note that it is part of "laboratory lore" that pigeons will not peck at unlit keys without special training.

The three lower conditions depicted in Figure 12.1 are controls for various nonassociative effects; that is, effects possibly produced by CS (key light) and US (food) presentations that are not attributable to their being associated. None of these nonassociative control procedures produced much pecking, so we shall not worry about them further.

The exciting result of Brown and Jenkins' experiment was the surprising finding that the fixed-trial procedure, totally lacking any operant contingency between pecks and food, was very nearly as effective as the other three forward-pairing conditions that had included an explicit contingency. Evidently, pairing alone of key light and food had been sufficient to generate and maintain pecking, a result which strongly suggests that classical conditioning has the power to generate key pecking behavior of pigeons in the Skinner box. If this is true, it not only provides a demonstration that our apparatus may record other behavioral processes than the one that it was designed to record, but it also shows that classical conditioning processes can exert a considerable influence on behavior (key pecks of pigeons) that had hitherto been thought of as being exclusively operant in character.

12.2
Could Autoshaping be Disguised Operant Behavior?

The results from Brown and Jenkins' fixed-trials, forward-pairing procedure seem difficult to explain by any direct operant contingency. Nevertheless, some hidden instrumental contingency might have existed, imbedded in the procedure. For instance, it might be thought that perhaps the bird's eye had first been "caught" by the key light coming on. The bird might have then naturally advanced towards the key as a part of an investigatory chain of behavior. As the bird advanced towards the key, the food magazine delivered food, and so that investigatory behavior received reinforcement, albeit fortuitously. On the next trial, the bird might be still closer to the key "investigating" it, when food arrived, and that adventitious reinforcement would strengthen still more this advancing towards the key. Eventually, the bird might actually look at and then reach out with a peck and contact the key, just at the moment that food arrived. Since a strike on the key is presumably a bird's end point of "investigating" the key, this seems a plausible, if slightly fanciful, way of developing a *post hoc* operant account of autoshaping.

Before we turn to an ingenious experimental test of this operant explanation of autoshaping, let us take time to ask ourselves what it means exactly to call a piece of behavior, "operant" behavior. Skinner's word captures the idea that this kind of behavior seems to operate on the environment to modify the subject's environment. In this sense too, Thorndike referred to this kind of behavior as "instrumental"; it is instrumental in producing changes in the organism's environment.

It has always been tempting to go further with this purely descriptive label and connect it, either explicitly or implicitly, with older categories of action. So it has happened that Skinner's elaboration of operant behavior was heralded as the first quantitative-experimental attack on skeletal behavior, voluntary behavior, on purpose, on will, and though unspoken, perhaps on consciousness itself. Nonetheless, such equations are clearly gratuitous. If we find a piece of behavior that happens to be under the control of its consequences at this particular time, under these particular conditions, with this particular reinforcement, and in this particular situation, then we are justified in talking about what we are seeing there as "operant behavior." Indeed, assuming that we keep reminding ourselves of these particular contextual conditions, we might even want to go so far as to talk about the operant "nature" of this particular behavior.

But beyond that, we cannot go with certainty, for our data say nothing about other conditions, at other times, and with other reinforcers. For instance, none of our previous hundreds of studies and tens of thousands of feet of cumulative records concerning the key pecking of pigeons for food justify the unqualified statement that the key pecks of pigeons are an "operant." To say this implies that such behavior is *only* susceptible to its consequences, clearly an untested assumption. The Brown and Jenkins' experiment surprises us only because we were inclined to identify operants with particular topographies; for example the beak movements involved in pecking. Any instance of key pecking may or may not be operant behavior, since it is a class of behavior whose occurrence is a function of many variables, only one of which is its consequences. We already know that key pecks are a function of motivational and emotional variables, about which we will speak in later chapters; but it has come as a shock to some to find that the frequency of occurrence of such behavior might also be so greatly influenced by purely associative factors.

The Brown and Jenkins' experiments seem the first solid demonstration of this kind of control which, while in no way invalidating our general laws of operant conditioning, do cause us to exercise extreme caution in casually explaining everyday human and animal acts as necessarily the result of unobserved reinforcement contingencies. Extrapolate we must, if our laboratory preparations are to have general significance for our world at large;

but autoshaping remains a lesson to us than when we forget our assumptions, we can be in for some rude reminders.

12.3

Omission Training

Is there a way to definitely rule out the possibility that the behavior that Brown and Jenkins observed in their fixed trials-forward pairing experiment was due to unprogrammed chance reinforcement of key pecking? There does indeed exist an ingenious test of the account. Imagine a procedure in which we pair a key light with food, *except* on those trials when a peck to the key actually occurs. If this procedure, in which key pecks actually prevent food delivery, still generates some key pecking, we should feel rather sure that no fortituous operant conditioning of key pecking could be involved.

In Section 10.10, we cited Sheffield's (1965) finding that salivation to a CS paired with food persisted, even when not-salivating was operantly reinforced, as evidence that classical conditioning was independent of operant conditioning. Williams and Williams (1969) employed the same logic to subject autoshaped responses to omission training and establish their independence of operant conditioning. In Williams and Williams' procedure, a 6-sec key light CS was followed by 4-sec access to grain US, unless the pigeon pecked the key when lit; in that case, the light went out and no grain was presented. Twelve out of thirteen pigeons responded on more than 10 per cent of CS presentations, and most of these responded at a high rate and thus prevented many of the potential reinforcers or US's. Data from a similar study of omission training following autoshaping, by Hearst (1975), appear in Figure 12.2. By responding in more than 70 per cent of the trials, Hearst's pigeons lost an average of more than 70 per cent of their programmed food

FIGURE 12.2.
Percentage of trials containing pecks during autoshaping, and subsequent omission training for a group of 6 pigeons (adapted from Hearst, 1975).

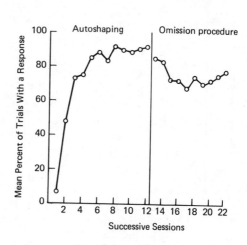

presentations. This is certainly good evidence for the associative nature of autoshaping, as is data on ommission training of approach behavior, collected by Browne, Peden, and Hearst (reported in Hearst, 1975). Their procedure resembled that of Williams and Williams, except that the response key was located on the left wall, 35 cm from the feeder. If the pigeon came within 25 cm of the key, an "approach response" was recorded, and if this occurred during the CS, the key light was terminated and no grain was delivered. The results from six pigeons are shown in Figure 12.3. Once again, high rates of response were recorded, only slightly lower than when the birds were subsequently transferred to autoshaping.

Pecking and approaching food are clearly a highly prepared sequence in Seligman's (1970) terms. Autoshaped behavior has been found rather less resistant to omission training when the measured response has been lever pressing by rats. Ridgers and Leslie (1975) used a clear plastic lever, as illustrated in Figure 12.4, in place of the conventional metal lever in a Skinner box. Illumination of this lever for 7 sec served as a CS that was followed by a US of a food pellet for a hungry rat. Ridgers and Leslie found that this procedure resulted in autoshaped lever pressing, but when omission training was subsequently introduced, pressing declined slowly to near-zero. Although the operant contingency was shown to be effective because the operant (not-pressing) increased in frequency, CS orientation and approach

FIGURE 12.3. Percentage of trials with a key-approach response over successive blocks of sessions in a group of 6 pigeons that were first exposed to omission training for key-approach during 40 sessions, and then transferred to autoshaping (Hearst, 1975).

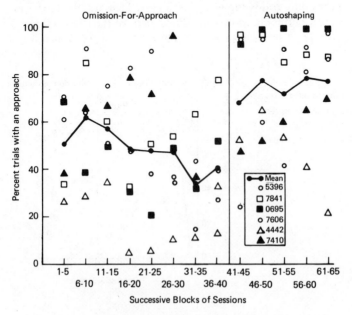

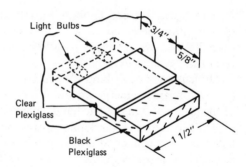

FIGURE 12.4.
A clear plastic lever that can be internally illuminated. This device enables autoshaping experiments to be conducted with rats which parallel those done with pigeons and illuminated keys (from Boakes, 1977).

were still observed during omission training. As these responses were not reinforced (nor were they punished) by the operant contingency, they must have persisted because of the continued association between the CS (illuminated lever) and the US (food pellets).

Clearly, the relative effectiveness of the (operant) response contingency and the (classical) stimulus contingency varies with the species and with details of the situation. There can be no doubt, however, that *both* operate during omission training.

12.4

Is Autoshaping Classical (Pavlovian) Conditioning?

In Chapter 10, we drew the conclusion that the amount of conditioning in a classical-conditioning procedure was influenced both by the temporal and predictive relationships between CS and US. We also concluded that while a simple stimulus substitution rule (predicting that the conditioned response would be identical with the unconditioned response to the US) did not accurately predict the nature of the conditioned response, a modification of this stating that all responses conditioned to the CS are components of the response to the US was the best approximation. If autoshaping results from a classical-conditioning process, we might expect to find a pattern of temporal and topographical results that parallels these Pavlovian temporal and topographical results.

Gamzu and Williams (1973) showed that pecking at a key light CS occurred both when the CS and the US (food) were explicitly paired, and when the US occurred more often during the CS than in its absence. However, when the US occurred equally often in presence or absence of the CS, or when it occurred only in the absence of the CS, no autopecking occurred. These results show that, like Pavlovian-conditioned responses, autoshaped pecking occurs only when the CS *predicts* the US.

The temporal factors important in classical Pavlovian conditioning have been shown to affect autoshaping in similar ways. Baldock (1974) found that rate of acquisition of pecking declined as the CS duration was increased from

4 sec to 32 sec. Terrace, Gibbon, Farrell, and Baldock (1975) found that rate of acquisition increased as the intertrial interval was increased from 10 sec to over 200 sec, which again parallels findings from classically conditioned responses, such as eyeblinks.

Difficulties of describing autoshaped responses in purely Pavlovian terms, however, begin to emerge when we start to consider the topographical nature of the behavior. On the one hand, some autoshaping studies, using a variety of US's, show a remarkable correspondence between the conditioned behavior and the unconditioned response to the US; on the other hand, there are striking features of the conditioned behavior that are not reported in Pavlovian studies.

Instances of the close correspondence between conditioned pecking and the unconditioned pecking with two different US's are illustrated in Figure 12.5. These high-speed photographs show that, when the key light CS signals food presentation, pecks are brief and forceful with the beak open. When the CS signals water presentation to a thirsty pigeon, however, the pigeon moves its head laterally across the key, with a slight opening and closing of the beak. In each case, the behavior closely resembles the consummatory behavior, or unconditioned response, to the US. Jenkins and Moore (1973) elegantly demonstrated that the topography of pecking did not depend on the animals' being solely deprived of either food or water, since their animals were both hungry and thirsty. In Jenkins and Moore's experiment, illumination of the left key signaled water, and illumination of the right key signaled food. These two different CS's were presented alternately during the same session, and the two different consummatory behaviors were almost exclusively directed at their appropriate CS's.

Characteristic features of autoshaped behavior are simply not investigated or reported in classical Pavlovian studies. Two of these features are *CS-approach* and *CS-contact*. Critics of the original Brown and Jenkins' autoshaping study argued that the behavior observed was not classically conditioned, because nothing in classical-conditioning theory predicts that pecks should be directed at the key. We will leave until later the question of why the CS is approached and contacted in autoshaping studies, but there is no doubt that it happens. The strength of the tendency to approach a CS signaling food is well demonstrated in the so called "long box" studies. A long box is like a Skinner box, except that it is considerably longer (5 feet or so), and the response key and the food magazine can be situated some distance apart.

Hearst and Jenkins (1974) describe a study in which the box was 152 cm × 46 cm, with response keys on the end walls, and a grain magazine in the middle of one of the side walls. Once a minute, a 5-sec CS was presented, (for example, a green key at one end) and followed by 4-sec access to grain. Equally often, another 5-sec stimulus (for example, a red key at the other end) was presented, but not followed by food. Out of seven birds given 10 sessions in this long box apparatus, six began to approach and peck at the

FIGURE 12.5. Typical food and water autoshaped responses as they appear at the moment of key contact. Left column shows behavior on 4 trials when the key light signaled water. Right column shows behavior of the same subject, in the same session, on 4 trials when the key light signaled food (Jenkins and Moore, 1973).

green CS when presented, even though it was 91 cm (nearly 3 feet) from the grain magazine. The red key was rarely approached. Autoshaped behavior developed in the first or second session and persisted until the end of training. Only two birds showed a decline towards the end of the experiment.

Hearst and Jenkins argue that this demonstration of the persistence of CS approach and contact is especially impressive, because CS approach often resulted in the food being lost altogether, since the bird often found itself 3 feet away from the food hopper, pecking the green key when food arrived. By the time the bird turned around and walked over to the food hopper, its 4-sec duty cycle had elapsed, and reinforcement was no longer available.

Using the long box highlights CS approach behavior, but it obviously occurs in every study in which the CS is actually pecked. We have already noted that Pavlovian studies, and others discussed in Chapter 10, do not report this approach behavior. However, we have to recall that Pavlov's harnessed dogs were physically unable to approach their CS's. We need not leave to speculation what might happen if Pavlovian subjects are released from their harnesses, as a very early experiment by Zener (1937) provides exactly this information. When released following restrained salivary conditioning, Zener's dogs did indeed approach the bell used as the CS. Zener's results give us a beautiful, early anticipation of autoshaping. However, in 1937, such results simply had no general interest, for they preceded all the work that later followed on free operant conditioning. It is in the context of operant control by reinforcement that associative control of approach to CS's has a meaning, and creates a problem to be understood.

The results we have cited so far in this section show impressive parallels between classical Pavlovian response-conditioning and autoshaping. There exist strong temporal similarities in the way that intertrial CS-US intervals control both phenomena. US predictability by the CS seems to be a required feature of both processes for behavior to occur and persist. The topographies of the behaviors studied in each appear so different, mainly due to arbitrary apparatus constraints. Perhaps we may now feel safe to conclude, at the very least, that autoshaping, and what we have called classical conditioning since the turn of the century, are two features of the same behavioral process. This conclusion is certainly not weakened by the difficulty we discussed in Chapter 10 in defining the exact behavioral results of Pavlov's classical procedure. This difficulty in predicting the response to expect in any new, untested classical-conditioning experiment poses problems for the design of a critical experiment that would tell us, once and for all, whether or not autoshaping should be labeled an instance of classical conditioning. On the other hand, by letting go of this pressure to subsume one phenomenon by the other, and rather interpreting both as related effects of a common procedure, we put ourselves in the favorable position of using the new autoshaping techniques to enhance and greatly broaden our knowledge of the associative process we have traditionally called "classical conditioning."

There will, of course, be differences in the outcome of the unrestrained autoshaping situation and the more restricted, classical Pavlovian procedures that are related to the distinctive features of autoshaping. For example, we noted earlier that Brown and Jenkins' "dark key" procedure did not produce much keypecking, although it is formally similar to trace conditioning, an effective Pavlovian technique. The reason for this however, can be found in the idea that autoshaping results in pecking at a *localized* CS signal predicting food. In the "dark key" procedure, it is the absence of a light that really predicts reinforcement, and this absence is not a localized stimulus. The crucial importance of a localized, discrete CS for autoshaping was demonstrated cleverly by Wasserman (1973). He found that if the experimental chamber was in complete darkness between CS (key light) presentations, autoshaping was retarded. This was because the key light was now the sole illumination for the whole box. Thus, when it came on, all of the interior was suddenly illuminated, and its role as a localized stimulus was diffused. Wasserman did report that some pigeons made pecking movements at reflections of the key light, or other distinctive features on the walls of the box that did appear when the box lit up, indicating that autoshaping certainly did occur, but now not invariably directed to the key itself.

12.5
Sign-Tracking: A General Phenomenon

So far, we have discussed the autoshaping key pecking of pigeons and identified its characteristic features. It turns out that this behavior is an instance of a more general phenomenon, common to many species, CS's and US's. We propose to follow Hearst and Jenkins (1974) and call it *sign-tracking*:

> Sign-tracking refers to behavior that is directed toward or away from a stimulus (CS) as a result of the relation between that stimulus and the reinforcer (US), or between that stimulus and the absence of the reinforcer . . . This label would cover not only the autoshaping paradigm but also several other phenomena in the field of animal and human learning . . . The word "tracking" is meant to be flexible in its application, it can refer to an organism's orientation, approach or contact responses directed towards signs of particular reinforcers (US's), as well as to an organism's withdrawal responses directed away from signs that a reinforcer is not coming. Among other advantages, the word "sign" implies the importance of stimulus-reinforcer (CS-US) correlations rather than the traditional law of effect. A sign predicts the presence or absence of some other environmental event, and it apparently achieves this capacity via procedures also used in conventional classical conditioning (Hearst and Jenkins, 1974, p. 4).

Sign-tracking certainly occurs in many situations. Although the most detailed information available is still from pigeons autoshaped with food, the basic effect has been seen with pigeons given water or presented with a mate, with rats given food pellets, brain stimulation, sucrose, or water, with monkeys given food, with cats given food, and with other species, including humans. The CS's used have mostly been visual, as these are readily localized, but positive results have been obtained with auditory CS's, where animals approach loudspeakers.

The Jenkins "long box" experiment made sign-tracking appear bizarre behavior: the pigeons pursued the signal, even though it reduced their access to the food. However, a moment's reflection shows that it is the experiment that is bizarre, not the pigeon's behavior. In such a situation, the experimenter has separated the sign from the thing signified, an event which seldom happens in the normal environment. The most important feature of most localized signals of significant events is that they come from the same direction as the event. For example, a pigeon's diet consists largely of grain, and this means that it must direct its pecking at the place where it sees grain: the sight of grain *directs* pecking as well as eliciting it. A pigeon fitted with "spectacles" so that grain on the left appeared in the right-hand visual field, would have great difficulty in learning this "unnatural" relationship between signal and food, and those in Jenkins' experiment are faced with a similar problem. Moreover, the omission-training studies with different species have found sign-tracking to be remarkably persistent in situations where it interferes with reinforced-operant behavior. The persistence of associative processes does not prove that they are all-important, or that operant conditioning is a myth, rather they show how two independent behavioral processes interact. In natural situations, both operant conditioning and sign-tracking are complementary and act concurrently to mold the individual's behavior to a variety of circumstances.

Our appreciation of the significance of sign-tracking for human behavior is in its infancy, but many real-life situations have already evolved so that signs are optimally placed. "Exit" and "Stop" are always placed in the appropriate location; buttons on machinery light up when due to be pressed. Human experimental psychologists are well aware that when response and signaling stimulus are "incompatible" (for example, left light being lit requires right button to be pressed), performance deteriorates dramatically.

12.6

Interactions With Operant Behavior

Sign-tracking has obvious implications for the practice, if not the theory, of operant conditioning. The most widely used apparatus for many years has been a pigeon Skinner box, in which the operant is defined as a contact with a localized visual stimulus (the key). The data reviewed here clearly indicate that key pecking will be facilitated when the key light is predictive of food (or other appetitive stimuli). It has also been found that an aversion to the key develops if its illumination signals the absence of food. For example, Wasserman, Franklin, and Hearst (1974) found that where there was a *negative contingency* between CS (key light) and US (food), pigeons moved away from the key when lit (see Figure 12.6). We can conclude that *the probability of the operant response will be strongly influenced by the associative properties of the manipulandum.* (Manipulandum is the general term for the devices upon which operant responses are made: keys, levers, etc.)

Several consequences follow from this conclusion:

1. Studies solely concerned with operant contingencies should control for

FIGURE 12.6. Approach–withdrawal ratios of 8 individual pigeons. The approach–withdrawal ratio was calculated as: total time on the same side as the keylight CS divided by total trial (CS) time. A ratio of .50 indicates no control by the CS. Each bird was placed on positive contingency, negative contingency, or CS-alone training for 21 sessions (left panel), and then 7 birds were switched to a different condition for 9 or 21 sessions (right panel) (adapted from Wasserman, Franklin, and Hearst, 1974).

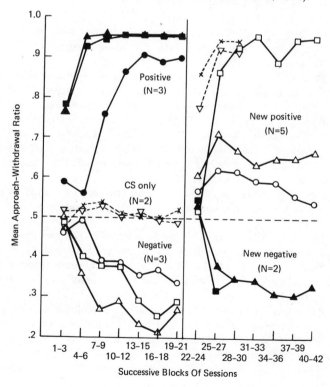

the associative properties of the manipulandum. This should lead, and is leading, to the range of stimuli and responses studied in the laboratory being broadened.

2. Apparent species differences in operant experiments may be the result of apparatus differences. While illuminated keys are usually used for pigeons, rats generally have metal levers to press and stimuli are presented elsewhere in the apparatus, from lights or loudspeakers. Stimulus-directed activity will then interact with operant behavior in quite a different fashion. Examples of the role of apparatus differences in apparent species differences will be found in Parts Four and Five.

3. Associative phenomena, studied in operant-conditioning situations, may critically depend on CS-directed behavior. It has long been realized that associative processes influence behavior seen in operant situations, but associative processes were not known to generate CS-directed behavior. Consequently, experiments were not controlled to see whether CS type and location was critical. Recently various associative phenomena in operant situation have been reanalyzed and the importance of CS-directed behavior has been demonstrated.

References for Chapter 12

Baldock, M. D. Trial and intertrial interval durations in the acquisition of autoshaped key pecking. Paper read to Eastern Psychological Association, Philadelphia, 1974.

Boakes, R. A. Performance on learning to associate a stimulus with positive reinforcement. In H. Davis and H. M. B. Hurwitz (Eds.) *Operant-Pavlovian interactions*. Hillsdale, N. J.: Lawrence Erlbaum, 1977.

Brown, P. L., and Jenkins, H. M. Autoshaping of the pigeon's key peck. *Journal of the Experimental Analysis of Behavior*, 1968, **11**, 1–8.

Gamzu, E., and Williams, D. R. Associative factors underlying the pigeon's key pecking in autoshaping procedures. *Journal of the Experimental Analysis of Behavior*, 1973, **19**, 225–232.

Hearst, E. Pavlovian conditioning and directed movements. In G. M. Bower (Ed.) *The psychology of learning and motivation*, Volume 9. New York: Academic Press, 1975.

Hearst, E., and Jenkins, H. M. *Sign-tracking: The stimulus-reinforcer relation and directed action*. Austin, Tex.: Psychonomic Society, 1974.

Jenkins, H. M., and Moore, B. R. The form of the auto-shaped response with food or water reinforcers. *Journal of the Experimental Analysis of Behavior*, 1973, **20**, 163–181.

Ridgers, A., and Leslie, J. C. Autoshaping and omission training in the rat. Paper read to Experimental Analysis of Behavior Group, Exeter, England, 1975.

Seligman, M. E. P. On the generality of the laws of learning. *Psychological Review*, 1970, **77**, 406–418.

Sheffield, F. D. Relation between classical conditioning and instrumental learning. In

W. F. Prokasy (Ed.) *Classical conditioning*. Englewood Cliffs, N.J.: Prentice-Hall, 1965.

Terrace, H. S., Gibbon, J., Farrell, L., and Baldock, M. D. Temporal factors influencing the acquisition of an autoshaped key peck. *Animal Learning and Behavior*, 1975, **3**, 53–62.

Wasserman, E. A. The effect of redundant contextual stimuli on autoshaping the pigeon's key peck. *Animal Learning and Behavior*, 1973, **1**, 198–206.

Wasserman, E. A., Franklin, S., and Hearst, E. Pavlovian appetitive contingencies and approach vs withdrawal to conditioned stimuli in pigeons. *Journal of Comparative and Physiological Psychology*, 1974, **86**, 616–627.

Williams, D. R., and Williams, H. Auto-maintenance in the pigeons: Sustained pecking despite contingent nonreinforcement. *Journal of the Experimental Analysis of behavior*, 1969, **12**, 511–520.

Zener, K. The significance of behavior accompanying conditioned salivary secretion for theories of the conditioned response. *American Journal of Psychology*, 1937, **50**, 384–403.

PART FOUR

Environmental Control

The prototypical classical-conditioning demonstration involves a dog, restrained in a harness, salivating in response to a buzzer or flashing light that is paired with food delivery. The prototypical demonstration of operant conditioning involves a rat in a Skinner box pressing a lever from time to time and receiving a food pellet. At first sight, there are more differences than similarities between these two situations; the delivery of food seems to be the only common factor.

   Suppose we now alter the operant-conditioning procedure so that a buzzer sounds or a light flashes at intervals, and only in the presence of that stimulus is the rat's lever pressing reinforced. We have introduced a discriminative stimulus (S^D) and greatly increased the similarity with the classical-conditioning procedure. Although a CS is said to *elicit* a conditioned response, while an S^D *sets the occasion* on which a response will be reinforced, both types of stimulus come to control a response as the result of a conditioning history. They both exert *stimulus control* over the conditioned response. This means that a particular response is more likely to occur in the presence of the stimulus than in its absence.

   Control of behavior by aspects of

the environment is a defining feature of all conditioning. Even when there is no explicitly programmed S^D during operant conditioning, there is still a restricted set of stimuli that specify the occasions on which the response can be reinforced. These may be simply the stimuli associated with being in the apparatus and having access to the manipulandum. The next two chapters are concerned primarily with two questions about environmental or stimulus control. First, which features of a highly complex environment come to control behavior? Second, how does discrimination training affect stimulus control?

We will be primarily concerned with laboratory techniques that enable us to tease the important variables apart, but the analysis of stimulus control is far from being an abstract exercise that makes no contact with everyday behavior. The stimulus control of behavior is evidenced by countless everyday observations. A dog will not beg for food in the absence of a human, a child learns to cry only when a parent is home to reinforce crying, and we are unlikely to ask for a glass of water when nobody is in the room to hear. More complex examples can be found in our social behavior. We might tell a joke in a bar we would not tell in church, we will accept insults from a person in a powerful position that would provoke verbal retaliation from anyone else. There is no doubt that human behavior is under very sophisticated stimulus control.

CHAPTER 13

Stimulus
Control

It is a convenient shorthand for experimental psychologists to describe the stimuli used in their experiments in terms of the physical properties of those stimuli. Thus, we talk of light energy with a given wavelength, tones of certain frequencies, pressures on the skin measured in force units. However, the effective stimulus, the one that influences the subject's behavior, differs from the experimenter-defined stimulus in two ways:

1. The effective stimulus has only those properties than can be perceived by the subject. It makes perfectly good sense to speak of a projector displaying a field of ultraviolet radiation on a screen, but as we will be unable to see it (although a honey bee could) it is not a stimulus for us because it could not enter into a relationship with our behavior. More subtly, if your arm is jabbed by the points of two needles, you will only feel one prick if the needles are close enough together. In this case, the

distance between the two is below the *threshold* for its detection.

2. At any given time, behavior may be influenced by some, but not all, of the stimulus properties potentially perceivable by the subject.

We can summarize these two restrictions on the effective stimulus as what the subject *can* learn about the stimulus, and what the subject *does* learn about the stimulus. In terms of the classical divisions of psychology, these topics fall into the areas of *perception* and *learning*, respectively. In this chapter, as elsewhere in this book, we are primarily concerned with learned behavior, but we start by considering some aspects of stimulus perception.

13.1
Stimulus Dimensions

The prevailing environment of an organism may be considered to be the pattern or configuration of all energies, present at any given time, that are capable of entering into lawful relationships with behavior. These energies are only a small subset of the energies studied by physicists. They are confined, at most, to those that can be detected by the specialized anatomical structures, *receptors*, that organisms have for receiving certain energies and for transforming them into electrical nerve impulses. The eye is specialized for the reception of a limited range of electromagnetic radiation, the ear for a limited range of air-pressure vibrations, the tongue and nose for certain chemical energies. Receptors in the skin detect mechanical pressure and thermal changes. There are receptors within the muscles and joints of the body that detect the movement of the muscle and joints in which they are embedded. A complete specification of the patterns of electromagnetic, mechanical, chemical, and thermal energies, impinging on an organism's receptors at any time, can rarely be undertaken. Fortunately, it is not usually necessary, as behavior can come under the selective control of only limited parts or features of the energy configurations that make up what we call the environment.

A stimulus is a part of the environment and can be described in terms of its *physical dimensions*. In manipulating the visual environment, for instance, we

FIGURE 13.1. The regular wavelike character of pure light. Wavelength (λ), the difference between successive wavecrests, is inversely proportional to the frequency in time of the waves, and is correlated with what we call the color, or hue, of the light. Amplitude is related to light intensity, or brightness.

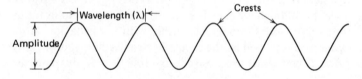

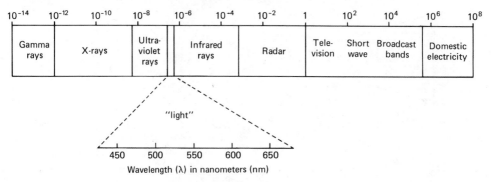

FIGURE 13.2. The electromagnetic spectrum. Note that the region that we can detect, and that can enter into relationships with behavior ("light"), is relatively small.

frequently confine our experimental changes to one of the fundamental dimensions by which physicists describe light. For our purposes, light may be considered to be a limited range of electromagnetic disturbance, radiated at 186,000 miles/sec in wave form. Light waves may be represented as in Figure 13.1. Wavelength (λ, pronounced "lambda") is one important stimulus dimension to which the different responses we call colors have been attached. The wavelengths that we call light comprise the very small portion from about 450 to 650 nanometers of the entire electromagnetic spectrum. In Figure 13.2 a more complete electromagnetic dimension of λ is shown.

Nearly all animals respond to differences in amplitude or intensity of light waves, but only a limited number of species have receptors specialized for detecting changes in λ. Pigeons, men, snakes, and monkeys are examples of animals that do. Others, such as the rat and dog, are said to be color-blind because differences in λ alone cannot control differential responding. The receptor we call the eye can be compared to a camera, for they have certain functional similarities (see Figure 13.3). Both admit light through an adjustable diaphragm; in the eye, this diaphragm is called the iris. Both the eye and the camera have lenses through which light passes and which serve to focus the light onto a sensitive surface. In the camera, that surface constitutes the emulsion of the film. In the eye, the surface consists of nerve cells making up the retina. These retinal cells transform light into nerve impulses. The structural analogy between the visual system and photography goes no further than this; the image projected on to the retina is not inspected by another eye.

The wavelengths that occur in the rainbow and perceived by us as colors (red, orange, yellow, green, blue, indigo, violet) are called pure spectral lights because they contain only one wavelength. They can be produced in the laboratory by a device called a monochromator. Most lights, including reflected light that reaches the eye from surfaces such as tables, chairs, blackboards, and lawns, are far from pure in this sense. Generally, even the

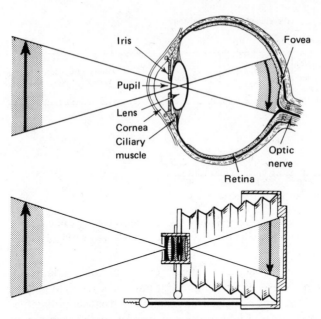

FIGURE 13.3. The eye compared functionally and schematically with a camera (after Wald, 1950).

light from a homogeneously colored surface or a lamp is made up of a large mixture of different wavelengths. Those wavelengths that are predominant usually determine the color-naming response we make. Some mixtures of light, however, are not named by their predominating wavelengths. the word "purple" is never used to name a pure spectral light of one wavelength. "Purple" is the color name for a mixture of red and blue. The lights we call white and the surfaces we call gray radiate heterogeneous mixtures of nearly all visible wavelengths. No single wavelength predominates in such lights, but the label "colorless" often given them would seem a misnomer.

Visual stimulus dimensions are not confined to different wavelength distributions and intensities of isolated patches of light. Relevant dimensions that can control behavior may be defined to include spatial combinations of the fundamental dimensions of wavelength and intensity. For instance, the relative intensities of two adjacent light regions can be a powerful controlling stimulus dimension, determining the brightness response that an observer will make to a portion of the pattern. A look at Figure 13.4 will show that when the amount of light reflected from the background surround varies, different brightness responses occur to the unchanging center triangle; that is, the observer will report different brightnesses of the triangle. (This phenomenon is called brightness contrast.) In fact, to produce an unchanging brightness response to the triangle, one would have to vary it in such a way that, as the surround intensity is raised (surround made lighter), the triangle would also have to be raised proportionately in intensity (triangle made

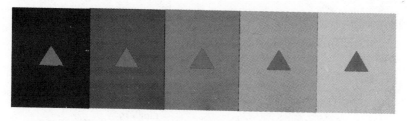

FIGURE 13.4. An example of how relations between two parts of the visual field influence responses (after Boring, Langfeld, and Weld, 1948).

lighter, also). In the situation illustrated by Figure 13.4, an identical brightness response to the different triangles is obtained only when the *ratio* of intensities of triangle to surround is the same (Wallach, 1948). The functional control of the brightness response to the triangles in Figure 13.4 is clearly located in a compound-environmental variable. As this lawfulness between environment and behavior is precisely the basis on which we assign the status of stimulus to environmental events, we need not be embarrassed to call this compound variable a stimulus. This designation, of course, does not preclude that with other contingencies prevailing, the triangle alone, or the surround alone, may also function as individual stimuli.

Sound stimuli, like light stimuli, may also be analyzed into a set of constituent dimensions. Sound bears a superficial resemblance to light in displaying certain wave properties. But the waves of sound are slowly propagated (700 ft/sec) disturbances in air pressure, rather akin to the waves in the sea that are the products of disturbances in surface water pressure. Both sound and sea-waves are *longitudinal waves,* the air or water is temporarily displaced in the direction of propogation of the wave energy, while electromagnetic radiation (light) is a *transverse wave,* and thus can be depicted as in Figure 13.1.

Changes in the amplitude of sound waves produce changes in the intensity of the energy, and are associated with different loudness responses. Figure 13.5 indicates various sound intensities in terms of a logarithmic scale called decibels; the figure provides some common examples of the sources of these intensities.

The wavelength dimension proves useful in further describing sound stimuli. Sound, however, is conventionally described by the number of crests or cycles per second (called Hertz, Hz) rather than by λ. The number of Hertz, or the *frequency* of the sound, is the dimension on which responses of pitch naming are based. Man is capable of making differential pitch responses over the range of about 20 to 20,000 Hz. Other animals, such as dogs and bats, have been shown to detect frequencies two or three times our maximum upper-frequency limit. The way in which pitch responses vary with frequency is illustrated by Figure 13.6, which gives the principal frequency of various notes of the piano. The harmonic scale is not an *interval scale* of Hertz; this means that the difference in frequency between adjacent notes (for

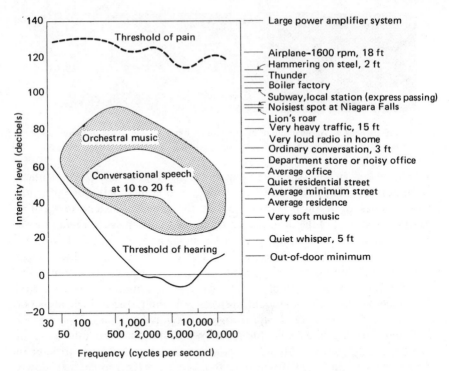

FIGURE 13.5. The intensity of some familiar sounds (after Lewis, 1963).

example B and C) is not a constant number of Hertz. Rather, it is a ratio scale. This means that the ratio between them is a constant. Specifically (with reference to Figure 13.6):

$$\frac{A_2}{B_2} = \frac{A_1}{B_1} = \frac{A}{B}$$

and

$$\frac{A_1}{A_2} = \frac{A}{A_1} = \frac{B}{B_1} = 2$$

As the distance from A_2 to A_1 is an octave, this means that the frequencies of each octave on the piano are twice those of the one immediately below it.

Just as a pure light containing only one λ is rare, so too, is a pure tone containing only one frequency. Tuning forks and electronic oscillators are sources of pure tones. The tones of musical instruments contain a mixture of frequencies, and the pitch (our response) is generally determined by the predominant frequencies. Everyday sounds, such as barks, traffic roar, speech, and music, represent very complex admixtures of many different frequencies. Sound containing a fairly generous distribution of all audible frequencies in approximately equal intensities (such as applause and radio static) is termed *white noise*, on an analogy with white light.

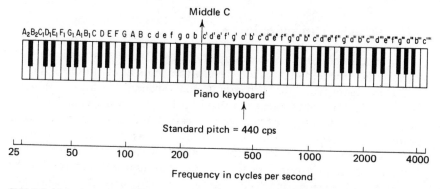

FIGURE 13.6. Sound frequencies of piano tones (after Boring, Langfeld, and Weld, 1948).

Dimensions have been conceptualized for describing the energies that make up the chemical, mechanical, and thermal portions of our environments. Smell and taste responses are based on differential changes in concentration, and molecular structure of gases in the nose, and solutions on the tongue, respectively. Changes in surface temperature are detected by certain receptors that are situated in the skin.

Describing the stimuli arising from muscle and tendon movements, generated by receptors called *proprioceptors*, poses experimental problems. Measurement of internal environmental changes is difficult without surgically invading the organism. The location of proprioceptors makes such internal environmental changes relatively inaccessible for either measurement or manipulation. In practice, internal stimuli are, therefore, more often inferred than actually observed. However, the biofeedback techniques described in Section 4.5 probably involve the acquisition of differential responding to internal proprioceptive stimuli.

Note that in this discussion, we use one set of terms to describe stimulus dimensions, and another set to describe corresponding behavioral responses. Although there are lawful correlations between these stimulus and response dimensions (described at length in the branch of psychology called psychophysics), labels for stimuli and responses should not be confused. Frequency and intensity of light energy are stimulus dimensions; color and brightness are response dimensions. Frequency and intensity of sound energy are stimulus dimensions; pitch and loudness (or volume) are response dimensions. Smell, taste, temperature, and weight are response terms associated with the stimulus dimensions of chemical structure, thermal energy, quantitative force, and so on. Recognition of the difference between the terms appropriate for describing stimuli and those for describing responses will prevent a great deal of confusion and unnecessary argument.

13.2
Stimulus Generalization

The importance of having quantitative dimensions available with which to describe and manipulate the environments of organisms is shown clearly in quantifying the behavioral phenomenon known as *stimulus generalization*. This phenomenon is seen in crude form when a child learning to speak refers to all furry objects as "cats," and calls all male adults "Daddy." It is exemplified in our own behavior when we hail a stranger mistakenly because he appears to resemble a friend. In such examples, similarity of stimuli seem clearly involved, but until we can specify the quantitative dimensions on which to relate such objects as cats, rabbits, and fur coats, a precise evaluation of the degree of similarity of any two stimulus situations is difficult. The availability of stimulus dimensions of the sort described in the previous section permits a more systematic study of this kind of similarity, which may be experimentally reinterpreted as follows. After a response has been strengthened in the presence of a particular environmental configuration, it will also occur, but to a lesser extent, when the environment is changed slightly in some way. The response may cease to occur at all when the change in the environment is large, or if critical features are eliminated.

The phenomenon of generalization is obviously very important. It would be highly maladaptive if conditioning mechanisms produced responses that were so specifically linked to the training stimulus (S^D or CS) that the response disappeared if some small "irrelevant" feature of the stimulus changed. Conversely, it would be equally inappropriate if huge changes in the stimulus produced no change in the response. That would, in fact, represent an absence of stimulus control; stimulus control being defined as the presentation of the stimulus reliably increasing (or decreasing) the probability of the behavior.

The method of studying stimulus generalization is simple in principle. After an operant response has been conditioned, variations are made in some well-controlled aspect of the environment and the strength of responding at various values is measured. This is called *generalization testing along a particular stimulus dimension*. Simple though it sounds, a detailed examination reveals several complications.

Let us consider a specific example. This uses the apparatus shown in Figure 13.7. This is a modified Skinner box in which pure light from a monochromator illuminates the pecking key. The monochromator permits the precise selection and presentation of any one of a very large number of visible wavelengths. The apparatus also includes provision for rapidly changing from one wavelength to another. In an experiment performed by Guttman and Kalish (1956), birds were shaped to peck the disk which was transilluminated by a yellow-green light (see Figure 13.2) of 550 nm (nm = nanometer = 10^{-7} m: a measure of λ, wavelength). Following some continuous-reinforcement training, the birds were shifted to a variable-

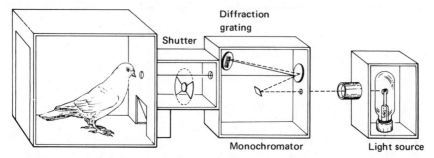

FIGURE 13.7. A pigeon Skinner box fitted with an optical system to project pure light onto the pecking key (after Guttman, 1956).

interval schedule (VI 1 min). When behavior had stabilized under VI, tests were made to determine to what extent the specific 550 nm light on the disk was controlling behavior. This test consisted of an extinction procedure in which the birds were exposed to a randomized series of successive 30-sec presentations of 11 different wavelengths, only one of which was the 550 nm actually used in training. No other changes were made in the bird's environment. The procedures can be stated thus:

1. Continuous reinforcement $S^D_{550\ nm} : R \rightarrow S^+$
2. Training on VI schedule $S^D_{550\ nm} : R \rightarrow S^+$
                                      after average
                                        of 1 min

3. Extinction tests $S_{550\ nm} : R \nrightarrow$
                       $S_{570\ nm} : R \nrightarrow$
                       $S_{510\ nm} : R \nrightarrow$ etc.

When the numbers of extinction responses emitted under each of the different stimuli were calculated, they formed the curve in Figure 13.8. This indicates that the birds gave the maximum number of extinction responses only at their training stimulus, and gave progressively fewer responses at the test stimuli located progressively farther away from the training stimulus along the λ dimension. This gradation of responding, seen when response strength is assessed in environments somewhat different from the environment in which original conditioning took place, is known as the *generalization gradient*.

The Guttman-Kalish technique illustrates nicely how procedures such as schedules of reinforcement and extinction can be combined to assess fundamental behavioral phenomena. For example, consider the purpose of the VI schedule in training. A glance back to Figure 5.18 will confirm that VI produces a very great persistence in the face of extinction. Several thousand responses may occur before the extinction rate begins to decline appreciably. In generalization, we are concerned with the spread of response strength to stimulus conditions other than those under which reinforcement actually

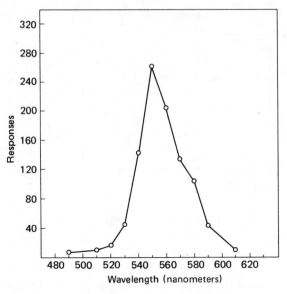

FIGURE 13.8. Responses emitted in the presence of 11 different wavelengths, projected one at a time onto the pecking key. Responses to all wavelengths were extinguished. Previous training took place only at 550 nm (Guttman, 1956).

took place. To make the necessary tests to assess this spread, we must never reinforce in the presence of the new, somewhat different stimulus conditions; otherwise, any responding that we might observe could be attributable to direct reinforcement in the presence of the new stimuli. But the use of the extinction procedure weakens behavior. How can we test as many as 11 different stimulus values in the face of this weakening? The solution to this problem lies in (1) making the presentation of each different test stimulus short (about 30 sec), (2) randomizing the order of presentation of the different test stimuli, and in (3) using a *VI* schedule in training to develop a persistence of several thousand potential extinction responses before marked signs of weakening begin to occur.

The results of Figure 13.8 illustrate the value of representing stimuli quantitatively. Suppose the experiment of Guttman and Kalish had been performed before it was known that light could be represented by waves and measured by wavelength. If the pigeon had been trained to peck at a disk covered with green paper, and then tested during extinction with green and then other colored papers on the disk, say blue, violet, red, orange, and yellow, differences in responding to these various colors would certainly have occurred. But consider whether a graph such as Figure 13.8 could have been drawn. The fact that no quantitative (numerical) dimension existed for relating the different colors one to another, would have precluded such a functional representation. In our hypothetical example, we have no basis for interpolating values of response strength between any two colors actually used. In the function of Figure 13.8 we did this easily, just by connecting response strengths for two quantitatively adjacent stimulus values with a straight line. This interpolation by straight lines enables us to predict the amount of generalization to lights not even used in the actual experiment. The best that we might have been able to do with an experiment conducted prior to the discovery of the numerical specifications of light by its wavelength would have been to draw a bar graph of the sort shown in Figure 13.9. In the absence of a better rationale, the colors of Figure 13.9 are arranged alphabetically along the abscissa. The fact that no independent variable can be assigned to the x axis of Figure 13.9 shows how deficient such a representation would have been. Here we are provided with some notion of the importance of quantitative dimensions in specifying and relating the independent variables in science. Moreover, the example is useful in showing how one science (psychology in this instance) often borrows the methods and findings of another (physics in this instance) and exploits them for its own uses in contexts entirely different from those in which the methods were originally developed.

The shape of the generalization gradient is not an invariant property of the stimulus dimension studied, even for one species or one individual. It is found to vary with the reinforcer used, the reinforcement schedule and even the training stimulus selected. Blough (1961) found the gradients of Figure 13.10 when he trained three groups of birds at 530 nm, 550 nm, and 570 nm, respectively. As the figure indicates, the actual shape of the obtained gradient varies depending on where the training stimulus lies on the λ dimension. At 530 nm, the bulk of the gradient lies to the left of the training stimulus; at 550 nm, on the other hand, it lies to the right. Only 570 nm shows a symmetrical gradient. Note that the gradient around 550 nm in Figure 13.10 differs somewhat from the one originally obtained by Guttman and Kalish in 1956 (and shown in Figure 13.8). The reason for the difference appears to be that Blough introduced an added precaution in taking his data. Because it is known that the pigeon's eye is more sensitive to some wavelengths than

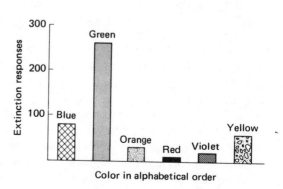

FIGURE 13.9.
Hypothetical numbers of responses emitted in extinction to various colors after training in the presence of green.

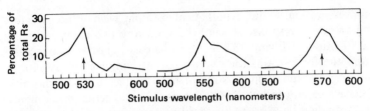

FIGURE 13.10. Generalization gradients around each of three different training wavelengths. Eight birds contributed to the curves—two at 530 nm, four at 550 nm, and two at 570 nm (Blough, 1961).

others, he used slightly different intensities of each test stimulus. The shape of Blough's gradients suggests that there are circumscribed *regions* along the λ spectrum in which generalization occurs more readily. "Trained near the middle of such a region the bird would generalize within the region, producing a symmetrical, flat-topped gradient. Trained at the edge of such a region, the bird would generalize into the region; in the other direction, its curve would fall more rapidly, to yield an asymmetrical gradient" (Blough, 1961, p. 38). The three curves of Figure 13.10 suggest that two such regions are centered at approximately 515 nm and 570 nm, respectively. It is tempting to equate the presence of these regions with the bands of colors that the human being discriminates in the spectrum. These and other results indicate that the study of behavioral generalization holds promise for elucidating fundamental properties of the eye of infrahuman organisms.

13.3
Some Implications of Generalization

Early in the preceding section, we briefly noted a few non-laboratory examples of stimulus generalization. The examples of children confusing one situation with another through indiscriminate responding are cases in which generalization appears to hinder the adaptation of an organism to its world. But generalization is equally often a very useful property of behavior. For instance, skills learned in one environmental situation can be used in new environmental situations. Having learned to catch a ball thrown from a distance of 5 ft, we will catch it pretty well at 10, 20, and maybe even 40 ft. Parents who teach their children to say "thank you" at home are implicitly relying on generalization to see to it to that "thank you" will be emitted outside the home. Our educational system is predicated on the assumption that the skills acquired in school will spread to environments outside the school. Still, the generalization *gradient* is there to remind and caution educators that the more closely a training situation resembles the situation in which the behavior will later be needed, the more effective will be the training. Schools and other agencies use this principle when they make the teaching situation as near to "real life" as possible.

The results shown in Section 13.2 support the inevitable conclusion that reinforcement is somewhat specific to the state of the environment prevailing when it occurs. The term "somewhat" is given precise meaning in the shape of the generalization gradients that can be observed when controlled changes in one or two physically specified stimulus dimensions are made. Generalization of this sort is a static concept. Unlike many of our previously familiar behavioral phenomena, generalization itself is not a process. That is, it is *not* a change in behavior over time with a fixed procedure held constant. Rather, it is a phenomenon that can be observed after operant or classical conditioning by the use of a certain sequence of operations. In a true behavioral process, *time* appears as the independent variable. But in the generalization gradients, the difference between training and test stimuli is the independent variable. Though static in this sense, we shall see in the next chapter how the generalization of conditioning combines with the generalization of extinction in discrimination training to yield a fundamental behavioral process.

Laboratory findings in generalization carry certain implications for an old philosophical problem, that of the meaning of *similarity*. C. E. Osgood's lucid comments are instructive of the manner in which the experimental method in psychology can occasionally provide a fresh reinterpretation of traditional philosophical problems.

> Suppose we ask (as has been asked in many an introductory class in philosophy), Which is more nearly similar to a red square—a green square or a red circle? The empirically oriented psychologist quickly tires of discussing matters like "the relatedness of unique qualities" and dashes off to the laboratory to "find out". After setting up a reaction, any reaction, to the red square, he tests his human subject for generalization to the green square and the red circle. Does the red circle show more generalization? If so, the red circle is more nearly similar to the red square than the green circle! Does this mean that we now have an object scale for measuring "similarity"? *Only when we are interested in similarity as defined by the behavior of an organism.* And it must be a specific type of organism, at that, since similarity for the rat, thus defined (or for the Australian Bushman, for that matter), would not necessarily parallel those for Western *Homo sapiens.*
>
> This brings up a minor matter of psychological jargon that most of us take periodic cognizance of but never observe in totality. We follow the impetus of our language and say that "there is more generalization between these two stimuli *because* they are more nearly similar," and then (like the brash young psychologist cited above) claim that "these two stimuli are more nearly similar *because* there is more generalization between them." Both statements are quite valid, depending on one's definition of similarity. Using a wave-frequency analyzer, we may measure the *physical* similarity

(nearness on the frequency continuum) of two tones and then measure generalization as a function of this similarity. Conversely, we may use a group of organisms as measuring instruments for the similarity of tones, as in psychophysics, which is really measuring physical continua in terms of generalization and discrimination. Observe carefully, however, that there is no guarantee that the two measures of similarity will be parallel; in fact, they seldom are. The clearest illustration of this lies in the phenomenon of *octave generalization*. For both the rat and the human, at least, generalization of response to tones one octave apart is greater than sound more nearly "similar." But, of course, there are those who would say that the concept of similarity is meaningful only in terms of the behavior of organisms. In this case, we must be content with as many modes of similarity as there are species, and cultures within species (Osgood, 1953, p. 361).

13.4
Stimulus Salience

Various factors determine whether a particular stimulus dimension will acquire control over behavior. Among these are discrimination training, which is the subject of the next chapter, and the *salience* of that stimulus dimension. By salience, we mean roughly, "likelihood of being noticed and responded to". Even within one stimulus dimension, certain stimulus values may be more likely to be responded to. Blough's (1961) data (Section 13.2) provide an example, and Hailman (1969) was able to demonstrate the adaptive value of this phenomenon. He measured the unconditioned pecking behavior of newly hatched gull chicks elicited by various monochromatic stimuli. He obtained a function that peaked sharply and resembled a generalization gradient. The peak corresponds to the color of the adult gull's beak and reflects the chicks' tendency to peck at their parents' beaks.

Innate stimulus preferences like this can easily confound experiments on stimulus control. If we wish to be sure that the subjects of an experiment are indifferent to the stimuli used, then we must do a generalization test *before* experimental training. If all the stimuli are responded to equally at this stage, then we can regard them as psychologically equivalent for the subjects.

The *modality* of a stimulus (the sensory system that responds to it) can also determine whether or not it acquires control over a conditioned response. Recall that in interoceptive conditioning (Chapter 11) a rat presented with a taste or visual/auditory CS would acquire a response to the taste CS if the US was interoceptive, and to the visual/auditory CS if the US was exteroceptive, but not *vice versa*. Similarly, in autoshaping (Chapter 12) visual CS's have been much more effective than auditory CS's.

In operant conditioning, the modality of S^D has not generally been regarded as important, but differential control of operant behavior by stimulus modalities can be demonstrated. Avoidance learning (see Chapter 16) in rats, for example, proceeds more quickly with auditory than with visual S^D's (Frontali and Bignami, 1974).

Practical problems of stimulus salience can arise in experiments on stimulus control using "single stimulus" training techniques, such as that used by Guttman and Kalish (1956) (Section 13.2). Recall that during VI training, the stimulus conditions for the pigeons were constant. Subsequent tests showed that the pigeons generalized their responding along the wavelength dimension of the light projected onto the pecking key. Guttman and Kalish could have tested stimulus control by varying the brightness of the key, the size of the key, or even the size of the Skinner box, but they assumed that wavelength would be salient and would come to the control pecking at the key.

It turned out that they were right, but the phenomenon of *overshadowing* suggests that if a stimulus dimension is not the most salient of those present, it will *not* acquire control over responding. Pavlov (1927) demonstrated that if a compound CS, consisting of one intense and one weak component, was used in classical conditioning with dogs, very often no conditioned response was seen to the weaker component of the CS when it was presented by itself. He thus described it as overshadowed by the intense CS. Going back to the single-stimulus training situation, if the training stimulus is effectively weaker than other stimuli present, this may result in a flat generalization gradient on subsequent test, showing a lack of control by the training stimulus (or the dimension of the training stimulus tested).

Van Houten and Rudolph (1972, and reported in Mackintosh, 1977) have demonstrated this effect in two experiments with pigeons. In the first experiment, one group of pigeons was reinforced for pecking a key illuminated with white light and in the presence of a 30-mph flow of air, while another group had the same conditions, except that the key was unilluminated and the box was dark. Subsequent tests showed that air-flow speed controlled responding in the second group, but not the first. The second experiment was similar, but now a 1,000 Hz tone was presented to both groups while key pecking for food. Again, one group had a white illuminated key, while the other had an unilluminated key in a dark box.

The results are shown in Figure 13.11. As in their earlier experiment, the presence of the visual stimulus prevented control being acquired by the other modality. The other stimulus did acquire control, however, when no visual stimulus was presented.

Very often, human behavior does come under the control of several features (or dimensions) of a complex stimulus. A child may learn that buses in his or her hometown are red, have six wheels, two decks, and a rear door, that they are very noisy, and smell of diesel oil. Visiting another town and seeing rather different vehicles, the child may still correctly identify them as buses. His or her response "bus" is not attached to only one (or very few) of

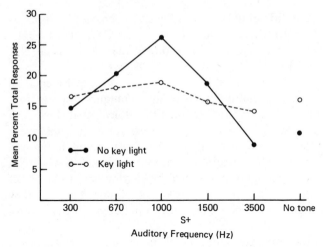

FIGURE 13.11. Van Houten and Rudolph's data on the relative gradients of auditory frequency generalization in pigeons after responses to 1000 Hz have been reinforced, either in the dark or with an illuminated key light (Mackintosh, 1977).

the stimulus features. With autistic children, on the other hand, a phenomenon has been demonstrated that resembles overshadowing. Lovaas and Schreibman (1971) trained normal and autistic children to pull a lever on an *FR*4 schedule for candy, with a compound auditory and visual discriminative stimulus:

$$S^D_{\substack{Auditory \\ + visual}} : R \overset{FR4}{\to} S^+_{Candy}$$

After acquisition (which took longer for the autistics); the children were tested with the auditory and visual components of S^D, separately. Most of the normals responded on 100 per cent of trials of both types, while the autistics tended to respond differentially, some responding on 100 per cent of one type of trial and none of the other. This abnormal acquisition of stimulus control may underlie various aspects of autistic behavior.

13.5
Temporal Control

Staddon (1972) distinguishes between two types of stimulus control: *situational control* and *temporal control*. A stimulus exercises situational control if its presence modifies the probability of the response occurring, but does not specify the moment of occurrence. We have discussed various examples of this type of control already. Staddon proposes to distinguish between this type of control and that which exists when the stimulus occurs at a certain point in time and can be shown to determine the *time* of occurrence of the response.

Consider the example of a pigeon on a multiple schedule of *FI* food reinforcement and extinction (*mult FI* EXT), where a red key light signals *FI* (S^D) and a green key light signals extinction (S^Δ). The key color exerts situational control because the color determines the rate of response, but reinforcer presentations exert temporal control in the *FI* component. As each reinforcer presentation will be followed by a postreinforcement pause in which responding is inhibited, reinforcer presentation controls the *time* at which responding occurs (or ceases to occur).

Staddon (1975) demonstrated that situational control and temporal control are independent. After training on *FI* 1 min, hungry pigeons were placed on a schedule where a visual stimulus of 3 vertical lines on the response key was presented just before food delivery on *FI* 1 min. Following training on this, generalization test sessions were introduced. In these sessions, various line-tilt stimuli (the vertical lines rotated through different angles) were presented at the end of the *FI*. The results, illustrated in Figure 13.12, lower panel, showed that line orientation controlled responding. When the visual stimuli were presented, a generalization gradient was obtained with maximum responding at vertical orientation of the lines. Line orientation thus exerted *situational control*, but it did not acquire the temporal control exerted by reinforcer presentation on an *FI* schedule, because responding *after* visual stimulus presentation did not depend on the line orientation. Food still exerted temporal control because, as can be seen in Figure 13.12, upper panel, response rates were consistently lower following food than following visual stimulus presentation alone. In other phases of this complex experiment, he was able to show temporal control in the absence of situational control.

Temporal control can be extremely precise, as illustrated in a study by J. C. Leslie (unpublished data) using *VI* and random interval (*RI*) schedules. Technically, a *VI* schedule is one in which a set of interreinforcement intervals (each having a specific value) is presented in a mixed order. An *RI* schedule is a special *VI* schedule in which the intervals are genuinely random; that is, there is a constant probability of reinforcement being made available in each unit of time. Thus, on *RI* 30 sec, there might be a probability of 1/30 of reinforcement being set up in each second. *RI* 30 sec and *VI* 30 sec appear very similar, but there is an important difference. On the *VI* schedule, but not the *RI* schedule, the *probability of a reinforcement being set up* (that is, a reinforcer being available for the next response) *increases with time since reinforcement*. On the *RI* schedule, it is a constant. Figure 13.13 shows the rate of response as a function of time since reinforcement for a rat on equivalent *RI* and *VI* schedules of food reinforcement.

Temporal control is shown in two ways. In both conditions, rate of response increases rapidly from zero immediately after reinforcement to a peak after a few seconds, and then falls to an intermediate rate. On the *RI*

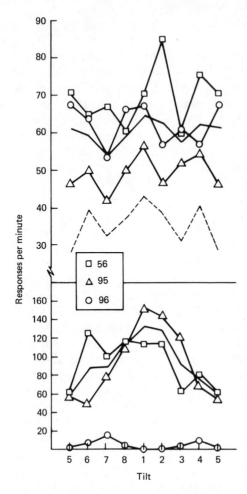

FIGURE 13.12.
Lower panel: Line-tilt generalization gradients for three birds after pairing of stimulus tilt 1 with food. Upper panel: Response rates for the birds after each line-tilt stimulus. Heavy line is mean curve, dashed line is mean rate after food (Staddon, 1975).

schedule, that rate then remains constant, but on the *VI*, it increases slowly but steadily. Thus, in each case, the local rate of responding reflects changes in the local probability of reinforcement. This is an example of very precise temporal control.

Temporal control bridges the gap between response emission (situational control) and response elicitation (reflex control). It accounts for those instances where the time of occurrence of a response is predictable, but not tied to the onset of the stimulus. Temporal control also occurs in classical conditioning, where temporal conditioning and inhibition of delay (Section 10.3) are examples.

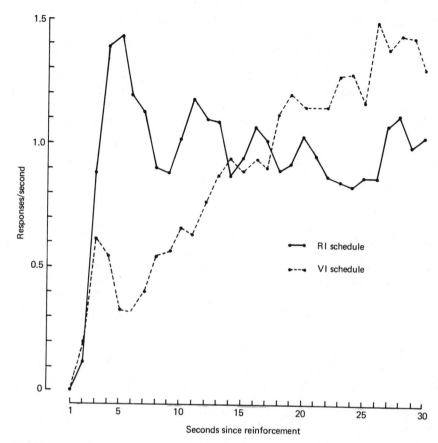

FIGURE 13.13. Local rate of responding as a function of time since reinforcement for a single rat trained first on an *RI* schedule and then on a *VI* schedule with an equivalent rate of reinforcement (J. C. Leslie, unpublished data).

References for Chapter 13

Blough, D. The shape of some wavelength generalization gradients. *Journal of the Experimental Analysis of Behavior*, 1961, **4**, 31–40.

Boring, E. G., Langfeld, H. W., and Weld, H. P. *Foundations of psychology*. New York: Wiley, 1948.

Frontali, M., and Bignami, G. Stimulus nonequivalences in go/no-go avoidance discriminations: sensory, drive, and response factors. *Animal Learning and Behavior*, 1974, **2**, 153–160.

Guttman, N. The pigeon and the spectrum and other complexities. *Psychological Reports*, 1956, **2**, 449–460.

Guttman, N., and Kalish, H. I. Discriminability and stimulus generalization. *Journal of Experimental Psychology*, 1956, **51**, 79–88.

Hailman, J. P. Spectral pecking preference in gull chicks. *Journal of Comparative and Physiological Psychology*, 1969, **67**, 465–467.

Lewis, D. J. *Scientific principles of psychology*. Englewood Cliffs, N.J.: Prentice-Hall, 1963.

Lovaas, O. I., and Schreibman, L. Stimulus overselectivity of autistic children in a two stimulus situation. *Behaviour Research and Therapy*, 1971, **9**, 305–310.

Mackintosh, N. J. Stimulus control: Attention factors. In W. K. Honig and J. E. R. Staddon (Eds.) *Handbook of operant behavior*. Englewood Cliffs, N.J.: Prentice-Hall, 1977.

Osgood, C. E. *Method and theory in experimental psychology*. New York: Oxford University Press, 1953.

Pavlov, I. P. *Conditioned reflexes*. London: Oxford University Press, 1927.

Staddon, J. E. R. Temporal control and the theory of reinforcement schedules. In R. M. Gilbert and J. R. Millenson (Eds.) *Reinforcement: Behavioral analyses*. New York: Academic Press, 1972.

Staddon, J. E. R. Limitations on temporal control: Generalization and the effects of context. *British Journal of Psychology*, 1975, **66**, 229–246.

Van Houten, R., and Rudolph, R. The development of stimulus control with and without a lighted key. *Journal of the Experimental Analysis of Behavior*, 1972, **18**, 217–222.

Wallach, H. Brightness constancy and the nature of achromatic colors. *Journal of Experimental Psychology*, 1948, **38**, 310–324.

CHAPTER 14

Discrimination

Having examined which aspects of a complex stimulus acquire control over behavior, how that control generalizes to related stimuli, and the types of control a stimulus can exert, we turn to the closely related set of issues concerned with discrimination. We now ask: (1) What is a discrimination? (2) What techniques can be used to analyze it? (3) What are the behavioral effects of discrimination training?

14.1

The Discrimination Paradigm

The prototype of all discriminations is the paradigm defined by the simplest case. This involves one response (R) class and two stimulus conditions. The response is reinforced in one of the stimulus conditions (S^D)

and is extinguished in the other stimulus condition (S^Δ). The result is that the probability of responding in S^D comes to exceed that in S^Δ. Eventually, the probability of responding in S^Δ falls to operant level or below.

The contingencies involved can be represented thus:

$$S^D: R \rightarrow S^+ \text{ and } S^\Delta: R \nrightarrow$$

Where

$\rightarrow$ is followed by

$\nrightarrow$ has no programmed consequences.

S^Δ is also used to denote conditions of *less* reinforcement, as well as zero reinforcement (extinction). Thus, S^D might be associated with *VI* 1 min food reinforcement for a hungry organism, while S^Δ signaled *VI* 5 min. In this case, we would simply expect S^D to maintain a higher probability of response than S^Δ.

Note that although we have defined discrimination as an operant paradigm, there is a closely related classical conditioning paradigm. In Section 9.3, we defined the *differentiation paradigm*, in which one CS (CS+) is followed by food (or another US) while another is also presented but never followed by the US:

$$CS+ \rightarrow US_{food} \text{ and } CS- \nrightarrow$$

We say that differentiation has occurred if, after a number of CS+ and CS− presentations, a greater response is elicited by CS+ than CS−. In parallel with the operant procedure, the response to CS− often tends towards zero with extended training. These related operant and classical procedures turn out to have very similar behavioral consequences.

Like reinforcement and extinction, discrimination is both a procedure and a behavioral process with a specified outcome. This reflects the fact that behavioral phenomena are neither pieces of behavior nor sets of environmental conditions, but interactions between the two.

Our formal definition of discrimination corresponds quite closely to our everyday use of the term. Discriminations are demonstrated at the human level by the ability to "tell two or more things apart." Some of us, for instance, discriminate the paintings of Monet from those of Manet, butter from margarine, two sets of similar fingerprints, or two similar Morse code characters. In "telling these things apart," we are doing nothing more nor less than showing differential responding in their respective presences.

Our simple discrimination paradigm takes no account of variations in complexity of discriminations. It merely states the necessary condition; namely, that two stimulus situations be differentially associated with reinforcement. However, human discriminations vary considerably in the number of stimulus situations and response alternatives involved, as the following examples show. In every case, the necessary condition of differential reinforcement (and behavior) associated with different environments is met.

1. The discriminating moviegoer does not go to every film that arrives at his or her neighborhood cinema. He or she goes (R) to some (S_A), and does not go (absence of R) to others (S_B).
2. We say that some groups of people are discriminated against when they are treated differently from the way that other people are treated. That is, the discriminated group (S_A) is treated one way (R_A), and other people (S_B) are treated another way (R_B).
3. The professional winetaster can discriminate a variety of wines that all taste the same to the novice. The professional's discrimination is evidenced by his or her ability to give a unique name (R_1, R_2, R_3, ... $R_{1,000}$) to each one of a thousand different wines (S_1, S_2, S_3, ... $S_{1,000}$).
4. In the fine discriminations that a watchmaker must make as he or she places (R_y) each one of a dozen tiny screws into its proper place (S_x), the difference between correct and incorrect positioning is measured in fractions of millimeters.

Each of these four examples illustrates a progressively more complex level of discrimination. In the technical discussions that follow, refer back, when necessary, to the corresponding example for intuitive support.

14.2
Simple Discrimination Training Techniques

In analyzing the simplest of all possible discriminations, we find that an organism emits a certain behavior with high strength in one situation, and does not emit that behavior in another situation. The basic operation for establishing such a discrimination between two situations is to reinforce a given operant in the presence of, or after, one stimulus (S^D); but to withhold reinforcement for that same operant in the presence of, or after, another stimulus (S^Δ, pronounced "ess-delta"). Two stimuli used in this fashion are called a pair of discriminative stimuli, one positive (S^D), the other negative (S^Δ).

In experimental practice, the procedure is usually complicated by the addition of several control techniques. Some of these insure that the discrimination is formed between the two desired stimuli and not some other spurious environmental changes. Others provide ways and means for quantitative and continuous measurement of response strength during the discrimination process. The need for these refinements can be seen in the simple example of providing a peanut for each chain pull that a monkey makes during a 3-min period in which a green light is on, then turning off the light and withholding peanuts for chain pulling during the next 3 min . . . . , and so on, repeatedly. Three faults can be detected in this experiment:

1. If the S^Δ interval is held constant, then a time discrimination can be made, allowing responding to come under the control of the fixed time

period of S^A, and not the environmental properties of S^D. Periods of reinforcement and nonreinforcement could acquire *temporal control* of responding, analogous to the effect of the reinforcer on an *FI* schedule (Section 12.5).

2. In this procedure, the reinforcement is continuous in S^D. This means that each of a series of responses is reinforced and *rate* of response becomes a meaningless measure. For all practical purposes, the rate is determined entirely by how long it takes the animal to eat each peanut. Thus, any changes that might occur in response strength during S^D go undetected.

3. The monkey could close its eyes, never look at the lights, and still make a good discrimination by just responding sporadically. The first occurrence of a reinforcement for a sporadic response would signal that all further responses would be reinforced for a while. Similarly, the first failure of a response to be reinforced would signal that all further responses would be extinguished for a while. Thus, the animal could base a discrimination on the presence or absence of reinforcement, rather than on the presence or absence of the green light. Formally, the reinforcer could acquire *situational control* (Section 12.5).

Herrick, Myers, and Korotkin (1959) employed an instructive procedure with rat subjects in studying discrimination between randomly alternating light (S^D) and dark (S^A) periods. To avoid fault *1*, they used variable-length S^A periods (30, 60, or 90 sec). To avoid fault *2*, and obtain a meaningful response-rate measure during the formation of the discrimination, they used *VI* 30-sec reinforcement in S^D. The *VI* schedule in S^D also precluded a discrimination based on reinforcement or nonreinforcement fault *3* since (*i*) failure to be reinforced did not necessarily signal S^A, and (*ii*) the obtaining of a reinforcement did not signal that subsequent responses would necessarily be reinforced.

To help simplify inspection of the behavioral process that results from a discrimination procedure of this sort, responses in S^D and responses in S^A may be recorded on separate cumulative recorders. The S^D recorder runs only while S^D is in effect, and the S^A recorder runs only in S^A. Figure 14.1 shows one rat's records of lever pressing from sessions 1, 6, 11, 21, and 40 on Herrick, Myers, and Korotkin's procedure. The reinforced response was lever pressing. Day *1* is essentially a generalization test: the rat had been trained originally in S^D and then on day *1*, S^A was introduced for the first time in alternation with S^D. Figure 14.1 indicates that S^D and S^A rates were nearly identical on day *1*; complete generalization of response rate from S^D to S^A occurred. As discrimination training was continued, however, the S^D and S^A rates drew apart. S^D slope appears to increase, and S^A slope continues to decrease throughout the 40 days of the discrimination procedure.

The observed increase in rate during S^D across sessions occurs because a shift from continuous to *VI* reinforcement always produces a gradual increase in rate. The sequence of changes in S^A is most interesting. Remember

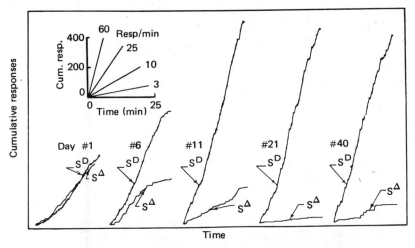

FIGURE 14.1. Sample cumulative records from daily sessions of one rat during forty days of discrimination training (Herrick, Myers, and Korotkin, 1959).

that responding is never reinforced in S^Δ. Despite this, complete generalization (equal response rates) occurred on Day *1*, and some responding was still present on Day *40*. Clearly, the visual discrimination was not "easy" for this rat. It is possible for discriminations to be acquired without many responses to S^Δ ("errors").

The results of *differentiation training* in classical conditioning are very similar in several ways. The results of two experiments by Pavlov with dogs were given in Table 10.2 and are reproduced graphically in Figure 14.2. As with operant discrimination, a response to CS− occurs initially as a result of generalization from CS+, but is then extinguished. In these examples discriminations were acquired much more rapidly than in Herrick, Myers and Korotkin's experiment. Many factors undoubtedly contributed to this, but one important influence was the previous experience of Pavlov's dogs. Typically, the dogs were used in many experiments and made many discriminations. Extensive experience of discrimination training produces subjects that learn a new discrimination very quickly.

14.3
Simultaneous Discriminations

So far, we have considered cases where S^D and S^Δ are presented *successively*. Where an operant procedure is used, this is a multiple schedule (Chapter 5). Discrimination training can also take place when several responses are available *simultaneously* but have different consequences; this is then a concurrent schedule (Chapter 5). It can be arranged by providing two manipulanda in a Skinner box, as are shown in Chapter 5. However, various other sorts of apparatus have been devised.

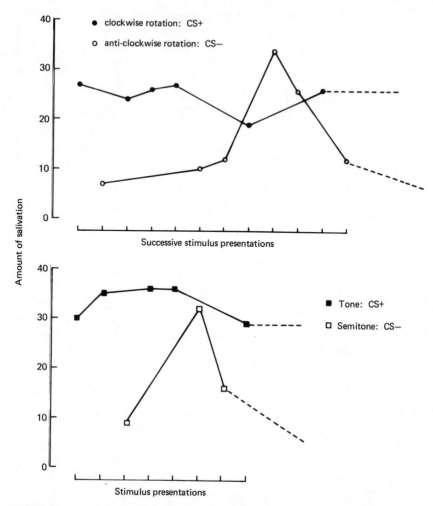

FIGURE 14.2. Data of Pavlov (1927) on the development of two discriminations by individual dogs in salivary conditioning experiments. Dotted lines indicate Pavlov's verbal report on the subsequent course of training. In each case, responding to CS− gradually decreased to zero, while responding to CS+ was maintained.

Most of these are inherently simpler than the Skinner box, measuring only choice between response alternatives and not providing any information about the probability of the selected response. Two examples are given in Figures 14.3 and 14.4. Lashley's jumping stand (Figure 14.3) involves a hungry rat jumping across a gap and through one of two windows covered by cards on which designs are displayed.

In preliminary training, the elevated platform is close to the windows, both of which are open, the cards having been removed. The rat has only to step from the platform through either window to reach food located at the

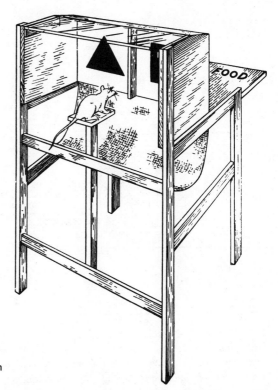

FIGURE 14.3.
One form of Lashley's jumping
stand for testing discrimination
in rats (after Lashley, 1938; from
Munn, 1950).

rear of the apparatus. When the rat has eaten, it may be picked up and returned to the elevated platform for another trial. Gradually, the jumping stand is moved further away from the windows until a true jump response has been successively approximated (shaped). Then the cards that will be used as discriminative stimuli are gradually inserted to cover the windows; at first partially, and then completely. One card (for example, the triangle) will be supported lightly by a spring that releases it if the rat jumps against it; after the jump, the rat finds itself facing a delicious bowl of bran mash. The other card (for example, the square) is locked in place, however, so that if the rat jumps against it, the animal falls into the net below. This consequence serves as punishment for that jump, in addition to providing an extinction trial. The behavioral effects of punishment (response-contingent delivery of aversive stimuli) are described in Chapter 16. Lashley thought that it would hasten the suppression of responding to S^{Δ}. This is true in general, but it also serves to make the whole apparatus aversive to the subject and it is sometimes difficult to get any jumping in the Lashley jumping stand.

We can expand the discrimination paradigm to describe this type of simultaneous discrimination. Consider an experiment in which two cards are used:

$$\boxed{-} \qquad \text{and} \qquad \boxed{+}$$

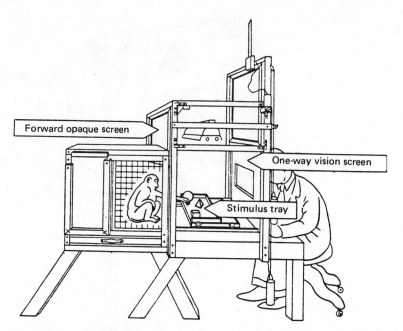

FIGURE 14.4. The Wisconsin General Test Apparatus. The experimenter can retract the stimulus tray, shuffle the objects on the tray, place food in wells under some of the blocks, and then present the tray again. The subject may then push aside any one block and pick up the food (if any) in the well underneath (Harlow, 1949).

These cards will be randomly alternated from side to side on successive trials, and whichever window contains $\boxed{+}$ will always be unlocked, while whichever window contains the $\boxed{-}$ will always be locked. The rat will adjust to a procedure of this sort in a few dozen trials, as shown by a gradual increase from 0.5 to 1.0 in the probability of responses to the correct card.

Describing the contingencies entailed in such discriminations is not difficult; the key is first to evaluate all possible stimulus situations. The individual cards are *not* stimuli, in and of themselves. Their particular pattern and relative positions only help define the stimulus situation at any time. In the present example, prior to jumping, there are two possible stimulus situations;

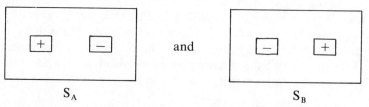

$$S_A \qquad\qquad\text{and}\qquad\qquad S_B$$

Since the experimenter will endeavor to hold every other feature in the rat's environment constant from trial to trial, we do not bother to include these constant features in the description of the two stimulus situations. Let us call the two situations S_A and S_B. If we ignore the net, the contingencies are:

$$S_A: R_L \rightarrow S^+ \text{ and } R_R \nrightarrow$$
$$S_B: R_R \rightarrow S^+ \text{ and } R_L \nrightarrow$$

Where

R_R = jump to right card
R_L = jump to left card

Comparing this with the description of simple discrimination (Section 14.1), shows that this is a double discrimination. The terms S^D and S^Δ are always *relative* to a given response, and must be carefully qualified if the discrimination is not simple. In the present example, we might reasonably say that S_A is the S^D for jumping left as well as the S^Δ for jumping right. Equally, S_B is the S^D for R_R and the S^Δ for R_L. In general, when referring to any particular situation as an S^D or S^Δ, the response class for which it serves should be stated, or at least, implied by the context.

Discriminations may be further complicated by specifying contingencies for more than just one or two response classes. In the Wisconsin General Text Apparatus (shown in Figure 14.4), right, left, and center-reaching movements are frequently specified. Food may be placed in shallow wells located under any of three objects. The arrangement of these objects serves to define discriminative stimuli. If the monkey is presented with the task of choosing a cube rather than a pyramid or a sphere, and assuming that each object must be present on each trial, then the possible stimulus situations are

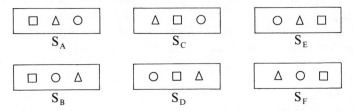

arranged in three groups, depending on the spatial location of the cube.

It should be apparent that, as the number of specified responses and stimuli increases, discriminations of any degree of complexity desired may be studied in the laboratory.

14.4

The Effects of Discrimination Training

The discrimination paradigms we have described have been used many times to successfully establish differential responding to two or more stimulus situations. Consequently, we know that they specify sufficient conditions for a discrimination to develop. But given that a subject successfully discriminates between two stimulus conditions, it does not follow that *every* difference between the two conditions controls responding.

Recall from Section 13.4 that more *salient* stimuli gain control of responding at the expense of others, even when both are equally associated with reinforcement. In the experiments of Rudolph and Van Houten described there, we saw that pitch or air-flow did not gain control over responding (that is, variations in those stimulus dimensions did not produce a generalization gradient peaked at the training stimulus value) when a visual stimulus was also present, but *dimensional control* did develop when the visual stimulus was removed. Other studies have shown that discrimination training, with presence and absence of tone or air flow as S^D and S^Δ, is sufficient to establish control by these dimensions. We may, therefore, conclude that differential reinforcement along a stimulus dimension results in dimensional control when that dimension is the only one that distinguishes S^D from S^Δ. If S^D and S^Δ differ along several dimensions, control may be established by the most salient dimension.

Discrimination training procedures can be classified as *intradimensional* or *interdimensional*. In intradimensional training, S^D and S^Δ lie on the *same* stimulus dimension (for example, two different wavelengths of light). This technique provides us with information about the effects of the *interaction* of reinforcement at S^D with extinction at S^Δ on values along that stimulus dimension. In interdimensional training, S^D and S^Δ are located on *independent* stimulus dimensions. For example, in an experiment with pigeons reinforced for key pecking, S^D could be green key illumination, while S^Δ is an oblique white line on a dark key. This technique enables us to obtain separate generalization gradients about S^D and S^Δ along the corresponding dimensions. The most important effect of intradimensional training is *peak shift*, while interdimensional training results in *inhibitory stimulus control*.

14.5
Peak Shift

Hanson (1959) gave four groups of pigeons intradimensional training with wavelength of light to key peck for food. In each case, S^D was 550 nm, while S^Δ was 555, 560, 570, and 590 nm for different groups. They were trained until responding during S^Δ reached zero, and then given a generalization test with stimuli ranging from 480 to 620 nm.

The results are shown in Figure 14.5. (A control group that received only S^D is included). The peak of the generalization gradient was *shifted* from 550 nm to around 540 nm for all four experimental groups. It had shifted away from S^Δ. A related demonstration was produced by Thomas and Williams (1963). In their study, S^Δ was located on the dimension between *two* S^D's. S^Δ was 560 nm while S^D was 540 or 580 nm. When these stimuli were used in an

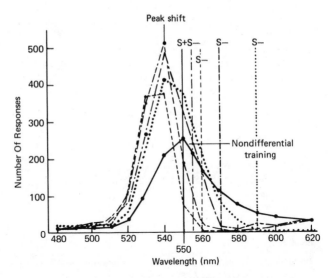

FIGURE 14.5. Effects of intradimensional discrimination training on the stimulus-generalization gradient for different groups of pigeons. For all groups, S^D (shown as $S+$) was 550 nm. For different groups, S^Δ (shown as $S-$) was 555, 560, 570, or 590 nm. A control group received nondifferential reinforcement at 550 nm (Hanson, 1959).

otherwise similar procedure with pigeons, a double peak shift was found in the generalization test. The peaks were at 530 and 590 nm. As Figure 14.6 shows, this result was consistently obtained in nine individual subjects.

These results are counterintuitive: the peaks in responding occur at stimulus values that have never been reinforced. The simplest and best-supported explanation is provided by Spence's (1937) theory of discrimination learning. Spence's theory is represented diagrammatically in Figure 14.7. He assumed that there is a strong tendency to respond at S^D and this generalizes along the training dimension. Similarly, there is a strong tendency to inhibit the response at S^Δ and this, too, generalizes along the training dimension. On this model, the tendency to respond (or probability of response) at any point on the dimension is obtained by subtracting the inhibitory effect, generalizing from S^Δ, from the excitatory effect, generalizing from S^D. Only when the excitation exceeds the inhibition, will any responding be seen.

Figure 14.7 shows that given some simple assumptions about the shape of the excitatory and inhibitory gradients, Spence's model predicts peak shift when S^D and S^Δ lie on the same stimulus dimension.

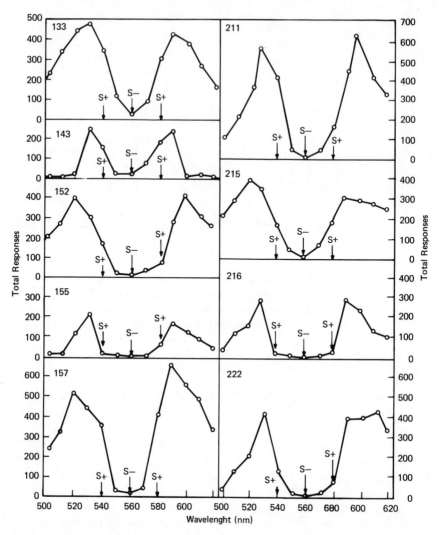

FIGURE 14.6. Generalization gradients for nine pigeons, reinforced for pecking at 560 nm and extinguished at both 540 nm and 580 nm (Thomas and Williams, 1963).

14.6
Inhibitory Stimulus Control

We have described instances of stimulus control where the *maximum* point on the generalization gradient occurs at S^D (or in the case of peak shift, near S^D), but stimulus control also exists when the *minimum* of the gradient, occurs at S^Δ. Only when S^D or S^Δ lie on independent dimensions, is it possible to sort out the excitatory (response-facilitating) effects of S^D from the

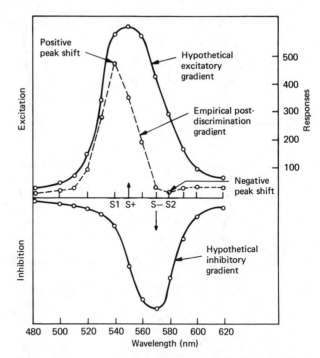

FIGURE 14.7. Hypothetical gradients of excitation and inhibition suggested by Spence. The excitatory peak is at S^D ($S+$) and the inhibitory peak is at S^Δ ($S-$). The net effect on behavior is shown as the "empirical postdiscrimination gradient" and the peak is shifted to S1 (from an original figure by M. Klein in Rilling, 1977).

inhibitory (response-suppressing) effects of S^Δ. If we vary a stimulus dimension on which S^Δ lies and which is independent of S^D (in the sense that all stimuli on that dimension are equally unlike S^D), and find an inverted generalization gradient with a minimum at S^Δ, then we can say that S^Δ exerts *inhibitory stimulus control*.

It can be very difficult to demonstrate inhibitory stimulus control, because responding may be at a very low level at all values along the S^Δ dimension. After all, this dimension has never been associated with reinforcement. One method of avoiding this problem is to measure *resistance to reinforcement* during generalization testing. Instead of responses to all stimuli being extinguished at this stage, they are all reinforced at equal rates, and this procedure is continued for several sessions.

Hearst, Besley, and Farthing (1970) trained hungry pigeons to peck a blank white key (S^D) for *VI* food reinforcement, and alternated periods with the white key with periods of extinction, with a thin black line bisecting the white key (S^Δ). When the number of responses to S^Δ was less than 4 per cent of

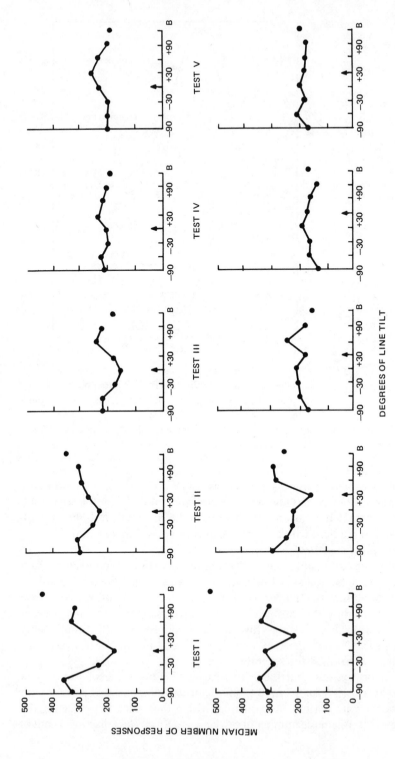

FIGURE 14.8. Median line-tilt gradients for groups of pigeons on successive generalization tests with *VI* reinforcement at all stimulus values. The upper group (9 subjects) was trained with S$^\Delta$ (S$^-$) at 0°; for the lower group (8 subjects), it was at 30° (Hearst, Besley, and Farthing, 1970).

the number to S^D, a generalization procedure was introduced. Various line tilts were presented for 30 sec at a time, and the *VI* reinforcement schedule was always in effect. The results for five successive sessions of this procedure for two groups, trained with different angled lines at S^Δ, are shown in Figure 14.8.

For both groups, a U-shaped gradient, with a minimum at the training S^Δ value, is seen on the first two sessions. By the fifth session, the curve has flattened out. This is not surprising, because the birds are now being trained *not* to discriminate on this dimension as reinforcement is available at every value presented. Note that in the first session, all values of the line tilt stimulus suppress responding below the S^D value (shown as *B*). This shows that the overall effect of the line stimulus is inhibitory. This effects has also dissipated by the fifth test session.

Such demonstrations of a gradient with a minimum at S^Δ confirm the predictions made by accounts of discrimination, such as Spence's (1937), which assume that a stimulus associated with extinction acquires inhibitory properties (see Figure 14.7). Similar predictions are made by theories of classical conditioning, from Pavlov's (1927) to very recent ones (for example, Rescorla and Wagner, 1972). These assume that a CS associated with the *absence* of the US comes to actively inhibit the conditioned response, rather than merely failing to elicit the conditioned response. It seems that stimuli associated with operant extinction acquire similar properties.

14.7
The Implications of Stimulus Control

In the last two chapters, we have examined how features of the physical environment gain control over conditioned behavior, both when behavior is reinforced in one stimulus situation, and when it is reinforced in one situation and extinguished in another. We have seen that a stimulus can acquire situational or temporal control and excitatory or inhibitory control over behavior, and that the excitatory and inhibitory influences of two stimuli can interact. All in all, the data show that conditioned behavior can be very sensitive to the *immediate* stimulus conditions.

We saw in Parts Two and Three that the contingencies of operant and classical conditioning can exert powerful and long-lasting influences on behavior, but they are essentially slow-acting processes. A considerable period of time may be required before the behavior is acquired, and still longer before a stable rate or pattern of behavior is established. It is equally true that it takes some time to bring a response under stimulus control, but once it is established, dramatic and *instant* effects can be produced by stimulus presentations.

Stimulus control techniques, therefore, give us the tools to both predict and understand the rapid changes in complex behavior that stimulus presentations can produce, and the powerful maintaining effects that stimuli can have in the apparent absence of any reinforcement. Orne (1962) obtained the latter effect in a task designed to be annoying, tiring, and boring. College students were given 2,000 papers, each requiring 224 addition sums. After instructions had been given, the subject was deprived of his or her watch and the experimenter said, "Continue to work, I will return eventually." After $5\frac{1}{2}$ hours, the experimenter gave up, because the subjects were still working. This compliance reflects an extraordinary degree of control by stimuli associated with the experiment.

The ability of discriminative stimuli to produce rapid changes in behavior suggests that controlling the availability of S^D's will effectively control the amount of behavior produced. This technique has been used most effectively to modify *excessive behaviors*, such as overeating and drinking too much alcohol. These therapeutic applications of stimulus control techniques are described in Part Eight.

References for Chapter 14

Hanson, H. M. Effects of discrimination training on stimulus generalization. *Journal of Experimental Psychology*, 1959, **58**, 321–334.

Harlow, H. F. The formation of learning sets. *Psychological Review*, 1949, **56**, 51–65.

Hearst, E., Besley, S., and Farthing, G. W. Inhibition and the stimulus control of operant behavior. *Journal of the Experimental Analysis of Behavior*, 1970, **14**, 373–409.

Herrick, R. M., Myers, J. L., and Korotkin, A. L. Changes in S^D and S^Δ rates during the development of an operant discrimination. *Journal of Comparative and Physiological Psychology*, 1959, **52**, 359–363.

Lashley, K. S. The mechanism of vision XV. Preliminary studies of the rat's capacity for detail vision. *Journal of Genetic Psychology*, 1938, **18**, 123–193.

Munn, N. L. *Handbook of psychological research on the rat.* Boston, Mass.: Houghton Mifflin, 1950.

Orne, M. T. On the social psychology of the psychological experiment: With particular reference to demand characteristics and their implications. *American Psychologist*, 1962, **17**, 776–783.

Pavlov, I. P. *Conditioned reflexes.* London: Oxford University Press, 1927.

Rescorla, R. A., and Wagner, A. R. A theory of Pavlovian conditioning: Variations in the effectiveness of reinforcement and non-reinforcement. In A. H. Black and W. F. Prokasy (Eds.) *Classical conditioning II: Current research and theory.* New York: Appleton-Century-Crofts, 1972.

Rilling, M. Stimulus control and inhibitory processes. In W. K. Honig and J. E. R. Staddon (Eds.) *Handbook of operant behavior.* Englewood Cliffs, N.J.: Prentice-Hall, 1977.

Spence, K. W. The differential response in animals to stimuli varying within a single dimension. *Psychological Review*, 1937, **44**, 430–444.

Thomas, D. R., and Williams, J. L. A further study of stimulus generalization following three-stimulus discrimination training. *Journal of the Experimental Analysis of Behavior*, 1963, **6**, 171–176.

PART FIVE

Aversive Contingencies

The first step in our systematic account of operant behavior was the definition of simple operant conditioning in Section 2.8. It was defined there as the presentation of a response-contingent stimulus, which produced a number of characteristic response changes that included an increase in response frequency. We called the stimulus in that paradigm a *positive reinforcer*, and to this point in our text, have restricted the account of operant behavior to those situations involving such positive reinforcement.

Little more than casual observation is needed, however, to detect the operation of another kind of reinforcement, defined by the operant conditioning that occurs through the response-contingent *removal* of certain environmental events. We see that birds find shelter during rainstorms, dogs move to shady spots when the summer sun beats down upon them, and people close windows when the roar of traffic is loud. In these instances, behavior is emitted that removes or terminates some environmental event: rain, heat or light, and noise. These observations suggest the existence of a distinctive class of reinforcing events. Because the operation that defines these events as reinforcing (their removal) is opposite in character to that of positive reinforcers (defined by their presentation), they are known as *negative reinforcers* (S^-). In general, negative reinforcers constitute those events whose *termination*, or reduction in intensity, will strengthen and maintain operants.

In the laboratory, aversive stimuli have typically taken the form of electric shocks, prolonged immersion in water, and certain intensities of light, sound, and temperatures. These are the events that, in common parlance, we call "annoying," "uncomfortable," "painful," "unpleasant," "noxious," and "aversive." Of these terms, we adopt the word "aversive" as a technical synonym for negative reinforcement. Aversiveness suggests the key notion of "averting," "moving away from," or "escaping from" a situation.

In the chapters that follow, we shall describe several important experimental paradigms—escape, avoidance, and punishment—as *procedures with a characteristic outcome*. In all of these procedures, negative reinforcers (aversive stimuli) operate as the special response-contingent stimuli that are used in characteristic ways in each procedure to produce its characteristic outcome.

We shall also consider classical-conditioning procedures, where the US has aversive properties. Pavlov (1927) first studied such conditioning, noting that most such US's elicit unconditioned defense reactions.

As in the preceding chapters of this book, we shall seek in Part Five to identify basic processes of operant and classical conditioning, to describe their action and interaction in particular situations, and to establish the contribution of species-typical behavior patterns to the outcome of experiments.

CHAPTER 15

Escape

We may justifiably regard the acquisition of behavior that leads to escape from (or termination of) an aversive stimulus as a fundamental behavioral process. After all, if an organism is not equipped to escape from potentially, physically damaging stimuli, its survival is endangered.

15.1

A Definition of Escape

We need a clear definition of escape in order to distinguish it from other aversive procedures that will be introduced later. In the *escape procedure*, a stimulus is presented, and termination of that stimulus is contingent upon the occurrence of a specified operant response. If this contingency results in an increase in frequency of the response and in the other associated behavioral changes described in Section 2.8, this is an instance of *escape learning*. We can also conclude that the stimulus presented is an *aversive stimulus*, and that it is a *negative reinforcer* for the response specified because its *termination* was the crucial event.

We can represent the escape procedure symbolically by the following three-term relation:

$$S^- : R_1 \rightarrow S_o \ (or\ S^- : R_1 \nrightarrow S^-)$$

where

S^- = aversive stimulus
R_1 = specified operant
S_o = absence of aversive stimulus
$\rightarrow$ = leads to
$\nrightarrow$ = leads to removal of

Note the following important points:

1. Escape learning, as defined here, is a form of operant conditioning.
2. The stimulus is designated as aversive, and its termination as negatively reinforcing, on the basis of the results of the experiment. The experiment can, therefore, be seen as a *test* of the aversiveness of the stimulus.
3. The aversive stimulus is also a discriminative stimulus.

Typically, an experiment involves a number of escape trials, each terminating after a correct response or a fixed period of exposure to the stimulus, separated by intertrial intervals in which no stimuli are presented.

15.2
Procedures Used in Escape Training

Various simple procedures have been used for escape training. An early study by Muenzinger and Fletcher (1936) used the apparatus shown in Figure 15.1. A rat was placed in a T-shaped maze that contained an electrically charged grid floor. The floor was wired so that as long as the animal remained on the grid, a continuous shock was administered to its paws. A cover over the maze (not shown) prevented the rat from escaping the shock by jumping out of the apparatus. One escape route remained; the animal could find safety by running consistently to a designated arm of the T.

Behavior in the T-maze is usually measured on each trial by timing the rat from start to safe, or by tallying the "incorrect" turns ("errors") into the nonsafe arm of the T. On early trials, the rat is equally likely to run right or left, but as acquisition of the response of turning to the safe side proceeds, responses to the "incorrect" side decrease. We see the average trend for 25 rats in Figure 15.2. We may infer from the declining error curve in Figure 15.2 that,

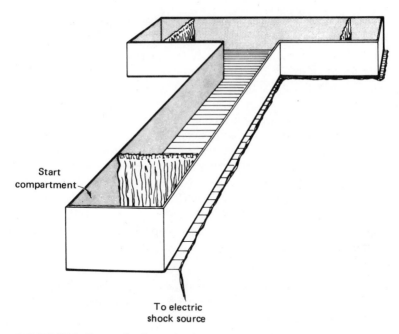

Start
compartment

To electric
shock source

FIGURE 15.1. T-maze for the study of escape behavior (after Muenzinger and Fletcher, 1936).

FIGURE 15.2. Percentage of incorrect turns in 100 trials of escape training (after Muenzinger and Fletcher, 1936).

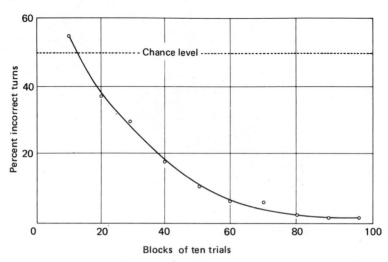

after 100 trials of escape training, acquisition of the turning response leading to safety has occurred.

More recent studies of escape have generally used apparatus in which a long series of trials (S⁻ presentations) can be presented at appropriate intervals without the subject having to be removed. In the Skinner box, for example, bar presses can be arranged to terminate electric shocks coming from the grid floor. But the most common apparatus for the study of escape conditioning has been the *shuttle box* of Figure 15.3. This box is simply a two-compartment chamber, where the measured operant response is movement from one chamber to the other (usually movement in either direction counts as a response). Movement is detected by spring switches under the floor, or by photocells. The aversive stimulus (S⁻) is usually pulsed electric shock, delivered through the grid floor. Escape behavior is rapidly acquired in this apparatus, possibly because the required operant response (running) is closely related to the unconditioned behavior elicited by the shock.

FIGURE 15.3. A shuttle box designed to study aversive contingencies with rats. When the shutter is raised, the rat can jump the hurdle to get into the other half of the apparatus (after Miller, 1951).

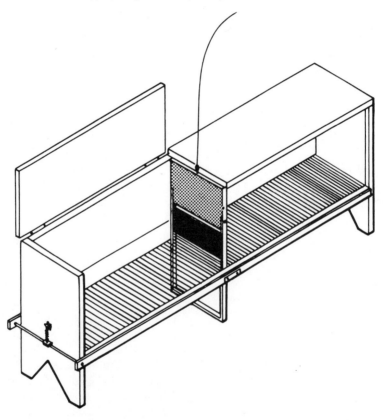

Most studies have employed rats as subjects and electric shock as the S⁻.
These choices were made because it is relatively easy to deliver a controlled
shock to a rat through the grid on which it is standing. Other stimuli (for
example, noise or blasts of air) are less easy to control, and other species
present a variety of methodological problems. So we must be ready to expect
some surprises when the escape paradigm is used with other species and other
stimuli.

15.3

Parameters of Escape Training

Dinsmoor and Winograd (1958) elegantly demonstrated schedule
control of escape behavior, and the influence of shock intensity. In their
study, rats learned to press a lever which turned off electric shocks
intermittently delivered through the grid floor. Following a lever press, there
was a 2-min intertrial interval (ITI), during which responses had no effects
and no shocks were delivered.

When shock presentation elicited a lever press with a low and consistent
latency (that is, escape learning had occurred), a *VI* 30-sec contingency was
introduced. The ITI remained 2 min, but during shock, responses were now
effective in escaping shock only after shock had been on for an average
duration of 30 sec. This intermittent-reinforcement procedure produced a
moderate and sustained rate of bar pressing in the presence of shock. The
pattern of behavior resembled *VI* food-reinforced responding.

Dinsmoor and Winograd explored the effects of varying intensities of
shock on this baseline of *VI* escape responding. Their technique was to begin a
session with a given intensity of shock present, say 100 uamps (1 uamp =
10^{-6} amp), observe the frequency of responding for a long enough period to
obtain a reliable rate measure, then change to a different value of shock, say
400 uamps, and repeat the process. In a 2-hr session they were thus able to
obtain escape rate measurements from as many as six different shock-
intensity values. A typical session appears in Figure 15.4.

When the overall function of response rate against shock intensity is
plotted, Figure 15.5A results. This function was obtained from the same rat
whose cumulative curves appear in Figure 15.4. Figure 15.5A indicates that,
over the range studied, as shock intensity increased, escape response rate
continuously increased as well.

Figures 15.5B and 15.5C document the results of similar experiments with
other aversive agents. Figure 15.5B illustrates the effects of increasing the
intensity of a sound on *VI* lever-pressing escape rate of cats. The results of
Figure 15.5C were obtained from a group of rats whose pushing of a panel on
FI contingencies terminated lights of various intensities. Both the (B) and (C)
panels of Figure 15.5 demonstrate that maxima in escape behavior occur if
the aversive-stimulus intensity is made very great. the decline in responding

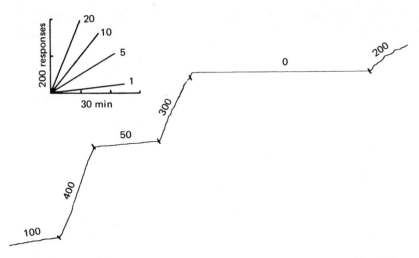

FIGURE 15.4. Cumulative *VI* escape responding at different shock intensities during the same session. Shock intensities are given in µamps (Dinsmoor and Winograd, 1958).

associated with very intense aversive events is not well understood; it is thought to be due to a general suppressive (emotional) effect of strong aversive stimuli.

Since we are interested in possible parallels between negative and positive reinforcement, we may ask to what variable in the field of positive reinforcement does aversive stimulus intensity correspond? Superficially, the intensity of a negative reinforcer seems analogous to the magnitude of a positive reinforcer. Intensity of S^- and magnitude of S^+ are both stimulus properties of the reinforcer, and increases in both variables generate increases in responding. But closer analysis of the functional role that these

FIGURE 15.5. Escape response rates as a function of the intensities of three different aversive stimuli [(A) Dinsmoor and Winograd, 1958; (B) Barry and Harrison, 1957; (C) Kaplan, 1952)].

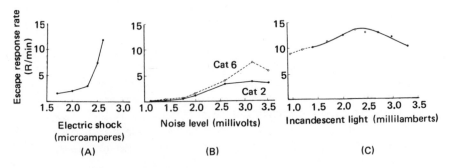

two variables play in negative and positive reinforcement, respectively, suggests that the analogy is only superficial. The principal effect of raising the intensity of a light, or a sound, or a shock, from a low to a high value, is that the reinforcement of behavior is made possible through termination of the new intensity. Increasing the intensity of an S^- has, therefore, the logic of a reinforcement-establishing operation; it makes possible the strengthening of behavior. Thus, in the presence of a weak intensity of light, a rat will not show conditioning of a response that terminates the light; so too, with a small value of food deprivation, a response that produces food will not be strengthened. Conversely, high values of both shock intensity and food deprivation make it possible to use shock termination and food presentation as reinforcers for conditioning operants. Thus, shock intensity is better described as a *motivational* variable, than as a reinforcement magnitude variable (see Part Seven).

An operant need not completely terminate an aversive stimulus to exhibit strengthening. Merely reducing the level of stimulus intensity is often sufficient to condition and maintain operant behavior. Small reductions in electric intensity, when contingent upon lever pressing, form the basis of a procedure for measuring the level of aversive stimulation that rats will tolerate (Weiss and Laties, 1959, 1963). In this procedure, each lever press produces a small decrement in the intensity of a prevailing aversive shock. A fixed period of time without a single lever press produces a small increment in the intensity of the stimulus. The relations between R and S^- are schematically illustrated in Figure 15.6. The first R emitted in Figure 15.6 reduces the intensity of S^- by one step. A second R follows closely on the heels of the first R, and the intensity falls another step. The criterion time then elapses without a response occurring, as a result of which, S^- is incremented one step. A further such period elapses without an R, and yet another increment in S^- occurs. The next 6 R's occur frequently enough to drive the aversive intensity down to zero. Subsequently, the intensity rises three steps anew in the absence of further emitted responses.

This procedure acts to bring about a state of equilibrium. The organism

FIGURE 15.6. Hypothetical data from a shock-intensity reduction procedure.

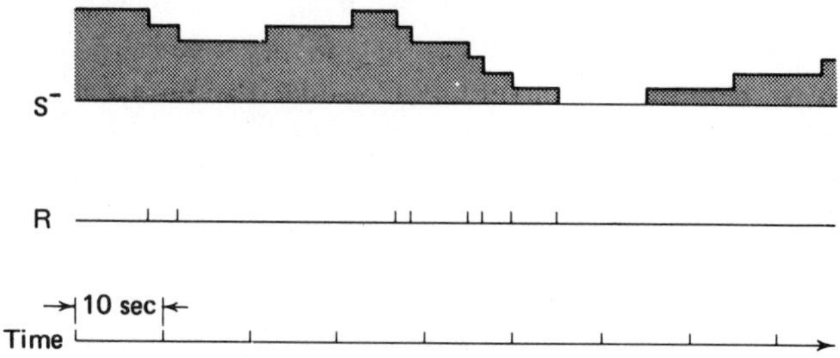

maintains a rate of responding that holds the S⁻ intensity within a small range of (usually low) intensities. When S⁻ is electric shock, this equilibrium is spoken of as the *shock-tolerance level*. The actual level maintained varies with a number of procedural parameters, and is sensitive to the administration of certain pharmacological agents, such as analgesics and anaesthetics. Figure 15.7 illustrates the typical behavioral stability that this procedure generates. In addition, the figure shows the behavioral result of intravenous administration of a small quantity of morphine to a rhesus monkey, working on such a procedure. (Figure 15.7 amounts to a much reduced and extended record of the S⁻ contour of Figure 15.6.) Injection of morphine is rapidly followed by a rise in shock tolerance to a new intensity level, which is held throughout the remaining 40 min shown. The effect confirms the well-known clinical properties of morphine, and suggests that the procedure provides a useful experimental tool for measuring the analgesic properties of various drugs.

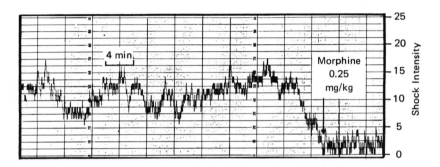

FIGURE 15.7. Effect of intravenously administered morphine sulfate, 0.25 mg/kg, on shock-tolerance level. Record reads from *right to left* (Weitzman, Ross, Hodos, and Galambos, 1961).

15.4
Bar Holding During Escape Training

In our discussions of the effects of positive reinforcement in Chapter 7, we frequently encountered behavior that was not directly specified in the programmed reinforcement contingency. It developed and then interacted with the reinforced operants, sometimes in competition and sometimes to enhance them. Analogous interactions occur in negative reinforcement procedures, too.

Bar press (lever press) rates of rats in shock-escape training remain rather low, and very often, the period in between presses is occupied by the rat standing over the bar, holding it down. This *bar-holding* behavior is never explicitly reinforced, and is absent when the same apparatus is used for positive reinforcement. We, therefore, need to explain why it is so common during escape training.

Consider these two explanations: (1) The rat holds the bar because this positions the animal optimally to escape the next shock; (2) Bar holding occurs because it is closely related to the rat's repertoire of *species-typical aversive behaviors*, or unconditioned responses to aversive stimulation.

The first explanation, that bar holding is indirectly reinforced because S^- is terminated more rapidly, was supported by the observations of Campbell (1962). He simply compared the speed (latency) with which S^- (shock) was terminated on trials on which the rat was holding the bar at the moment of shock onset with speed on other trials. He found that shock offset was indeed faster when preceded by bar holding. A direct test of this idea was carried out by Dinsmoor, Matsuoka, and Winograd (1958). They found that if the rat was required to release the bar, press it, and then release it again before shock terminated, holding declined to around 50 per cent of its level than when the rat had merely to release it and then press it. Introducing a penalty for bar holding at the time of S^- presentation was thus effective in reducing bar holding. In a second experiment, bar holding prior to S^- presentation resulted in a 0, 1.5, or 3-sec delay before a press-release sequence could produce escape. Bar holding declines as a function of the delay. At 3-sec delays, very little bar holding occurred over the course of 200 training trials.

Even though bar holding shows itself modifiable by these kinds of special response-shock offset contingencies, it is still possible that in typical escape procedures that lack these contingencies, its occurrence mainly reflects species-typical, unconditioned aversive behavior. Freezing, or immobility, is a highly probable, unconditioned response of rats to foot shocks and other aversive agents. In natural settings, the adaptive value of aversive-produced immobility seems clear. Small rodents are preyed upon by larger carnivorous mammals and birds of prey, usually at night. If the rat freezes before the predator sees it, it may be safe from detection and attack. As the escape procedure involves regular presentation of aversive stimuli, we would not be surprised if freezing becomes a highly probable behavior. Furthermore, since the aversive stimulus repeatedly occurs in the same situation (the apparatus), it seems likely that freezing gets classically conditioned to apparatus cues signaling shock, such as the bar.

It is, therefore, possible that the bar holding observed represents largely classically-conditioned freezing on the bar. Davis (1977) points out that in many escape-training studies, bar holding occupies the greater part of the session and is only interrupted when shock is delivered. Davis also found that bar holding diminished greatly if the bar was designed so that the rat could not comfortably freeze on it. This strongly suggests that bar holding is the result of an interaction between a species-typical response topography (freezing), the physical characteristics of the operandum, and the position in which the rat finds itself, immediately after having emitted a reinforced escape response.

The "bar-holding story" has been told here, not because bar holding has especial intrinsic interest, but because this apparently puzzling behavior provides further evidence that we cannot understand the organism we observe unless we are prepared to take into account *all* of its relevant behavioral processes and their interactions.

15.5
Overview

In this chapter, we have defined and described effective procedures for studying escape training. We have also outlined some representative results, and drawn parallels with positive reinforcement. The effectiveness of escape training demonstrates that operant behavior can be maintained by *removal* of a stimulus (a negative reinforcer), as well as by presentation of a stimulus (a positive reinforcer). Either procedure can be used to define a set of reinforcing stimuli and/or a class of characteristic, contingent behavior modifications. The existence of negative reinforcement greatly extends the scope of operant conditioning. Potentially, there are as many significant behavioral phenomena associated with negative reinforcement as have been demonstrated with positive reinforcement. Knowledge of these negative-reinforcement phenomena will greatly enhance our ability to account for everyday behavior, and to suggest new ways of analyzing behavioral problems.

The possible role of classical conditioning in situations designed to evaluate negative reinforcement was illustrated by the example of bar holding by rats during escape training. Bar holding probably develops from unconditioned shock-elicited freezing, and is then conditioned and maintained because it facilitates speedy escape responses. This interaction reminds us that we can never understand all the effects of an operant-reinforcement contingency unless we include (1) The species-typical behavioral tendencies of the organism in the experimental situation, (2) The role of clandestine classical conditioning, (3) The detailed effects, direct and implicit, of the contingency itself.

References for Chapter 15

Barry, J. J., and Harrison, J. M. Relations between stimulus intensity and strength of escape responding. *Psychological Reports*, 1957, **3**, 3–8.

Campbell, S. L. Lever-holding and behavior sequences in shock-escape. *Journal of Comparative and Physiological Psychology*, 1962, **55**, 1047–1053.

Davis, H. Response characteristics and control during lever-press escape. In H. Davis and H. M. B. Hurwitz (Eds.) *Operant-Pavlovian interactions*. Hillsdale, New Jersey: Lawrence Erlbaum, 1977.

Dinsmoor, J. A., Matsuoka, Y., and Winograd, E. Barholding as a preparatory response in escape-from-shock training. *Journal of Comparative and Physiological Psychology*, 1958, **51**, 637–639.

Dinsmoor, J. A., and Winograd, E. Shock intensity in variable interval escape schedules. *Journal of the Experimental Analysis of Behavior*, 1958, **1**, 145–148.

Kaplan, M. The effects of noxious stimulus intensity and duration during intermittent reinforcement of escape behavior. *Journal of Comparative and Physiological Psychology*, 1952, **45**, 538–549.

Miller, N. E. Learnable drives and rewards. In S. S. Stevens (Ed.) *Handbook of Experimental Psychology*. New York: Wiley, 1951.

Muenzinger, K. F., and Fletcher, F. M. Motivation in learning, VI. Escape from electric shock compared with hunger-food tension in the visual discrimination habit. *Journal of Comparative Psychology*, 1936, **22**, 79–91.

Pavlov, I. P. *Conditioned reflexes*. London. Oxford University Press, 1927.

Weiss, B., and Laties, V. G. Titration behavior on various fractional escape programs. *Journal of the Experimental Analysis of Behavior*, 1959, **2**, 227–248.

Weiss, B., and Laties, V. G. Characteristics of aversive thresholds measured by a titration schedule *Journal of the Experimental Analysis of Behavior*, 1963, **6**, 563–572.

Weitzman, E. D., Ross, G. S., Hodos, W., and Galambos, R. Behavioral method for study of pain in the monkey. *Science*, 1961, **133**, 37–38.

CHAPTER 16

Avoidance

Consider the escape paradigm applied to the example of someone walking in the rain:

$$\underset{\substack{\text{rain}\\\text{falling}}}{S^-} \quad : \quad \underset{\substack{\text{put}\\\text{up umbrella}}}{R} \quad \rightarrow \quad \underset{\substack{\text{rain}\\\text{avoided}}}{S_o} \quad (\text{or } S^- : R \nrightarrow S^-)$$

This seems to be a clear case of escape behavior; putting up the umbrella is reinforced by escape from the rain. Consider, however, another behavioral element of this incident; the fact that our hypothetical subject was carrying an umbrella. Can we explain the "umbrella carrying response" in terms of an operant reinforcement contingency? It seems likely that umbrella-carrying on a showery day is reinforced by the *avoidance* of getting wet that would otherwise occur. We can thus state:

$$\underset{\substack{\text{showery} \\ \text{day}}}{S^D} \quad \underset{\substack{\text{carry an} \\ \text{umbrella}}}{: R} \quad \rightarrow \quad \underset{\substack{\text{rain avoided}}}{S_o}$$

Note the differences between this three-term relation and the one for escape. The discriminative stimulus (S^D) for making the response is not now an aversive stimulus as well: it need not actually be raining when we leave the house for us to take an umbrella. Furthermore, the consequence of making the response is rather different. In the escape paradigm, S^- offset occurs as soon as the response is made. In the avoidance paradigm, *S^- is prevented from occurring* by the response.

Avoidance behavior is a pervasive and important phenomenon, but its analysis has posed problems for the behavioral scientist. As an introduction to these problems, let us consider an early study which demonstrated that avoidance behavior involved negative reinforcement.

16.1
Avoidance Behavior Is Not Classically Conditioned

Early studies of behaviors generated and maintained by aversive stimuli assumed that the observed behavioral effects were some kind of classical conditioning. This assumption was challenged in a pair of important experiments carried out in the late 1930's. Brogden, Lipman, and Culler (1938) placed guinea pigs in individual activity wheels. A 1,000 Hz tone was presented to the animal, and 2 sec later, a shock was administered through the floor of the cage. If the guinea pig ran in the wheel while the tone was on, and caused it to turn an inch or more, then shock was not delivered. The guinea pigs learned to turn the wheel, and thereby avoid shock on almost every trial. Figure 16.1 relates the observed increasing percentages of trials with a wheel-turning response to the average day that each particular percentage was attained.

In this procedure, there existed a pairing between stimuli such as we discussed earlier, under the topic of classical conditioning. The tone, which could act as a CS, reliably preceded a shock, which is a powerful US that elicits wheel turning as an unconditioned response. To test the possibility that their results could be explained in terms of classical conditioning, Brogden, Lipman, and Culler carried out a second experiment. They simply used the same stimuli, apparatus, and subjects, but in a classical-conditioning procedure. Thus, tone-shocks were presented in a fixed sequence, and wheel-turning responses had no effects.

The results of the second experiment are shown in Figure 16.2. The average percentage of trials on which a wheel turn occurred, rose erratically to around 40 per cent, and then declined towards 20 per cent. Comparison with Figure 16.1 shows a striking difference. Clearly, the results of the first

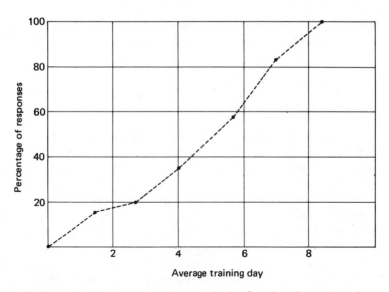

FIGURE 16.1. Acquisition of avoidance behavior. Data from four guinea pigs (after Brogden, Lipman, and Culler, 1938).

FIGURE 16.2. Percentage of trials with a wheel turn in a classical conditioning procedure (after Brogden, Lipman, and Culler, 1938).

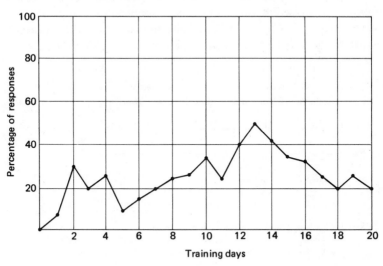

experiment could not be explained in terms of classical conditioning, alone, because the explicit classical-conditioning procedure, using exactly the same stimuli, maintained a much lower response rate. We may, therefore, conclude that the response contingency in the first experiment somehow contributed greatly to the acquisition and maintenance of wheel turning. Apparently, *wheel turning was reinforced by shock avoidance.*

16.2
A Definition of Avoidance

In an avoidance procedure, a stimulus is programmed to occur unless a specified operant response occurs. Occurrence of that response cancels or postpones these stimulus presentations. If this contingency results in an increase in frequency of that response, then *avoidance learning* has occurred, and the stimulus has *negative reinforcement properties* for that response. Notice that the avoidance procedure supplements the escape paradigm in giving us a second, independent way of discovering negative reinforcers, and thus for defining *aversive stimuli.*

Representing avoidance diagrammatically is awkward, because the crucial element is the postponement or cancelation of an event which has not yet occurred. Figure 16.3 illustrates time lines for two types of *avoidance schedule.* (The aversive stimuli are assumed to be electric shocks.) In *free operant avoidance* (Figure 16.3A), shocks occur at regular intervals, the shock-shock (S-S) interval, unless an operant response occurs. If it does, the next shock is postponed for a period of time, the response-shock (R-S) interval. On this schedule, no shocks will ever be delivered if each response follows the preceding one within the response-shock interval. In *discriminated avoidance* (Figure 16.3B), a discriminative signal (S^D) precedes each shock delivery. A response during the warning S^D cancels the shock delivery

FIGURE 16.3. Timelines illustrating the procedures of: (A) free operant avoidance; (B) discriminated avoidance; (C) escape.

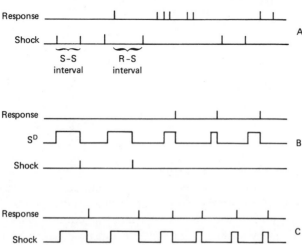

and (usually) terminates the S^D. Responses during the intertrial interval have no effect. Every shock will be avoided if one response occurs during each S^D. This was the procedure used by Brogden, Lipman, and Culler (1938). For purposes of comparison, Figure 16.3C illustrates the escape procedure described in Section 15.1.

16.3
Discriminated Avoidance

Some data on the acquisition by rats of a lever-press response to avoid foot shock are shown in Figure 16.4. After an intertrial interval which averaged 10 min, a 1,000 Hz tone S^D was presented. If the lever was pressed during the S^D, it was terminated and shock was avoided. This study also involved an escape contingency. If the rat failed to make the avoidance response within 60 sec, shock was delivered continuously until a response occurred (Hoffman and Fleshler, 1962). Figure 16.4 shows that the average response latency for the group of rats declined steadily across sessions, while the number (percentage) of avoidance responses increased. Both latency and number of responses reached an *asymptote* in the seventh session and showed little further change. The third measure shown is the number (percentage) of intertrial intervals (S^Δ) in which a response occurred. Comparison of the avoidance curve with the interval responding curve gives a classic example of the development of a discrimination. S^D responding increases first, then S-delta responding increases. Then, as S^D responding continues to increase, S-delta responding reaches a peak, thereafter declining towards zero. The acquisition of avoidance behavior and its discriminative control thus proceeds in the fashion familiar to us from many types of positively-reinforced behavior.

In discriminated avoidance, the response generally has *two* consequences: S^D termination, and shock avoidance. What happens when only one of these consequences is provided for the response? Kamin (1957) trained four groups of rats in a shuttle box (see Figure 15.2) under the following conditions. One group could avoid shock and terminate the S^D, if they "shuttled" during the S^D (discriminated avoidance group). Another group could neither terminate the S^D nor avoid shock, no matter what they did (classical-conditioning group). A third group could avoid shock if they responded during S^D, but S^D duration was unaffected by responses (pure shock-avoidance group). A final group could terminate the S^D by responding during the S^D, but a shock was still delivered at the scheduled time (S^D termination group). The results for all four of these groups are shown in Figure 16.5. Note that Kamin's first two groups are the same as Brogden, Lipman, and Culler's (1938) groups; and despite the different apparatus and species, Kamin replicated the earliest results. Thus, the discriminated-avoidance group acquired and maintained a much higher level of responding than the classical-conditioning group.

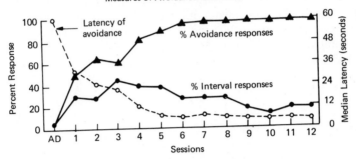

Measures of Avoidance: Bar Press

FIGURE 16.4. Three measures of behavior during acquisition of a discriminated, lever-press avoidance response. Data are from a group of 12 rats (Hoffman and Fleshler, 1962).

More interesting data yet were revealed by the pure shock-avoidance group and the S^D-termination group. As Figure 16.5 shows, both of these groups maintained a level of performance, intermediate between the discriminated-avoidance group and the classical-conditioning group. This suggests that, while pure shock avoidance *per se* produces a certain level of responding, the S^D-termination contingency also enhances responding. So the removal or absence of the S^D for the avoidance response appears to be a reinforcing event, an idea to which we shall return shortly.

FIGURE 16.5. Avoidance behavior of the four groups of rats in Kamin's experiment (after Kamin, 1957).

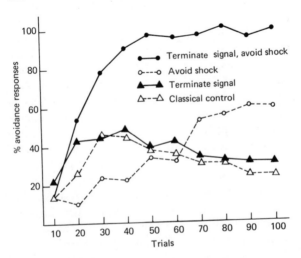

16.4

Free Operant Avoidance

Free operant avoidance is, as its name implies, a procedure in which a response occurring at any time serves to postpone or eliminate programmed shocks. No signals are ever presented to warn the subject of impending shocks. This schedule, first devised by Sidman (1953), leaves the animal free to respond at any time, and without any external cues as to when to make that response.

An example of the acquisition of a lever-pressing response by a rat on Sidman's avoidance schedule is shown in Figure 16.6. In this case, both the R-S and S-S intervals were 30 sec. After an initial period where many shocks were delivered, the rat developed fairly rapidly a sustained moderate rate of responding, which resulted in shocks being delivered only occasionally (Verhave, 1959). This means that only rarely did the rat pause for more than 30 sec (the R-S interval) or fail to respond within 30 sec of receiving a shock (the S-S interval).

This is a remarkable performance when you consider that when the rat is successful, nothing happens. That is, since no external stimulus consequences are presented, the only feedback from making a response constitute kinaesthetic aftereffects and whatever small noise the lever makes. Compare this situation with the discriminated-avoidance schedule, where an explicit S^D

FIGURE 16.6. Cumulative records of lever press avoidance during training of a rat in free-operant avoidance. Hatch marks indicate shocks. The first record is at the bottom of the figure (Verhave, 1959).

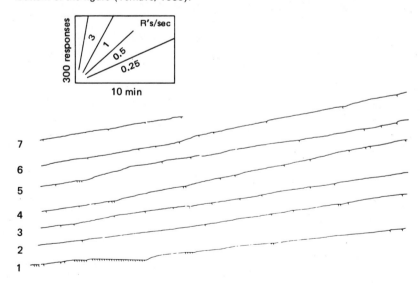

signals the time to respond, and S^D termination usually follows completion of the response.

The precise control of the subject's behavior that can be established on the Sidman avoidance schedule is illustrated in Figure 16.7. This figure shows the probability of responding at any time as a function of the time since the last response for a rat on various, free operant-avoidance schedules (Sidman, 1966). These curves resemble in many ways positive reinforcement, fixed-interval (FI) scallops (see Figure 5.5), even though the FI scallop is plotted as a function of time since *reinforcement* rather than, as in this case, time since a response. The data in Figure 16.7 illustrate transitions between one set of

FIGURE 16.7. An animal's temporal discrimination before and after changes in the R-S interval. Response probability is calculated as number of responses at time *t* divided by number of responses at *t* or later (Sidman, 1966).

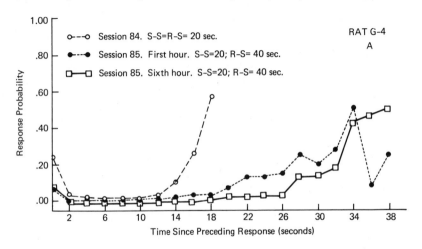

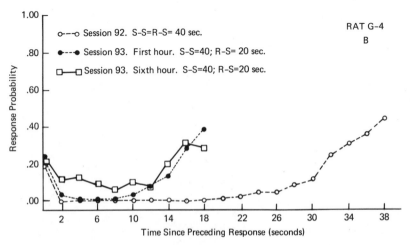

schedule values and another. Within the first hour on the new schedule, behavior changes so that responding is improbable, except toward the end of the R-S interval. By the sixth hour, a smooth curve has developed.

These data constitute clear evidence for *temporal control* of avoidance responding (c.f., Section 13.5) and the transitions can be made without many shocks being delivered. Sidman (1966) reports that during the transition shown in Figure 16.7A, only eight shocks occurred in the first hour on the new schedule. It appears that the passage of time since making a response acts as a discriminative stimulus that determines when the next response will occur.

Temporal discriminations are, however, not a necessary condition of successful performance on Sidman avoidance schedules, since rats can successfully avoid on schedules where the R-S and S-S intervals are variable and such discriminations rendered impossible. Consequently, we cannot attribute responding in general on free operant avoidance to the action of temporal discriminations. Rather, temporal discriminations develop whenever shocks are delivered at specific times since a response or a shock. The subject capitalizes on that information to respond as efficiently as possible.

16.5
What Reinforces Avoidance Behavior?

Everyday descriptions of avoidance behavior are couched in purposive terms. We say that we turn the wheel of a skidding car opposite to the direction of the skid *to* avoid a crash, that one builds a bridge in a certain way *to* avoid its collapsing, that a deer flees *in order to* avoid a pursuing wolf. The term "to," or "in order to," imputes a certain purposive quality to the behavior. The purpose of a given act, and hence its apparent explanation, is given in a statement of the aversive or undesirable consequences that might have occurred, had the act not averted them. Purposive or teleological explanations are generally rejected by scientists on the grounds that such explanations purport to let a future (and, therefore, nonexistent) event be the cause of a present (existing) event; and because purposive explanations add nothing to the bare facts. To say, for instance, that a stone falls to the ground *in order* to return to its natural resting place, the earth, tells no more than the purely descriptive statement: stones fall to the earth. And yet, by seeming to be a sufficient explanation, the teleological statement tends to discourage further examination of the phenomena, thus postponing a functional analysis.

When faced with the facts of avoidance behavior, behavior theorists have persistently sought to explain them by a mechanism that was clearly nonteleological. However, in attempting to frame an account of avoidance behavior that was analogous to simple operant conditioning or escape behavior, they struck a serious problem. In both simple operant conditioning (Section 2.8) and escape learning (Section 15.1), behavior is strengthened by making a stimulus change consequent upon that behavior. In avoidance learning, however, the reinforcing stimulus is present neither after the response nor before it. Rather, it occurs intermittently in the absence of responding.

There are two routes to a solution of this problem. Either some stimulus, or stimulus change, must be identified which is a consequence of responding and acquires the power to reinforce avoidance responses; or we accept the facts of avoidance behavior as a pristine, irreducible, primitive process, thereby abandoning any attempt to explain them further at the behavioral level. Although some theorists (for example, Herrnstein, 1969) have called for the adoption of the latter strategy, in three of the following sections we examine the role of various possible stimulus events that are found in avoidance learning, and which could serve to reinforce the behavior that develops. Only if avoidance behavior proves refractory to the explanatory power in our familiar and established behavioral processes, will we then be willing to confer upon it the special status of a new principle requiring no explanation.

16.6
Removal of Discrete Conditioned Aversive Stimuli

Some avoidance behavior could be reinforced by the removal of discrete, punctate, conditioned aversive stimuli. This interpretation seems appropriate especially in discriminated avoidance. Suppose we assume that avoidance learning proceeds by two distinct stages. In stage 1, an S^D becomes repeatedly paired with shock. This occurs on early shock trials, before actual successful avoidance behavior has begun to occur. At that time, through classical conditioning, the S^D becomes a conditioned aversive stimulus. Now the organism is set for stage 2. Any response that now happens to result in the removal of this conditioned aversive stimulus will be reinforced, and a conditioning process set into operation that is properly viewed as a form of escape learning.

In its simplest form, as outlined here, this two-factor account, derived originally from discriminated avoidance studies that it handles quite well, falls short of explaining all types of avoidance. We want to examine some of the problems posed for two-factor avoidance theory, for their solution obliges us to expand our ideas of reinforcement and to deploy new concepts.

One problem we notice is that, as avoidance learning progresses, we observe the S^D to elicit less and less fear from the subject. A well-trained rat subject typically nonchalantly approaches the avoidance lever as late as possible after the S^D appears, and seemingly without any emotion, depresses the lever, avoiding shock. This objection to a two-factor account, however, is really not a systematic one, for we defined an aversive stimulus not by its ability to elicit emotional responses, but by its ability to support escape behavior. Although it may come as a surprise that the rat loses its fear to the stimulus that signals shock, it does continue to respond in a way that indicates that the signal remains operationally aversive.

A more serious problem arises when we try to explain Sidman avoidance, which contains no explicit S^D, by a theory based on escape from S^D's paired with shocks. Attempts have been made to postulate interoceptive and temporal stimuli that, although not directly observed, could play a role similar to the exteroceptive stimuli of discriminated avoidance. Although temporal discriminations can, and probably do, play a role in Sidman avoidance with fixed R-S and S-S intervals, they cannot, as we pointed out, explain avoidance learning when these intervals are variable. The problem with hypothetical proprioceptive cues is just that they have remained hypothetical. And the various studies that have attempted to surgically eliminate as many of these as possible (Taub and Berman, 1968) have found avoidance learning and maintenance remarkably unaffected. So invoking hypothetical, conditioned aversive stimuli seems a rather unattractive way of preserving two-factor theory. If we want two-factor theory to work here, we are going to have to find some observable event or events that could serve to motivate and reinforce the avoidance response.

One other possible problem with the theory of avoidance that we are considering in detail here might seem to be the prediction that avoidance behavior, once conditioned, should show a cyclic tendency to extinguish and then recondition. Such cycles seem predicted because, whenever avoidance behavior does occur, the association between S^D and S^- is broken. Breaking that association eventually renders the S^D ineffective as a conditioned aversive stimulus; hence, it no longer can reinforce an operant avoidance response. Yet at precisely the moment when that occurs, and the subject fails to avoid, the S^D-S^- pairing is reinstated, and S^D can once again support avoidance learning. Actually, such cycles do occur, especially in rats' bar pressing under Sidman avoidance of brief mild electric foot shock. But we know, too, that much human avoidance behavior seems protected in some way from these extinction cycles. One burn from a hot stove may suffice to condition a lifetime of wariness. The rat of Figure 16.8 also shows a high degree of resistance to extinction. Following training on a free-operant avoidance of shock schedule, this animal responded steadily for over two hours and made over 1,000 responses. However, such robust performances need not vitiate the cyclic prediction of two-factor avoidance theory. Rather, the cycles may simply have become so extended through progressively more intermittent pairings that their period now exceeds the lifetime of the organism, or the patience of the observer.

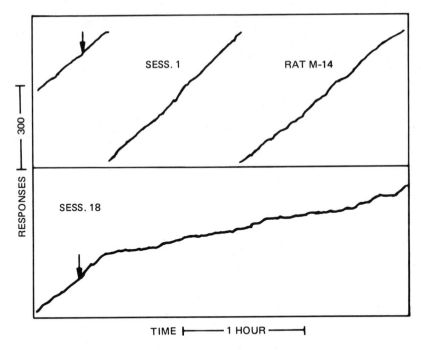

FIGURE 16.8. Cumulative records of a rat's performance during the first and the eighteenth session in which extinction was introduced after free-operant avoidance. Extinction began at the arrowed point (Boren and Sidman, 1957).

16.7
Safety Signals

The difficulties in locating stimuli which might reinforce avoidance behavior oblige a closer examination of the shock-free periods that occur in a situation where shocks sometimes occur. These periods are called, appropriately, *safety signals*. In classical defense conditioning, if there exists a CS paired with shock (a CS$^+$), then there must of logical necessity exist some other stimulus which is *not* paired with that shock, or paired with it less often (a CS$^-$). Moreover, there is considerable evidence showing that these CS$^-$'s develop classical inhibitory properties.

In a discriminative avoidance procedure, the *absence* of the S^D can function as a safety signal, because shocks are only delivered during or at the end of the S^D. Alternatively, an independent *feedback* stimulus can be made contingent upon the successful completion of the avoidance response. In either case, response-contingent safety signals may function to reinforce avoidance responses.

The reinforcing properties of these safety signals have been demonstrated in a number of ways. For instance, operant conditioning will occur when a response can alter a situation from one in which a number of shocks are delivered unpredictably, to one where that same number of shocks are signaled. Thus, Badia, Culbertson, and Harsh (1973) trained rats on a procedure where shocks were delivered at variable intervals with a mean of 2 min. If a lever press occurred, a *correlated stimulus* light was presented for 3 min. Any shocks programmed during the light were preceded by a 5-sec tone. Badia *et al* found that the lever press response was rapidly acquired, the subjects spending nearly all the session with the light on, and their shocks being preceded by a warning tone. Remarkably, preference for this condition over the alternative, involving unsignalled shock, persisted even when the signaled shocks were made much longer or much stronger than the unsignaled shocks. Representative results of the effects of both of these variables are shown in Figure 16.9. The unsignaled shocks were always 0.5 sec and 1.0 mA, but either the duration (upper panel) or the intensity (lower panel) of the signaled shocks were systematically increased. Even shocks that were nine times as long or three times as intense were preferred if they were signaled. It, therefore, appears that the presentation of the correlated stimulus had powerful reinforcing properties. The correlated stimulus can be regarded as a safety signal, because it signals that no shock will be delivered unless the warning tone occurs. The correlated stimulus, alone, is thus a signal of safety, a shockfree period.

It seems clear that safety signals *can* exert powerful effects on behavior, but it does not necessarily follow that they are crucial in avoidance behavior. Few studies of avoidance have included an external stimulus that could function as a safety signal. However, Cicala and Owen (1976), training rats in discriminated avoidance in a shuttle box, found that a group given a feedback stimulus (safety signal) contingent upon the avoidance response, acquired the response as quickly as a group in which S^D terminated when a response was made. Since both of these groups learned more slowly than a group given *both* a feedback stimulus and S^D termination, we conclude that safety signals certainly can affect avoidance behavior.

16.8
Shock-Density Reduction

Every avoidance paradigm entails response-contingent shock density reduction. But how might shock-density reduction reinforce avoidance behavior? Suppose the density of shock is x shocks/min when the organism is doing R_A, and $x + \Delta x$ when the organism is doing something else, R_B. Then R_A will receive reinforcement when it occurs, because it moves the organism from a higher aversive state, associated with R_B, to the lower aversive state, associated with and following R_A. This analysis, developed by Anger (*in press*), notes that *all* the movements of a rat, in a box where lever pressing avoids or postpones shock, become aversive because they encounter,

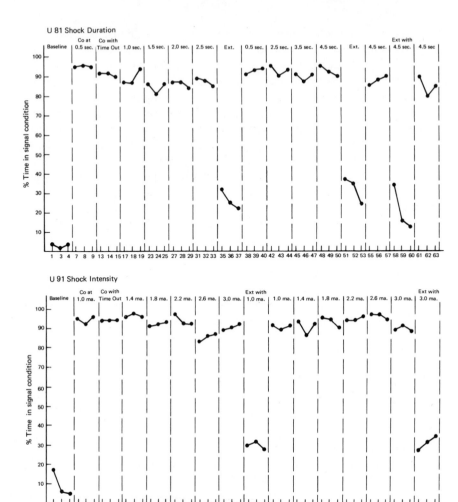

FIGURE 16.9. Upper panel: Percentage of session time spent in signaled shock schedule for the last three sessions in each condition for an individual rat. Signaled shock duration is given at the top of each column. Lower panel: Equivalent data from an individual rat when shock intensity was varied (Badia, Culbertson, and Harsh, 1973).

at one time or another, shocks. But even so, lever pressing represents R_A, the *least* aversive behavior, because it, and the period of time immediately after it, are associated with the lowest shock density. And, just as rats can discriminate lights, tones, and times especially associated with shocks, and escape these events, so too, rats can discriminate their own movements especially associated with shocks and escape them.

Anger's account draws strong support from the procedure of Herrnstein

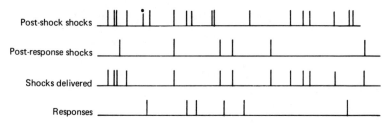

FIGURE 16.10. A response-contingent, shock-frequency reduction procedure. At any moment, actual shock density is determined either by a post-shock programmer, or by a post-response programmer. If the last event was a shock, the shocks programmed by the post-shock generator are delivered. If the last event was a response, the shocks programmed by the post-response generator are delivered (after Herrnstein and Hineline, 1966).

and Hineline (1966), illustrated in Figure 16.10. On this unusual schedule, there were no fixed temporal relations between responding, not-responding, and shock delivery. Instead, responding produced periods of time in which shocks were relatively less frequent. Herrnstein and Hineline found that this schedule both produced and maintained the lever-press avoidance response by rats, despite the fact that responses were sometimes immediately followed by shock. In this experiment, we find direct empirical support for the notion that the occurrence of an operant response correlated with a reduction in shock density can generate an increase in frequency of that response.

De Villiers (1974) substantiated and expanded this conclusion by his finding that the rate of response of rats on a *VI* avoidance schedule (in which lever presses cancelled the delivery of shocks scheduled at variable intervals) was a graded function of the obtained reduction in shock density. The results of de Villiers study, illustrated in Figure 16.11, provided a good fit to the equation

$$R_1 = \frac{kr_1}{r_1 + r_o}$$

where R_1 = lever press response rate, r_1 = rate of reinforcement measured as observed decrements in shock density, r_o = other unknown reinforcers for other behaviors in that situation, and k = a constant.

This is Equation 2 of Chapter 6, the equation Herrnstein (1970) derived to describe behavior where a single response is *positively* reinforced. Thus, de Villiers demonstrated that avoidance is related to shock density reduction in the same orderly manner that positively reinforced behavior is related to reinforcement rate. Here then, is powerful support for the notion that avoidance behavior is quantitatively reinforced by the amount of reduction from a higher to a lower shock density it produces.

How does the organism detect such differences in shock density? Again, we must appeal to the animal's ability to discriminate its own behavior.

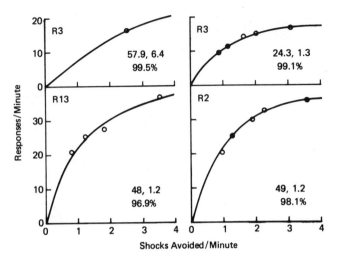

FIGURE 16.11. Rate of responding as a function of shock-frequency reduction for four rats responding on *VI* schedules. The value of *k* and r_o are shown with the percentage of the variance in response rate accounted for by the curve fitted to the data (de Villiers, 1974).

Although there are no tones or lights systematically correlated with the higher or lower shock densities, lever presses *are* systematically correlated with the latter, and all other behaviors emitted by the subject are systematically correlated with the former. In discriminating different shock densities, the rat is displaying its ability to discriminate different degrees of conditioned aversiveness of its own behavior.

16.9
Delay of Shock

In the avoidance procedures we have described, the operant response has two effects. It reduces shock density, but it also increases the average delay to the next shock. These are normally interwoven in avoidance procedure, but when cleverly separated, it turns out that delay of shock can have powerful reinforcing effects by itself.

Hineline (1970) devised an ingenious schedule in which a response could produce shock-delay without affecting overall shock density (see Figure 16.12). Hineline's procedure consisted of a 20-sec cycle, which began with an electrically-driven retractable lever being inserted into a previously empty Skinner box. If no response occurred, a shock was delivered to the rat in the 8th sec, and the lever was withdrawn at the end of the 10th sec. If the rat pressed the lever before 8 sec, however, the lever was immediately withdrawn

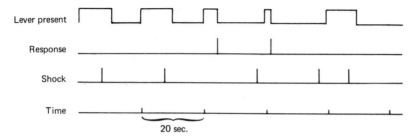

FIGURE 16.12. Hineline's (1970) procedure where a response produces delay of shock without shock-frequency reduction. A response delays shock from the 8th to the 18th sec of the 20-sec cycle. The lever is retracted when a response is made.

and shock was postponed until the 18th sec of the cycle. So, whether the rat pressed or did not press, it received one shock every 20 sec. Yet this procedure maintained responding in all of the 5 rats exposed to it; negative reinforcement occurred without shock-density reduction.

Even more striking results were obtained by Gardner and Lewis (1976), in a procedure similar to that of Badia *et al.*(1973) that is described in Section 16.7. Rats were exposed to unsignaled, unpredictable shock, at average intervals of 30 sec. If a lever press occurred, a correlated stimulus consisting of two lights and a clicking noise was presented for 3 min. During this stimulus, 6 shocks were presented (the same overall rate as when the correlated stimulus was not present), but all 6 occurred in a 5-sec period, which occurred either 10 sec, 88 sec, or 165 sec after the onset of the correlated stimulus. The procedure is illustrated in Figure 16.13.

Gardner and Lewis found that preference for the correlated stimulus was an increasing function of the time at which shock was delivered in the correlated stimulus. Thus, long delays of shock were reinforcing, although

FIGURE 16.13. The procedures for Gardner and Lewis's (1976) three groups. In each case, the correlated stimulus came on if a response was made, and stayed on for 3 min.

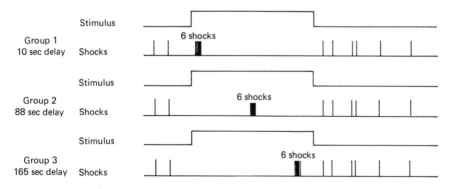

shock density was held constant. The results of all their subjects are shown in Figure 16.14. A second experiment showed that rats would respond for a correlated stimulus associated with a shock density, $1\frac{1}{2}$ or 2 times greater than the baseline schedule, if the first $2\frac{1}{2}$ min of the 3-min stimulus period were shock-free.

Although shock delay and shock frequency (or density) are confounded in most avoidance situations, the results of this section strongly suggest that delay of shock may have a powerful reinforcing effect in many avoidance schedules.

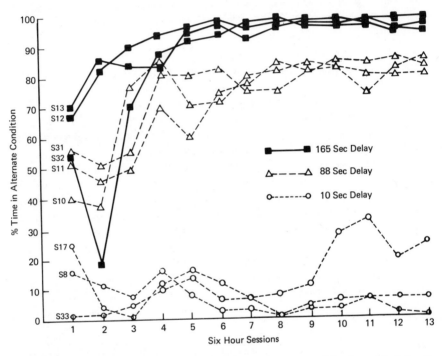

FIGURE 16.14. Percentage of time in the correlated stimulus condition for subjects in all three delay groups (Gardner and Lewis, 1976).

16.10
Failure of the Avoidance Contingency

We have seen that negatively reinforced behavior can be maintained by conditioned aversive stimulus termination, safety signal presentation, shock density reduction, and delay of shock. Even so, avoidance behavior sometimes fails to develop where one or more of these inducing factors are present. To understand such failures, we have to remind ourselves that there exists great variability in the ease with which different operants can be conditioned to escape or avoid electric shock. Some operants, such as standing still, condition extremely easily in rats and other rodents, often in a single trial. Other operants, among them, shuttling and lever pressing in rats, remain more difficult to condition, even though they are the most commonly studied.

We can begin to understand some of these puzzling failures and difficulties when we look closely at the topographical properties of responses selected for the study of avoidance, and then look in turn at what their adaptive function has been in the evolutionary history of that species. Although the response of running in the rat to avoid shock has generally been studied in shuttle boxes, we might well have selected a runway, instead, had we given thought to the role that running plays in the normal repertoire of that species. In a runway, the animal runs from start box to goal box and is then removed. On every trial, successful or not, it runs away from the shock source. But in the shuttle box, when the subject fails to avoid a shock and escapes it by running, this subject must, on the next trial, run to the very place where it last received shock. This analysis gives us some idea of why shuttle-box running can take a very long time to condition, whereas one-way runway avoidance is acquired in very few trials.

Every avoidance procedure involves not only a negative reinforcement contingency, but also the necessary ingredients for aversive classical conditioning. Aversive stimuli are repeatedly paired with either apparatus cues or S^D's. Recall from Chapter 7 and Chapter 12 that analogous situations, involving positive reinforcers, frequently lead to species-typical appetitive behaviors being conditioned, and interacting with operant performances. Similarly, we must expect to find *species-typical aversive behaviors* elicited by avoidance situations. Bolles (1970) has emphasized this factor by suggesting that *only* behaviors compatible with these species-typical aversive behaviors are free to occur in such situations. In his view, whatever instrumental conditioning that occurs must, of necessity, involve behavior deriving from, or highly compatible with, these species-typical aversive reactions.

Species-typical aversive behaviors represent those unconditioned behaviors that occur naturally in response to attack. In rats, the most readily identifiable ones comprise freezing, flight, and attack. Running is evidently a component of flight, so we might expect rapid acquisition of an avoidance response that involves running movements. However, flight means running *away from* the dangerous situation (the aversive CS). Here is another reason why one-way runway avoidance conditions more rapidly than shuttling back and forth in a shuttle box. The latter is retarded by an unconditioned tendency to keep away from places where aversive stimuli have been received.

When we apply this analysis to lever pressing, we look for a natural, species-typical aversive behavior, derivative from either attack, flight, or freezing. Flight is impossible in a Skinner box (though rats do jump at the ceiling), and attacking the grid floor where shocks are delivered has no effect on the shocks (though bar biting does occur). However, freezing in just the right spot, namely on the lever, does aid the animal in escaping shocks rapidly. So it seem plausible, that out of this freezing on the bar that represents a transition stage prior to the acquisition of avoidance, develops the presses that eventually anticipate the shock, and hence define successful avoidance.

We may safely conclude that the general pattern of interaction of operant behavior with species-typical behavior appears the same for avoidance as for positive-reinforcement procedures. Only careful analysis can distinguish the species-typical components of behavior observed during avoidance from the outcome of implicit reinforcement contingencies. More generally, the prominence of interfering species-typical behavior in negative-reinforcement studies indicates that only by allowing such an analysis to inform our design of apparatus and procedures can we expect to tease apart the contributions of the various interacting processes.

16.11
Summary

Our understanding of avoidance behavior and related effects of negative reinforcement hinges on a dissection of various independent sources of negative reinforcement. Experimental work over the past 30 years has gradually elaborated the following crucial factors: (1) termination of S^D's associated with shock, (2) presentation of safety signals, (3) reduction in shock density, and (4) delay of shock.

Classical conditioning exerts the same potent influence in negative reinforcement procedures that it does in positive reinforcement. Once again, we had to drive home the moral that instituting an operant-conditioning procedure gives no guarantee that all of the behavior observed to develop is the result of an operant-conditioning process.

Many everyday situations correspond loosely to the avoidance schedules of the laboratory. We work to avoid the privations of poverty, we break off a conversation to avoid embarrassment, we travel at a time when transportation is less crowded, we postpone telling a friend bad news. However, it is often difficult to establish whether a behavior is maintained by negative or positive reinforcement. For example, is etiquette maintained by social approval (a positive reinforcer), or by avoidance of social disapproval (a negative reinforcer), or both? Lacking an exhaustive experimental analysis, it is very difficult to answer this type of question authoritatively. Even so, our increasingly sophisticated understanding of negative reinforcement is commencing to give us a more accurate picture of the possible roles it plays in everyday human behavior.

References for Chapter 16

Anger, D. *Two-factor theory and the avoidance puzzles* (in press).

Badia, P., Culbertson, S., and Harsh, J. Choice of longer or stronger signalled shock over shorter or weaker unsignalled shock. *Journal of the Experimental Analysis of Behavior*, 1973, **19**, 25–32.

Bolles, R. C. Species-specific defense reactions and avoidance learning. *Psychological Review*, 1970, **77**, 32–48

Boren, J. J., and Sidman, M. A discrimination based upon repeated conditioning and extinction of avoidance behavior. *Journal of Comparative and Physiological Psychology*, 1957, **50**, 18–22.

Brogden, W. J., Lipman, E. A., and Culler, E. The role of incentive in conditioning and extinction. *American Journal of Psychology*, 1938, **51**, 109–117.

Cicala, G. A., and Owen, J. W. Warning signal termination and a feedback signal may not serve the same function. *Learning and Motivation*, 1976, **7**, 356–367.

de Villiers, P. A. The law of effect in avoidance: A quantitative relationship between response rate and shock frequency reduction. *Journal of the Experimental Analysis of Behavior*, 1974, **21**, 223–235.

Gardner, E. T., and Lewis, P. Negative reinforcement with shock-frequency increase. *Journal of the Experimental Analysis of Behavior*, 1976, **25**, 3–14.

Herrnstein, R. J. Method and theory in the study of avoidance. *Psychological Review*, 1969, **76**, 49–69.

Herrnstein, R. J. On the law of effect. *Journal of the Experimental Analysis of Behavior*, 1970, **13**, 243–266.

Herrnstein, R. J., and Hineline, P. N. Negative reinforcement as shock-frequency reduction. *Journal of the Experimental Analysis of Behavior*, 1966, **9**, 421–430.

Hineline, P. N. Negative reinforcement without shock reduction. *Journal of the Experimental Analysis of Behavior*, 1970, **14**, 259–268.

Hoffman, H. S., and Fleshler, M. The course of emotionality in the development of avoidance. *Journal of Experimental Psychology*, 1962, **64**, 288–294.

Kamin, L. J. The effects of termination of the CS and avoidance of the US on avoidance learning: An extension. *Canadian Journal of Psychology*, 1957, **11**, 48–56.

Sidman, M. Two temporal parameters of maintenance of avoidance behavior by the white rat. *Journal of Comparative and Physiological Psychology*, 1953, **46**, 253–261.

Sidman, M. Avoidance behavior. In W. K. Honig (Ed.) *Operant behavior: areas of research and application.* New York: Appleton-Century-Crofts, 1966.

Taub, E. and Berman, A. J. Movement and learning in the absence of sensory feedback. In S. J. Freedman (Ed.) *The Neuropsychology of spatially oriented behavior.* Homewood, Illinois: Dorsey, 1968.

Verhave, T. Avoidance responding as a function of simultaneous and equal changes in two temporal parameters. *Journal of the Experimental Analysis of Behavior*, 1959, **2**, 185–190.

CHAPTER 17

Punishment and Conditioned Aversive Stimuli

In the last chapter, we saw how operant responses could remove or reduce aversive states. In this chapter, we turn to *punishment*, a procedure in which aversive stimuli are made contingent upon behavior. Because response suppression is a prominent consequence of that punishment procedure, we shall also want to consider closely, classical-conditioning procedures where a CS paired with an aversive stimulus acquires the ability to suppress operant behavior.

The modification of behavior by contingent presentation of aversive stimuli represents an extremely controversial subject. Punishment is an emotive word, and much progressive thinking in education, psychotherapy, child rearing, penal reform, relationship-improvement programs, and even radical social change is based on the premise that our first step must be to eliminate punishment. The validity of this claim depends on what is meant by punishment, the effects (direct and indirect) that punishment has, and ethical considerations.

17.1

A Definition of Punishment

We define punishment in a similar way to the way that we defined escape and avoidance, as a procedure with a characteristic outcome. In the punishment procedure, a stimulus is made contingent upon a specified response. If there occurs a variety of characteristic effects, one of which is a *reduction in frequency* or suppression of that response, then we say that punishment has occurred, and that the contingent stimulus is a punisher, a punishing stimulus, or an aversive stimulus. We can represent the procedure as

$$R \rightarrow S^-$$

where

R = the specified response, and
S^- = an aversive stimulus.

Aside from response suppression, this procedure does have very characteristic effects associated with it, and it is in part a description and explication of these effects which this chapter addresses.

Clearly, the punishment paradigm supplements escape and avoidance procedures as an independent way of assessing the aversiveness of contingent stimuli. However, note that, parallel with all other operant procedures, the effect of the consequent stimulus depends on the particular situation, the particular response selected for study, and other contextual variables. We cannot assume, for example, that the verbal command, "Sssh!", which effectively silences a child talking in church, will also have this effect in a schoolroom. Neither can we assume that a stimulus identified as an effective punisher for one operant will necessarily effectively punish another operant behavior, or that a stimulus found aversive from escape or avoidance procedures will necessarily act as a punisher. In practice, the ubiquitous punishers in laboratory experiments have been, almost exclusively, electric shock.

In ordinary language, the word "punishment" is used ambiguously. It can either mean the delivery of an aversive stimulus contingent upon a response, as here, or simply the delivery of an aversive stimulus in no particular relation to behavior. We have removed this ambiguity, and we shall see later in this chapter that there are important behavioral differences between the two procedures. We depart from ordinary language in specifying that punishment has only occurred when a particular behavioral *effect* is seen.

17.2

Is Punishment Effective?

Early laboratory work on punishment appeared to support the conclusion that punishment yields only a transient effect on operant behavior. Skinner (1938) trained hungry rats to press a lever for food on a fixed-interval schedule. Lever pressing was then extinguished through the withholding of food. Some of the rats were punished during the first 10 min of extinction. The punishment was in the form of a sharp slap delivered by the lever itself to the forepaws after each press. The slap was a rapid and forceful reverse movement of the lever, transmitted to it by a hammer that struck it sharply after each press. The effects of this 10-min slapping contingency can be seen in Figure 17.1, which shows the extinction processes for two groups of rats, with and without punishment. The punishment had an immediate effect, and the number of responses for that group remained lower for the first day. On the second day, however, responding recovered and reached the same total as for the unpunished group. (Note the spontaneous recovery of both groups at the beginning of the second session.)

These data suggest that punishment has only a temporary suppressive effect, rather than permanently decreasing responding. Further support for this view came from an influential series of experiments by Estes (1944). Using a similar experimental design to Skinner's, except that the punisher was electric shock, Estes replicated the finding shown in Figure 17.1. He also found that severe shock delivery tended to suppress not only punished lever pressing, but *all* activity for a period of time. Estes, therefore, concluded that the suppression from response-contingent punishment represented a special case of a general suppressive effect of electric shock, independent of any programmed response contingency. Estes argued that, by classical con-

FIGURE 17.1. The effects of mild punishment (slapping) on the operant extinction process (Skinner, 1938).

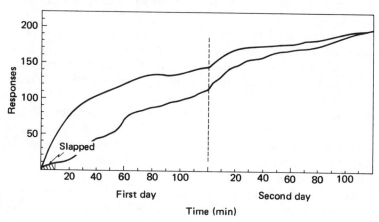

ditioning, apparatus cues paired with shock became a CS that elicited an emotional anxiety state of the organism, which was reflected in generalized operant suppression.

Estes' theory predicted little or no *selective* suppression on the response being punished. This response declined in frequency simply because *all* behavior was suppressed. We shall see in the next section, however, that the results of many newer experiments embarrass this view. We review these data in the next section, and in Section 17.8 show how two-factor theory integrates both the new and old results.

Actually, response-suppression due to response-contingent shock proves more selective than Estes' early experiments indicated. We now know that the response class on which shock is made contingent becomes the most suppressed, even though suppression may often spill over to related operants and even general activity. An echo of Estes' analysis, however, remains in more recent theories of punishment, which draw our attention to selective classical-conditioning processes that are embedded in all punishment procedures, and on which a full understanding of the effects of punishment are based.

17.3
Selective Effects of Punishment

If Mongolian gerbils are placed in a response chamber with a food bin, drinking tube, and a small roll of adding machine paper, when food and water deprived, they will spend about 25 min of a 30-min session eating, drinking, or paper shredding. Muyesu-Kaisha Mainavi (reported by Dunham, 1971) studied the effects of punishing one of these responses on the unpunished behaviors. Nine gerbils were divided between three groups. Group *E* was punished for eating, group *P* was punished for paper shredding, and group *D* was punished for drinking. In each case, a brief shock was delivered at 2-sec intervals, from the onset of the punished activity until it stopped.

This procedure was repeated each time that activity occurred. The probability of each behavior, before the introduction of shock and during punishment sessions, is shown in Figure 17.2 for all the subjects.

Inspection of preshock data reveals that paper shredding was the preferred activity for all the gerbils, while eating was usually a poor second, and drinking, third. When shock was introduced, all subjects showed a new behavior. This was grid biting, and it was elicited by the shock. As the punishment procedure was designed to effectively suppress the selected response, Dunham (1971) was most interested in the changes in the unpunished behavior.

One feature is common to all subjects: *at least one unpunished behavior increased in frequency during punishment.* Not only did punishment

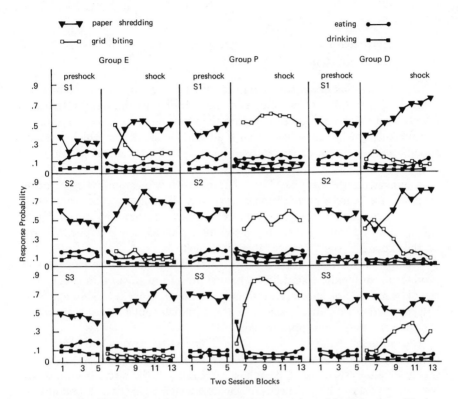

FIGURE 17.2. Effects of punishing one of three responses in gerbils. Note that grid-biting did not occur prior to the introduction of shocks (Dunham, 1971).

selectively suppress one response, rather than producing general suppression as Estes (1944) claimed, but also some response actually became more frequent. Dunham (1971) noted that after the initial disruption, it was the most frequent unpunished behavior that increased in probability, and thus filled the time made available by suppression of the punished behavior.

Note that when eating or drinking was punished, it was generally paper shredding, previously the most frequent behavior, that showed an increase. If, however, paper shredding was itself punished, then grid biting became the predominant activity. This is remarkable, because there was *no* grid biting before the introduction of shock. Dunham argued that in every case it was the response which is most frequently associated with the absence of shock that increased through a negative reinforcement process. In group *P*, this was grid biting, because paper shredding had previously been so frequent that there was now a high frequency of shock, and thus, of grid biting.

As well as providing information about changes in unpunished behavior, this study emphasizes the highly selective nature of the effects of punishment.

17.4

Response-Dependent and Response-Independent Aversive Events on Concurrent Chains

A two-link concurrent chain schedule proves valuable in comparing preferences for different procedures and situations. Rachlin and Herrnstein (1969) used this technique to compare the reinforcing value of a response-contingent punishment schedule with another schedule, in which periodic shock was delivered independently of responses. Their general procedure is shown in Figure 17.3.

A hungry pigeon was placed in a chamber with two response keys. During the first link "choice period", both keys were illuminated with white light. Pecking on the left key occasionally resulted in that key turning red, signaling a *VI* 1-min food reinforcement plus a shock delivery schedule now on that key. The right key was then darkened.

Pecking on the right key during the first link darkened the left key and produced a different second link schedule of reinforcement and shock. The right key second link shock schedule entailed noncontingent shocks, while the left key second link shock schedule was a punishment procedure in which shocks were contingent upon pecks.

The animals' behavior in the first link, where two white keys were presented, is going to tell us something about which of these two different shock schedules the animal likes the least. In link 1, the bird can choose, by restricting part or all of its pecks to one key, which of the two second links it

FIGURE 17.3. The concurrent chain procedure. An example of one of Rachlin and Herrnstein's (1969) procedures.

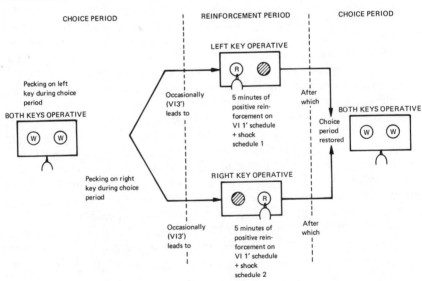

wishes to experience. An important aspect of this technique is its separation of the behavioral effects of punishment suppression from the *choice* of punishment versus free shock. In the chained procedure of Figure 17.3, it would be possible for punishment in the second link to strongly suppress these red key pecks, yet the bird might still choose, in link 1, to more often produce that punishment schedule in preference to some free shock schedules programmed for the other key that yielded less suppression in link 2.

Rachlin and Herrnstein varied the rate of free shock (x) in right key link 2 over a wide range, comparing the various values of x with the same fixed punishment schedule on the left key. They found that the punishment schedule did suppress responding in the left second link, much more than the same average density of periodically delivered free shock in the right second link. Yet, they discovered that pigeons' choice of second links was always determined by the second link associated with a lower shock density, independent of whether that shock came inevitably, or in the form of punishment.

This important result tells us that we cannot assess response strength or relative reinforcing value in aversive situations merely by referring to the rate of the target operant. Punishment has an instrumental suppressive effect that goes beyond the generalized effect of the shocks having lowered the overall attractiveness of the situation. Just as we observed in Chapter 6, in attempting to assess response strength under *VR* or *DRL* schedules that affect response rate by their shaping constraints, so too, punished rates of response will also reflect a combination of instrumental shaping and reinforcement value. The behavior in Rachlin and Herrnstein's second links reflected the former, and the behaviors in the first link reflected the latter. Thus, their technique amounts to a valuable separation procedure, not unlike the use of a centrifuge in chemistry that separates mixtures containing substances of different specific gravities.

17.5
Punishment and Discrimination

Having demonstrated that punishment is a more effective technique for selective response suppression than free shock, how can we explain the effect, illustrated in Figure 17.1 and replicated by Estes (1944) in several ways, that punishment during extinction seems to have little influence on overall resistance to extinction?

Recall again that a procedure can have more than one behavioral effect. In Skinner's (1938) and Estes' (1944) experiments, extinction and punishment were introduced at the same time. The punishing stimulus, therefore, probably became a *discriminative stimulus*, cueing extinction for the rat. This interpretation is supported by the finding that when punishment was no longer presented, the rate of responding increased. This may have been because the subjects had discriminated between the reinforcement period, signaled by nonpunishment, and the extinction period, signaled by punishment. If they had, we would expect an increase in rate when punishment ceased, because they then returned to the reinforcement condition. (Of course, responding would soon decline again through extinction).

By this analysis, the effect found by Estes is not paradoxical, but simply the result of the acquisition of stimulus control by the punishment condition. Azrin and Holz (1966) made the following test. Pecks at a white key of hungry pigeons were reinforced on a *VI* 2-min schedule with food. After a large number of sessions on this schedule, "pseudopunishment" was introduced. Each response produced a 400-msec flash of green light on the key and concurrently food reinforcements were discontinued. The results are shown in Figure 17.4. Responding rapidly decreased to near-zero. This "pseudopunishment" was now discontinued, but extinction was still in effect. As soon as the green flash no longer followed responding, there was a dramatic increase in response rate prior to a second decline. Thus, Azrin and Holz's neutral stimulus had the same effects as shock in Estes' experiment; it accelerated extinction, but responding recovered when it was removed.

Even clearer evidence of the potential discriminative properties of punishment comes from another study of Holz and Azrin (1961). The food-reinforced pecking of pigeons during a discriminative stimulus (S^D) was also punished with shock, while in another stimulus (S$^\Delta$), there was neither

FIGURE 17.4. Response rate of a pigeon on a *VI* 2-min schedule of food reinforcement during reinforcement, extinction plus a response-produced brief green light, and extinction without this added contingency (Azrin and Holz, 1966).

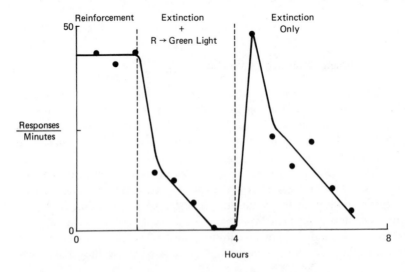

reinforcement nor punishment. In tests, punishment during S^Δ produced substantial increases in response rate. Shock had become associated with reinforcement. Such experiments seem to provide clues to masochistic human behavior. Perhaps masochism, the seeking out of aversive stimuli, results from a history of aversive stimuli being associated with positive reinforcement.

17.6
Punishment of Human Behavior

Punishment can be shown to modify human behavior under laboratory conditions. We need not employ painful shocks, since we can rely on the aversiveness of loss of potential reinforcements. Bradshaw, Szabadi, and Bevan (1977) examined the effects of a punishment contingency on the performance of humans pressing buttons for points on a *VI* schedule. The points could be exchanged for money at the end of the experiment. After initial training, multiple *VI* schedules were used and a *VR*34 punishment contingency was superimposed on alternate sessions. Reinforcement on the *VI* schedules were always signaled by 100 msec green light flash and the addition of one point to the score on a counter in front of the subject. When punishment occurred, a red light flashed on for 100 msec and one point was subtracted from the counter.

The results from their three subjects are shown in Figure 17.5. Without punishment, response rate was a negative accelerated function of reinforcement rate in each component of the multiple schedule, and the data are a good fit to Herrnstein's Matching Law. (Equation 5 of Chapter 6 is the appropriate one). During punishment, the maximum (asymptotic) response rate was greatly reduced for all subjects, but the data were still a good fit to Equation 5. This shows a consistent and extremely orderly effect of punishment on human operant performance. Note that the effects of positive reinforcement, shock avoidance (Chapter 16), and punishment can all be described by the Matching Law.

Laboratory demonstrations, along with our everyday experience, suggest that punishment is a pervasive and important behavioral process. Like positive reinforcement, negative reinforcement, and classical conditioning, the sufficient conditions for its occurrence are frequently met in the natural environments of humans as well as of other organisms. As Azrin and Holz (1966) point out, to "eliminate punishment from the world" would involve elimination of *all* contact between the individual and the physical world, because there are so many naturally occurring punishment contingencies. We learn *not* to do a great many things. These include touching hot surfaces, falling out of bed, shutting our fingers in doors, and all the ways we avoid natural aversive consequences.

If we agree that the contingencies of punishment specified by the physical

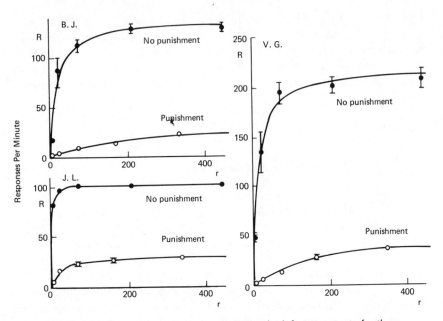

FIGURE 17.5. Relationship between response rate and reinforcement rate for three human subjects, with and without a punishment contingency. Data are the means of three sessions. The bars give standard errors of the means (Bradshaw, Svabadi, and Bevan, 1977).

world are not eradicable, can we and should we minimize the number of punishment contingencies operated by individuals and institutions upon individuals? We can distinguish between those that involve painful stimuli and those that involve response-cost or time-out. "Time-out" refers to all procedures which involve temporary prevention of access to positive reinforcers. In everyday life, these include removal of attention (being ignored), withdrawal of privileges, and levying fines. Many experimental studies, such as that by Dunham (1971) (see Section 17.3), have shown that painful stimuli elicit aggressive behaviors and these can become predominant. Clearly, this is highly undesirable and would seem to be sufficient reason to reject the use of punishment contingencies that involve painful stimuli, if alternatives can be found.

There is a more subtle problem that applies to *all* types of punishment contingency that are administered by another individual or an institution. Through classical conditioning, the agent may itself become aversive, or the aversive properties of the situation may result in avoidance learning. The punishment contingency will then be ineffective, because it will no longer make contact with the individual's behavior. Instead, the individual will refuse to have anything to do with the other individual or the institution.

Against the drawbacks of punishment, must be set any advantages it may have over alternatives. Its chief advantage is undoubtedly the rapidity with which response suppression can be produced. It is often pointed out that an equivalent change can be produced by positive reinforcement without undesirable side-effects, but reinforcing an alternative response may not have as specific or rapid effects on the behavior to be eliminated. If a child persists in running off the sidewalk into the path of vehicles, socially administered punishment may be the only way of preventing the "natural" punishment contingency from having more drastic effects.

17.7
Maintenance of Behavior by Response-Produced Shock

In Section 17.1, we defined punishment both as a procedure and an effect. Punishment has not occurred if behavior is not suppressed by it. This makes it difficult to categorize instances where a schedule of response-produced shock, that normally suppresses responding, actually maintains it. Nevertheless, it can happen.

We have already seen one example in Section 17.5, where response-contingent shock in the S^D component resulted in shock acquiring discriminative properties and increasing the rate of response. Even more remarkable are situations in which behavior is maintained by response-produced shock and *no other reinforcement*. Typically, such behavior is observed when the subject is transferred from an avoidance schedule, or a schedule of response-independent shock, to a schedule of response-produced shock.

Morse, Mead, and Kelleher (1967) presented unavoidable shocks every 60 sec to restrained monkeys. Each shock presentation elicited biting at the collar and leash holding the monkey, similar to the grid biting shown by Dunham's (1971) gerbils. After a number of sessions, the schedule was altered so that shocks were now delivered on an FI 30-sec schedule, contingent upon the biting response, or 60 sec after the previous shock, if no response was made. Results for one monkey are shown in Figure 17.6. Responding was maintained, most shocks being delivered by the FI schedule. Furthermore, the "scallop" characteristic of positively reinforced behavior gradually appeared, and if shock was discontinued, responding extinguished. It is clear that after an appropriate history, shock presentation can maintain FI behavior in a similar fashion to food presentation.

This remarkable behavioral phenomenon is not fully understood, but it seems that response-contingent aversive events can acquire discriminative properties on schedules, and then maintain behavior. It may be that in procedures like Morse, Mead, and Kelleher's, the subject's behavior is telling us that it prefers to deliver its own shocks, contingent on responding, rather than wait and have the experimenter do it by zapping it when it may not be expecting it. The monkey seems to act as we sometimes do, when we ask

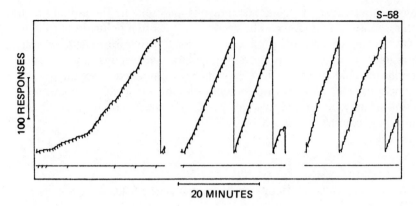

FIGURE 17.6. Leash pulling by a monkey on a schedule of *FI* 30-sec shock or response-independent shock after 60 sec. Data are from the 1st, 2nd, and 18th sessions (Morse and Kelleher, 1970).

directly to hear the bad news, rather than wait and have it come when we are not braced or prepared for it. Although Rachlin and Herrnstein's experiment of Figure 17.3 suggested otherwise, it may well be that under some conditions, response-produced shock actually is somewhat less aversive than the same frequency of free shock.

17.8
Aversive Classical Conditioning

Escape, avoidance, and punishment procedures all involve programmed relationships between responses and aversive stimuli. The other general class of aversive contingencies involves relationships between neutral (conditioned) stimuli and aversive stimuli. These are, of course, varieties of classical conditioning. However, they were not explicitly discussed in Chapter 10, where our examples are mainly of appetitive classical conditioning.

In the previous two chapters, we noted the effects that classical conditioning can have in escape or avoidance. In punishment, too, the particular stimuli, consisting especially of the behavior of carrying out the punished response, are reliable predictors of shock and should, therefore, come to elicit species-typical aversive behaviors, such as flight, attack, and freezing. Indeed, this tendency of stimuli paired with shocks to elicit freezing when flight is impossible, as it is in small experimental compartments, formed the basis of Estes' (1944) early theory of punishment suppression.

Estes' theory, however, ignored the selective associations that the lever-pressing behavior had with shock, and it failed on that account to explain the effects of shock that many later experiments demonstrated were selective to the punished response.

In punishment, the behavior involved in initiating and completing the punished response also represents the stimuli most closely and consistently paired with shock. We already saw, in our discussion of avoidance, that animals can and do discriminate differences in aversiveness of their own behavior. Similarly, when punishment exerts a suppressive effect, we may infer that the subject is actually avoiding its own aversive behavior, the punished behavior, by emitting responses incompatible with it. So when the rat starts to initiate a response sequence that will be punished, but aborts it part way through, it effectively escapes its own aversive behavior and thereby avoids shock (Millenson and Macmillan, 1975).

This account represents an extension of two-factor theory, very similar to the one we employed in the previous chapter for avoidance. Indeed, punishment has been appropriately termed *passive avoidance*, for two-factor theory says that the response suppression we observe, is actually due to the conditioning of incompatible avoidance responses. Aside from neatly accounting for the facts of punishment, this extension of two-factor theory succeeds in unifying all three fundamental aversive paradigms: escape, avoidance, and punishment.

Aversive classical conditioning is studied directly when contingencies are arranged between CS's and aversive US's. Many aspects of the resultant process parallel appetitive classical conditioning. Indeed, many Pavlovian phenomena were originally demonstrated with aversive conditioning. The responses most often studied were salivation and leg flexion in dogs, and eyeblinks and heart rate in humans and other species. However, all these paradigms involve *restrained* organisms. If freely-moving subjects are used, some effects are seen in aversive classical conditioning that distinguish it from appetitive classical conditioning.

These effects are twofold: species-typical aversive behaviors, and suppression or disruption of ongoing behavior can be elicited by the aversive CS. In some situations, these are two sides of the same coin, because the elicited aversive behaviors interfere with the ongoing behavior; but in others, disruption occurs during an aversive CS that cannot be attributed to species-typical aversive behaviors. The latter case is called *conditioned suppression*.

As the analysis of species-typical, aversive behavioral repertoires must be repeated for each species of interest, data are accumulating only slowly. However, a fair amount of information is available about the laboratory rat, the experimental psychologist's favorite subject, and piecemeal data on other species have been recorded. It is widely agreed that freezing, defecation, flight (running away), and aggression are components of the rat's aversive repertoire. Of these, defecation and freezing can be conditioned to a CS associated with shock, (Hunt and Otis, 1953), and components of aggressive behavior are seen if a pair of rats receive a CS that has been paired with shock (Ulrich, 1967). As an aversive, CS readily elicits flight in one-way avoidance (Section 16.10); we may conclude that species-typical aversive behaviors of the rat can be classically conditioned. This strengthened the claim that they are a significant factor in escape, avoidance, and punishment training.

Our lack of detailed information about the human behavioral repertoire makes it difficult to assess the role of species-typical behavior. However, the pioneer behaviorist, J. B. Watson, suggested that our emotional responses are acquired through classical conditioning of species-typical behavior. His investigations are described in Chapter 23.

17.9
Conditioned Suppression

Hunt and Brady (1951) trained liquid-deprived rats to press a lever for water reinforcement on a *VI* schedule. When response rate on this schedule had become stable, a clicker CS was presented periodically for 5 min, and immediately followed by a brief electric shock US to the rat's feet.

Some of the typical behavioral changes that ensued are shown in the cumulative lever-pressing records in Figure 17.7. The first CS presentation had little discernible effect. but the accompanying US (denoted by S in panel B) temporarily slowed the response rate. After a number of CS-US pairings, the CS suppressed responding almost totally, but responding recovered as soon as the US had been delivered. Because suppression of responding during the CS is dependent on a conditioning history, it is called conditioned suppression.

The conditioned-suppression procedure, first developed by Estes and Skinner (1941), has proved to be a very sensitive behavioral technique. The effect of the CS is usually described in terms of the degree of suppression of the positively reinforced behavior relative to the non-CS periods. Measured in this way, conditioned suppression increases with magnitude of the US, decreases with length of the CS, and is in general, such a sensitive indicator of classical-conditioning parameters that it has often been treated as the best method of studying classical-conditioning effects (for example, Rescorla, 1968).

If the reinforcement schedule maintaining the operant response is varied, conditioned suppression can be dramatically altered. Blackman (1968) trained hungry rats on a multiple schedule of food reinforcement. In one component (*DRL* 15 sec), very low rates of responding were reinforced, while the other (*FI*) maintained much higher levels of responding. When a CS followed a mild shock, response rate *increased* in the *DRL* component while being suppressed in the *FI* component. With more intense US's responding was suppressed in both components. The data are shown in Figure 17.8 in terms of the *ratio* of response rate during the CS to response rate in non-CS periods. Values of the suppression ratio greater than 1.0 indicate increases in response rate rather than suppression.

The sensitivity of the conditioned-suppression technique has lead to its

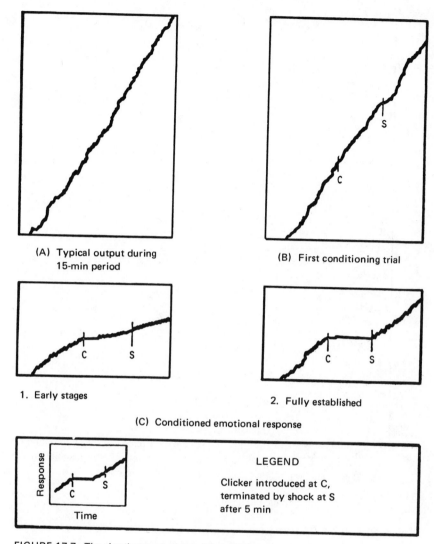

(A) Typical output during
15-min period

(B) First conditioning trial

1. Early stages

2. Fully established

(C) Conditioned emotional response

FIGURE 17.7. The development of conditioned suppression in a thirsty rat, lever pressing for water on a *VI* schedule (Hunt and Brady, 1951).

widespread use in evaluation of drug effects (Millenson and Leslie, 1974). The drugs tested have mostly been those known clinically to reduce anxiety, because conditioned suppression has often been treated as a model of fear or anxiety. We will assess this idea in Chapter 23.

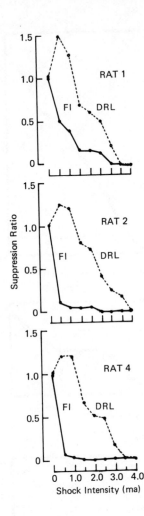

FIGURE 17.8.
Conditioned suppression (calculated as rate during CS divided by rate at other times) of *DRL* responding and *FI* responding for three rats (Blackman, 1968).

References for Chapter 17

Azrin, N. H., and Holz, W. C. Punishment. In W. K. Honig (Ed.) *Operant behavior: areas of research and application*, New York: Appleton-Century-Crofts, 1966.

Blackman, D. E. Conditioned suppression or acceleration as a function of the behavioral baseline. *Journal of the Experimental Analysis of Behavior*, 1968, **11**, 53–61.

Bradshaw, C. M., Svabadi, E., and Bevan, P. Effects of punishment on human variable-interval performance. *Journal of the Experimental Analysis of Behavior*, 1977, **27**, 275–280.

Dunham, P. J. Punishment: Method and theory. *Psychological Review*, 1971, **78**, 58–70.

Estes, W. K. An experimental study of punishment. *Psychological Monographs* 1944, **57**, (Whole No. 263).

Estes, W. K., and Skinner, B. F. Some quantitative properties of anxiety. *Journal of Experimental Psychology*, 1941, **29**, 390–400.

Holz, W. C., and Azrin, N. H. Discrimination properties of punishment. *Journal of the Experimental Analysis of Behavior*, 1961, **4**, 225–232.

Hunt, H. F., and Brady, J. V. Some effects of electro-convulsive shock on a conditioned emotional response ("anxiety"). *Journal of Comparative and Physiological Psychology*, 1951, **44**, 88–98.

Hunt, H. F., and Otis, L. S. Conditioned and unconditioned emotional defecation in the rat. *Journal of Comparative and Physiological Psychology*, 1953, **46**, 378–382.

Millenson, J. R., and Leslie, J. C. The conditioned emotional response (CER) as a baseline for the study of anti-anxiety drugs. *Neuropharmacology*, 1974, **13**, 1–9.

Millenson, J. R., and MacMillan, A. St.C. Evidence for abortive responding during punishment. *Learning and Motivation*, 1975, **6**, 279–288.

Morse, W. H., and Kelleher, R. T. Schedules as fundamental determinants of behavior. In W. N. Schoenfeld (Ed.) *The theory of reinforcement schedules*. New York: Appleton-Century-Crofts, 1970.

Morse, W. H., Mead, R. N., and Kelleher, R. T. Modulation of elicited behavior by a fixed-interval schedule of electric shock presentation. *Science*, 1967, **157**, 215–217.

Rachlin, H., and Herrnstein, R. J. Hedonism revisited: On the negative law of effect. In B. A. Campbell and R. M. Church (Eds.) *Punishment and aversive behavior*. Englewood Cliffs, N. J.: Prentice-Hall, 1969.

Skinner, B. F. *The behavior of organisms*. New York: Appleton-Century-Crofts, 1938.

Ulrich, R. E. Pain-aggression. In G. A. Kimble (Ed.) *Foundations of conditioning and learning*. New York: Appleton-Century-Crofts, 1967.

PART SIX

Complex Behavior

The principles elaborated in the preceding chapters permit us to describe and classify a large fraction of the learned behavior of animal and human organisms. But were we to terminate our account of behavior with the phenomena of operant conditioning, classical conditioning, environmental control, and aversive contingencies, we would still be forced to admit that the bulk of complex human behavior had been left untouched. The activities that might be classified as complex human behaviors are, of course, extremely diverse, and in this part we have arbitrarily selected three categories. These are concept acquisition, problem solving, and modeling.

In each case, we will set out to specify carefully the definition of the behavioral category, and examine the extent to which we can relate it to the simple principles of behavior outlined in earlier chapters. We do not claim that *all* complex behavior can be allocated to one of the three categories we shall discuss. Rather, the developments in these areas should be seen as steps towards the analysis of complex behavior in general, demonstrating that we have by no means reached the limit of behavioral analysis.

CHAPTER 18

Concept
Acquisition

To "acquire a concept" or "form a concept" sounds like an abstract mental process, with no obvious behavioral connotations. Consideration of what it means to "have a concept", however, suggests that concept acquisition is closely related to the behavioral process of *discrimination*.

If a child has the concept of "school", he or she will apply this name to educational establishments, but not to other large public buildings, as he or she may have done when younger. We can say that the response "school" is under the *discriminative control* of features common to schools and not found in other buildings. An experimental investigation would be necessary to find out which features are important.

We begin with a consideration of a simple, animal discrimination learning paradigm, which shares certain important properties with human concept acquisition. This will enable us to identify the term *concept* with certain precise features of behavior, and having anchored this key word, a number of simple human experiments will further elaborate the logic of concept behavior. This groundwork completed, we will briefly consider some of the complex human behavior associated with terms such as understanding, meaning, and perception.

18.1
Simple Learning Sets

In Chapter 14 (Discrimination), we noted that one class of discriminations entailed two situations and two responses, and we described experimental apparatus useful for setting such contingencies. One such apparatus, the Wisconsin General Test Apparatus, was shown in Figure 14.4. In the WGTA, a monkey or other primate subject may be presented with several objects on a movable tray, one object concealing a peanut in a well beneath it. Suppose two objects to be in use, a solid wooden cross and a solid wooden U-shaped object. The peanut is always to be found under the cross figure, whether the latter appears on the left or on the right. The two possible contingencies may be diagrammed as[1]

$$S_{+u}: R_L \rightarrow S^+ \text{ and } S_{u+}: R_R \rightarrow S^+$$

where S_{+u} means that the cross is on the left, and S_{u+} means that the objects are reversed. Any "incorrect" responses have no consequences except the removal of the tray, while "correct" responses (those specified above) produce the peanut (S^+). A learning trial consists of presentation of one of the two possible contingencies. Either a correct or an incorrect response terminates the trial, and the next trial follows after a short intertrial interval.

From what we know about discrimination, we may be sure, given a number of such trials, that a behavioral process will take place. During the early trials, the animal's behavior will not be under the control of the cross object, and hence incorrect R's will occur (reaching towards u). Eventually, however, as more trials are given, the animal's behavior will gradually come under the control of the location of the cross. Since this process is a gradual one, tens to hundreds of trials, depending on species and individual differences, may be necessary to reach an asymptotic value of near or at 100 per cent "correct" responses.

So far, we have merely described a set of 2S-2R discrimination contingencies. Let us call a single such set of contingencies a discrimination *problem*. Suppose, once the discrimination process has reached its asymptote, we present a new set of contingencies. That is, suppose we present a new discrimination problem. We choose the new problem so that it differs from the old contingencies only in the objects used to make up its 2 S's; for

[1] Throughout this chapter R_L, R_C, and R_R refer to reaching left, center, and right.

example, a solid wooden sphere and an inverted wooden cone. The problem is otherwise identical. What will be the nature of this *new* discrimination process? In fact, it is very similar to the first process. The animal begins by performing little better than chance would predict; but it eventually comes to choose the correct object (now a sphere) on each and every trial. Closer inspection of these two processes might reveal, however, a slightly more rapid shift toward the asymptote in the second case.

This comparison of two successive discrimination processes suggests an interesting, general experimental design. Evidently we are not limited to one, or two, or even a few, such discrimination problems. We can continue to present new problems, one after the other, as long as we can find different objects and as long as our patience holds out. Fortunately for the latter, we discover that as we do present more and more problems, the discrimination processes become appreciably more rapid. Although tens to hundreds of trials may have been necessary to reach asymptotic performance on the early problems, perhaps less than a half-dozen trials are necessary for errorless performance by the time 100 discriminations have been learned. Eventually, after several hundred problems, we discover a remarkable outcome. The monkey is now able to solve any new problem of this sort immediately. If, by chance, it chooses the correct object on trial 1, it thereafter continues to choose the correct object. If, by chance, it chooses the wrong object on trial 1, it reverses its response pattern immediately and chooses the correct object from trial 2 on. In both cases, the monkey's performance is nearly always perfect by trial 2. In effect, presentation of a long series of similar problems has eradicated the gradual discrimination process. We are left with an animal that solves new discriminations immediately.

The preceding example illustrates the development of a *learning set* (L-set), a general paradigm studied extensively and named by H. F. Harlow. Figure 18.1 displays more precisely the results of the L-set procedure obtained from typical rhesus monkey subjects. Each curve in Figure 18.1 is the average of a number of discrimination processes. The processes are shown through trials 1 to 6 only. The key just below the graph tells exactly which discriminations are averaged in each curve. Figure 18.1 thus shows in detail the changes in the form of successive averaged discrimination processes. Discrimination process 1 to 8 is gradual and $\int$ shaped, and it is clear that its asymptote would lie well beyond the 6 acquisition trials shown. The average process for problems 9 to 16 is less gradual; the curve is steeper and will reach its asymptote more quickly. Subsequent processes are still steeper, until, after 232 problems, there is no "process" as such. There is only the result: on trial 2, the monkey is nearly always correct.

It is this behavioral result of presenting successive similar discrimination contingencies—an acquired ability to solve any one of a class of similar discrimination problems with maximum efficiency—that is usually described as a learning set (L-set). The acquired nature of such an ability suggests that it may have a characteristic process of its own. And indeed, the curve that

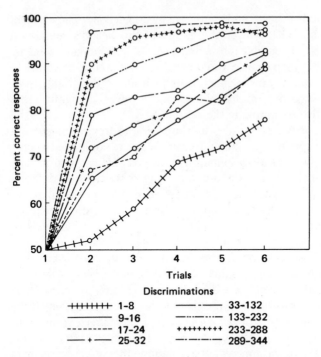

FIGURE 18.1. Changes in successive blocks of discrimination
processes. The curves are the average scores of eight monkeys
(after Harlow, 1949).

describes the development of an L-set can be derived from Figure 18.1, if we
use the performance on trial 2 as an index of its progress. Maximum
efficiency for solving this sort of discrimination would be indicated by
errorless performance on trial 2. It should be clear that performance on trial
1 cannot possibly be above 50 per cent correct. In advance, the monkey has
no basis for discriminating which of two new objects is correct, and so it will
pick the correct object on a chance, 50-50 basis only. Figure 18.2 shows the
performance level on trial 2 as a function of the number of problems
previously presented. The figure is, then, a convenient description of the
L-set acquisition process. An important feature of the process shown in
Figure 18.2 is its gradual and continuous character. *Thus, the ability to solve a
discrimination problem in one trial is itself acquired by a gradual process.*

In contrasting the discrimination processes of Figure 18.1 and the L-set
process of Figure 18.2, note that in discrimination, the independent time
variable over which the behavior changes with continued exposure to a
constant procedure is called trials. In the L-set process, on the other hand,
the independent time variable over which the behavior changes is called
problems. Note also that the *result* of each individual process of Figure 18.1

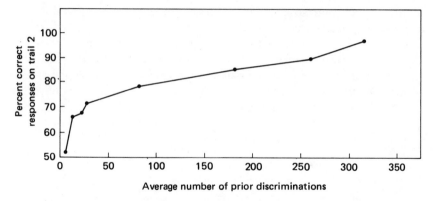

FIGURE 18.2. An L-set process derived from the data of Figure 18.1 based on performance on trial 2.

is called a discrimination; but the *result* of the process of Figure 18.2 is an L-set—the ability to solve a type of discrimination immediately.

We must not suppose that L-sets are restricted to the particular type of discrimination described in our example. In the discriminations of Figures 18.1 and 18.2, behavior is gradually brought under the control of one of two objects—the object that covers the peanut reinforcer in trial 1. But the general notion of an L-set consists of an acquired ability to solve discriminations of a given class on first contact. Thus, bringing behavior under the control of the larger of two objects, the green or the triangular one of two objects, constitutes other simple 2S-2R L-sets which may conveniently be established by a procedure similar to that described. In general, we may assume that the L-set procedure is applicable whenever it is possible to devise a set of *related* discrimination problems. After the animal has been exposed to a subset of these problems, it may eventually acquire the ability to solve them all.

Formally, the L-set *procedure* involves presenting a series of related discrimination problems to the organism. The successive discrimination processes change from slow and gradual to sudden and abrupt. The final *outcome* is that new, but related, discriminations are acquired very quickly. The term L-set usually refers to this result or outcome.

18.2
Effects of Species on L-set Acquisition

Harlow (1959) has summarized investigations of L-set formation, using various species of organisms, including children. Children tested in L-set procedures typically surpass chimpanzee and monkey subjects in overall performance, but they, too, exhibit a continuous L-set acquisition process. Primates lower on the phylogenetic scale than rhesus monkeys—squirrel monkeys and marmosets, for example—show a more gradual L-set acquisition process than Figure 18.2 depicts, Even after 1,000 or more problems, the asymptote of their L-set process is significantly lower than perfect L-set performance. Other animals, like rats and cats, show some steepening in successive discrimination processes, but they never reach sophisticated L-set results within the limits of the experiments that have been performed. A summary from five species is shown in Figure 18.3.

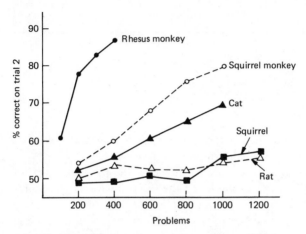

FIGURE 18.3. Performance of various species on a series of visual discrimination problems (from Mackintosh, 1977; after Warren, 1965).

These data suggest that true L-sets are a privileged ability of primates. Such a conclusion would have to be treated with great caution, in view of the many methodological difficulties in establishing comparable arrays of discriminations for different species, but anyway, has turned out to be wrong. Herman and Arbeit (1973) have shown that a bottle-nosed dolphin is capable of performing from 86 to 100 per cent correct on Trial 2 of each problem of an auditory learning-set task. The experimental study of learning continues both to erode the number of behaviors attributable only to man and to "upgrade" many species not previously suspected of "higher" learning abilities.

18.3
More Complex L-Sets

We have avoided using the term "concept" in the preceding discussions, but it seems natural to wonder whether an organism possessing an L-set for the larger of two objects, or for the green one of two objects, might reasonably be said to exhibit the concept "larger of two," or "green one of two." Such speculations would find themselves in good company, for Harlow hypothesized that "all concepts such as triangularity, middle-sizedness, redness, number, and smoothness evolve only from L-set formation" (Harlow, 1959, p. 510). We postpone, for the moment, a rigorous definition of the term concept, and merely suggest that the "concept" acquired in Figure 18.1 and 18.2 is "the object of two which had the peanut under it on the previous trial." Its verbal description is longer than those concepts mentioned by Harlow; a single-word identifier is lacking, perhaps because the contingencies that comprise this concept are rare in the world outside monkey behavior laboratories. An example of a more complex L-set will prove useful in illuminating the close relation between L-sets and concepts.

An important class of L-sets consists of "oddity" discriminations. In these discriminations, a group of objects is presented. Reinforcement is contingent upon picking out a single object which differs in some way from the other objects of the group. Such a discrimination might consist of the contingencies shown in Table 18.1. These entail two kinds of objects, six situations, and three responses. Once the primate subject has acquired the discrimination at a certain criterion level, a new problem is presented. Two new object types are used in the new problem, but the contingencies remain such that the position of the odd-shaped one of three is again correlated with reinforcement. After a series of many such problems, the monkey acquires an L-set which we could call "choosing the odd-shaped one of three." The well-trained subject in Figure 18.4 is demonstrating the behavior typifying this L-set. The sophisticated performance of the rhesus monkey is achieved only after the presentation of many similar problems. These results indicate the degree to which L-set procedures can succeed in bringing the operant behavior of animals under the control of rather subtle relationships existing within situations.

Such behavioral control in humans is often the basis upon which we assign the word "concept." For instance, we agree that a child has the concept of ownership when he or she can discriminate his or her own possessions from those of anyone else. We say that a child has the concept of a noun phrase when he or she can pick out the noun phrases from unfamiliar sentences.

TABLE 18.1. A set of oddity contingencies.

	Situations	Reinforced response
S_1	○ △ △	
S_2	△ ○ ○	R_L
S_3	△ ○ △	
S_4	○ △ ○	R_C
S_5	△ △ ○	
S_6	○ ○ △	R_R

FIGURE 18.4.

Similarly, we credit the child with the concept of equality of number when he or she can identify equal quantities in unfamiliar settings, as when he or she can match the number of beads in one jar to the number of apples on a table. However, these illustrations are, at best, merely suggestive. Clearly, we require a more rigorous definition of a "concept" if we wish to examine in detail the relation between L-sets and concepts. It will prove fruitful, therefore, to turn to some of the earliest concept-formation experiments with human subjects. It is here that we find an explicit attempt to translate human concept formation into behavioral terms, with the systematic question, "What does a person *do* when he or she is said to exhibit a concept?" When that question can be given a satisfactory answer, we shall be in a position to determine the procedures by which such conceptual behaviors are acquired.

18.4
Simple Human Concept-Formation Experiments

C. L. Hull (1920) took as his point of departure for the study of concept formation, the history by which a child comes to acquire the concept of "dog."

A young child finds himself or herself in a certain situation, reacts to it by approach, say, and hears it called "dog." After an indeterminate intervening period, the child finds himself or herself in a somewhat different situation, and hears that called "dog." Later he or she is in a somewhat different situation still, and hears that called "dog" also. Thus, the process continues. The "dog" experiences appear at irregular intervals (Hull, 1920, p. 5). As a result of these "experiences," a time arrives when the child is said to have the concept of dog. Hull's interpretation of this concept was a "characteristic more or less common to all dogs and not common to cats, dolls, and 'teddy bears' " (Hull, 1920, p. 6).

If a concept consists of a characteristic common to a diverse group of situations, it should be possible to set up laboratory conditions to study how behavior comes under the control of the common characteristics of a group of situations. As the elements for his experimental concepts, Hull chose the 144 Chinese characters shown in Figure 18.5. The unfamiliarity of these characters to his American university student subjects assured that none of the experimental concepts could have been previously acquired. In order to produce groups of situations containing a common characteristic, groups of characters were selected containing certain common elements. Note, for instance, that in Figure 18.5 all the characters in row 1 have embedded in their different, overall structures, the common brush strokes ⺅. In

FIGURE 18.5. The 144 Chinese characters used by Hull to study concept acquisition. The verbal identifying response and the common element are shown for each series (Hull, 1920).

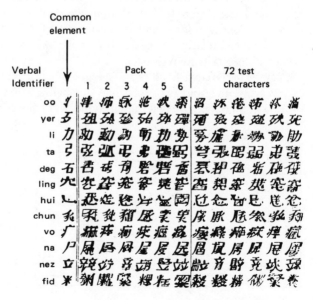

general, each character in a given horizontal row is related to every other character in that same row via the possession of some common element. In the experiment, the characters were combined into packs (vertical columns of Figure 18.5) so that each pack contained one, and only one, of the characters having a particular common element. Subjects were then shown the characters of pack 1, one at a time, and were asked to give the appropriate verbal identifying response as shown under the left column in Figure 18.5. The correct name was spoken by the experimenter a few seconds after presentation of each character. The subject's task was to name the character before the experimenter did so. The first trial was, of course, unique, for it acquired the subject with the set of verbal identifiers. When the criterion of two perfect trials had been reached, that is, when the subject had correctly named all the characters of pack 1 twice in a row, the characters of pack 2 were presented until they were all identified, then those of pack 3, and so forth, through pack 6.

Once the subject had learned to identify these 72 Chinese characters (6 packs × 12 characters per pack), the experimenter made a generalization test. He presented the remaining 72 characters, but no longer spoke the identifier. Is the subject capable of identifying them, even though he or she has never seen them before? Hull found that the subjects correctly identified over 70 per cent of these new characters. In fact, correct identifications were often made, even though the subject was unable to verbalize the rule for inclusion in the particular class.

In Hull's experiment, each member of a given S class had a certain brush stroke in common. Smoke (1932) pointed out that concepts in the real world rarely, if ever, consist of a class of situations with such explicit common elements. Concept formation more generally would seem to involve a response under the control of *relationships* common to a group of stimulus patterns. Consider, for example, the figures of Figure 18.6 generated by a rather artificial relation suggested by Smoke. All the figures in the left-hand box of Figure 18.6 are members of the S^D class named "dax," while none of the figures in the right-hand box of Figure 18.6 is a "dax" figure. The rule for "dax" is a circle and two dots; one dot being inside the circle, the other outside it. Smoke found that human subjects readily acquired the generalized

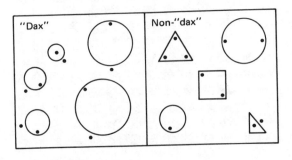

FIGURE 18.6.
Samples of "dax" S^D's and non-"dax" S^Δs (from Kimble and Garmezy, 1963; after Smoke, 1932).

behavior of categorizing "dax's" from other patterns, even though their only prior "discrimination training" was a presentation of some appropriately labeled "dax's" and non-"dax's", with instructions to note the differences. Though they were frequently unable to verbalize the rule for class inclusion, subjects could still correctly identify new instances of "dax" which they had never seen before.

In both the Hull and Smoke experiments, subjects are said to acquire certain concepts. We may now ask in what way these experiments demonstrate concept learning:

1. In both the Hull and Smoke experiments, subjects acquire the ability to pin a common verbal label on any member of a class of situations.
2. The acquired behavior generalizes to new situations to which the subjects have never before been exposed.
3. The class of situations is bound together by some common relationship—a brush stroke, or a complicated geometric rule.

From these findings, we are led to two conclusions about concept behavior. First, an organism is said to exhibit a concept when it can identify any member of a set of related situations. Second, the organism can acquire that ability via an explicit reinforcement history, or instructions relying on a previous reinforcement history, in the presence of a subset of the situations.

We are now in a position to see the relation of the L-set paradigm to concept formation. The L-set procedure is merely a systematic way of ordering a reinforcement history that leads to concept behavior. Though the monkeys do not speak, the behavior they acquire from L-set procedures seems precisely analogous to what human subjects in concept-formation experiments do, using verbal responses. The monkey picks the odd object from a set of objects it may never have seen previously. The human picks the "dax" from a set of patterns which he or she may never have seen previously. In real life, it would seem that we rarely acquire our concepts by the orderly advance from one related problem to another, the sequence characteristic of L-sets. The child in school, at home, and at play acquires his or her concepts concurrently, and in a far more haphazard fashion than any laboratory procedure arranges. Nevertheless, when the child can identify a new dog as a dog, or a new social situation as one that requires "company manners," he or she is engaging in behaviors of the sort produced by the various procedures we have described.

Note that the term concept, as described, does not refer to a thing. Like discrimination, conditioning, and extinction, the term refers to certain behavioral facts and certain relationships between behavior and environment. The word "concept" denotes the behavioral fact that a given response is under the control of a class of related S^D's. An interesting corollary of this definition is that it does not separate a concept from a discrimination. We may recall that a discrimination is a name for the behavioral fact that an S^D has come to control an operant response. But we know that generalization renders it impossible to discover a perfect case of discrimination in which only a single S^D controls a response. Prolonged discrimination training may narrow down the class of environmental events that sets the occasion for the response, but the class remains a class. If we have been trained to say "yellow" in the presence of a certain wavelength of light, the probability of the "yellow" response remains high when slight changes in wavelength are made. Such results, indicating the persistence of generalization even after long discrimination training, are expressions of the limitations on the capacity of the organism to make infinitely fine discriminations.

If a concept also refers to a class of S^D's controlling the emission of a response, how does it differ from a discrimination? Evidently the difference is one only of degree; at its borders the distinction is fuzzy and arbitrary. It is, therefore, plausible to speak either of the concept of yellow, or of the *discrimination* of yellow. Our word usage in a particular case will be determined merely by the broadness of the class of controlling S^D's. If the class of S^D's seems relatively narrow, we call the behavior a discrimination; if it seems relatively wide or broad, we are more likely to call the behavior a concept.

While the notion of broadness *per se* is too imprecise to permit a rigorous distinction between concepts and discriminations on the basis of the behaviors exhibited, it does suggest that the distinction between the two can be made procedurally. Suppose we were interested in training an organism to make finer and finer discriminations between a given triangle (S^D) and all other triangles. Our procedure would be to present triangles gradually more and more similar to the S^D triangle, while withholding reinforcement in their presence. In effect, we sharpen the discrimination by broadening the class of experienced S^Δ's. In forming the *concept* of triangularity, on the other hand, we would present and reinforce responses to triangles similar to the original triangle, thus broadening the S^D class. This is just what Hull did for "oo," Smoke did for "dax," and Harlow did for oddity. All these procedural variants serve gradually to build up the aggregation of S^D's that control a given response, by the behavior saying "oo," saying "dax," or selecting the odd-shaped object. The procedures for forming concepts and discriminations begin similarly with reinforcement in the presence of a single S^D, but they diverge thereafter to achieve their different effects. Discrimination training narrows the class of controlling S^D's, while concept formation broadens the class of controlling S^D's. Keller and Schoenfeld's (1950) "discrimination between classes, generalization within classes" is a handy phrase for summarizing the behavior characteristic of a concept, and reminds us of the processes that went into its evolution.

18.5

Arbitrary S^D Classes: Disjunctive Concepts

In the previous sections, we have alleged that when the behavior of organisms comes under the discriminative control of the members of a broad class of S^D's, these organisms are demonstrating conceptual behavior. In the concepts discussed, the controlling S^D classes may be described as a set of stimuli bound together by a common relation of spatial arrangement or topological structure. Thus, however unique each animal that constitutes the S^D class "cat" may be, each member of this class shares certain physical relations in common with every other member. the same holds true for the Chinese characters grouped in the "oo" concept, the "dax" figures, and so forth. In general, such common relations characterize our object concepts such as "house," "book," "table," and the printed letter "E." In other concepts, such as "bigger than," "comes from," "to the right of," "is a member of," "leads to," and "threeness," the common relations binding all the S^D's are not spatial structure, but other types of relations that are named by the very verbal responses they occasion. Thus, "bigger than" is a verbal response that names the relation shared by the members of the controlling S^D class.

It should be apparent that relational concepts are very pervasive. Nevertheless, behavior frequently may be observed to come under the control of broad classes of stimuli whose members seem to lack common stimulus relations. An obvious physical stimulus relation, for instance, is absent in the S^D's for "food." A carrot, a pea, a leaf of spinach, and a glass of milk appear as extremely diverse objects. From its visual characteristics alone, a pea is more like a marble than it is like a leaf; a carrot is more like a stick than it is like a glass of milk. A similar heterogeneity is present in the white crystals of iodine, the red liquid bromine, and the colorless gas known as chlorine, which partially constitute the class "halogen." The set of situations collected in Figure 18.7 all control stopping behavior, yet they bear little resemblance to one another.

Evidently, dissimilarity in the members of a broad S^D class is no deterrent to their ability to control a similar response. We may demonstrate experimentally the control illustrated by broad, but heterogeneous, S^D classes with an L-set procedure. If we train a monkey to choose *either* the triangular *or* the spherical of two objects and agree never to present a triangle and a sphere together, the monkey's behavior will come under the control of "triangles *or* spheres." Moreover, the control will generalize to both new triangles and new spheres. Here, the controlling S^D class consists of two very different subclasses. The triangular members are all bound together by their common geometrical relation, and the spherical members by theirs. Yet a common relation is lacking *between* spheres and triangles. By extending the procedure to additional diverse S^D's, we may broaden the monkey's S^D class to an indefinite list of heterogeneous objects. If we are careful to keep the new S^D

FIGURE 18.7. Physically different stimuli that all control the same
response: stopping (Goldiamond, 1966).

elements unrelated to the old ones, there will be no reason to expect the
monkey to generalize to any novel S we decide to add to the class.

The examples of everyday heterogeneous S^D classes, and the behavior of
the monkey cited in the last paragraph, illustrate what are known as
disjunctive concepts. The members of the S^D class are *either* triangles *or*
spheres; *either* carrots, *or* peas, *or* spinach, *or* milk, ...; *either* a policeman at
an intersection, *or* a red light; and so forth. In each case, a response is under
the control of a broad class of S^D's, and therefore, meets one of the important
criteria of concept behavior; nevertheless, the lack of a single common
relation, a thread linking all the members of the class, prevents the
generalization to new members that is typical of other concepts.

The difficulty in bringing in new members of a disjunctive S^D class on the
basis of generalization may be one of the reasons why mankind is sometimes
said to abhor disjunctive concepts (Bruner, Goodnow, and Austin, 1956).
Fortunately, it is frequently possible to find an *underlying* relation among the
members of a disjunctive S^D class that can provide the basis for
generalization. For example, different though foods may be in appearance,
all have the common property of being substances which are ingested by
living organisms and changed into vital bodily constituents. Similarly,
bromine, chlorine, and iodine have the common property of combining with
metals to form white crystalline salts which, in fact, are closely related to each
other.

In these and many other disjunctive concepts, an underlying relation is revealed by the behavioral operation that transforms the originally heterogeneous and diverse members of an S^D class into a new set of homogeneous and similar members. These new situations share a common relation, and that relation provides the basis for normal generalization. Sometimes the operation that is required is simple. To discover whether a certain substance is a food, we need merely ingest it and wait for the resulting transformed situation. To discover whether some new substance is a halogen, we let it interact with sodium and see whether a white crystalline "halogenic" salt is produced.

More frequently, resolving disjunctive classes into underlying relational concepts may be arduous. A significant part of scientific activity consists in trying out operations on superficially unlike events in the hope of transforming them into situations that are, in fact, similar. Much of this book is devoted to illustrating underlying relations discovered in behavioral events that, on the surface, look very different. A bird pecking a disk and a student voicing an opinion are shown to have an underlying relation.

Searches for underlying relations are by no means confined to science. Consider the long attempt to discover the absolute standard for great art or great music. Such a standard, if it could be found, would be a rule for relating the extremely diverse instances of what we identify as good art or music. The failure to find such rules may force us in exasperation to conclude that good music is what the critics say is good; or, to cite an illustration from psychology, intelligence is sometimes said to be "what the intelligence tests measure." No one has yet found an operation to perform on paintings or musical compositions that generate a set of situations in which the great and the mediocre are unequivocally distinguished. The concept of greatness remains disjunct. "When to stop" also retains a certain arbitrariness. No operation can be found to transform the diverse elements of Figure 18.7 into those exhibiting a common stimulus relation. The class is man-made and the choice of stimulus elements arbitrary. For this reason, there is no basis for generalization when a new S is introduced; all one can do is test each new instance as it comes along, determining class inclusion by the reinforcement contingencies alone. Such a class is built in much the way that we built the monkey's concept of "triangle-or-sphere."

In the final analysis, the only relation common to all kinds of disjunctive concepts is that their dissimilar members govern the same response. Some disjunctive concepts, for example, food and halogens, have the further property that their diverse members can be so transformed as to show a common underlying relation. Other disjunctive concepts, such as great music and intelligence, *may* have an underlying relation; others still, such as the experimental "sphere-or-triangle" concept, remain entirely arbitrary and dissimilar.

18.6
Concepts, Meaning, and Understanding

The meaning of a word has long been held to be related to concept formation, but the lack of a systematic framework for describing concepts has hampered an analysis of the exact relationship. In his discussion of how a child evolves the concept of a dog, Hull equated the formation of the concept with the idea of meaning. A child has the meaning of a dog when he or she can appropriately identify new objects as dogs. We may agree that appropriate use of a verbal response to identify the members of a concept's S^D class is part of what is meant by having the meaning for the verbal response. But we are likely to feel that something is missing in equating meaning with discriminative behavior. Consider the concept of milk. Would we be willing to agree that a child has the meaning of milk when he or she can correctly identify bottles of milk, glasses of milk, and spilled milk? The child might be said to have a limited meaning of milk if all he or she can do is identify instances of the S^D class, but we shall be inclined to say that his or her understanding of the concept does not go very deep. Analogously, a chimpanzee may be trained to pick out triangles from any group of objects, but few psychologists would be willing to use terms like meaning or understanding in describing the observed behavior. Meaning and understanding are, however, things we try to teach in schools. Science and art are sometimes said to be quests for them. Hence, it may be appropriate to ask what further behaviors may be involved when an organism is said to have the meaning of, or to understand, a concept.

We must first examine the notion that an organism may acquire a concept which is itself made up of two or more concepts. In the present terminology, a response (verbal or otherwise), may be controlled by a broad S^D class, which can itself be partitioned into two or more S^D classes, each controlling its own unique response. Consider, for instance the concept "ice," which we shall take as equivalent to "frozen water." The S^D class for ice is evidently the intersection of the set of frozen objects and the set of water objects. Few of our everyday concepts are as simple as this, but the majority of the concepts acquired by human organisms do lend themselves to analysis in terms of other concepts. Thus, an operant is the ⟨set of responses⟩ under ⟨the control of⟩ their ⟨consequences⟩. A harbor is a ⟨sheltered⟩ ⟨body of water⟩ with ⟨piers⟩. Father is a ⟨male⟩ ⟨parent⟩. We may even invent such concepts, as in the example: tiglon = the ⟨offspring⟩ of a ⟨male⟩ ⟨tiger⟩ and a ⟨female⟩ ⟨lion⟩.

Whenever the S^D classes of a concept are made up of the intersection, or what is more often called the conjunction, of two or more S^D classes, we speak of the concept as a *conjunctive* concept. The compound nature of a conjunctive concept suggests an experimental question; namely, whether a prior history with its component concepts affects the acquisition of such a conjunctive concept. An experiment by Kendler and Vineberg (1954) indicates that when its components are previously conceptualized, a concept based on their conjunction is more quickly acquired. The experiment involved sorting cards, reinforced as "right" or "wrong", according to a rule that varied between three groups of subjects. Two groups sorted by shape, one by color. After acquiring this concept, each group learned another concept (size, color, or shape). Finally, all subjects were reinforced for sorting into four piles on the basis of the conjunctive concepts consisting of size and shape. Performance on this task was best if the subjects had previously been trained on *both* these concepts, not as good if they had been trained on one, and worst if they had not been trained on either. The rate of acquisition of the conjunctive concept was, therefore, directly related to the number of component concepts previously learned.

In Kendler and Vineberg's final concept task, two component concepts (size and shape) were related by conjunction to form a new concept (size-shape). Conjunction is, however, only one of the many ways that concepts may be related, and it is an analysis of such interconcept relations that is most pertinent for the meaning or understanding of a concept. We argued earlier in this section that a child who could identify instances of the concept milk, or a monkey who could press a lever whenever it was presented with a triangle, cannot fully be said to exhibit all the behavior necessary for us to class it as exhibiting understanding. The kind of additional behavior that seems required is represented schematically in Figure 18.8 for the concept of milk.

Figure 18.8 is explicated as follows. Each of the circles of the diagram refers to a class of S^D's of the sort we have previously described. Thus, the child, for whom Figure 18.8 might be said to be a meaningful structure, can identify bottles of milk, cups of milk, spilled milk, and so on. But he or she can also identify (with different verbal responses) cows of various sorts, cereals of one kind or another, cheeses, ice creams, and milkmen. If he or she is a high school student studying nutrition, then he or she is likely to be able to identify fluids, butterfat, and calcium, too. But, equally important, the sophisticated human organism can give a *relational* identifier for a compound situation consisting of one S^D from milk and one from any of the other S^D classes indicated. This further conceptual skill is indicated by the lines between circles with the statements describing the relation. Each relational statement is, however, also a concept; indeed, it is the sort of concept we have met frequently in previous sections. The training required for such relational concepts as "comes from" and "is a component of" is precisely analogous to the training given the monkey when such concepts as the "odd one," "the taller," the "one rotated 90 degrees," were acquired. A child is said to have a more complete meaning of milk, or a more complete understanding of the concept of milk, therefore, when he or she can identify the relations between members of the S^D class making up milk and the members of various other S^D classes.

It should be clear that the structural representation of meaning of Figure

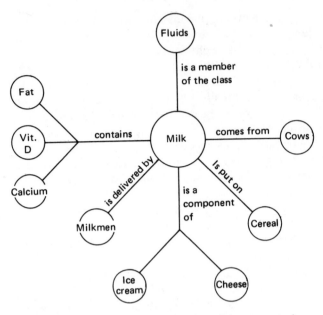

FIGURE 18.8. A schematic representation of the concept of milk and its relation to several other concepts.

18.8 is artificially isolated. We have, in fact, shown only the relations between a single concept and a group of others, neglecting the interrelationships of each peripheral concept to the others, and to all other concepts the organism exhibits. A complete representation of the conceptual repertoire of any given individual would seem an insurmountable task, though a limited sample of concepts and their interrelations might feasibly be described.

Figure 18.8 does give us a way of crudely representing varying degrees of understanding. The more dense the interconnections, and the more S^D classes that can be tied together, the more likely we are to say that an individual understands a concept. The understanding a child has of milk differs principally from that of the dairy manager, or the nutrition expert, in the smaller number of concepts to which the child can relate milk. My understanding of my car is very incomplete compared with that of my garage mechanic, who can relate the word car to thousands of other S^D classes, including, in particular, what we call the parts of the vehicle. Yet his or her understanding may end with the mechanics of engines. An interesting case is provided by the physicist, who may be able to analyze such concepts as friction, acceleration, work, and energy at a far more basic level than could the mechanic. But when his or her car refuses to start, the physicist will be helpless in repairing it unless he or she also possesses such concepts as rocker arm, spark plug, cylinder, distributor, and their various interrelations. The interrelationships between concepts for any given individual depend on that individual's past history: the automobile driver's contingencies are affiliated with a certain set of situations, the mechanic's with another, and the physicist's with still another. The differences between their conceptual repertoires suggest a distinction in level, though it is often very difficult in practice to establish the relative levels of concepts.

18.7

The Perceptual Constancies

The notion of a "thing" as an unchanging entity is so strongly ingrained that it may come as a surprise that things as primitive as objects may be described as concepts. Consider that the face of a friend is not a single visual stimulus. At times, it appears in shade; at other times, in sunlight. At times, it is smiling; at times, frowning. Sometimes you see the profile; at other times, you see the front view. Yet, profile and front view are themselves a collection of profiles and front views, no single one of which is ever exactly repeated. In spite of the fact that you never see the same face twice, you have no difficulty identifying your friend. In technical language, your friend is a broad class of S^D's, and you respond similarly to all the members.

Consider the object shown in Figure 18.9. All four sketches represent "the same door," yet the various patterns that reach the eye, and that constitute the four situations we call "door," are vastly different. It is clear that for doors, or any other object we wish to imagine, our concept of the given object consists not of a single situation, but a broad class of situations. The examples we have just given are instances of what might be called *object constancy*. In spite of rather marked changes in the situation, we retain a constant response in the presence of all its variants.

What kind of concept is represented by object constancy? Taken individually, the four sketches of Figure 18.9 suggest that the object concept is disjunctive, since these four situations look so different. But Figure 18.9 is only a sample of the infinite set of situations ranging from open to shut, all of which control the response "door." And all of these situations are related, one to the other, by the fact that one "door" situation may be continuously

FIGURE 18.9. Four members of the S^D class "door" (Gibson, 1950).

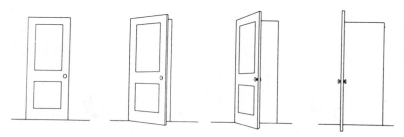

transformed into another. Such a series of transformations relates the situations of any given object.

Object constancy is merely one of a class of what are generally called perceptual constancies. Another example is shown by the two pieces of coal resting on white paper illustrated in Figure 18.10. We call the coal "black" and the paper "white", regardless of the absolute intensity of light that either the coal or the paper alone reflects. In shadow, the piece of coal in the left panel of Figure 18.10 reflects only 1 millilambert of light, while the same piece of coal in the sun (right panel of Figure 18.10) reflects 100 times as much light. Still we call the coal black, even though now it reflects more than ten times as much light as did the white paper in the shade. The neutral color response (shade of gray) depends on the relative illumination of the object to its background or immediately surrounding region. Thus, "black" appears as a concept since it is the response in the presence of a broad class of related S^D's: object 1 unit of light, background 9 units of light; object 10 units, background 90 units; object 100, background 900; and so forth.

A final example is provided by the phenomenon known as *size constancy*. As a person walks towards you, you are unlikely to report that his or her visual image is increasing in size. Yet, as he or she approaches, the person's image is growing in size on your retina in a way that is approximately inversely proportional to his or her distance from you. Within limits, you will report the person as the same size, regardless of the size of his or her image on your retina. It turns out that one's concept of size is dependent on an S^D class, where the rule for class inclusion is a complex function of the retinal size of the object plus the values of numerous other visual variables that vary with the distance of an object. Figure 18.11 shows that the concept of constant size is not controlled by constant retinal size. The three cylinders of Figure 18.11 are all the same size (measure them), but we tend to class them as progressively larger from left to right, because of the changes in linear perspective, one of the variables that ordinarily changes progressively with distance.

It is, of course, no accident that object, neutral-color, and size constancies have developed. Reinforcement contingencies are very often correlated with

FIGURE 18.10. A case of neutral color constancy. A piece of coal rests on a sheet of white paper (Hochberg, 1964).

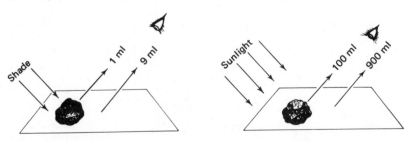

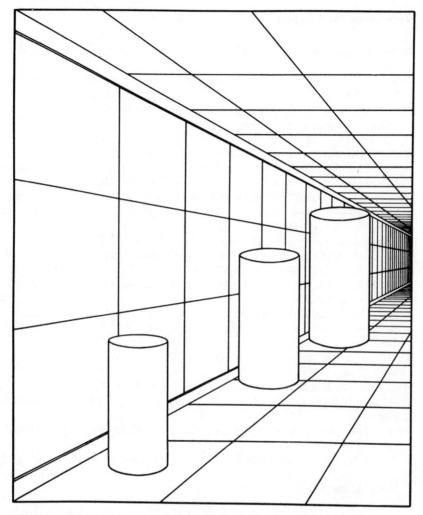

FIGURE 18.11. Size response as influenced by distance cues (Gibson, 1950).

"objects" (a bird had best keep clear of all the situations we call "cat" if it is to live to a ripe old age), as well as the compound stimulus variables controlling achromatic color constancy and size constancy. It is rarely of use to regard an object as changing its color or size when its illumination or distance changes. On the other hand, it is very useful to classify that animal moving rapidly towards you as "big", even though its image size is still very small. Our concepts mirror the reinforcing contingencies of nature, though it remains an interesting speculation whether these perceptual concepts are generally reacquired in each individual's past history, or whether, having been so well acquired by his or her ancestors, they are now a permanent part of the person's visual behavior.

References for Chapter 18

Bruner, J. S., Goodnow, J. J., and Austin, G. *A study of thinking.* New York: Wiley, 1956.

Gibson, J. J. *The perception of the visual world.* Cambridge, Mass.: The Riverside Press, 1950.

Goldiamond, I. Perception, language, and conceptualization rules. In B. Kleinmuntz (Ed.) *Carnegie Institute of Technology annual symposium on cognition.* New York: Wiley, 1966.

Harlow, H. F. The formation of learning sets. *Psychological Review,* 1949, **56**, 51–65.

Harlow, H. F. Learning set and error factor theory. In S. Koch (Ed.) *Psychology: A study of a science,* Volume 2. New York: McGraw-Hill, 1959.

Herman, L. M., and Arbeit, W. R. Stimulus control and auditory discrimination learning sets in the bottlenose dolphin. *Journal of the Experimental Analysis of Behavior,* 1973, **19**, 379–394.

Hochberg, J. E. *Perception.* Englewood Cliffs, N.J.: Prentice-Hall, 1964.

Hull, C. L. Quantitative aspects of the evolution of concepts. *Psychological Monographs,* 1920, **28**, (Whole No. 123).

Keller, F. S., and Schoenfeld, W. K. *Principles of psychology.* New York: Appleton-Century-Crofts, 1950.

Kendler, H. H., and Vineberg, R. The acquisition of compound concepts as a function of previous training. *Journal of Experimental Psychology,* 1954, **48**, 252–258.

Kimble, G. A., and Garmezy, N. *Principles of general psychology.* New York: Ronald Press, 1963.

Mackintosh, N. J. stimulus control: Attention factors. In W. K. Honig and J. E. R. Staddon (Eds.) *Handbook of operant behavior.* Englewood Cliffs, N.J.: Prentice-Hall, 1977.

Smoke, K. L. An objective study of concept formation. *Psychological Monographs,* 1932, **42** (Whole No. 191).

Warren, J. M. Primate learning in comparative perspective. In A. M. Schrier, H. F. Harlow, and F. Stollnitz (Eds.) *Behavior of nonhuman primates,* Volume 1. New York: Academic Press, 1965.

CHAPTER 19

Problem
Solving

The term "problem" has arisen occasionally in previous discussions. Thorndike placed cats in a puzzle box containing a latch that could be opened by various movements (Figure 1.4). Cats lacking a previous history with the contingencies of this apparatus were said to be faced with a problem— escaping from the box. The acquisition of any instrumental, or operant, behavior can thus be said to contain elements of problem solving. In the learning sets of the last chapter, we described the successive sets of discrimination contingencies presented during training as a series of discrimination problems. Monkeys solve these problems, and as a result, achieve the ability to solve new and similar problems with increasing efficiency.

19.1

The structure of a Problem and the Nature of a Solution

The problems faced by Thorndike's cats and Harlow's monkeys differed in several respects, but particularly, in the contingencies extant. The contingencies set for the cats were predominantly response differentiations; those for the monkeys, stimulus discriminations. It seems that the notion of a "problem" does not denote any particular class of reinforcement contingencies. Both discriminations and differentiations can be problems. Whether a set of contingencies is or is not to be construed as a problem for an organism, depends upon the behaviors that are at strength when the organism first faces the problem situation. Thorndike's cats evidently found the puzzle box a problem on their early trials. Eventually, as the behavior that led to opening the latch was repeatedly reinforced, the situation lost its problematic character. No sooner were the cats placed in the box, than they were out again. A similar development occurs in L-set formation. A monkey with a well-formed oddity L-set solves any new oddity discrimination immediately. The oddity situation can no longer be described as a "problem" for this organism.

These simple ideas are not limited to the artificial problems set animals in psychological laboratories. For a second grader

$$
\begin{array}{r}
25 \\
-18 \\
\hline
\end{array}
$$

constitutes a problem, but a year or so later, that will no longer be the case. Similarly, you may not find $\int e^{-3x}dx$ a problem, depending on whether you possess certain skills usually taught in first-year calculus texts. At the extreme end of the continuum, we may all be said to find "how to end wars" a problem, since a universal solution remains to be demonstrated. In summary, no class of contingency, nor any particular contingency, can be described as a problem until we know what behavior the organism has available in the presence of that contingency. Let us now attempt to describe this view more rigorously. To do so, we shall find the concepts of chaining, introduced in Chapter 8, useful.

In a chain of behavior, an organism emits operants in a sequential order. The particular order is governed by the consequences set for each individual operant. In solving a division problem, a well-trained child performs multiplication, subtraction, borrowing, carrying, and so on, in a certain sequence that is dependent on the result of various discriminations. A child without the component skills cannot perform the required chain. This second child illustrates the possibility that in any given situation, there may not exist any chain at strength that will produce the situation associated with reinforcement. This may arise in one of two related ways:

1. The organism has not in the past acquired a part or all of the chain necessary to lead it from the present situation, S_A, to the reinforcing situation, S_B, though such a chain may be known to other organisms.
2. No known chain exists whose execution guarantees the transformation of S_A to S_B.

Let us now examine several representative problems. The puzzle-box problem reveals a number of interesting features in problem solving. The cats were placed in an initial situation, the locked box, S_A. A number of behaviors were immediately generated. The cats thrashed about, meowed, put their paws through the bars, scratched at large openings, looked in various directions, and so forth. These behaviors may represent operants generalized from a past history within similar situations. When confined to a small space in the past, the cat usually escaped by looking around the environment, advancing towards any opening, scratching at loose parts of the environment, and so on. Some other behaviors, such as meowing are undoubtedly built into the structure of the cat. Regardless of how they became established, a number of behaviors, $R_1, R_2, R_3, R_4, \ldots$, arise in the initial problem situation. Furthermore, though these behaviors are not random, they are not yet patterned into the well-ordered sequence that is emitted when the cat "solves the problem." Eventually, one of these R's may succeed in opening the latch; when that happens, the cat has transformed the situation from door closed to door open.
We can describe this as:

$$S_{A(door\ closed)}: \quad \begin{array}{l} R_1 \\ R_2 \\ R_3 \\ R_4 \to S_{(door\ open)}: R_{(go\ through\ door)} \to S_{B\ (out\ of\ box)} \\ \cdot \\ \cdot \\ \cdot \end{array}$$

In the new situation, $S_{(door\ open)}$, the cat produces a well-established response sequence and advances through the open door. This simple problem illustrates several important aspects of problem solving in general. (1) An organism brings a set of responses $(R_1, R_2, R_3, \ldots)$ to the situation, either by virtue of its past history with similar situations, or by virtue of its genetically determined response to situations of that type. (2) These R's are not all equally likely to occur; some (scratching at openings, meowing) exist at higher strength than others (exploring the roof of the box, standing still). (3) Once a given response succeeds in transforming the situation into a familiar one, a well-established sequence can carry the animal to the reinforcing situation, S_B.

19.2

Trial and Error, or Insight?

Thorndike, as others before him, referred to the first two aspects described as *trial-and-error* responding. The animal emitted ("tried") many responses in the problem situation, most of them being "errors"; eventually it chanced upon the "correct" R, and thereby achieved "success." Kohler (1925) very early criticized this characterization of problem solving. He argued that Thorndike's situation was not representative of problems in general. The cats, maintained Kohler, could not initially observe the relation between the latch and the open box. But many actual problems, he argued, permit the organism to observe more aspects and relations in the situation than was the case for these cats. Kohler, therefore, set animals the following problem (Figure 19.1). A banana was located outside an ape's cage. There were two hollow bamboo sticks inside the cage, but neither stick was long

FIGURE 19.1. Köhler's two-stick problem.

enough to reach the banana. One stick, however, was smaller in diameter and could easily be inserted into either end of the other stick, thereby making a single stick long enough to reach the banana. Kohler's apes, when placed in this situation, initially exhibited behaviors that had been reinforced in the past. They extended one or the other stick, moving it back and forth just short of the banana. After a certain amount of extinction, this responding weakened. At this point, some animals were observed to sit quietly for a time, after which, they suddenly put the two sticks together and drew in the banana.

> Sultan first of all squats indifferently on a box, which has been left standing a little back from the railings; then he gets up, picks up the two sticks, sits down again on the box and plays carelessly with them. While doing this, it happens that he finds himself holding one rod in either hand in such a way that they lie in a straight line; he pushes the thinner one a little way into the opening of the thicker, jumps up and is already on the run towards the railings ... and begins to draw a banana towards him with the double stick (Kohler, 1925, p. 27).

Kohler called this sudden solution an *insight* and suggested that it was a typical property of problem solving. He maintained that Sultan and other subjects solved the problem because the structure of the problem became readily apparent, and not because the behavior of putting the two sticks together was an operant of high strength in the situation. Birch (1945), however, was able to show that a certain past history is critical in solving this kind of problem. Kohler had not specified his apes' past histories in detail.

Birch undertook to see whether prior stick manipulation was essential. He took a group of apes who had never had experience with sticks and set them identical problem contingencies. Contrary to Kohler's finding, none of these subjects was able to solve the problem in a 30-min session. Birch then allowed the apes several sessions of play with short, straight sticks. He observed the animals gradually come to use the sticks as extensions of their arms for poking, prying, digging, raking, and other similar operations. On a second test, all the animals solved the two-stick problem in less than half a minute. The conclusion is inescapable. Previous manipulation of sticks contributes to the solution of a problem requiring this as a component skill; the logical structure of the situation will not aid an organism that possesses no skills in utilizing that structure.

The chained nature of the component behaviors constituting the solution to a problem helps us explain the sudden character of solutions observed by Kohler and others. Once the organism has produced a situation that is the cue for a well-established sequence of behavior, the problem has ended. Once Sultan turned those two short sticks into one long one, the problem had come to an end; for we may reasonably suppose that Sultan had had a previous history of raking in objects with sticks of varying lengths.

19.3
Puzzles

In studying human problem solving, psychologists have set their subjects a variety of tasks. Some of these have been in the form of puzzles. A well-known puzzle is shown in Figure 19.2. The subject is instructed to draw through each of the nine dots with four straight lines without taking his or her pencil off the paper and without retracing a line. Lines can cross each other if necessary. Most subjects meet the problem with a set of operants for connecting up points by drawing around the periphery. This sequence fails, however, and another response at high strength usually emerges—the drawing of a diagonal. This new behavior is of little aid, since the diagonal plus three peripheral lines still leave one dot unaccounted for. Very quickly, then, the subject exhausts his or her usual repertoire for dealing with such "problems"; it is at this point that he or she will agree that it is, indeed, a puzzle. A solution to the nine-dot problem consists of the extension of the lines beyond the confines of the dot matrix.

That such a simple solution requires such a great deal of time, and frequently is not achieved at all, points to an important feature of puzzles. Many problems or puzzles are difficult to solve because they tend to control very strong but inappropriate responses. Puzzles frequently resemble past situations in which certain responses were appropriate and reinforced. The nine-dot problem, for instance, is very similar to a situation containing only eight dots (imagine the center dot of Figure 19.2 to be missing), which could easily be "solved" by drawing four lines along the periphery. The repeated emission of inappropriate behavior in a problem situation is usually called set, used in the sense that we say someone is "set in his ways." Confining line-drawing responses to the boundaries of the nine-dot matrix is an example of such a set. Many problems can only be solved by unusual responses, so it is frequently useful to instruct problem solvers in such a way that their

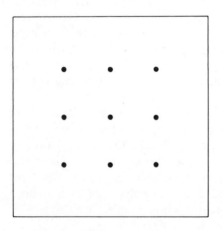

FIGURE 19.2.
The nine-dot puzzle. (For answer see p. 356.)

variability of behavior increases. It is easy to demonstrate that set is under the control of the organism's reinforcement history. Luchins (1942) asked subjects to solve a number of numerical problems calling for the measurement of quantities of water by means of several measuring jars. Table 19.1 shows eleven of these problems. Problem *1* was an introductory example. The subject was shown that in order to obtain 20 units of water (the value in the rightmost column), he or she would have to fill the 29-unit jar and pour 3 units from it, 3 times. The subject then worked at the other ten problems. Note that (excluding the introductory example) all problems, except number 9, conform to the rule *B* minus *A* minus *2C*: first, fill the large jar, *B*; then, pour off 1 *A*-jarful and 2 *C*-jarfuls. Problems *7* to *11*, however, have an alternative solution, using only two jars, which might be interpreted as a simpler chain of behavior. Nevertheless, subjects from grade school to university graduate level rarely used the two-jar solutions. Their reinforcement history on problems *2* to *6* brought the three-jar sequence to such high strength that it dominated all other chains.

The idea of set appears in the celebrated two-string problem of Figure 19.3. The initial situation, S_A, consists of two strings hanging from the ceiling of an otherwise practically bare room. The terminal reinforcing situation, S_B, consists of the two ends of the strings tied together. However, the distance between the strings is too great for the subject to reach over and grasp one string while holding on to the end of the other. In one version of the problem, the only loose object present in the experimental room was an electromagnetic relay. A solution to the problem is shown in Figure 19.4. The subject has attached the relay to the string and has set the weighted string in motion as a pendulum. Once caught, the end of the swinging string can be joined to the other string, and the two strings can easily be tied. Subjects

TABLE 19.1. Luchins (1942) Water-Jar Problems.

Problem number	Capacities of Jars			Required amount
	A	*B*	*C*	
1	29	3	—	20
2	21	127	3	100
3	14	163	25	99
4	18	43	10	5
5	9	42	6	21
6	20	59	4	31
7	23	49	3	20
8	15	39	3	18
9	28	76	3	25
10	18	48	4	22
11	14	36	8	6

FIGURE 19.3.
The two-string problem. The two strings are to be tied together, but they are too far apart for one to be held while the other is grasped.

FIGURE 19.4.
A solution to the two-string problem. The subject has tied the relay to one string and, using it as a weight, has set the string swinging.

given a prior session, in which they were instructed in using the relay as an electrical-circuit component, were markedly deficient at solving this problem (Birch and Rabinowitz, 1951). Here again, a certain past history (using the electrical component as an electrical component) overrode the behaviors needed for solving the problem (using the electrical component as a weight).

As a final example, consider the matchstick problems of Figure 19.5. The matchstick problems illustrate a feature common to many problems, namely, that the solution to be arrived at is specified only in general form. The legend of Figure 19.5 tells what general properties the solution must have; it does not specify in detail the terminal situation, S_B. Except for the nine-dot problem, our previous problems and puzzles specified the exact reinforcing situation, S_B, rather than its general structure. The monkey solved the problem when the banana was in the cage; the two-string problem was solved when the strings were tied together. But the matchstick problems are solved only when the box count is the required number. For these problems, there are several acceptable solutions, with many ways to arrive at them.

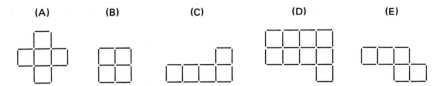

FIGURE 19.5. Katona's (1940) matchstick problems. In A, B, and C, move three matches to produce a new figure that has one less square than the original figure. In D, produce a new figure with only five squares by moving three matches. In E, move two matches to produce a figure with four squares, (For answer see p. 356.)

19.4
Heuristic Search Strategies

Our general characterization of problems emphasized their chained, or component, nature. But analysis of most of the sample problems from the previous sections does not require detailed chaining. Let us, therefore, broaden the concept of a "problem." Consider the combination lock of Figure 19.6. Most combination locks of this type have 50 or 100 discrete positions, but 5 will suffice for our illustration. A person, for whom such a lock bars the entrance to some reinforcing situation, may be said to be faced with a problem if he or she does not have the sequence of behaviors available to open the lock. However, if this person tries every combination, he or she will eventually succeed. This is probably the notion of trial-and-error behavior that Kohler and other psychologists attributed to Thorndike, when they criticized his analysis of problem solving as lacking the elements for a structured solution. Yet Thorndike never reported that the cats engaged in every possible behavior in every possible sequence. In fact, the cats confined their attention to the slots and moving parts of the puzzle box, exhibiting a highly *selective* set of behaviors. But a combination-lock problem illustrates much purer trial-and-error responding. Thus, a lock with 50 numbers, which opens when the correct sequence of 3 numbers is dialed, will require $50^3/2$

FIGURE 19.6.
A five-position combination lock.

($=62,500$) sequences to be tried on the average before it will open. If each sequence takes 6 sec to dial, the average time to open such a lock would be about 4 days' continuous work. It is obvious why such a lock serves as a protection, even though nearly everyone could follow the procedure of trying every combination.

An upside-down tree structure is a useful way of representing the behavior sequences in this kind of problem (Figure 19.7). The circles or nodes in a tree structure represent the situations that may be produced by various responses available to the organism. Thus, the top node is the original situation, with no number dialed as yet. The first 5 possible numbers are shown as nodes one level lower. Analogously, the 25 nodes at the next level represent the set of situations that result from dialing yet another number. The possibilities at the lowest level, reached by dialing a third number, are so numerous (125) that we can conveniently represent only a sample of these in the diagram. In the tree of Figure 19.7, the lines represent the operant dialing responses of the organism. The structure gives us a way of representing the possible situations that may arise when all the available responses in a problem are specified, and all their resulting consequences known. It is apparent from inspection of Figure 19.7 that a person who wishes to open this lock is going to have to make his or her way through very many branches before chancing upon the correct one.

Many other problems can be represented in the form of a tree of operant sequences and their resulting situations. If a simple 5 numeral turn lock can lead to so many possible branches (125), we may well wonder how an individual ever solves really difficult problems, such as finding a good move in chess, integrating a function, proving a theorem in logic. The possible situations resulting from only a dozen distinct types of responses carried to a sequence level of 12 is 12^{12}. Evidently, pure trial and error could never suffice to solve a problem of any difficulty.

FIGURE 19.7. A tree structure representing some of the behaviors and resulting situations arising from dialing the numbers of the lock in Figure 19.6. The "combination" (3, 5, 4) is shown as dotted lines joining the filled circles.

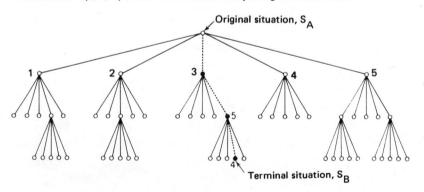

Suppose that there were some way for the problem solver to limit his or her alternative operations. That is, suppose that in Figure 19.7, the individual was told that the first number in this kind of lock is usually 3. His or her search then might be profitably limited to the small portion of the tree stemming from the node 3. In general, problems that are soluble do have associated with them various rules or *heuristics* that permit the organism to narrow down his or her response topography to a certain likely set of operations. These heuristics are generally characterized as rules of thumb that help limit the behavior sequence. Their use does not guarantee a solution, but it does frequently aid in finding a solution. We may think of Thorndike's cats as exhibiting such heuristics when they confined their attention to the slots and moving parts of the puzzle box. In the past, such responses paid off more frequently than other behaviors, either for the individual or for the species. A possible heuristic for the combination-lock problem might be to note that people sometimes fasten a lock and leave the last number of the combination still standing. This is not invariably true, but it might serve as a useful heuristic.

In complex problems, it is helpful to be able to diagnose whether progression towards or recession away from the solution is occurring; that is, whether one is "getting warmer." As one moves away from S_A, it is often possible to interpret the intermediate situations (nodes) as bringing one either close to or further away from the terminal situation, S_B. Suppose we blindfold a person, confine him or her to a large room, and tell the person that his or her task is to throw a dart into a bull's-eye. The location of the box of darts and of the target is unknown to the person. We permit our subject two responses, walking, and throwing darts. We agree to advise him or her, however, after every step taken, whether or not he or she is getting closer to the dart box. Furthermore, once he or she gets there and starts throwing darts, we shall advise this person as to whether his or her successive throws are closer or farther from the target. This is just a version of the "you're getting warmer" game, and if our target is not too small, our subject will solve this problem quickly. But it is obvious that a person who is not supplied with the progressive S^D's ("advice") along the way may never solve the problem.

In general, an analysis of problem solving takes the form of (1) noting the suitable heuristics that narrow the response topography to be used and the situations that are worth exploiting; (2) noting the important intraproblem discriminations that must be made in order to detect whether a response has moved the organism closer to or further away from the terminal situation.

If these are indeed the critical components of problem-solving behavior, it ought to be possible to incorporate them into the structure of a machine which could then solve similar problems. The behavior of such a machine might be of interest for several reasons. First, it could act as a check on the sufficiency of the set of heuristics and discriminations we might hypothesize to be necessary for any given set of problems. Second, by varying features of the machine, we might discover ways to develop a more efficient problem solver, and then apply these discoveries to educational practice. Because of its rapidity of operation (25,000 or more operations per sec), the digital computer is ideally suited for the exploration of such models of problem solving. Representations of situations can be programmed, various operations corresponding to organismic responses can be simulated, and a strategy for successively transforming one situation into another can be built into the machine. Newell and Simon (1963) have described a computer program called the General Problem Solver (GPS) for treating certain puzzles and problems. The program uses a variety of heuristic search strategies and discrimination tests for evaluating whether newly created situations represent progress toward the terminal situation, S_B.

One of their problem environments is the domain of symbolic logic. The machine may be asked to prove that $(R \supset \sim P) \cdot (\sim R \supset Q)$ is equivalent to $\sim (\sim Q \cdot P)$. The machine is given the same information that a college student subject is faced with, namely, a dozen rules for transforming symbols by adding terms, deleting terms, changing connectives, changing signs, changing groupings, and so forth. The program that turns the computer into a problem solver provides it with the ability to apply these rules (respond), and to discriminate differences among the situations it produces. Perhaps most important, the program provides it with a number of heuristics to guide its search through a problem tree. One useful heuristic restrains GPS from trying to transform a situation (node) if that situation is more difficult to transform than a previous situation (node) was. GPS has its own built-in criteria of difficulty of transformation. GPS expects differences between its successively generated situations, S_1, S_2, $S_3 \ldots$, and the terminal situation, S_B, to decrease as GPS proceeds to work its way through a series of transformations. If that does not prove to be the case, GPS returns to a higher level (back towards S_A) and sets off along a new branch. Another heuristic forces GPS to abandon a branch when it gets below a given depth (the vertical dimension in Figure 19.7) and situation S_B has not yet turned up. GPS seems to solve its problems about as well as the college student subjects and, more important perhaps, often makes the same kinds of errors. Other programs for solving geometric proofs, playing chess and checkers, performing integration, and balancing assembly lines have been devised, all making use of the ideas of heuristic search strategies.

19.5
Rules as Solutions to Problems

In the combination lock problem, the statement "try every possible combination" is a *rule* guaranteeing its eventual (but not rapid) solution. The heuristic search strategies described above are "rules of thumb" designed to save time in reaching a solution. If an individual can solve problems of a particular type, he or she is said to *know the rules* for their solution.

"Knowing the rules" is clearly related to "having the concept", discussed in Chapter 18. Correctly identifying dogs, is like being able to state a rule specifying what will count as a dog. However, there are important differences. First, accurate use of concepts does not imply that the user will be able to produce a verbal rule. Second, once a rule has been stated, it may exert control over behavior directly.

If a three-number sequence is required to open a combination lock, and the sequence is always such that the third number is twice the second number, which is the same as the first, then once this rule is acquired, it will be used. The rule provides for very efficient problem solution. However, *learning the rule is not the same as responding to the reinforcement contingencies.* There are many types of human behavior that are influenced by reinforcement contingencies without the individual knowing rules or even thinking them relevant. The baseball pitcher pitches with great accuracy without being able to articulate the rules governing his or her own movements or the flight of the ball in the air.

With human subjects, it is possible to carry out concept formation experiments, as described in Chapter 18, and concurrently ask them to verbalize the rule. They are asked to specify which features of a stimulus determine its allocation to a particular category. These procedures are called *concept identification.*

Bruner, Goodnow, and Austin (1956) presented subjects with the 81 cards shown in Figure 19.8. These cards varied in four ways: (1) the number of figures (1, 2, or 3), (2) the color of the figures (red, green, or black), (3) the

FIGURE 19.8. A set of cards used to study concept identification. The forms varied in number, shape, color, and number of borders (Bruner, Goodnow, and Austin, 1956).

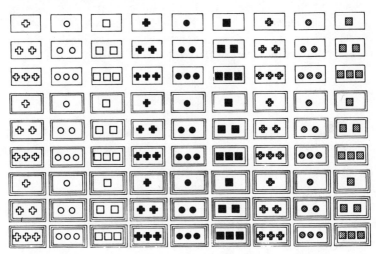

shape of the figures (cross, circle, or square), and (4) the number of borders (1, 2, or 3). The subjects were first shown a given card (say the one with three red circles and two borders, 3RO2b) and told that this was a positive instance of a concept that they were to identify. The subjects were then advised that they could choose additional cards from the 80 remaining to obtain more information. After each choice, they were advised whether the particular card they chose was or was not an instance of the concept. When the task consisted of identifying conjunctive concepts (red circles, two green figures, and so on), the majority of subjects adopted a strategy which consisted of choosing cards that varied in one, and only one, dimension from the known, initial positive card. In this way, each selection eliminated one or more concepts. An example of the kinds of choice sequences made using this strategy might·be as follows:

3R O 2b (+)	the initial given positive example.
2R O 2b (+)	first choice: eliminate "three" figures as a relevant element.
3G O 2b (−)	second choice: retain "red" as a relevant element.
3R +2b (−)	third choice: retain "circle" as a relevant element.
3R O 1b (+)	fourth choice: eliminate "two borders" as a relevant element.

Ergo: concept is "red circles."

Bruner, Goodnow, and Austin were able to show that a number of variables, such as whether the concept was conjunctive or disjunctive (see Chapter 18), the manner in which the 81 cards were displayed, and the number of examples the subjects were permitted to choose, affected the type of systematic strategy employed.

Dennis, Hampton, and Lea (1973) used a related technique to examine identification of *polymorphous concepts*. Formally, in an *m*-out-of-*n* polymorphous rule, there are *n* relevant conditions of which *m* must be satisfied. An example is given in Figure 19.9. The rule here is: A member of *A* possesses at least two of the properties symmetric, black, and circular. (All other stimuli are members of *B*). Arguably most of our "real world" concepts

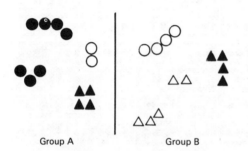

FIGURE 19.9.
Patterns determined by a two-out-of-three polymorphous rule (Dennis, Hampton, and Lea, 1973).

Group A   Group B

are of this type. For example, a person will have many features common to people in general, but no one feature is *necessary*.

In their first experiment, college students were asked to sort packs of cards showing either rows of shapes (as in Figure 19.9), typewritten letters, or random shapes into two piles (*A* and *B*). After each response, the experimenter told them whether their allocation of a card to a pile was right or wrong. On different trials, the subjects were required to sort the cards by a conjunctive rule (for example, *A*'s are black and composed of circles), or disjunctive rule (for example, *A*'s are black or composed of triangles), or a polymorphous rule such as the one previously described. They sorted a pack of 48 cards and the response measured was the number of cards sorted before the last error, where an error is putting a card in the wrong pile. Dennis, Hampton, and Lea found that the median number of cards sorted was 9, 28, and 40 for the conjunctive, disjunctive, and polymorphous rules, respectively. This shows that the polymorphous concept was the most difficult to acquire, then the disjunctive, then the conjunctive.

In a second experiment, each subject was given four examples in each category (*A* and *B*) and asked to state the rule. Again, each subject was tested with cards divided according to a conjunctive, disjunctive, and polymorphous rule. They were given a maximum of 10 min to solve the problems. The median solution times were 34 sec, 2 min 35 sec, and 10 min, respectively. This means that typically the subjects *failed* to state the polymorphous rule within 10 min, although the disjunctive rule was produced fairly quickly and the conjunctive rule very quickly. Comparison between their first and second experiments suggests that polymorphous conceptual behavior in response to reinforcement contingencies is acquired only slightly more slowly than conjunctive and disjunctive conceptual behavior, but polymorphous *rules* take a great deal longer to acquire than the other types. This points out that contingency-shaped behavior does not depend on prior acquisition of the corresponding rules.

This view is supported by experiments with pigeons. Using food reinforcement for key pecking, pigeons have been trained to successfully discriminate between color slides with and without people in them, although the people were at all sorts of positions, angles, distances, and so forth (Herrnstein and Loveland, 1964). "Person" is clearly a polymorphous concept, as previously defined. Furthermore, Lea and Harrison (1978) trained pigeons in a similar procedure to discriminate on the basis of a 2-out-of-3 polymorphous concept, similar to the ones used by Dennis, Hampton, and Lea. If pigeons can acquire polymorphous concepts, but humans have great difficulty in stating polymorphous rules, we can only conclude that acquisition of the rule is not a necessary condition for solving this sort of problem.

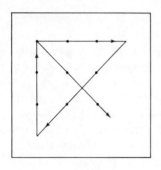

(A)   (B)   (C)   (D)   (E)

References for Chapter 19

Birch, H. G. The relation of previous experience to insightful problem solving. *Journal of Comparative Psychology*, 1945, **38**, 367–383.

Birch, H. G., and Rabinowitz, H. S. The negative effect of previous experience on productive thinking. *Journal of Experimental Psychology*, 1951, **41**, 121–125.

Bruner, J. S., Goodnow, J. J., and Austin, G. *A study of thinking*. New York: Wiley, 1956.

Dennis, I., Hampton, J. A., and Lea, S. E. G. New problem in concept formation. *Nature* (London); 1973, **243**, 101–102.

Herrnstein, R. J., and Loveland, D. H. Complex visual concept in the pigeon. *Science*, 1964, **146**, 549–551.

Katona, G. *Organizing and memorizing: studies in the psychology of learning and teaching*. New York: Columbia University Press, 1940.

Kohler, W. *The mentality of apes*. New York: Harcourt, Brace, 1925.

Lea, S. E. G., and Harrison, S. N. Discrimination of polymorphous concepts by pigeons. *Quarterly Journal of Experimental Psychology*, 1978, **30**, 521–537.

Luchins, A. S. Mechanization in problem solving: the effect of *Einstelling*. *Psychological Monographs*, 1942, **54**, (Whole no. 248).

Newell, A., and Simon, H. GPS, a program that simulates human thought. In E. A. Feigenbaum and J. Feldman (Eds.) *Computers and thought*. New York: McGraw-Hill, 1963.

CHAPTER 20

Modeling

The experimental analysis of behavior has been mostly concerned with the factors that govern the *performance* of a behavior, and less concerned about how that behavior is *acquired*. For this reason, operants selected for study have usually been simple acts which can be completed in a very short space of time (lever pressing, key pecking, button pressing, and so on). Similarly, although it is acknowledged that classical conditioning can simultaneously produce diverse effects on behavior, investigators have normally looked in detail at a single, relatively simple, aspect of behavior (salivation, eyeblinks, heart-rate, and so forth). Thus, neither operant nor classical-conditioning techniques are oriented to the analysis of the *acquisition of complex behavioral sequences*. However, it is a compelling fact that humans readily acquire such sequences, and do so very rapidly.

Many examples of such behavior seem to depend on *observation*. The new factory worker is shown how the machine works by the foreperson, he or she can then operate it himself or herself *immediately* with reasonable efficiency. His or her subsequent improvement towards being a skilled operator depends on feedback (reinforcement) from the machine and from co-workers, but the rapid initial acquisition is hard to explain by operant principles. We might crudely conceptualize it thus:

S^D:	R	$\rightarrow$	S^+
operation of	copying		successful
machine by	foreperson's		operation of
foreperson	behavior		machine

While this might suffice to explain why "copying foreperson's behavior" is *performed*, it does not provide a mechanism for its *acquisition*. How does the worker manage to execute a long and complex behavior sequence that he or she has not produced previously or been reinforced for?

The only operant principle that might provide an explanation is *chaining* (see Chapter 8). Behavior chains are sequences that are reinforced when completed. They can be long and complex, but they are established through a relatively lengthy piecing together, shaping, process which involves *explicit reinforcement*. In our present example, however, there is only a single demonstration (trial) and no explicit reinforcement for either worker or foreperson.

If an observer acquires a new response pattern or behavior sequence by observation of another individual, this is an instance of *modeling*. There are three types of modeling influence. The first, and most striking, is the one we have described. This can be called the *response acquisition effect* of modeling. Observation of a model may also lead to the inhibition or facilitation of already learned behavior. For example, observing someone else making jokes about a taboo subject and gaining approval may lead to the observer telling similar jokes. We will call this the *response modulation effect*. The third modeling effect occurs when the behavior of others functions as a discriminative stimulus for the same type of behavior by the observer. If the person walking along the street in front of you suddenly stops and gazes up into the sky, it is very likely that you will do the same when you reach that point in the street. This is the *response facilitation effect*. It differs from the response modulation effect in that the *consequences* of the model's behavior are important in response modulation, but not in response facilitation. If your companion makes a joke about religion which is followed by an embarrassed silence, this will tend to inhibit similar behavior on your part. Response facilitation, on the other hand, can occur without the observer seeing the consequences of the model's behavior. The response facilitation effect differs from the response acquisition effect because response facilitation does not involve any "new" behavior. Rather, the subject produces behavior already in his or her repertoire. In both cases, however, the model's behavior functions as a *discriminative stimulus* for the same behavior by the subject.

The response facilitation effect is well known to ethologists. The coordinated behavior of flocks or herds of animals is controlled in this fashion. Psychologists, on the other hand, have been primarily concerned with the response acquisition and response modulation effects. These differ in that the former is an effect on *learning* (the acquisition of behavior), while the latter is an effect on *performance* (the probability of the behavior occurring in a particular situation). The learning/performance distinction is generally an important one in psychology, but in both operant and classical-conditioning, performance is the focus of interest.

Before attempting an analysis of modeling processes, we will describe a study that demonstrates the effectiveness of modeling, both on response acquisition and response modulation.

20.1
Children's Behavior After Observing Aggressive Models

Bandura and associates carried out a series of studies showing the powerful effects on children of short periods of observing adults or children modeling specific behaviors. In a typical study (Bandura, 1965), children (aged 42 to 71 months) watched film of an adult who produced several, novel, physical and verbal aggressive behaviors.

The film lasted 5 min and involved an adult approaching an adult-sized plastic doll and ordering it out of the way. Then the model (the adult) laid the doll on its side, sat on it, and punched it on the nose. This was followed by hitting it on the head with a mallet and then kicking it round the room. Finally, the model threw rubber balls at the doll. Each act of physical aggression was accompanied by a particular verbal aggressive response. Following this performance, the children observing the film saw one of three closing scenes. Either another adult appeared with candies and soft drinks and congratulated the model, giving the model food and drink (model-rewarded group), or the second adult came in and reprimanded the model, while spanking the model with a rolled-up magazine (model-punished group). For a third group of children, the film ended before the second adult arrived (no-consequences group).

Immediately after watching the film, each child was taken to a room containing a similar large doll, a mallet, balls, and a number of other toys not seen in the film. The child spent 10 min in this room, where they could be observed through a one-way mirror. The experimenter then entered, carrying soft drinks and pictures. These were offered to the child as rewards if he or she could imitate what the model had done in the film. Each modeled behavior was reinforced with a drink or a picture.

The results from both parts of the experiment are shown separately for boys and girls in Figure 20.1. There were 11 subjects in each of the six groups. The most notable feature of the data is the generally high level of modeling behavior. After watching a short film, a number of conditions produced

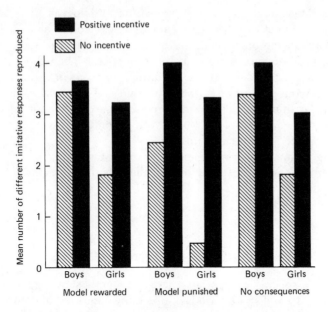

FIGURE 20.1. Mean number of matching responses performed by children as a function of consequences for the model, sex of child, and whether or not the child was reinforced for modeling ("positive incentive" or "no incentive") (Bandura, 1965).

mean levels of between 3 and 4 different modeled behaviors out of a possible maximum of 8 (4 physical acts and 4 verbal behaviors). Apart from this, the sex of the children, the consequences for the model, and the consequences for the children all influenced behavior.

Figure 20.1 shows that in the first observation period, when no reinforcement was provided, the boys reproduced more of the model's aggressive acts than the girls. In the second period, however, when modeling was reinforced, all groups considerably increased modeling behavior and the differences between the sexes were largely eliminated. These two phases demonstrate (1) that some modeling occurs without reinforcement for the subjects (this is the *response acquisition* effect), (2) some modeled responses are acquired that may not be performed unless explicitly reinforced, and (3) the sex difference in aggressive behavior diminishes when aggression is reinforced.

In the first observation period, the amount of modeled behavior was also influenced by the observed consequences of the behavior for the model. If the model had been seen to be punished for the aggressive behavior, the children showed less aggression. The effect was particularly dramatic for the girls in the model-punished group. They modeled an average of less than 0.5 aggressive acts in the first period, but increased this to more than 3.0 when subsequently reinforced for aggressive acts. This exemplifies a powerful *response modulation* effect; performance of aggressive behavior was jointly influenced by the observed consequences for the model and the available consequences for the subject.

20.2
The Status of the Model

In Bandura's (1965) study, observation of the adult model for a short period of time was a sufficient condition for the children to imitate some of the model's behavior without reinforcement or explicit instructions. This is a remarkable finding and suggests that modeling may be responsible for the acquisition of many social and complex behaviors. After all, we spend a great deal of time observing the behavior of others. However, we obviously do not acquire *all* the behavior we observe, and some models must be more likely to be imitated than others.

It turns out that models with demonstrated high competence, who are experts or celebrities, are more likely to be imitated. The age, sex, social power, and ethnic status of the model also influence its effectiveness (Bandura, 1969). The *nurturance* of the model has been experimentally manipulated. This has been defined by whether or not the model behaves warmly towards and reinforces the subject (observer). Nurturance does affect modeling behavior, nurturant models being imitated more, but aversive activities are not facilitated (Mischel and Grusec, 1966) and aggressive behavior is modeled anyway by children, even if the model is nonnurturant (Bandura and Huston, 1961).

Multiple modeling, the same behavior, demonstrated by several different models, produces more modeling behavior in the observers. For example, Bandura and Menlove (1968) studied the effects on children with severe fears of dogs of watching a series of graduated films in which either one model displayed progressively more intimate interactions with a single dog (single model condition), or several models interacted with numerous dogs (multiple model condition). A range of dog-approach behaviors were examined before treatment (watching the films), after treatment, and one month later (a follow-up). The most extreme involved the child being asked to climb into a playpen with a dog, pet it, and scratch it, and remain alone in the room under these conditions.

The effects on this behavior for a group of children given a single model, a group given multiple models, and a control group given films without modeling are shown in Figure 20.2. On this measure, there were no significant differences after treatment, but at one-month follow-up, the mutiple model group did significantly better. As less extreme measures of dog-approach showed that both single and multiple model groups improved over the controls (both at post-test and follow-up), we can conclude that

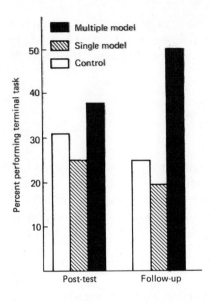

FIGURE 20.2.
Percentage of children achieving terminal approach behavior to dogs, after treatment and one month later, as a function of treatment condition (Bandura and Menlove, 1968).

given multiple modeling, the children's behavior to dogs went on improving after treatment.

Overall, observers tend to model behavior shown by high status models, behavior of models that are nurturant towards them, and behavior observed in several models. Modeling, therefore, can produce a "group identification" effect whereby behavior, initially shown by leaders, is rapidly transmitted to the whole group. This effect is readily observed in groups of adolescents.

20.3
Does Modeling Involve Reinforcement?

Bandura (1969) describes modeling as "no-trial learning" because response acquisition can occur without the subject being reinforced. As modeling effects cannot be described as classical conditioning either, Bandura concludes that there is a *modeling process* that can be distinguished from both operant and classical-conditioning processes. Bandura's analysis of modeling is complex, but it involves the following components:

1. Sensory Conditioning. Modeling stimuli elicit perceptual responses in observers that become sequentially associated and integrated through temporal contiguity. These perceptual response sequences can subsequently guide reproduction of matching responses.
2. Attention to the model's behavior is crucial and depends on the model's status (see Section 20.2). This is a precondition for the modeling stimuli to elicit perceptual responses.

3. Modeled behavior will be highly probable when reinforced, but readily suppressed by punishment contingencies.

A central, and plausible, tenet of this approach is that although reinforcement contingencies influence the performance of modeled behavior, they are not necessary for the acquisition of modeled behavior which can occur through sensory conditioning alone. There is an alternative explanation, however, despite the "no-trial learning" effect.

It is possible that modeling is maintained by *conditioned reinforcement*. We all have a history of being reinforced for behavioral similarity, or matching the behavior of a model. During language acquisition by a young child, for example, parents often spend long periods of time coaxing the child to repeat a particular word or phrase. When the child finally produces the appropriate utterance, this *behavioral similarity* is immediately reinforced.

As behavioral similarity is often paired with reinforcement in this way, it could become a conditioned reinforcer (see Chapter 8). If behavioral similarity does have conditioned reinforcing properties, this might explain how modeling behavior can occur in experimental and clinical studies, even though it is not apparently reinforced. The paradigm would be:

$$S^D \quad : \quad R \quad \rightarrow \quad S^+$$

S^D	R	S^+
model's	imitate	behavioral
behavior	model	similarity

where the last term is a conditioned reinforcer. Behavioral similarity would only acquire and retain conditioned reinforcing properties if it was explicitly reinforced in a variety of situations. Nonreinforced modeling in the test situation can then be described as generalized imitation, because modeling behavior is generalizing from reinforcement to nonreinforced situations.

Gladstone and Cooley (1975) were able to demonstrate conditioned reinforcing effects of behavioral similarity. Children were given the opportunity to model a behavior sequence (that is, act as models) and then operate a bell, a horn, or a clicker. If the appropriate one of these responses was made, the experimenter (acting as the observer) immediately imitated the behavior the child had modeled. The other two responses had no consequences. If behavioral similarity has reinforcing properties, the child-model should select the response that resulted in imitation by the experimenter-observer.

The results in Figure 20.3 show that this did happen. Each of the four subjects gradually switched to the response currently reinforced. When a child had selected the reinforced response (horn, bell, or clicker) on at least 16 out of 20 consecutive trials, the reinforced response was changed (for example, from horn to bell). The children's behavior always changed in accordance with the contingencies.

This study demonstrates reinforcing effects of behavioral similarity, and raises the possibility that these effects are involved in all modeling situations.

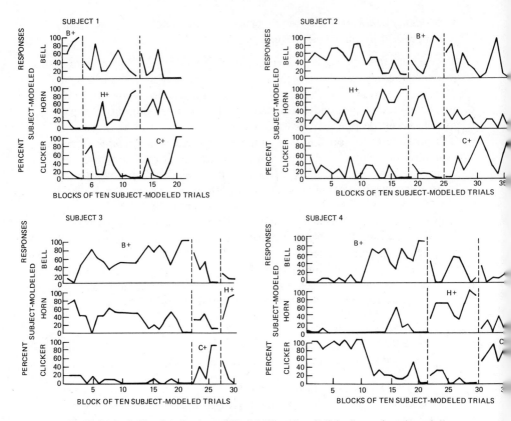

FIGURE 20.3. Subject's selection of "bell," "horn," or "clicker" as a function of the experimenter-modeled response. A plus (+) following the letters B, H, and C indicates which noisemaker was the experimenter-modeled response (Gladstone and Cooley, 1975).

If this is true, however, we still have to explain how behavioral similarity is achieved by the observer. As we pointed out earlier, the sudden production of integrated behavior sequences is one of the most striking features of response ecquisition through modeling. This feature can be accounted for by Bandura's notion of sensory conditioning, but not by operant reinforcement principles.

20.4
Modeling Verbal Behavior

Several aspects of verbal behavior are more readily described in terms of modeling, than in terms of the behavioral processes we introduced in earlier chapters. In particular, the rapid acquisition of language by children and the speedy adoption of new accents, mannerisms, and slang by adults probably depend primarily on modeling.

Harris and Hassemer (1972) showed that observation by children of adults using either simple or complex sentences was sufficient to induce the children to shorten or lengthen their own sentences correspondingly. In this study, a child (observer) and an adult (model) sat together and were asked to make up sentences about simple pictures presented on cards. In different phases, the model used long sentences (more than 10 words) or short sentences (less than 5 words) for the descriptions. For boys and girls of two different ages (second and fourth grade), speaking in Spanish or English, the sentence length was greater when the model used longer and more complex sentences. This effect occurred even though these young children always produced comparatively short sentences. The children's sentences were rated for complexity, and this was also found to increase when the model's sentences were longer and more complicated.

This study is important because no explicit reinforcement was provided, but systematic modeling effects were still obtained. In remedial education, modeling is often used in conjunction with reinforcement of behavioral similarity. This combination of techniques produces powerful effects on behavior, as we will see in Section 20.6.

20.5
Concept Formation

In Chapter 18, we saw how concepts could be acquired through selective reinforcement. Concept acquisition can also be greatly enhanced by modeling, Rosenthal and Kellogg (1973) compared the effects of verbal instructions, demonstration (modeling), and reinforcement in acquisition of a concept involving number and color by retardates. Given three red disks, for example, the subject was required to make three, 3-marble triangles from red marbles, while when given two blue disks, two blue, 3-marble triangles were required.

Baseline rates, prior to instruction or demonstration, were zero (no correct solutions). Verbal instructions (for example, "If I show you one white disk, you make one white triangle by putting three white marbles together," and so on) produced a low level of correct performance. Demonstrations of the correct solutions without the model saying anything, however, produced much higher levels, which generalized to some extent to a related task. The absolute levels of responding varied considerably because groups of retardates of differing abilities were tested. However, the group of highest ability ("prevocational") produced an average of 11 out of 12 correct, after visual demonstration.

In this study, half the subjects in each condition were reinforced with candy for every correct solution. This had no discernible effect on performance, that is, reinforcement did not increase the frequency of correct solutions. This is interesting, but perhaps not surprising. Given the small number of trials (12 in each phase of the experiment), reinforcement was unlikely to enable the subject to select the correct concept from among many possibilities. Modeling, on the other hand, demonstrates the concept directly. In our everyday experience, there are many situations that represent "problems" of the types described in Chapter 19. If, however, one is "shown the answer", that is, appropriate behavior is modeled, acquisition of the solution is instantaneous and the situation is no longer regarded as posing a problem. Indeed, someone who demonstrates the solution of a problem being solved for entertainment will be accused of spoiling the fun.

20.6
Reinforcement of Modeling

Given that operant reinforcement and modeling can both modify the behavioral repertoire, the joint operation of both should be a highly effective method of altering behavior, and so it has proved. It is particularly suitable for conditions of *behavioral deficit*. A behavioral deficit means that an individual simply lacks a class of behavior common in other individuals. Behavior deficits have a peculiar influence on the relationship between the individual's behavior and the contingencies of reinforcement provided by the society in which he or she lives. Normally, the incidence of a class of behavior, for example, talking, is continuously modified by the social environment. Someone who never speaks, however, *fails to make contact with these contingencies*. Their situation is quite different from that of a low-frequency talker, whose talking may have been suppressed by verbal punishment, or may subsequently increase as a result of reinforcement. The nontalker will be neither reinforced nor punished.

Behavioral deficits, then, represent a severe type of behavior problem. Baer, Peterson, and Sherman (1967) attempted to alleviate this problem in three retardates (aged 9 to 12 years) with very large deficits that included failure to imitate any behavior. Subjects were taught a series of discriminated operants of this form:

S^D	:	R	$\rightarrow$	S^+
"Do this" followed by demonstration by model		behavioral similarity by subject		food

As no imitative behavior occurred initially, shaping was used. This involved assisting the subject, physically, to make the appropriate sequence of actions, and then delivering food reinforcement. (Sessions were always conducted at meal times). The amount of assistance was gradually reduced.

After initial training, imitation of some of the model's demonstrated responses were never reinforced and these responses thus formed an S^Δ class. Following S^D—S^Δ training, all imitation was extinguished. Reinforcement was now delivered if *no* imitation occurred for a specified period after the model's demonstration. (This is a *DRO* schedule, meaning the *d*ifferential *r*einforcement of *o*ther behavior than the previously reinforced response). The results for a representative subject are shown in Figure 20.4. Reinforcement maintained a high level of S^D responding, but also a high level of S^Δ responding. When the *DRO* schedule was introduced, both rates declined gradually to zero. Responding to S^D and S^Δ recovered when reinforcement for S^D was reintroduced.

Baer, Peterson, and Sherman's procedure had powerful effects. Responding to S^D was maintained at a high level by reinforcement and suppressed by the *DRO* contingency. Modeling was undoubtedly critical, as well, because reinforcement alone could not account for the high levels of responding shown by these subjects. Remember that prior to the experiment, they had a *very* limited behavioral repertoire. The procedure also generated a high level of S^Δ responding, and extended S^D—S^Δ training failed to suppress responding to S^Δ.

The S^Δ responding represents a "failure to discriminate" in operant terminology, which might have resulted from the discrimination being difficult because both S^D and S^Δ classes were demonstrated by the same model. Bandura and Barab (1973) replicated this result with a single model, but found that S^Δ responding was suppressed if there was one model for S^D

FIGURE 20.4. Reinforced imitative responses and nonreinforced imitative responses for a single child during reinforcement, *DRO*, and reinforcement conditions (Baer, Peterson, and Sherman, 1967).

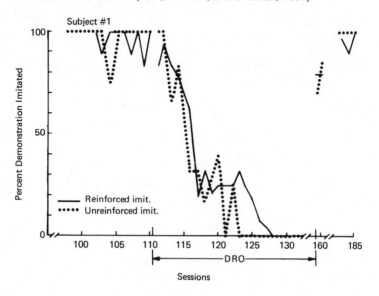

and a different model for S^{Δ}. The fact of "discrimination failure" when a single model is used is important, because it is a further demonstration of the response acquisition effect; under appropriate conditions observers will imitate the behavior of a model, even when there is no explicit reinforcement for imitations.

References for Chapter 20

Baer, D., Peterson, R., and Sherman, J. The development of imitation by reinforcing behavioral similarity to a model. *Journal of the Experimental Analysis of Behavior*, 1967, **10**, 405–416.

Bandura, A. Influence of model's reinforcement contingencies on the acquisition of imitative responses. *Journal of Personality and Social Psychology*, 1965, **1**, 589–595.

Bandura, A. *Principles of behavior modification*. New York: Holt, Rinehart & Winston, 1969.

Bandura, A., and Barab, P. Processes governing disinhibitory effects through symbolic modeling. *Journal of Abnormal Psychology*, 1973, **82**, 1–9.

Bandura, A., and Huston, A. C. Identification as a process of incidental learning. *Journal of Abnormal and Social Psychology*, 1961, **63**, 311–318.

Bandura, A., and Menlove, F. L. Factors determining vicarious extinction of avoidance behavior through symbolic modelling. *Journal of Personality and Social Psychology*, 1968, **8**, 99–108.

Gladstone, B. W., and Cooley, J. Behavioral similarity as a reinforcer for preschool children. *Journal of the Experimental Analysis of Behavior*, 1975, **23**, 357–368.

Harris, M. B., and Hassemer, W. G. Some factors affecting the complexity of children's sentences: the effects of modeling, age, sex and bilingualism. *Journal of Experimental Child Psychology*, 1972, **13**, 447–455.

Mischel, W., and Grusec, J. Determinants of the rehearsal and transmission of mental and aversive behaviors. *Journal of Personality and Social Psychology*, 1966, **3**, 197–205.

Rosenthal, T. L., and Kellogg, J. S. Demonstration versus instructions in concept attainment by mental retardates. *Behaviour Research and Therapy*, 1973, **11**, 299–309.

PART SEVEN

Motivation and Emotion

The principles of behavioral analysis that we have enumerated are concerned with the changes in the behavior of an organism that arise out of the contingencies between stimuli (which result in classical conditioning), or between behavior and its consequences (which result in operant conditioning). After a period of exposure to a contingency, behavior reaches a steady state. We do not subsequently expect systematic behavioral changes to result from the contingencies, unless the contingencies themselves are changed; as for instance, when we extinguish an operant response, after having previously reinforced it. Of course, stimulus control may have been acquired by a discriminative stimulus, in which case, its presentation will substantially affect behavior; but in unchanging stimulus conditions, we might expect behavior to remain constant.

Actually, behavior typically changes despite constant contingency pressure and constant stimulus conditions. Increases or decreases in deprivation of a reinforcer, the effects of repeatedly emitting a similar behavior over and over again, and simply the mere passage of time markedly alter the probability of certain classes of behavior. In addition to the various classes of determinants that we have encountered so far, these dynamic effects suggest that there exist other important determinants of behavior. Historically, these other determinants have generally been labeled as *motivational variables,* and from our point of view, they define a broad class of influences concerned with changes in the reinforcing value of the controlling reinforcers we are studying.

A special class of these motivational variables seem to be those falling in the field of *emotional behavior.* Agreement for such a classification is far from universal, however, since a persistent, and still unsolved, problem in emotion has been achieving a satisfactory definition of just what constitutes emotional behavior. In the last chapter of this part of the book, we will attempt a behavioral translation of emotion. We shall refer to the acute motivational changes elicited by abrupt stimulus changes, "emotional", and the behavioral states arising from those changes, "emotional states." We will then show how affective phenomena are related and ordered by these definitions.

CHAPTER 21

Motivation and Drive

Historically, "motivation" and associated words like "drive" and "incentive" have loosely been synonymous with the causes of behavior. Since we shall wish to restrict and limit motivation to a particular *class* of causes, this tradition obliges us to consider first what is meant by cause and effect in science, in general, and in psychology, in particular.

21.1
Cause, Effect, and Scientific Law

The terms "cause" and "effect" have a long history of usage in philosophical, as well as scientific, attempts to explain nature. The terms are part of our everyday language for describing aspects of hurricanes, revolutions, epidemics, assassinations, and airplane crashes, as well as more pedestrian events. We may, therefore, be surprised to discover, in turning to the contemporary scientific literature, that these terms are conspicuously missing. In their place, we can find reference only to relationships between variables, correlations of events, and "laws" relating phenomena. It is not that the scientist has lost interest in the causes of his or her phenomena, it is simply that all the scientist finds upon performing experiments are relations between events or variables. For him or her, finding the causes of a phenomenon y has become equivalent to finding which other variables, u, v, w, x, and so forth are systematically (*functionally*) related to y.

Every science is filled with examples of functional relationships that purport to replace more ordinary notions of cause and effect. Consider Hooke's law: so long as the elastic limit is not exceeded, the extension of a body is directly proportional to the force applied to it. The law may be summarized as the relation between two variables, *Force → Extension*. The relation would be more extensively described by a graph, in which units of force (the independent variable) are plotted against units of extension (the dependent variable). We may, if we wish, consider the cause of any particular extension to be the particular force acting on the body. But in calling the force the cause of extension, we add no additional information to the functional relation itself. In fact, while the law describes the exact form of the relationship for a host of forces and extensions, the assignment of cause is confined to the logical statement—*if* a force, *then* extension.

In the relationship

Heat water to 212°F → Water boils

the application of heat may be considered to be the cause of the boiling. But if we persist in asking "why" water boils when heated sufficiently, we shall be referred to further functional relationships between the vapor pressure of water and temperature. At exactly 212°, we are told, the vapor pressure of water equals that of the atmosphere. This may or may not satisfy our curiosity about boiling water, but in any case, the form of the answers we shall obtain to all further "why" questions will always be the same—more functional relationships.

Relationships are equally central to the explanatory process in biological science. The mating of male and female white-eyed fruit flies invariably yields white-eyed offspring.

Mate white-eyed parents → white-eyed offspring

A functional relationship exists between the color of the parents' eyes and the color of the offspring's eyes.

All these functional relationships exhibit a common logic. If we regard the antecedent variable in these relationships as x, and the consequent that is produced as y, their logic seems to be

If x, then y

and its corollary

If not y, then not x

Thus *if* a force (*x*) is applied, *then* we shall observe extension (*y*). But *if* no extension was observed (*not y*), *then* force must not have been applied (*not x*). Similarly, *if* the temperature of the water rises to 212° (*x*), *then* water will boil (*y*). Furthermore, *if* the water is not boiling (*not y*), *then* the temperature must be below 212° (*not x*). Finally, *if* both parents have white eyes (*x*), *then* all offspring will have white eyes (*y*). But *if* the offspring's eyes were not white (*not y*), *then* the parents could not both have had white eyes (*not x*).

We must not be disappointed to learn that scientific laws give an accurate representation of nature only when certain conditions are met. Scientific laws hold in context, sometimes broad, sometimes narrow, depending on the generality of the particular relation; but no scientific law is true under *all* conditions. Beyond the elastic limit, Hooke's law fails, and extension is no longer proportional to the applied force. Unless certain variables, such as atmospheric pressure and purity of the water, are held constant, water does not boil at 212°. Irradiation of the parent fruit flies complicates hereditary relationships.

In the laws described, the *x* and *y* terms of the functional relationships are concepts based on *observable* quantities. The intimacy by which such concepts are tied to observables is the reason that such laws are said to be *empirical*. We may observe and measure events which we conceptualize as forces and extensions of bodies, temperatures and states of water, sexual reproduction and eye-color of fruit flies. The kinds of explanation afforded by empirical laws are to be contrasted with prescientific and nonscientific explanations. Prior to the discovery of laws relating microorganism activity to disease, illness was often attributed to the presence of demons lodged within the body. Animal and human behavior was long believed to be due to animal spirits and souls. In these prescientific explanations, illness and behavior were related to hypothetical events (demons, souls), which were free to take on almost any property the theorist wished to give them. The lack of restrictions placed on the hypothetical nature of these concepts made it possible for them, in principle, to explain everything; yet, their immunity to disconfirmation by any procedure put them in the paradoxical position of, in fact, explaining nothing.

In contrast to the emptiness of such fictional explanations, the functional relationship of science possesses powerful abilities for the prediction, interpretation, and control of nature. When a functional law exists between *x*, and *y*, knowing the value of *x*, we may *predict* the value of *y*. Having the law in hand, whenever we suspect that we see *x* and *y* acting in the everyday world, we are in a position to *interpret* actual nonlaboratory events. Finally, if we can manipulate *x*, then we have the means of *controlling y*. In the model of the functional relationship, we have the power and versatility of the scientific enterprise revealed in a striking way.

21.2
Fiction and Nonfiction in the Causation of Behavior

In the introduction to this part, we pointed out that the external determinants we class as conditioning variables are by no means the only causes of behavior. We identified a class of internal determinants called motivational variables as another set of important factors. Both conditioning and motivational variables can be treated as real or "nonfictional" causes of behavior in that they can be shown to enter into functional relationships with behavior, of the type described in the previous section. If we examine traditional, more loosely stated, accounts of behavior, however, we find at least three classes of "fictional" causes of behavior. Each class is unreal or fictional because it violates at least one of the principles for establishing empirical scientific laws.

In one, behavior is explained by reference to observable events that are fortuitously correlated with it, such as the position of the planets at birth, the direction of lines in the palm, the relative prominence of various bumps on the skull. Although both behavior and the "causal agent" are observable, any relation between them is nonsystematic and, therefore, qualifies as "chance" rather than "lawful."

In the second, behavior is frequently attributed to events supposedly located in the central nervous system (the brain and spinal cord). When we say a man is clever because he has brains, that he cannot work because his nerves are exhausted, or that he needs his head examined when he acts strangely, we are invoking causal events apparently located inside the nervous structure. In practice, however, actual observation of these events is rarely made. In these examples, the nervous system exists only as a repository for fictional explanations of behavior. The properties of the hypothetical causes are specified in only the grossest manner, and no specific relations are either observed or theorized between them and the observed behavior.

In the third, behavior is commonly "explained" by hypothetical, inner mental processes. We are said to close a door because we "want" it closed, to whistle a tune because we have an "urge" to whistle, to read a book because we "feel" like reading. Because such statements seem so natural and harmless, we are unlikely to notice that they imply a form of cause and effect which differs markedly from the laws of the preceding section. Yet in each, an unobservable inner "want", "urge", or "feeling" is being subtly assigned the status of a cause of some behavior. Here again, these "causes" are given no independent properties which might be related either by theory, or by observation to the actual behavior to be explained. The "want" and the "urge" are fictional, because they are inferred entirely from the behavior which they are proposed to explain.

The emergence of a scientific psychology is, to a large extent, a shift from fictional to functional causes of behavior. We need only to examine the various procedures and processes of previous chapters to find a number of functional relationships between environmental variables and behavior. It is important to realize that, in turning to motivational variables, we are not dealing with fictional causes of behavior, but extending the range of functional relationships. The independent variables of motivation can be measured just as objectively as those of conditioning.

21.3
Temporal Fluctuations in Behavior

We have identified motivated behavior with behavior that shows fluctuations with time, although the external environment is unchanged. When behavior is observed in natural conditions, this temporal fluctuation is one of its most obvious features.

In Man, the sleeping-waking cycle is readily observed at all ages. Its development is schematically illustrated in Figure 21.1. Sleep has several features that characterize motivated behavior:

1. It shows a regular *cycle*. From a knowledge of the pattern for an individual, we can make an accurate prediction about whether he or she will be awake at a particular time.
2. The probability of sleep onset increases with *deprivation*. Attempts to keep oneself awake become increasingly difficult with time, once one's usual waking period is exceeded. Some experimental data for rats,

FIGURE 21.1. Cycles of sleep at different ages (Kleitman, 1963).

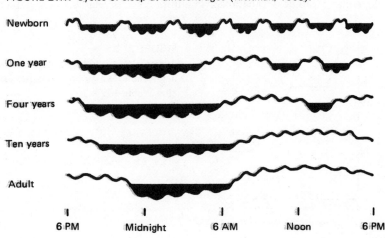

Newborn

One year

Four years

Ten years

Adult

6 PM   Midnight   6 AM   Noon   6 PM

relating latency of sleep onset to sleep deprivation, are shown in Figure 21.2.

3. Deprivation of sleep results in the opportunity for sleep to become *reinforcing*. We will forego social activities, favorite television shows, and sex in order to go to sleep.

4. It is related to physiological imbalances. Complex restorative processes take place during sleep and prolonged sleep deprivation results in death.

Given that a class of behavior shows cyclic fluctuations, increases with deprivation, reinforces other behavior when in a state of deprivation, and is related to biological tissue balances, we may draw the following diagram to reflect these facts:

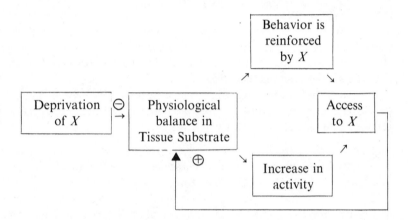

A variant of this causal sequence was proposed by Hull (1943) as a general model for the activation and control of behavior. The model predicts, in the case of feeding, for example, that food deprivation results in a buildup of a particular biological imbalance. The imbalance is related to the depletion of

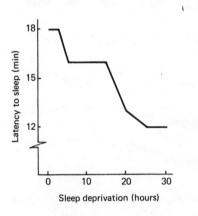

FIGURE 21.2.

Average latency to fall asleep following sleep deprivation for a group of rats (Bolles, 1967; after Webb, 1957).

various products that derives from food digestion and assimilation. By neural and hormonal mechanisms, that are only gradually becoming clearer to neurophysiologists, this physiological imbalance is detected by the brain which, in turn, increases general activity and makes food a reinforcer. These two effects jointly raise the probability of food being obtained and eaten. Consumption of food reduces deprivation of food, thus the physiological imbalance is reduced, and the cycle begins anew.

(Note, however, that Hull's hypothesis that activity increases does not hold for the example of sleep.)

The preceding diagram defines a negative feedback loop (see Section 5.6) since the output of the system, in this case, food-obtaining behavior, feeds back into the system and modifies the state of the system. The loop here is a negative one, because the feedback of eating opposes the effects of food deprivation. This opposition is illustrated by the + and − notations in the diagram.

21.4
Drive

"Hungry", "thirsty", "bored", and "sexy" are terms that we often apply to ourselves and others. Each term implies a high frequency of not one, but several, sorts of behavior. A hungry person is more likely to eat than others, but he or she is also more likely to ask for food, approach a restaurant, enter a supermarket, and so on. Similarly, a person may be thirsty because it is some time since he or she drank any liquid, but if this person eats salt or sits in a very hot room, his or her thirst will increase. We are thus led to the conclusion that organisms are at certain times in highly motivated states, which are determined by several sorts of stimuli, and result in several sorts of behavior. These highly motivated states, one of which exists for each primary reinforcer of the species under consideration, are generally correlated with the physiological imbalances discussed in the previous section.

Drive concepts are potentially very useful to experimental psychologists because they reduce the number of functional relationships that have to be established. Consider the following model of thirst:

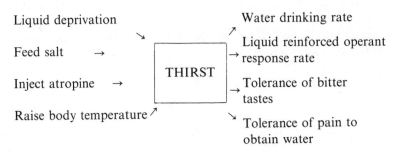

On the left, are four operations, and on the right, four types of behavior. We could establish the functional relationship between each operation and each behavior, giving us $4 \times 4 = 16$ relationships. If however, we create an intervening variable, thirst, which is functionally related to all four antecedent operations, and in turn, is characterized by particular changes in all four types of behavior, we need only establish $4 + 4 = 8$ relationships. These latter 8 relationships will be of the form:

$$D = f(E) \text{ and } B = f(D)$$

while the former 16 relationships would all be of the form:

$$B = f(E)$$

where

D = drive level
E = aspect of environment
B = class of behavior
$f(\ )$ = is a function of the variable in the brackets

In constructing a scientific theory, we wish to be as parsimonious as possible; that is, we wish to have the smallest number of explanatory principles that is required to account for the facts. However, the *validity* of the drive concept depends on all of its behavioral effects *covarying* with changes in each of the drive-enhancing operations. If, for example, we find that increases in liquid deprivation increase water drinking rate and liquid-reinforced operant rate, but not tolerance of bitter tastes, while feeding salt increases tolerance of bitter tastes and rate of liquid-reinforced operants, but not water drinking rate, then we must abandon or modify the drive concept.

A drive defined in this way is said to be an *intervening variable*. This variable we have created is an abstraction devised to summarize our understanding of the complex influences of the environment on behavior. An intervening variable has no properties other than its defining relationships with environmental variables and behavior, and no spatial location. "Drives" have the property of describing the characteristic features of motivated behavior defined in the previous section. So their associated reinforcers should show temporal fluctuations and increase with appropriate deprivation. The reinforcing value of access to the drive-reducing stimulus and general activity should change in direct response to the drive-inducing operations. Finally, if we follow Hull, drive level should reflect certain biological imbalances in the organism's tissues.

In summary, a drive is an intervening variable with these properties:

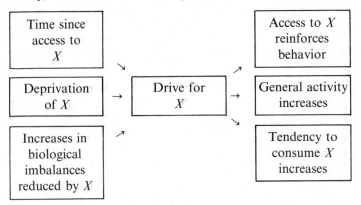

21.5
Patterns of Feeding and Drinking

The utility of drive concepts can only be assessed by a detailed empirical examination of these predicted relationships. It is readily demonstrated that given continuous access to food or water, or to an operant response reinforced with food or water, many animals show a clear cycle of feeding or drinking.

The eating pattern of a mouse on a continuous reinforcement schedule is shown in Figure 21.3. Each lever press produced a small pellet of food. The cycle is quite long. A "meal" consists of 3–5 hr sustained pressing and eating and this is followed by a "pause" of up to 6 hr.

Left to drink water whenever it chooses, the rat produces characteristic cycles of drinking and no drinking, as the cumulative drinking curves of Figure 21.4 indicate. There is relatively little drinking between 6 a.m. and 6 p.m., the daylight hours. Drinking then gradually increases and is usually at its peak around midnight.

Studies in which access to food or water has been noncontinuous have shown that a 24-hr cycle can be seen that is independent of the current deprivation state. For example, Bousfield (1935) found that delaying a feeding period that normally occurred at the same time each day, actually *decreased* food intake.

21.6
Cycles of Activity

"Energy" and "motivation" are closely related concepts. Highly motivated people work vigorously and energetically, and we might ascribe their energy to their motivation; for example, "he works energetically

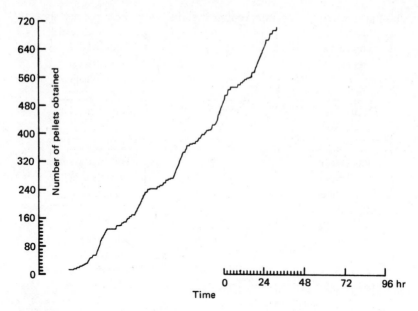

FIGURE 21.3. Cyclical feeding pattern of a single mouse (Anliker and Mayer, 1956).

FIGURE 21.4. Cumulative drinking curves for four rats. The graph shows periods of drinking and nondrinking of distilled water which was constantly available (Young and Richey, 1952).

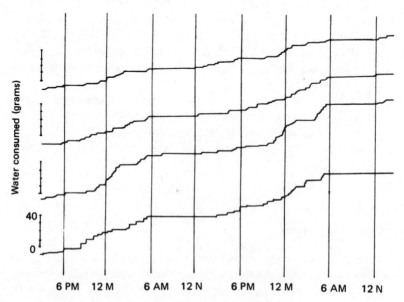

because he is highly motivated." Hull built this statement into his formal theory of drive by implying that increases in general activity are part of the meaning of increases in drive. We will examine two possible relationships between drive and activity.

1. When drive increases, for example, through deprivation, general activity increases.
2. Where a cyclic change in general activity is observed, there exists a corresponding drive.

An apparatus known as the running wheel (or activity wheel) has been in use since the beginning of the century for the study of general activity in small mammals (rats, hamsters, mice). The wheel (Figure 21.5) is frequently attached to the organism's living cage, and the animal is free to enter the wheel at any time and run. The question of whether motivation is related to activation is approached in a straightforward way by studying the relation of various drive operations to running activity in the wheel.

Another apparatus that records a somewhat different set of general activities than the wheel is the stabilimeter (Figure 21.6). The stabilimeter

FIGURE 21.5. A running wheel.

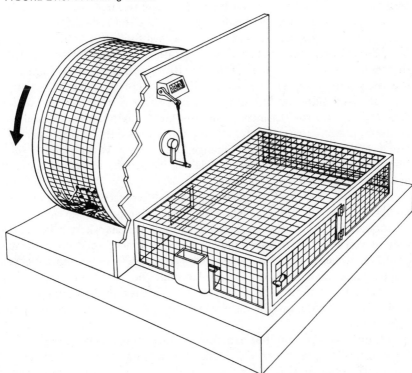

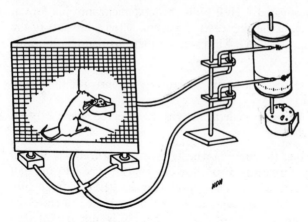

FIGURE 21.6. A stabilimeter for recording movements of small
animals (Harlow, 1948).

consists of a cage (often triangular) whose floor is mounted above a
pneumatic suspension system. Slight movements about the cage, and shifts in
balance by the animal, tilt the floor slightly, changing the air-pressure
balance. These changes are transmitted to recording pens that permit a
permanent record of activity to be kept. The movements recorded are not
necessarily the same type as the movements in wheel running.

Both types of apparatus have been used with food deprivation to test the
first prediction. It turns out that the apparatus used substantially influences
the result. In stabilimeter cages, rats' activity levels increase only slightly with
food deprivation, but *environmental stimulation* greatly increases activity in
food-deprived subjects. In running wheels, there is a clear effect of food
deprivation and a smaller increase in response to environmental stimulation.
In these studies, environmental stimulation means either a short period of
visual and auditory stimulus change, or a high background level of
stimulation (such as is produced by placing the activity recording apparatus
in the middle of a busy laboratory).

Two factors contribute to these apparatus differences. First, Bolles (1967)
points out that the running wheel and the stabilimeter cage are sensitive
to topographically different behaviors, and he has shown that under
food deprivation there are complex changes in the relative frequencies
of different behaviors. Food-deprived rats move around more *and* rest
quietly more than undeprived rats. Second, the wheel-running response
produces a lot of audiovisual feedback. This means that the running wheel is
probably more similar to the stabilimeter cage *with* additional environmental
stimulation.

Results of a representative experiment using running wheels are shown in
Figure 21.7. Here we see mean amounts of running for a group of rats in a
"normal" environment and for a group given extra environmental

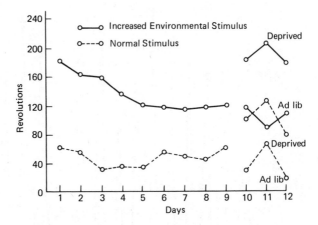

FIGURE 21.7. Amount of running by groups of rats in Hall's (1956) experiment (from Gross, 1968).

stimulation. As the figure shows, the stimulated group was consistently about twice as active. After 9 days, food was removed from half the subjects in each group. An equivalent and substantial rise in activity was seen in both conditions.

There is, therefore, evidence that food deprivation results in increases in activity, but the effect is relatively fragile (that is, it can be obscured by other effects) and a steady increase in activity with deprivation has rarely been obtained. However, using *body weight loss* as an index of deprivation, rather than hours without food, Duda and Bolles (1963) found a good correlation between body weight loss and amount of wheel running.

We now know enough about the physiology of digestion to trace the connection between deprivation and activity. During deprivation, the blood glucose levels fall, glucose is released from the liver where it is stored as glycogen, and there is an increase in secretion of adrenalin which assists the conversion of glycogen to glucose. As adrenalin also increases reactivity to sensory stimuli and facilities motor activity (Gross, 1968), we can presume that adrenalin secretion is intimately related to the observed increases in general activity. This analysis of the "physiological pathway" suggests that activity increases may be indirect "by-products" of various physiological changes, rather than direct products of deprivation states.

Deprivation of a reinforcer often results in significant changes in general activity. Is the converse true? That is, can we use observed changes in general activity to infer that reinforcement values have changed correspondingly? In particular, where a cyclic change in general activity is observed, will we find a parallel drive cycle? Figure 21.8 depicts a pronounced cycle in wheel running. This is the activity cycle of a mature female rat and it is correlated with cycles in sexual hormone secretion and ovulation (called the estrous cycle). It can be

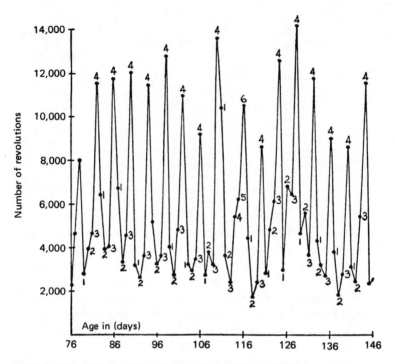

FIGURE 21.8. Typical activity of a female rat (Richter, 1927).

seen that approximately every 4 days, the female rat is extremely active. Corresponding physiological measurements show that it is precisely during this active period that ovulation occurs, rendering the female maximally susceptible to insemination. During this period, the female is said to be "in heat" and is then most receptive to sexual advances from the male. During the low-activity portions of the cycle, however, the female is likely to resist copulation and fight off advances by the male. Thus, for the female rat, there exists an intimate correlation between general activity and other behavioral and physiological aspects of "sex drive".

We should be careful, however, not to presume that all activity in the female rat is sexually drive-related. We know, for instance, that the basic activity cycle is not a response to sexual deprivation. If the female remains unmated, the activity cycle goes up and down again repeatedly. From the days marked 4 on Figure 21.8, there is a large drop to the following day 1, although deprivation has increased since no sexual behavior has occurred.

General activity is probably related to more than one motivational system (food *and* sex), and may even partially reflect an independent drive just for activity. In the aforementioned examples, we found that general activity increased only slightly with duration of food deprivation, and that the hormonal estrous cycle dramatically altered general activity, but was unrelated to sexual deprivation duration.

21.7
Physiological Aspects of Motivation

We have had little occasion to mention the properties of the nervous system in the present treatment of behavioral principles. This neglect should not be taken as a disinterest in the nervous structures and functions that underlie the various behavioral processes. Rather, it stems from the recognition that the tremendous volume of information which constitutes behavioral science must of necessity be partitioned into somewhat arbitrary divisions. Psychology, sociology, and anthropology constitute such divisions; so do the hybrid disciplines of behavior genetics and physiological psychology. Although we have elsewhere noted that the laws of behavior cannot be subsumed or replaced by laws of physiology (or chemistry, or mechanics, or particle physics), the nervous system is intimately involved in all behavioral phenomena. Indeed, many of the behavioral phenomena we have described have been used as techniques for assessing the effects of alterations in the nervous system.

Natural phenomena transcend the arbitrary boundaries of disciplines. Thus, behavior involves a complex of physical, biochemical, physiological, psychological, and sociological events. The position we have adopted is dictated by convenience: psychology concerns itself with lawful relations between environment and behavior. Laws relating behavior to nervous function carry us outside the strictly psychological province into physiology studies; they contribute to our knowledge of behavior *and* physiology, hence the designation physiological psychology. In the present text, however, physiological psychology cannot be treated in any degree of depth. We elect to introduce certain of its findings in the context of motivation, because the picture that is emerging of the physiological mechanisms underlying motivated behavior helps in understanding the behavioral concept of drive. Physiological studies promise to give aspects of drive a physical referent in various anatomical structures, and to tie together a number of environmentally diverse drive operations by discovering their common effects within the organism.

EATING AND DRINKING MECHANISMS. In the gradual elaboration of the bodily mechanisms associated with eating, we find a representative example of the search for physiological events underlying behavioral phenomena. More precisely, that search concerns itself with certain internal events and processes that accompany changes in the reinforcing power of food. The state of the stomach was thought, from antiquity to recent times, to play a major role in the control of feeding. The fact that "hunger pangs" often accompanied reports of great hunger in humans led to investigations of the relationship between hunger pangs, stomach contractions, and hunger. Cannon and Washburn (1912) studied stomach contractions, using an ingenious technique in which a human subject swallowed a small rubber balloon. Once in the stomach, the balloon was inflated, and any stomach contractions that occurred squeezed the balloon. The resulting air-pressure variations within the balloon were, in turn, transmitted to a pen-recording device. The subject depressed a telegraph key whenever he felt hunger pangs. Cannon and Washburn showed that the contractions were closely correlated with reports of hunger pangs, and concluded that these contractions were the *cause* of hunger. The hypothesis won immediate attention, because it seemed to offer such a simple and straightforward mechanism for hunger and eating. But it was soon shown that patients lacking stomachs altogether ate in normal ways, and reported "hunger" even though they never had stomach contractions. The implications behind these observations were extended in experiments which showed that rats ate normally, even though the nerves from the stomach were surgically isolated from the brain. Other observations showed that hunger contractions were abolished by the first morsels of food, yet eating continued long after the contractions had ceased. In the end, the stomach-contraction theory of hunger had to be abandoned, for it failed to explain enough of the facts.

A more complicated mechanism was indicated by the early experiments of Tschukilshew (cited in Templeton and Quigley, 1930), in which blood transfusion from food-deprived animals to well-fed animals augmented the stomach motility of the recipient. More recent experiments have shown that transfusing the blood between hungry and satiated rats (Figure 21.9) affects the food intake of these animals. Feeding and fasting appear to change some aspect of the blood, which could, in turn, affect brain mechanisms, leading to a reduction in hunger drive. One theory (Mayer, 1953) holds that a possible mediating variable is the relative arterial to venous glucose concentration, and that the cells in the brain where this concentration may be "metered", lie in a restricted region of the hypothalamus (Figure 21.10).

Independent experimental work has confirmed that certain structures in the hypothalamus are intimately related to the control of eating. Rats with

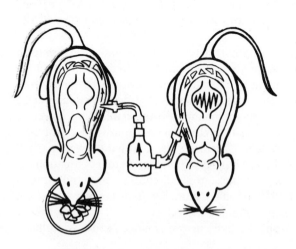

FIGURE 21.9.
When blood is transfused between hungry and satiated rats, food intake is altered (Sanford, 1961).

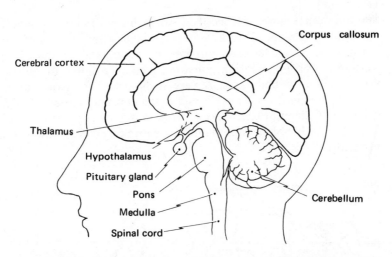

FIGURE 21.10. Schematic diagram of the human brain (Rosenzweig, 1962).

damage in the ventromedial region of the hypothalamus, overeat and grow obese. Electrical stimulation of this brain region also has effects on food-motivated behavior. Tiny electrodes can be implanted in the brain with fairly precise localization, yet without damaging surrounding structures. The electrodes are guided into brain tissue through a hole drilled in the skull, then secured in a plastic block that is cemented to the skull, covering the hole. Finally, the scalp is resewn. Following a few days of recovery from the operation, such an implanted animal regains complete health. The animal appears in no way inconvenienced by the addition of the electrodes, and lives normally. Through the implanted electrodes, minute electrical currents can be applied to the brain structure where the tips of the electrodes lie. The behavioral effects of such electrical current are then measured. When the ventromedial region of the hypothalamus is so stimulated, food intake decreases. Other areas in the brain have been found where stimulation causes a "satiated" animal to begin eating. The picture of physiological mechanisms behind deprivation and eating is complex and still fragmentary. No single bodily structure is all-important. The stomach, the blood, the brain, and probably other bodily systems interact to determine when food shall be consumed.

An analogous experimental history can be narrated for drinking mechanisms, but we can only indicate it briefly. The earliest explanations centered on the role of the relative dryness of throat and mouth membranes, and the importance of salivary secretions. Dry mouth and pharynx were equated with thirst. Later work showed that salivation could not be crucial, since animals both drank and ceased to drink normally, even when their salivary ducts were tied off. Conversely, in experiments in which the water that dogs drank never reached their stomachs, but ran out from a fistula in the throat (Figure 21.11), water-deprived dogs continued to drink indefinitely, although their throats and mouths were thus being kept constantly wet. Experimental attention gradually shifted to the role of the water content of body cells. A very slight deficit from the normal water concentration in the body's cells and blood appears to be a critical factor in drinking (Gilman, 1937). Recent work has focussed on localizing brain centers in the hypothalamus that regulate drinking and cessation of drinking behavior.

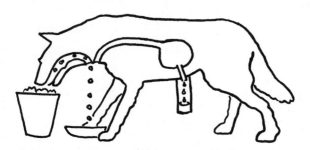

FIGURE 21.11. (From Rosenzweig, 1962).

If these physiological measures of motivation are taken to reflect various biological balance systems of the organism, we can conclude that relationships can be established between physiological imbalances and behavioral aspects of drive. However, no one physiological variable has been found that uniquely correlates with hunger or thirst. Instead, various physiological variables are related in complex ways to various aspects of motivated behavior.

References for Chapter 21

Anliker, J., and Mayer, J. Operant conditioning technique for studying feeding patterns in normal and obese mice. *Journal of Applied Physiology*, 1956, **8**, 667–670.

Bolles, R. C. *Theory of motivation*. New York: Harper & Row, 1967.

Bousfield, W. A. Quantitative indices of the effects of fasting on eating behavior. *Journal of Genetic Psychology*, 1935, **46**, 476–479.

Cannon, W. B., and Washburn, A. L. An explanation of hunger. *American Journal of Psychology*, 1912, **29**, 441–452.

Duda, J. J., and Bolles, R. C. Effects of prior deprivation, current deprivation, and weight loss on the activity of the hungry rat. *Journal of Comparative and Physiological Psychology*, 1963, **56**, 569–571.

Gilman, A. The relation between blood osmotic pressure, fluid distribution, and voluntary water intake. *American Journal of Physiology*, 1937, **120**, 323–328.

Gross, C. G. General activity. In L. Weiskrantz (Ed.) *Behavioral Change*. New York: Harper & Row, 1968.

Hall, J. F. The relationship between external stimulation, food deprivation, and activity. *Journal of Comparative and Physiological Psychology*, 1956, **49**, 339–341.

Harlow, H. F. Studying animal behavior. In T. G. Andrews (Ed.), *Methods of Psychology*. New York: Wiley, 1948.

Hull, C. L. *Principles of behavior*. New York: Appleton-Century-Crofts, 1943.

Kleitman, N. *Sleep and wakefulness*. Chicago: University of Chicago Press, 1963.

Mayer. J. Glucostatic mechanism of regulation of food intake. *New England Journal of Medicine*, 1953, **249**, 13–16.

Richter, C. Animal behavior and internal drives. *Quarterly Review of Biology*, 1927, **2**, 307–343.

Rosenzweig, M. The mechanisms of hunger and thirst. In L. Postman (Ed.) *Psychology in the making*. New York: Knopf, 1962.

Sanford, F. *Psychology, a scientific study of man*, Belmont, Calif.: Wadsworth, 1961.

Templeton, R. D., and Quigley, J. P. The action of insulin on the mobility of the gastro-intestinal tract. *American Journal of Physiology*, 1930, **91**, 467–474.

Webb, W. B. Antecedents of sleep. *Journal of Experimental Psychology*, 1957, **53**, 162–166.

Young, P. T., and Richey, H. W. Diurnal drinking patterns in the rat. *Journal of Comparative and Physiological Psychology*, 1952, **45**, 80–89.

CHAPTER 22

Motivation and Reinforcement

We saw in the previous chapter that various classes of motivated behavior are influenced by deprivation, related to physiological imbalances, show cyclic patterns, and are associated with changes in general activity. However, these relationships differ qualitatively and quantitatively for different motivated behaviors. Thus, the relationships of a particular class of motivated behavior to its physiological correlates and its environmental antecedents tends to be specific to that class. In a biological context, this conclusion is unsurprising, for each primary motivational system serves a different function for the organism. The natural environment demands different types of behavior for obtaining and eating food than for obtaining and drinking water, or for obtaining access to a mate.

There is one relationship that we did not examine in detail in the previous chapter that is often considered to apply to all motivated behavior. This is the relationship between reinforcement and motivation, and it has been stated in two ways:

1. Reinforcement occurs when a physiological imbalance is reduced, therefore, such reduction is a necessary property of reinforcing stimuli (Hull, 1943).
2. The reinforcing value of a stimulus depends on the organism being in an appropriate state of deprivation. Reductions in deprivation should reduce the reinforcing value of the stimulus.

The first statement makes a stronger claim; in fact, it represents a theory of reinforcement. It states that presentation of a stimulus will have reinforcing effects only if a physiological imbalance is reduced directly by the stimulus. Thus, reinforcing stimuli are identical with physiological imbalance-reducers. It is, of course, quite in keeping with the observation that repeated presentations of the reinforcer result in satiation, the cessation of reinforced behavior.

The second statement of the relationship between reinforcement and motivation makes the weaker claim that there is a functional relationship between deprivation level and reinforcing value. The term "reinforcing value" represents a quantification of the idea that the effectiveness of a stimulus as a reinforcer can vary considerably. Presentation of a single food pellet to a rat that has just finished eating the daily food ration may have no discernible effect, while presenting a similar pellet to the same rat, when 36 hrs deprived of food, can produce dramatic behavioral changes. Saying that there is a functional relationship between deprivation and reinforcing value does not imply that deprivation changes are the *only* method of altering reinforcing value, but it is usually taken to imply that repeated access to the reinforcer will reduce its reinforcing value to zero.

In this chapter, we will describe methods of measuring satiation and reinforcing value as a prelude to evaluating the two stated relationships between reinforcement, motivation and deprivation.

22.1
Satiation

When we deprive an organism of a class of primary reinforcers for a fixed period of time, and then permit access to the reinforcer, we may observe the effect that our deprivation operation has had upon behavior. In the case of food and water, the actual behavior of consuming the reinforcer is often of interest. After a period of deprivation, an animal eats and drinks a certain quantity of food or water, and then ceases. We say that the process conveniently takes the form of the change in rate of a continuously reinforced response that produces food or water. Since each response is reinforced, the rate of eating is indexed by the rate of emission of this response.

Food-satiation curves do not all take the same form, but the most common form seems to be that of a constant rate of eating, followed by a fairly abrupt cessation (Smith and Smith, 1939; Reese and Hogenson, 1962). In Figure 22.1, several satiation curves from a pigeon pecking a key for grain are shown. The curves were taken after various lengths of food deprivation, as indicated.

In their decline in rate, satiation curves may bear a superficial resemblance to extinction curves. The form of a satiation curve is, however, characterized

FIGURE 22.1. Individual food-satiation curves. Curves are labeled with number of hours of prior food deprivation. A pip above the curve indicates that the bird did not eat following that pecking response (Reese and Hogenson, 1962).

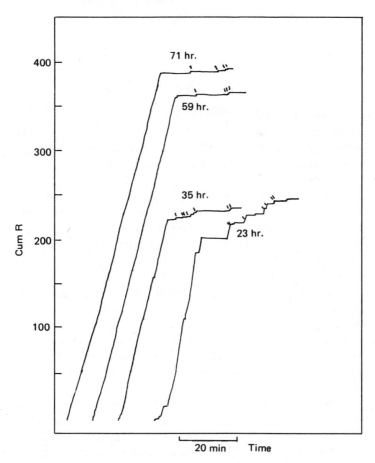

by a much more abrupt cessation of rate (see Figure 22.1). Furthermore, if the chain of acquired behavior is examined in detail, it will be found to remain intact as the process progresses. The extinction process, on the other hand, is associated with a marked disintegration of the chain of behavior.

The satiation effect is readily obtained with primary reinforcers for a wide range of species and we can define a *satiation paradigm*. Given an operant response previously reinforced with a primary reinforcer, and a state of deprivation such that that reinforcer currently has reinforcing value, the procedure is:

$$R \rightarrow S^+$$
primary reinforcer used
in previous training

This results in a fairly constant rate of responding, and then an abrupt cessation of responding. At this point, we say satiation has occurred. Note that this procedure is operationally identical with reinforcement and with punishment; it is the outcomes that distinguish between them.

22.2
Measurements of Reinforcing Value

There is no way to measure the reinforcing value of stimuli, save by measuring the behavioral effects of those stimuli when they are made contingent upon operant responses. Thus, many of the familiar behavioral measures of previous chapters, such as response rate and resistance to extinction, will be useful in assessing the strength of reinforcers. A curious implication of this versatility follows. The behavior that the experimenter chooses to measure cannot, alone and in itself, determine what phenomenon is under study. Lever pressing, key pecking, and vocalizing, "I'm hungry," take on meaning only when they are associated with other events. More generally, this is the reason why the very discipline of psychology cannot be defined solely as the study of behavior, but is more appropriately considered the study of behavior as it is related to the environment. In earlier chapters, the response rates of representative operants were used frequently to study conditioning, extinction, discrimination, chaining, and other phenomena, depending on the particular procedure that was being imposed on the organism when the behavior was being measured. Now we discover yet another use for operant measures. When conditioning parameters are held constant, and the behavior is related to drive operations, the properties of the behavior being emitted serves as a measure of the relative reinforcing value (or strength) of primary reinforcers. Note carefully how this experimental strategy is the converse of one in previous chapters, where drive operations were always held constant, and reinforcement contingencies were manipulated. Using that methodology, the rate of behavior was generally taken to represent the strength of behavior. In motivational methodology, the rate of behavior will often be taken to represent the strength of the reinforcer. Evidently, the "meaning" of behavior is derived only by considering the variable or variables to which the behavior is being related. We discuss herewith a number of behavioral techniques that have been used to measure the primary reinforcing value of stimuli, and therefore, by inference, motivation. At the same time, we illustrate a variety of different responses and primary reinforcers.

RESISTANCE TO SATIATION. Our intuitions tell us that the "thirstier" we are, the more water we can consume, and the "hungrier" we are, the more food we can eat. How can we quantify these impressions? One way is to examine the properties of the satiation process in relation to the duration of time that an individual has been previously denied access to all the reinforcers in a certain class. In effect, we look at satiation curves obtained at various degrees of deprivation. Suppose, after a period of deprivation, we set a contingency so that some arbitrary chain of behavior can lead to reinforcement. Then, either the time it takes the organism to reach some arbitrary low-rate criterion, or the number of reinforced responses emitted before reaching the low-rate criterion, would provide a measure of the *resistance to satiation*. It is evident that if continuous reinforcement is used, and if each reinforcement is held constant in amount, this last measure is equivalent to the amount of the reinforcer consumed. Resistance to satiation is calculated analogously to resistance to extinction (Section 3.4). Using the resistance-to-satiation method, Siegel (1947) measured the amount of water drunk by rats in a 5-min period as a function of how long the animals had been deprived of water. The relationship obtained is shown in Figure 22.2.

FIGURE 22.2. Amount of drink by rats in a five-min test period as a function of the number of hours of deprivation of liquids (after Siegel, 1947).

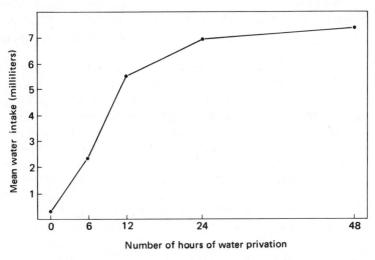

Number of hours of water privation

From 0- up to 48-hr deprivation, the resistance to satiation, as measured by the amount of water consumed, increased. The *rate of increase*, however, appears to fall off after 12 hr. Similar results may be obtained for food deprivation. At very long periods of deprivation, however, the amount of food eaten will decline, presumably as a result of shrinkage of the stomach and inanition. Within limits, however, resistance to satiation increases as deprivation time increases.

Resistance to satiation, although a useful technique, is not always entirely satisfactory for measuring reinforcing value. One difficulty lies in the physiological complications that occur at long deprivation times, sometimes causing reduced intake. Another difficulty arises if we wish to know how strong the reinforcer is at various points in the satiation process. At any level of deprivation, an organism may eat or drink at a constant high rate until the process comes to an abrupt halt (Figure 22.1). Hence, the momentary strength of the reinforcer is difficult to assess by inspection of the satiation process. Satiation curves tend to differ principally in their point of termination, rather than in their slopes (Figure 22.1). Hence, we are forced to wait until satiation has been reached to know how hungry or thirsty the animal was at the beginning.

RATE OF INTERMITTENTLY REINFORCED RESPONSES. A more generally useful technique for measuring reinforcement value is to observe the rate of response generated by the organism when behavior is being intermittently reinforced. An interval schedule, for instance, can be arranged to provide a low enough reinforcement rate so that behavior can be maintained, without the occurrence of satiation, for a very long period. Skinner (1938) used this technique to assess the behavioral effects of feeding specified amounts of food to rats, prior to testing. Rats were at first deprived of food for 23 hr and then, on various days, fed different amounts of food just prior to testing on interval contingencies. The results for one of these rats appear in Figure 22.3. The numbers associated with each curve refer to the amount of food in grams fed the rat previously. It is clear that the more the rat was fed immediately prior to working, the lower the response rate on the schedule.

Clark (1958) studied the effects of various degrees of food deprivation on "stabilized" *VI* response rates of rats. Several different *VI*'s were used. Clark obtained the curves of Figure 22.4 when he plotted the rats' response rate against hours of deprivation. The effect of increasing deprivation was to increase the response rate under all *VI* schedules. The way in which the deprivation and reinforcement schedule interacted to determine the response rates of Figure 22.4 is of some interest. The similarity in shape of the curves of Figure 22.4 means that deprivation interacted with the *VI* schedule so that, at all deprivation levels, the ratio of the rate at one *VI* to that of the rate at another *VI* was a constant. For example, at 5-hr deprivation, the rate of *VI*-3 min was about 4 responses/min, and at *VI*-1 min, it was 2.5 times that, about

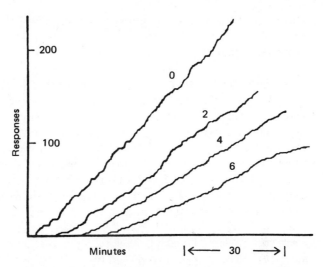

FIGURE 22.3. Four daily records for one rat under interval contingencies, 23-hr deprived then fed different amounts of food (0, 2, 4, or 6 grams) immediately prior to testing (Skinner, 1938).

FIGURE 22.4. *VI* response rate as a function of deprivation time on *VI* 1-min, *VI* 2-min and *VI* 3-min schedules (Clark, 1958).

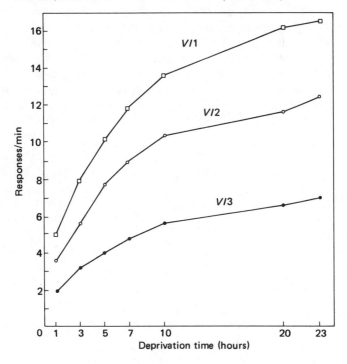

10 responses/min. When deprivation was increased to 20 hr, the two rates were approximately 6 and 15, respectively, so that the *VI*-1 min rate was still 2.5 times greater than the *VI*-3 min rate.

RESISTANCE TO EXTINCTION. The rate of response during extinction, and other measures of resistance to extinction (Section 3.4) have frequently been used to measure the behavioral effects of deprivation and other deprivation-like operations. Crocetti (1962) trained 7-hr, food-deprived rats to press a lever for food. The subjects were then distributed into five groups, and each group was extinguished after a different duration of deprivation. In Figure 22.5, the total number of responses emitted by each group after 3 hr of extinction is shown. The curve shows the usual increase in response rate as deprivation time increases; but observe that the shape of this curve differs from those of Figure 22.4. Differences such as these raise the systematic problem of which behavioral index best represents reinforcement value. At present, there is no clear-cut solution to this problem, and theorists are often forced to take the position that the measures that correlate the best with each other represent reinforcing value best.

ACQUISITION. We might expect that with an increase in the power of the reinforcer, there would be a concomitant increase in the speed of the acquisition process. When the acquisition entails a long chain of responses (for instance, behavior in a runway), or a discrimination, this prediction is verified. Broadhurst (1957) ran rats in the underwater equivalent of a *Y*-maze. Rats were submerged in a start box and confined there for a few seconds, then permitted to swim underwater to the choice point. There they were presented with a light-dark discrimination, with contingencies of the sort discussed in relation to the Lashley jumping stand (Section 14.3). If, at the choice point, the rat then swam to the bright side, it found an unlocked door that led out to dry land. If, however it swam to the incorrect side, it

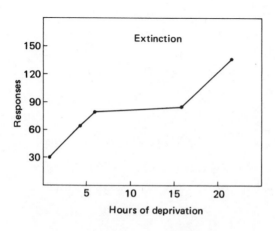

FIGURE 22.5.
The relation of hours of food deprivation to the number of bar-pressing responses during extinction (after Crocetti, 1962).

encountered a locked door, and had to swim back to the choice point, and then down the other branch of the Y to get out.

Broadhurst varied the intensity difference between the two parts of the visual choice-point stimulus. The greater this difference, the easier the discrimination task (Frick, 1948). Hence, a large difference in the illumination corresponds to an "easy" discrimination; a small difference in the illumination corresponds to a "difficult" discrimination.

The results of the acquisition are shown in Figure 22.6. The number of correct choices in 100 acquisition trials is shown for the two discriminations. When the illumination difference was large ("easy" discrimination), we may summarize the results by saying that the longer the deprivation time for air, the more efficient was the acquisition performance. But when a small illumination difference was used ("difficult" discrimination), acquisition was most efficient at a middle value (2 sec) of air deprivation, and less efficient at both shorter and longer deprivations. If this result can be generalized, it appears that with difficult tasks, it is possible to have too much motivation for optimum performance. Certainly, the differences in shape between the two curves of Figure 22.6 indicate that the acquisition method must be used cautiously as a measure of reinforcing strength. For instance, a rather

FIGURE 22.6. Number of correct discrimination choices in 100 acquisition trials as a function of prior air deprivation. The data are for two discriminations varying in difficulty (after Broadhurst, 1957).

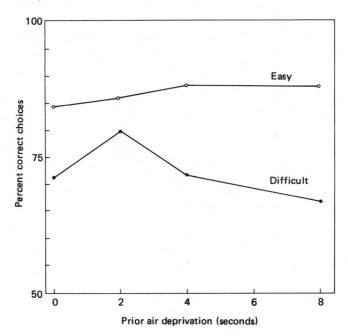

different result was obtained in a situation requiring a straight underwater swim without discrimination contingencies. Then over the range of prior air deprivations from 0 to 10 sec, rats swam faster, the greater the previous air deprivation.

OVERCOMING OBSTRUCTIONS. The more reinforcing a stimulus, the more obstructions, barriers, and hindrances an organism would be expected to overcome to produce the reinforcer. That is the rationale for the Columbia Obstruction Box shown in Figure 22.7. A rat is placed in the start box and an electrically charged grid is interposed between it and food, water, or a mate located in the goal box. (The rat has previously been trained to run to the goal box without receiving any electric shocks). If the rat crosses the grid, it is given brief access to the reinforcer, and then returned to the start box for another trial. The number of crossings of the electrified grid in 30 min provides a measure of the strength of the behavior. Warden (1931) investigated several primary reinforcers and deprivation procedures with this apparatus. He believed it was a way of comparing objectively the maximum strengths of the various primary reinforcers. One interesting set of Warden's functions appears in Figure 22.8. From these, we see that if deprivation operations are carried out long enough, the behavior that leads to the reinforcer rises to a maximum strength, then eventually declines. Warden thought that the relative heights of the maxima could be interpreted to mean that the water and food drives were stronger than the sex drive. But is such a conclusion justified? We must remember that behavioral functions depend on many variables other than the particular one that the experimenter happens to be investigating. Reinforcement value, in particular, depends on such factors as the quality and quantity of the reinforcement. Warden's conclusion assumed that somehow these factors had been equated for sex, food, and water, so that deprivation

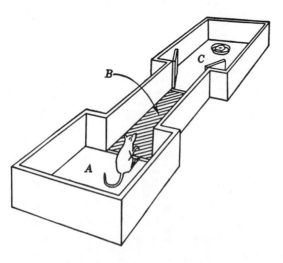

FIGURE 22.7.
The Columbia Obstruction Box. A charged grid (B) lies between the rat's compartment (A) and a reinforcer in the goal box (C) (after Warden, 1931, from Harlow, 1948).

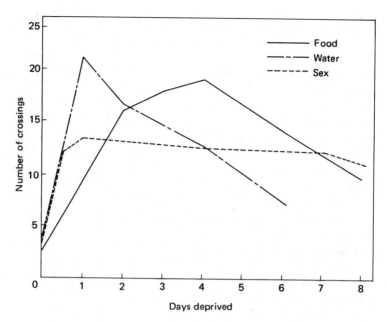

FIGURE 22.8. The number of crossings of a charged grid as a function of days of deprivation of the appropriate primary reinforcer (after Warden, 1931).

was the only *variable* in the situation. But in what sense, except the most trivial, can (say) a 10-sec exposure to a female rat, a dish of water, and a piece of cheese be said to be equal? And even if some way were found to equate two reinforcers, the satiation processes associated with each class of reinforcer are almost certainly so different that the average crossings in a 30-min session would reflect a different composite of reinforcement values for each reinforcer. These considerations indicate that Warden's ranking of water, food, and sex drives probably should not be taken too seriously. The question of which drive is the strongest may not even have experimental meaning.

MAXIMUM-WORK TECHNIQUE. The maximum-work technique is similar in outlook to the obstruction box, but avoids one of the latter's undesirable side effects—contamination of the results by emotional effects of electric shocks. The maximum-work technique is based on the idea that the stronger the reinforcer, the more work an individual will do to obtain it. Hodos (1961) devised an ingenious procedure in which an organism works on a ratio schedule of reinforcement, in which the actual value of the ratio is progressively increased with each successive reinforcement. In one experiment, the session began with a ratio of 2, and each successive reinforcement increased the ratio by an additional 2, so that animals were required to emit 2 responses for the first reinforcement, 4 for the second, 6 for the third, and so on. A ratio is eventually reached which is so high that the animal refuses to go on working. The point at which this occurs is named the "breaking point", defined in Hodos' work as 15 min of no responding. Using rat subjects, and sweetened condensed milk as reinforcement, Hodos manipulated the deprivation schedule of his subjects by feeding them each day, only enough food to keep their body weights at a fixed percentage of their free-feeding weights. Thus, a rat kept at 80 per cent of its normal body weight is strongly deprived; a rat kept at 95 per cent of its normal body weight is only mildly deprived. This procedure is commonly used to control deprivation in experimental subjects, and is thought by some to give slightly better control of motivation than maintaining subjects at a fixed duration of deprivation, say 23 hr. We noted earlier that Duda and Bolles (1963) obtained a good correlation between percentage body weight and general activity, while other investigations found less clear relationships using hours of deprivation. The measure of behavior used by Hodos was the number of responses in the last completed ratio prior to the breaking point. This final ratio is the maximum ratio that the rat would complete under the conditions of the experiment. Figure 22.9 shows that as the rats were more deprived, they completed a larger maximum ratio. We interpret this to mean that with greater deprivation, the rat will put out more total work.

ADULTERATION OF REINFORCER. When we are only slightly hungry, we are very selective about what we will eat. Eventually, as we grow increasingly hungry, our standards of what we will accept go down. If we are starving, we will eat almost anything. These impressions suggest that deprivation might control the quantity of an unpalatable substance that can

FIGURE 22.9. Maximum ratio run leading to milk that rats will emit as a function of degree of food deprivation (Hodos, 1961).

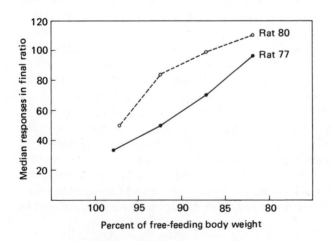

be mixed with food, before the organism stops working for or consuming the adulterated food.

If a small area of a rat's brain is experimentally destroyed (lesioned) in the ventromedial nuclei of the hypothalamus (see Figure 21.10), the animal, once recovered from surgery, eats voraciously. In 2 months' time, it will double its weight if given continuous access to food (Teitelbaum, 1955). Though such "operated" rats will eat enormous quantities of food and grow obese, Miller, Bailey, and Stevenson (1950) had earlier shown that these rats would not work as hard to obtain food on ratio schedules as would normal rats. This is one of several findings that amount of food consumed (resistance to satiation) and work done for food are not perfectly correlated. Miller, Bailey, and Stevenson took the ratio findings to mean that the obese rats were not as "hungry" as normal rats, though if food were freely available, they would eat relatively much more of it.

Teitelbaum used the method of adulterating the rat's food with a fixed, small amount of quinine (a substance that humans find bitter) to further examine Miller, Bailey, and Stevenson's interpretation. He found that during the 2 months after the operation, as the rats were growing obese, the quinine did not deter their abnormally large consumption of food. In other words, during this period in which the rats grew very fat, food was a strong reinforcer. But once the rats had become obese, an amount of quinine, too small even to affect the normal rat's food consumption, completely deterred the obese animals from eating. It appears that food is less reinforcing for the fully obese rat than it is for the normal rat. Even so, if given continuous access to nonadulterated food, the obese animal will eat a great deal more—its resistance to satiation is higher than normal.

SUMMARY. This review of methods of measuring the value of various primary reinforcers shows that most measures increase with deprivation and reach a maximum. This supports the idea that reinforcing value increases with deprivation, but we also noted that different measures of the same reinforcer correlate imperfectly. This means that the reinforcing value of a particular stimulus may change, depending on the method that is used to measure it. This result fits into the pattern we observed in the preceding chapter. While various measures of motivated behavior change in orderly fashion with environmental changes, they are not as closely related as would be predicted by the assumption that they are all reflections of the same drive state.

22.3
Brain Stimulation Reinforcement

At the beginning of this chapter, we noted that two relationships between reinforcement and motivation have been suggested: either that reinforcement occurs only when a physiological imbalance is reduced (Hull,

1943), or that reinforcing value is a function of deprivation. The evidence we have reviewed, in general, supports both these viewpoints. Satiation can be obtained by allowing continued access to a primary reinforcer, and reinforcing value usually increases with deprivation. If, however, these are inherent properties of reinforcers, there should be no exceptions; any stimulus that is a reinforcer should show satiation and deprivation effects. We now examine a possible exception.

Olds and Milner (1954) implanted electrodes deep in the rat's brain, with the aim of seeing whether stimulation in a region associated with sleep would facilitate or hinder simple operant acquisition. The investigators were surprised to find that the stimulation itself had a marked effect on the rat's behavior.

> In the test experiment we were using, the animal was placed in a large box with corners labeled A, B, C and D. Whenever the animal went to corner A, its brain was given a mild electric shock by the experimenter. When the test was performed on the animal . . . it kept returning to corner A. After several such returns on the first day, it finally went to a different place and fell asleep. The next day, however, it seemed even more interested in corner A.
>
> At this point we assumed that the stimulus must provoke curiosity; we did not yet think of it as a reward. Further experimentation on the same animal soon indicated, to our surprise, that its response to the stimulus was more than curiosity. On the second day, after the animal had acquired the habit of returning to corner A to be stimulated, we began trying to draw it away to corner B, giving it an electric shock whenever it took a step in that direction. Within a matter of five minutes the animal was in corner B. After this, the animal could be directed to almost any spot in the box at the will of the experimenter. Every step in the right direction was paid with a small shock; on arrival at the appointed place the animal received a longer series of shocks (Olds, 1956).

Evidently, the brain stimulation was acting like a reinforcer with which operant behavior could be quickly shaped. Eventually, the animal was placed in a Skinner box (Figure 22.10) and allowed to stimulate its own brain at whatever rate it chose. High rates of response were emitted on continuous reinforcement. The similarities between brain-stimulation reward and more conventional, positive reinforcers, such as food and water, are pronounced. Like other positive reinforcers, brain-stimulation reinforcement maintains FR operants, generates high resistance to extinction after intermittent contingencies, and permits powerful schedule control (Pliskoff, Wright, and Hawkins, 1965). Additional work by Olds and others indicates that there is not one but a number of places in the brain where electrical stimulation exerts reinforcing effects (Olds, 1962). Many of these are the very places at

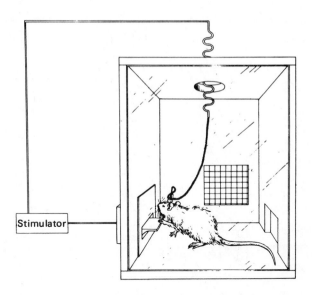

FIGURE 22.10. Rat self-stimulating in a Skinner box (after Olds, 1956).

which stimulation has been found in other studies to elicit eating, drinking, and other drive-related activities.

The peculiarities of brain-stimulation reinforcement become apparent when we look for satiation and deprivation effects. The results of an experiment in which a rat was given unlimited access to a response that was continuously reinforced with brain stimulation are shown in Figure 22.11. This animal emitted 26 lever presses per min for 26 hr before stopping. It was sleep and exhaustion that then intervened, rather than satiation. Even more remarkably, Valenstein and Beer (1964) recorded an overall rate of 30 responses per min for a 20-day period.

Not only does brain stimulation reinforcement appear relatively insatiable, but also, its reinforcing value remains continuously high. Rats have been shown to lever press for brain stimulation in preference to food and water, even when 48-hrs food or water deprived, and to tolerate cold or pain while obtaining brain stimulation. Its reinforcing value is not "infinite", however, because conventional reinforcers will be preferred to brain stimulation, if they are large enough, or if a weak current is used for brain stimulation.

Deprivation appears to have no effect on response rates maintained by brain-stimulation reinforcement. Characteristically, a constant rate of response is seen for the whole time that the reinforced response is available. However, if stimulation at that location in the brain also elicits eating, then brain-stimulation-reinforced response rate will increase with food de-

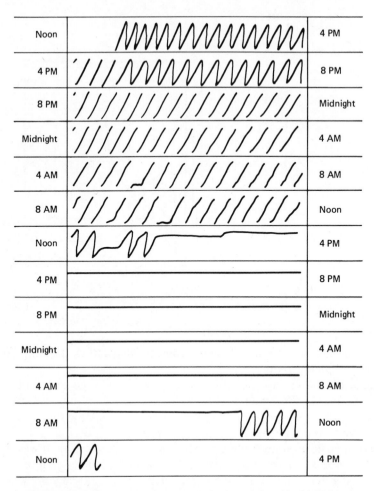

Noon		4 PM
4 PM		8 PM
8 PM		Midnight
Midnight		4 AM
4 AM		8 AM
8 AM		Noon
Noon		4 PM
4 PM		8 PM
8 PM		Midnight
Midnight		4 AM
4 AM		8 AM
8 AM		Noon
Noon		4 PM

FIGURE 22.11. Persistence of operant behavior reinforced with brain stimulation. Data are consecutive cumulative records from a single rat (Olds, 1958).

privation, and decline with food satiation and other treatments that depress eating (Mogenson and Cioé, 1977).

Overall, it appears that brain-stimulation-reinforcement is not influenced by deprivation and satiation of brain stimulation, but can be influenced by deprivation and satiation of another reinforcer, for example, food, water, or sex. It is as if brain stimulation "short circuits" a motivational system, and produces the reinforcing effects of the conventional reinforcer without any of its other effects (for example, satiation). This is a plausible account of the data, but it suggests that the usual relationships between satiation and deprivation are not necessary features of reinforcing stimuli.

22.4
Insatiable Behavior

The foregoing analysis could be objected to on the grounds that the brain stimulation reinforcement technique is both abnormal and "unbiological". It would, perhaps, be unwise to draw general conclusions about behavior from a technique that involves a drastic, and poorly understood, intervention in the brain. The case would be strengthened if a similar divorce could be demonstrated between reinforcing effects, on the one hand, and satiation and deprivation effects, on the other hand, for more conventional reinforcers. We will, therefore, describe two further examples: air licking in rats and water ingestion in doves.

Hendry and Rasche (1961) found that water-deprived rats would make an operant response for the opportunity to lick at a stream of air. This stimulus is presumably reinforcing to thirsty rats, because of the local cooling effect on the tongue. However, it tends to *increase* water deprivation because of evaporation from the tongue. Hendry and Rasche found that air licking did not satiate, but if the rats were no longer water deprived, they stopped air licking. This is a further example of the separation of reinforcing from satiation effects. When the subjects are thirsty, air has the reinforcing, but not the satiating effects of water.

The magnitude of these effects were quantified in a subsequent study by Oatley and Dickinson (1970). They tested groups of rats reinforced with water, low-pressure air, or high-pressure air, after varying periods of water deprivation. The results are shown in Figure 22.12. There are three points of interest. First, licking low-pressure air maintained substantially higher rates than water reinforcement. Second, air licking was an increasing function of water deprivation. Third, air licking showed no tendency to satiate over the 60-min session. Air licking is, therefore, reinforcing, and sensitive to water deprivation and satiation, but insensitive to air-licking deprivation and satiation.

The air-licking procedure involves presenting an unusual stimulus that has some of the properties of a conventional reinforcer, but not others. Similar effects have been obtained in a very different species by allowing a conventional reinforcer to have some of its usual effects, but not others. McFarland (1969) performed a surgical operation on Barbary doves, and inserted a tube (an esophageal fistula) so that water could be placed directly into the gut, without stimulating receptors in the mouth. After postoperative recovery, the doves were trained, while thirsty, to key peck for continuous reinforcement with water, which they drank in the normal fashion. Once this response had stabilized, responses to that key were extinguished, while responses to a second, concurrently available key were reinforced. Half of the subjects received water reinforcement by mouth in this phase (as in the previous phase). These subjects rapidly transferred their responding to the second key. The other half were reinforced with water delivered straight into

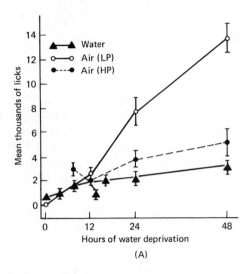

(A)

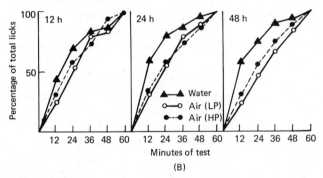

(B)

FIGURE 22.12. Amount of air licking for groups of rats in Oatley and Dickinson's (1970) experiment. Panel (A): Mean number of licks for water, low- or high-pressure air as a function of water deprivation. Panel (B): Cumulative percentages of licks over a 1-hr test period. The parameter is hours of water deprivation (from Gray, 1975).

the gut. Although these doves were still thirsty, and could still obtain water by making the operant response, they failed to respond on the second key.

It appears from these results that water is only reinforcing to thirsty doves when received in the mouth. In the next phase of the experiment, key pecks were reinforced with water simultaneously delivered by the normal route and directly into the stomach. In different conditions, the doves received 0.05 ml to mouth and 0.05 ml to gut, 0.1 ml to mouth and 0.1 ml to gut, or 0.1 ml to mouth, only. (He could not test them with water to gut only as reinforcer, because the earlier part of the experiment showed that this will not maintain behavior). McFarland recorded the total amount of water drunk before key pecking stopped, that is, the amount of water needed for satiation, and found that it was identical for all three conditions. This means that satiation resulted only from the amount of water in the gut, whichever route it arrived by, while reinforcement had already been shown to occur only when water was ingested through the mouth.

The results described in this section and the preceding one show that reinforcing effects *can* be independent of deprivation and satiation. The results described in the earlier sections of this chapter showed, however, that reinforcement and satiation are *normally* correlated. It seems that the reinforcing value of a stimulus does not always increase with deprivation, and satiation with that stimulus will not always reduce its reinforcing value. We must, therefore, conclude that a reinforcer does not have its effects *because* there is a deprivation state, or *because* it produces satiation.

22.5
Response Deprivation

If the relationship between a reinforcer and motivational variables is not a necessary one, what can we say about the nature of reinforcers? In Section 2.7, we briefly described Premack's (1965) approach to this problem. Premack demonstrated that if a rat was deprived of water, it would run in a wheel for water reinforcement; while if it was deprived of activity, it would drink water to obtain access to the wheel. The reinforcement relation was thus *reversible*.

Premack surmised that *response probabilities* determine which response of a pair will reinforce which at a particular moment. Premack's principle states that the more probable response of a pair will reinforce the less probable. This technique for obtaining these probabilities is to allow free access to both responses, simultaneously. The probability of each behavior is defined as the proportion of time spent on it. These probabilities are then used to predict the outcome, when access to one is restricted. For example, if feeding is more probable then wheel running, then when small amounts of feeding (small food deliveries) are made contingent upon running, running should increase in frequency (running will be reinforced).

This account of reinforcement shifts the emphasis from the reinforcing *stimulus* to its associated *response*. Other theories of reinforcement have presumed that this consumatory response was simply a way of the organism interacting with the reinforcing stimulus. The importance of the consumatory response, independent of the effects of the stimulus, is underlined by the results of the preceding section. There, we saw that given a deprivation state (for example, thirst), a stimulus (for example, an air stream) that elicits the appropriate consumatory response is reinforcing, even if it does not reduce the deprivation state. Conversely, a stimulus that reduces the deprivation state is not reinforcing if it does not elicit the appropriate consumatory response.

Timberlake and Allison (1974) have modified and extended Premack's approach by use of the *response deprivation principle* (Eisenberger, Karpman, and Trattner, 1967). This principle states that reinforcement will occur when

$$\frac{O}{C} > \frac{P_o}{P_c}$$

where

$\quad$ O $\quad$ = the amount of the *operant* response required for access to the contingent response.

$\quad$ C $\quad$ = the amount of access to the *contingent* response when the operant requirement is completed.

$\quad$ P_o = response probability of the operant response.

$\quad$ P_c = response probability of the contingent response.

$\quad$ > $\quad$ = greater than.

Response probabilities of the two responses are obtained in the way recommended by Premack; that is, the proportion of time spent on each when *both* are freely available. Note that this differs from the measurement of *operant level*, which is assessed when only the operant response is available. In this terminology, Premack's principle states that reinforcement will occur if $P_c > P_o$; it takes no account of O and C.

Evidence that the stronger response-deprivation condition must be met for reinforcement to occur comes from one of Premack's (1965) own experiments. In this, the operant response, wheel running, had a lower probability than the contingent response, licking water. And so, $P_c > P_o$ (conventionally, we would describe the subjects as water deprived). The schedule of the experiment required only a small amount of the operant response for access to a large amount of the contingent response. Thus, O was small, relative to C. Under these conditions, there was no increase in the running response; that is, reinforcement did not occur.

According to the response deprivation principle, not only is Premack's principle (that reinforcement will occur if $P_c > P_o$) not sufficient, but neither is it necessary. Provided that O is greater than C by a sufficient magnitude, the operant response will be reinforced, even if $P_o > P_c$. Translating into Premack's experimental paradigm, wheel running might be reinforced by licking, if the operant-response requirement (O) exceeded the amount of access to the contingent licking response (C), even if the response probability of running (P_o) was actually higher than that of licking (P_c), when the subject was given free access to both.

Allison and Timberlake (1974) tested this prediction, using drinking of two saccharin solutions by rats as the operant and contingent responses. First, they established that the rats spent more time drinking 0.4 per cent solutions than 0.3 per cent solutions, and designated the *less* probable response as the contingent response.

Thus

$$\text{Operant response} = \text{drinking 0.4 per cent solution}$$
$$\text{Contingent response} = \text{drinking 0.3 per cent solution}$$

and $P_o > P_c$, so reinforcement should *not* occur in this situation, according to Premack's principle. Then, they established a contingency that required 80 sec of 0.4 per cent licking for 10 sec access to 0.3 per cent solution.

Thus

$$O = 80 \text{ sec}$$
$$C = 10 \text{ sec}$$

This schedule satisfied the response-deprivation condition

$$\left(\text{because } \frac{O}{C} = 8 > \frac{P_o}{P_c} \right) \text{ and reinforcement } \textit{did} \text{ occur.}$$

Notice that in this exposition of the response-deprivation account of reinforcement, attention has shifted from the question, "Why is a reinforcing stimulus effective?" to the related question, "How can we predict when reinforcement will occur?" This shift suggests that the role of motivational factors may not be to set the occasion on which reinforcing stimuli have particular effects, but rather to modify response probabilities. The various data discussed in this chapter are consistent with this view.

References for Chapter 22

Allison, J., and Timberlake, W. Instrumental and contingent saccharin licking in rats: Response deprivation and reinforcement. *Learning and Motivation*, 1974, **5**, 231–247.

Broadhurst, P. L. Emotionality and the Yerkes-Dodson law. *Journal of Experimental Psychology*, 1957, **54**, 345–352.

Clark, F. C. The effect of deprivation and frequency of reinforcement on variable interval responding. *Journal of the Experimental Analysis of Behavior*, 1958, **1**, 221–228.

Crocetti, C. P. Drive level and response strength in the bar-pressing apparatus. *Psychological Reports*, 1962, **10**, 563–575.

Eisenberger, R., Karpman, M., and Trattner, J. What is the necessary and sufficient condition for reinforcement in the contingency situation? *Journal of Experimental Psychology*, 1967, **74**, 342–350.

Frick, F. C. An analysis of an operant discrimination. *Journal of Psychology*, 1948, **26**, 93–123.

Gray, J. A. *Elements of a two-process theory of leaving*. London: Academic Press, 1975.

Harlow, H. F. Studying animal behavior. In T. G. Andrews (Ed.) *Methods of psychology*, New York: Wiley, 1948.

Hendry, D. P., and Rasche, R. H. Analysis of a new non-nutritive reinforcer based on thirst. *Journal of Comparative and Physiological Psychology*, 1961, **54**, 477–483.

Hodos, W. Progressive ratio as a measure of reward strength. *Science*, 1961, **134**, 943–944.

Hull, C. L. *Principles of behavior*. New York: Appleton-Century-Crofts, 1943.

McFarland, D. J. Separation of satiating and rewarding consequences of drinking. *Physiology and Behavior*, 1969, **4**, 987–989.

Miller, N. E., Bailey, C. J., and Stevenson, J. A. F. Decreased "hunger" but increased food intake resulting from hypothalamic lesions. *Science*, 1950, **112**, 256–259.

Mogenson, G., and Cioé, J. Central reinforcement: A bridge between brain function and behavior. In W. K. Honig and J. E. R. Staddon (Eds.). *Handbook of operant behavior*. Englewood Cliffs, N.J.: Prentice-Hall, 1977.

Oatley, K., and Dickinson, A. Air drinking and the measurement of thirst. *Animal Behavior*, 1970, **18**, 259–265.

Olds, J. Pleasure centers in the brain. *Scientific American*, Oct. 1956, **195**, 105–116.

Olds, J. Satiation effects in self-stimulation of the brain. *Journal of Comparative and Physiological Psychology*, 1958, **51**, 675–678.

Olds, J. Hypothalamic substrates of reward. *Physiological Review*, 1962, **42**, 554–604.

Olds, J., and Milner, P. Positive reinforcement produced by electrical stimulation of septal area and other regions of rat brain. *Journal of Comparative and Physiological Psychology*, 1954, **47**, 419–427.

Pliskoff, S. S., Wright, J. E., and Hawkins, T. D. Brain stimulation as a reinforcer: intermittent schedules. *Journal of the Experimental Analysis of Behavior*, 1965, **8**, 75–88.

Premack, D. Reinforcement theory. In D. Levine (Ed.) *Nebraska Symposium on motivation*. Lincoln, Neb.: University of Nebraska Press, 1965.

Reese, T. W., and Hogenson, Marilyn J. Food satiation in the pigeon. *Journal of the Experimental Analysis of Behavior*, 1962, **5**, 239–245.

Siegel, P. S. The relationship between voluntary water intake, body weight loss and numbers of hours of water privation in the rat. *Journal of Comparative and Physiological Psychology*, 1947, **40**, 231–238.

Skinner, B. F. *The behavior of organisms*. New York: Appleton-Century-Crofts, 1938.

Smith, M. F., and Smith, K. U. Thirst-motivated activity and its extinction in the cat. *Journal of General Psychology*, 1939, **21**, 89–98.

Teitelbaum, P. Sensory control of hypothalamic hyperphagia. *Journal of Comparative and Physiological Psychology*, 1955, **48**, 156–163.

Timberlake, W., and Allison, J. Response deprivation: An empirical approach to instrumental performance. *Psychological Review*, 1974, **81**, 146–164.

Valenstein, E. S., and Beer, B. Continuous opportunity for reinforcing brain stimulation. *Journal of the Experimental Analysis of Behavior*, 1964, **7**, 183–184.

Warden, C. J. *Animal motivation studies*. New York: Columbia University Press, 1931.

CHAPTER 23

Emotional
Behavior

One of the oldest of distinctions is the broad classification of human behavior into emotions and passions, on the one hand, and rational and voluntary acts, on the other. Yet, this venerable and compelling dichotomy has done little to further the experimental analysis of the behaviors regarded as emotional. Too often, these have remained merely behaviors that could not be explained by known causes. Emotion has, in effect, been a wastebasket category of behavior, and the various phenomena discarded there have shown a strong resistance to systematic integration. Indeed, many present-day psychologists, discouraged by the persistent failures to formulate a positive concept of emotional behavior, would like to drop the term "emotion" altogether from the conceptual vocabulary of the science. They would prefer to construe emotional phenomena as special states of motivation or general activity. None of these attempts proves completely satisfactory because, as we shall see, a careful conceptual dissection of emotional behavior reveals certain unique features, not incorporated by other unifying behavioral rubics. In the present account, therefore, we retain the concept of emotion, using it to refer to certain widespread changes in behavior that result from the application of well-defined environmental operations. But before elaborating these relationships, we discuss a number of traditional solutions to the problems that have been assigned to the field of emotion.

23.1
Is Emotion a Cause of Behavior or a Behavioral Effect?

Prior to the end of the nineteenth century, emotion was thought of as an internal state of the organism that, when induced, caused appropriate behavior on the part of the organism. Thus, in the traditional or classical view, emotion was a cause of behavior. When, for example, a deer saw a bear (a stimulus), fear (a bodily state) was aroused, and was followed by an appropriate response, running. Similarly, a person when thwarted (a stimulus operation), became angry (bodily state), and their anger made them aggressive, a class of behavior.

The overt behaviors supposedly induced by emotional states were classified very early, and Charles Darwin wrote a classic treatise describing their biological usefulness. Fear, for instance, in inducing caution, must have saved the life of many an animal in evolutionary history. So too, anger might have been useful in destroying certain physical barriers preventing the completion of a chain of behavior leading to a reinforcer of biological significance. Other emotions, such as joy, Darwin thought useful for the purpose of communicating to other nearby organisms that no aggressive action would be forthcoming, and therefore, cooperative, sexual, and other behaviors would now be safe and reinforced. Darwin described the elaborate postures and respondents by which the emotions of rage, fear and joy are "expressed" in animals (Figure 23.1). Well-defined response patterns could be identified, which were, in some respects, peculiar to the species, and yet showed common elements between species. The curl of a person's lip in rage, revealing his or her canine teeth, was construed as a vestige of the retraction of the animal's gum preparing its sharp teeth to attack an aggressor. We rarely bite in anger today, but this vestigal pattern is with us still.

Darwin's account emphasized what we might call the topographical features of emotional behavior. William James, writing at the end of the nineteenth century, was more interested in the *sequence* of cause and effect in emotion. In particular, he was concerned with refuting the idea that internal states cause emotional behavior. James proposed that the bodily changes in emotion (the physiological reactions) were not the cause of overt behavior at all, but were the result of the patterns of behavior which were directly elicited by the situation. "Common sense says, we lose our fortune, are sorry

FIGURE 23.1. Hostility and friendliness in animals. (1) Hostility in the dog. (2) Friendliness in the dog. (3) Hostility in the cat. (4) Friendliness in the cat (from Darwin, 1872, after Young, 1961).

and weep; we meet a bear, are frightened and run; we are insulted by a rival, are angry and strike" (James, 1890). James argued, however, "that the more rational statement is that we feel sorry because we cry, angry because we strike, afraid because we tremble and not that we cry, strike, or tremble, because we are sorry, angry, or fearful, as the case may be" (James, 1890). Thus, James reversed the classic sequence of events in emotion.

In James's account, as well as in all traditional ones, the "feeling" of emotion, be it a cause or an effect, played a critical role:

> What kind of an emotion or fear would be left if the feeling neither of quickened heart-beats nor of shallow breathing, neither of trembling lips nor of weakened limbs, neither of goose-flesh, nor of visceral stirrings, were present it is quite impossible for me to think. Can one fancy the state of rage and picture no ebullition in the chest, no flushing of the face, no dilation of the nostrils, no clenching of the teeth, no impulse to vigorous action . . . ? In like manner of grief, what could it be without its tears, its sobs, its suffocation of the heart, its pang in the breastbone? (James, 1890).

James' description implied that the bodily states accompanying emotional behaviors offered a basis on which to define the emotions.

In the 1920's and 1930's, Walter Cannon, a physiologist, disputed James' suggestion that emotions were distinguished by special bodily states. Cannon argued that (1) the physiological states for many different emotions were very similar, and could not be distinguished; rage and anxiety, for instance, produce identical changes in many responses; (2) The responses of emotion occur in nonemotional states, such as exposure to an icy wind, heavy exercise, and fever; (3) The drug, adrenalin, when injected into humans, produces the changes typical of fear (dilation of the bronchioles, constriction of blood vessels, liberation of sugar from the liver, increase in heart rate, cessation of gastrointestinal function, and so on) yet, the individuals so injected give no reports of emotion (Cannon, 1927).

Cannon adduced other evidence to prove that the "feeling" of emotion could not be the result, solely, of the bodily changes that occur in emotional situations, and then offered a theory of his own. The internal events we report as "feelings" are mediated by a special region of the brain, the thalamus. His hypothesis was based on the effects of lesions and the electrical stimulation of this brain region on emotional behavior.

23.2
Three Concepts of Emotion

PRIVATE EVENTS. Despite the differences among the theories of Darwin, James, and Cannon, in each one unobservable private events ("feelings"), accessible only to the individual experiencing the emotion, occupy a prominent position. The diagrams of Figure 23.2 summarize these historical views. (Read → as "leads to.")

A methodological problem emerges in determining how to treat the so-called "feelings" of emotion, those events so vividly described by James on page 415. We may all agree that such feelings do, indeed, characterize emotion, but how are we to measure and control them? And in the absence of direct observation, how can we even be sure that the feeling of fear that Smith says he has is the same as the feeling of fear that Jones says he has? An individual

FIGURE 23.2. Schematic representation of three historical theories of emotional causation.

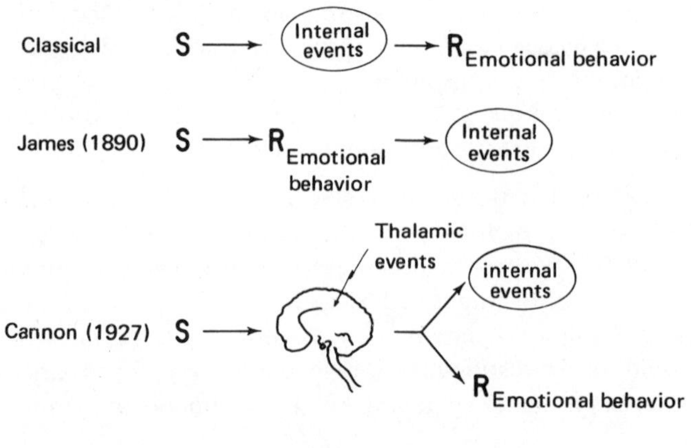

acquires such verbal responses as "I am afraid", "I am sorry," "I am happy," through reinforcement by parents and other adults when, as a child, he vocalized these statements in the presence of certain environmental situations. For example, seeing a child tremble and cry in the presence of an unfamiliar object, a parent might be inclined to say, "you are afraid," and the child could thereby acquire the response, "I am afraid." An analogous history would prevail for other "emotions". But the community, shaping our verbal repertoire of "emotion" words, never looks inside us to make reinforcement contingent on discriminative responding in the presence of a particular and well-specified physiological state. Whatever the internal S^D elements may be that were present at the time of early reinforcement, they are *presumably* the same internal events that are present when the adult later reports his or her emotional state; but those discriminative events are private, and remain forever private for each of us.

The inaccessibility of our feelings to others' scrutiny does not render them altogether irrelevant. As hints to the individual scientist, for where and when to look for the significant variables, relationships, and concepts of emotional behavior, they remain invaluable. It is as scientific data that they fail to meet the observability criterion of "science", for this criterion stipulates that the data on which "science" builds its laws, shall be accessible to all who wish to observe them. When emotion—like learning, memory, motivation, and other psychological phenomena treated in previous chapters—finds a translation in behavioral terms that everyone can validate, the stage is set for its experimental analysis.

The problem of private events is particularly emphasized in emotion, simply because overt emotional behavior is frequently accompanied by intense and widespread visceral (stomach, heart, lungs, and so forth) and glandular changes. Whether or not these events are strongest when behavior is said to be "emotional", the methodology of emotion study remains fundamentally the same as that of the other behavioral processes. The feelings that may accompany visceral events always present the problem of privacy, and hence, of scientific exclusion, however vivid they may be to the person experiencing them. A reasonable assumption is that the inaccessible private events we call feelings are correlated with particular physiological states, which are accessible to observation, given the necessary instrumentation. To turn to the inside of the organism and investigate the properties of physiological processes concomitant with overt behavior, is indeed, commendable, and plays an important part in developing a comprehensive picture of any behavioral phenomenon. But such physiological investigation does not replace the need for firm information about behavior and its environmental determinants.

REFLEX PATTERNS. If we turn our attention away from private events, we discover that the problem of the sequence of situation, feeling, and behavior no longer concerns us in the way it did James and Cannon. Since the actual feelings are not measurable or directly manipulable, whether they come before, after, or at the same time as behavior is not of critical interest to us. J. B. Watson, the man who prepared psychology in so many ways for modern behavior analysis, seems to have been among the first to see this, and in his writings viewed emotions as special patterns of responses elicited initially by unconditioned stimuli. These patterns, he suggested, could be attached to previously neutral stimuli via classical-conditioning procedures. From studies on newborn babies, Watson concluded that there were only three such patterns that legitimately qualified as emotions, patterns X, Y, and Z. Table 23.1 summarizes Watson's scheme. Evidently, the three primary emotional patterns in Table 23.1, X, Y, and Z, are the prototypes of what we more usually call, rage, fear, and joy. According to Watson, all other emotions were based on these three, as mixtures or combinations brought about by complex, Pavlovian conditioning procedures.

Watson arranged a simple demonstration to show how conditioning extends the controls of emotion. To an infant, Albert, aged 11 months,

TABLE 23.1. The Watsonian Definition of the Infants' Emotions as Reflex Patterns (Compiled by Tolman, 1923).

Stimuli	Elicited behavior
Rage (X)	
Hampering the infant's movements by holding its face or head; or holding its arms tightly to its sides	Crying, screaming, body stiffening Co-ordinated slashing or striking movements of hands and arms Feet and legs drawn up and down Holding breath
Fear (Y)	
Suddenly removing all means of support (dropped from the hands to be caught by an assistant) Loud sound Sudden push or slight shake (when just falling asleep or just waking up) Sudden pulling of supporting blanket (when just going to sleep)	Sudden catching of breath Clutching (grasping reflex) Blinking of eyelids Puckering of lips Crying
Joy (Z)	
Stroking or manipulation of an erogenous zone Tickling, shaking, gentle rocking Patting Turning on stomach across attendant's knee	If the infant is crying, it stops crying A smile appears Gurgling and cooing

Watson showed a rat (CS), never previously feared, and paired the presence of the rat with a few presentations of a sudden loud sound (US), produced by striking a steel bar with a hammer. The sound frightened the infant (Watson's syndrome Y), and served as the unconditioned stimulus in a Pavlovian paradigm. Eventually, the rat (CS) came to elicit a conditioned response in Albert that was very similar to Y behavior: crying, whimpering, withdrawal, and so on. The conditioned form of fear may or may not be exactly identical to unconditioned fear. To emphasize this point, the conditioned response, based on unconditioned fear reflexes, is often referred to as *anxiety*. In later experiments, Watson showed that this conditioned anxiety could be slowly extinguished by the usual method—presentation of the CS (the rat) without the US (the loud sound).

One of the important advances of Watson's treatment of the emotions over that of his predecessors was that he asked the question, what are the external causes of emotional behavior? As Watson himself remarked, "It never occurred to James, or any of his followers for that matter, to speculate, much less experiment, upon the genesis of the emotional forms of response" (Watson, 1930, p. 142). Watson's demonstration that emotions were allied to classical-conditioning principles was a key first step to their experimental analysis. In the present chapter, we will show that a variety of emotional phenomena can be described in terms of classical conditioning.

WIDESPREAD BEHAVIORAL CHANGES. Another conceptual step must be taken to simplify the experimental analysis of emotional phenomena. Watson subscribed to the view (as had Darwin) that the primary emotions were complex, unconditioned response patterns, and he picked out three such patterns as "fundamental." But what justification did he have for confining himself to just these particular three? A loud sound, for example, a pistol shot at close range, will produce the startle pattern (Figure 23.3) and a host of other reflex responses. The pattern is completed in about $\frac{1}{2}$ sec, and contains many of the features of a brief bout of emotion. But why is it not called an emotion? So too, the cough, the hiccup, the sneeze, the tearing of the eye to a dust particle, the allergic symptoms called hay fever, the panting and flushing of heavy exercise, and indigestion from overeating, all involve complex patterns of responses. Yet, few would be disposed to call them emotions. What is special about the X, Y, Z reactions that they, rather than these other patterns, should be raised to special status and called "emotions"? No satisfactory answer has ever been given to this question. Useful criteria that might distinguish emotional reflexes from nonemotional reflexes have never been found. In their absence, we may suppose that the definition of emotion lies elsewhere than in the special characteristics of certain reflex patterns.

A prime feature of all emotions is the disruption, disturbance, enhancement, or general change that takes place in any of a host of arbitrary behaviors, in which an individual might be engaged at the moment when

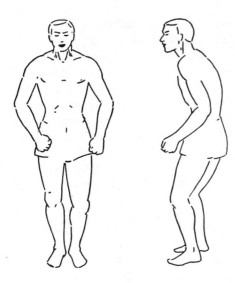

FIGURE 23.3.
The startle response to a pistol shot
(Landis and Hunt, 1939).

what we call an emotional situation occurs. Indeed, a person made afraid is more easily identified by the marked depression of all of his or her usual activities than by special cardiac, respiratory, or digestive changes. An angry person is the epitome of a person disrupted. The very angry person is unlikely to go on with what he or she was doing before the individual was made angry. Now, the person turns to new behaviors; he or she is especially likely to damage things near him or her, to make verbal retorts, and to emit operants with unusual force. Give a child a promise of an especially attractive activity, and the child may literally jump for joy. Many of the child's present behaviors are temporarily disrupted, others may be enhanced. It is the special character of these widespread changes, not of the reflex patterns, nor of the bodily states, that will prove the most convenient framework for the study of the emotions.

The operations that bring about these widespread changes consist of two main types: (1) the presentation, or termination, of powerful primary reinforcers, and (2) the presentation of stimuli which have previously been associated with such powerful reinforcers through classical conditioning. The widespread changes in many operant behaviors associated with these operations could well be interpreted as simultaneous changes in the reinforcing value of practically all of the organism's primary reinforcers. Destruction and damage take on such strong reinforcing value for the angry individual that, momentarily, nothing else is important. The person who is afraid or grief-stricken, loses his or her appetite and sexual desire. People in love are often so wrapped up in their newfound reinforcers that they "live on love" exclusively for a time, neglecting to eat or engage in other routine activities. It would appear that emotion, like motivation, classifies a set of operations that modulate the reinforcing value of primary reinforcers, and change the general activity of the organism. There are, of course, differences in the kinds of operations historically assigned to the two fields. The universal antecedent operations associated with motivation are deprivation and satiation. In emotion, the antecedent operations are abrupt stimulus changes. Moreover, fear, anger, and joy imply diffuse, nonspecific changes in the value of all reinforcers; hunger and thirst imply somewhat more specific changes in a more restricted set of reinforcers.

This third concept of emotion, as a generalized disruption of ongoing behavior, produced by presentation of powerful reinforcers or CS's associated with them, has the advantage that it is couched in terms of variables that are used in the analysis of other behavior, and can be studied in the laboratory.

23.3
Conditioned Suppression as a Model of Anxiety

In Section 17.9, we described the conditioned-suppression procedure devised by Estes and Skinner (1941). As this involves the presentation of a CS associated with an aversive US, and results in disruption of the ongoing operant behavior, it conforms to the concept of emotion previously described. Indeed, conditioned suppression has, on occasion, been described as a conditioned emotional response, conditioned fear, or conditioned anxiety. These terms have been applied because, (a) signals of impending aversive events (aversive CS's) correspond to many situations that would usually be described as frightening; and (b) subjects appear frightened during such CS's.

Both these reasons for treating conditioned suppression as a model of anxiety are open to objection. Not all frightening situations are easily described in terms of aversive CS's, and "looking frightened" is a poorly defined behavioral category. By carrying out experiments on conditioned suppression, we cannot prove or disprove the thesis that emotional behavior is involved, since this is a matter of definition. We can see, however, whether variables that exert powerful influences on conditioned suppression are ones that we would plausibly expect to affect emotional behavior.

We noted in Section 17.9 that conditioned suppression is sensitive to classical-conditioning parameters (increasing with US magnitude and decreasing with CS duration) and to the schedule of reinforcement of the operant response, DRL responding, being facilitated under certain conditions. We can add here that conditioned suppression is sensitive to food deprivation and reinforcement magnitude (Leslie, 1977), and that if a localized CS is used, a sign-tracking effect may be observed, with the subject refusing to approach the aversive CS (Karpicke, Christoph, and Hearst, 1977). None of these effects conflicts particularly with the behavioral effects we normally describe as, or attribute to, fear. Translating the effects into ordinary language, and assuming that conditioned suppression is a measure of fear, the data say that fear increases with the magnitude and proximity of an aversive event, that it can disrupt complex behavior sequences, that the effect of a particular frightening stimulus depends on current motivation and reinforcement for other activities, and that subjects will steer clear of a localized, fear-provoking stimulus.

Conditioned suppression combines several behavioral processes that are, in principle, dissociable, but it is a reasonable, working hypothesis that most of these processes also occur together in the fear-provoking situations that people experience. The consensus that conditioned suppression does have important features in common with human fear or anxiety has lead to its widespread use in the analysis of anti-anxiety drugs. All of the major classes of drugs that are effective in alleviating clinical anxiety (phenothiazines, reserpine, benzodiazepines, meprobamate, and barbiturates) have been shown to reduce conditioned suppression, although their effectiveness depends on the method of drug administration (Millenson and Leslie, 1974).

23.4

Aggression

Recall from Section 3.3 that the transition from reinforcement of key pecking by a pigeon to extinction can result in aggression directed at another pigeon. (Azrin, Hutchinson, and Hake, 1966) It turns out that a wide variety of situations, involving periods of nonreinforcement, can elicit aggression. This effect has even been demonstrated on *VI* schedules, where periods of nonreinforcement are less regular than on *FI* or *FR* schedules (where the postreinforcement pause is associated with nonreinforcement, and suppresses operant responding). Dove, Rashotte, and Katz (1974) trained pigeons to key peck for food on a series of *VI* schedules. A stuffed pigeon was always accessible, and attacks upon it were recorded. The results for one pigeon are shown in Figure 23.4. Attacks increased in frequency as the mean interval lengthened, and the lowest panel of Figure 23.4 shows that there was a strong tendency for attacks to occur in the immediate postreinforcement period, when there was zero probability of reinforcement. Although there is no programmed external stimulus associated with nonreinforcement in procedures such as this, subjects have to learn that certain periods in the schedule predict nonreinforcement before aggression occurs. We can, therefore, conclude that *CS's associated with nonreinforcement elicit aggression.*

This simple fact about aggression was elevated to the status of an all-embracing theory by the *frustration-aggression hypothesis* (Miller, 1941). This states that *every* instance of aggression is preceded by a state of frustration, and frustration is elicited by extinction or nonreinforcement. This says no more than our previous statement, except that frustration is said

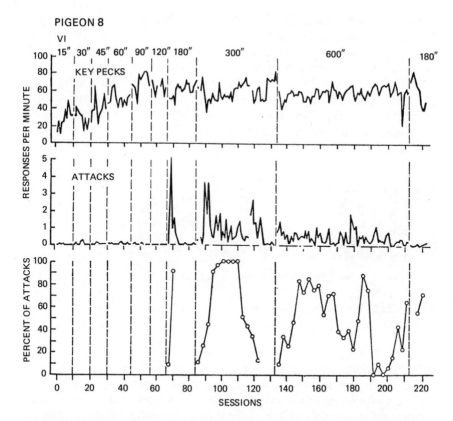

FIGURE 23.4. The top two panels show key peck rate and attack rate in each session for a pigeon on several *VI* food-reinforced schedules. Each point in the bottom panel is the median percent attacks occurring immediately after reinforcement, (before any reinforcement was scheduled by the *VI* schedule in effect) (from Dove, Rashotte, and Katz, 1974).

to be *necessary* for aggression. This is incorrect, because there is at least one other general class of events that elicit aggression; the presentation of highly aversive or painful stimuli.

Perhaps you recall the fairy story in which two sleeping giants are tricked into fighting with each other by their diminutive prisoner, who escapes during the ensuing melée. His technique was to throw rocks at the giants, which hurt them and woke them up. On waking, each giant saw only the other giant present, blamed him for the attack, and began to retaliate. An analogous effect can be demonstrated in the laboratory. If two rats are placed together in a box, and a painful electric shock is delivered through the grid floor, "reflexive fighting" occurs; that is, they attack each other in response to the shock from the floor (Ulrich and Azrin, 1962).

The amount of aggression produced by an "aggressor" increases with the amount of shock received, but it is also related to the behavior of the "target". Hynan (1976) found that the position of a restrained rat affected the frequency with which it was attacked by another, freely moving rat, that was shocked intermittently. The positions are shown in Figure 23.5. The supine position resembles a submissive posture, and resulted in more attacks than the upright, threat posture. It was also found that shocking the target rat could reduce attacks on it when supine, presumably because the target rat then showed components of the threat posture.

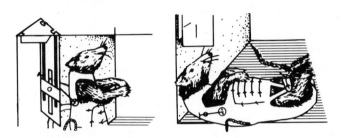

FIGURE 23.5. Positions of "target" rat in Hynan's (1976) experiment.

These findings correspond fairly well with our everyday assumptions about the origins of aggression. Experimentally, aggression has been seen when CS's for nonreinforcement or extinction are presented, or when painful stimuli are delivered. In the latter case, aggression increases with the magnitude of the painful stimuli and is sensitive to the behavior of the other, submissiveness tending to increase aggression.

23.5

Positive Conditioned Suppression: A Further Classical-Operant Interaction

If a classically-conditioned CS is presented to a subject engaged in reinforced-operant behavior, we call this procedure a classical-operant interaction. It can be seen as a technique for using changes in *operant* performance to monitor the effects of a *classical* CS. The conditioned-suppression procedure, just introduced as a model of anxiety, is clearly a classical-operant interaction. Such interactions have many parameters, but two seem to be particularly important; the type of event signaled by the CS, and the type of reinforcement for the operant response. Some interactions are described in terms of these variables in Table 23.2.

This is not an exhaustive list, but includes those interactions for which we have a fair amount of data. Note that this crude, classificatory system ignores several important determinants of behavior, including the reinforcement schedule, the nature of the operant response, and the nature of the CS which, if localized, may result in sign tracking. However, classifying classical-operant interactions by just these two variables, gives us a relatively small number of categories that we may be able to relate to emotional behavior.

We have already discussed the first two examples in Table 23.2, and seen that each procedure and the associated behavioral changes correspond reasonably well to our use of the emotion words given in the right-hand column. The third example, an appetitive CS, presented during the performance of a positively-reinforced operant, is labeled, "elation" or "joy", on the assumption that these emotions are produced by signals of impending appetitive or "nice" events. However, while the behavioral consequences of CS's associated with aversive US's or nonreinforcement correspond well with what we describe as fearful or aggressive behavior, the behavioral effects of appetitive signals do not seem to correspond to joyful or happy behavior.

We typically associate "positive emotions" with energization of behavior, but the presentation of an appetitive CS typically results in *positive conditioned suppression*; that is, the operant is suppressed. In one informative experiment, Miczek (1973) compared the effects of aversive and appetitive CS's on the same food-reinforced *VI* responding by rats. He also examined the effects of various doses of chlordiazepoxide (a drug in the benzodiazepine group which, we noted earlier, reduces suppression to an aversive CS). The results, given in Figure 23.6, show that both CS's suppress *VI* responding, when no drug is given (condition *C*). This effect is seen as a suppression ratio of substantially less than 0.5, because the ratio is calculated as response rate

TABLE 23.2.

Event signaled by CS	Nature of operant reinforcement	Behavioral outcome	Common name of "emotion"
aversive US	positive	operant suppression	anxiety/fear
nonreinforcement	positive	attack on conspecifics	anger
appetitive US	positive	operant suppression or sign tracking	elation?
aversive US	negative	operant suppression or acceleration, depending on experimental details	—
appetitive US	negative	operant suppression	—

during CS/rate during CS plus baseline rate, and will equal 0.5 if CS rate is the same as baseline rate. With increasing doses of chlordiazepoxide, suppression to the aversive CS systematically reduces, but suppression to the appetitive CS is unaffected.

Miczek thus replicated the finding that an appetitive CS may suppress positively reinforced behavior, but also showed that this suppression is a different kind from that produced by an aversive CS. The complexities of the appetitive CS on positively reinforced behavior interaction are further illustrated in an experiment by Lolordo, McMillan, and Riley (1974). In experiments with pigeons reinforced with food, they demonstrated that response rate could be greatly *increased* by presentation of a prefood CS, but only if that CS occurred *on the response key*. Thus, sign-tracking effects (Chapter 12) can reverse the positive-conditioned suppression effect.

Rather than try to unravel the complexities of these data, we will simply point out the implications. When a procedure that seems formally similar to

FIGURE 23.6. Effects of chlordiazepoxide on baseline response rate of rats on a *VI* schedule (lower panel), and conditioned suppression (upper panel) produced by a prefood and a preshock CS (from Miczek, 1973, redrawn by Blackman, 1977).

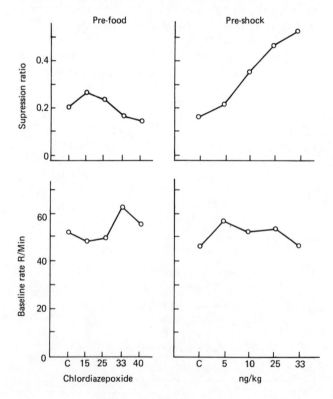

human emotional situations has behavioral consequences that are unlike the human behavior we associate with the emotion in question, the utility of the procedure as a model of emotion is reduced. This does not mean that classical-operant interactions are not plausible models of emotional behavior; indeed, we have already seen that they provide good models of fear and aggression. However, the plausibility of an interaction being used as a model of an emotion depends upon its having generally appropriate behavioral consequences.

The problems raised here underline the fact that emotional behavior is best characterized in terms of the situation *and* the resulting behavioral change. Neither a class of situations (for example, a CS associated with an aversive US), nor a particular behavioral change (for example, operant suppression) is necessary and sufficient to be called emotional.

Table 23.2 also includes the effects of aversive and appetitive CS's on negatively reinforced behavior. These also result in complex behavioral changes that are not easily identified with any human emotion. The extension of the experimental analysis of emotional behavior depends not only on the study of procedures like these, but also on clearer statements of what emotion words *mean* as applied to human behavior. If we cannot agree about what constitutes "boredom", and under which circumstances it occurs, for example, we cannot proceed to its experimental analysis.

23.6

The Autonomic Nervous System

Sir Charles Sherrington remarked that of the places where physiology and psychology meet, one is emotion. Certainly, no analysis of emotion would be complete without outlining the great physiological changes that take place.

The idea that each emotion is associated with a unique pattern of autonomic responses appears in the passage by William James, cited earlier (p. 000). However, attempts to record these patterns have not been very successful. Generally, more similarities than differences between emotions have been identified. It is true, though, that large, autonomic response changes characterize emotional behavior.

Autonomic responses are internal changes mediated by the *autonomic* ("self-regulating") nervous system (ANS), depicted diagrammatically as Figure 23.7.

The ANS carries electrical impulses *from* the brain and spinal cord *to* the visceral organs, never the reverse. The ANS breaks down functionally into two divisions. One of these is called the *sympathetic* system, and is shown as dotted lines in Figure 23.7. The other, *parasympathetic* division ("para" means alongside of), lies anatomically above and below the sympathetic division. It is shown by solid lines in Figure 23.7.

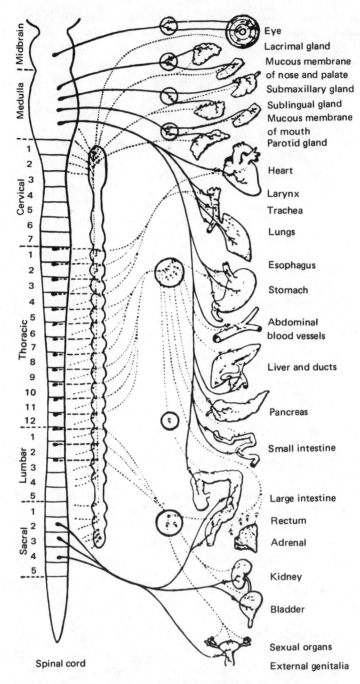

FIGURE 23.7. The right side of the human autonomic nervous system (Kimble and Garmezy, 1963).

The following facts are of importance. First, many autonomic responses have been successfully classically conditioned. Over the past half-century, Russian investigators have shown that the functioning of nearly every organ in the diagram is susceptible to classical-conditioning procedures.

A second point of interest is in the function of the two divisions of the ANS. Note that parasympathetic fibers (solid lines) typically come from *unique* origins, and go straight to their destination without interconnecting or interacting. This anatomical fact is reflected in the physiological fact that different parts of the parasympathetic system operate individually. The sympathetic fibers (dotted lines), however, go first to a common junction chain (the long vertical structure shown along the right side of the spinal cord in Figure 23.7), where they interact before they go on to the organs. This anatomical organization results in the sympathetic system operating as a unit.

Finally, we can observe that each individual organ in Figure 23.7 has dotted and solid lines leading to it and is, therefore, subject to influences from both the sympathetic and the parasympathetic divisions. But the effects on each organ of these two divisions are not the same. In fact, they are typically opposite. This is partly because the two divisions liberate different chemicals at their terminal points. Table 23.3 summarizes some of the main effects of the two divisions of the autonomic system.

At one time, it was thought that anxiety or fear involved sympathetic effects, primarily, while anger principally involved parasympathetic effects. It is now known that the picture is much more complex, and that all emotional operations activate *both* divisions. If there are physiological differences between emotions, they must consist of different patterns of sympathetic and parasympathetic action. These patterns are sometimes called the *autonomic substrate* of the emotions.

Inducing a particular physiological state does not necessarily result in a particular emotion, although it can make *some* emotion more likely. Schacter and Singer (1962) injected college students with adrenalin, which produces pronounced autonomic changes, and placed them in either irritating or amusing situations. Students given the drug became more angry and more euphoric, respectively, in these situations than undrugged controls. Providing the autonomic substrate facilitates emotion, but the nature of the emotion is specified by the *situation*.

23.7
Stress

The set of pronounced autonomic changes produced by adrenalin was discovered by Cannon (1932), and termed the "emergency reaction". It results from aversive stimuli, or CS's for aversive events or nonreinforcement. Its biological function is to mobilize the body's resources for swift

TABLE 23.3. Effects of the Autonomic Nervous System (after P. T. Young, 1961).

Sympathetic nerves	Bodily structures	Parasympathetic nerves
Dilates the pupil	Iris	Constricts the pupil
Inhibits secretion	Salivary glands	Facilitates secretion
Erects (pilomotor reflex)	Hair	
Augments secretion	Sweat glands	
Constricts	Surface arteries	
Accelerates	Heart	Inhibits
Dilates bronchioles	Lung	Contracts bronchioles
Secretes glucose	Liver	
Inhibits gastric secretion and peristalsis	Stomach	Facilitates gastric secretion and peristalsis
Constricts, giving off erythrocytes	Spleen	
Secretes adrenalin	Adrenal medulla	
Inhibits smooth-muscle activity	Small intestine	Facilitates smooth-muscle activity
Constricts	Visceral arteries	
Relaxes smooth muscle	Bladder	Contracts smooth muscle to empty
Relaxes smooth muscle	Colon and rectum	Contracts smooth muscle to empty
Constricts, counteracting erection	Arteries of external genitals	Dilates, causing erection
Contracts at orgasm	Vasa deferentia	
Contracts at orgasm	Seminal vesicles	
Contracts at orgasm	Uterus	

action. Heart rate increases, the number of red blood cells circulating is increased, glycogen stored in the liver is released into the blood as glucose, respiration deepens (that is, air volume increases), and a number of other changes occur that allow for sudden action and its consequences.

If *stress* is prolonged, that is, the organism is exposed to the stimuli provoking the emergency reaction, repeatedly or for a long time, longer-term responses occur. Some of these responses are mediated by adreno-cortico-trophic hormone (ACTH), released from a subcortical brain structure beneath the hypothalamus called the anterior pituitary. ACTH continues the energy mobilization started by the emergency reaction, but prolonged stress also tends to produce gastric ulcers.

The stress reaction is clearly biologically adaptive, because it enables threatened animals to expend energy in escaping from the situation. However, the "fight or flight" that it facilitates is rarely appropriate behavior for people in modern life. If the boss insults you or treads on your foot, neither hitting him or her, nor running away, is an appropriate response. However, we still have the ancient physiological responses that, until a few dozen generations ago, were essential for our survival. The socially programmed suppression of those responses appears to act as a principle factor in stomach ulcers and other psychosomatic illness that are related to prolonged unrelieved stress.

23.8
The Meaning of Emotional Behavior

We have repeatedly emphasized the importance of both stimulus and response in defining emotional behavior. This is a further example of the general principle noted in Section 22.2; a piece of behavior can only be understood with reference to its controlling variables.

This principle is of practical, as well as theoretical, significance. We typically observe behavior and make inferences about its causes, but because we cannot see histories of reinforcement or classical conditioning, we tend to assume that a particular class of behavior is under one type of control whenever it occurs. For example, if a baby cries, we may assume that it is in distress. This may, indeed, be the case, but it is also likely that crying in the presence of adults has been repeatedly reinforced by attention. Diagrammatically, it may be an unconditioned response:

$$US_{pain} \rightarrow R_{crying}$$

Or it may be a discriminated operant:

$$S^D_{adults \atop present} : R_{crying} \rightarrow S^+_{attention}$$

It is impossible to decide between these alternatives without more information, perhaps obtained by intervention in the situation, but we often uncritically tend to jump to a conclusion without adequate evidence. This is equivalent to saying that only the nature of the response is important in describing emotional behavior.

Emphasizing only the stimulus aspects of emotion, results in similar error. An example here is the assumption that CS presentation *must* be an emotional event, and that its effects on operant behavior must be interpreted as emotional. We saw, earlier, the problems that this attitude creates for the understanding of positive-conditioned suppression.

The realization that responses, normally classified as emotional, can be under the control of nonemotional variables, gives us an insight into many, apparently pathological behaviors. Patients showing the excessive fears that are called phobias may have suffered classical conditioning, in which the phobic stimulus was associated with traumatic events. A fetishist obsessed with shoes, or a transvestite, may each have unusual reinforcement histories.

The "meaning" of a piece of behavior depends heavily on the experiences of the individual displaying it. It is hard for us to accept that hysterical laughter or furniture smashing by patients in mental institutions may be under the same sort of control as the normal, social and emotional behavior of our associates. However, the principles described in this book imply that, even if the origins of the behavior differ, it will still be susceptible to the same controlling variables. This implication opens up a wide field of therapeutic possibilities.

References for Chapter 23

Azrin, N. H., Hutchinson, R. R., and Hake, D. F. Extinction-induced aggression. *Journal of the Experimental Analysis of Behavior*, 1966, **9**, 191–204.

Blackman, D. E. Conditioned suppression and the effects of classical conditioning on operant behavior. In W. K. Honig and J. E. R. Staddon (Eds.) *Handbook of operant behavior*. Englewood Cliffs, N.J.: Prentice-Hall, 1977.

Cannon, W. B. The James-Lange theory of emotions: a critical examination and an alternative theory. *American Journal of Psychology*, 1927, **39**, 106–124.

Cannon, W. B. *The wisdom of the body*. New York: Norton, 1932.

Darwin, C. *The expression of the emotions in man and animals*. London: Murray, 1872.

Dove, L. D., Rashotte, M. E., and Katz, H. N. Development and maintenance of attack in pigeons during variable-interval reinforcement of key pecking. *Journal of the Experimental Analysis of Behavior*, 1974, **21**, 563–570.

Estes, W. K., and Skinner, B. F. Some quantitative properties of anxiety. *Journal of Experimental Psychology*, 1941, **29**, 390–400.

Hynan, M. T. The influence of the victim on shock-induced aggression in rats. *Journal of the Experimental Analysis of Behavior*, 1976, **25**, 401–409.

James, W. *Principles of psychology*, Volume 2. New York: Holt, 1890.

Karpicke, J., Christoph, G., Peterson, G., and Hearst, E. Signal location and positive versus negative conditioned suppression in the rat. *Journal of Experimental Psychology: Animal Behavior Processes*, 1977, **3**, 105–118.

Kimble, G. A., and Garmezy, N. *Principles of general psychology*. New York: Ronald Press, 1963.

Landis, C., and Hunt, W. A. *The startle pattern*. New York: Farrar and Rinehart, 1939.

Leslie, J. C. Effects of food deprivation and reinforcement magnitude on conditioned suppression, *Journal of the Experimental Analysis of Behavior*, 1977, **28**, 107–115.

Lolordo, V. M., McMillan, J. C., and Riley, A. L. The effects upon foodreinforced pecking and treadle-pressing of auditory and visual signals for response-independent food. *Learning and Motivation*, 1974, **5**, 24–41.

Miczek, K. A. Effects of scopolamine, amphetamine, and benzopliazepines on conditioned suppression. *Pharmacology, Biochemistry and Behavior*, 1973, **1**, 401–411.

Millenson, J. R., and Leslie, J. C. The conditioned emotional response (CER) as a baseline for the study of anti-anxiety drugs. *Neuropharmacology*, 1974, **13**, 1–9.

Miller, N. E. The frustration-aggression hypothesis. *Psychological Review*, 1941, **48**, 337–342.

Schacter, S., and Singer, J. E. Cognitive, social and physiological determinants of emotional state. *Psychological Review*, 1962, **69**, 379–399.

Tolman, E. C. A behavioristic account of the emotions. *Psychological Review*, 1923, **30**, 217–227.

Ulrich, R. E., and Azrin, N. H. Reflexive fighting in response to aversive stimulation. *Journal of the Experimental Analysis of Behavior*, 1962, **5**, 511–520.

Watson, J. B. *Behaviorism*. Revised Edition. Chicago: University of Chicago Press, 1930.

Young, P. T. *Motivation and emotion*. New York: Wiley, 1961.

PART EIGHT

Behavior Modification

In this final part we turn from the identification and analysis of behavioral processes in the laboratory to the operation of those processes in the world outside. There are many areas of human life and endeavor where we seek to modify behavior. It may be the behavior of our children, our peers, our pupils, or even ourselves. In all these cases, and in clinical attempts to cope with behavior problems, we employ the techniques of reinforcement, punishment, discrimination, modeling and so forth that we have encountered in the preceding parts of this book.

We cannot avoid using these techniques. Our behavior is part of a social environment that arranges contingencies, establishes associations between stimuli, and provides models for the behavior of other individuals. These behavioral processes are pervasive and will operate continuously, regardless of the wishes of the individuals that make up society. Even if, for example, we believe that "arranging contingencies is manipulative and dehumanizing" and seek *not* to arrange contingencies, such expressed opinions may serve as models for pupils or as punishing stimuli for those that disagree.

We therefore have two alternatives. Either we allow events to take their traditional course and make no attempt to use the principles of behavioral analysis that we have derived from laboratory studies, or we apply behavioral principles to the situations and behavior we observe in the world around us attempting to influence people's actions in accord with our own values. The latter application of scientific principles to influence others is called, appropriately, the technology of *behavior modification.*

The technology of behavior modification seeks to apply techniques derived from laboratory studies of behavior to the analysis, understanding, and control of human behavior in everyday situations. Its potential range of application is enormous because so much of our behavior, particularly our social behavior, modifies the behavior of others. However, the success of a particular behavior modification technique can never be guaranteed. Even though a phenomenon is highly reliable in the laboratory, we cannot know whether it will *generalize* to a very different non-laboratory situation until we have conducted an empirical test. Laboratory research thus suggests possible behavior modification techniques that may be effective for a particular type of behavior. These techniques will then be adapted in the light of results.

Although still in its infancy, behavior modification has already been applied to a wide range of behaviors, making an exhaustive review beyond the scope of the present book. Instead we attempt to convey the flavor of behavior modification by presenting some representative techniques and findings from two general areas. These are education and the treatment of disturbed behavior.

CHAPTER 24

Education

A significant conceptual contribution of behavior analysis to educational practice is the emphasis on the *specification of objectives*. Operant conditioners are sometimes caricatured as "animal trainers." This description is intended to be disparaging, but it does highlight an important and characteristic feature of operant conditioning. The animal trainer trains his pupils to do something very specific. The dolphin jumps through a hoop, the seal balances a ball on its nose, and the elephant stands on its hind legs. The animal trainer, like the operant conditioner, uses the techniques he has available with subtlety and skill to select just those responses he wants.

Although the athletics coach may be seen in a similar role to this, the teacher's intellectual and conceptual activities are usually described in a vaguer fashion. The teacher is said to seek to produce an "all-round education," or to "foster creativity"; he or she believes that "every child's strengths should be developed." These goals are certainly desirable, but they remain very unclear. They omit to state the assessment and criteria we might apply to decide whether the teacher or the school has succeeded. Yet traditional educational objectives do not need to stay unspecifiable. Translating complex concepts into a list of objective criteria has always been possible (although lengthy), but there has been resistance in principle to this "mechanistic" or reductionist approach. Subtle general concepts seem to imply or hint at more than any particular individual's list of simple objectives contains. Yet subtlety and objectivity need not be antagonistic. Part of the salutary effect in sitting down and translating what we mean by "fostering creativity" is the gain in our own understanding. And our students are bound to gain as we pass along that increased understanding to them.

Specifying minimally what we want our students to learn represents only a first, although, crucial step in an educational technology. The impact of "progressive" education, which avoids coercion and aversive contingencies, has been to challenge the assumption that the methods of teaching are irrelevant. Making the material interesting and challenging, encouraging discovery, and providing a variety of options all seem ideas which fit well with what we have learned in the laboratory from our animal studies. Animal studies show how important is control of the environment, how much more behavior can be generated when the reinforcer suits the response, and how serious are the by-products of aversive control.

24.1

The Classroom

To their continual consternation, schoolteachers find much of their time occupied with problems of discipline, gaining the attention of the class, and dealing with disruption. Indeed the roles of school teacher and college teacher are usually regarded as quite different because the success of the former depends almost entirely on their ability to cope with these problems, while the success of the college teacher depends mostly on teaching skills and academic knowledge. If we go into a typical school classroom as a behavior analyst, we begin by identifying and classifying some relevant behaviors, both of the teacher and of the students, that we then might attempt to modify through reinforcement techniques. To do that, of course, we shall have to discover what the students actually do find reinforcing. We have to keep an open and objective mind about what might or might not be reinforcing, and what might or might not constitute an operant response class. For instance, we might think *a priori* that when a teacher shouts at a pupil for interrupting or throwing spit balls that the shout might be punishing. Actually, it might well be reinforcing, since it does constitute attention, albeit negative. So too, the observed behaviors have to be critically analyzed. A child may disrupt a class for many reasons: to gain attention, out of boredom, because the material seems too hard or too uninteresting or too easy, to curry peer approval, or as displaced aggression from home to school. Each reason implies a different controlling contingency, and treating them all as a single class of "disruptive behaviors" will inevitably prove simplistic and ineffective. Nevertheless, all the techniques we use to promote an environment favorable for learning are designed to bring the children's behavior into contact with contingencies that will promote studying and discourage competing behavior. In the last analysis we have only the teachers' and students' behaviors, consequences, and their relationships, with which to deal.

Consider this study carried out in a secondary school classroom by McAllister, Stachowiak, Baer and Conderman (1969) as an example of a behavioral analysis that employed a combination of reinforcement and punishment on two separate and distinct classes of behavior. These workers defined and recorded the frequency of four behaviors in two classes: inappropriate talking, inappropriate turning round, verbal reprimands by the teacher, and praise by the teacher. These actions were recorded as occurring or not occurring for each one minute interval in a class period. After 27 days, the teacher in one class began to administer verbal punishment for inappropriate talking (for instance, "John, be quiet"), and when periods of quiet occurred she socially reinforced the whole class (for instance, "Thank you for not talking"). The results in Figure 24.1 show that the amount of inappropriate talking steadily declined from around 24 per cent to 5 per cent. On the 54th day the same contingencies were applied to turning around. As Figure 24.2 shows, the frequency of this behavior fell rapidly from around 15 per cent to a very low level.

FIGURE 24.1. Effects on the class of measures to reduce talking, introduced on Session 27 (from McAllister, Stachowiak, Baer, and Conderman, 1969).

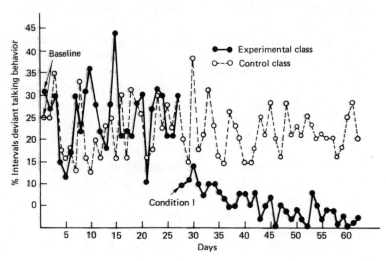

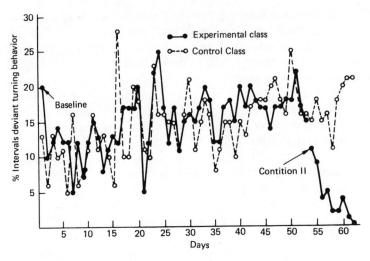

FIGURE 24.2. Effects on the class of measures to reduce "turning round," introduced in Session 54 (from McAllister, Stachowiak, Baer, and Conderman, 1969).

24.2
Group Contingencies

The experiment described in Section 24.1 constitutes a demonstration of *group contingencies* modifying behavior, where the group as a whole co-operated before reinforcement was delivered. In a group contingency some consequence for the whole class or group of students is made contingent upon the non-occurrence of a class of behavior in any member of the group, or alternatively on the occurrence of a class of behavior in every member of the group.

Group contingencies in the classroom are of course commonplace. These can involve positive reinforcement ("When you have all finished your work, you will all get some apple juice") or punishment ("until you are all quiet none of you may go"). But making rather vague group contingencies more explicit often has value. Gallagher, Sulzbacher and Shores (1967, described by Axelrod, 1977) introduced a group contingency for a class of five emotionally disturbed boys who showed a variety of disruptive behaviors in a classroom. The "target" behavior was seat leaving. During the initial baseline phase, the boys left their seats without permission an average of seventy times a day. They were then told that there would be a 24-min "Coke break" at the end of the day if they never left their seats without permission. For each infringement, however, 2 min would be deducted from the break. The teacher wrote the numbers "24, 22, 20, 18, 16, 14, 12, 10, 8, 6, 4, 2, 0" on the chalkboard, and then crossed off a number each time somebody left their seat without permission. Thus if there was one infringement during the day the break was 22 min, for two infringements it was 20 min, and after twelve or more there was no break. Over the 15 days in which the group contingency was in effect the average number of seat-leavings fell to 1.0 per day and other disruptive behavior decreased.

24.3
Individual Contingencies

Tribble and Hall (1972) introduced positive reinforcement contingencies for one pupil (John) who performed poorly on his daily mathematics assignments. Over a fifteen-day baseline period John completed an average of 21 per cent of the work each day. He was then told that if he finished 60 per cent the teacher would mark "+" on his paper. John could then take the paper to his mother who would exchange it for a "surprise." John's performance on baseline, in the "surprise at home" phase, and subsequent phases of the study are shown in Figure 24.3.

The reinforcing effects of "surprise" were clearly transitory. After 100 per cent performance on the first day, John's mathematics achievement plummeted and on the fourth day fell below the 60 per cent level required for reinforcement. The investigators then adopted a strategy that is often important in human behavior modification: *They changed the reinforcer.* From day 20, John was reinforced for completing 100 per cent of his math problems within 20 min of the beginning of the period by playing "engineer." This involved the entire class going outside to play, with John as engineer leading the train of pupils.

This reinforcement contingency maintained 100 per cent performance on 10 of the 11 days that it was in effect. Subsequently, extinction resulted in deterioration to the original baseline level, but 100 per cent performance returned as soon as the "engineer" contingency was reintroduced. As these highly effective procedures did not involve any attempt to improve John's knowledge of mathematics, we may conclude that the improved performance resulted from raising the reinforcing value of completing the mathematics assignments relative to behaviors that normally competed successfully with it.

Individual contingencies can also be applied simultaneously to several individuals. Alexander and Apfel (1976) examined several aspects of such a situation. The subjects were a class of five boys with "behavior disorders" aged between 7 and 13. During most class periods the boys were reinforced at the end of 15 min intervals for attentive behavior during that interval. The reinforcer was "play money" that could later be exchanged for candy, small toys, or free time. (This is a type of *token economy*; see Section 25.1.) The investigators found that while attention was maintained by this schedule, it did not generalize to a 1-hr period of "communicative skills." In this time the

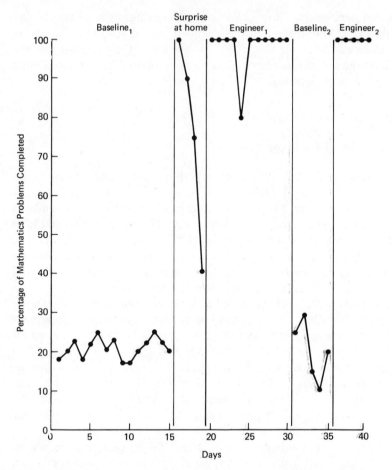

FIGURE 24.3. Percentage of mathematics problems completed by John when no specific reinforcement was arranged (Baseline) and under two reinforcement contingencies ("Surprise at home" and "Engineer") (Tribble and Hall, 1972).

children watched science experiments, played games, or did art projects and tokens for attending were not given out until the end of the hour. Consequently, a variable-interval (*VI*) reinforcement schedule was introduced to see whether attention could be maintained during this time by more immediate reinforcement.

In the baseline and subsequent conditions, an observer noted every 3 min whether each boy was engaged in nonattentive motor behavior (for example, hitting or pinching), verbal behavior (for example, yelling or name-calling), or daydreaming. This method of categorizing behavior is called "time sampling". The mean amount of attending is shown in Figure 24.4, while the frequency of inattentive behaviors for each subject is shown in Table 24.1.

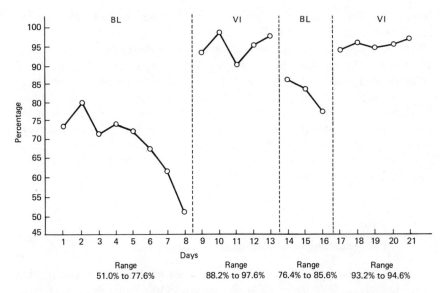

FIGURE 24.4. Average percentage of time spent attending during alternated baseline (BL) and variable-interval reinforcement (VI) phases (Alexander and Apfel, 1976).

Following 8 baseline sessions, token reinforcement for attending was introduced by the teacher on a *VI* 3 min schedule. Figure 24.4 and Table 24.1 show that attending markedly increased while all classes of inattentive behavior became less frequent. During subsequent return-to-baseline (Days 14 to 16), in which tokens were again given at the end of the hour, there was

TABLE 24.1. Average frequencies of disruptive behaviors per 45 minutes in successive baseline (BL) and variable interval reinforcement (VI) phases (Alexander and Apfel, 1976).

Subjects	Nonattending behaviors	BL	VI	BL	VI
1	Daydreaming	3.3	.2	2.7	.2
2	Motor	4.6	1.2	3.3	.6
	Verbal	4.1	1.8	3.3	.4
3	Motor	8.4	2.0	4.0	.8
	Verbal	5.8	1.4	2.3	.4
	Daydreaming	2.4	.4	1.6	1.0
4	Motor	2.4	.2	.3	.0
	Verbal	2.0	.4	.3	.4
5	Motor	8.9	2.4	4.0	.8
	Verbal	2.8	2.2	2.7	.8

some reduction in attention, but it immediately recovered when the *VI* schedule was again introduced.

This study provides a clear indication that a single teacher can implement an intermittent reinforcement schedule for a group of pupils that will maintain a high level of attention. The use of an intermittent reinforcement schedule will produce greater resistance to extinction than continuous reinforcement and increase the likelihood of generalization to other situations. Alexander and Apfel (1976) point out that the only difference between baseline and *VI* conditions was the distribution of reinforcements in time. When reinforcement was more immediate (on the *VI* schedule) there was a dramatic improvement in performance.

24.4
Programmed Individual Instruction

So far we have only considered behavior modification's contribution to the negative side of the educational process, optimizing conditions for the instructional activities more conventionally labeled "education" to take place. This casts the behavior modifier in role of a custodian rather than a educator. A more important contribution of behavior modification constitutes the improvement of the actual techniques of instruction.

Nineteenth-century educational techniques tended to treat a class of children as a unit. Pupils recited multiplication tables in unison, read through the same book at the same speed, and so on. This method is convenient for the teacher because he or she can address the whole class at once, but it is far from ideal for the students. Typically some are always "lagging behind" and thus never fully understand the lessons of the day, while others are being "held back" and thus become bored and soon lose interest. How can we approach this problem without assigning a teacher to each child? Recent technological developments based on operant principles suggest some innovations that merit close attention.

Skinner (1968) suggested that teaching could be radically improved by the introduction of:

1. A step-by-step program of instruction in which only a very small and identifiable piece of information is added at each step.
2. A question and answer format in which immediate reinforcement (feedback) is provided for correct answers.
3. A system in which the student only progresses to the next stage once he or she has achieved the objectives of the earlier stages. These recommendations are intended to ensure that the student progresses as fast as possible without "skipping" things he or she does not understand, and without the aversive consequences of "being wrong." The latter is achieved by breaking down the subject matter into sufficiently small steps that error becomes highly unlikely.

This set of features characterizes *programmed instruction*, either in the form of programmed texts or teaching machines. A programmed text is a sort of half-way house between a conventional text book and a teaching machine. In it, a page is divided into a sequence of panels or *frames*. Each frame contains a brief statement, followed by another statement with a word or phrase missing. The student's task is to read through the text at his own speed and supply the missing phrase in each frame before going on to the next one. The answer is contained in information in that frame or one or more of the earlier ones. The student can check his solution against the correct answer, usually printed elsewhere on the same page. A skilfully-written programmed text will systematically build up the students knowledge, help him recall the material presented earlier, and retain his interest.

One problem with programmed texts is that the student may look at several frames at once, or leave some out, thereby breaking up the sequential structure. The *teaching machine*, in which only one panel is available at any time, prevents this difficulty. Depending on its sophistication, such a machine could also provide a record of the student's progress that could then be used for his own and the teacher's assessment.

24.5
Programmed Concept Acquisition

In line with Skinner's recommendations given above, a teaching machine incorporates three essential aspects: 1. Material is presented to the student in small discrete portions, called *frames*. 2. This material sets the occasion for some discriminative operant on the part of the student, such as writing a word or sentence, completing a blank, or choosing an answer. 3. Provision is made for immediately reinforcing the behavior emitted by making available the correct "answer" as soon as the student has responded, thus permitting him to advance to the next frame. One such machine is shown in Figure 24.5 In this version, frames are written on a rotary disk, and one frame at a time appears in the center window. After reading the frame, the student writes his or her response on a paper strip exposed through the opening on the right. She or he then lifts a lever at the front of the machine, thus moving what has been written under a transparent cover and revealing the correct response in the center window. The individual frames are organized in small sequential steps. The student can move at his or her own pace through the succession of frames constituting the program, making very few errors.

It is useful to classify the verbal subject matter constituting a frame into two types of statements, rules and examples, (Evans, Homme and Glaser, 1962). A rule may be considered to be a general specification or definition of an S^D class, whereas an example may be considered to be an instance of one

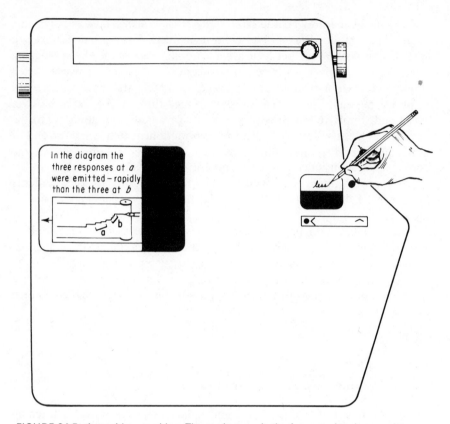

In the diagram the
three responses at *a*
were emitted – rapidly
than the three at *b*

less

FIGURE 24.5. A teaching machine. The student reads the frame and makes a written response, then moves a lever to uncover the correct answer for comparison with his response (after Skinner, 1958).

of the members of the S^D class. An instructional program may be viewed as an arrangement of various rules and examples, with portions of each rule or example missing, thus requiring behavior on the part of the learner for completion. It should be apparent that a presentation of a subset of examples associated with a given rule is analogous to the presentation of a subset of individual S's from a broad S^D class and the reinforcement of a given identifying response, such as occurs in experimental studies of *concept acquisition* (these were described in Chapter 18).

Consider the four frames of a student program for teaching certain concepts of imagery in poetry shown in Figure 24.6. Prior to these frames, the concepts of image, object, and likeness had been taught by examples. Frames 48, 49, and 50 are three examples from the S^D class which is to be identified as *simile*. Note that each frame is so arranged that the contextual cues enhance the probability of the required response. The three frames used as S^D's for simile have certain similarities but also certain differences. Since

48. An image that expresses a likeness between objects of different classes, but does not mean exactly what it says, is called a *simile*. The image "the girl is like a flower" is a _____. *Answer. simile*
49. Because it expresses a likeness between objects of different classes, but does not mean exactly what it says, the image "the man's face lit up like the sun" is a _____. *Answer. simile*
50. A simile is not only introduced by the word like, but by the words as, as if, or as when. Thus the image "the man is as red *as* a beet" is a _____. *Answer. simile*
51. On the other hand, a phrase which expresses identity between two objects, but does not mean exactly what it says, is not a simile. Thus the image "her eyes are stars" (is/is not) a simile. *Answer. is not*

FIGURE 24.6. Four frames of a program designed to teach concepts concerned with imagery in poetry (courtesy of Susan Stitt).

the programmer desires the concept of simile to be as broad as possible, the reinforcement contingencies are set in the presence of a wide variety of examples from the S^D class. Frame 51, however, is an S^Δ instance. In human as well as animal concept acquisition, it is important to present situations which are not members of the S^D class and withhold reinforcement for the response or, as in this case, reinforce an incompatible response. Frame 51 helps establish what a simile is not.

Another example of concept formation is shown in the frame of Figure 24.7. Later on in this program, the student will encounter pictures of other organisms with and without six legs, and with many other features that vary. But the word "insect" will be cued and reinforced only in the presence of pictures of six-legged organisms. Eventually, the concept of insect will generalize to the broad class of organisms with six legs, via this history with a subset of the members.

Still another example in the field of behavior analysis itself is provided in the frames of Figure 24.8. The concept to be acquired is that of a response event. Note that the four frames provide S^D and S^Δ instances for the concept. Eventually, a frame will appear in which the programmer will ask the learner to induce the general definition from his past history with numerous examples.

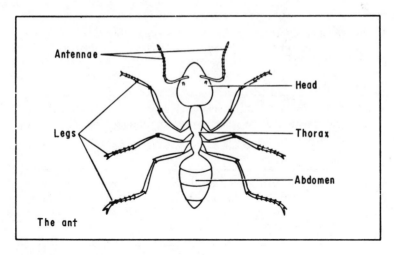

FIGURE 24.7. A frame illustrating a member of the S^D class "insect" (Lysaught and Williams, 1963).

The examples of concept formation via programmed instruction show how control of a verbal response (simile, insect, response-event) by a broad class of S^D's can be brought about by systematic presentation of examples, with reinforcement for the desired verbal response. It is clear that the concepts evolved are compound concepts made up of others. "Simile" is composed of certain relations between the concepts of object, image, and likeness; "insect" is the conjunction of organism and six legs; response event is a compound of action and actor. In a complete program, each concept to be acquired is established via a suitable set of contingencies with a subset of its members, and many of the acquired concepts are then related to each other via suitable compound examples. It is this web of concepts which appears to be the hallmark of true understanding of a subject matter.

Programming concept acquisition raises a number of systematic questions concerning the role of certain variables that the programmer has under his control. The programmer may control the number of S^D examples and S$^\Delta$ counter-examples; he or she may control their diversity and their sequences. In developing a number of different concepts, he or she may choose one concrete multi-dimensional example, presenting it from various points of view, or the programmer may use numerous simpler examples, presenting each from a single point of view.

Supposing we have introduced programmed instruction by teaching machine into a classroom, have we made the teacher redundant? Not in the least. By assigning the presentation of the material and the assessment of the students' progress to the machine, the teacher is free to deal with the special problems of individuals as they arise. The teacher thus retains the more interesting parts of his or her task and loses the drudgery.

1. Your being born *was* *not* a "response-event" for you. Your throwing your rattle out of your crib *was* a "response-event" for you.

   Check those sentences below that describe a response event for the person or animal *named* in it. (Note: You can check any number of sentences.)

   a. ☐ Clara dyed her hair red.   a
   b. ☐ Herman died.
   c. ☐ John had a cavity.
   d. ☐ Harold went to the dentist.   d
   e. ☐ The cat meowed.   e

2. When you hit someone, it is *your* response-event. When the other person hits you back, it *is* *not* your response-event.

   For each sentence below, check the box if it describes a response-event for the organism named in it.

   a. ☐ Philip ran fast.   a
   b. ☐ Gregory was run over.
   c. ☐ Alice cheated on the exam.   c
   d. ☐ Mary was caught cheating.
   e. ☐ The canary lost all its feathers.
   f. ☐ The dog caught the fudge on the first bounce.   f

3. Check the statements that describe response-events for *you.*

   a. ☐ You solved a hard math example.   a
   b. ☐ Your teacher gave you a good report card.
   c. ☐ You are a dentist.
   d. ☐ You are studying to be a dentist.   d

4. The sentence "A cat runs" refers to a response-event.
   The sentence "A person runs" refers to a response-event.
   The sentence "A color runs" does not refer to a response-event.

   Check the response-events below:

   a. ☐ The hurricane struck here yesterday. (for the hurricane)
   b. ☐ Tom struck Harry. (for Tom)   b
   c. ☐ Tom struck Harry. (for Harry)
   d. ☐ The clock struck ten. (for the clock)
   e. ☐ You eat a carrot. (for you)   e
   f. ☐ A mosquito bites you. (for you)
   g. ☐ A mosquito bites you. (for the mosquito)   g

FIGURE 24.8. A series of frames designed to establish the concept of response-event. The correct responses are indicated by the small letters to the right of the frame (Mechner, 1963).

24.6

Mental Retardation

The definition of mental retardation is a complex issue, perhaps because the same term is applied to individuals with a wide variety of intellectual and social deficits. Some cases of mental retardation can be clearly attributed to brain damage, genetic abnormalities, or disease. There remain many, however, that are not readily categorized.

Behavior modification has had a considerable impact in this area because it directs attention away from sterile debate about subdivisions of mental retardation and towards programs that can effect genuine behavioral change. If we take our educational and therapeutic objective to be improving the retardate's behavior so as to make it more similar to that of the general population, then arguments about the ontogeny of retardation are rendered irrelevant.

The primary problems of retardates are *behavioral deficits*. They lack many of the skills that the normal individual takes for granted. Bandura (1969) has pointed out that behavioral deficits result in a complete loss of contact between the individual and the contingencies that normally maintain that class of behavior in the community. If a retarded child never speaks, then none of the many subtle contingencies that affect the verbal behavior of the rest of us will influence that child. We could say that his or her verbal behavior has an operant level of zero and thus can never be reinforced. What is required is a technique of establishing that class of behavior and raising it to a sufficient level that it will be maintained subsequently by the everyday contingencies of reinforcement.

Two of the techniques we introduced in earlier chapters are particularly relevant here. These are *shaping* and *modeling*, and both have been extensively used with retardates. We will briefly describe two examples. Watson (1973) shaped a retarded child to take off a short-sleeved pullover shirt. In accordance with the principles used in laboratory work, the child was first taught to perform the last element in the chain of behaviors, for example, to take the shirt off his left wrist. Gradually, across several sessions, the chain was built up with each completion (that is, reaching the last element from wherever he started) being reinforced. Watson also describes a similar technique for training the child to dress himself completely. Initially, the child is fully dressed except for his shoes and he is reinforced for putting them on. Later he has to put on both shoes and socks for reinforcement, and so on.

Our second example is a case study reported by Neisworth and Smith (1973). A six year old girl cried every day at "nap time," thus disrupting a group of children. A package of measures were introduced:

1. Positive reinforcement: Verbal praise every time she stopped crying.
2. Extinction: Crying was ignored.
3. Reinforcing incompatible behavior: The other children were reinforced for ignoring the crying.

4. Modeling: The other children were reinforced for lying quietly on their cots.

The effect on amount of time spent crying are shown in Figure 24.9. The crying disappeared rapidly and permanently.

Progress with retarded children is undoubtedly slow, but it is real. Through skilful management of environmental contingencies, small positive steps can be taken by retardates towards a richer and more successful life. Behavior modification does not offer a magic cure, but it does offer genuine improvements.

The use of behavior modification with retardates shifts the burden of responsibility away from doctors, psychiatrists, and other professionals onto parents, nurses, attendants and even siblings. Only the people who are with the retardate day in and day out can implement a comprehensive behavior modification program. It is being increasingly realized that a small expenditure on training "lay behavior modifiers" can pay much bigger dividends that massive investments in clinics and institutions. This is a heartening sign because it suggests that the trend towards shutting away all "difficult" people in institutions may now be reversed, and they may be increasingly cared for in the community.

The use of behavior modification with retardates is not only an important therapeutic advance, but also facilitates a functional analysis of behavioral development. Modification of retarded behavior requires a detailed description of the behavioral repertoire and results in an assessment of the

FIGURE 24.9. Amount of crying before and after a package of measures was introduced to eliminate this behavior (Neisworth and Smith, 1973).

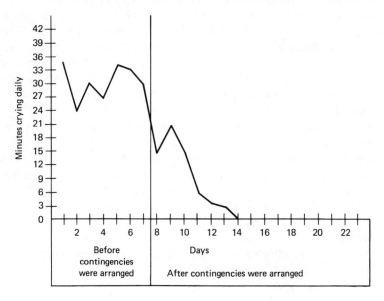

sensitivity of various classes of behavior to environmental contingencies. These can be seen as steps towards a thoroughgoing descriptive account of human behavioral development.

24.7
Intelligent Behavior

"Intelligence" is a word that enjoys a very wide currency in the English-speaking world, though it was rarely used until the eighteenth century. Perhaps this is because intelligence refers not to the possession of any particular skill, but rather to the possession of a known or hypothetical collection of skills that may not have been thought of collectively in preindustrial society. Psychologists have become heavily involved in the study of intelligence, but not, as one might suppose, in the analysis of the skills constituting intelligent behavior. Rather they have been the originators and distributors of *tests of intelligence*. Indeed, psychologists since 1905 have often been in the curious "position of devising and advocating tests for measuring intelligence and then disclaiming responsibility for them by asserting that 'nobody knows what the word really means'" (Wechsler, 1958). In order to understand this paradox we must briefly look at the history of intelligence testing.

In 1904, the psychologist Alfred Binet was commissioned by the French Minister of Public Instruction to devise a test which would pick out those children whose academic aptitudes were so low that they needed to be placed in "special schools." Binet's resulting test was a series of problems using pictures, wooden blocks, peg boards, and other materials that were administered to one child at a time. The test was successfully adopted by the French school system and versions of it were rapidly implemented in the United States. Intelligence testing in the U.S. received a terrific boost during the First World War, when the armed forces decided that all inductees should be given pencil-and-paper tests in order to categorize them and thus allocate them to various tasks. The large numbers of inductees necessitated development of group tests that could be administered simultaneously to many individuals.

Intelligence testing has survived and prospered because its results have proved useful to the educational institutions it has served. It is therefore unsurprising that test scores are usually good predictors of scholastic achievement; this merely tells us that the tests measure skills required in school; it does not necessarily mean that the tests accurately measure all the skills we class as intelligent behavior. As intelligence test items are usually selected empirically (by a method outlined later in this section) rather than as measures of specific skills that are defined independently of the test, the contents of intelligence tests are best explained by looking at examples of items. A sample set of items is shown in Figure 24.10.

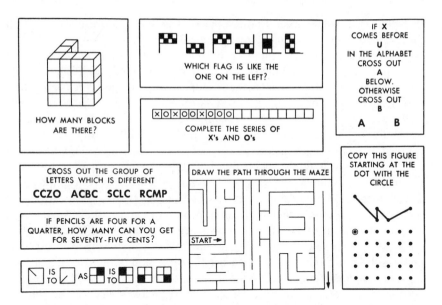

FIGURE 24.10. Sample items of the sort used in group tests of intelligence (Kimble and Garmezy, 1962).

The different items require a variety of skills. Some problems rely heavily on language skills, others involve discrimination and perceptual skills. For the most part there is an attempt to use items that test general problem-solving and the ability to apply broad concepts. Items requiring specific factual knowledge are avoided on the grounds that specific learning experiences of individuals should not determine test scores. This rule was often honored in the breach by early test-constructors. The test used by the U.S. Army in the First World War included such multiple choice items as "The Brooklyn Nationals are called the Giants . . . Orioles . . . Superbas . . . Indians" (Kamin, 1974). The recent Italian, or even English, immigrant would tend to appear "stupid" on such a measure.

The best approximation appears to be that intelligence tests are *intended* to measure a general set of cognitive or problem-solving skills that are independent of specific learning experiences or particular cultural back-grounds. It is not clear whether these criteria are met by the existing tests for two reasons: First, the set of skills has not been specified and so it is impossible to decide whether a test adequately measures them. Second, as all skills are acquired through specific learning experiences in particular cultural contexts, it is difficult to see how the requirements of independence from these factors can be established. Before examining the other issues in this complex area, we must outline the way in which a test is developed and the way individual scores on the test are calculated.

The test-constructor's first task is to collect test items, the problems or questions that will be posed to the subjects. The selection is usually based on material from previous tests plus supplementary material. New material may be introduced because older items proved ambiguous or unreliable, or to test skills not previously included. The total range of skills tested inevitably depends on the test constructor's judgement. In the Wechsler Adult Intelligence Scale, for example, eleven named subtests make up the full scale. These are: information, comprehension, arithmetic, similarities, digit span, vocabulary, digit symbol, picture completion, block design, picture arrangement, and object assembly (for details see Wechsler, 1955). Does this cover *all* relevant skills? Probably not, but in the absence of a general account (or definition) of intelligent behavior, it is impossible to answer this question. Test construction also raises questions of balance. If some skills are tested more often than others, then individuals proficient in those skills will be rated as more intelligent than individuals proficient in other skills. Wechsler gives equal weight to each of his subtests, but this does not solve the problem because different subtests may measure the same skill (scores on subtests are highly correlated) and some skills may be accurately reflected by specific subtests while others are not. These various problems led to the famous remark that "Intelligence is what the tests test" (Boring, 1923).

Whatever intelligence is, one of the most obvious facts that emerges from intelligence testing is that the number of problems (or types of problems) a child can solve increases with his or her age. Consider the data in Figure 24.11 from five individuals tested repeatedly up to the age of 25 years. Their scores, reflecting the number of problems they could solve, increase continuously, although for some of them the increases are tapering off by age 25. The population at large shows a sharp tapering off in the late teens, and generally small changes occur between the ages 20 and 50.

The orientation of intelligence-testers towards allocating individuals to relative categories, rather than examining the specific sets of skills acquired, led them to develop *relative measures* of intelligence. An individual's test score is related to that of his peers rather than treated as an important datum in its own right. One reason for doing this is that it avoids the assumption that the range of skills measured by the particular test used is definitive or exhaustive of "intelligence." Instead, the individual is given a score indicating his or her performance on this (perhaps not wholly representative) test relative to other individuals of the same age. The score generally used is the "intelligence quotient" or IQ, defined as

$$IQ = 100 \times \frac{\text{obtained score on test}}{\text{average score for that age-group}}$$

For adults it is generally assumed that changes with age are negligible, and a single "typical adult" score is used as the divisor (actually Wechsler [1955] does not make this assumption). Clearly the mean IQ will be 100, and IQ tests are generally designed so that the distribution of scores is approxi-

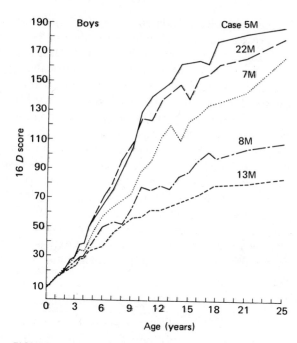

FIGURE 24.11. Problem-solving scores of five boys as a function of age (Bayley, 1955).

mately *normal*. This means that they conform to the bell-shaped curve shown in Figure 24.12. If scores are normally distributed, then 34 per cent of them will fall between the mean and a point one standard deviation above (or below) the mean and 48 per cent will lie between the mean and a point two standard deviation above (or below) the mean. Conventionally, IQ scores are adjusted so that the standard deviation is 15. This means that 2 per cent of people in the population will score more than the mean plus two standard deviations, or $100 + (15 \times 2) = 130$. These various relationships between the distributor of test scores, percentiles and IQ's are shown in Figure 24.12.

FIGURE 24.12.
Relations among test scores, percentiles and IQ scores (after Cronbach, 1963).

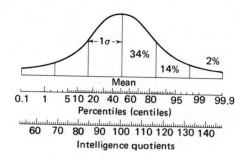

IQ scores are calculated *relative to a population*. If an individual's IQ exceeds 130 this places him or her in the top 2 per cent of the population for which the test was standardized. Standardization involves obtaining scores from large samples of individuals of a particular age in order to calculate an age-group average score to put in the IQ equation given above. In selecting the standardization sample, the test-constructor should ideally take account of all variables within the population that he believes to be determinants of test scores. We have already pointed out that age is taken into account. Another undoubtedly relevant variable is amount of schooling. Wechsler (1955) included people with different amounts of schooling in roughly the same proportions as they existed in the population at large in the standardization of the Wechsler Adult Intelligence Scale. This sample is thus representative of the population with respect to this variable. This does not, however, *control* for the effect of amount of schooling on IQ scores, as Wechsler (1958) points out. This could only be done by establishing average scores for people with different amounts of schooling. We could then calculate IQ as:

$$IQ = 100 \times \frac{\text{obtained score on test}}{\substack{\text{average score for group with} \\ \text{this individual's amount of schooling}}}$$

for an adult, where we assume that age is not important. This standardization has not been done and so this variable remains confounded with IQ scores. Neither has this exercise been carried out with respect to race (or ethnic group), socioeconomic status, family background or any other of the variables that may strongly influence the particular set of skills acquired by an individual. As we shall see in the next section, this poses great limitations on the interpretation of IQ scores.

Because there is a good correlation between IQ scores and scholastic achievement, as we noted earlier, it is reasonable to use them to make school "streaming" decisions and the like. However, a correlation *for the population* between IQ scores and another variable does not enable us to conclude that an *individual's* IQ is stable. In fact there is evidence that the IQ scores of a large proportion of the population change considerably during childhood and adolescence. McCall, Appelbaum and Hogarty (1973) report data from longitudinal study in which a large group of predominantly white middle-class children were given IQ tests on up to 17 occasions between the ages of $2\frac{1}{2}$ and 17 years. Data, in terms of IQ scores, for the 80 subjects (38 of them male) for whom relatively complete records were available are shown in Figure 24.13. The subjects have been placed in six groupings according to the trends shown in IQ scores; there are no other differences between the groupings. Cluster 1 includes 36 subjects that showed minimal systematic deviation, although some individuals produced a considerable range of scores. Clusters 2–5 each have a characteristic pattern and the ranges of scores

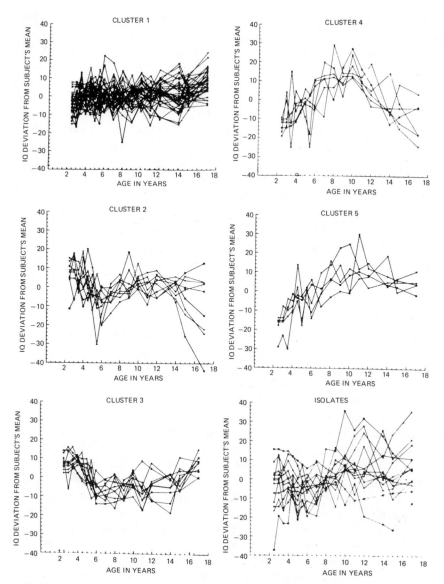

FIGURE 24.13. IQ scores of 80 individuals, calculated as a deviation from their personal mean score, as a function of age from 2½ to 17 years. Individuals are grouped in clusters according to the trends in their scores (McCall, Appelbaum, and Hogarty, 1973).

of individuals are generally greater, frequently exceeding 30 IQ points. The "isolates" are individuals who show variation that does not conform to the other patterns. Some of their ranges are enormous; the greatest recorded was 74 IQ points. Recall from Figure 24.12 that 68 per cent of the population have IQ's between 85 and 115, while 96 per cent have IQ's between 70 and 130.

A change in IQ of around 30 points therefore represents an enormous change in the position of that individual relative to the standardization populations. McCall and associates obtained an *average* range of 28.5 points in their study.

Clearly it is invalid to assume that a single assessment of IQ at a particular age will remain accurate for a number of years. A curious feature of the McCall data is the dramatic drops in IQ that certain individuals recorded. These might lead us to assume that these individuals were becoming "less clever." If by that is meant that they could not solve problems that they dealt with successfully at an earlier date, this is probably untrue. The chief cause of declining IQ will be a failure to increase problem-solving skills as fast as the average member of the population. The paradox that IQ can decline while skills improve is highlighted by the study of retardates. Their skills increase with age, but not as fast as those of the normal population. Consequently, their IQ's fall steadily.

24.8
The Interpretation of IQ

We have seen that there are numerous problems to be overcome before an IQ score can safely be presumed to accurately reflect an individual's intelligence, and that the existing tests do not deal with all the problems. We can only say that an IQ score reflects the individual's position relative to the standardization population on the skills that the test used requires. The standardization population is not homogeneous; it contains people whose backgrounds vary in many ways that might influence IQ scores. For example Wechsler (1955) included representatives of categories of geographic origin, race, urban or rural residence, occupation, and educational history in roughly the same proportions as they occur in the U.S. population at large. This ensured that his standardization sample was representative of the U.S. population with respect to these variables, but, as was pointed out in the previous section, it does not control for them. The problems that this raises for the interpretation of IQ scores are best dealt with by considering an hypothetical example.

Suppose that an investigator records the IQ scores of 400 16-year-old children. Half of these children come from urban environments and the other half from rural environments; otherwise the groups are made as similar to each other as possible. It is found that the urban group has a mean IQ of 105, while the rural group has a mean IQ of 95. If this is the only information available in the published report of the study (and often it is), how are we to interpret it?

Here are some possibilities:

1. The rural group are less intelligent, because of:
    a Environmental differences; perhaps lower nutritional levels retard

brain development, or schools are less well-equipped, or family environments are unhelpful, or cultural facilities are lacking.

or *b* Genetic differences; these are not directly observed but it is possible that they exist and affect intelligence. If they do exist, they may have been brought about by selective migration away from rural areas, by rural in-breeding, or there may be genetic differences for historical reasons, the urban and rural populations being descended from different stock.

or *c* An interaction of environmental and genetic factors. The possibilities here are innumerable.

2. The rural population develop problem-solving skills move slowly and reach "intellectual maturity" later. Thus, measured at 16 years, they score lower on IQ. This difference could be due to:

   a Environmental factors

   b Genetic factors

or *c* An interaction of the two.

3. The IQ test accurately reflected the skills and knowledge of the urban population, but not those of the rural population. The results therefore tell us that rural children have less urban skills, but not whether they are less intelligent.

4. The IQ scores reflect the degree to which the children share the culture and value system of the test-constructor. The rural children are not less intelligent, they merely have less in common with the test-constructor.

Before discussing these alternatives, it is very important to note that *if we are only given the mean IQ scores, we cannot decide between these alternatives.* The considerable debate about the significance of some between-group differences therefore remains at the level of speculation about causes, rather than demonstration of causes. Drawing inferences from population statistics is very different from demonstrating functional relationships in the laboratory.

The proposed interpretations of our hypothetical rural–urban difference are all of the following form: The IQ score differences tell us that the children differ with respect to characteristic X, differences in X are due to factor Y. What one considers "X" and "Y" to stand for depends on the general account of intelligence one adopts, and there is a wide range of choice in this because, as pointed out earlier, we have not devoted as much effort to analyzing intelligent behavior into its component skills as we have to trying to rank people according to their possession of those skills. However, there is one particular general account or theory of intelligence that has attracted a great deal of attention.

On this theory, the *hereditarian thesis*, IQ tests measure intelligence (X), which is a relatively fixed potential of the individual to acquire problem solving and related skills, and intelligence is largely determined by the genetic endowment (Y) of the individual. According to the hereditarian thesis, a substantial between-group difference in IQ will only be obtained if there is a difference between the groups in the relative frequencies of genes that affect intelligence. An acrimonious dispute has surrounded the application of the hereditarian thesis to differences in mean IQ scores of blacks and whites, and of various social classes in the United States. Hereditarians maintain that the mean differences reflect real differences, with some racial groups or social classes being genuinely superior in intelligence to others, and that changes in the environment will not be able to substantially narrow the gaps.

We have already seen that IQ scores are complex data and that the interpretation of between-group differences is more complex still. We would therefore be justified in merely noting that the hereditarian thesis is one example of this speculative activity, and passing on to other matters. However, the social and political implications of the hereditarian analysis oblige us to look at it in more detail.

We will consider the two steps in the hereditarian analysis separately. Firstly, it is maintained that IQ scores reflect intelligence, and secondly that intelligence is largely genetically determined. The belief that IQ scores reflect intelligence is common to all those who use IQ tests, but, as we have already seen, it is an assumption. It cannot be tested unless there is some independent definition of intelligence. Such a definition will follow from a better understanding of behavioral development in general and the development of problem solving skills in particular, but it is not available at present.

Opponents of IQ tests believe that the tests measure in part nonintellectual skills of one sort or another. It may be claimed that they test knowledge taught in schools and available in middle-class homes, or that they embody the values of the establishment. An example of how this may happen is given by Kamin (1974) from the widely-used Stanford-Binet IQ test developed by Terman (1916). Fourteen-year-olds were asked to explain this incident: "My neighbor has been having queer visitors. First a doctor came to his house, then a lawyer, then a minister. What do you think happened there? ". Terman scored an explanation involving a death as correct, but failed this explanation: "Somebody was sick; the lawyer wanted his money, and the minister came to see how he was." Clearly, Kamin (1974) points out, Terman categorizes the child as stupid if he or she does not assume that lawyers always have honorable intentions. Of course, not all IQ test items are as obviously biased as that, but unbiased items (if they exist) can only be identified with reference to a clear definition of intelligent behavior.

Most arguments for and against the hereditarian thesis have centered on the second step of the analysis: the assertion that intelligence (whatever it is) is largely genetically determined. All of an organism's structures, functions and activities are generated by a complex interaction between hereditary and environmental factors. The genetic endowment, or *genotype*, determines many features of the individual but the development of these features depends critically on an appropriate environment at every stage. We may, however, be able to point to "details" that appear to be attributable solely to genotype or environment. As examples consider the blood group and native language of an individual. Blood group is not susceptible to environmental influence, while native language depends entirely on the verbal community in which the individual is raised. Such observations imply that there may be a continuum of *sensitivity to the environment* along which human characteristics can be arranged. In the absence of direct measurements of the genotype, we can take evidence of insensitivity of a characteristic to the environment as evidence for strong genetic determination. A trivial example will underline the idea. Most adult humans have two legs. Subjecting them to rigorous programs of exercise or restricting will greatly modify the strength of their legs without changing the number. "Strength of legs" is thus a human characteristic sensitive to the environment, while "number of legs" is insensitive to the environment.

If a quantitative index of environmental sensitivity could be found, then it might possibly be applied to intelligence (assuming that intelligence can be treated as an observable characteristic) to estimate the relative importance of genotype and environment. Hereditarians (for example, Jensen, 1969, and Herrnstein, 1973) believe that heritability, a concept developed in quantitative genetics, represents such an index. Great controversy surrounds this measure which reflects the environmental and genetic components of variation in a *population* (Lewontin, 1970). Whatever its validity, we as psychologists remain concerned with the behavior of *individuals*, and the ways and means by which it can be optimally modified. One day we may perhaps eventually discover something corresponding to the "limits of educability," but if we do the discovery will come from the application of psychological techniques, not through quantitative genetics. However, it seems far more likely that with increasing knowledge, we shall probably discover that what we called "limits" were inherent in our present limited understanding, rather than residing within the child. As Schoenfeld (1974) puts it:

> Behavioral limits and "physical" ones even more so, are inferred from performance rather than the other way round. The 4-minute mile was thought to be a physiological limit for runners until it was broken, and it is now merely a good day's performance (pp. 22–23).

References for Chapter 24

Alexander, R. N., and Apfel, C. H. Altering schedules of reinforcement for improved classroom behavior. *Exceptional Children*, 1976, **43**, 97–99.

Axelrod, S. *Behavior modification for the classroom teacher*. New York: McGraw-Hill, 1977.

Bandura, A. *Principles of behavior modification*. New York: Holt, Rinehart & Winston, 1969.

Bayley, N. On the growth of intelligence. *American Psychologist*, 1955, **10**, 805–818.

Blackwood, R. O. *Operant control of behavior*. Akron, Ohio: Exordium Press, 1971.

Boring, E. G. Intelligence as the tests test it. *The New Republic*, 1923, **34**, 35–36.

Cronbach, L. J, *Educational psychology.* New York: Harcourt, Brace and World, 1963.

Evans, J. L., Homme, L. E., and Glaser, R. The ruleg system for the construction of programmed verbal learning sequences. *Journal of Educational Research*, 1962, **55**, 513–518.

Gallagher, P. A., Sulzbacher, S. I., and Shores, R. E. A group contingency for classroom management of emotionally disturbed children. Paper presented at the Kansas Council for Exceptional Children, Wichita, 1967.

Herrnstein, R. J. *IQ in the meritocracy.* Boston: Little, Brown, 1973.

Jensen, A. R. How much can we boast IQ and scholastic achievement? *Harvard Educational Review*, 1969, **39**, 1–123.

Kamin, L. J. *The science and politics of I.Q.* New York: Lawrence Erlbaum, 1974.

Kimble, G. A., and Garmezy, N. *Principles of general psychology.* Second edition, New York: Ronald Press, 1963.

Lewontin, R. Race and intelligence. *Bulletin of the Atomic Scientists*, March, 1970, 2–8.

Lysaught, J. P., and Williams, C. M. *A guide to programmed instruction.* New York: Wiley, 1963.

McAllister, L. W., Stachowiak, J. G., Baer, D. M., and Conderman, L. The application of operant conditioning techniques in a secondary school classroom. *Journal of Applied Behavioral Analysis*, 1969, **2**, 277–285.

McCall, R. B., Appelbaum, N. I., and Hogarty, P. S. Development changes in mental performance. *Child Development Monographs*, 1973, **38**, (3), 1–94.

Mechner, F. *Science, education and behavioral technology.* New York: Basic Systems, 1963.

Neisworth, J. T., and Smith, R. M. *Modifying retarded behavior.* Atlanta, Georgia: Houghton Mifflin, 1973.

Schoenfeld, W. N. Notes on a bit of psychological nonsense: "Race differences in intelligence". *Psychological Record*, 1974, **24**, 17–32.

Skinner, B. F. Teaching machines. *Science*, 1958, **128**, 969–977.

Skinner, B. F. *The technology of teaching.* New York: Appleton-Century-Crofts, 1968.

Terman, L. M. *The measurement of intelligence.* Boston: Houghton Mifflin, 1916.

Tribble, A., and Hall, R. V. Effects of peer approval on completion of arithmetic assignments. In F. W. Clark, D. R. Evans, and L. A. Hamerlynck (Eds.) *Implementing behavioral programs for schools and clinics.* Champaign, Illinois: research Press, 1972.

Watson, L. S. *Child behavior modification: A manual for teachers, nurses and parents.* New York: Pergamon, 1973.

Wechsler, D. *Wechsler Adult Intelligence Scale manual.* New York: Psychological Corp., 1955.

Wechsler, D. *The measurement and appraisal of adult intelligence.* Baltimore: Williams & Wilkins, 1958.

CHAPTER 25

Behavior
Therapy

What is the cause of abnormal behavior? A century ago the most common answer was madness. Today we are more likely to regard such behavior as the symptoms of a special disease, mental illness. Yet this newer explanation is just as fictitous as the devil of earlier times who drove people mad, because there is no actual evidence of any disease other than the behavior we wish to explain.

In the late nineteenth century, medicine made great strides in discovering the physical correlates of diseases. These discoveries lead to the extrapolation that there exist "psychic diseases" which underlie abnormal behavior, in the same way as viruses and bacteria underlie the symptoms of measles, influenza, and other familiar illnesses. Just as the doctor does not treat measles by covering up the spots, so, it was argued, we cannot treat abnormal behavior without penetrating to the underlying causes. The psychoanalysts, beginning with Sigmund Freud in Vienna, believed these causes to be intrapsychic conflicts resulting from early experiences. In their view these conflicts must be identified and resolved by careful probing interviews, conducted by a trained therapist, before any real behavioral changes could occur. Any attempt to treat behavior directly, they believed, could be positively dangerous and result in *symptom substitution*, where one abnormal behavior is suppressed and the underlying intrapsychic disorder expresses itself in a new, and perhaps more bizarre form.

This *medical model* of behavioral pathology had the virtue of bringing the emotional suffering of human beings out of the darkness of fear and superstition and into the objective light of science. But the fruitful period of that model has probably expired. True, there do exist a few behavioral syndromes which have been found to have a purely organic basis, and thus can accurately be described as illnesses. But for the majority of those symptom packages we call *neuroses* and *psychoses*, no organic causes have been identified, the intrapsychic causes remain speculative, and the abnormal behavior remains substantially unchanged by the treatments of traditional Western medicine.

Behavior modification offers a completely different conceptual scheme and suggests a wide range of therapeutic possibilities. On this view, disturbed, disorderly, or bizarre behavior represent primary data, rather than symptoms of underlying causes. If, as we have argued throughout this text, the behavioral processes identifiable in the psychological laboratory operate in the real world, then all behavior that occurs must be influenced by them. The distinction between abnormal and normal behavior must therefore be an arbitrary one, since all behavior is generated and maintained by the same (normal) processes. Of course, some behavior is abnormal or unusual in a statistical sense. And some behavior is abnormal simply because it is undesired, either by the person who exhibits it, or by his or her society. We shall argue here that unusual abnormal behavior results either from prolonged punitive, oppressive, contradictory, and confusing contingencies, or from prolonged insufficient or inappropriate reinforcement in the history of the individual; and further, that these particular contingencies and reinforcer deficits can be identified and then changed or countered.

Suggestive evidence of the existence of such historical factors is provided by Laing and Esterson (1970). These two British psychiatrists produced detailed reports on the families of eleven women aged between fifteen and forty who were admitted to mental hospitals and diagnosed as "schizophrenic," but who had normal intelligence and showed no sign of brain damage or other relevant organic disorder. On the basis of very extensive case investigations, involving many interviews with members of the family in various combinations, Laing and Esterson argued persuasively that these women were not "mad" as a result of "mental illness" (such as schizophrenia), but that their bizarre behavior was the result of bizarre contingencies prevailing in their family environments. Most of the women's parents had made extreme or unusual demands of them, starting in adolescence, but the fact of these demands was vigorously denied by the parents.

In one case, many normal patterns of adolescent (and later, adult) behavior were attributed to mental illness by the parents, or their occurrence was flatly denied. For example, the daughter believed that she was emotionally disturbed from the ages of eight to fourteen, that she masturbated from the age of fifteen, and she stated that she still masturbated. All these claims were denied, including the one referring to her present behavior, and this disagreement was used as evidence for the daughter's unreliable memory. Her poor memory was in turn attributed to her mental illness. Laing and Esterson's analysis showed that in such instances the parent's denials were largely based on their wishes to believe that these events did not happen, and that the daughter's statements were probably true. There is thus every reason to believe that the bizarre or deviant behavior seen in Laing and Esterson's sample of "schizophrenic" women resulted from the lies implicit in the contingencies established in the family.

Behavior therapy is behavior modification applied to the categories of behavior traditionally dealt with by clinical psychologists and psychiatrists. Its techniques, as we shall see, usually derive directly from processes discovered in the laboratory. As with behavior modification in general, there is no guarantee that a particular technique will work. The intervention of a therapist for a short period of time has to compete with other contingencies that may have been in effect for many years. In this context, behavior therapy has been remarkably successful in its short history.

Because behavior therapy techniques are derived from scientific investigations of behavior, they lend themselves to scientific evaluation and scrutiny. The general strategy follows this pattern: evaluation of existing behavior; specification of desired behavioral change; treatment (that is, application of behavior therapy); assessment of obtained behavioral change. The use of observable behavior to define both the existing state of the person and the desired change in them makes assessing the therapy's effectiveness easy in principle. This contrasts with the evaluation of psychoanalytic treatment, where assessment of change can become a most mysterious process, not open to inspection by anyone but the psychotherapist. Where direct comparisons of behavior therapy and psychoanalytic therapy have been made, and both have been assessed in terms of overt behavioral change, behavior therapy has generally been found more effective. Interestingly, many controlled studies have found no effect of psychoanalytic therapy at all (Rachman, 1971).

25.1
Token Economies for Institutionalized Groups

The behavior modification approach leads us to suspect that the behavior of patients in an institution is a product not only of their experiences prior to entering the institution, but also of the environment inside the institution. Patients in the long-stay wards of psychiatric institutions are often lethargic, dependent and depressed. These same patients are also designated as schizophrenic, a broad category of "mental illness" or psychosis referring to people showing bizarre behaviors, paranoia, hallucinations, emotional deficits, and who have a poor prognosis for recovery.

Is the inactivity and depression of the long-stay patients a result of organic causes and their past histories, or is it the result of the contingencies prevailing in the ward? Several lines of circumstantial evidence suggests the latter. Institution staff generally have very low expectations of their charges and may be actually punitive towards self-assertiveness. Conversely, the caring orientation of the paramedical professions leads them to reinforce dependency by patients and ignore patients who appear not to require attention.

The idea that there are a set of reinforcement contingencies maintaining the observed behaviors was put to the test by Ayllon and Azrin (1965). They devised a *token economy* and implemented it in a hospital psychiatric ward. A token economy is characterized by two key features:

1. Tokens are made contingent upon a range of *target behaviors*.
2. The tokens can be exchanged for a variety of *back-up reinforcers*.

In Ayllon and Azrin's original study the target behaviors were various work activities in the hospital, the tokens were dispensed by hospital staff, and the back-up reinforcers were selected for individual patients by the Premack Principle. Recall from Sections 2.7 and 22.5 that Premack (1965) states that high frequency, or preferred, activities will reinforce low frequency activities. This method of identifying reinforcers is particularly useful with long-stay psychiatric patients for whom many conventional reinforcers are ineffective. Reinforcers used included privacy, going for walks, and religious services.

Once they had established the token economy on the ward, Ayllon and Azrin carried out a series of studies with clear-cut results. One of their findings is shown in Figure 25.1. In this study the entire ward of 44 patients were alternately reinforced for participation in work activities (first and third phases) or given the same number of tokens independent of their behavior, thus breaking the contingency (second phase). Clearly, this behavior rapidly extinguished in the group once the contingency was broken.

Following this pioneer study, many others have replicated and extended Ayllon and Azrin's findings. Target behaviors can be simple self-help skills (washing, dressing etc), social behavior, or complex tasks taking the

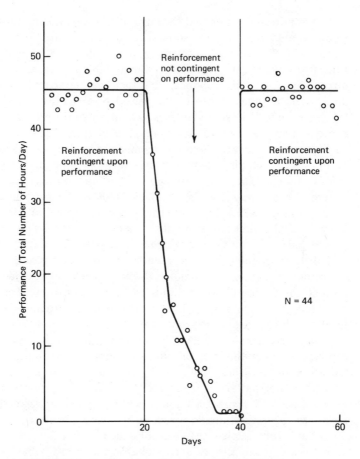

FIGURE 25.1. Total number of hours a group of 44 patients participated in rehabilitative activities under conditions of both contingent and noncontingent reinforcement (Ayllon and Azrin, 1965).

patients away from the ward. Many studies report generalized improvements in the patients' behavior and marked increases in activity. Interestingly, reductions in bizarre behavior have been reported even when no explicit contingency has been placed on these behaviors.

Perhaps the most difficult task in implementing a token economy is training (or more often, retraining) the ward staff. As pointed out earlier their professional attitudes generally dispose them to reinforce dependency, acquiescence and inactivity. The staff have to be shown why it is important to make the "good things in life" *contingent* on behavior rather than freely available. Their full co-operation is vital, particularly because the attention of staff is usually the most potent reinforcer in the institutional context.

It is important to note that the introduction of a token economy does not entail a reduction in "living standards" of the patients. Indeed, there is no reason why the patients' access to preferred activities should not increase. Ethical problems can arise if the patients fail to increase the frequency of target behaviors. This may mean that their creature comforts and privileges do actually decline relative to the period prior to the introduction of the token economy. This should be seen as a failure of the program to provide an effective reinforcer or conditioning process rather than a failure of the patient, and further efforts should be made to identify significant reinforcers or an effective shaping routine. It may turn out, however, that no stimulus short of food or sleep following deprivation functions as a reinforcer for the patient. Ayllon and Azrin (1965) noted that 8 of the 44 patients contributing the data of Figure 25.1 showed no behavior change at all with the contingency. They concluded that they had failed to identify effective reinforcers for these patients, all of whom showed extreme social withdrawal.

Token economies have a number of interesting implications. Like classroom management techniques (Section 24.1) they provide an improved behavioral "background" against which further more complex change programs can be developed. Like programs for retardates, they involve the people carrying out day-to-day care as behavior modifiers. Additionally, they can have striking effects on discharge rates of patients not normally expected to leave the hospital, and can improve the morale of ward staff (Atthowe and Krasner, 1968).

In this brief outline of token economies for institutionalized groups we have shown how restructuring an environment without greatly altering its resources can have dramatic effects on behavior. The results are all the more remarkable because they have been obtained with groups of people regarded as suffering from serious and probably incurable behavioral disorders. Whether or not there is an incurable organic component to these disorders, we have seen that there is an environmental component which is readily "cured."

25.2

Fears and Phobias

Fear is not in itself abnormal behavior. On the contrary, as we noted in Chapter 22, fears represent adaptive stress reactions in most species. Although they are often maladaptive in contemporary human society, they remain an extremely common feature of human behavior. Some very interesting data were collected in an early study by Jersild and Holmes (1935). Figure 25.2 shows their data on the relative frequency of various fears of children at ages from 0 to 71 months. With age, the fears of physical events diminish (left panel), and fears of imaginary objects increase (right panel).

We would expect that in the course of daily experience children and adults

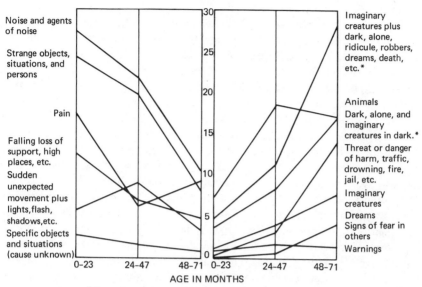

* Starred items represent a cumulative tally of two or more categories that also are depicted separately.

FIGURE 25.2. Relative frequency of children's fears (Jersild and Holmes, 1935).

acquire and extinguish fears through the classical conditioning process described in Chapter 23. However some fears, called *phobias*, are unusually strong and do not seem to extinguish or habituate in the normal course of events.

It appears that phobias can be acquired in several ways. These are: traumatic classical conditioning in which the US is highly aversive (such as might occur during warfare); modeling of phobic behavior (often by parents); and instructions and misinformation (again usually by parents). Rachman (1977) points out that certain phobias are far more common than would be expected on the basis of traumatic experiences, while others are less common than might be expected. For example, on the one hand Agras, Sylvester and Oliveau (1969) found that snake-phobias were twice as common as dentist-phobias in the population of a small city, although painful contact with the dentist was far more likely. On the other hand, air raids in England during the Second World War, which were widely predicted to produce mass panic, had a negligible effect on the incidence of fear-related clinical problems.

Seligman (1971) suggests that these disparities result from *preparedness* (see Chapters 11 and 12) of people to acquire fear of certain stimuli. In parallel with other highly prepared responses, these fears are highly resistant to extinction and thus classified as phobias. Certainly many phobias relate to stimuli of probable historical significance for the species, including darkness, deformities, snakes and dogs.

Behavior therapy has been widely and successfully used in the treatment of phobias. The techniques used include the familiar ones of modeling and reinforcement, but also *systematic desensitization*. The methods of desensitization were largely developed by Joseph Wolpe (1958, 1973). Because of the high success rate of desensitization, and its consequent clinical importance, we will describe Wolpe's (1973) methods in some detail.

Prior to treatment, Wolpe administers questionnaires that ask questions about general emotionality, specific situations that elicit anxiety, and self-sufficiency. The questionnaire responses are used to enable the therapist to identify possible organic causes of the problem, which are then treated separately, and to make decisions about which areas should be treated with the highest priority. It turns out that many sufferers from phobias have several semi-independent areas of anxiety. In such a case the most severe and incapacitating phobia will be treated first. The next stage is an initial "probing" interview. In this the therapist seeks to establish an objective but permissive emotional climate, to reassure the patient that all phobic behavior can be eliminated, to correct any misconceptions, and to encourage assertive behavior. The correction of misconceptions about the world can be very important; phobic patients sometimes believe that real dangers exist in the situations that frighten them (for example, the presence of certain animals). This contrasts with the more common finding that phobic patients realize that their fears are largely imaginary or exaggerated. The interviews are in general oriented towards obtaining details of the situations that cause anxiety, finding out when it started, and what the probable causes were.

After these initial procedures, systematic desensitization proceeds in four stages: training in deep muscle relaxation; the establishment and use of a scale of subjective anxiety; the construction of anxiety hierarchies; counterposing relaxation and anxiety-evoking stimuli from the hierarchies.

DEEP MUSCLE RELAXATION. The subject is instructed to tense and then relax various groups of muscles. This technique, developed by Jacobson (1938), enables the subject to bring relaxation under voluntary control. It takes a number of sessions before the subject is proficient.

SUBJECTIVE ANXIETY SCALE. Wolpe trains the subject to assign numbers between 0 and 100 to their current level of anxiety. After a little practice, most people can do this readily.

CONSTRUCTING ANXIETY HIERARCHIES. Items causing anxiety are collected from the interview and questionnaire material, and from additional questioning on topics that make the subject anxious. As an example Wolpe (1973, p. 110) gives the following "raw list of fears," numbering twenty in all: high altitudes, elevators, crowded places, church, darkness, being alone, sexual relations (pregnancy), walking, death, accidents, fire, fainting, falling back, injections, medications, the unknown, losing one's mind, locked doors, amusement park rides, and steep stairways. With assistance from the subject, Wolpe classified these as:

Acrophobia	Claustrophobia	Agoraphobia
high altitudes	elevators	being alone
amusement park rides	crowded places	walking
steep stairways	church	
	darkness	
	locked doors	

Illness	Objective fears
fainting	sexual relations (pregnancy)
falling back	death
injections	accidents
medications	fire
	the unknown
	losing one's mind

Wolpe treats the objective fears as non-neurotic and attempts to eliminate them through correcting misconceptions and providing reassurance.

A *hierarchy* is next constructed for each of the other groups. Each hierarchy will contain more elements than those given here. A variety of situations which contain the same basic feature, for instance, crowds of various sizes, may be used. They will be ranked in order from the least anxiety-provoking to the most. It is important that the first member of a hierarchy evokes only a very low level of anxiety. The items in a hierarchy can be very specific, for example, the sight of a dead dog 50 yards away. Numerical parameters are frequently used in hierarchies; for instance, for a social phobia the stimuli of being in the room with one person, two people, three people, and so on, might be items in the same hierarchy.

COUNTERPOSING RELAXATION WITH ANXIETY-EVOKING STIMULI. This is the final and clinically effective step. The subject is told to relax and from then on is asked to report his subjective anxiety level at intervals. The therapist then asks him or her to imagine some neutral scenes, prior to imagining items from the hierarchies. Each time a scene is imagined, the subject indicates when the image is clearly formed and the therapist then says "stop the scene" 5 to 7 sec later. Immediately after termination of the image the subject reports how much it disturbed him on the subjective anxiety scale.

Using these methods the therapist works up through a hierarchy (or several hierarchies concurrently), presenting each item several times. According to Wolpe, the number of presentations required to reduce the anxiety-evoking properties of an item increases monotonically as the hierarchy is ascended. Difficulties with therapy can occur if the subject cannot relax or has difficulty imagining the situations. Relaxation problems can sometimes be overcome by using anxiolytic drugs, and imagery problems may be dealt with by using real-life situations.

Desensitization has been widely used, particularly for phobias, and with great success. After reviewing the literature, Paul (1969) concludes ". . . desensitization is the first psychotherapeutic procedure in history to withstand rigorous evaluation" (p. 146). Many types of phobias and fears have been treated, but particularly those involving concrete phobic stimuli, such as snakes, rats, heights, and enclosures. Experimental studies and clinical trials with desensitization have shown that it can work without the origin of the phobia being established; that symptom substitution does not occur; that relaxation is not effective by itself; and that it can be automated so that no relationship with the therapist is established (Rachman, 1971).

Why does this rather esoteric procedure so effectively reduce anxiety? Wolpe (1958, 1973) suggests that *counter-conditioning through reciprocal inhibition* is involved. The idea is that the anxiety-provoking stimuli are paired with another response, relaxation, and that consequently anxiety is inhibited and on subsequent occasions the same stimuli elicit less anxiety. Wolpe treats anxiety as a high level of autonomic activity combined with neuromuscular tension. The e both can be inhibited by muscular relaxation. As anxiolytic drugs that affect only the central nervous system (rather than muscular activity) are effective in desensitization (Lang, 1969), it may be that the inhibition of anxiety occurs at a central rather than peripheral level. An alternative theoretical account of desensitization is that the procedures of relaxation and graded presentation of stimulus hierarchies allow the subject to be exposed to phobic stimuli and the anxiety evoked by them to be extinguished. Extinction of anxiety does not normally occur because the subject avoids the stimuli.

There have been some reports of behavior therapy treatments for phobias that are even more effective than systematic desensitization. Bandura, Blanchard and Ritter (1969) carried out a study involving 48 adults with snake phobias to compare the effects of various behavioral treatments. The major response measure was a behavioral test of snake-avoidance consisting of a graded series of 29 performance tasks, these ranged from approaching the snake in a glass case up to allowing it to crawl in their laps while keeping their hands passively at their sides.

After snake avoidance assessment the subjects were assigned to one of four treatments.

1. Systematic desensitization.
2. Symbolic modeling. They observed a 35 min film showing people engaging in progressively more threatening interactions with a snake.

3. Graduated live modeling and guided participation. After watching the experimenter handle the snake, the subjects were encouraged to gradually do the same both with the experimenter's help and then by themselves.
4. Control. No treatment given.

Treatments were given twice a week until subjects reached a criterion of snake-tolerance, or for a maximum of $5\frac{1}{4}$ hours. Systematic desensitization tended to take longer than the other treatments.

Once treatment was concluded the behavioral test of snake-avoidance was readministered. The results are shown in Figure 25.3. Live modeling with guided participation clearly had the greatest effect (note that maximum score possible was 29), while the other treatments produced smaller improvements. Other measures of fear and attitudes showed a similar pattern.

On this evidence, live modeling with guided participation is an extremely effective fear-reducing procedure. This is an important finding, particularly because it involves only a simple restructuring of a natural instructional situation.

FIGURE 25.3.
Mean number of approach responses performed by subjects before and after receiving their respective treatments (Bandura, Blanchard, and Ritter, 1969).

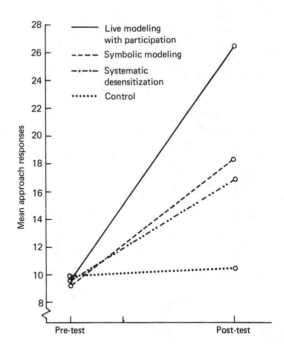

25.3

Depression

Depression is a frequent and debilitating behavior disorder which almost everyone suffers at some time. It is, however, hard to describe behaviorally. Perhaps for this reason a plethora of conflicting diagnostic categories have been devised, treatments are few and poorly understood, and so depression has evaded experimental analysis almost entirely. Recently, however, research workers have devised two behavioral paradigms in animals that parallel features of depression. These are *helplessness training*, and *activity-cycle disruption*.

In a series of studies on traumatic avoidance training in dogs Maier, Seligman, and Solomon (1969) found that exposure to inescapable and highly aversive electric shocks greatly interfered with subsequent avoidance in a shuttlebox. Whereas naive dogs jump around vigorously when shocked in the shuttlebox and soon make the avoidance response, pre-shocked dogs rapidly stop running around and passively take the shock. Maier, Seligman and Solomon called this behavior "learned helplessness" and attributed it to a distinctive learning process. On their account the dogs learn in the first phase that no response produces shock-offset, and thus "not-responding" is conditioned. This "not responding" then persists later when the avoidance contingency is introduced. The magnitude of the effect is considerable, as can be seen in Figure 25.4. This summarizes data from 117 dogs, 82 given

FIGURE 25.4. Median latencies of avoidance responses for groups of dogs that were naive or given prior inescapable shock. A latency of 60 sec was an arbitrary maximum, representing a failure to respond (Maier, Seligman, and Solomon, 1969).

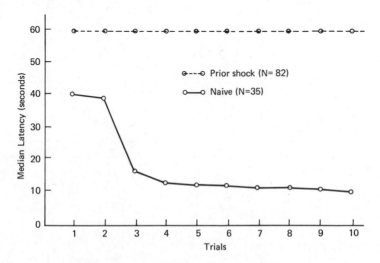

inescapable shock prior to avoidance training. Shock terminated automatically after 60 sec. After 10 trials, the median performance of the prior-shock dogs is still failure to respond within 60 sec. In contrast to this, the naive dogs appear to reach an asymptotic median latency of 10 sec within 5 trials.

Seligman (1975) argues that learned helplessness parallels features of human depression, and that depressed individuals have several behavior patterns in common with experimentally helpless animals. These include lowered initiation of operant behavior, difficulty in learning that responses have outcomes, lowered aggression, loss of appetite, and characteristic physiological changes. Support for these views includes experimental studies with humans showing that exposure to inescapable noise or depression interferes with problem-solving performance in a way that exposure to equivalent escapable noise does not (Miller and Seligman, 1975).

Seligman's hypothesis is important because it suggests that we may be able to use learned helplessness as an *animal analog* of depression, and thus be able to discover parameters of depression by experimental studies of helplessness. Most existing treatments of depression are pharmacological, and it has already been shown that helplessness and depression have similar biochemical correlates. Studies of helplessness may be able to suggest new behavioral treatments. Indeed, Seligman (1975) has shown that forced exposure to the reinforcing consequences of responding is effective in overcoming helplessness in dogs, and he reports a parallel study with human depressives. Depressed individuals were persuaded to engage in verbal tasks of increasing difficulty and were praised for successful completion of each task. Within an hour all 24 depressed subjects had graduated to making an impromptu speech, a very rare activity during depression, and 19 out of 24 showed a large self-rated elevation in mood.

A completely different approach to the behavioral analysis of depression was taken by Baltzer and Weiskrantz (1975). They noted that clinical depression is often associated with disturbances of sleep patterns and other diurnal rhythms. Clinically it is not possible to determine the relationship between two behaviors observed to occur together. Are sleep disruption and depression aspects of one process, or is sleep disruption an unimportant "side-effect" of depression? Their strategy was to experimentally disturb the diurnal pattern of activity (and hence sleep) in rats and to measure the effects of known anti-depressant drugs and other behaviorally active drugs on the course of activity pattern disruption. If anti-depressant drugs minimize the disruption of the activity pattern, it would suggest that depression and sleep disturbance are importantly related.

Rats were maintained in activity cages on a 12-hr light, 12-hr dark schedule. The behavior measured was simply the amount of activity in the light period, L, and the amount of activity in the dark period, D. From this the "periodicity" of their activity was calculated as the proportion of activity in the light: $L/L + D$. Rats are more active during the dark and values of

L/L+ D were typically around 0.15. Following a number of days on this schedule, the light-dark cycle was reversed by extending one dark period to 24 hrs and then returning to 12 hr light and dark period. This resulted in a temporary increase in L/L+ D which gradually dissipated. The time course of this effect is shown in Figure 25.5. The behavioral measure is the relative change in L/L+ D, calculated as

$$\frac{(L/L+D)_{\text{postreversal}} - (L/L+D)_{\text{prereversal}}}{(L/L+D)_{\text{prereversal}}}$$

It is shown as a percentage in Figure 25.5, which presents data for a group of 7 rats not given a drug but injected with inactive saline (this is a routine control procedure in pharmacological experiments), and for two other groups given daily injections of antidepressant drugs. The saline group showed a very large change initially and a persistent disruption lasting until around Day 13 after light-dark reversal.

Baltzer and Weiskrantz tested rats in this procedure with 3 antidepressant drugs (imipramine, maprotiline, pargyline), 3 anxiolytic drugs (chlordiazepoxide, chlorpromazine, reserpine), and one stimulant (*d*-amphetamine). Only *d*-amphetamine affected L/L+ D prior to reversal, reducing the proportion of activity in the light, but the data of interest were the measures of relative change in L/L+ D following reversal. On this measure, all the groups given antidepressant drugs showed less disruption than the saline controls, while the other drugged groups did not differ significantly from the controls. These

FIGURE 25.5. Disruption in proportion of activity in light period (L/L+D) following reversal of light-dark cycle for a control group of rats (saline) and two groups given daily doses of anti-depressants (Imipramine and Pargyline) (Baltzer and Weiskrantz, 1975).

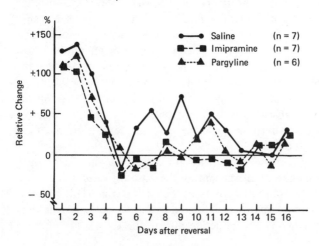

calculations were based on Days 5 to 16 postreversal. The nature of the difference is illustrated for the two antidepressant groups shown in Figure 25.5.

These results are interesting because they suggest the possibility that antidepressant drugs have their effects by treating disrupted diurnal rhythms. A more conservative suggestion is that sleep disruption and depressed behavior are intimately related and depend on the same environmental events. The Baltzer and Weiskrantz technique will not only prove useful in testing drugs for anti-depressant properties but may also be used to shed further light on variables controlling depression.

25.4
Sexual Dysfunctions

Miller and Haney (1976) define sexual dysfunction as "a notably diminished or unsatisfying response in the presence of appropriate sexual stimuli." In clinical work, dysfunctions are often defined in terms of dissatisfied couples.

In men, sexual dysfunctions are usually classified into erectile impotence, and either premature or retarded ejaculation. In women, dysfunctions take the form of orgasmic problems, low sexual tension, and vaginismus (Masters and Johnson, 1970; Kaplan, 1974).

Because sexuality is such a complex phenomenon, the precise causation of the various dysfunctions has proven difficult to isolate. Wolpe (1958) conceptualized sexual problems in terms of an incompatibility between anxiety and sexual arousal. He dealt with it by *in vivo* systematic desensitization (extinction) of the anxiety, in conjunction with a program of graded homework assignments which amounted to progressive shaping of appropriate sexual responses.

The most significant and probably still most influential work in the area of sex therapy remains that of Masters and Johnson (1970). Their research included large samples and long-term follow-ups. To date most successful behavioral treatments are variations on their theme. Masters and Johnson emphasized "spectatoring," or obsessively watching one's performance in order to see how well one is doing. In their therapy, couples were always treated together by two therapists, one male and one female. Where a partner was unavailable "surrogate partners" were provided. At round table discussions, an exhaustive sexual and medical history was taken. The medical model was discouraged so that clients would not view themselves as abnormal. The role of spectatoring was discussed. In order to reduce performance anxiety, subjects were asked to refrain from actual coitus.

The first behavioral step of therapy was *sensate focus 1*, where partners caressed each other non-genitally and gave each other feedback regarding pleasure. The second step was termed *sensate focus 2*, which included genital caressing. The key idea in sensate focusing, both genital and nongenital, is to direct time and attention to the complex *act* of love making, and give the couple permission to enjoy, expand, and elaborate the various behavioral components of the sexual chain of behavior, of which orgasm is only the final consumatory response.

The work of Lobitz and LoPicollo (1972) and Kaplan (1974) directly complements and builds on that of Masters and Johnson. These workers also treat sexual dysfunctions as learned phenomena maintained by anxiety and a nonreinforcing environment. In addition, they emphasize the lack of skills, knowledge, or communication between partners as contributing factors. In some of their work, motivation has been maintained by the drawing up of a financial contract. Data regarding sexual activity is recorded daily. They encourage fantasy to enhance arousal to the partner, and to take attention away from performance. Many of their programs have included masturbation training, including the use of vibrators for women. Similar techniques were used by Hartman and Fithian (1972) who also showed their clients films from which they could model sexual behaviors.

An "anything goes" approach to sex therapy appears indicative of current trends. As the media increasingly publicizes sexuality, and as the womens' movement becomes more vocal, permissible therapeutic options change. At some point, however, theory and practice must merge if we are to fully understand and deal with all the complexities of sexual function and dysfunction in human beings.

25.5
Alcoholism

Alcoholism is arguably our most serious social problem, but until recently very little was known of its causes. Traditionally, a variety of "neurotic personality disorders" have been proposed to explain alcoholism. These include inferiority complexes, latent homosexuality and emotional immaturity. However, surveys (Syme, 1957) have failed to find any substantial personality differences between alcoholic and nonalcoholic groups. It is therefore reasonable to assume that there are environmental conditions that can establish and maintain excessive drinking in any individual.

Bandura (1969) points out that cultural influences produce great variations in drinking habits and can override any other factors. For example, it is sometimes assumed that members of minority groups under stress will tend to drink, but Jews have a very low rate of alcoholism despite their long history of persecution. This is because there is a very narrow range of stimulus conditions under which drinking is sanctioned in the Jewish culture.

More specific influences can be seen within families and peer groups.

Although it is possible that the "transmission" of heavy drinking from parent to child has a genetic basis, it is certain that drinking patterns are modeled within families and peer groups. Additionally, many subcultures generously reinforce excessive drinking. This support is probably essential if an adolescent is to continue to drink heavily despite the aversive after-effects of alcohol.

Once heavy drinking is established other contingencies operate. Metabolic changes take place in the body such that abstinence from alcohol produces *withdrawal symptoms* which are extremely aversive. Once this state of pharmacological addiction is reached a great deal of drinking must occur simply to avoid withdrawal symptoms.

Apart from its direct effects, the social and side effects of alcoholism are disastrous. The alcoholic is frequently reduced to destitution, losing his family, his friends, and his job. Malnutrition is also common because alcoholics tend not to eat. Improvement in these various aspects of life are among the therapeutic objectives in the treatment of alcoholism. Successful treatments for alcoholism take three forms, two of them behavioral and one pharmacological.

The first successful behavioral technique used was *aversion therapy*. This generally involves pairing stimuli associated with drink with aversive events such as nausea. These studies, which generally conform to a classical conditioning paradigm, produce a 50 to 60 per cent nondrinking rate one year after treatment. This is good relative to the success rate of psychotherapeutic treatments and can be improved by "booster" sessions. However, aversion therapy has several drawbacks. Patients may become averse to the whole situation and fail to attend for treatment, aversion may develop only to those drinks and stimuli used in therapy, and ethical problems are raised by the repeated administration of aversive events.

Antabuse and disulfiram drugs can be administered. These drugs suppress drinking because they interact with ingested alcohol to produce violent illness. Their use produces a similar success rate to aversion therapy. As drugs are comparatively cheap and easy to administer, this might seem like the final answer to the problem, but there are disadvantages. The drugs can have severe side-effects which may require the subject to stop treatment. The subject may also stop for the obvious reason that they make drinking highly aversive. We can conceptualize the situation as one of *discriminative punishment*. When the drug is taken (S^D) drinking is punished, but when it is not taken this contingency is removed (S^Δ). On this analysis it is not surprising that alcoholics taking the drug tend to stop taking it from time to time and go on "drinking binges" (Bandura, 1969). The drug does not solve the psychological problem of reducing the reinforcing value of drink.

The third and most exciting approach to treatment employs operant conditioning and the management of environmental contingencies. Several programs have attempted to drastically modify the vocational, marital and social life of alcoholics so that reinforcement for abstinence is increased, and to maximize the opportunities for behavior incompatible with drinking. In a study of this type, Hunt and Azrin (1973) obtained not only sustained reductions in drinking in a group of alcoholics, but also reductions in unemployment, institutionalization, and the amount of time spent away from home.

Contingency management systems resembling token economies have been organized within hospital clinics. Bigelow, Cohen, Liebson and Faillace (1972) allowed alcoholics in the clinic access to various privileges provided they did not drink more than a specified amount each day. The residents were able to remain within the set limit 90 per cent of the time. This suggests, contrary to popular belief, that alcoholics can learn to control their own drinking. Sobell and Sobell (1973) confirmed this finding in a study where shaping alcoholics to reduce their drinking rate formed one part of a complex behavior modification package that produced excellent results.

The results of these programs seem very encouraging when set against the dismal prospects for alcoholics in most medical or psychiatric treatments. As in other areas of behavior modification, the people directly involved in contact with the patient are the most important agents of behavioral change. We should note in passing that where a recovery from alcoholism is attempted while the patient remains in the community, the costs can be considerable. Time and money are inevitably required for the all-embracing program of visits, contacts with relatives, and other forms of follow-up required after the actual treatment. It is not surprising that expense is incurred, however, because the therapist is attempting to restructure the whole environment of the alcoholic.

25.6
Self-Control

We frequently use the term "self-control" to describe our own behavior or that of others. One is said to require self-control to give up smoking, or overeating, or to study in the face of alternative attractions. However, the term seems to have mentalistic connotations that we have rejected throughout this book. Can self-control be given meaning in behavioral terms?

Rachlin and Green (1972) performed an ingenious experiment with pigeons that showed apparent self-control in these lowly organisms. Hungry birds were placed on a two-key concurrent chain procedure (see Section 17.4). In the first component both keys were lit with white light and responding on either key was reinforced on an FR 15 schedule with access to a second component. If the ratio was completed on the left key, the pigeon was given 10 sec blackout followed by a choice between a red key and a green key. A peck at the red key was immediately followed by 2 sec access to food, while a peck at the green key produced by 4 sec of blackout followed by 4 sec access to food. If the ratio was completed on the right key in the first component instead, only the green key was illuminated in the second component after the 10 sec blackout. Again a peck on this produced 4 sec blackout followed by 4 sec food. Overall, this schedule involved an initial choice between a situation where 4 sec food will be available in 14 sec, and a situation where 2 sec food will be available after 12 sec or 4 sec food after 14 sec. In the latter case a second choice is made after 10 sec between the two alternatives.

The pigeons completed the ratio on the right key on 65 per cent of trials. That is, they usually selected the component with the guaranteed *longer* delay of reinforcement (14 sec) leading to greater (4 sec) reinforcement. When they did select the other component, however, they always selected the smaller immediate reinforcement when the red and green keys were presented. Rachlin and Green argue that this represents the pigeon "making a commitment" in the first component that results in eventual greater reinforcement. When the pigeon fails to make the commitment and responds on the left key, it subsequently chooses the immediate and smaller reinforcement. Arguably, the pigeon shows self-control when it makes the commitment and opts for the longer delay of reinforcement.

In this experiment the deferred reinforcement exerted greater control over the pigeon's behavior that the more immediate reinforcement. No reference to the pigeon's "mental power" is necessary. Similarly, the situations where we invoke "self-control" are those where behavior has both immediate and deferred consequences. Overeating may be immediately reinforcing, while fasting will produce long-term improvements in health and social approval. It is easier to go to a party than stay home and study, but the latter will be reinforced by good performance in the end-of-year examinations.

A variety of self-control techniques are finding increasing use in behavior therapy. These typically involve *self-monitoring* and *control of discriminative stimuli*. In the studying example, the student might record the amount of time he spends studying each day on a chart above his desk, thus monitoring his own behavior and using it as a discriminative stimulus that may maintain it. He may also remove the record player and other distractions from the room as these are discriminative stimuli that set the occasion for other activities.

An effective behavioral package for the treatment of obesity was designed by Stuart (1971). It included several self-control features which are shown in Table 25.1. Cue elimination and cue suppression are instances of control of discriminative stimuli, while several self-monitoring activities are included in the cue strengthening section. The Table also includes reinforcing consequences arranged by the therapist and others. Stuart's results for two groups of overweight women are shown in Figure 25.6. Initially, one group (Treatment) were given the procedure in Table 25.1 plus diet and exercise plans. The other group ("self-control") were given diet and exercise plans and asked to practice "self-control" of eating. Ironically this latter group showed no weight loss at all until they were transferred to the treatment

TABLE 25.1. Sample procedures used to strengthen appropriate eating and to weaken inappropriate eating (Stuart, 1971).

Cue elimination	*Cue suppression*	*Cue strengthening*
1. Eat in one room only 2. Do nothing while eating 3. Make available proper foods only: (a) shop from a list; (b) shop only after full meal 4. Clear dishes directly into garbage 5. Allow children to take own sweets	1. Have company while eating 2. Prepare and serve small quantities only 3. Eat slowly 4. Save one item from meal to eat later 5. If high-calorie foods are eaten, they must require preparation	1. Keep food, weight chart 2. Use food exchange diet 3. Allow extra money for proper foods 4. Experiment with attractive preparation of diet foods 5. Keep available pictures of desired clothes, list of desirable activities
Reduced strength of undesirable responses		*Increase strength of desirable responses*
1. Swallow food already in mouth before adding more 2. Eat with utensils 3. Drink as little as possible during meals		1. Introduce planned delays during meal 2. Chew foods slowly, thoroughly 3. Concentrate on what is being eaten
Provide decelerating consequences		*Provide accelerating consequences*
1. Develop means for display of caloric value of food eaten daily, weight changes 2. Arrange to have deviations from program ignored by others except for professionals 3. Arrange to have overeater re-read program when items have not been followed and to write techniques which might have succeeded		1. Develop means for display of caloric value of food eaten daily, weight changes 2. Develop means of providing social feedback for all success by: (a) family; (b) friends; (c) co-workers; (d) other weight losers; and/or (e) professionals 3. Program material and/or social consequences to follow: (a) the attainment of weight loss subgoals; (b) completion of specific daily behavioral control objectives

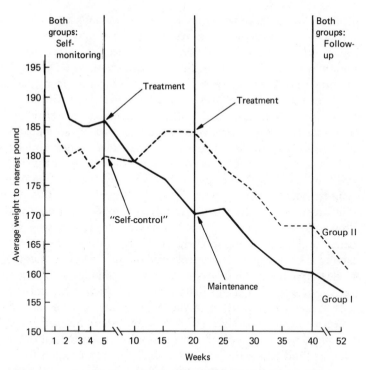

FIGURE 25.6. Average weight of two groups of women before and during use of Stuart's package of measures (Stuart, 1971).

condition. Clearly instructions to exercise self-control have no effect by themselves. When combined with Stuart's package of techniques, however, a considerable weight loss can be achieved.

25.7
Ethics

The behavior therapist is often caricatured as a manipulator who tortures, bribes, or brainwashes helpless victims to obtain the behavior he or she wants. The foregoing sections should demonstrate that such a judgment is unrepresentative, for it does not fit with the facts about the practice of behavior therapy. Rather it depends on two assumptions about behavior therapy and other forms of treatment. These are, first, that behavior therapy is an attempt to influence behavior; and second, that it is necessarily a coercive method. We believe that the first of these is true, but is common to all psychiatric and psychotherapeutic techniques, while the second is false.

"Dealing with disordered behavior," "curing mental illness," "facilitating self-actualization," and "treating abnormal behavior" are all descriptions of attempts to influence behavior. Evidently, working to achieve change is not distinctive to behavior therapy. What is perhaps distinctive is the *overt specification of behavioral objectives*. All therapists have objectives, although they may be unable or unwilling to state them. The client of the behavior therapist, however, enjoys a measure of protection from the imposition of unstated therapist objectives because it is the client who normally specifies them. Psychoanalysts, on the other hand, have been criticised for *covertly* requiring the client's behavior to change towards societal norms (Brown, 1973). Similarly, the pursuit of a "cure" by a medically-oriented therapist may involve unstated expectations of socially conventional behavior.

Many behavior therapy techniques involve the implementation of reinforcement contingencies by the therapist for the client. Because reinforcement contingencies involve events traditionally described as "rewards" and "punishments," behavior therapy is seen as coercive. In behavioral terms coercion corresponds roughly to one person (or agency) having a large degree of control over the reinforcers of another individual, while that individual has no countercontrol (Skinner, 1972) over this powerful person or agency. On this definition, the behavior therapist who contracts with a client to treat him in the hope of attaining a specified behavioral objective is not coercive. He does establish reinforcement contingencies, certainly, but only because the client allows him to. If primary reinforcers such as food and water are to be used, the client makes these available by attending therapy in an appropriate state of deprivation. If the client finds the procedures more aversive than he or she will tolerate, the client is free to drop out, which may have the additional consequence of terminating payments to the therapist. In various ways the client exerts *countercontrol*; his or her behavior provides reinforcing consequences for the therapist. Cooperation, rather than coercion, characterizes such a relationship.

As soon as countercontrol is removed, ethical issues become much more problematical. If a token economy is introduced, do institutionalized patients have any choice about their participation? Furthermore, are the behavioral objectives selected for the patients' benefit, or to further the smooth running of the institution? Who specifies these objectives anyway? These are real problems that could only be answered by detailed consideration of particular cases. *However the problems do not arise from the use of behavior therapy*. Rather, they arise from placing individuals in situations where they lack countercontrol. Szasz (1961, 1977) has brilliantly illustrated the plight of individuals classified as mentally sick. Because both the behavior and the wishes of the "mentally sick" are said to be affected by their "illness," their wishes have often been blatantly disregarded while a therapist assumes absolute power. Once medical and psychiatric authorities adopted this medical model their clients were placed in a position to be coerced and oppressed. On an optimistic view, the introduction of behavior therapy may improve the possibilities of countercontrol by making the control processes more visible to patients and staff. On a pessimistic view, the situation may worsen as behavior therapy is used for the more effective coercion of patients. Like all scientific techniques and principles, whether we use behavior therapy for good or evil depends on our values.

When ethical issues have been raised, it has often been objected that behavior therapy is a set of techniques and not an ethical system (for example, Bandura, 1969). However, while it is true that behavior therapy techniques are in themselves value-free, ethical issues will invariably come up in the practice of therapy. This is an inevitable consequence of attempting to change behavior, rather than of the particular methods involved. The primary ethical questions are: who desires the behavior to be changed, and why do they wish it to be changed? The humanistic answers to these questions are: the individual with the behavior; and, because it causes personal distress. The authors regard it as unethical to modify the behavior of individuals purely to conform with social conventions. Complex ethical questions do arise, however, when the client's wishes conflict with the therapist's personal views. In this case the therapist may still be able to act as his or her client's consultant or servant in employing behavioral techniques in the service of the client's aims. When the therapist cannot in good conscience do this, his or her only realistic option is to decline to work with the client.

25.8

Prospects

Initial successes in behavior therapies were greeted enthusiastically. Here at last, it was thought, were scientifically-based techniques, and ones that actually work. Against a background of comparatively ineffective therapies based on a diversity of conflicting theories, this enthusiasm was not surprising. However, the early successes led to overambitious claims. These in turn led to a reaction, and claims that behavior therapy was no more scientific nor any more effective than traditional forms of therapy.

Now that sufficient time has elapsed to gain a perspective on behavior therapy, it is possible to see its contributions and its limitations. The existing techniques certainly do not provide "instant cures" for all forms of abnormal behavior, but they have been able to make a significant impact on a considerable range of problems. The label "scientific" does not guarantee success to a form of therapy; it does, however, direct investigators towards *evaluating* and *improving* therapeutic techniques in the light of results. In behavior therapy a technique is never justified because a theory states that it is "correct," for it is generally recognized that a technique can only be judged by its results.

Behavior therapy tends to take the form of a package of measures, all relating to similar objectives. This strategy is adopted for the good reason that it produces clear changes in behavior. It has, however, postponed discovery of crucial components of therapeutic techniques. Systematic desensitization, for example, has been extensively researched, but its "active ingredients" have proved difficult to isolate. This is inconvenient for our theoretical understanding of behavior therapy, but we may be taking too simplistic a view. Just as behavior is generated and maintained by a complex of contingencies in the natural environment, it may be only complex changes in the environment that will reliably produce behavioral change.

There seems little doubt that behavior therapy will continue to grow in sophistication, complexity, and scope. As behavior therapies become more refined we can hope that their results will begin to provide us with information about the behavior principles from which they are derived, thereby nourishing the reciprocity between theory and practice.

References for Chapter 25

Agras, S., Sylvester, D., and Oliveau, D. The epidemiology of common fears and phobias. *Comparative Psychiatry*, 1969, **10**, 151–156.

Atthowe, J. H., and Krasner, L. A preliminary report on the application of contingent reinforcement procedures (token economy) on a "chronic" psychiatric ward. *Journal of Abnormal Psychology*, 1968, **73**, 37–43.

Ayllon, T., and Azrin, N. H. The measurement and reinforcement of behavior of psychotics. *Journal of the Experimental Analysis of Behavior*, 1965, **8**, 357–383.

Baltzer, V., and Weiskrantz, L. Antidepressant agents and reversal of diurnal activity cycles in the rat. *Biological Psychiatry*, 1975, **10**, 199–209.

Bandura, A. *Principles of behavior modification*. New York: Holt, Rinehart & Winston, 1969.

Bandura, A., Blanchard, E., and Ritter, B. The relative efficacy of desensitization and modeling approaches for induced behavioral, affective, and attitudinal change. *Journal of Personality and Social Psychology*, 1969, **13**, 173–199.

Bigelow, G., Cohen, M., Liebson, I., and Faillance, L. Abstinence or moderation? Choice by alcoholics. *Behaviour Research and Therapy*, 1972, **10**, 209–214.

Brown, P. (Ed.) *Radical psychology*. London: Tavistock, 1973.

Hartman, W. E., and Fithian, M. A. *Treatment of sexual dysfunction*. California: Center for Marital and Sexual Studies, 1972.

Hunt, G. M., and Azrin, N. H. A community-reinforcement approach to alcholism. *Behaviour Research and Therapy*, 1973, **11**, 91–104.

Jacobson, E. *Progressive relaxation*. Chicago: University of Chicago Press, 1938.

Jersild, A. T., and Holmes, F. B. Methods of overcoming children's fears. *Journal of Psychology*, 1935, **1**, 75–104.

Kaplan, H. *The new sex therapy*, New York: Bruner-Mazel, 1974.

Laing, R. D., and Esterson, A. *Sanity, madness and the family*. London: Tavistock, 1970.

Lang, P. J. The mechanics of desensitization and the laboratory study of human fear. In C. M. Franks (Ed.) *Behavior therapy: Appraisal and status*. New York: McGraw-Hill, 1969.

Lobitz, W. C., and LoPiccolo, J. New methods in the behavioral treatment of sexual dysfunction. *Journal of Behavior Therapy and Experimental Psychiatry*, 1972, **3**, 256–272.

Maier, S. F., Seligman, M. E. P., and Solomon, R. L. Pavlovian fear conditioning and learned helplessness: Effects on escape and avoidance behavior of (a) the CS-US contingency and (b) the independence of the US and voluntary responding. In B. A. Campbell and R. M. Church (Eds.) *Punishment and aversive behavior.* New York: Appleton-Century-Crofts, 1969.

Masters, W. H., and Johnson, V. *Human sexual inadequacy.* Boston: Little Brown, 1970.

Miller, H. L., and Haney, J. R. Behavior and traditional therapy applied to pedophiliac exhibitionism: a case study. *Psychological Reports*, 1976, **3**, 1119–1124.

Miller, W., and Seligman, M. E. P. Depression and learned helplessness in man. *Journal of Abnormal Psychology*, 1975, **84**, 228–238.

Paul, G. L. Outcome of systematic desensitization. II: Controlled investigations of individual treatment, technique variations, and current status. In C. M. Franks (Ed.) *Behavior therapy: Appraisal and status.* New York: McGraw-Hill, 1969.

Premack, D. Reinforcement theory. In D. Levine (Ed.) *Nebraska symposium on motivation.* Lincoln, Neb: University of Nebraska Press, 1965.

Rachlin, H., and Green, L. Commitment, choice, and self-control. *Journal of the Experimental Analysis of Behavior*, 1972, **17**, 15–22.

Rachman, S. *The effects of psychotherapy.* Oxford: Pergamon, 1971.

Rachman, S. The conditioning theory of fear-acquisition: A critical examination. *Behaviour Research and Therapy*, 1977, **15**, 375–387.

Seligman, M. E. P. Phobias and preparedness. *Behavior Therapy*, 1971, **2**, 307–320.

Seligman, M. E. P. *Helplessness: On depression, development, and death.* San Francisco: Freeman, 1975.

Skinner, B. F. *Beyond freedom and dignity.* New York: Bantam, 1972.

Sobell, M. B., and Sobell, L. C. Alcoholics treated by individualized behavior therapy: One year treatment outcome. *Behaviour Research and Therapy*, 1973, **11**, 599–618.

Stuart, R. B. A three-dimensional program for the treatment of obesity. *Behaviour Research and Therapy*, 1971, **9**, 177–186.

Syme, L. Personality characteristics and the alcoholic. A critique of current studies. *Quaterly Journal of Studies on Alcohol*, 1957, **18**, 288–301.

Szasz, T. S. *The myth of mental illness: Foundations of a theory of personal conduct.* New York: Hoeber-Harper, 1961.

Szasz, T. S. *The theology of medicine.* New York: Harper & Row, 1977.

Wolpe, J. *Psychotherapy by reciprocal inhibition.* Palo Alto, Calif: Stanford University Press, 1958.

Wolpe, J. *The practice of behavior therapy.* Second Edition. New York: Pergamon, 1973.

BIBLIOGRAPHY

Agras, S., Sylvester, D., and Oliveau, D. The epidemiology of common fears and phobias, *Comparative Psychiatry*, 1969, **10**, 151–156.

Alexander, R. N., and Apfel, C. H. Altering schedules of reinforcement for improved classroom behavior. *Exceptional Children*, 1976, **43**, 97–99.

Allison, J., and Timberlake, W. Instrumental and contingent saccharin licking in rats: Response deprivation and reinforcement. *Learning and Motivation*, 1974, **5**, 231–247.

Anger, D. A. *Two-factor theory and the avoidance puzzles.* (in press).

Anliker, J., and Mayer, J. Operant conditioning technique for studying feeding patterns in normal and obese mice. *Journal of Applied Physiology*, 1956, **8**, 667–670.

Anrep, G. V. Pitch discrimination in the dog. *Journal of Physiology*, 1920, **53**, 367–385.

Antonitis, J. J. Response variability in the white rat during conditioning, extinction and reconditioning. *Journal of Experimental Psychology*, 1951, **42**, 273–281.

Atthowe, J. M., and Krasner, L. A preliminary report on the application of contingent reinforcement procedure (token economy) on a "chronic" psychiatric ward. *Journal of Abnormal Psychology*, 1968, **73**, 37–43.

Axelrod, S. *Behavior modification for the classroom teacher*. New York: McGraw-Hill, 1977.

Ayllon, T., and Azrin, N. H. The measurement and reinforcement of behavior of psychotics. *Journal of the Experimental Analysis of Behavior*, 1965, **8**, 357–383.

Ayllon, T., and Azrin, N. H. *The token economy*. New York: Appleton-Century-Crofts, 1968.

Azrin, N. H., and Holz, W. C. Punishment. In W. K. Honig (Ed.) *Operant behavior: areas of research and application*, New York: Appleton-Century-Crofts, 1966.

Azrin, N. H., Hutchinson, R. R., and Hake, D. F. Extinction-induced aggression. *Journal of the Experimental Analysis of Behavior*, 1966, **9**, 191–204.

Badia, P., Culbertson, S., and Harsh, J. Choice of longer or stronger signalled shocks over shorter or weaker unsignalled shock. *Journal of the Experimental Analysis of Behavior*, 1973, **19**, 25–32.

Baer, D., Peterson, R., and Sherman, J. The development of imitation by reinforcing behavioral similarity to a model. *Journal of the Experimental Analysis of Behavior*, 1967, **10**, 405–416.

Baldock, M. D. Trial and intertrial interval durations in the acquisition of autoshaped key pecking. Paper read to Eastern Psychological Association, Philadelphia, 1974.

Baltzer, V., and Weiskrantz, L. Antidepressant agents and reversal of diurnal activity cycles in the rat. *Biological Psychiatry*, 1975, **10**, 199–209.

Bandura, A. Influence of model's reinforcement contingencies on the acquisition of imitative responses. *Journal of Personality and Social Psychology*, 1965, **1**, 589–595.

Bandura, A. *Principles of behavior modification*. New York: Holt, Rinehart and Winston, 1969.

Bandura, A., and Barab, P. Processes governing disinhibitory effects through symbolic modeling. *Journal of Abnormal Psychology*, 1973, **82**, 1–9.

Bandura, A., Blanchard, E., and Ritter, B. The relative efficacy of desensitization and modeling approaches for induced, behavioral, affective and attitudinal change. *Journal of Personality and Social Psychology*, 1969, **13**, 173–199.

Bandura, A., and Huston, A. C. Identification as a process of incidental learning. *Journal of Abnormal and Social Psychology*, 1961, **63**, 311–318.

Bandura, A., and Menlove, F. L. Factors determining vicarious extinction of avoidance behavior through symbolic modelling. *Journal of Personality and Social Psychology*, 1968, **8**, 99–108.

Barry, J. J., and Harrison, J. M. Relations between stimulus intensity and strength of escape responding. *Psychological Reports*, 1957, **3**, 3–8.

Bayley, N. On the growth of intelligence. *American Psychologist*, 1955, **10**, 805–818.

Bigelow, G., Cohen, M., Liebson, I., and Faillace, L. Abstinence or moderation? Choice by alcoholics. *Behaviour Research and Therapy*, 1972, **10**, 209–214.

Birch, H. G. The relation of previous experience to insightful problem solving. *Journal of Comparative Psychology*, 1945, **38**, 367–383.

Birch, H. G., and Rabinowitz, H. S. The negative effect of previous experience on productive thinking. *Journal of Experimental Psychology*, 1951, **41**, 121–125.

Blackman, D. E. Conditioned suppression or acceleration as a function of the behavioral baseline. *Journal of the Experimental Analysis of Behavior*, 1968, **11**, 53–61.

Blackman, D. E. *Operant conditioning: An experimental analysis of behaviour.* London: Methuen, 1974.

Blackman, D. E. Conditioned suppression and the effects of classical conditioning on operant behavior. In W. K. Honig and J. E. R. Staddon (Eds.) *Handbook of operant behavior.* Englewood Cliffs, N.J.: Prentice-Hall, 1977.

Blackwood, R. O. *Operant control of behavior.* Akron, Ohio: Exordium Press, 1971.

Blough, D. The shape of some wavelength generalization gradients. *Journal of the Experimental Analysis of Behavior*, 1961, **4**, 31–40.

Blough, D. S. New test for tranquilizers. *Science*, 1958, **127**, 586–587.

Boakes, R. A. Performance on learning to associate a stimulus with positive reinforcement. In H. Davis and H. M. B. Hurwitz (Eds.) *Operant-pavlovian interactions.* Hillsdale, N.J.: Lawrence Erlbaum, 1977.

Bolles, R. C. *The theory of motivation.* New York: Harper & Row, 1967.

Bolles, R. C. Species-specific defense reactions and avoidance learning. *Psychological Review*, 1970, **77**, 32–48.

Boren, J. J., and Sidman, M. A discrimination based upon repeated conditioning and extinction of avoidance behavior. *Journal of Comparative and Physiological Psychology*, 1957, **50**, 18–22.

Boring, E. G. Intelligence as the tests test it. *The New Republic*, 1923, **34**, 35–36.

Boring, E. G. *A history of experimental psychology.* New York: The Century Company, 1929.

Boring, E. G., Langfeld, H. W., and Weld, H. P. *Foundations of psychology.* New York: Wiley, 1948.

Bousfield, W. A. Quantitative indices of the effects of fasting on eating behavior. *Journal of Genetic Psychology*, 1935, **46**, 476–479.

Bradshaw, C. M., Svabadi, E., and Bevan, P. Effects of punishment on human variable-interval performance. *Journal of the Experimental Analysis of Behavior*, 1977, **27**, 275–280.

Branch, M. N., and Gollub, L. R. A. detailed analysis of the effects of d-Amphetamine on behavior under fixed interval schedules. *Journal of the Experimental Analysis of Behavior*, 1974, **21**, 519–539.

Breland, K., and Breland, M. The misbehavior of organisms. *American Psychologist*, 1961, **61**, 681–684.

Broadhurst, P. L. Emotionality and the Yerkes-Dodson law. *Journal of Experimental Psychology*, 1957, **54**, 345–352.

Brogden, W. J., Lipman, E. A., and Culler, E. The role of incentive in conditioning and extinction. *American Journal of Psychology*, 1938, **51**, 109–117.

Brown, P. (Ed.) *Radical psychology.* London: Tavistock, 1973.

Brown, P. L., and Jenkins, H. M. Autoshaping of the pigeon's key peck. *Journal of the Experimental Analysis of Behavior*, 1968, **11**, 1–8.

Bruner, J. S., Goodnow, J. J., and Austin, G. *A study of thinking.* New York: Wiley, 1956.

Bullock, D. H., and Smith, W. C. An effect of repeated conditioning-extinction upon operant strength. *Journal of Experimental Psychology*, 1953, **46**, 349–352.

Campbell, S. L. Lever-holding and behavior sequences in shock-escape. *Journal of Comparative and Physiological Psychology*, 1962, **55**, 1047–1053.

Cannon, W. B. The James-Lange theory of emotions: a critical examination and an alternative theory. *American Journal of Psychology*, 1927, **39**, 106–124.

Cannon, W. B. *The wisdom of the body*. New York: Norton, 1932.

Cannon, W. B., and Washburn, A. L. An explanation of hunger. *American Journal of Psychology*, 1912, **29**, 441–452.

Capehart, J., Viney, W., and Hulicka, I. M. The effect of effort upon extinction. *Journal of Comparative and Physiological Psychology*, 1958, **51**, 505–507.

Catania, A. C. Concurrent operants. In W. K. Honig (Ed.) *Operant behavior: areas of research and application*. New York: Appleton-Century-Crofts, 1966.

Catania, A. C. Reinforcement schedules and psychophysical judgements: A study of some temporal properties of behavior. In W. N. Schoenfeld (Ed.) *The theory of reinforcement schedules*. New York: Appleton-Century-Crofts, 1970.

Catania, A. C., and Reynolds, G. S. A quantitative analysis of the responding maintained by interval schedules of reinforcement. *Journal of the Experimental Analysis of Behavior*, 1968, **11**, 327–383.

Centers, R. A laboratory adaptation of the conversational procedure for the conditioning of verbal operants. *Journal of Abnormal and Social Psychology*, 1963, **67**, 334–339.

Chomsky, N. A review of Skinner's Verbal Behavior. *Language*, 1959, **35**, 26–58.

Cicala, G. A., and Owen, J. W. Warning signal termination and a feedback signal may not serve the same function. *Learning and Motivation*, 1976, **7**, 356–367.

Clark, F. C. The effect of deprivation and frequency of reinforcement on variable interval responding. *Journal of the Experimental Analysis of Behavior*, 1958, **1**, 221–228.

Cohen, I. A note on Herrnstein's equations. *Journal of the Experimental Analysis of Behavior*, 1973, **19**, 529–530.

Conant, J. B. (Ed.) *Harvard case histories in experimental science*. Cambridge: Harvard University Press, 1957.

Cook, A. Habituation of a freshwater snail (*Limnaea stagnalis*). *Animal Behaviour*, 1971, **19**, 463–474.

Cowles, J. T. Food-tokens as incentives for learning by chimpanzees. *Comparative Psychology Monographs*, 1937, **14**, 1–96.

Crocetti, C. P. Drive level and response strength in the bar-pressing apparatus. *Psychological Reports*, 1962, **10**, 563–575.

Cronbach, L. J. *Educational psychology*. New York: Harcourt, Brace Jovanovich, 1963.

Cumming, W. W., and Schoenfeld, W. N. Behavior under extended exposure to a high-value fixed interval reinforcement schedule. *Journal of the Experimental Analysis of Behavior*, 1958, **1**, 245–263.

Darwin, C. R. *The expression of the emotions in man and animals*. London: Murray, 1873.

Davis, H. Response characteristics and control during lever-press escape. In H. Davis and H. M. B. Hurwitz (Eds.) *Operant-pavlovian interactions*. Hillsdale, N.J.: Lawrence Erlbaum, 1977.

Dennis, I., Hampton, J. A., and Lea, S. E. G. New problem in concept formation. *Nature* (London), 1973, **243**, 101–102.

Dennis, W. *Readings in the history of psychology*. New York: Appleton-Century, 1948.

deVilliers, P. A. The law of effect in avoidance: A quantitative relationship between response rate and shock frequency reduction. *Journal of the Experimental Analysis of Behavior*, 1974, **21**, 223–235.

deVilliers, P. A. Choice in concurrent schedules and a quantitative formulation of the law of effect. In W. K. Honig and J. E. R. Staddon (Eds.) *Handbook of operant behavior*. Englewood Cliffs, New Jersey: Prentice-Hall, 1977.

Dews, P. B. Free-operant behavior under conditions of delayed reinforcement. I. CRF-type schedules. *Journal of the Experimental Analysis of Behavior*, 1960, **3**, 221–234.

Dinsmoor, J. A., Matsuoka, Y., and Winograd, E. Barholding as a preparatory response in escape-from-shock training. *Journal of Comparative and Physiological Psychology*, 1958, **51**, 637–639.

Dinsmoor, J. A., and Winograd, E. Shock intensity in variable interval escape schedules. *Journal of the Experimental Analysis of Behavior*, 1958, **1**, 145–148.

Dove, L. D., Rashotte, M. E., and Katz, H. N. Development and maintenance of attack in pigeons during variable-interval reinforcement of key pecking. *Journal of the Experimental Analysis of Behavior*, 1974, **21**, 563–570.

Duda, J. J., and Bolles, R. C. Effects of prior deprivation, current deprivation, and weight loss on the activity of the hungry cat. *Journal of Comparative and Physiological Psychology*, 1963, **56**, 569–571.

Dunham, P. J. Punishment: Method and theory. *Psychological Review*, 1971, **78**, 58–70.

Ebbinghaus, H. *Memory* (Translated by H. A. Ruger and C. E. Bussenius). New York: Teachers College, 1913.

Eckerman, D. A., and Lanson, R. N. Variability of response location for pigeons responding under continuous reinforcement, intermittent reinforcement and extinction. *Journal of the Experimental Analysis of Behavior*, 1969, **12**, 73–80.

Egger, M. D., and Miller, N. E. Secondary reinforcement in rats as a function of information value and reliability of the stimulus. *Journal of Experimental Psychology*, 1962, **64**, 97–104.

Eisenberger, R., Karpman, M., and Trattner, J. What is the necessary and sufficient condition for reinforcement in the contingency situation? *Journal of Experimental Psychology*, 1967, **74**, 342–350.

Estes, W. K. An experimental study of punishment. *Psychological Monographs* 1944, **57**, (Whole No. 263).

Estes, W. K., and Skinner, B. F. Some quantitative properties of anxiety. *Journal of Experimental Psychology*, 1941, **29**, 390–400.

Evans, J. L., Homme, L. E., and Glaser, R. The ruleg system for the construction of programmed verbal learning sequences. *Journal of Educational Research*, 1962, **55**, 513–578.

Falk, J. L. Production of polydipsia in normal rats by an intermittent food schedule. *Science*, 1961, **133**, 195–196.

Falk, J. L. The nature and determinants of adjunctive behavior. *Physiology and Behavior*, 1971, **6**, 577–588.

Fantino, E. Conditioned reinforcement: Choice and information. In W. K. Honig and J. E. R. Staddon (Eds.) *Handbook of operant behavior*. Englewood Cliffs N.J.: Prentice Hall, 1977.

Farmer, J. Properties of behavior under random interval reinforcement schedules. *Journal of the Experimental Analysis of Behavior*, 1963, **6**, 607–616.

Fearing, F. *Reflex action: A study in the history of physiological psychology*. Baltimore: Williams and Wilkins, 1930.

Ferster, C. B., and Skinner, B. F. *Schedules of reinforcement*. New York: Appleton-Century-Crofts, 1957.

Findley, J. D., and Brady, J. V. Facilitation of large ratio performance by use of conditioned reinforcement. *Journal of the Experimental Analysis of Behavior*, 1965, **8**, 125–129.

Fleshler, M., and Hoffman, H. S. A progression for generating variable-interval schedules. *Journal of the Experimental Analysis of Behavior*, 1962, **5**, 529–530.

Frick, F. C. An analysis of an operant discrimination. *Journal of Psychology*, 1948, **26**, 93–123.

Frick, F. S., and Miller, G. A. A statistical description of operant conditioning. *American Journal of Psychology*, 1951, **64**, 20–36.

Frontali, M., and Bignami, G. Stimulus nonequivalences in go/no-go avoidance discriminations: sensory, drive, and response factors, *Animal Learning and Behavior*, 1974, **2**, 153–160.

Gallagher, P. A., Sulzbacher, S. I., and Shores, R. E. A group contingency for classroom management of emotionally disturbed children. Paper presented at the Kansas Council for Exceptional Children, Wichita, 1967.

Gamzu, E., and Williams, D. R. Associative factors underlying the pigeon's key pecking in autoshaping procedures. *Journal of the Experimental Analysis of Behavior*, 1973, **19**, 225–232.

Garcia, J., Green, K. F., and McGowan, B. K. X-ray as an olfactory stimulus. In C. Pfaffman (Ed.), *Taste and olfaction*, Volume 3. New York: Rockefeller University Press, 1969.

Garcia, J., Hankins, W. G., and Rusiniak, K. W. Behavioral regulation of the milieu inteme in man and rat. *Science*, 1975, **185**, 824–831.

Garcia, J., Kimmeldorf, D. J., and Hunt, E. L. The use of ionising radiation as a motivating stimulus. *Psychological Review*, 1961, **68**, 383–395.

Garcia, J., and Koelling, R. A. Relation of cue to consequence in avoidance learning. *Psychonomic Science*, 1964, **4**, 123–124.

Garcia, J., McGowan, B. K., and Green, K. F. Biological constraints on conditioning. In A. H. Black and W. F. Prokasy (Eds.) *Classical conditioning II*. New York: Appleton-Century-Crofts, 1972.

Gardner, E. T., and Lewis, P. Negative reinforcement with shock-frequency increase. *Journal of the Experimental Analysis of Behavior*, 1976, **25**, 3–14.

Gardner, R. A., and Gardner, B. T. Teaching sign language to a chimpanzee. *Science*, 1969, **165**, 664–672.

Garrett, H. *Great experiments in psychology.* New York: Appleton-Century-Crofts, 1951.

Gibson, J. J. *The perception of the visual world.* Cambridge. Mass.: The Riverside Press, 1950.

Gilbert, R. M., and Keehn, J. D. (Eds.) *Drugs, drinking, and aggression.* Toronto: University of Toronto Press, 1972.

Gilbert, T. F. Fundamental dimensional properties of the operant. *Psychological Review,* 1958, **65**, 272–282.

Gilman, A. The relation between blood osmotic pressure, fluid distribution, and voluntary water intake. *American Journal of Physiology,* 1937, **120**, 323–328.

Gladstone, E. W., and Cooley, J. Behavioral similarity as a reinforcer for preschool children. *Journal of the Experimental Analysis of Behavior,* 1975, **23**, 357–368.

Goldiamond, I. Perception, language, and conceptualization rules. In B. Kleinmuntz (Ed.) *Carnegie Institute of Technology annual symposium on cognition.* New York: Wiley, 1966.

Gormezano, I., Schneiderman, N., Deaux, E. B., and Fuentes, I. Nictitating membrane: Classical conditioning and extinction in the albino rabbit. *Science,* 1962, **138**, 33–34.

Grant, D. A., and Norris, E. B. Eyelid conditioning as influenced by the presence of sensitized Beta-responses. *Journal of Experimental Psychology,* 1947, **37**, 423–433.

Gray, J. A. *Elements of a two-process theory of learning.* London: Academic Press, 1975.

Gross, C. G. General activity. In L. Weiskrantz (Ed.) *Behavioral change.* New York: Harper and Row, 1968.

Guilford, J. P. *General psychology.* Princeton: D. Van Nostrand, 1939.

Gustavson, C. R., Garcia, J., Hankins, W. G. and Rusiniak, K. W. Coyote predation control by aversive conditioning. *Science,* 1974, **184**, 581–583.

Guthrie, E. R., and Horton, G. P. *Cats in a puzzle box.* New York: Rinehart, 1946.

Guttman, N. The pigeon and the spectrum and other complexities. *Psychological Reports,* 1956, **2**, 449–460.

Guttman, N., and Kalish, H. I. Discriminability and stimulus generalization. *Journal of Experimental Psychology,* 1956, **51**, 79–88.

Hailman, J. P. Spectral pecking preference in gull chicks. *Journal of Comparative and Physiological Psychology,* 1969, **67**, 465–467.

Hall, G. S., and Hodge, C. F. A sketch of the history of reflex action. *American Journal of Psychology,* 1890, **3**, 71–86; 149–173; 343–363.

Hall, J. F. The relationship between external stimulation, food deprivation, and activity. *Journal of Comparative and Physiological Psychology,* 1956, **49**, 339–341.

Hanson, H. M. Effects of discrimination training on stimulus generalization. *Journal of Experimental Psychology,* 1959, **58**, 321–334.

Harlow, H. F. Studying animal behavior. In T. G. Andrews (Ed.), *Methods of psychology.* New York: Wiley, 1948.

Harlow, H. F. The formation of learning sets. *Psychological Review,* 1949, **56**, 51–65.

Harlow, H. F. Learning set and error factor theory. In S. Koch (Ed.) *Psychology: A study of a science,* Volume 2. New York: McGraw-Hill, 1959.

Harris, M. B., and Hassemer, W. G. Some factors affecting the complexity of children's sentences: the effects of modeling, age, sex and bilingualism. *Journal of Experimental Child Psychology,* 1972, **13**, 447–455.

Hartman, W. E., and Fithian, M. A. *Treatment of sexual dysfunction*, California: Center for Marital and Sexual Studies, 1972.

Hayes, C. *The ape in our house*. New York: Harper and Row, 1951.

Hayes, K. J., and Hayes, C. In G. J. D. Wayne (Ed.), *The non-human primates and human evolution*. Detroit: Detroit University Press, 1955.

Hearst, E. resistance-to-extinction functions in the single organism. *Journal of the Experimental Analysis of Behavior*, 1961, **4**, 133–144.

Hearst, E., Besley, S., and Farthing, G. W. Inhibition and the stimulus control of operant behavior. *Journal of the Experimental Analysis of Behavior*, 1970, **14**, 373–409.

Hearst, E. Pavlovian conditioning and directed movements. In G. M. Bower (Ed.) *The psychology of learning and motivation*, Volume 9. New York: Academic Press, 1975.

Hearst, E., and Jenkins, H. M. *Sign-tracking: The stimulus-reinforcer relation and directed action*. Austin, Tex.: Psychonomic Society, 1974.

Hefferline, R. F., and Keenan, B. Amplitude-induction gradient of a small-scale (covert) operant. *Journal of the Experimental Analysis of Behavior*, 1963, **6**, 307–315.

Hemmes, N. Pigeon's performance under differential reinforcement of low rates schedules depends upon the operant. *Learning and Motivation*, 1975, **6**, 344–357.

Hendry, D. P., and Rasche, R. H. Analysis of a new non-nutritive reinforcer based on thirst. *Journal of Comparative and Physiological Psychology*, 1961, **54**, 477–483.

Herman, L. M., and Arbeit, W. R. Stimulus control and auditory discrimination learning sets in the bottlenose dolphin. *Journal of the Experimental Analysis of Behavior*, 1973, **19**, 379–394.

Herrick, R. M. The successive differentiation of a lever displacement response. *Journal of the Experimental Analysis of Behavior*, 1964, **7**, 211–215.

Herrick, R. M., Myers, J. L., and Korotkin, A. L. Changes in S^D and S^Δ rates during the development of an operant discrimination. *Journal of Comparative and Physiological Psychology*, 1959, **52**, 359–363.

Herrnstein, R. J. Relative and absolute strength of response as a function of frequency of reinforcement. *Journal of the Experimental Analysis of Behavior*, 1961, **4**, 267–272.

Herrnstein, R. J. Method and theory in the study of avoidance. *Psychological Review*, 1969, **76**, 49–69.

Herrnstein, R. J. On the law of effect. *Journal of the Experimental Analysis of Behavior*, 1970, **13**, 243–266.

Herrnstein, R. J. Quantitative hedonism. *Journal of Psychiatric Research*, 1971, **8**, 399–412.

Herrnstein, R. J. *IQ in the meritocracy*. Boston: Little, Brown, 1973.

Herrnstein, R. J. Formal properties of the matching law. *Journal of the Experimental Analysis of Behavior*, 1974, **21**, 159–164.

Herrnstein, R. J., and Hineline, P. N, Negative reinforcement as shock-frequency reduction. *Journal of the Experimental Analysis of Behavior*, 1966, **9**, 421–430.

Herrnstein, R. J., and Loveland, D. H. Complex visual concept in the pigeon. *Science*, 1964, **146**, 549–551.

Hineline, P. N. Negative reinforcement without shock reduction. *Journal of the Experimental Analysis of Behavior*, 1970, **14**, 259–268.

Hochberg, J. E. *Perception.* Englewood Cliffs, N.J.: Prentice-Hall, 1964.

Hodos, W. Progressive ratio as a measure of reward strength. *Science,* 1961, **134**, 943–944.

Hoffman, H. S., and Fleshler, M. The course of emotionality in the development of avoidance. *Journal of Experimental Psychology,* 1962, **64**, 288–294.

Holz, W. C., and Azrin, N. H. Discriminative properties of punishment. *Journal of the Experimental Analysis of Behavior,* 1961, **4**, 225–232.

Horn, G., and Hill, R. M. Responsiveness to sensory stimulation of units in the superior colliculus and subadjacent tectotegonental regions of the rabbit. *Experimental Neurology,* 1966, **14**, 199–223.

Hull, C. L. Quantitative aspects of the evolution of concepts. *Psychological Monographs,* 1920, **28**, (Whole No. 123).

Hull, C. L. *Principles of behavior.* New York: Appleton-Century-Crofts, 1943.

Hull, J. H. Instrumental response topographies of rats. *Animal Learning and Behavior,* 1977, **5**, 207–212.

Hunt, G. M., and Azrin, N. H. A community reinforcement approach to alcoholism. *Behavior Research and Therapy,* 1973, **11**, 91–104.

Hunt, H. F., and Brady, J. V. Some effects of electro-convulsive shock on a conditioned emotional response ("anxiety"). *Journal of Comparative and Physiological Psychology,* 1951, **44**, 88–98.

Hunt, H. F., and Otis, L. S. Conditioned and unconditioned emotional defecation in the rat. *Journal of Comparative and Physiological Psychology,* 1953, **46**, 378–382.

Hurwitz, H. M. B. Periodicity of response in operant extinction. *Quarterly Journal of Experimental Psychology,* 1957, **9**, 177–184.

Hynan, M. T. The influence of the victim on shock-induced aggression in rats. *Journal of the Experimental Analysis of Behavior,* 1976, **25**, 401–409.

Irwin, O. C. Infant speech: Development of vowel sounds. *Journal of Speech and Hearing Disorders,* 1952, **17**, 269–279.

Iversen, I. H. Interactions between reinforced responses and collateral responses. *The Psychological Record,* 1976, **26**, 399–413.

Jacobson, E. The electrophysiology of mental activities. *American Journal of Psychology,* 1932, **44**, 677–694.

Jacobson, E. *Progressive relaxation.* Chicago: University of Chicago Press, 1938.

James, W. *Principles of psychology,* Volume 2. New York: Holt, 1890.

Jenkins, J. G., and Dallenbach, K. M. Oblivescence during sleep and waking. *Journal of Experimental Psychology,* 1924, **35**, 605–612.

Jenkins, H. M., and Moore, B. R. The form of the auto-shaped response with food or water reinforcers. *Journal of the Experimental Analysis of Behavior,* 1973, **20**, 163–181.

Jensen, A. R. How much can we boast IQ and scholastic achievement? *Harvard Educational Review,* 1969, **39**, 1–123.

Jersild, A. T., and Holmes, F. B. Methods of overcoming children's fears. *Journal of Psychology,* 1935, **1**, 75–104.

Kamin, L. J. The effects of termination of the CS and avoidance of the US on avoidance learning: An extension. *Canadian Journal of Psychology*, 1957, **11**, 48–56.

Kamin, L. J. *The science and politics of I.Q.* New York: Lawrence Erlbaum, 1974.

Kantor, J. R. *The scientific evolution of psychology.* Vol. 1. Chicago: Principia Press, 1963.

Kaplan, H. *The new sex therapy.* New York: Brunner/Mazel, 1974.

Kaplan, M. The effects of noxious stimulus intensity and duration during intermittent reinforcement of escape behavior. *Journal of Comparative and Physiological Psychology*, 1952, **45**, 538–549.

Karpicke, J., Christoph, G., Peterson, G., and Hearst, E. Signal location and positive versus negative conditioned suppression in the rat. *Journal of Experimental Psychology: Animal Behavior Processes*, 1977, **3**, 105–118.

Katona, G. *Organizing and memorizing: Studies in the psychology of learning and teaching.* New York: Columbia University Press, 1940.

Kelleher, R. Schedules of conditioned reinforcement during experimental extinction. *Journal of the Experimental Analysis of Behavior*, 1961, **4**, 1–5.

Kelleher, R. Conditioned reinforcement in second-order schedules. *Journal of the Experimental Analysis of Behavior*, 1966, **9**, 475–485.

Keller, F. S., and Schoenfeld, W. N. *Principles of psychology.* New York: Appleton-Century-Crofts, 1950.

Kendler, H. H. *Basic psychology.* New York: Appleton-Century-Crofts, 1963.

Kendler, H. H., and Vineberg, R. The acquisition of compound concepts as a function of previous training. *Journal of Experimental Psychology*, 1954, **48**, 252–258.

Kimble, G. A. *Hilgard and Marquis' conditioning and learning.* New York: Appleton-Century-Crofts, 1961.

Kimble, G. A., and Garmezy, N. *Principles of general psychology.* New York: Ronald Press, 1963.

Kimmel, H. Instrumental conditioning. In W. F. Prokasy and D. C. Raskin (Eds.) *Electrodermal activity in psychological research.* New York: Academic Press, 1973.

Kleitman, N. *Sleep and wakefulness.* Chicago: University of Chicago Press, 1963.

Kohler, W. *The mentality of apes.* New York: Harcourt, Brace, 1925.

Kramer, T. J., and Rilling, M. Differential reinforcement of low rates: A selective critique. *Psychological Bulletin*, 1970, **74**, 225–254.

Kuhn, T. *The structure of scientific revolutions.* Chicago: University of Chicago Press, 1970.

Laing, R. D., and Esterson, A. *Sanity, madness and the family.* London: Tavistock, 1970.

Landis, C., and Hunt, W. A. *The startle pattern.* New York: Farrar and Rinehart, 1939.

Lang, P. J. The mechanics of desensitization and the laboratory study of human fear, In C. M. Franks (Ed.) *Behavior therapy: Appraisal and status.* New York: McGraw-Hill, 1969.

Lashley, K. S. The mechanism of vision. XV. Preliminary studies of the rat's capacity for detail vision. *Journal of Genetic Psychology*, 1938, **18**, 123–193.

Lea, S. E. G., and Harrison, S. N. Discrimination of polymorphous concepts by pigeons. *Quarterly Journal of Experimental Psychology*, 1978, **30**, 521–537.

Leslie, J. C. Effects of food deprivation and reinforcement magnitude on conditioned suppression. *Journal of the Experimental Analysis of Behavior*, 1977, **28**, 107–115.

Lewis, D. J. *Scientific principles of psychology*. Englewood Cliffs, N.J.: Prentice-Hall, 1963.

Lewontin, R. Race and intelligence. *Bulletin of the Atomic Scientists*, March, 1970, 2–8.

Lisina, M. I. The role of orientations in converting involuntary to voluntary responses. In L. G. Voronin *et al.* (Eds.) *The orienting reflex and exploratory behavior*. Moscow, 1958.

Lobitz, W. C., and LoPiccolo, J. New methods in the treatment of sexual dysfunction. *Journal of Behavior Therapy and Experimental Psychiatry*, 1972, **3**, 256–272.

Lolordo, V. M., McMillan, J. C., and Riley, A. L. The effects upon food-reinforced pecking and treadle-pressing of auditory and visual signals for response-independent food. *Learning and Motivation*, 1974, **5**, 24–41.

Long, Lillian D. An investigation of the original response to the conditioned stimulus. *Archives of Psychology*, (New York) 1941, No. 259.

Lovaas, O. I., and Schreibman, L. Stimulus overselectivity of autistic children in a two stimulus situation. *Behavior Research and Therapy*, 1971, **9**, 305–310.

Luchins, A. S. Mechanization in problem solving: the effect of *Einstellung*. *Psychological Monographs*, 1942, **54**, (Whole No. 248).

Lynn, R. *Attention, arousal and the orientation reaction*. Oxford: Pergamon, 1966.

Lysaught, J. P., and Williams, C. M. *A guide to programmed instruction*. New York: Wiley, 1963.

Mackintosh, N. J. Stimulus control: Attention factors. In W. K. Honig and J. E. R. Staddon (Eds.) *Handbook of operant behavior*. Englewood Cliffs, N.J.: Prentice-Hall, 1977.

Maier, S. F., Seligman, M. E. P., and Solomon, R. L. Pavlovian fear conditioning and learned helplessness: Effects on escape and avoidance behavior of (a) the CS–US contingency and (b) the independence of the US and voluntary responding. In B. A. Campbell and R. M. Church (Eds.) *Punishment and aversive behavior*. New York: Appleton-Century-Crofts, 1969.

Masters, W. H., and Johnson, V. *Human sexual inadequacy*. Boston: Little Brown, 1970.

Max, L. W. Experimental study of the motor theory of consciousness. IV. Action-current responses in the deaf during awakening, kinaesthetic imagery and abstract thinking. *Journal of Comparative Psychology*, 1937, **24**, 301–344.

Mayer, J. Glucostatic mechanism of regulation of food intake. *New England Journal of Medicine*, 1953, **249**, 13–16.

McAllister, L. W., Stachowiak, J. G., Baer, D. M., and Conderman, L. The application of operant conditioning techniques in a secondary school classroom. *Journal of Applied Behavior Analysis*, 1969, **2**, 277–285.

McCall, R. B., Appelbaum, N. I., and Hogarty, P. S. Developmental changes in mental performance. *Child Development Monographs*, 1973, **38**, (3), 1–84.

McFarland, D. J. Separation of satiating and rewarding consequences of drinking. *Physiology and Behavior*, 1969, **4**, 987–989.

Mechner, F. *Science, education and behavioral technology*. New York: Basic Systems, 1963.

Miczek, K. A. Effects of scopolamine, amphetamine, and benzopliazepines on conditioned suppression. *Pharmacology, Biochemistry and Behavior*, 1973, **1**, 401–411.

Millenson, J. R. Random interval schedules of reinforcement. *Journal of the Experimental Analysis of Behavior*, 1963, **6**, 437–443.

Millenson, J. R., and Hurwitz, H. M. B. Some temporal and sequential properties of behavior during conditioning and extinction. *Journal of the Experimental Analysis of Behavior*, 1961, **4**, 97–105.

Millenson, J. R., and Leslie, J. C. The conditioned emotional response (CER) as a baseline for the study of anti-anxiety drugs. *Neuropharmacology*, 1974, **13**, 1–9.

Millenson, J. R., and Macmillan, A. St. C. Abortive responding during punishment of bar-holding. *Learning and Motivation*, 1975, **6**, 279–288.

Miller, H. L., and Haney, H. R. Behavior and traditional therapy applied to pedophiliac exhibitionism: A case study. *Psychological Reports*, 1976, **39**, 1119–1124.

Miller, N. E. The frustration-aggression hypothesis. *Psychological Review*, 1941, **48**, 337–342.

Miller, N. E. Learnable drives and rewards. In S. S. Stevens (Ed.) *Handbook of experimental psychology*. New York: Wiley, 1951.

Miller, N. E. Learning of visceral and glandular responses. *Science*, 1969, **163**, 434–445.

Miller, N. E., Bailey, C. J., and Stevenson, J. A. F. Decreased "hunger" but increased food intake resulting from hypothetical lesions. *Science*, 1950, **112**, 256–259.

Miller, N. E., and Dworkin, B. R. Visceral learning: Recent difficulties with curarized rats and significant problems for human research. In P. A. Obrist *et al.* (Eds.) *Cardiovascular psychophysiology*, Chicago: Aldine, 1974.

Miller, W., and Seligman, M. E. P. Depression and learned helplessness in man. *Journal of Abnormal Psychology*, 1975, **84**, 228–238.

Mischel, W., and Grusec, J. Determinants of the rehearsal and transmission of mental and aversive behaviors. *Journal of Personality and Social Psychology*, 1966, **3**, 197–205.

Mogenson, G., and Cioé, J. Central reinforcement: A bridge between brain function and behavior. In W. K. Honig and J. E. R. Staddon (Eds.) *Handbook of operant behavior*. Englewood Cliffs, N.J.: Prentice-Hall, 1977.

Moore, B. R. The role of directed Pavlovian reactions in simple instrumental learning in the pigeon. In R. A. Hinde and J. Stevenson-Hinde (Eds.) *Constraints on learning*. London: Academic Press, 1973.

Morse, W. H., and Kelleher, R. T. Schedules as fundamental determinants of behavior. In W. N. Schoenfeld (Ed.) *The theory of reinforcement schedules*. New York: Appleton-Century-Crofts, 1970.

Morse, W. H., Mead, R. N., and Kelleher, R. T. Modulation of elicited behavior by a fixed-interval schedule of electric shock presentation. *Science*, 1967, **157**, 215–217.

Mostofsky, D. (Ed.) *Stimulus generalization*. Stanford: Stanford University Press, 1965.

Mowrer, O. H., and Jones, H. M. Extinction and behavior variability as functions of effortfulness of task. *Journal of Experimental Psychology*, 1943, **33**, 369–386.

Muenzinger, K. F., and Fletcher, F. M. Motivation in learning. VI. Escape from electric shock compared with hungerfood tension in the visual discrimination habit. *Journal of Comparative Psychology*, 1936, **22**, 79–91.

Munn, N. L. *Handbook of psychological research on the rat.* Boston, Mass.: Houghton Mifflin, 1950.

Nachman, M. Some stimulus conditions affecting learned aversions produced by illness. Paper read at 3rd International Conference on the Regulation of Food and Water Intake, Philadelphia, 1968.

Neisworth, J. T., and Smith, R. M. *Modifying retarded behavior.* Boston, Mass.: Houghton Mifflin, 1973.

Newell, A., and Simon, H. GPS, a program that simulates human thought. In E. A. Feigenbaum and J. Feldman (Eds.) *Computers and thought.* New York: McGraw-Hill, 1963.

Notterman, J., Schoenfeld, W. N., and Bersh, P. J. Conditioned heart rate response in human beings during experimental anxiety. *Journal of Comparative and Physiological Psychology,* 1952, **45**, 1–8.

Oatley, K., and Dickinson, A. Air drinking and the measurement of thirst. *Animal Behavior,* 1970, **18**, 259–265.

Olds, J. Pleasure centers in the brain. *Scientific American,* Oct. 1956, **195**, 105–116.

Olds, J. Satiation effects in self-stimulation of the brain. *Journal of Comparative and Physiological Psychology,* 1958, **51**, 675–678.

Olds, J. Hypothalamic substrates of reward. *Physiological Review,* 1962, **42**, 554–604.

Olds, J., and Milner, P. Positive reinforcement produced by electrical stimulation of septal area and other regions of rat brain. *Journal of Comparative and Physiological Psychology,* 1954, **47**, 419–427.

Orne, M. T. On the social psychology of the psychological experiment: With particular reference to demand characteristics and their implications. *American Psychologist,* 1962, **17**, 776–783.

Osgood, C. E. *Method and theory in experimental psychology.* New York: Oxford University Press, 1953.

Paul, G. L. Outcome of systematic desensitization. II. Controlled investigations of individual treatment, technique variations, and current status. In C. M. Franks (Ed.) *Behavior therapy: Appraisal and status.* New York: McGraw-Hill, 1969.

Pavlov, I. P. *Conditioned reflexes.* London: Oxford University Press, 1927.

Pavlov, I. P. *Lectures on conditioned reflexes.* New York: International Publishers, 1928.

Perin, C. T. Behavior potentiality as a joint function of the amount of training and the degree of hunger at the time of extinction. *Journal of Experimental Psychology,* 1942, **30**, 93–113.

Pliskoff, S. S., Wright, J. E., and Hawkins, T. D. Brain stimulation as a reinforcer: intermittent schedules. *Journal of the Experimental Analysis of Behavior,* 1965, **8**, 75–88.

Premack, D. Reversibility of the reinforcement relation. *Science,* 1962, **136**, 255–257.

Premack, D. Reinforcement theory. In D. Levine (Ed.) *Nebraska symposium on motivation.* Lincoln, Nebraska: University of Nebraska Press, 1965.

Premack, D. Catching up with commonsense or two sides of a generalization: Reinforcement and punishment. In R. C. Glaser (Ed.) *The nature of reinforcement.* New York: Academic Press, 1971.

Premack, D., and Premack, A. J. Teaching visual language to apes and language-deficient persons. In R. L. Schiefelbusch and L. L. Lloyd (Eds.) *Language perspectives-acquisition, retardation and intervention*. New York: Macmillan, 1974.

Rachlin, H., and Green, L. Commitment, choice, and self-control. *Journal of the Experimental Analysis of Behavior*, 1972, **17**, 15–22.

Rachlin, H., and Herrnstein, R. J. Hedonism revisited: On the negative law of effect. In B. A. Campbell and R. M. Church (Eds.) *Punishment and aversive behavior*. Englewood Cliffs, N.J.: Prentice-Hall, 1969.

Rachman, S. *The effects of psychotherapy*. Oxford: Pergamon, 1971.

Rachman, S. The conditioning theory of fear-acquisition: a critical examination. *Behavior Research and Therapy*, 1977, **15**, 375–387.

Reese, T. W., and Hogenson, Marilyn J. Food satiation in the pigeon. *Journal of the Experimental Analysis of Behavior*, 1962, **5**, 239–245.

Rescorla, R. A. Probability of shock in the presence and absence of CS in fear conditioning. *Journal of Comparative and Physiological Psychology*, 1968, **66**, 1–5.

Rescorla, R. A. Second-order conditioning: Implications for theories of learning. In F. J. McGuigan and D. B. Lumsden (Eds.) *Contemporary approaches to conditioning and learning*. Washington, D.C.: V. H. Winston & Sons, 1973.

Rescorla, R. A., and Wagner, A. R. A theory of Pavlovian conditioning: Variations in the effectiveness of reinforcement and non-reinforcement. In A. H. Black and W. F. Prokasy (Eds.) *Classical conditioning II: Current research and theory*. New York: Appleton-Century-Crofts, 1972.

Revusky, S. H., and Garcia, J. Learned associations over long delays. In G. Bower (Ed.) *The psychology of learning and motivation*, Volume 4. New York: Academic Press, 1970.

Reynolds, G. S. *A primer of operant conditioning*. Second Edition. Glenview, Ill.: Scott, Foresman, 1975.

Rheingold, H. L., Gewirtz, J. L., and Ross, H. W. Social conditioning of vocalizations in the infant. *Journal of Comparative and Physiological Psychology*, 1959, **52**, 68–73.

Richter, C. Animal behavior and internal drives. *Quarterly Review of Biology*, 1927, **2**, 307–343.

Ridgers, A., and Leslie, J. C. Autoshaping and omission training in the rat. Paper read to Experimental Analysis of Behavior Group, Exeter, England, 1975.

Rilling, M. Stimulus control and inhibitory processes. In W. K. Honig and J. E. R. Staddon (Eds.) *Handbook of operant behavior*. Englewood Cliffs, N.J.: Prentice-Hall, 1977.

Romanes, G. J. *Animal intelligence*. (4th ed.) London: Kegan Paul, 1886.

Rosenthal, T. L., and Kellogg, J. S. Demonstration versus instructions in concept attainment by mental retardates. *Behavior Research and Therapy*, 1973, **11**, 299–309.

Rosenzweig, M. The mechanisms of hunger and thirst. In L. Postman (Ed.) *Psychology in the making*. New York: Knopf, 1962.

Routh, D. K. Conditioning of vocal response differentiation in infants. *Developmental Psychology*, 1969, **1**, 219–226.

Rozin, P. Central or peripheral mediation of learning with long CS-UCS intervals in the feeding system. *Journal of Comparative and Physiological Psychology*, 1969, **67**, 421–429.

Rozin, P., and Kalat, J. W. Specific hungers and poison avoidance as adaptive specializations of learning. *Psychological Review*, 1971, **78**, 459–486.

Sanford, F. *Psychology, a scientific study of man*. Belmont, Calif.: Wadsworth, 1961.

Schacter, S. Some extraordinary facts about obese human and rats. *American Psychologist*, 1971, **26**, 129–144.

Schacter, S., and Singer, J. E. Cognitive, social and physiological determinants of emotional state. *Psychological Review*, 1962, **69**, 379–399.

Schoenfeld, W. N., Antonitis, J. J., and Bersh, P. J. A preliminary study of training conditions necessary for secondary reinforcement. *Journal of Experimental Psychology*, 1950, **40**, 40–45.

Schoenfeld, W. N. Notes on a bit of psychological nonsense: "Race differences in intelligence." *Psychological Record*, 1974, **24**, 17–32.

Schwartz, B., and Williams, D. R. Discrete-trials spaced responding in the pigeon: the dependence of efficient performance on the availability of a stimulus for collateral pecking. *Journal of the Experimental Analysis of Behavior*, 1971, **16**, 155–160.

Seligman, M. E. P. On the generality of the laws of learning, *Psychological Review*, 1970, **77**, 406–418.

Seligman, M. E. P. Phobias and preparedness. *Behavior Therapy*, 1971, **2**, 307–320.

Seligman, M. E. P. Introduction. In M. E. P. Seligman and J. L. Hager (Eds.) *Biological boundaries of learning*. New York: Meredith, 1972.

Seligman, M. E. P. *Helplessness: On depression, development, and death*. San Francisco: Freeman, 1975.

Sevenster, P. Incompatibility of response and reward. In R. A. Hinde, and J. Stevenson-Hinde (Eds.) *Constraints on learning*. London: Academic Press, 1973.

Sheffield, F. D. Relation between classical conditioning and instrumental learning. In W. F. Prokasy (Ed.) *Classical conditioning*. New York: Appleton-Century-Crofts, 1965.

Sherrington, C. *The integrative action of the nervous system*. New Haven, Conn.: Yale University Press, 1906 (Second Edition, 1947).

Shettleworth, S. J. Food reinforcement and the organization of behavior in the golden hamster. In R. A. Hinde, and J. Stevenson-Hinde (Eds.) *Constraints on learning*. London: Academic Press, 1973.

Shimp, C. P. Short-term memory in the pigeon: relative recency. *Journal of the Experimental Analysis of Behavior*, 1976, **25**, 55–61.

Sidman, M. Two temporal parameters of maintenance of avoidance behavior by the white rat. *Journal of Comparative and Physiological Psychology*, 1953, **46**, 253–261.

Sidman, M. *Tactics of scientific research*. New York: Basic Books, 1960.

Sidman, M. Avoidance behavior. In W. K. Honig (Ed.) *Operant behavior: areas of research and application*. New York: Appleton-Century-Crofts, 1966.

Siegel, P. S. The relationship between voluntary water intake, body weight loss and numbers of hours of water privation in the rat. *Journal of Comparative and Physiological Psychology*, 1947, **40**, 231–238.

Skinner, B. F. The concept of the reflex in the description of behavior. *Journal of General Psychology*, 1931, **5**, 427–458.

Skinner, B. F. *The behavior of organisms*. New York: Appleton-Century-Crofts, 1938.

Skinner, B. F. A review of C. L. Hull's Principles of Behavior. *American Journal of Psychology*, 1944, **57**, 276–281.

Skinner, B. F. The nature of the operant reserve. *Psychological Bulletin*, 1940, **37**, 423.

Skinner, B. F. *Current trends in experimental psychology*. Pittsburgh: University Press, 1947.

Skinner, B. F. Are theories of learning necessary? *Psychological Review*, 1950, **57**, 193–216.

Skinner, B. F. *Science and human behavior*. New York: Macmillan, 1953.

Skinner, B. F. A case history in scientific method. *American Psychologist*, 1956, **11**, 221–233.

Skinner, B. F. The experimental analysis of behavior. *American Scientist*, 1957, **45**, 343–371.

Skinner, B. F. *Verbal behavior*. New York: Appleton-Century-Crofts, 1957.

Skinner, B. F. Teaching machines. *Science*, 1958, **128**, 969–977.

Skinner, B. F. A case history in scientific method. In S. Koch (Ed.) *Psychology: a study of a science*. Volume 2. New York: McGraw-Hill, 1959.

Skinner, B. F. *The technology of teaching*. New York: Appleton-Century-Crofts, 1968.

Skinner, B. F. *Beyond freedom and dignity*. New York: Bantam, 1972.

Slobin, D. I. (Ed.) *The ontogenesis of grammar*. New York: Academic Press, 1971.

Smith, J. C., and Roll, D. L. Trace conditioning with X-rays as the aversive stimulus. *Psychonomic Science*, 1967, **9**, 11–12.

Smith, M. F., and Smith, K. U. Thirst-motivated activity and its extinction in the cat. *Journal of General Psychology*, 1939, **21**, 89–98.

Smith, R. F. Behavioral events other than key striking which are counted as responses during pigeon pecking. Doctoral dissertation, Indiana University, 1967.

Smoke, K. L. An objective study of concept formation. *Psychological Monographs*, 1932, **42** (Whole No. 191).

Sobell, M. B., and Sobell, L. C. Alcoholics treated by individualized behavior therapy: One year treatment outcome. *Behavior Research and Therapy*, 1973, **11**, 599–618.

Sokolov, Y. N. *Perception and the conditioned reflex*. Oxford: Pergamon Press, 1963.

Spence, K. W. The differential response in animals to stimuli varying within a single dimension. *Psychological Review*, 1937, **44**, 430–444.

Spencer, H. *The principles of psychology*. New York: D. Appleton, 1878.

Staddon, J. E. R. Temporal control and the theory of reinforcement schedules. In R. M. Gilbert, and J. R. Millenson (Eds.) *Reinforcement: Behavioral analysis*. New York: Academic Press, 1972.

Staddon, J. E. R. Temporal control, attention and memory. *Psychological Review*, 1974, **21**, 541–551.

Staddon, J. E. R. Limitations on temporal control: Generalization and the effects of context. *British Journal of Psychology*, 1975, **66**, 229–246.

Staddon, J. E. R., and Simmelhag, V. The superstition experiment: A re-examination of its implications for the principles of adaptive behavior. *Psychological Review*, 1971, **78**, 3–43.

Stevens, S. S. Mathematics, measurement, and psychophysics. In S. S. Stevens (Ed.) *Handbook of experimental psychology*. New York: John Wiley, 1951.

Stuart, R. B. A three-dimensional program for the treatment of obesity. *Behavior Research and Therapy*, 1971, **9**, 177–186.

Syme, L. Personality characteristics and the alcoholic. A critique of current studies. *Quarterly Journal of Studies on Alcohol*, 1957, **18**, 288–301.

Szasz, T. S. *The myth of mental illness: Foundations of a theory of personal conduct*. New York: Hoeber-Harper, 1961.

Szasz, T. S. *The theology of medicine*. New York: Harper and Row, 1977.

Taub, E., and Berman, A. J. Movement and learning in the absence of sensory feedback. In S. J. Freedman (Ed.) *The neuropsychology of spatially oriented behavior.* Homewood, Illinois: Dorsey, 1968.

Teitelbaum, P. Sensory control of hypothalmic hyperphagia. *Journal of Comparative and Physiological Psychology,* 1955, **48**, 156–163.

Templeton, R. D., and Quigley, J. P. The action of insulin on the mobility of the gastro-intestinal tract. *American Journal of Physiology,* 1930, **91**, 467–474.

Terman, L. M. *The measurement of intelligence.* Boston, Mass.: Houghton Mifflin, 1916.

Terrace, H. S., Gibbon, J., Farrell, L., and Baldock, M. D. Temporal factors influencing the acquisition of an autoshaped key peck. *Animal Learning and Behavior,* 1975, **3**, 53–62.

Thomas, D. R., and Williams, J. L. A further study of stimulus generalization following three-stimulus discrimination training. *Journal of the Experimental Analysis of Behavior,* 1963, **6**, 171–176.

Thorndike, E. L. Animal intelligence. *Psychological Review Monograph Supplement,* 1898, No. 8.

Thorndike, E. L. *Animal intelligence: Experimental studies.* New York: Macmillan, 1911.

Thorpe, W. H. The comparison of vocal communication in animals and man. In R. A. Hinde (Ed.) *Non-verbal communication.* Cambridge: Cambridge University Press, 1972.

Timberlake, W., and Allison, J. Response deprivation: An empirical approach to instrumental performance. *Psychological Review,* 1974, **81**, 146–164.

Tolman, E. C. A behavioristic account of the emotions. *Psychological Review,* 1923, **30**, 217–227.

Toulmin, S., and Goodfield, J. *The architecture of matter.* New York: Harper and Row, 1962.

Tribble, A., and Hall, R. V. Effects of peer approval on completion of arithmetic assignments. In F. W. Clark, D. R. Evans and L. A. Hammerlynck (Eds.) *Implementing behavioral programs for schools and clinics.* Champaign, Illinois: Research Press, 1972.

Trowill, J. A. Instrumental conditioning of the heart rate in the curarized rat. *Journal of Comparative and Physiological Psychology.* 1967, **63**, 7–11.

Ulrich, R. E. Pain-aggression. In G. A. Kimble (Ed.) *Foundations of conditioning and learning.* New York: Appleton-Century-Crofts, 1967.

Ulrich, R. E., and Azrin, N. H. Reflexive fighting in response to aversive stimulation. *Journal of the Experimental Analysis of Behavior,* 1962, **5**, 511–520.

Valenstein, E. S., and Beer, B. Continuous opportunity for reinforcing brain stimulation. *Journal of the Experimental Analysis of Behavior,* 1964, **7**, 183–184.

Van Houten, R., and Rudolph, R. The development of stimulus control with and without a lighted key. *Journal of the Experimental Analysis of Behavior,* 1972, **18**, 217–222.

Van Twyver, H. B., and Kimmel, H. D. Operant conditioning of the GSR with concomitant measurement of two somatic variables. *Journal of Experimental Psychology,* 1966, **72**, 841–846.

Verhave, T. Avoidance responding as a function of simultaneous and equal changes in two temporal parameters. *Journal of the Experimental Analysis of Behavior,* 1959, **2**, 185–190.

Verplanck, W. S. The control of the content of conversation. *Journal of Abnormal and Social Psychology,* 1955, **51**, 668–676.

Wald, G. Eye and camera. *Scientific American,* August 1950, **182**, 32–41.

Wallach, H. Brightness constancy and the nature of achromatic colors. *Journal of Experimental Psychology,* 1958, **38**, 310–324.

Warden, C. J. *Animal motivation studies.* New York: Columbia University Press, 1931.

Warren, J. M. Primate learning in comparative perspective. In A. M. Schrier, H. F. Harlow, and F. Stollnitz (Eds.) *Behavior of nonhuman primates,* Volume 1. New York: Academic Press, 1965.

Wasserman, E. A. The effect of redundant contextual stimuli on autoshaping the pigeon's key peck. *Animal Learning and Behavior,* 1973, **1**, 198–206.

Wasserman, E. A., Franklin, S., and Hearst, E. Pavlovian appetitive contingencies and approach vs. withdrawal to conditioned stimuli in pigeons. *Journal of Comparative and Physiological Psychology,* 1974, **86**, 616–627.

Watson, J. B. Psychology as the behaviorist views it. *Psychological Review,* 1913, **20**, 158–177.

Watson, J. B. *Behavior, an introduction to comparative psychology.* New York: Holt, 1914.

Watson, J. B. Is thinking merely the action of language mechanisms? *British Journal of Psychology,* 1920, **11**, 87–104.

Watson, J. B. *Behaviorism.* Revised Edition. Chicago: University of Chicago Press, 1930.

Watson, L. S. *Child behavior modification: a manual for teachers, nurses, and parents.* New York: Pergamon, 1973.

Wawrzyncyck, S. Badania and parecia *Spirostomum ambiguum* major. *Acta Biologica Experimentalis* (Warsaw), 1937, **11**, 57–77.

Webb, W. B. Antecedents of sleep. *Journal of Experimental Psychology,* 1957, **53**, 162–166.

Wechsler, D. *Wechsler Adult Intelligence Scale manual.* New York: Psychological Corp., 1955.

Wechsler, D. *The measurement and appraisal of adult intelligence.* Baltimore: Williams & Wilkins, 1958.

Weiss, B., and Laties, V. G. Titration behavior on various fractional escape programs. *Journal of the Experimental Analysis of Behavior,* 1959, **2**, 227–248.

Weiss, B., and Laties, V. G. Characteristics of aversive thresholds measured by a titration schedule. *Journal of the Experimental Analysis of Behavior,* 1963, **6**, 563–572.

Weiss, T., and Engel, B. T. Operant conditioning of heart rate in patients with premature ventricular contractions. *Psychosomatic Medicine,* 1971, **33**, 301–321.

Weissman, N. W., and Crossman, E. K. A comparison of two types of extinction following fixed-ratio training. *Journal of the Experimental Analysis of Behavior,* 1966, **9**, 41–46.

Weitzman, E. D., Ross, G. S., Hodos, W., and Galambos, R. Behavioral method for study of pain in the monkey. *Science,* 1961, **133**, 37–38.

Wilcoxon, H. C., Dragoin, W., and Kral, P. A. Illness induced aversions in rat and quail: Relative salience of visual and gustatory cues. *Science*, 1971, **171**, 826–828.

Williams, J. B. Resistance to extinction as a function of the number of reinforcements. *Journal of Experimental Psychology*, 1938, **23**, 506–522.

Williams, D. R., and Williams, H. Auto-maintenance in the pigeons: Sustained pecking despite contingent nonreinforcement. *Journal of the Experimental Analysis of Behavior*, 1969, **12**, 511–520.

Willis, J. W., Hobbs, T. R., Kirkpatrick, D. G., and Manley, K. W. Training counselors as researchers in the natural environment. In E. Ramp and G. Semb (Eds.) *Behavior analysis: areas of research and application.* Englewood Cliffs, N. J.: Prentice-Hall, 1975.

Wolfe, J. B. Effectiveness of token-rewards for chimpanzees. *Comparative Psychology Monographs*, 1936, **12**, 1–72.

Wolfle, H. M. Conditioning as a function of the interval between the conditioned and the original stimulus. *Journal of General Psychology*, 1932, **7**, 80–103.

Wolin, B. R. Difference in manner of pecking a key between pigeons reinforced with food and with water. Paper read at conference on the Experimental Analysis of Behavior, 1948.

Wolpe, J. *Psychotherapy and reciprocal inhibition.* Stanford: Stanford University Press, 1958.

Wolpe, J. *The practice of behavior therapy.* New York: Pergamon, 1973.

Wyckoff, L. B., Jr. The role of observing responses in discrimination learning: Part I. *Psychological Review*, 1952, **59**, 431–442.

Young, P. T. *Motivation and emotion.* New York: Wiley, 1961.

Young, P. T., and Richey, H. W. Diurnal drinking patterns in the rat. *Journal of Comparative and Physiological Psychology*, 1952, **45**, 80–89.

Zeaman, D., and Smith, R. W. Review of some recent findings in human cardiac conditioning. In W. F. Prokasy (Ed.) *Classical conditioning.* New York: Appleton-Century-Crofts, 1965.

Zener, K. The significance of behavior accompanying conditioned salivary secretion for theories of the conditioned response. *American Journal of Psychology*, 1937, **50**, 384–403.

Zimmerman, D. W. Durable secondary reinforcement: method and theory. *Psychological Review*, 1957, **64**, 373–383.

Zimmerman, D. W. Sustained performance in rats based on secondary reinforcement. *Journal of Comparative and Physiological Psychology*, 1959, **52**, 353–358.

AUTHOR INDEX

Autonomic nervous system, 427–430
Autonomic responses, 45–46, 174–175, 427–430
Autoshaping, 209–219
Aversion therapy, 479
Aversive stimulus, 264, 266, 280, 295, 299–300
Avoidance, 277–297
Awareness, 43, 84

Babbling, 40, 42
Back-up reinforcer, 466
Backward conditioning, 181, 204
Bait-shyness, 198
Bar holding, 272–274
Baseline, see Behavioral baseline
Behavior meter, 132
Behavior modification, 69, 435–436, 444, 464–465
Behavior therapy, 463–486
Behavioral baseline, 29, 443
Behavioral deficit, 366
Behavioral dimension, 78
Behavioral disorders, 441–442, 468; see also Abnormal behavior
Behavioral similarity, 363–364, 366–367
Behaviorism, 13–15
Biofeedback, 86–87, 233
Bodily state, in emotion, 414–416, 430
Body weight loss, 383, 402; see also Deprivation
Brain stimulation reinforcement, 403–406
Brightness contrast, 230–231
Brief stimulus presentation, 153–154

CRF, see Continuous reinforcement
CS, 180; see also Localized CS
CS+, 185, 248, 288
CS−, 185, 248, 288; see also Classical conditioning
Causes, in science, 371–374
Causes of behavior, 374–375, 386, 414–416
Chaining, 54, 62, 160–163, 342–343, 358
Choice, 304–305
Classical conditioning, 165, 177–196
  of appetitive behavior, 134–135
  and autonomic responses, 429
  and aversion therapy, 479
  aversive, 264, 299, 310–312
  and avoidance, 278–280, 295–296
  and conditioned suppression, 421
  and emotion, 418–419
  and environmental control, 225
  extinction, 49
  and inhibitory control, 261
  Pavlov's investigations, 7–9
  and phobias, 429
  and positive conditioned suppression, 424–425
  and sign tracking, 208
  and taste aversion, 198, 201, 204–205
  and temporal control, 244

Classical-operant interactions, 312–314, 421–422, 424–427
Classroom behavior, 438–441, 468
Claustrophobia, 471
Columbia obstruction box, 400–401
Concept acquisition, 317, 319–339, 365–366, 445–449
Concept formation, see Concept acquisition
Concept identification, 353–355
Concurrent chain, 304–305
Concurrent schedule, 104–106, 120–128, 251
Conditioned aversive stimulus, 286–288, 310–312
Conditioned emotional response, see Conditioned suppression
Conditioned reflex, 7–9, 21, 178–180; see also Classical conditioning
Conditioned reinforcement, 146–160
Conditioned reinforcer, 146–152, 154–156, 160, 363
Conditioned response, 190–191, 225
Conditioned stimulus, 180; see also Classical conditioning
Conditioned suppression, 311–314, 421–422
Conditioned taste aversion, 198–202
Conjunctive concepts, 334–335, 354
Contiguity, temporal, 186
Contingencies of reinforcement, see Reinforcement contingencies
Contingency, 29–30, 186–187, 196
Contingency management, 479–480
Contingent response, 410
Continuous reinforcement, 89, 92
Correlated stimulus, 289–290, 293–294
Counterconditioning, 472
Countercontrol, 484–485
Covert behavior, 162–163; see also Private events
Crying, 225, 450–451
Cumulative recorder, 17–18, 30–31, 90
Cycles of behavior, 375–377, 379–384, 391, 474–476

Deep muscle relaxation, 470
Delay conditioning, 181
Delay of shock, 292–294
Depression, 474–477
Deprivation, 375–377; see also Hunger; Thirst
  and activity, 383
  of air, 398–400
  and drive, 379
  of food, 383, 396–398, 402
  and overcoming obstructions, 400–401
  and reinforcement, 392, 409
  and response rate, 396–398
  of sleep, 375–377
  of water, 407–408
Descartes, R., 4–6, 9–10, 20, 170
Desensitization, see Systematic desensitization